I0306000

SUNY Series in
Religious Studies

Harold Coward, Editor

Dattātreya
The Immortal Guru, Yogin, and Avatāra

Dattātreya
The Immortal Guru, Yogin, and Avatāra

A Study of the Transformative and Inclusive Character of a Multi-Faceted Hindu Deity

Antonio Rigopoulos

STATE UNIVERSITY OF NEW YORK PRESS

Production by Ruth Fisher
Marketing by Anne M. Valentine

Published by
State University of New York Press, Albany

Printed in the United States of America

For information, address the State University of New York Press, State University Plaza, Albany, NY 12246

Library of Congress Cataloging-in-Publication Data

Rigopoulos, Antonio, 1962–
Dattātreya : the immortal guru, yogin, and avatāra : a study of the transformative and inclusive character of a multi-faceted Hindu deity / Antonio Rigopoulos.
p. cm. — (SUNY series in religious studies)
Includes bibliographical references and index.
ISBN 0-7914-3695-0 (hc : alk. paper). — ISBN 0-7914-3696-9 (pb : alk. paper)
1. Dattātreya (Hindu deity) I. Title. II. Series.
BL 1225.D3R55 1998
294.5'2113—dc21 97-21244
CIP

10 9 8 7 6 5 4 3 2 1

vibhur-nityānandaḥ śruti-gaṇa-śirovedya-mahimā
yato janmādyasya prabhavati sa māyā-guṇavataḥ /
sadā-dhāraḥ satyo jayati puruṣārthaika-phala-daḥ
sadā dattātreyo viharati mudā jñāna-lahariḥ //

All-pervading eternal happiness, the glory to be recognized as supreme among the multitude of revealed texts,

comes from the narration from birth onward of this One: He manifests through the attributes of His illusory power.

Glory to the ever-supporting One, the True, the One granting the foremost fruit of the aims of human life!

Always Dattātreya roams about with joy, He who is the flood of knowledge.

Datta-laharī 1

Contents

Guide to Pronunciation ix

Preface xi

Acknowledgments xv

1. The Genealogy of Dattātreya 1
2. Purāṇic Mythology of Dattātreya 27
3. Dattātreya in Minor *Upaniṣads* 57
4. Dattātreya in the Literature of the Mahānubhāvas 89
5. The *Guru-caritra* and the Rise of the Dattātreya Cult 109
6. Eknāth, Dāsopant, and the Unfolding of the Dattātreya Movement 135
7. The *Tripurā-rahasya* 169
8. The *Avadhūta-gītā* 195
9. The Development of Dattātreya's Iconography 223

Conclusion 249

General Bibliography 265

Selected Bibliography on Dattātreya and His Movement 285

Index 297

Guide to Pronunciation

In Sanskrit and Marāṭhī the short *a* is pronounced like the English *u* in *but;* the long *ā* is like the *a* in *father.* The short *i* is like the *i* in him; the long *ī* is like the *ea* in *heat.* The short *u* is like the *u* in *pull;* the long *ū* is like the *u* in *rule.* As for the other vowels, *e* is pronounced as the *a* in *cable; ai* as the second *i* in *divine; o* as the *o* in *hotel; au* as the *ow* in *power.* The letter *ṛ* is also a vowel and should be pronounced as the *ri* in *ring.*

Consonants are pronounced as in English, with the following cases being noted: *c* is pronounced as in *church; ś* and *ṣ* are similar to the sound *sh* in *shine.*

The aspirated consonants should be pronounced distinctly: *th* as in *hothouse; ph* as in *top hat; gh* as in *doghouse;* and *bh* as in *clubhouse.*

The underdotted consonants *ṭ, ṭh, ḍ, ḍh, ṇ,* and *ṣ* are not common phonemes in English and are produced by curling the tongue slightly backward toward the roof of the mouth.

The underdotted *ṃ* and the overdotted *ṁ* and *ṅ* are nasals.

The letter *w* is sometimes found as the incorrect transliteration of Sanskrit and Marāṭhī *v.*

In Hindī words, the final *a* is often dropped.

Perso-Arabic words are transliterated according to standard rules.

In the case of commonplace names and modern Indian States, the diacritical marks are generally dropped (e.g. Bombay rather than Mumbaī, Maharashtra rather than Mahārāṣṭra, etc.).

Preface

This study presents the main phases in the making of the Hindu deity Dattātreya, from its Purāṇic emergence as an immortal Guru, Yogin, and Avatāra, up to its celebration as the *trimūrti* of Brahmā, Viṣṇu, and Śiva. Focusing on the origin and development of this particular deity, one is brought into touch with virtually all major religious strands of that complex network of religions called Hinduism. Its assimilative force is witnessed by the variety of communities which appropriated Dattātreya from within an overall nondual philosophical framework: from the world of antinomian Tantrism to the world of Brahminical ritual orthodoxy, passing through the renunciatory milieux of Yoga, the Mahānubhāva sect, *Vaiṣṇava* devotionalism, *Śaiva* asceticism, Śāktism and Devī worship. Although one might envision the presence of plural Dattātreyas, construed in different ways within each given community, I would rather opt for the existence of a single multifaceted deity, constantly absorbing new traits in an ongoing process of cross-fertilization. Significantly, Dattātreya's catalyzing force extends beyond the boundaries of Hinduism, also being linked to popular Sufism and Jainism.

Following the ascendance of Dattātreya to the top of the Marāṭhī pantheon—truly a triumphant *vijaya*—affords a recognition of the synthetic spirituality which this deity inspired and attracted. It also illustrates the Maharashtrian reworking of religious influences from both the north and the south of India, as well as the synthesizing of *Śaiva* and *Vaiṣṇava* motifs. Although Maharashtra is the heartland of Dattātreya devotion, his presence is attested to throughout the Indian subcontinent, especially in southern States such as Karnataka, Andhra Pradesh, Kerala, and Tamilnadu, but also in Gujarat and even in Nepal.

The adaptation and assimilation of a "lord of Yoga" exhibiting Tantric, antinomian traits, into the more sanitized and *bhakti*-oriented views of the *Purāṇas* is of special relevance. The basic relationship between *Tantra* and *Purāṇa* is of great importance for understanding medieval Indian spirituality. Dattātreya's presence in both types of canons makes him a case study for understanding this complex link. Furthermore, the unfolding of the Dattātreya icon illustrates the development of Yoga as a synthetic and inclusive body of ideologies and practices. Although fundamentally a *jñāna-mūrti*, Dattātreya is a "honey bee" Yogin: one whose character and teachings are developed by gathering varieties of Yoga's flowers. For all religious groups whose propensity it is to include ideas, practices, and teachings from the ocean of traditions, Dattātreya is truly a paradigm.

The scarce attention paid to this remarkable figure by most Western scholars of Indian religions contrasts sharply with the deity's ubiquitous presence and social permeability. The only three scholarly monographs on Dattātreya are the following: Sri Jaya Chamarajendra Wadiyar Bahadur, *Dattātreya: The Way and the Goal* (London: George Allen & Unwin, 1957; reprint, Delhi: Motilal Banarsidass, 1982); R. C. Dhere, *Datta Sampradāyācā Itihāsa* (2d ed. Puṇe: Nilakanth Prakashan, 1964; 1st ed. 1958); Hariprasad Shivprasad Joshi, *Origin and Development of Dattātreya Worship in India* (Baroda: Mahārāja Sayajirao University of Baroda Press, 1965). For its wealth of information on the Dattātreya movement and its cult-centers, mention must also be made of P. N. Joshi, *Śrī-dattātreya-jñān-koś* (Bombay: Surekha Prakashan, 1974).

Devotion to Dattātreya cuts through the social and religious strata of Indian society: among his adepts one finds Brahmins, Muslims, untouchables, Mahānubhāvas, Yogins, thieves, philosophers, prostitutes, ascetics, and so forth. There appears to be no religious milieu, at least in Maharashtra, in which Dattātreya is not in some way or other involved. Through the study of this single *mūrti*, one is offered a rich fresco of Hindu religion as well as an appreciation of Marāṭhī integrative spirituality: precisely this richness and complexity of themes constitute Dattātreya's distinctive mark. Adopting a contextualized approach, this study is inevitably concerned with all primary religious dimensions: myth, doctrine, ritual, philosophy, mysticism, and iconography. Its aims are to provide the following: (1) an introductory yet comprehensive monograph of a rather neglected Hindu god (2) an analysis of the amalgam of religious motifs which have contributed to the molding of this exemplary Maharashtrian deity, and (3) a representative case, useful for comparative work with other Hindu gods.

In an attempt to present not the history of the Dattātreya icon but rather some of the crucial phases in the deity's unfolding, chapter 1 begins by offering a sketch of Dattātreya's genealogy and Purāṇic birth, focusing on the Vedic mythical antecedents of his "parents," Atri and Anasūyā, and "brothers," Soma and Durvāsas.

Chapter 2 treats the Epic and Purāṇic mythology of Dattātreya, his foremost legendary feats and their variants. Though subsequently identified as an Avatāra of Viṣṇu, Dattātreya first emerged in the *Mahābhārata* as a powerful Ṛṣi granting boons, notably a thousand arms to Arjuna Kārtavīrya. In Purāṇic literature, particularly in the *Mārkaṇḍeya Purāṇa*, he is depicted as a master of Yoga tinged with Tantrism, teaching his art to his pupil Alarka. These seminal Epic and Purāṇic themes, in which both heterodox and orthodox Brahminical discourses are discernable, determine Dattātreya's synthetic personality. Subsequent *sampradāyas* and religious literature will enlarge upon these narratives, recreating the basic myths in a variety of ways.

Chapter 3 is devoted to Dattātreya's place in late sectarian *Upaniṣads*—probably reflecting older traditions and beliefs—in which he is often mentioned in the role of Yoga teacher, identified as the archetypal Avadhūta or Paramahaṃsa ascetic. These *Upaniṣads* are important crossover texts bridging Yoga traditions as well as establishing the *Vaidika/Tāntrika* connection.

Chapter 4 describes Dattātreya's place in the literature of the thirteenth-century Yogic Mahānubhāva sect. Here is the first roughly datable testimony of the deity's presence in Maharashtrian religious life: Dattātreya is worshipped as one of the five manifestations (Pañca-Kṛṣṇas) of the supreme God, Parameśvara. The Mahānubhāvas probably adopted the deity through the influence of western Indian branches of Nātha Yogins. Besides presenting a reelaboration of Dattātreya's Purāṇic myths, Mahānubhāva texts show how the deity is associated with important *śakti-pīṭhas*, such as Mahur and Kolhāpur, also attesting to Dattātreya's link with Śaṅkara and his Daśanāmī order.

Chapter 5 illustrates the rise of the modern Marāṭhī Datta *sampradāya* from the two seminal figures, Śrīpāda Śrīvallabha (c. 1323–53) and Nṛsiṃha Sarasvatī (c. 1378–1458), the veritable founder of the sect. It describes the three principal sites connected with Nṛsiṃha Sarasvatī (Audumbar, Narsobāvāḍī, and Gāṇagāpūr) and their ritual activities, including the non-Brahminical practice of exorcism of the seemingly possessed. Sarasvatī Gaṅgādhar narrates the lives of both Śrīpāda Śrīvallabha and Nṛsiṃha Sarasvatī in the sixteenth-century work *Guru-caritra*, the sacred text of the *sampradāya*. Precisely in this period Dattātreya's triadic iconographic motif emerges. The main objective of Nṛsiṃha Sarasvatī was the awakening of Brahminical orthodoxy and the reinforcement of Vedic ritualism to counter Islamic dominance as well as Tantric excesses.

Chapter 6 focuses upon the unfolding of the Dattātreya movement while giving special attention to the biographies and hagiographies of two important figures: Eknāth (1533–99) and Dāsopant (1551–1615). Besides observing the synthesis of *Śaivism* and *Vaiṣṇavism* within the Dattātreya cult, one cannot fail to note the enduring link of the Datta movement with both Nāthism and Sufism.

Chapter 7 analyzes the *Tripurā-rahasya*, which presents Dattātreya as the teacher of *Śākta* nondualism to his disciple Paraśurāma thus showing the deity's connection with Devī worship. Dattātreya's *upadeśa* is conveyed through the narration of some delightful tales, favorites of the Vedānta mystic Ramaṇa Maharṣi (1879–1950).

Chapter 8 examines the *Avadhūta-gītā*, an important work of Nātha inspiration which confirms Dattātreya's role as the archetypal Guru and Avadhūta. The core of the *Avadhūta-gītā*'s *upadeśa* rests upon the attainment of *sama-rasya*, a condition of natural spontaneity and equanimity, true mark of the liberated soul.

Chapter 9 traces the various stages in the development of Dattātreya's iconography, from its first *ekmukhī* characterization to its modern trifacial, six-armed form, in which Dattātreya is accompanied by four dogs, said to represent the four Vedas, and by a cow, identified as Kāmadhenu and believed to symbolize Mother Earth. The immediate, comprehensive *darśana* of the deity best conveys the fusion of *Vaiṣṇava* and *Śaiva* motifs in Dattātreya's worship.

The conclusion highlights the contemporary vitality of Dattātreya's cult which is evidenced not only by the ongoing relevance of pilgrimage sites such as Gāṇagāpūr in northern Karnataka and other major shrines but also by the activities of saintly figures and religious groups such as the Sāī Bābā movement and the Marāṭhī Navnāth *sampradāya*. An examination of Dattātreya's encounter with the West through the missionary zeal of Śrī Purohit Svāmin, coupled with an appraisal of Dattātreya's "hidden presence" in the poetry of William Butler Yeats (1865–1939) and T. S. Eliot (1888–1965), closes the study.

Acknowledgments

This book grew from its original dissertation format, discussed at the Religious Studies Department of the University of California, Santa Barbara, in September 1994. My deep appreciation goes to my committee, composed of Gerald James Larson, Ninian Smart, and Barbara Holdrege, who, with their vast knowledge and wisdom, criticisms, and suggestions, patiently guided me throughout my research. My thanks also go to the personnel of the library of the University of California, Santa Barbara.

In the United States, I further wish to thank Philip Lutgendorf of the University of Iowa and William Powell of the University of California, Santa Barbara, for their valuable advice, as well as my former colleagues and friends in the graduate program at Santa Barbara: Corinne Boyle, Jeffrey Brodd, Ann Dion, Steve Heim, Knut Jacobsen, Kimberly Labor, Ramdas Lamb, Richard Merkel, Tracy Pintchman, Stefano Predelli, Cybelle Shattuck, Kerry Skora, and Brian Wilson.

I thank all those who assisted me during my sojourn and field-research in India during autumn 1991, and in general, all Dattātreya devotees, who taught me about their *iṣṭa-devatā* and the lives of Datta Avatāras. In particular, the Agravāl family for once again offering me hospitality in Bombay and generously providing me with transportation and all necessities. Special gratitude goes to my guide, Kṛṣṇa Bāpūrāo Deśmukh of Khāmgāon, who accompanied me to various sanctuaries and pilgrimage places, among them, Solāpur, Gāṇagāpūr, Paṇḍharpur, and Tuḷjāpūr. For my research in Andhra Pradesh, thanks go to the nuns and priests of the Social Service Center of Vijayavādā, the Satya Sāī Bābā Puttaparthi Saṃsthān, and Count Gianandrea Gropplero of Troppenburg.

It is a pleasure to acknowledge the many suggestions received from a host of scholars in Italy: Giuliano Boccali, Gian Giuseppe Filippi (who provided valuable iconographic material), Franco Michelini-Tocci, Antonio Rigo, Giovanni Torcinovich, and Stefano Zacchetti, all of the University of Venice; Enrico Fasana of the University of Trieste; Alberto Pelissero, Stefano Piano, and Mario Piantelli of the University of Turin. I also wish to thank my friend Ivano Battain for his help in the preparation of the photographs in this volume.

An earlier version of the first chapter of this book, "The Genealogy of Dattātreya," was published in 1993 in the *Annali di Ca' Foscari*, 32, no. 3, of the University of Venice.

During a seminar on Dattātreya held in the winter of 1995 as well as on many other occasions, various students of the University of Venice proved helpful and supportive, stimulating my own interest with their questions. In particular, I'd like to mention Sonia Calza, Monia Marchetto, Valentina Moretti, Gianni Pellegrini, Corrado Puchetti, and Claudia Ramasso.

At the Giorgio Cini Foundation of Venice, thanks go to Ernesto Talentino, Alfredo Cadonna, and the secretary of the Institute *Venezia e l'Oriente*, Carla Bonò.

I especially wish to express deep thanks to the State University of New York Press and its former director, William D. Eastman, for his constant encouragement and support.

Finally, personal thanks to my beloved Emanuela Botta, who always inspired me along the way, and to my dear parents, Eleutherios and Sally Rigopoulos, for their wholehearted support as well as for my mother's refined editing skills.

All these splendid individuals deserve whatever merit may accrue from this book. However, they are exempted of any consequences resulting from its defects; those are mine alone.

A. R.
Venice, Italy

1

The Genealogy of Dattātreya

In this introductory chapter, as a first tessera of Dattātreya's complex mosaic, the focus is on the principal myths concerning the deity's father, mother, and two brothers as well as on the circumstances attending Dattātreya's birth.[1] The rich fresco of Dattātreya's background helps us to situate the deity within his appropriate mythical and religious context. The main legendary themes from which these figures emerged set the scene for the unfolding of Dattātreya's icon in the following chapters. Whatever foreshadowings of Dattātreya appear in the Epics, it is only in the *Purāṇas* that his mythical characterization arises. In these vast encyclopedic collections of post-Vedic religion, Dattātreya does not materialize out of thin air but is born within a family and is part of a lineage. The *Purāṇas* inform us that Dattātreya was born to Anasūyā and the Ṛṣi Atri, her husband,[2] as a fragment of Viṣṇu or as the Viṣṇu portion of the *trimūrti,* when Brahmā, Viṣṇu, and Śiva consented to be born as three sons, known as Soma, Dattātreya, and Durvāsas, from the womb of Anasūyā.[3]

Let us first consider the figure of Atri, Dattātreya's "father." Throughout the Epics and *Purāṇas,* he as well as all Ṛṣis is revered as a mind-born son of Brahmā the Creator or as one of the ten Prajāpatis, the lords of creation. Moreover, the common refrain in Vedic, Epic, and Purānic texts is that Ṛṣis are born from fire. Consider the example of *Bṛhaddevatā* 5.97–103, recounting the birth of Atri as well as that of Aṅgiras and Bhṛgu. We are told that once the goddess Vāc appeared to Ka and Prajāpati as they were sacrificing. At her sight they became excited and spilled their semen, which was scattered into the fire by the wind-god Vāyu. From the coals Aṅgiras was born and from the flames Bhṛgu. Vāc then insisted on having a third son and this was Atri. Another version of this myth is found in *Nirukta* 3.17. Here, Prajāpati sacrifices his seed into the fire. From the flames Bhṛgu is born and Aṅgiras rises from live coals. Then the two just born say: "Seek the third in this very place." Thus, Atri is found. From this story, the *Nirukta* offers the rather puzzling etymology of Atri as meaning "not three." However, Atri almost surely designates a devourer, being derived from the verbal root *ad,* to eat, to devour. *Atrin,* a cognate of Atri, is an adjective frequently used to describe demons in the *Ṛg Veda*. The term *atri* itself is once used (*Ṛg Veda* 2.85) as an attribute of Agni, probably meaning "devourer." This suggests that Atri may have originally represented some form of Agni.

In Vedic literature the classic list of the seven Ṛṣis, believed to dwell in the northern region of the Indian subcontinent, comprises Viśvāmitra, Jamadagni, Bharadvāja, Gotama, Atri, Vasiṣṭha, and Kaśyapa.[4] The number may have been suggested by that of the seven priests reported in *Ṛg Veda* 2.1.2. *Śatapatha Brāhmaṇa* 2.1.2.4 associates the Ṛṣis to the seven stars in the constellation of Ursa Major and states that they were originally bears. Such identification is partly due to the equal number in the two cases and also because of the similarity of sound between *ṛṣi* and *ṛkṣa,* which in the *Ṛg Veda* means both star (1.24.10) and bear (5.56.3). Atri, the fifth Ṛṣi in the Vedic list of seers, is identified with Alioth (epsilon Ursae Majoris), the only "unpaired" star of the Great Bear. The other six are latitudinally divided in three pairs: Dubhe (alpha) and Merak (beta) identify Viśvāmitra and Jamadagni, Phekda (gamma) and Megrez (delta) identify Bharadvāja and Gotama, Mizar (zeta) and Alkaid (eta) identify Vasiṣṭha and Kaśyapa. Thus, Atri figures as the "loner" or "born alone."[5] On a human, microcosmic level, Atri, as an "eater" (*atti*), is said to correspond to the mouth or voice (*vāc*), whereas the other six Ṛṣis or "three twins" are said to correspond to the *prāṇas*.[6]

In later Epic and early Purāṇic literature, a second list of the seven Ṛṣis, now believed to dwell chiefly in the southern region of India, came to supersede the first. The reasons for this change can be traced to influences exerted by members of particular Brahmin *gotras* from southern regions, particularly the region of the western Deccan during the rule of the Sātavāhanas[7] and their successors. This second list comprises Aṅgiras, Atri, Vasiṣṭha, Marīci, Pulastya, Pulaha, and Kratu.[8] Atri and Vasiṣṭha are the only Ṛṣis who appear in both of the main lists. Their *gotras* are also listed independently from all others.

In Vedic mythology Atri is a Maharṣi author of many hymns, composed especially in praise of Agni, Indra, the Aśvins, and the Viśvadevas.[9] Atri is one of the seers most frequently mentioned in the *Ṛg Veda,* and its fifth *maṇḍala* is attributed to the family of the Atris. Atri is spoken of as a Ṛṣi belonging to the five tribes (*Ṛg Veda* 1.117.3), and he is mentioned along with Manu[10] and other ancestors of the human race (1.39.9). Agni is said to have helped Atri (7.15.5). Indra, having heard Atri's prayer (8.36.7), also helped him by opening the cowstall for him and the Aṅgirases[11] (1.51.3). A characteristic myth about Atri in the *Ṛg Veda* is connected with the Aśvins, his chief protectors. They deliver Atri from darkness (6.50.10, 7.71.5), rescuing him out of a burning chasm with all his host (1.116.8, 1.117.3). The Aśvins made the burning chasm agreeable for him (1.112.7, 8.62.7, 10.39.9) and prevent fire from burning him (8.62.8). They rescue Atri who is in the heat (10.80.3) and protect him from the heat with coolness (1.119.6; 8.62.3). Once they are said to have rejuvenated Atri (10.143.1–2).

The most important episode about Atri in Vedic mythology, subsequently taken up in the Epics and *Purāṇas*, is the one in which he found and replaced the sun when it was afflicted by the demon of eclipses, Svarbhānu:[12]

> The demon Svarbhānu struck the sun with darkness; Indra destroyed him, and Atri found the hidden sun, Atri placed the eye of the sun in the sky.[13]

Other Vedic versions similarly relate that Atri replaced the sun in the sky and repelled the darkness by his speech.[14] Since Atri restored light to the worlds, the Ātreyas are supposed to officiate at sacrifices and to receive the first sacrificial salary, before members of other exogamous clans (*gotras*).[15] The basic transformation which the Ṛṣi brings about in his performance of asceticism and *tapas* is the production of heat in the body. The "fire" of his *tapas* is such that he is thought to be transmuted into fire (Agni) itself, burning the worlds and illuminating them with his body. Consequently, one of the powers acquired by the Ṛṣis was to bring light to the world, taking the place of either the sun or the moon. In this connection, Atri may be viewed as a manifestation of Agni, personification of the sacrificial fire who carries the offerings to the deities of the celestial realms.[16]

Later versions in the *Purāṇas* also relate Atri's rescue of the sun, adding that Atri himself spread brilliance and that he stopped the sun from falling by uttering the words "may all be well with you" (*svasti te'stu*).[17] As it is typical of Ṛṣis in Purāṇic literature, the savior-figure Atri achieves his goal through powerful speech. In other accounts, Atri himself took the place of the sun, becoming the sun itself. The *Mahābhārata* relates that Atri is he who, when the sun was destroyed, ascended upwards.[18] One passage relates that he became both the sun and the moon:

> Svarbhānu pierced the sun and moon with arrows, whereupon the gods were engulfed in darkness and began to be struck down by the demons. They caught sight of Atri performing *tapas* in a

wood, and asked him to help them; Atri asked how he could protect them, and they replied: "Become for us the moon, the destroyer of darkness, and the sun, the destroyer of demons." Thereupon Atri created light through his *tapas*, and made the worlds bright and without darkness; he overcame hosts of the gods' enemies through his own *tejas*,[19] and the gods saw that the demons were being burnt by Atri.[20]

Further versions say that, due to the length and power of his asceticism, Atri's body became as brilliant as the moon: his lustre spread over the sky and flooded the worlds with light whence ten goddesses conceived and gave birth to Soma.[21] It is also reported that through his *tapas* the moon flooded forth from his eyes and illumined the universe with its luster.[22] In these latter accounts, Atri's connection with the moon is probably derived from his role as the father of Soma, *soma* being another name for the moon.

In the *Mahābhārata*, Atri is said to have gone to Videha to instruct King Nimi on the performance of the *śrāddha* rites.[23] On another occasion, Atri went to King Vainya to gain wealth to distribute to his sons and servants before retiring to the forest. He praised the king as the foremost of all sovereigns. But the Ṛṣi Gautama objected, saying that such an honor was reserved only for Indra. The dispute was finally resolved in Atri's favour by Sanatkumāra.[24] Ṛṣis are often depicted as being the recipients of gifts from kings. In *Bṛhaddevatā* 5.28–36, we read of how Atri received 10,320 cows and a golden wagon with two oxen from King Tryaruṇa Aikṣvāka, 100 oxen from King Aśvamedha, and much wealth from King Trasadasyu.

In the *Rāmāyaṇa*, when Rāma, with Lakṣmaṇa and Sītā, leaves Ayodhyā, he is offered hospitality at the hermitage of Atri and Anasūyā on the Citrakūṭa mountain. Here Rāma learns how in olden times, through her *tapas*, Anasūyā caused the river Gaṅgā to flow past their hermitage during a hundred-year drought.[25] In some *Purāṇas*, Atri's *āśrama* is located in the Himalayas near the source of the river Airāvatī. The seer is depicted as a strict vegetarian: even the animals around his hermitage are vegetarian and tame, due to the Ṛṣi's influence.[26] The *Matsya Purāṇa*, narrating the journey of the Brahmin Purūravas,[27] describes Atri's hermitage thus:

> On that mountain there is a charming hermitage where all desires are granted and whose trees drop fruit fit for the chief of gods. That supreme hermitage, where black bees are always buzzing, encircles the mountain like a necklace. Visited by the

wives of the gods, it destroys all sins. There, heaps of snow, shining like the orb of the moon, are piled up here and there by playful monkeys. The hermitage is surrounded on all sides by valleys filled with snow and rocky caves always hidden from mankind.

After worshipping Bhava, the mighty King Purūravas, lord of Madra, reached the hermitage. . . . Adorned with hundreds of beautiful flowers, radiant, brilliant, conferring bliss, it was built by the sage Atri himself.[28]

Atri is also said to have performed *tapas* for obtaining a son in various locales: on mount Ṛkṣakula, on the banks of the river Nirvindhyā, on the banks of the river Narmadā, and in the Kāmada forest in the south, by the Citrakūṭa mountain. Ātreyas are said to be peoples of northern countries.[29]

In the list of Śiva's thousand names—taken from the *Anuśāsana Parvan* of the *Mahābhārata* (13.17.31–153)—the seventy-first praises the god as "the adorer of Atri's wife" (*atryā namaskartā*). Swami Chidbhavananda renders the verse thus:

> Adoration to Him who paid homage to Anasūyā the wife of Atri for begetting two illustrious sons, Dattātreya and Durvāsas.[30]

Atri's wife Anasūyā (literally "the nonenvious one")[31] is identified either as a daughter of Dakṣa and Prasūti or of Kardama and Devahūti.[32] In the Epics and *Purāṇas*, Anasūyā is celebrated as a model of virtue and chastity, the ideal wife. Through her chastity she stores up great power and performs exceptional feats. In the *Mahābhārata* we read of how Anasūyā once abandoned Atri in a fit of anger, and, after a *tapas* of fasting and sleeping on wooden boards for three hundred years, she obtained from Śiva the boon of having a son without sexual intercourse with her husband.[33] The *Rāmāyaṇa*, after narrating how Anasūyā, through the power of her *tapas*, caused the Gaṅgā to flow past their hermitage in the Citrakūṭa mountain, also reports that she once made "ten nights one" in order to help a female friend who had been cursed that she would become a widow the next day. "Morrow shall not be," said Anasūyā, and she extinguished the curse by making ten nights one.[34] The sixteenth chapter of the *Mārkaṇḍeya Purāṇa* takes up this episode in its presentation of the birth of Soma, Dattātreya, and Durvāsas. Here, Anasūyā has the opposite function of helping to restore the light of the sun. The story is worth recounting in brief.[35]

In ancient times there lived in Pratiṣṭhāna a Brahmin named Kauśika, a leper who was prone to all sorts of vices. He had a chaste and pious wife, identified with Śāṇḍilī by tradition,[36] who was devoted to him in spite of his bad character. Kauśika was attached to a prostitute in the town and spent most of his time in her company, without caring for Śāṇḍilī. The day came when Kauśika had no money and was rejected by the prostitute. Śāṇḍilī received him warmly at home and took great care of him. One day, however, Kauśika ordered his wife to lead him back to the other woman. Obediently, Śāṇḍilī took Kauśika on her shoulders and started for the prostitute's house in the dark. Along the way they found sage Māṇḍavya, who had been impaled on a pointed pole *(śūla)* by the guards of the ruling king, having been wrongly accused of theft.[37] On account of his Yogic powers, he was still hanging there alive. Kauśika, afraid of thieves in the darkness, pushed away Māṇḍavya, impaled on the stake, causing him to curse that Kauśika would die at sunrise.[38] On hearing this, Śāṇḍilī was shocked. She sent a touching appeal to the sun not to rise at all, so that her husband would not die. The sun complied with the wish of this chaste woman and the activities of the world stopped. Thus the gods in heaven did not get their share of oblations as sacrifices were not performed by the people. The entire cycle of sacrifices, rain, grain, and so forth came to a standstill, and there was chaos in the whole universe.[39] The gods then went to Brahmā who directed them to propitiate Anasūyā, a chaste woman who was performing a great penance with her husband Atri. Brahmā said:

> Majesty is subdued by majesty indeed, and austerities also by austerities, O ye immortals! . . . Hence do ye, through desire that the sun should rise, propitiate Atri's faithful wife Anasūyā who is rich in austerities.[40]

Accordingly, all gods with Brahmā, Viṣṇu, and Śiva went to the hermitage of Atri and Anasūyā and requested Anasūyā to help them.[41] The kind-hearted Anasūyā showed her readiness to accompany them. She met with Śāṇḍilī and a pleasant conversation began between the two on the theme of a wife's devotion to her husband. Anasūyā explained how, for Śāṇḍilī's sake alone, the entire universe was in peril. Śāṇḍilī agreed to reconsider the problem. Anasūyā promised that her husband would have a new life, free of leprosy and all evils. Thus Śāṇḍilī cheered the world with the light of the sun, while Anasūyā preserved the life of Śāṇḍilī's husband by her power of chastity. The gods, grateful for Anasūyā's services, offered her a boon. She then asked that the *trimūrti* of Brahmā, Viṣṇu, and Śiva be born to her, and that she and her husband be exempted from *saṃsāra*. The gods granted the boon and departed.

Time went by, and one day Atri mentally enjoyed Anasūyā, seductive and perfect in form, who had just bathed after her menstruation.[42] A powerful wind brought the change that was produced in her, the effect of Atri's mental impregnation.[43] Soma, characterized by passion and also known as Candra, was born as a portion of Brahmā; Dattātreya, the Brahmin in whom goodness predominated, as Viṣṇu incarnated; and Durvāsas, in whom darkness prevailed, as a portion of Śiva. Thus the three deities took their births and fulfilled the promise made to Anasūyā.[44] It is said that Durvāsas issued from his mother's womb prematurely, just seven days after conception, from rage on seeing that the king of the Haihayas was offending Atri: in his anger, he wanted to burn up the king.[45] Afterward, Soma ascended to heaven, and Durvāsas, practising the vow of "madness" (*unmatta*),[46] left his mother and father and wandered the world. Dattātreya, depicted as the benefactor of the docile, protected offspring from destruction by the malignant Daityas. Identified as a lordly Yogin who nevertheless enjoyed sense-objects, Dattātreya, wishing to be without attachments, immersed himself in a lake for innumerable years.[47]

In other Purāṇic versions we are told of how, when Atri and Anasūyā sought to obtain a son through *tapas*, the *trimūrti*, pleased with their asceticism, agreed to become their sons.[48] The story of how the *trimūrti* tested Anasūyā's chastity in Atri's absence, requesting that she serve them food while naked, is very popular though not found in the main *Purāṇas*. First, Anasūyā sprinkled some water over her guests, transforming them into three babies. Then, she willingly took off her clothes and started breast feeding them. Thus through the power of her perfect purity she succeeded in complying with the gods' wish. Informed by sage Nārada of their husbands' whereabouts, the three goddesses Sarasvatī, Lakṣmī, and Pārvatī came to Atri's hermitage requesting that the Ṛṣi's wife restore their husbands to their original forms. The chaste wife of Atri consented, and the gods invited the divine couple to ask for a boon. Atri and Anasūyā expressed the desire that the *trimūrti* itself be born to them as their children, and thus it was that Soma, Datta, and Durvāsas were incarnated.

In a later form of the myth, however, Anasūyā, in a fit of anger after they raped her, cursed Brahmā, Viṣṇu, and Śiva to become her sons and to be worshipped as head, feet, and *liṅga*. In this way Anasūyā was able to avert a potentially dangerous hierogamy by transforming it into a sexless maternal relationship.[49] Once again we find the belief that only through single-minded devotion to asceticism may the greatest creative potency and power be obtained.

Now for some astrological interpretations of Dattātreya and his "family."[50] In his work *The Orion; or, Researches into the Antiquity of the Vedas* (1893), Bāl Gaṅgādhar Ṭiḷak—upholding the idea that in Vedic times the vernal equinox was in the constellation of Orion—supports an astrological understanding according to which the *trimūrti* would be represented by the three stars (*tristri*) of Orion. Mṛga-śiras is the fifth lunar mansion (*nakṣatra*)[51] and contains three stars—lambda, phi^1, and phi^2 Orionis—also known as Orion's head. Ṭiḷak observes:

> Later writers describe this trinity as represented by the three-headed Dattātreya, followed by the Vedas in the form of dogs . . . I think we can have no difficulty in identifying this personified Trinity with Orion having three stars in the head and closely followed by the dog (Canis) at its foot.[52]

This is an allusion to Dattātreya's modern iconography, in which the deity bears the three heads of Brahmā, Viṣṇu, and Śiva and is surrounded by four dogs—the four brightest stars of the constellation of Canis Major—representing the four *Vedas* (note that the deity, in modern iconography, is also usually accompanied by a cow representing Mother Earth). It's highly probable that devotees also came to identify Dattātreya's three heads with Orion's belt, also known as "the arrow": delta Orionis (Mintaka), epsilon Orionis (Alnilam), zeta Orionis (Alnitak).[53] The middle star of the belt, that is, epsilon Orionis, would then certainly have identified Viṣṇu, Dattātreya's core identity: a supergiant about 1,600 light-years away from us, it is forty thousand times more luminous than the sun.

The story of Dattātreya's birth presents some analogies with one of the tales about the birth of the giant Orion, the wild hunter celebrated in Greek mythology and later identified with the sky asterism.[54] According to *Apollodorus Mythographus* 1.4.3, the three gods Zeus, Poseidon, and Hermes came one day under disguise to the house of Irieus or Enopion, who was then old and childless.[55] Being pleased with him and his hospitality, the gods decided to grant him a boon. The man wished to have a child, despite his age. The gods then placed their semen inside the skin of a sacrificed bull, telling the man to bury it in the earth. From this powerful amalgam with Mother Earth, Orion was born nine or ten months later as a giant springing out from the ground. Despite the obvious differences and the absence of any links between the mythologies of Orion and Dattātreya, it is perhaps not superfluous to note how in this story Orion, like Dattātreya, is the exceptional offspring—not begotten through natural human intercourse—of a boon granted by a divine triad to an old, childless, and devout man.

The interpretation of "later writers" to which Ṭiḷak refers probably antedates a more elaborate one concerning Atri, Anasūyā, and the birth of Soma, Datta, and Durvāsas reported by Hariprasad Shivprasad Joshi:

> The myth of Dattātreya is possibly based on the peculiar position of three constellations, that is, Mṛga, Ārdrā, and Punarvasu. The Mṛga star represents a cradle with three babes, Ārdrā literally means a gem, Anasūyā, while Punarvasu means a house or hermitage. Sirius, the brightest star in front of Orion or Mṛga, is Atri. Just near Orion we have Canis Major consisting of four stars, which represent the four dogs symbolizing the four Vedas, and the cow is possibly evolved out of Lupus. It is also possible that these dogs represent the four largest planets with their moons, since instances have been known of these planets having been discerned with the naked eye.[56]

This interpretation, fascinating as it may be, is certainly not to be viewed as the original basis for the Dattātreya myth. Rather, it demonstrates the vitality of the myth itself, which in the course of centuries has given rise to various interpretations, including this astrological reading. As noted above, Mṛga is the fifth lunar mansion and contains three stars: lambda, phi^1, and phi^2 Orionis. Ārdrā is the sixth lunar mansion, containing the star alfa Orionis (Betelgeuse), tenth in the list of the most luminous stars. Punarvasu is the seventh lunar mansion, containing the stars alfa and beta Geminorum (Castor and Pollux). The cradle with the *trimūrti* is represented by lambda, phi^1, and phi^2 Orionis. Of these three stars, lambda Orionis, also known as Heka, is the most luminous, being nine thousand times brighter than the sun. Most probably, devotees identify lambda Orionis with Datta, whereas the smaller stars phi^1 and phi^2 are thought to represent the newborn Soma and Durvāsas. Of course, another possibility is that by the expression "the Mṛga star" (i.e., Orion), Joshi refers not to the three stars of the constellation according to traditional Hindu astrology, but rather to the three stars of Orion's belt, which thus correspond to the three "brothers" Soma, Datta, and Durvāsas.

Ārdrā, identified with Anasūyā, is said to mean a gem, probably because of the brilliance of alfa Orionis. On the other hand, Sirius (alfa

Canis Majoris) is the brightest star in the sky. Significantly, the luminosity of alfa Orionis which equals Anasūyā is matched with that of Sirius which equals Atri.[57] Punarvasu is said to mean the abode of Atri and Anasūyā, perhaps because of the rectangular shape of Gemini's constellation. Canis Major is not, as Joshi reports, a small constellation consisting of only four stars. Sirius aside, the four most luminous stars possibly representing Datta's dogs are beta (Mirzam), gamma (Muliphein), delta (Wezen), and epsilon Canis Majoris (Adhara). It should be noted that *Lupus* is probably a misprint for *Lepus*, the name of the small constellation of the Hare situated just below Orion. The cow would thus be symbolized by alfa (Arneb) or beta Leporis (Nihal).

The mythological origins of Dattātreya's "brother" Soma—in Purāṇic accounts usually revered as a form of Brahmā—are identified with the *soma* sacrifice, the ritual preparation and drinking of the juice of an hallucinogenic climbing plant (Asclepias acida), main element of the Ṛg Vedic liturgy.[58] All the 114 hymns of the ninth book, besides 6 in other books, are dedicated to the praise of the *soma* plant, thought to be the nectar of happiness, long life (*āyus*), and immortality (*amṛta*). It is also celebrated in portions of 4 or 5 other hymns, and as a dual divinity with Indra, Agni, Pūṣan, and Rudra,[59] in about 6 other hymns. The name of *soma*, in its simple form and in compounds, occurs hundreds of times in the *Ṛg Veda*. Judged by the standard of frequency, the deified Soma is, after Indra and Varuṇa,[60] third in order of importance among the Vedic gods: he is primeval, all-powerful, healer of all diseases, bestower of riches, lord of other gods, and identified with the supreme being. Soma is the support of the three worlds, all sacrifices being rooted in him. In post-Vedic literature, Soma is a name for the moon (*candra*), poetically regarded as being "drunk up" by the gods, thus waning until it is filled up again by the sun (*sūrya*). In *Chāndogya Upaniṣad* 5.10.4 it is stated that the moon is king Soma, the food of the gods, and is drunk up by them. Even in the *Brāhmaṇas* the identification of Soma with the moon is commonplace. Clearly the qualities of the *soma* juice are transferred to the moon, which is revered as *oṣadhi-pati*, lord of herbs, and as the guardian of sacrifices, stars, and healing plants.

Though the early Epic does not connect Soma to Atri the following lineage of the lunar race came to be established: Brahmā, Atri, Soma, Budha, Purūravas, Āyu.[61] The *Harivaṃśa*[62] clearly relates Soma to Atri, declaring that Soma the *rājarāj* was son of Atri, born of his tears, and Atri was his *hotṛ*. Similarly, *Matsya Purāṇa* 23.1–10 narrates that once Brahmā told Atri to create, and Atri performed great *tapas* for creation. Thus a great bliss entered his eyes, in which Śiva dwelled together with his consort. Tears flowed down from Atri's eyes, flooding the universe with light. The ten quarters of the sky, taking the form of a woman, received that embryo in their belly. After three hundred years they released it, and Brahmā made it into a youth, Soma. Wendy Doniger O'Flaherty comments: "The tears, a seed substitute, are ultimately transformed back into Soma, the Upaniṣadic source of all seed."[63]

In the *Mahābhārata* and the *Rāmāyaṇa*, the moon god Soma is less important than his rival luminary the sun, though he is supposed to be higher in space, larger, and better endowed with rays (*aṅśu*). He belongs to a lower class of deities, for Soma is one of the group of the eight Vasus, three of whom, moon, wind, and fire, are retained in the Epic list.[64] The moon in both the Epics is celebrated by its natural characteristics, as a delighter of eyes and heart. *Mahābhārata* tradition identifies the twenty-seven *nakṣatras*, Dakṣa's mythical daughters representing the lunar mansions, as Soma's wives. Soma, however, paid such attention to the fourth, the beautiful Rohiṇī,[65] that the others became jealous and appealed to their father. Dakṣa's intervention was fruitless, and he cursed his son-in-law who remained childless and ill with consumption. This moved his wives to pity, and they interceded with their father. Even though Dakṣa could not cancel his curse, he modified it so that Soma's decay would be periodical, not permanent. Hence the waxing and waning of the moon.

Another myth narrates how Soma performed the *rāja-sūya*, thus becoming so arrogant and licentious that he carried off Tārā, the wife of Bṛhaspati, and refused to give her up even at the command of Brahmā: this gave rise to a wide-spread quarrel (*tārakā-maya*).[66] The sage Uśanas, out of enmity to Bṛhaspati, sided with Soma, and he was supported by the Dānavas, the Daityas, and other foes of the Devas.[67] Indra and the gods in general sided with Bṛhaspati. A fierce battle ensued and the earth was shaken to its center. Soma had his body cut in two by Śiva's *triśūla*, and hence he is also known as Bhagnātma (broken-bodied). Brahmā finally stopped the fight, compelling Soma to restore Tārā to her husband. The result of this intrigue was the birth of a child, whom Tārā, after great persuasion, declared to be the son of Soma, and to whom the name Budha was given: from him originated the lunar race.[68]

In Purāṇic mythology Soma is commonly called the son of the Ṛṣi Atri and his wife Anasūyā, but not all authorities agree. One calls him son of Dharma,[69] another attributes paternity to sage Prabhākara, of Atri's race. Soma is also said to have been produced at the churning of the ocean in another *manvantara*. According to the

Purāṇas, Soma's vehicle is a three-wheeled chariot drawn by ten horses as white as snow.

Durvāsas, Dattātreya's second "brother," is an extraordinary figure who deserves his own book. Prototype of the wild, antinomian ascetic, he was born from Śiva's anger and is believed to be the manifestation of the furious, ferocious aspect of Maheśvara. Among the various stories of his birth,[70] all of which present him as an emanation or part (*aṁśa*) of Śiva, the one in the *Brahmāṇḍa Purāṇa* deserves notice. During a quarrel between Brahmā and Śiva, Śiva's appearance became so frightening that the gods fled in terror. Pārvatī,[71] his wife, also intimidated by him, cried, "It has become impossible for me to live with you!" (*durvāsaṃ bhavati me*). Śiva then realized that his anger was the cause of useless suffering and deposited it in the belly of Anasūyā, from whom the sage Durvāsas was born.[72]

The 278th epithet of Śiva's thousand names honors the great god as "the one clothed in rough skin" (*durvāsaḥ*), and Swami Chidbhavananda comments: "Durvāsas is the angry element in Nature."[73] The *Mahābhārata* portrays Durvāsas as a disagreeable guest, a bald ascetic of ferocious temper. He is universally noted for his irascible temper and many fall under his curse.[74] For instance, he cursed Śakuntalā for keeping him waiting at the door, thus causing her separation from King Duṣyanta.[75] However, Durvāsas also bestowed blessings from time to time.[76] In a famous episode in the *Mahābhārata*, he blessed Kuntī by giving her a *mantra*, so that she became a mother by the sun.[77] In the same Epic, Kṛṣṇa himself offers a vivid description of Durvāsas:

> [Formerly] I put up in my house the Brahmin Durvāsas, who was green and tawny, clad in rags *(cīravāsāḥ)*, who had a stick of *Bilva (Aegle marmelos)*, a long beard; he was emaciated, taller than the tallest man; he wandered over all the celestial and human worlds, singing this verse at congregations and in public squares:
>
> "Who would invite the Brahmin Durvāsas to dwell in his house? He becomes enraged with everyone even at the slightest transgression; he that would give me shelter should not anger me."
>
> As no one took notice of him, I invited him. Sometimes he would eat food sufficient for many thousands of persons, sometimes very little, and [sometimes] he would not return home; he would laugh and weep without any visible reason;[78] no one at that time was equal to him in years; [one day] he burnt all the

> beds and coverlets and all the well-adorned damsels, and then went out; then he asked for rice-milk (*pāyasa*); having previously caused every kind of food and drink to be kept ready, I had hot rice-milk be brought; having eaten some, he ordered me to smear my limbs with the remnant, which I did; then he smeared Rukmiṇī,[79] and had her yoked to a chariot. Ascending that chariot, he set out of my house striking her with the hook, and proceeded along the high road. . . . As Rukmiṇī tottered, he struck her [with the whip]; then he leapt down from the chariot and fled towards the south on foot, followed by us. Then he became gratified because I had subdued my anger, and said:
>
> "As long as gods and men continue to entertain a liking for food, so long will everyone cherish the same liking for thee; so long as there will be righteous [men] (*puṇyāḥ*) in the worlds, so long will thy fame last; agreeable thou shalt be to all persons; whatever articles of thine have been broken or burnt or destroyed, thou shalt see restored or even better; thou wilt have no fear of death through such parts of thy body as have been smeared [with the rice-milk]; thou ought to have smeared also the soles of thy feet."[80]

On another occasion Kṛṣṇa is said to have entertained him hospitably, though omitting to wipe the fragments of food from the sage's foot. At this Durvāsas grew angry and foretold Kṛṣṇa's death.[81]

The most popular myth relates Kṛṣṇa's death to a curse which Durvāsas pronounced against the whole of the Yādava clan.[82] During a religious festival, the young men decided to play a trick on the sage. They dressed a young boy as a girl, and tied an iron pot on his belly to make him look pregnant. They took him to Durvāsas and asked if he could tell them the sex of the future child. But the clairvoyant seer immediately realized their mischief, lost his temper, and cursed them all saying that whatever came forth from that "pregnancy" would utterly ruin all the Yādavas. The frightened youths rushed to Kṛṣṇa to ask for advice. He told them to destroy the pot, so that not even a tiny piece remained. Inadvertently, they failed to destroy a very small piece; this they tossed into the sea. It was swallowed by a fish, later caught by a hunter called Jaras, meaning "old age." Having found the piece of iron when slitting the fish open, the hunter decided to use it as an arrowhead. Where the iron filings fell, there grew a thick cluster of hard canes. Some time later, the Yādava youths came to this very spot, drunk and riotous. A quarrel broke out, soon turning into a murderous fight. Some of them tore up the canes and used them as weapons, others beat and strangled each other: not one walked away alive from that place of slaughter. In the fight, Pradyumna, Kṛṣṇa's beloved son, and Balarāma,[83] Kṛṣṇa's brother, were both killed. In deep sorrow, Kṛṣṇa wandered off to the forest and lay down in a thicket to rest, keeping his foot on his knee. The hunter who had caught the fish saw Kṛṣṇa's foot and mistook it for a deer. He shot an arrow that pierced Kṛṣṇa's heel, his only vulnerable point. The poison coursed through Kṛṣṇa's veins, and he died after forgiving the hunter. The arrowhead had been made from the piece of iron the hunter had retrieved from the fish's belly. Thus, all the Yādavas perished and Durvāsas' curse was fulfilled.

Commonly portrayed as a devout *Śaiva* in the *Purāṇas*, Durvāsas is particularly associated with the *Śaiva Āgamas*.[84] According to the *Harivaṃśa*, Kṛṣṇa himself was taught the sixty-four nondual *Āgamas* by Durvāsas, who is the revealer of them in this *kali* age.[85] The *Śaiva Siddhānta* venerates Durvāsas and identifies him with Āmardaka, although he sometimes figures as his predecessor.[86] According to Somānanda, historical founder of the *Pratyabhijñā* school of Kashmiri *Śaivism*, Durvāsas was the father of Tryambaka, the first Guru within the mythic *sampradāya* of "the doctrine of recognition."[87] It is said that Tryambaka received the teachings of *Śaiva* nondualism from Durvāsas, who in turn had learnt them on Mount Kailāsa from Śrīkaṇṭha, a form of Śiva.[88] Tryambaka appears in other accounts relative to the origins of Kashmiri *Śaivism*. According to these accounts, Durvāsas was instructed by Śrīkaṇṭha so that he might spread the wisdom of *Trika*, the essence of all *Śaiva* scriptures.[89] Durvāsas then generated from his mind three perfected Yogins, namely, Tryambaka, Āmardaka, and Śrīnātha, who taught *Śaiva* monism, dualism, and unity-in-difference (*bhedābheda*).[90] The *sampradāya* founded by Tryambaka is said to have been none other than that of *Trika*.[91] Finally, it should be noted that within the Devī *Āgamas* Durvāsas is known as Krodha-bhaṭṭāraka, and revered as one of the promulgators of the *Śrī-vidyā* tradition of southern Śāktism.[92] Durvāsas is particularly celebrated within the Tripurā cult, the *Śākta* tradition centered on the worship of the goddess Tripurā.[93]

This overview of the mythical and religious background of Dattātreya's family and birth has been intended as a descriptive portrayal of Dattātreya's genealogy. It evidences the richness and complexity of the context in which the deity is placed—veritably linked to an impressive variety of religious and symbolical motifs—and brings me now to the heart of this research, namely, the examination of the Purāṇic myths concerning Dattātreya.

Notes

1. The presentation of divine and semidivine figures taken at face value, is mainly based on the following reference books: Macdonell, *Vedic Mythology*; Hopkins, *Epic Mythology*; Dowson, *A Classical Dictionary of Hindu Mythology and Religion, Geography, History and Literature.*

2 . According to some accounts, Atri also married ten other wives, including Bhadrā (in some versions, Soma is Bhadrā's son), and begot the so-called Svastyātreyas from them. John E. Mitchiner offers an apt definition of the nature and functions of seers:

> The Ṛṣis are . . . above all those who are ever involved in movement (√ṛṣ): firstly, the inner movement of self-transformation through *tapas*, and secondly, the external movement of causing change, growth and increase in creation. The Ṛṣi traditions revolve around the complementary cycles of asceticism and creation; when one such cycle ends, the next begins, and the Ṛṣis are thus constantly building up and discharging their inner creative energy which is itself the energy and nature of *Brahman*. (*Traditions of the Seven Ṛṣis* [Delhi: Motilal Banarsidass, 1982], 313)

On the Vedic Ṛṣis, see also Elizarenkova, *Language and Style of the Vedic Ṛṣis*, 16–28.

3. See *Brahmāṇḍa Purāṇa* 3.8.82; *Mārkaṇḍeya Purāṇa* 16.88–90.

4. To Viśvāmitra, literally "friend of all," is attributed the authorship of the third *maṇḍala* of the *Ṛg Veda*. The Ṛṣi was born a Kṣatriya, but by intense austerities raised himself to the Brahmin caste. The most important legend concerning Viśvāmitra is the enduring struggle between him and the Brahmin Ṛṣi Vasiṣṭha, typifying the rivalry between the Brahmin and Kṣatriya castes for supremacy.

Jamadagni, a Brahmin descendant of Bhṛgu, was the son of Ṛcīka and Satyavatī. He married Reṇukā, daughter of the King Prasenajit of the solar race, and was the father of five sons, the youngest and most famous of whom was Paraśurāma. The *Mahābhārata* reports that Jamadagni mastered all the *Vedas*.

Bharadvāja, literally "bearing speed or strength." Many Ṛg Vedic hymns are attributed to Bharadvāja: 6.1–30, 6.37–43, 6.53–74, 9.67.1–3, 10.137.1. He was the son of Bṛhaspati and the father of Droṇa, preceptor of the Pāṇḍavas. In the *Rāmāyaṇa* it is narrated that he received Rāma and Sītā in his hermitage at Prayāg. On Bharadvāja, see Thaneswar Sarmah, *The Bhāradvājas in Ancient India*.

Gotama, literally "the largest ox," was Rahūgaṇa's son and belonged to the family of Aṅgiras. The composition of *Ṛg Veda* 1.74–93 is attributed to Gotama.

Vasiṣṭha, literally "most wealthy," was the possessor of the cow of plenty, who had the power of granting him all things he wished for. He is the author of the seventh *maṇḍala* of the *Ṛg Veda* and of several others hymns.

Kaśyapa, literally "having black teeth," is a Vedic seer to whom some hymns are attributed. According to the *Mahābhārata,* he married Aditi and twelve other daughters of Dakṣa, from whom he had numerous offspring.

5. See *Ṛg Veda* 1.164.15; *Atharva Veda* 9.9.16, 10.8.5.

6. See *Śatapatha Brāhmaṇa* 14.5.2.6; *Bṛhadāraṇyaka Upaniṣad* 2.2.3–4.

7. In the *Purāṇas,* also referred to as the Āndhras. The texts mention the names of thirty kings, whose rule lasted for about four centuries (first century B.C.E. to third century C.E.). Their capital appears to have been Pratiṣṭhāna on the upper Godāvarī river.

8. Many hymns of the *Ṛg Veda* are attributed to Aṅgiras. He is later identified as one of the lawgivers and as a writer on astronomy. He is also identified with Bṛhaspati, the regent of the planet Jupiter, or with the planet itself.

Marīci, literally "a ray of light." A son of Brahmā, he is the chief of the Maruts, the storm gods. In the Epics and in many *Purāṇas* he is presented as the father of Kaśyapa.

Pulastya was the medium through which some of the *Purāṇas* were revealed. He was father of Viśravas, from whom Kuvera and Rāvaṇa were born. All the *rākṣasas* are supposed to have sprung from him.

Pulaha is identified as one of the Prajāpatis whose wife was Kṣamā. They had three sons: Kardama, Arvarīvat, and Sahiṣṇu.

Kratu, literally "understanding," is intelligence personified.

9. Agni is one of the most ancient and sacred deities of the Hindu pantheon. He appears in three main forms: in heaven as the sun, in midair as lightning, on earth as fire. About two hundred hymns of the *Ṛg Veda* are dedicated to him. The very first Ṛg Vedic hymn begins with the celebration of Agni as the supreme messenger between gods and men.

Indra, the god of the firmament, is the atmosphere personified. In the *Vedas* he stands first among the gods. His weapon is the thunderbolt, but he also uses arrows, a great hook, and a net. The *soma* juice is his special delight. He governs the weather and dispenses the rain and fertility. Thus, he is constantly at war with Vṛtra, the demon of drought and inclement weather. More hymns are addressed to Indra than to any other deity in the *Vedas,* with the exception of Agni.

The Aśvins are literally "the owners of horses." The twin sons of Dyaus, the bright sky, the Aśvins are represented as ever young and handsome, of golden brilliancy, agile and possessed of many forms. They ride in a golden car drawn by horses or birds, as harbingers of dawn and deliverers from darkness. Throughout Vedic mythology, the twin gods are revered as miraculous physicians. Fifty-four hymns of the *Ṛg Veda* are dedicated to them.

In the *Vedas,* the Viśvadevas, whose name literally means "all the gods," form a class of deities of inferior order. They are often addressed as "preservers of men" or "bestowers of rewards."

10. Literally "the man," from root *man*, to think. This name refers to fourteen mythological progenitors of mankind and rulers of earth, each of whom holds sway for a period of no fewer than 4,320,000 years (*manvantara*). The first of these Manus was Svāyambhuva, who sprang from Svayambhū, the self-existent, identified with Brahmā. According to another account, this Manu sprang from the incestuous relationship of Brahmā with his daughter Śatarūpā. As the creator, this Manu produced the ten Prajāpatis or progenitors of mankind, also known as Maharṣis. The Manu of the present age is the seventh, Vaivasvata of the Kṣatriya race, son of Vivasvat the sun.

11. The descendants of Aṅgiras. They occur in hymns addressed to luminous deities, and, in a later period, become personifications of light, of luminous bodies, of celestial phenomena, and of sacrificial fires. The Aṅgirases are associated with Agni and often described as messengers between gods and men.

12. For a recent analysis of the Atri-Svarbhānu myth which challenges the interpretation of the solar eclipse, see Jamison, *The Ravenous Hyenas and the Wounded Sun: Myth and Ritual in Ancient India.*

13. *Ṛg Veda* 5.40.6–9.

14. *Atharva Veda* 13.2.4–36; *Gopatha Brāhmaṇa* 1.2.17; *Kauṣītaki Brāhmaṇa* 24.3; *Pañcaviṃśa Brāhmaṇa* 6.6.8–10, 14.11.14; *Śatapatha Brāhmaṇa* 4.3.4.21.

15. On Atri's *gotra*, see Brough, *The Early Brahmanical System of Gotra and Pravara: A Translation of the* Gotra-pravara-mañjarī *of Puruṣottama-paṇḍita*, 139–45.

16. For an overview of Atri in Vedic literature, see Gonda, *Vedic Literature.*

17. *Brahma Purāṇa* 13.9–11; *Liṅga Purāṇa* 1.63.71–73; *Skanda Purāṇa* 7.1.20.42–44.

18. *Mahābhārata* 1.114.39–42.

19. Literally "splendor," "brilliance," "fiery energy." The term may refer to the Ṛṣi's powerful semen.

20. See Mitchiner, *Traditions of the Seven Ṛṣis*, 259.

21. *Harivaṃśa* 20.1–14.

22. *Matsya Purāṇa* 23.3–6.

23. *Mahābhārata* 13.91.18ff.

24. *Mahābhārata* 3.183.1–32. For a list of the places in the *Mahābhārata* where Atri and the Ātreyas are mentioned, see Sörensen, *An Index to the Names in the Mahābhārata. With Short Explanations and a Concordance to the Bombay and Calcutta Editions and P. C. Roy's Translation*, 99-100.

25. See *Rāmāyaṇa* 2.117. On the sacred Citrakūṭa peak, see Dave, *Immortal India*, 2: 74–81. The Gaṅgā is mentioned only twice in the *Ṛg Veda*. The *Purāṇas*

represent the river flowing from Viṣṇu's toe. It was brought down to earth by the prayers of the saint Bhagīratha. On the Gaṅgā's mythology, see Piano, *Il mito del Gange: Gaṅgā-Māhātmya*. Jāhnavī, literally "the daughter of Jahnu," is one of the many names of the Gaṅgā derived from Jahnu, a sage descended from Purūravas. Disturbed in his devotions by the passage of the river, Jahnu drank up its waters. He afterwards relented and allowed the Gaṅgā to issue from his ear.

26. *Matsya Purāṇa* 119.55ff.

27. In the *Vedas*, a mythical personage connected with the sun and the dawn, existing in the middle of the universe. According to the *Ṛg Veda*, he was son of Ilā, and a beneficent pious prince, the hero of the story of Vikrama and Urvaśī.

28. Quoted from Dimmitt and van Buitenen, *Classical Hindu Mythology: A Reader in the Sanskrit Purāṇas*, 325–26. Bhava, literally "being," "existence," is a name of Rudra or Śiva. Madra is a country to the northwest of Hindustan.

29. Mount Ṛkṣakula, *Siva Purāṇa śatarudra-saṃhitā* 19.3–4; the river Narmadā, *Skanda Purāṇa* 5.3.103.1–109; the Kāmada forest, *Śiva Purāṇa koṭirudra-saṃhitā* 3.7; Ātreyas, *Mārkaṇḍeya Purāṇa* 57.39 and *Vāmana Purāṇa* 13.41ff.

30. Swami Chidbhavananda, *Śiva Sahasranāma Stotram: With Namavali, Introduction, and English Rendering*, 29. See also R. Anantakrishna Sastri, *Śiva Sahasranāma Stotra (Sanskrit Text): With an English Translation of Śrī Nīlakaṇṭha's Commentary*, 8.

31. It may be noted that the epithet *anasūya* is attributed by Kṛṣṇa to Arjuna in *Bhagavad-gītā* 9.1. It designates the perfect *bhakta* or devotee. In his commentary, Nīlakaṇṭha explains the term as *doṣāviṣkaraṇa-rahita*, that is, "devoid of any evil characteristic."

In one version of the Puṇḍalīka legend the *mātā-pitṛ-bhakti*—which will originate the founding myth of the Viṭṭhala cult at Paṇḍharpur—is said to have been taught by Anasūyā. The story goes that Puṇḍalīka once arrived at the *āśrama* of Dattātreya and he went to the door of the great *pati-vratā* Anasūyā to ask for food. Being engaged in serving her husband Atri, she kept Puṇḍalīka waiting and when she finally came out Puṇḍalīka was very angry at her. She then taught him about the three kinds of *bhakti:* the *bhakti* of a son toward his elderly relations, the *bhakti* of a disciple toward his Guru, and the *bhakti* of a servant toward his master. She said that if he would serve his elderly relations at home (*mātā-pitṛ-bhakti*), then Hṛṣīkeśa would come and give him a fortune. Then Puṇḍalīka when to Vārāṇasī, where he heard a *Purāṇa* praising Paṇḍharpur. Finally, he left Vārāṇasī and reached Paṇḍharpur carrying his father in a yoke (*kāvaḍa*). On this episode, see Sand, "*Mātāpitṛbhakti*: Some Aspects of the Development of the Puṇḍalīka legend in Marathi Literature," 142–43.

32. According to the *Mahābhārata*, Dakṣa, whose name literally means "able," "intelligent," sprang from the right thumb of Brahmā, and his wife from that deity's left thumb. The *Purāṇas* adopt this view of his origin but state that he married Prasūti. He had, according to different sources, twenty-four, fifty, or sixty daughters by her. An important event in the life of Dakṣa is the episode of his sacrifice, violently interrupted by Śiva.

Prasūti, literally "procreator." She is variously identified as the daughter of Priyavrata or of Manu Svāyambhuva.

In the Epics, Kardama, literally "shadow," is one of the Prajāpatis who sprang from Brahmā's shadow. He is also said to be a son of Pulaha or Dakṣa.

Devahūti, literally "invocation of the gods," is one of the daughters of Manu Svāyambhuva.

33. See *Mahābhārata* 13.14.93–96. A rare case in which Anasūyā rebels against her husband Atri. She said: "I shall no longer live under that ascetic."

34. See *Rāmāyaṇa* 2.117. On the drought episode, see also *Śiva Purāṇa koṭirudra-saṃhitā* 3.9–4.61.

35. A similar tale is found in *Brahmāṇḍa Purāṇa* 3.8.82ff. Here, Ugraśravas and Śīlavatī take the place of Kauśika and his wife.

36. In the *Mahābhārata*, Kauśika went to a hell of torment for having pointed out to robbers a road by which some persons were fleeing from them. These people were then pursued and killed by the criminals. In the same Epic, Śāṇḍilī is the name of a Brahmin woman worshipped as Agni's mother.

37. See *Mahābhārata* 1.107.2–17. Māṇḍavya is also known as Aṇīmāṇḍavya; the *Skanda Purāṇa* locates his hermitage on the banks of the river Narmadā. On the sage, see Utgikar, "The Story of Ṛṣi Aṇī-māṇḍavya in Its Sanskrit and Buddhist Sources."

Padma Purāṇa 6.141.24–45 states that this punishment was inflicted on Māṇḍavya because in his childhood he had put a living moth on a stake.

38. *Skanda Purāṇa* 6.137.1–15 narrates the same account, saying that Māṇḍavya continued to suffer on the pole but did not die. For this undeserved punishment, he cursed the god of justice Dharmarāja to be born as the Śūdra Vidura; see *Mahābhārata* 1.108.8–15.

39. Compare with the *locus classicus* of the *pravartitaṃ cakram* in *Bhagavadgītā* 3.14–16. For an English translation, see Edgerton, *The Bhagavad Gītā*, 19.

40. Pargiter, *The Mārkaṇḍeya Purāṇa*, 95. All quotes from the *Mārkaṇḍeya Purāṇa* are from Pargiter's translation.

41. The shrine of Dattātreya at Sucindram, in Tamilnadu, is believed to be the place where the three gods Brahmā, Viṣṇu, and Śiva revealed themselves to Atri and Anasūyā.

42. Sexual intercourse is prohibited during the menstrual period. Whoever approaches a menstruating woman (*rajasvalā*) must purify himself by fasting and eating *ghī* for three days; see Meyer, *Sexual Life in Ancient India: A Study in the Comparative History of Indian Culture*, 225–26.

43. Giving birth through one's powerful mind or inner eye is a feat often attributed to Ṛṣis, due to the intensity of their stored *tapas*. The top of the head and particularly the point in the middle of the forehead, are thought of as the reservoir in which semen (*retas*) is stored, and the Yogin or Ṛṣi may utilize it for the purposes of creation, without having sexual intercourse.

44. An allegorical interpretation of the *trimūrti*'s birth from Anasūyā has been offered by the Svāmin Satya Sāī Bābā (b. 1926) during the *Guru-pūrṇimā* festival of July 1993. The Svāmin has pointed out that as *asūyā*, that is, envy or jealousy, gives birth to the "three sons" of hatred (*dveśa*), anger (*krodha*), and greed (*lobha*), so Anasūyā gave birth to patient endurance (*sahana*) in the form of Brahmā or Soma, love (*preman*) in the form of Viṣṇu or Dattātreya, and knowledge (*sānubhūti*) in the form of Śiva Maheśvara or Durvāsas; see *Sanathana Sarathi* 36, no. 7 (July 1993): 171.

45. This king is probably to be identified with Arjuna Kārtavīrya. The Haihayas are a race to whom a Scythian origin has been ascribed. The *Viṣṇu Purāṇa* represents them as descendants of the Yadu race, but they are generally associated with outlying tribes.

46. Such antinomian characterization concealing his divine nature—which brings to mind the ritualized behavior of the *Śaiva* Pāśupatas—typically manifests through explosions of terrible wrath, revealing Durvāsas' *raudra* nature. For Durvāsas' *unmatta* portrayal, see also *Viṣṇu Purāṇa* 1.9.

47. The Daityas are descendents from Diti by the sage Kaśyapa. They are said to be demons and giants who warred against the gods and interfered with sacrifices. They are generally associated with the Dānavas.

Padma Purāṇa 2.12.51–60 narrates that Dattātreya, together with Durvāsas, practiced penance by remaining under water for ten thousand years.

48. See *Devī-bhāgavata Purāṇa* 4.16.6–9; *Śiva Purāṇa śatarudra-saṃhitā* 19.24–27; *Skanda Purāṇa* 5.3.103.1-109. Thus a popular tradition understands Atri's name as meaning "one who desires three sons."

49. See *Bhaviṣya Purāṇa* 3.4.17.67–78; *Cucīntira* (Sucindram) *Sthala Purāṇa* 2.1–7.26; *Tirumūrtti-malai Purāṇa* 6–7. For the *Bhaviṣya Purāṇa* account, see O'Flaherty, *Śiva: The Erotic Ascetic*, 226–27; O'Flaherty, *Hindu Myths: A Sourcebook Translated from the Sanskrit*, 53–55. For the south Indian variant, see O'Flaherty, *Sexual Metaphors and Animal Symbols in Indian Mythology*, 100–101. See also Das, *Temples of Tamilnad*, 7–15; Dave, *Immortal India*, 2:58–64. At the temple of Sucindram, Anasūyā receives regular worship: her *mūrti* is placed at the center of three *liṅgas* representing the *trimūrti*.

50. On Hindu astrology, see Pingree, *Jyotishastra: Astral and Mathematical Literature*. By the same author, see "Representation of the Planets in Indian Astrology." On the caste of village priests and astrologers (*jośī*), see Russell and Lal, *The Tribes and Castes of the Central Provinces of India*, 3:255-79.

51. Configurations of stars, marking twenty-seven or twenty-eight points on the ecliptic in which the moon rises in the course of a lunar month.

52. Tilak, *The Orion; or, Researches into the Antiquity of the Vedas*, 134–35.

53. The symbolic interpretations of the three stars of the belt are numerous in both Indo-European and Semitic cultures. They have been construed as the Group of Jacob, the Group of Peter, the three Kings, and the three Magi.

54. On Orion in Greek mythology, see Kerényi, *Die Mythologie der Griechen*, chap. 12.4. See also Graves, *Greek Myths*, chap. 41.

55. Irieus, from the Greek word *hyron*, "beehive," appears to be connected with bees and their nectar, the ambrosia of the gods. He is generally identified as a poor beekeeper. Enopion, from the Greek word *oinos*, "wine," is presented as a king.

56. Hariprasad Shivprasad Joshi, *Origin and Development of Dattātreya Worship in India*, 187.

57. Besides Sirius, Atri has been identified with epsilon Ursae Majoris, the sun, and the moon.

58. On the interpretation of the *soma* juice, see Gordon Wasson, "The Soma of the Rig Veda: What Was It?" On Soma, see Gonda, *Change and Continuity in Indian Religion*, 38–70.

59. Derived from the root *puṣ*, the term *pūṣan* means "prosperer." From Vedic literature, Pūṣan is closely connected with the sun. He bestows wealth and protection on men and cattle, chiefly as a pastoral deity. He is often associated with Soma as protector of the universe.

Rudra, literally "a howler," is from the root *rud*, "to cry." This god occupies a subordinate position in the *Ṛg Veda*, being celebrated in only three entire hymns, in part of another, and in one conjointly with Soma; his name occurs about seventy-five times. Rudra is the howling terrible god, the god of storms, the father of the Rudras or Maruts, sometimes identified with Agni. On the one hand, he is a destructive and malevolent deity, bringing disease upon men and cattle. On the other hand, he is a somewhat beneficient deity with healing powers. These opposite characteristics contribute to the molding of the great god Śiva.

60. The universal encompasser, the all-embracer. Varuṇa, together with Indra, is the greatest of the gods of the *Ṛg Veda*. One of the oldest of the Vedic deities, he is the personification of the encompassing vault of the sky, the

maker and upholder of heaven and earth. He is king of the universe, king of gods and men, possessor of unlimited knowledge, the supreme deity.

61. Budha, literally "wise," "intelligent"; personification of the planet Mercury. Āyu, literally "a living being"; name of the fire, as the first-born son of Purūravas and Urvaśī.

62. Probably composed around 400 C.E. in southern India, the *Harivaṃśa* is a poem of 16,374 verses narrating the genealogy of Hari or Viṣṇu. Though it is included in the *Mahābhārata*, it is of much later date and may be ranked alongside Purāṇic literature.

63. O'Flaherty, *Sexual Metaphors*, 40. For another version of this myth, see *Padma Purāṇa* 5.12.1–13.

64. The Vasus are a class of deities chiefly known as attendants of Indra. In Vedic times they appear as personifications of natural phenomena. According to the *Rāmāyaṇa* they were all children of Aditi.

65. Literally "the red one," from the color of Aldebaran, the principal star in the constellation of Taurus.

66. *Rāja-sūya*, literally "a royal sacrifice," is performed at the consecration of a king.
In the *Ṛg Veda*, Bṛhaspati, literally "lord of prayer or devotion," is the priest who intercedes with gods on behalf of men. He is also the *purohita* of the divine community.

67. Uśanas is the name of an ancient Ṛṣi with the patronymic Kāvya. In later times, he was identified with Śukra, the teacher of the Asuras, who presides over the planet Venus. The Dānavas, descendants from Danu by the sage Kaśyapa, were giants who warred against the gods.

68. See Hopkins, *Epic Mythology*, 90.

69. An ancient sage, sometimes classed among the Prajāpatis. He married ten or more of Dakṣa's daughters and had numerous progeny, all personifications of faculties, virtues, and religious rites.

70. See *Mahābhārata* 13.160.32–37, *Vāmana Purāṇa* 2.45-47.

71. Literally "she who dwells in the mountains." Since Epic times, Pārvatī has been considered a reincarnation of the goddess Satī, Śiva's first wife. In Hindu mythology, Pārvatī's main function is that of inducing Śiva into marriage, to absorb him into the wider circle of worldly life from which he is aloof as an ascetic. On Pārvatī's mythology, see Kinsley, *Hindu Goddesses: Visions of the Divine Feminine in the Hindu Religious Tradition*, 35–54.

72. For this and other myths relative to Durvāsas, see Mani, *Purāṇic Encyclopaedia: A Comprehensive Dictionary with Special Reference to the Epic and Purāṇic Literature*, 256-57. See also Dange, *Encyclopaedia of Purāṇic Beliefs and Practices*, 2:453–56.

73. Chidbhavananda, *Śiva Sahasranāma Stotram*, 53. See also Sastri, *Śiva Sahasranāma Stotra*, 22.

74. Durvāsas is often reported to curse the gods who are then defeated by the Asuras; see *Viṣṇu Purāṇa* 1.9, *Padma Purāṇa* 1.4.1–23, *Naiṣadha-carita* 16.31. The story goes that Durvāsas offered a garland of flowers to Indra, who placed it on his elephant, but the elephant flung it on the ground. Then Durvāsas became angry at this "insult" and cursed Indra saying that his sovereignty over the three worlds would be subverted. In *Skanda Purāṇa* 6.37.10, he cursed an assembly of Brahmins, and the same *Skanda Purāṇa* 7.4.2.35–49 describes how he cursed Rukmiṇī to be separated from Kṛṣṇa. *Brahma-vaivarta Purāṇa* 24.6–82 narrates the story of how Durvāsas even cursed his wife Kandalī, daughter of sage Aurva, to be turned into a heap of ashes, though he later felt remorse for his action.

75. Śakuntalā, the daughter of Viśvāmitra by the nymph Menakā, was left in a forest at birth and was nourished by birds until found by the sage Kaṇva. The marriage, separation, and reunion of Śakuntalā and King Duṣyanta, who met her on a hunting expedition, are the subject of Kālidāsa's celebrated play *Śakuntalā*.

Duṣyanta, a valiant king of the lunar race, was descended from Puru. From Śakuntalā he had a son, Bharata.

76. See *Mahābhārata* 3.260, where King Mudgala was granted salvation by Durvāsas for his firm conduct. See also *Varāha Purāṇa* 38.7–29, where Durvāsas blessed Satyatapas, a hunter, for his devotion, and *Śiva Purāṇa śatarudra-saṃhitā* 19.29–55, where he tested and offered boons to King Ambarīṣa and later even to Rāma. In *Bhāgavata Purāṇa* 9.4.35–55, however, Durvāsas was practically forced to forgive King Ambarīṣa—who had broken his vow—because of Viṣṇu's intervention. *Padma Purāṇa* 5.105.174–180 narrates how Durvāsas saved the gods from the evil consequences of having raped the wife of the Ṛṣi Gautama through the chanting of the *Śatarudrīya-mantra* and the granting of sacred ashes. The Devas smeared their bodies with ash, thus having their sins removed.

77. See *Mahābhārata* 1.111.6–19. Kuntī was the daughter of the Yādava Prince Śūra, king of the Śūrasenas, whose capital was Mathurā on the Yamunā. She was sister of Vasudeva and was given by her father to his childless cousin Kuntibhoja, by whom she was brought up. Thanks to Durvāsas's charm she obtained a son, Karṇa, without losing her virginity. She then married Pāṇḍu and bore three sons, Yudhiṣṭhira, Bhīma, and Arjuna, who were called Pāṇḍavas although they were said to be the sons of the gods Dharma, Vāyu, and Indra respectively.

78. Again a reference to Durvāsas's *unmatta* characterization. Such behavior is not uncommon among ascetics, especially *Śaiva*, often believed by ordinary people to be mad (*pāgal*).

79. Literally "adorned with gold." Daughter of Bhīṣmaka, king of Vidarbha. According to the *Harivaṃśa* she was sought in marriage by Kṛṣṇa, with whom

she fell in love. Rukmiṇī was his principal wife and bore him a son, Pradyumna, along with nine other sons and one daughter.

80. Quoted in Sörensen, *An Index to the Names in the Mahābhārata*, 275.

81. The narration of Kṛṣṇa's death is found in the sixteenth book of the *Mahābhārata*, the *Mausala Parvan*. *Viṣṇu Purāṇa* 1.9 states that Indra fell due to the imprecation of Durvāsas, who describes himself as one whose nature is a stranger to remorse.

82. The celebrated race into which Kṛṣṇa was born. The Yādavas led a pastoral life, though under Kṛṣṇa they established a kingdom at Dvārakā in Gujarat. All the Yādavas who were present in that city after the death of Kṛṣṇa perished when Dvārakā was submerged by the ocean. The few who were absent, however, are said to have perpetuated the race.

83. Pradyumna, literally "the preeminently mighty one," is the son of Kṛṣṇa and Rukmiṇī. Pradyumna was kidnapped when only six days old and thrown into the ocean by the demon Śambara. He was swallowed by a fish which was later caught and carried to Śambara's house. When the fish was opened, the child was discovered and Māyāvatī, mistress of Śambara's household, took him under her care. Pradyumna later challenged the demon to battle and killed him. Pradyumna married Māyāvatī as well as Kakudmatī, daughter of Rukmin, from whom he had a son named Aniruddha.

Balarāma, literally "Rāma the mighty one," is the elder brother of Kṛṣṇa. The *Mahābhārata* states that Viṣṇu took two hairs, a white one and a black one, and these became Balarāma and Kṛṣṇa respectively. Both children of Devakī, they grew up together. Among Balarāma's main exploits was the killing of the Asura demon Dhenuka. When Kṛṣṇa went to Mathurā, Balarāma accompanied him. In the *Mahābhārata* Balarāma, though inclining toward the side of the Pāṇḍavas, refused to take an active part in the battle.

84. Within the *mantra-pīṭha* of the Jayadrathayāmala canon, Bhairava states that the *Bhairava-tantra* was brought down to earth by eight sages, among whom is Durvāsas; see Dyczkowski, *The Canon of the Śaivāgama and the Kubjikā Tantras of the Western Kaula Tradition*, 110.

85. See Pandey, *Abhinavagupta: An Historical and Philosophical Study*, 63.

This present age is the last and worst of the four *yugas*. The *kṛta-yuga* or *satya-yuga*, the golden age, lasts 4,800 divine years; the *tretā-yuga*, 3,600; the *dvāpara-yuga*, 2,400; and the *kali-yuga*, 1,200 (each divine year lasts 360 human years). A complete cycle, called *mahā-yuga*, lasts 12,000 divine years. One thousand *mahā-yugas*, in turn, correspond to one day in the life of Brahmā, that is, one *kalpa*.

86. See Dunuwila, *Śaiva Siddhānta Theology: A Context for Hindu-Christian Dialogue*, 35, 43.

Āmardaka, whose name derives from Āmarda, literally "crushing," is the founder of dualist *Śaivism* according to the tradition of Kashmiri *Śaivism*. He is known as the founder of a major Siddhānta monastic center in Ujjāin that bears his name. Āmardaka is also a name of Kāḷ Bhairav, the terrible Śiva manifestation.

87. Although Tryambaka literally means "three-eyed," originally it probably meant "three-mothered," from the expression *ambe ambike 'mbālike*. It is a name attributed to one of the Rudras or to Śiva. Tryambaka is also the name of one of the celebrated twelve *liṅgas* of Śiva, on the banks of the Gomatī river.

The *Pratyabhijñā* or "school of recognition," the fullest expression of *Śaiva* nondualism, takes its name from the *Stanzas on the Recognition of Īśvara* (Īśvara-pratyabhijñā-kārikā) written by Utpaladeva, disciple of Somānanda, toward the beginning of the tenth century C.E. Somānanda's *Śiva-dṛṣṭi* is the first work of the Recognition school. For an overview of the *Pratyabhijñā* school, see Dyczkowski, *The Doctrine of Vibration: An Analysis of the Doctrines and Practices of Kashmir Shaivism*, 17–20.

88. Kailāsa, a mountain in the Himalayas, north of the Mānasa lake, is believed to be Śiva's paradise.

According to Abhinavagupta, the *Śaivāgama* is divided into two major currents: one originates from Lakulīśa, the other from Śrīkaṇṭha. The latter consists of the five streams which form the majority of the *Śaivāgama*; see *Tantrāloka*, 36.13b–17. On Śrīkaṇṭha's *Śaiva* Vedānta, classified as a *bhedābheda* system, see Pandey, *An Outline of History of Śaiva Philosophy*, 32-36.

89. See Chatterjee, *Kashmir Shaivaism*, 6 n. 1.

The religio-philosophical traditions of Kashmiri *Śaivism* are known as *Trika* (threefold), referring to the triad of *śiva*, *śakti*, and *aṇu*, or the triad of *pati*, *pāśa*, and *paśu*.

90. See *Tantrāloka* 36.11–12.

91. See Chatterjee, *Kashmir Shaivaism*, 6 n. 1.

92. In the *Tripurā-tāpinī Upaniṣad*, Durvāsas figures as one of the twelve sages linked to the *mantra* of *Śrī-vidyā*. Durvāsas is also credited with the authorship of texts such as the *Lalitā-stava-ratna* and the *Śakti-mahimna-stava*; see S. K. Ramachandra Rao, *Āgama-Kosha* (Āgama Encyclopaedia), 5:125.

93. The most important Tantric form of Śrī-Lakṣmī, Tripurā is associated with the ancient tradition of the Saubhāgya *saṁpradāya*, which we find in Kashmir but also in southern India and which developed between the Medieval period and the eighteenth century. An indirect relationship between Durvāsas and Tripurā may be suggested from the *Mahābhārata* variant of the myth of Śiva's destruction of the city of Tripura: after Śiva had pierced the city of the Asuras with his arrow, this was transmuted into the form of a child bearing five locks of hair (*pañca-śikha*) and came back landing in Pārvatī's lap. That child's name was Durvāsas (13.160.32).

2

Purāṇic Mythology of Dattātreya

After presenting the few but primary references to Dattātreya within the *Mahābhārata,* this chapter will focus on the Purāṇic myths characterizing the deity. The *Mārkaṇḍeya Purāṇa* account deserves special attention, being as it is the *locus classicus* of Dattātreya in the whole literature of the *Purāṇas.* Herein, Dattātreya's portrayal as an Avatāra of Viṣṇu and as a teacher of Yoga tinged with Tantrism represents the most important assimilative phase in the deity's early development. Since it is in the *Purāṇas* that Dattātreya's rise to avatārahood takes place, the various lists of divine "descents" in which he figures will be reviewed. Finally, the relationship between heterodox and orthodox elements in the making of Dattātreya's plural and composite identities will be examined.

The traditional interpretation of the name Dattātreya, reiterated throughout sectarian literature, is found in *Bhāgavata Purāṇa* 2.7.4: as the Ṛṣi Atri desired a son, Viṣṇu gave himself to him. *Śāṇḍilya Upaniṣad* 3.2.7–8 confirms this derivation of the name:

> Wherefore then is it known as Dattātreya? For the reason that by the self-effulgent Lord who was exceedingly satisfied, his own self was given [*datta*] to the sage Atri, who was undergoing the severest penance and was desirous of begetting a son; and for the reason that Atri's son was born of Anasūyā; for these reasons it is known as Dattātreya.[1]

I. M. P. Raeside has challenged this conception, arguing that *datta* plus *ātreya*—meaning "the given son of Atri"—is "a common though doubtless mistaken etymology of his name."[2] He notes that in the birth story of Soma, Datta, and Durvāsas, he is given just the name Datta and that, since Ātreya is also a name of Durvāsas, there seems to be some sort of conflation. The traditional etymology *datta* plus *ātreya* need not be considered wrong, however. Of course, Soma, Datta, and Durvāsas—as descendants of Atri—are all "Ātreyas." The name *Datta,* as a past passive participle, simply means "given," "granted":

Viṣṇu's special gift of himself to the noble Ṛṣi. We know that according to *Manu-smṛti* 9.168, Datta or Dattrima, "received by gift" meaning adopted, is one of the twelve types of sons in Hindu law. One might argue that the common appellation *Datta* was replaced with that of Dattātreya or even Datta Ātreya by subsequent authorities in an effort to specify his identity as Atri's son.

A second interpretation of the name Dattātreya, quite current among his followers, is "the one who gave up or surrendered (*datta*) the three (*treya*)." In this case, the number three is said to refer to the three *guṇas* which Dattātreya relinquished. The fact that Dattātreya is without or beyond the *guṇas* (*nirguṇa*) would then be exemplified by his naked appearance as *digambara* or "clad in space."

We find Dattātreya first mentioned in the *Mahābhārata* as a powerful Ṛṣi. Dattātreya's ascendance in status—his unfolding from Ṛṣi to deified Guru and Avatāra of Viṣṇu—takes place in the crucial passage from the Epic to the Purāṇic period.[3] Of course, we must always be aware of the possibility that the name *Dattātreya,* and especially the most generic appellation *Datta,* may have identified different figures in different texts and periods. After all, the existence of a plurality of Dattas is self-evident in the literature. For instance, even in the Buddhist *Jātakas* we find the story of one Datta or Bhūridatta who is identified with the Bodhisatta, that is, the Buddha himself (*Bhūridatta-jātaka,* no. 543). The second son of the Nāga King Dhataraṭṭha and his wife Samuddajā, this Datta curiously presents some analogies with our Dattātreya: his abode is under a lake; he attains fame due to his extraordinary wisdom (hence his name is changed from Datta to Bhūridatta, his wisdom being as wide as the earth); he is a great ascetic (he lies and fasts in anthills); he is praised as the embodiment of the *dhamma* and as the one who grants all desires.

In *Mahābhārata* 12.297, Parāśara presents a list of Ṛṣis, including one Datta, said to have been produced in "lowest wombs" and to have achieved higher status in society by means of austerities. If this text really referred to our Dattātreya— which is doubtful—we would infer that his mother (Anasūyā?) was of a low caste and that he came to be viewed as a Brahmin Ṛṣi in virtue of his *tapas.*[4]

F. E. Pargiter has even tried to trace the actual historical descent of Dattātreya, linked to King Arjuna Kārtavīrya, as follows. One Prabhākara (called Atri or Ātreya) married the ten daughters of Bhadrāśva or Raudrāśva and Ghṛtācī. From them, he had ten sons, the Svastyātreyas. The most important among Prabhākara's Svastyātreya descendants would have been Datta and Durvāsas. Four *gotras* descended from Datta were apparently widely renowned; namely, the Śyāvāśva, Mudgala, Balāraka, and Gaviṣṭhira.[5]

This "historical" reconstruction, however, appears questionable being inextricably linked to myth. Moreover, it must be remembered that the Purāṇic Dattātreya will be appropriated across the centuries by a variety of religious communities. This complicates the difficulty of tracing the significant phases of Dattātreya's development, as well as of individuating Dattātreya's "essential core," his *svabhāva*, if such a thing really exists.

In the *Mahābhārata, Udyoga Parvan* 36.1–21, the mendicant Ṛṣi Dattātreya gives instructions to the Sādhyas on the practice of self-control, and *Anuśāsana Parvan* 91.5 states that he was father of Nimi.[6] Dattātreya's major feat is that of having granted gifts, notably one thousand arms, to Arjuna Kārtavīrya (also known as Sahasrārjuna), son of Kṛtavīrya, a Haihaya king, ancestor of the Yādava race, who had propitiated him by means of austerities.[7] *Mahābhārata* 3.115.12–13 also mentions a "golden aerial chariot" whose march was irresistible; the Ṛṣi Dattātreya donated it to Kārtavīrya.[8]

The substance of the *Mahābhārata* myth relative to Arjuna Kārtavīrya is related to the important story of the extermination of the Kṣatriya race by Paraśurāma.[9] When the time came for Kārtavīrya to succeed to his father's throne, he refused to do so on account of the sins and evil nature of his subjects. On hearing this, the teacher Garga[10] advised him to propitiate the Ṛṣi Dattātreya, said to be on earth for the uplifting of the world. Garga told how Indra himself and other gods had obtained favors from him, achieving victory over the demon Jambha.[11] Kārtavīrya went to Dattātreya and, after serving him for many years, obtained four boons: (1) a thousand arms, (2) the elimination of evil and injustice even though performed by a great man, (3) sovereignty over all the world through righteousness, (4) invincibility over enemies, and death by the hands of a superior man. The story of Kārtavīrya's boons reaches its finest elaboration in chapters 18 and 19 of the *Mārkaṇḍeya Purāṇa*, where Dattātreya is presented as the lord of Yoga, addicted to sensual pleasure though not affected by it.[12]

Mārkaṇḍeya Purāṇa 17.18–25 reports that Dattātreya, to free himself of all attachments, plunged into a lake for innumerable years. Dattātreya wished to be forsaken by the assembly of Munis who were still on the banks of the lake awaiting his return. He emerged from the waters in the company of a beautiful woman. The text tells us that he made love with her (*maithuna*), indulged in liquor, and was addicted to singing and musical instruments. Despite this, the Munis did not abandon Dattātreya, interpreting his behavior as a way of dissimulating his supreme dispassion. Dattātreya, attended by his woman, continued to perform austerities and was meditated upon by all Munis longing for *mokṣa*.

In chapter 18, we are told how Arjuna Kārtavīrya, upon becoming king, resolved to rule worthily. Garga, his minister, advised him to propitiate Muni Dattātreya. Garga told him how, when the Daityas and Dānavas headed by Jambha had conquered all the gods, Indra followed Bṛhaspati's advice ("Deign to gratify with your faith Dattātreya, Atri's high-souled son, the ascetic, who is occupied in improper practices") and propitiated Dattātreya. Garga thus celebrates Dattātreya (18.12–13):

> The illustrious, who made his abode once in a bucket, who protects the three worlds, who is busied in religious devotion [*yoga*], who . . . looks impartially everywhere, who is a portion of Viṣṇu, the upholder of the world, incarnate on earth.[13]

As a "descent" or Avatāra of Viṣṇu, Dattātreya was enjoying himself with Lakṣmī, engrossed in sensuous pleasures and in drinking liquor.[14] However, the gods, headed by Indra, refused to acknowledge the words of Dattātreya, who protested his inability to help them, being himself unable to subdue his senses. The gods spoke (18.29):

> Thou art sinless [*anagha*], O lord of the world; no stain hast thou, into whose heart, purified by the ablution of learning, has entered the light of knowledge.[15]

Moreover, the virtuous gods recognized Dattātreya's woman as none other than the mother of the world. Dattātreya was finally forced to bestow his blessings upon them. He asked the gods to bring the demons before his sight, so that he might destroy them through the fire of his glance. It so happened that the demons penetrated Dattātreya's hermitage—where the gods, utterly defeated, had sought protection from their fury—and, seeing the beautiful Lakṣmī, were prey to lust. Now their only desire was to seize her: they placed Lakṣmī on a *pālkhī* above their heads and set off to their abodes. Because of this action, they were all rendered powerless by Dattātreya, who spoke to the gods (18.53–54):

> When mounted on the head, she [Lakṣmī] forsakes the man and thence resorts to another abode. And here, mounted on their head, she will now desert these Daityas.[16] Therefore seize your arms and slay these foes of the gods; nor fear them greatly; I have rendered them impotent; and through touching another's wife their merit is consumed, their might is broken.[17]

Thus the gods were able to slaughter the demons—who suddenly became powerless—regain heaven, and be free from affliction.

Finally, in chapter 19 of the *Mārkaṇḍeya Purāṇa*, King Arjuna Kārtavīrya, having heard the above story and accepted Garga's advice, proceeded to Dattātreya's hermitage. He worshipped him by massaging his feet and presenting him with food, water, honey, perfumes, garlands, and so on. Though pleased with the service, Dattātreya told his devotee that he would be unable to benefit him and that he should better look for some other bliss-bestower. At this, Arjuna Kārtavīrya, remembering Garga's speech, replied (19.7):

> Why dost thou beguile me, my lord, resorting to thy illusory devices. Sinless thou art, and this brāhman lady is the path of all existence.[18]

Then Dattātreya, mightily pleased that he had discovered his secret—after having assured the bestowal of supreme gratification, children, wives, wealth, and other blessings upon whoever worshipped him, especially through such offerings as meat (*māṅsa*), strong drink (*mada*), songs, and musical instruments (19.10–12)—asked Arjuna Kārtavīrya to choose whatever boon he wished for. The king then said (19.14–18):

> If my lord thou art gracious, then grant me supreme prosperity, whereby I may protect my people and may not incur iniquity. I desire to have knowledge in the customs of others, irresistibility in fight, and the dexterity of a thousand arms. May my paths be unimpeded on hill, in air, in water, and on land, and in all the hells! And may my death come from a superior man! And let me have moreover a guide to the right path when I stray from the path . . . let there be freedom from impoverishment in my country. . . . May my faith in thee be ever in truth unwavering![19]

Dattātreya granted Arjuna Kārtavīrya all the boons he wished for, adding that through his favor he would become a universal monarch. It is reported that on the very day that the king received prosperity from Dattātreya, he performed sacrifice to Dattātreya. Arjuna Kārtavīrya's subjects, having seen the king's prosperity, also offered sacrifices with great devotion (19.30–31).

Thus, Dattātreya appears as the type of Yogin who is in the world and yet outside of it, and who, though not mad, acts as if he were intoxicated or a lunatic (*unmatta*), dissimulating his true nature, as already seen in the case of his "brother" Durvāsas. It is significant that Dattātreya's disciple Kārtavīrya is also mentioned in later texts of Tantric ritual.[20] In our text, it is only when the aspirants for his favor declare that he and his Śakti, the world mother, are beyond *bhoga* and the sensuous realm that Dattātreya relents and grants them their requests. In this account, Kārtavīrya pleases Dattātreya by massaging his feet and serving him delicious food, without resorting to any kind of austerity or *tapas*. The *Viṣṇu Purāṇa* celebrates Kārtavīrya, claiming that no other king equalled him in sacrifices, liberality, austerities, and self-restraint. He is reported to have ruled for eighty-five thousand years with unbroken health, prosperity, strength, and valor.

King Kārtavīrya is said to have been the contemporary of Rāvaṇa. *Rāmāyaṇa* 7.31–33 narrates that when Rāvaṇa went to Arjuna's capital Māhiṣmatī on the Narmadā and heard of Arjuna Kārtavīrya's powers, the latter demonstrated them to him by blocking the river with his thousand arms. Fierce fighting ensued, in which Kārtavīrya caught hold of Rāvaṇa. *Viṣṇu Purāṇa* 4.11.4ff. also reports that Arjuna Kārtavīrya captured Rāvaṇa without difficulty and confined him like a wild beast.[21] The *Vāyu Purāṇa* further states that Kārtavīrya invaded Laṅkā and there took Rāvaṇa prisoner.

Kārtavīrya's death followed the visit he paid to the *āśrama* of Ṛṣi Jamadagni. Though the sage and his sons, including Paraśurāma, were away, his wife Reṇukā treated him hospitably. Kārtavīrya, however, cut down the trees around the hermitage and carried away the sacred cow, fulfiller of all desires, the Kāmadhenu Suśīlā or Surabhi, which Jamadagni had acquired through his *tapas*. Paraśurāma returned and, having discovered the crime, cut off Kārtavīrya's thousand arms and killed him. The sons of Kārtavīrya went in revenge to Jamadagni's *āśrama* and, in the absence of Paraśurāma, killed the Ṛṣi. When Paraśurāma found the lifeless body of his father, he laid it on a funeral pile, vowing that he would eliminate the whole Kṣatriya race. Thereafter, he killed all of Kārtavīrya's sons, clearing the earth of the Kṣatriya caste for the following twenty-one generations. During this period, Paraśurāma kept the blood of all the warriors he had killed in a lake near Kurukṣetra, in order to offer it to his ancestors. These, headed by Ṛcīka, finally appeared on the scene and invited him to stop the massacre. Paraśurāma, in order to expiate the killing of so many innocent Kṣatriyas, celebrated a great sacrifice (*mahā-yajña*) and donated his kingdom and all the lands he had conquered to Kaśyapa. He subsequently embraced a life of renunciation and meditation, retiring to the Mahendra mountain.[22]

In the *Purāṇas*, Dattātreya is frequently associated with the figure of Alarka.[23] *Brahma Purāṇa* (180.32), *Bhāgavata Purāṇa* (1.3.11), *Garuḍa Purāṇa* (1.1.19; 3.15.13), and *Mārkaṇḍeya Purāṇa* (16.12) refer to Dattātreya as a Guru expounding the path of *aṣṭāṅga-yoga* or even *ānvīkṣikī* (logic or systematic reflection) and *sutarka-vidyā* (the knowledge of good reasoning) to Alarka.[24] Gerald James Larson notes how Kauṭilya, the famous minister of Candragupta Maurya, refers in his *Ārtha-śāstra* treatise (c. 300 B.C.E.) to the dualist Sāṃkhya *darśana* as one of the three traditions of *ānvīkṣikī* (together with Yoga and the materialistic schools of Lokāyatas). Larson notes:

> The notion of *ānvīkṣikī* in these ancient contexts means something like the enumeration of the contents of a particular subject matter by means of systematic reasoning. The practice of *ānvīkṣikī* is not really "philosophy" in our usual sense of the term; it is, rather, a kind of general "scientific" inquiry by means of the systematic enumeration of basic principles. Such enumerations appeared in a variety of intellectual subject areas, including phonology, grammar, statecraft, medicine, law, cosmology, and iconography, and the compilations of these subject-areas enumerations sometimes came to be called "*tantras*."[25]

Dattātreya's Purāṇic role as a teacher of "good reasoning" and "systematic reflection," given the generic quality of these terms, does not prove his relation to a specific *darśana*, such as classical Yoga or Sāṃkhya, though such a possibility cannot be ruled out. For example, in Śrī Nīlakaṇṭha's commentary on the 269th name of Śiva's thousand names ("He who is reached through Sāṃkhya"; *sāṃkhya-prasādaḥ*), it is stated that Dattātreya is the teacher of Sāṃkhya.[26] Given Datta's peculiar role as Yoga teacher, his *ānvīkṣikī* doctrine might be related to the "systematic enumeration" of the basic principles of Sāṃkhya-Yoga (or of a "Tantricized" form of Yoga), such as the twenty-five *tattvas*, the eight *bhāvas*, the fifty *padārthas*, and so on. After all, we know that there even existed a specific Dattātreya "school of thought," the main ideas of which are summarized in the *Kathā-bodha*.[27] Most important of all, in Dattātreya *ānvīkṣikī* is related to soteriological concerns, that is, to the attainment of liberating knowledge. Thus *ānvīkṣikī* and *ātma-vidyā*, the science of the self, are integrated into what might be referred to as an *ānvīkṣikī ātma-vidyā*.

Chapters 37 to 43 of the *Mārkaṇḍeya Purāṇa* narrate the story of Dattātreya and Alarka.[28] Alarka was the fourth and last son of king Ṛtadhvaja Kuvalayāśva and his wife Madālasā. The latter was a great

Yoginī who had attained *ātma-vidyā*, which she imparted to her three elder sons, Vikrānta, Subāhu, and Śatrumardana, from their childhood. Thus they followed the path of renunciation (*nivṛtti-mārga*), becoming indifferent to worldly things. Alarka, however, was not given these spiritual instructions, because his father Ṛtadhvaja had expressed the desire that one son should "remain in the world," for the good of the kingdom and to offer oblations to the ancestors. Ṛtadhvaja thus requested Madālasā to instruct Alarka in the path of action and enjoyment (*pravṛtti-mārga*). Madālasā gave detailed instructions on the performance of the *śrāddha* ritual and taught Alarka about the duties of a king, the rules of *varṇas* and *āśramas*, the responsibilities of a householder, and the actions that are permitted and those which are forbidden. Ṛtadhvaja consecrated Alarka king, and Madālasā presented him with a golden ring containing a note of instructions. Ṛtadhvaja and Madālasā then retired to the forest to practise austerities. Alarka ruled in righteousness and peace for many years, cultivating the gratification of his desires, attached to pleasures and uncontrolled in his senses. His elder brother Subāhu, who roamed the forests and wished to teach him a lesson in detachment, concluded an alliance with the king of Kāśī to attack Alarka's kingdom so as to divest him of power. In the battle that followed, Alarka and his country were defeated by the king of Kāśī and his army. Disgusted by his downfall and deeply dejected, Alarka remembered the token ring containing the note given him by Madālasā. The note he found read (37.23–24):

> Association [*saṅga*] must be shunned by every soul; if to shun it be impossible, it should be formed with the good, for association with the good is a panacea. Love [*kāma*] must be shunned by every soul; if to eschew it be impossible, it should be displayed towards the desire for final emancipation from existence [*mumukṣāṃ prati*], for that desire is a cure therefore.[29]

Alarka then decided to seek relief from the stainless Muni Dattātreya. Questioned by Dattātreya on the reason and nature of his affliction, Alarka explained to that magnanimous Brahmin wherein lay his suffering—namely, in his attachment to the senses—and launched into a metaphysical speech on the soul, the mind, the body, and pleasure and pain. Dattātreya confirmed the validity of Alarka's utterances, saying (38.6–7):

> It is even so, O tiger-hero! as thou hast just declared. The thought "it is mine" is the root of pain; and the thought "it is naught of

Dattātreya, master of Yoga, with his disciple Alarka.

> mine" is the root of calmness. From my question indeed has this sublime knowledge sprung up in thee, who hast cast off the conviction "it is mine," as if it were the cotton of the seemul tree.[30]

Then, utilizing the parable of the tree, Dattātreya explained that only cutting down the tree of selfishness with the axe of learning—sharpened through the association with the good—can one travel along the path of *mokṣa* (38.14–16):

> Neither art thou, O king, nor am I a gross object consisting of the elements and of organs . . . the conscious soul [*kṣetra-jña*] is sublime, and the personal aggregate consists of qualities [*guṇa*].[31]

Alarka then asked Dattātreya to explain how to attain deliverance, that state devoid of qualities (*nirguṇa*) and of oneness with *Brahman*. It is precisely at this point—chapters 39 through 43—that Dattātreya's *upadeśa* on Yoga begins.[32] Indeed, it is as a teacher of Yoga that Dattātreya is best known in the *Purāṇas*.[33] The topics covered are: (1) the nature of Yoga; (2) different stages of Yoga practice; (3) the appropriate time and place for Yoga practice; (4) dangers resulting from the neglect of rules prescribed for Yoga exercises; (5) details concerning the practice of Yoga; (6) the Yogin's life; (7) description of the successful Yogin; (8) the composition, symbolical meaning and efficacy of the *oṃ* syllable designating supreme *Brahman*; (9) results of Yoga practice; and (10) the signs—partly natural phenomena, partly dreams—by which a Yogin is able to predict his own imminent death.[34]

In his *Encyclopedic Dictionary of Yoga*, Georg Feuerstein remarks that the Yoga which Dattātreya taught Alarka prescribes a ritualistic lifestyle for the Yogin, classified as a kind of *kriyā-yoga*.[35] In my opinion, however, it seems more appropriate to view Dattātreya's teachings in the light of *jñāna-yoga*. Though emphasis is placed on performing the correct ritual acts and Yogic exercises, Dattātreya's *upadeśa* insists on the fundamental assumption that union with *Brahman* is the goal. All Yogic procedures are a preparation to the adept's absorption in the self, the only key to liberation and freedom. The goal is achieved by following a path which utilizes the classic theme of *aṣṭāṅga-yoga* as its primary referent.[36] The original and more archaic philosophical framework of Yoga, the Sāṃkhyan dualism of *Puruṣa* and *Prakṛti*, is replaced by a nondual framework, teaching oneness with *Brahman* rather than *viveka-khyāti* and *kaivalya*. Whereas the Sāṃkhyan *tattvas* are utilized and/or presupposed, the metaphysical conclusions of Sāṃkhya-Yoga are substituted by Advaita metaphysics, postulating the identity of the *jīvātman* with the *paramātman*. The whole discussion on the *oṃ* syllable in chapter 42 of the *Mārkaṇḍeya Purāṇa*—recalling the exemplary exposition of the *Māṇḍūkya Upaniṣad*—highlights the nondual context of Dattātreya's Yoga as well as its focus on *jñāna* rather than on *karman* or *kriyā*. From the outset, Dattātreya presents himself as a *jñāna-yogin*: *mokṣa* or union with *Brahman* and separation from the *guṇas* of *Prakṛti* come from the practice of Yoga and are to be attained through knowledge. In turn, knowledge or *jñāna* is preceded by dispassion or *vairāgya*. The fact that Dattātreya's teachings are those of a *jñāna-yogin* is confirmed by his appearance as a key figure in other *jñāna*-type traditions, such as the nondual Śāktism of the *Tripurā-rahasya* in south India.

The Yogic means which Dattātreya enumerates and analyzes for reaching *mokṣa* are the classic ones (39.10–42): (1) restraining of breath (*prāṇāyāma*), which can be of three kinds, namely, slight, medium, and intense; (2) concentration of the mind (*dhāraṇā*) by focusing attention on the tip of one's nose; (3) withdrawal of the senses (*pratyāhāra*); and (4) deep meditation (*dhyāna*).

Chapter 41 is of particular interest. Herein, Dattātreya teaches Alarka the way a Yogin should live. The similarity with the lifestyle of the Avadhūta or Paramahaṃsa—which will be presented in chapter 3—is noteworthy. The Yogin should never become a guest and should seek his alms only among householders who have already eaten, that is, where the charcoal fire is extinguished. The ascetic should resort to high-souled Brahmin householders, learned in the *Vedas*, since the practice of seeking alms among men of no caste is the last livelihood a Yogin should seek. Such practice connects "the Brahmin Dattātreya" to a milieu of purity and orthodoxy. The virtuous alms—rice gruel, barley gruel, milk, buttermilk, fruit, roots, panic seed, grain, oil cake and meal—should be eaten only after offering oblations to the five vital airs.[37] Vowing himself to honesty, sanctity, self-sacrifice, uncovetousness, and harmlessness, the Yogin devotes himself to the knowledge of the self, to profound contemplation and final *samādhi*. Controlling his speech, actions, and mind, he should practise *dhyāna* in empty places, such as caves and forests.

In chapter 42, dedicated to the sacred *oṃ* syllable, Dattātreya links the letters *a*, *u*, and *m* to the three *guṇas*, whereas the "fourth" on top of the syllable—the half-instant—is said to be symbolic of *nirguṇa* and to be understood only by Yogins (42.13–14):

> By uttering the word *oṃ*, everything both existent and non-existent may be grasped. Now the first instant is short, the second is long, and the third is prolated, and the half instant is not cognisant to speech.[38]

The three letters are also said to represent the three *Vedas*, the three worlds, the three fires, and the *trimūrti*. When pronounced, the *oṃ* reaches the head, and the vibration conveys the feeling of ants moving over the body. Through meditation on the *oṃ*, the Yogin is said to attain perfect union with *Brahman*.

Having thus gained perfect knowledge, Alarka thanked Dattātreya, returned to the king of Kāśī and Subāhu, and relinquished his kingdom in their favor.

Bhāgavata Purāṇa 1.3.11 and *Garuḍa Purāṇa* 1.1.19, along with Alarka, mention Prahlāda[39] as receiving instructions from Dattātreya. *Bhāgavata Purāṇa* 7.13.11–46 narrates a dialogue between them in which Dattātreya explains the code of conduct pertaining to ascetics. The meeting takes place on the top of the Sahyādri (Western Ghats) on the banks of the Kāverī. Lying on the ground, concealed by a coat of dust covering his entire body, Dattātreya is described as observing the *ajagara* or python "mode of life" (eating anything people or animals bring to him unasked).

Prahlāda asks how he can be endowed with such a corpulent body despite his total lack of material comforts. Then, Dattātreya—identified as a Brahmin—offers a teaching on the need for detachment and cessation of all activities so as to achieve freedom from *saṃsāra*. He points out how the bee and the python are men's best teachers, since they offer a lesson in renunciation and contentment respectively. Equanimity is Dattātreya's key *upadeśa*. As he says:

> Remaining contented in mind, I enjoy what is ordained by fate, and I wear linen garments or silks or deerskin or rags or any other fabric that is offered to me.
>
> Sometimes I sleep on the bare ground; sometimes on grass or on a heap of leaves or on a slab of stone or in ashes; sometimes I lie inside a mansion on a rich bed over a precious bedstead as desired by God.
>
> Sometimes I take a bath with my body anointed with fragrant pigments. I put on rich garments and wear garlands and ornaments. Sometimes I ride in a chariot or on an elephant or on a horse and sometimes I wander stark-naked like an evil spirit, Oh King.

> I neither revile nor praise people who are of diverse nature. I pray for their welfare and bless them with their union with the Almighty Lord Viṣṇu.[40]

In closing, Dattātreya highlights the secrecy of his mode of life, said to be far different from secular as well as Śāstric canons of behavior. An affirmation which points at the antinomian character of his ascetic personality.

Dattātreya is also celebrated for granting offspring to childless kings. Thus, *Padma Purāṇa, bhūmi-khaṇḍa* 103.101ff., narrates how King Āyu, with his wife Indumatī, performed many rites in order to have a son, all in vain. At last, the king came to Dattātreya and worshipped him for a long time. Then, after many days, Dattātreya, who was in an intoxicated condition, asked the king to serve him meat and wine. Pleased with Āyu's devotion, Dattātreya gave the king a fruit to be taken to Indumatī, and when the latter ate it she conceived a male offspring, Nahuṣa. *Varāha Purāṇa* 10.18ff. mentions King Supratīka of the *kṛta-yuga*, who had two wives, named Vidyutprabhā and Kāntimatī. Since he had no son, Supratīka decided to go to Citrakūṭa to propitiate Dattātreya, the son of Atri. After pleasing him he fathered a son. This mention of Dattātreya with the Citrakūṭa mountain reminds us of the reference in *Rāmāyaṇa* 2.117.5ff., where Rāma, together with Sītā and Lakṣmaṇa, visited the *āśrama* of Atri and Anasūyā.

The *Skanda Purāṇa* narrates the story of a Brahmin named Durācāra who, owing to bad company, lost his Brahmin condition and was overpowered by Vetāla.[41] After wandering all over the earth, he finally came to the holy place of Dhanuṣkoṭi,[42] where he was freed from the clutches of Vetāla. He inquired about the sanctity of the place from the Ṛṣi Dattātreya, who lived there and was known as the best among Yogins. Dattātreya narrated the greatness of Dhanuṣkoṭi; Durācāra, pleased by the account, returned home deciding to live according to the way expounded by sage Dattātreya.[43]

Another little known story of Ṛṣi Dattātreya is recorded in legends relative to the Kṛṣṇaite shrine of Guruvāyur[44] in Kerala. King Janamejaya[45] had become a victim of leprosy during a snake sacrifice that he performed in order to avenge his father's death, brought about by the deadly serpent-demon Takṣaka. When he was unable to obtain relief through medicines, the sage Dattātreya advised him to worship an image of Śrī Kṛṣṇa. Janamejaya did so with single-minded devotion, doing penance for four months, and was cured. Dattātreya revealed to him that the image of Kṛṣṇa at Guruvāyur had originally been worshipped by Brahmā, who later had given it to Viṣṇu. Viṣṇu, in his descent as Kṛṣṇa, had brought the idol along with him to Dvārakā. Before ascending to heaven, Kṛṣṇa requested his devotee Uddhava[46] to retrieve the idol from the impending submergence of his capital and to install it in an equally holy spot. Uddhava entrusted the task to "Guru," the preceptor of the gods, and Vāyu, the god of wind. They ultimately decided to install the idol near a lake full of lotuses. This site was Guruvāyur, which came to be known as the "Dvārakā of the south."[47]

Finally, *Bhāgavata Purāṇa* 11.7.24–11.9.33 reports the dialogue between King Yadu and a young Avadhūta, which tradition identifies in twelve-year-old Dattātreya (*bāla-avadhūta*).[48] Dattātreya, once again identified as a Brahmin (though Yadu notes that he behaves as if being a dunce, a lunatic, or one haunted by a ghost), taught him the secret of happiness which lies in detachment, acquired by means of constant reflection (*manana*) and by careful observation of the laws of nature. The dialogue is couched within a nondual theological discourse. Dattātreya enumerates a list of his twenty-four "universal teachers"[49] comprising the five elements, the sun and the moon, the sea, twelve animals (seven between birds and insects, two reptiles, two mammals, and one fish), a prostitute, a child, a maiden, and a blacksmith. The connection of Yogins and Avadhūtas with animals[50] and the wilderness in general is exemplary of their life as renunciants living in woods or on the borders of society: for this reason they are usually envisioned as frightening, even demonic, beings.

Dattātreya's twenty-four Gurus are: earth, from which he learned firmness, forbearance, and the importance of doing good to others; air, from which he learned nonattachment and freedom; sky/ether, from which he learned that the self is all-pervading and yet has no contact with any object whatsoever; water, from which he learned purity, clearness, and coolness; fire, from which he learned austerity and the devouring flame of self-knowledge; moon, from which he learned impermanence and how the self is always perfect and changeless, unperturbed; sun, from which he learned how the *ātman*, though one, appears as many due to its reflections; pigeons, from which he learned the dangers of attachment (as when a householder of poor sense takes delight in conjugal life and, with his mind thus perturbed, goes to ruin along with the family); python or *boa constrictor*, from which he learned how to lie actionless and yet sleepless, giving up all efforts at obtaining food; sea, from which he learned to remain quiet and unmoved, as the deep sea remains unmoved even though hundreds of rivers flow into it; moth, from which he learned the danger of being enticed by women and thus of ruining himself like a moth flying into the fire; bee, from which he learned that he should only beg a little food from one house and then from another, without becoming a burden to the householder;[51] male elephant, from which he learned about the fettering bonds of passion and the pitfalls of lust; honey gatherer, from which he learned that hoarding is the root cause of all misery; deer, from which he learned not to fall prey to alluring melodies and captivating songs, creating erotic passions; fish, from which he learned not to develop greed for tasty food and the importance of subduing the sense of taste; the courtesan Piṅgalā,[52] from whom he learned that dejection may lead to self-inquiry, detachment, and freedom from hope; osprey, from which he learned that one who possesses and collects worldly goods will always live a life of struggle; child, from whom he learned the virtue of cheerfulness and freedom from anxiety and all material cares; maiden, from the noise of whose bangles he learned the values of solitude and silence; arrow maker or blacksmith, from whom he learned mind concentration, leading to complete absorption in the self; serpent, from which he learned that a renouncer should not be marked out by his behavior nor should he ever build a home for himself but rather live in holes, caves, or temples built by others; spider, from which he learned how Lord Nārāyaṇa creates, protects, and withdraws the universe, just like a spider extends through its mouth the cobweb from its heart, sports with it and again swallows it; wasp, from which he learned that one may attain to the semblance of whatever object his or her soul concentrates on with love, hate, or fear.[53]

Strangely enough, neither the dog nor the cow, figuring prominently in Dattātreya's modern iconography, is listed among the twenty-four Gurus. Young Dattātreya's point, namely, that the investigative and broad-minded adept may derive knowledge from the whole of nature, bears great interest. Such an attitude, which includes the imitation of animals[54]—envisioning a kind of "spiritual opportunism"—is the expression of a renunciatory, ascetic milieu. Herein, a disciple is allowed and sometimes even encouraged to have more than one Guru simultaneously.

The story of the pigeons (11.7.52–74) and especially the "lessons" derived from the moth (11.8.7–8), the elephant (11.8.13–14), and the deer (11.8.17–18) evidence a strong anti-feminine conviction which is typical of an ascetic, orthodox mentality and which we will find reiterated in the *Avadhūta-gītā*. He who falls prey of a householder's life and, above all, is attached to women and sex, is said to lose himself and fall into dark hell, since a woman is a man's "veritable death." On the other hand Dattātreya offers the story of the prostitute Piṅgalā, who repented and gave up all hopes, as an illustration of perfect dispassion leading toward *mokṣa* (11.8.22–44). Significantly, in this narration of Dattātreya's twenty-four Gurus relevant antinomian aspects of Datta's personality as found in the earlier *Mārkaṇḍeya Purāṇa*—his indulging in meat and sex, in music and intoxicants—have disappeared and are implicitly condemned.

In closing his *upadeśa*, the young Avadhūta points out that a wise person should take up the path of renunciation at the earliest and not in old age, so as to make the best use of the rare fortune of having been born in a human body.

As noted from the outset, if in the Epic period Dattātreya is portrayed as a powerful Ṛṣi, in later Purāṇic accounts he is elevated to the status of an Avatāra or divine manifestation. The lists of Viṣṇu's descents in the *Purāṇas* are numerous and varied. In fact, apart from shorter and longer lists, there is the belief that Viṣṇu's Avatāras are innumerable.[55] The Avatāra is believed to come on earth to maintain the cosmic order (*dharma*) and to support the forces of good when overpowered by evil.[56] Moreover, the Avatāra is always thought to have a unique purpose to accomplish, such as killing a demon.[57] The so-called Prādurbhāva and Vibhava manifestations are assimilable to the Avatāra, though often presented as subordinate, nontranscendent or partial descents, having more "personal" or occasional reasons for their appearance.[58] Over the course of time, the "principal" Avatāras of Viṣṇu were set at ten. According to some authorities the classic *daśa-avatāra* list—comprising Matsya, Kūrma, Varāha, Narasiṁha, Vāmana, Paraśurāma, Rāma, Kṛṣṇa, Buddha, and Kalkin—was systematized around the eleventh or twelfth century, but we know that the same list appears in an inscription at Mahābalipuram much earlier, around the latter half of the seventh century.[59] It may be hypothesized that the *daśa-avatāra* list had already found general acceptance before the eighth century.[60]

Though various *Purāṇas* do not mention Dattātreya in their lists of Avatāras, *Garuḍa Purāṇa* 1.1.19 and *Bhāgavata Purāṇa* 1.3.11—among the most authoritative *Vaiṣṇava* sources—mention him as the sixth Avatāra of Viṣṇu in a list comprising twenty-two descents. Sometimes Dattātreya appears to take Paraśurāma's place in the lists of descents. Such replacement may not be casual, considering Dattātreya's favorable disposition toward Kārtavīrya, who was killed by Paraśurāma to avenge the honor of his father Jamadagni.

Whereas *Matsya Purāṇa* 47.242 lists Dattātreya as the fourth *daśa-avatāra*,[61] *Brahma Purāṇa* 180.31 has him as the sixth Avatāra, while

213.106 of the same *Purāṇa* reports him as the fifth Prādurbhāva. Likewise, Dattātreya is viewed as a Prādurbhāva in *Devī-bhāgavata Purāṇa* 4.16. *Agni Purāṇa* 49.27, dealing with the characteristic features of Viṣṇu's Avatāras, refers to Dattātreya's image confirming his elevation to the status of a divine manifestation. *Matsya Purāṇa* 99.14 prescribes that a devotee should give away one in each month of the year the golden images of the ten manifestations as well as of Dattātreya and Vedavyāsa, along with a lotus of gold.

Sāttvata Saṃhitā 9.77-84, one of the earliest sources within the *Pāñcarātra* tradition[62] (which *Ahirbudhnya Saṃhitā* 5.50f. copies almost verbatim), places Dattātreya as the twenty-fifth principal Prādurbhāva or Vibhava within a list of thirty-eight descents. Provocatively, F. O. Schrader has argued:

> The list of . . . *avatāras* occurring in one of the very oldest *Saṃhitās* [the *Sāttvata Saṃhitā*] is older than the smaller lists found in later *Saṃhitās*, and older even than the *Mahābhārata* and *Nārāyaṇīya* lists, which appear to be mere selections.[63]

If Schrader's claim is correct—though I frankly doubt it—the inclusion of Dattātreya in the *Sāttvata Saṃhitā* would prove his rise to the status of divine manifestation at quite an early stage.[64] The later *Viśvak-sena Saṃhitā*, which follows the *Ahirbudhnya Saṃhitā*, excludes Kapila, Dattātreya, and Paraśurāma from its list of principal Prādurbhāvas, who are only regarded as Prādurbhāvāntara, that is, minor or dependent manifestations.[65] Even *Padma-tantra* 1.2.31f. lists Dattātreya as just an Āveśa Avatāra (Guṇa Avatāra), where the deity's attributes take possession of beings only occasionally.[66] However, the *Tantra-sāra-saṅgraha*, in its repertoire of Viṣṇu's forms to be worshipped in the sacred water-pot (*kalaśa*), includes Dattātreya in a list of thirteen together with the *daśa-avatāras*. In late classical literature, both Harṣa in *Naiṣadha-carita* 21.94 and Māgha in *Śiśupāla-vadha* 14.79 include our deity in the list of the ten Avatāras.[67] Finally, in the eleventh chapter of the *madhya-khaṇḍa* of the late *Bṛhaddharma Purāṇa*, a *Śākta Upapurāṇa*, we find Dattātreya listed as the sixth Avatāra of Viṣṇu in a list of twenty descents.[68]

From this survey we can gather that Dattātreya was viewed as an important manifestation of Viṣṇu. Although he was not included in the classic group of the *daśa-avatāras*, he was nevertheless variously considered a principal or dependent manifestation (sometimes within lists of ten, more frequently in longer lists). As noted above, all these names express the idea of a descent of Viṣṇu—either totally or partially, that is, as an *aṁśa*—into a human, animal, or human-animal form, though of course the Avatāric connotation is the most important, implying a fullness of divinity. According to *Brahma Purāṇa* 213.107–9, as well as to the *Viṣṇu-dharmottara Purāṇa* (pt. 1, chap. 25), the purpose of the Dattātreya manifestation was the restoration of *dharma* and of Vedic religion and rites, in harmony with Kṛṣṇa's definition of the function of an Avatāra:

> When all the Vedic knowledge with its branches and the sacrifices were lost, when the caste system was upset, when the religion was lowered down in position, when untruth gained the superiority over truth and when all the people and religion became restless, Dattātreya put everything in its right position.[69]

Shankar Mokashi-Punekar, partly following the interpretative framework of the Marāṭhī scholar R. C. Dhere,[70] has suggested that two diverging religious streams contributed to the molding of Dattātreya's cult: a heterodox one, under the influence of the Nātha schools and centered in northern India, and an orthodox Brahminical one, centered in western India, hieratic, duty bound, and *bhakti* oriented:

> Two significant and seemingly contradictory accounts of Dattātreya's personality and role are to be met with in Mārkaṇḍeya Purāṇa and Brahma Purāṇa respectively. They define the two concepts of the Dattātreya image held dear by two widespread Hindu devotional cults of a later period, both alive up to the present day: (a) The Nātha cult of northern India. . . . (b) The Dattātreya cult of western India.[71]

Moreover:

> The western India Datta cult fortified social order by a powerful revival of ritualism and duty-bound social consciousness; ascetics like Sripad Srivallabh, Nrsimha Saraswati . . . were the leaders of this movement. These two streams [the western India Datta cult and the Nātha cult], raised under the name and tutelage of the same teacher-deity, Dattātreya, certainly crossed each other's path and gained sustenance from each other, annexed devotees from unexpected families, places, traditions and castes, all over India.[72]

Mokashi-Punekar's intuition is basically correct when positing a distinction between a proto-Dattātreya, identified as a great Yogin, and a deutero-Dattātreya, grounded in later Purāṇic lore. Along these lines, one could argue either for the separate existence of at least two Dattātreyas—within two religious milieux separate in time and space—or for the existence of one Dattātreya, subsequently sanitized in Purāṇic literature. What is certain is that the composite *trimukhī* Dattātreya of later times is the outcome of an inextricable *miśra* or fusion of unorthodox *Śaiva* and orthodox *Vaiṣṇava* motifs.

Chronologically, the *Mārkaṇḍeya Purāṇa*, which presents the fullest account on Dattātreya, antedates the more heterogeneous *Brahma Purāṇa*.[73] In fact, whereas the *Mārkaṇḍeya Purāṇa* may be placed around the seventh century (making it possibly one of the oldest works in Purāṇic literature), the *Brahma Purāṇa* was probably composed around the thirteenth or fourteenth century.[74] Both F. Eden Pargiter and R. C. Hazra agree in dating chapters 10 through 44 of the *Mārkaṇḍeya Purāṇa*, which include the stories about Dattātreya, even earlier than the seventh century, that is, between the third and fourth century.[75] In any case, Mokashi-Punekar's contrasting of the *Mārkaṇḍeya* and *Brahma Purāṇas* does not appear applicable. The *Mārkaṇḍeya Purāṇa*, non otherwise than the *Brahma Purāṇa*, is couched within an overall Brahminical discourse, fitting even the antinomian Datta in a frame of purity and orthodoxy. The same can be said for the relevant *Bhāgavata Purāṇa* passages. I would argue that the older *Mārkaṇḍeya Purāṇa* retains traces of an archaic "Tantric" characterization of Dattātreya. Despite the attempt to sanitize the deity—as in the chapters of Dattātreya's *upadeśa* on Yoga—at various points in the *Purāṇa* Dattātreya is explicitly presented as enjoying meat, wine, and sex. He bears the dishonorable name of *madya-pa* or drinker of intoxicating liquors. It is also said that he should be worshipped with the offerings of meat, wine, perfume, and garlands to the accompaniment of music. As Pargiter himself notes:

> Indulgence in spirituous liquor and in sensual enjoyments is viewed with little or no disapprobation in the story of Dattātreya; and meat and strong drink are mentioned as most acceptable offerings in the worship of Dattātreya, as an incarnation of Viṣṇu.[76]

The very fact that Dattātreya is presented as a teacher and lord of Yoga favors a *Śaiva* characterization. The *Vaiṣṇava* names that the *Mārkaṇḍeya Purāṇa* uses to praise Dattātreya as an Avatāra of Viṣṇu are as numerous as those celebrating him as both a Muni and a Yogin. He is variously referred to as rich in austerities (*tapo-dhana*), best among the ascetics having taken the vow of silence (*muni-śreṣṭha*), great ascetic (*mahā-muni*), knower of Yoga (*yoga-vit*), lord of Yoga (*yogīśvara*), absorbed in Yoga (*yoga-yukta*), and so forth.[77] The *Purāṇa* attempts to avoid connecting Dattātreya with immoral, polluting behavior by furnishing a justification for his conduct. The text underlines Dattātreya's divine purity—analogous to the wind—as beyond all worldly contaminations, viewing the woman by his side as his powerful wife or Śakti. So it is said that he appears as if indulging in wine and sex and behaving in a weird manner only to avoid being pestered by people. His fondness for wine and women is explained by his will to test the devotees' faith. Certainly, the theme of disguising one's saintliness and even actively courting dishonor and insults—reaping good *karman* from being regarded as an evil person or a fool—is a well-known ascetic strategy, one of which the lost *Śaivite* sect of the Pāśupatas is the exemplary model.[78] Thus, the *Mārkaṇḍeya Purāṇa* minimizes the unorthodox aspects of Dattātreya's persona, though his overall portrayal reveals what appears to be an originally antinomian figure. Clearly, we witness a tension between the Yogic characterization of Dattātreya and the *Vaiṣṇava* tradition desirous to enforce purity and orthodoxy, especially in the case of an Avatāra (a Yogin) who is said to have come for the destruction of *adharma* and the reestablishment of *dharma*!

In conclusion, Dattātreya's orthodox, *Vaiṣṇava* portrayal is most likely to be regarded as posterior to his more basic identity as a heterodox, antinomian figure. Dattātreya traditionally plays an important part in Tantric literature. His connection with Yoga and Tantra, with the pan-Indian movement of the Nātha Yogins as well as with *Śaiva* sects such as the Aghorīs, will be discussed in the following chapters. The "first" or proto-Dattātreya was a Yogin—possibly a historical figure who became legendary—later adapted into the more sanitized and *bhakti*-oriented views of the *Purāṇas*.[79] Although this is by no means unusual, the basic link between *Tantra* and *Purāṇa* is of fundamental importance for the understanding of medieval Indian religions. The relationship between the more private ritualism and philosophy of Tantric Hinduism, and the public *bhakti sampradāyas* rooted in Purāṇic lore, is traceable in the main phases of the deity's development. Dattātreya's presence in both Tantric and Purāṇic types of religions, in both canons and cults, makes him thus a focal point for understanding this complex transition.

Notes

1. This passage is from T. R. Srinivasa Ayyangar's translation, *The Yoga Upanishads*, 490.

2. Raeside, "Dattātreya," 490.

3. There are very few exceptions to the *Vaiṣṇava* characterization of Dattātreya in the *Purāṇas*. Occasionally, however, he is reported as a *Śaiva* or as a devotee of Śiva.

4. For an interpretation of this passage, and on *tapas* as a criterion for *varṇa* distinctions, see Vora, *Evolution of Morals in the Epics (Mahābhārata and Rāmāyaṇa)*, 140ff.

5. See Pargiter, *Ancient Indian Historical Tradition*, 228–30.

6. The Sādhyas are a class of deities dwelling in the region between heaven and earth, representing the rites and prayers of the *Vedas*. Nimi was father of Śrīmat. The *Anuśāsana Parvan* states that Nimi, instructed by Atri, was the first to perform the *śrāddha* ritual for his deceased son; see Dakshina Ranjan Shastri, *Origin and Development of the Rituals of Ancestor Worship in India*, 127–28. On Nimi as Dattātreya's son, see *Rāmāyaṇa* 7.55.4f. (Kṛṣṇācārya's edition).

7. See *Mahābhārata* 3.115.8ff., 12.49.30ff., 13.137.5–6, 13.138.12, and 13.142.21. The references are to the BORI edition, which consigns the first two cases to an appendix or footnote as interpolations. The references to Dattātreya in the *Anuśāsana Parvan*, however, have remained. Raeside notes how the Kārtavīrya episode provides Madeleine Biardeau with a platform from which to launch one of her attacks on the "reconstructed" *Mahābhārata* text, although here she is not concerned with Dattātreya; see Biardeau, "The Story of Arjuna Kārtavīrya without Reconstruction." On Arjuna Kārtavīrya by Biardeau, see also "Études de mythologie Hindoue (4)." On Kārtavīrya's austerities, see *Mahābhārata* 2.14.11, 3.3.10. For a presentation of the role of Kārtavīrya within the legend of the Brahmin Paraśurāma in the *Mahābhārata*, see J. Muir, *Original Sanskrit Texts on the Origin and History of the People of India, their Religion and Institutions*, 1:442–79. For an overview of the major myths concerning Arjuna Kārtavīrya, see Mani, *Purāṇic Encyclopaedia*, Kārtavīryārjuna (Kārtavīrya).

8. For a list of the places in the *Mahābhārata* where Dattātreya is mentioned, see Sörensen, *An Index to the Names in the Mahābhārata*, 235.

9. Literally "Rāma with the axe," which he received from Śiva who instructed him in the use of arms. Both the Epics and *Purāṇas* refer to his skill in martial arts. Sixth Avatāra of Viṣṇu, Paraśurāma was a Brahmin, the fifth son of Jamadagni and Reṇukā. From his father's side he descended from Bhṛgu, from his mother's side from the royal race of the Kuśikas. The first act which

the *Mahābhārata* records is the beheading of his mother Reṇukā, in obedience to his father's command. She had angered Jamadagni by entertaining impure thoughts, thus he called upon each of his sons to kill her. Paraśurāma alone obeyed, thus receiving a boon from Jamadagni. He begged that his mother be restored to life in her pristine moral purity and that he become immortal and invincible in single combat. According to tradition, Paraśurāma manifested for the purpose of repressing the tyranny of the Kṣatriyas, and his most celebrated deed is the extermination of the warrior caste. Confronted by Rāma, Viṣṇu's seventh Avatāra, Paraśurāma recognized the former's superiority. Nowadays, Paraśurāma is mostly venerated in southern India, and in Kerala a calendar based on "the era of Paraśurāma" is still in use. The belief that he actually created Kerala and that he lives as an immortal in a cave in central India is widely held. For an analysis of the important Paraśurāma myth, see Shulman, *The King and the Clown in South Indian Myth and Poetry*, 110–29.

10. An ancient sage and one of the sons of King Vitatha. Garga is also the name of one of the oldest writers on astronomy.

11. Literally "one who crushes or swallows." Jambha is the name of several demons, and Indra is known with the epithet of *jambha-bhedin*—slayer of Jambha—for having killed him. *Bhaviṣyottara Purāṇa* 4.58, a late *Śākta Upapurāṇa*, narrates that Dattātreya saved the gods from the hands of Jambha, Śumbha, and other Daityas.

12. Dattātreya's connection with Arjuna Kārtavīrya is found in various *Purāṇas*. See *Agni Purāṇa* 4.14; *Brahma Purāṇa* 13.161; *Matsya Purāṇa* 43.15; *Padma Purāṇa* 6.71.199–212; *Viṣṇu Purāṇa* 4.11.13; *Viṣṇu-dharma Purāṇa* 30.

13. Pargiter, *The Mārkaṇḍeya Purāṇa*, 102.

14. For a similar Tantric characterization of Dattātreya, with eyes red due to spirituous liquor and devoid of sacred thread, see *Padma Purāṇa* 2.103.110–13.

Lakṣmī, literally "good fortune," "prosperity," is the goddess of fortune, wife of Viṣṇu, and mother of Kāma. According to legend she sprang from the foam of the ocean, in full beauty with a lotus in her hand, when it was churned by the Devas and Asuras. Another legend represents her as floating on a lotus flower at creation. On Śrī-Lakṣmī, see Kinsley, *Hindu Goddesses*, 19–34.

15. Pargiter, *The Mārkaṇḍeya Purāṇa*, 103. Dattātreya is often celebrated with the epithet *anagha* in the *Mārkaṇḍeya Purāṇa*; see also *Padma Purāṇa* 6.71.199–212.

16. *Mārkaṇḍeya Purāṇa* 18.49ff. mentions Lakṣmī's seven auspicious bodily parts, through which she grants her *prasāda*. If, however, Lakṣmī is located above a human's head, this is interpreted as a sign of misfortune.

17. Pargiter, *The Mārkaṇḍeya Purāṇa*, 105.

18. Ibid., 106.

19. Ibid., 107. *Brahmāṇḍa Purāṇa* 3.37–40 identifies Kārtavīrya's thousand arms with the thousand rays of Sudarśana, the celebrated disc of Viṣṇu.

20. See chap. 17 of the *Mantra-mahodadhi*. Among the Tantric texts in praise of Kārtavīrya mention should be made of the *Kārtavīryārjuna-kalpa*, the *Kārtavīryārjuna-pañjara*, the *Kārtavīryārjuna-sahasranāma* and the *Kārtavīryārjuna-yantra-lakṣaṇa*.

21. On the struggle between Rāvaṇa and Arjuna Kārtavīrya, see Bhosa's *Rāvaṇārjunīya*, an epic in twenty-seven cantos.

A story is also reported of Rāvaṇa going to Dattātreya's *āśrama*. The Ṛṣi had placed a water-pot (*kamaṇḍalu*), purified through the recitation of various *mantras*, in a safe place. Rāvaṇa succeeded in stealing the water-pot. When Dattātreya found out, he cursed the demon, saying that since the water, evoked by magic spells, had "fallen on Rāvaṇa's head," monkeys would in turn pollute his head by treading on it; see Mani, *Purāṇic Encyclopaedia*, 206.

22. See *Vāyu Purāṇa, dvitīya-khaṇḍa*, chap. 32. Late sectarian works such as *Śrī Datta Purāṇa* 4.8 and *Śrī Guru-līlāmṛta, jñāna-kāṇḍa*, chap. 26, add that Paraśurāma went to Dattātreya's *āśrama* together with his mother Reṇukā. She became a *satī*, immolating herself on the funeral pile, and Paraśurāma performed the *śrāddha* ceremony with Dattātreya as priest. In the *jñāna-khaṇḍa* of the *Tripurā-rahasya*, Dattātreya transmitted the highest knowledge of pure nondualism to Paraśurāma, accepting him as his disciple; see chap. 7.

23. On the other hand, chap. 30 of the *Āśvamedhika Parvan* of the *Mahābhārata*, describing how Alarka attained perfection in Yoga, does not mention Dattātreya. The name Alarka means "dog-howler." In *Mahābhārata* 12.3.12–13, Alarka appears as a worm who draws blood from Karṇa's thigh.

24. On Dattātreya's teaching of *ānvīkṣikī*, see R. G. Bhandarkar, *Vaiṣṇavism, Śaivism and Minor Religious Systems*, 42.

25. Gerald James Larson and Ram Shankar Bhattacharya, eds., *Encyclopedia of Indian Philosophies*, vol. 4, *Sāṃkhya: A Dualist Tradition in Indian Philosophy*, 4. On *ānvīkṣikī*, see Hacker, "Ānvīkṣikī." See also Halbfass, *India and Europe: An Essay in Understanding*, 273–86.

26. See R. A. Sastri, *Śiva Sahasranāma Stotra*, 21. A Marāṭhī follower of Śaṅkara's Advaita Vedānta, Nīlakaṇṭha lived around 1650 C.E.; see ibid., ii–iii. Dattātreya is also mentioned alongside with Kapila—unanimously identified as the "supreme sage" (*parama-ṛṣi*) within the Sāṃkhya tradition—in *Śaṅkara-dig-vijaya* 9.22, a late biography of Śaṅkara: Kapila, Dattātreya, Vyāsa, and Śaṅkara are defined as the teachers of the *satya, tretā, dvāpara*, and *kali* age respectively.

27. On this text, see Mukund Lāl Śāstrī, *Kathābodha*. See also Handiqui, *The Naishadhacarita of Śrīharsha (Cantos 1–22)*, 522.

28. The Purāṇic context is the following: fantastic birds, versed in the *Vedas*, relate their knowledge in answer to the questions of the sage Jaimini.

The birds reproduce a dialogue between Jaḍa and his father. When the latter asks the son how to be free from the wheel of *saṃsāra,* Jaḍa advises him to practise Yoga as taught by sage Dattātreya to King Alarka.

29. Pargiter, *The Mārkaṇḍeya Purāṇa,* 188–89.

30. Ibid., 191. See also *Garuḍa Purāṇa* 4.226.2.

31. Pargiter, *The Mārkaṇḍeya Purāṇa,* 192.

32. On Yoga in the *Mārkaṇḍeya Purāṇa,* see Ram Ugra Mishra, "Yoga in Mārkaṇḍeya Purāṇa."

33. *Bhāgavata Purāṇa* 2.7.4 says that by the dust of his lotus-like feet Yadus, Haihayas and others got their bodies purified and attained excellence in Yoga. *Bhaviṣyottara Purāṇa* 4.58 refers to Dattātreya's practice of Yoga in his hermitage on the Vindhya mountains. *Kāśī-khaṇḍa* 84.18 of the *Skanda Purāṇa* even mentions a *Dattātreya-tīrtha,* saying that a person bathing in its waters attains perfection in Yoga. The only exceptions to Dattātreya's portrayal as a Yogin, seem to be the *Liṅga* and *Kūrma Purāṇas;* see H. S. Joshi, *Origin and Development,* 55.

34. See Desai, *Ancient Indian Society, Religion, and Mythology as Depicted in the Mārkaṇḍeya-Purāṇa (A Critical Study),* 127–36.

35. See Feuerstein, *Encyclopedic Dictionary of Yoga,* Mārkaṇḍeya-Purāṇa.

36. See Patañjali's *Yoga-sūtra* 2.28–3.3.

37. These five vital airs are *prāṇa,* or the ascending breath issuing from the navel or the heart and including both inhalation and exhalation; *apāna,* or the breath associated with the lower half of the trunk; *vyāna,* or the diffuse breath circulating in all limbs; *udāna,* or the "up-breath" held responsible for eructation and speech, as well as concentration; and *samāna,* or the breath localized in the abdominal region where it is connected with the digestive processes. On the five vital airs, see Zysk, "The Science of Respiration and the Doctrine of the Bodily Winds in Ancient India."

38. Pargiter, *The Mārkaṇḍeya Purāṇa,* 206.

39. Literally "delight," "joy." A Daitya, son of Hiraṇyakaśipu and father of Bali, paradigm of the ideal *bhakta.*

40. *Bhāgavata Purāṇa* 7.13.39–42. This English translation is taken from Tagare, *The Bhāgavata Purāṇa,* pt. 1, 978–79.

41. A ghost or goblin. A spirit said to haunt cemeteries and to animate dead bodies.

42. Literally "the curved end of a bow." Possibly the name of a mountain to the north of Madhya-deśa.

43. See H. S. Joshi, *Origin and Development*, 64.

44. On this southern Indian locale, see Dave, *Immortal India*, 3:167–73.

45. A great king, son of Parikṣit and great-grandson of Arjuna. Vaiśampāyana recited the *Mahābhārata* to him.

46. A friend and counsellor of Kṛṣṇa. According to tradition he was Kṛṣṇa's cousin, being son of Devabhāga, the brother of Vasudeva.

47. For more details of this legend, see Vaidyanathan, *Temples and Legends of Kerala*, 153–59.

48. The conversation between Yadu and the Avadhūta is a dialogue within a dialogue. Originally, the exchange is between Kṛṣṇa and Uddhava, where the former imparts the highest knowledge.

The eldest among the five sons of King Yayāti, Yadu was the founder of the great line of the Yādavas. The younger brother Puru had succeeded Yayāti as king, taking Yadu's place. Yadu took this as an insult and retired to the forest where he met Dattātreya, whom he found perfectly contented even in the absence of any material possessions.

The symbolism of number twelve is one of completion, designating a fullness of time. For a recent study on numerology, see Schimmel, *The Mystery of Numbers*.

The term *avadhūta* comes from the root *dhū* plus *ava*, meaning "shaking off," "removing worldly ties." The Avadhūta is thus an ascetic who has shaken off worldly existence, having achieved liberating knowledge. For a beautiful portrayal of the Avadhūta, who leads the life of an *ajagara* and is despised by human society, see *Bhāgavata Purāṇa* 5.5.29–35. The Nāthas, as well as the Rāmānandīs, designate themselves as Avadhūtas. For a Nātha account on the Avadhūta, envisioned as the highest type of ascetic, see the sixth *upadeśa* of the *Siddha-siddhānta-paddhati* ascribed to Gorakhnāth. According to the medieval *Maṇḍala-brāhmaṇa Upaniṣad* (5.9), the Avadhūta is a Yogin accomplished in the practice of *nirvikalpa-samādhi* (exclusive concentration upon an entity without distinct and separate consciousness of the knower, the knowable, and the process of knowing). Known as a Paramahaṃsa, he is said to bring about the liberation of 101 generations in his family. *Mahā-nirvāṇa-tantra* 14.149 distinguishes between two types of Avadhūta: the perfect one called "Paramahaṃsa" and the still imperfect one known as a "wanderer," a "Parivrājaka." The Avadhūta ascetics are traditionally depicted as roaming about naked from place to place. On Dattātreya as a renunciant belonging to the Avadhūta class within the *Saṃnyāsa Upaniṣads*, see chap. 3. The Avadhūta as the perfect Yogin, is celebrated in the short poem *Avadhūta-gītā* attributed to Dattātreya. For a discussion on the *Avadhūta-gītā* and its textual tradition, see chap. 8.

49. Even Eknāth, in his *Eknāthī Bhāgavata* (7.341–344), makes Avadhūta (Dattātreya) narrate an account of his Gurus, enumerating twenty-four objects

as his models. Avadhūta remarks that the whole world may be viewed as one's teacher; see R. D. Ranade, *Mysticism in Maharashtra* (*Indian Mysticism*), 243.

50. Such connection is also described in *Mārkaṇḍeya Purāṇa* 43.48–58, where Dattātreya refers to various animals—ants, rats, ichneumons, lizards, sparrows, deer, etc.—as teachers of *vairāgya* and other virtues.

51. Compare with the kind of begging called *mādhūkara* to which renunciants resort, collecting food from any three, five, or seven houses at random, imitating bees gathering nectar. The ascetic should not accept alms with a view to storing them. He should use no other vessel than his palms and his stomach.

52. On the special role and function of prostitutes in Purāṇic literature, see Dange, *Encyclopaedia of Purāṇic Beliefs and Practices*, Prostitutes. On the caste of prostitutes (Kasbī, Tawaif, Devadāsī), see Russell and Lal, *The Tribes and Castes of the Central Provinces of India*, 3:373–84.

53. The twenty-fourth Guru, the wasp, exemplifies the ancient Indian belief that one can assume the form of another by focusing one's mind on it. *Bhāgavata Purāṇa* 11.9.22–23 states:

> On whatever a man focuses his entire mind through love, hate, or fear, he attains its form. A worm, contemplating the wasp who has brought him to his hive, O king, becomes like a wasp without losing its former shape.

On this same issue, see *Nārada-parivrājaka Upaniṣad* 155, 178.

For a modern exegesis of Dattātreya's twenty-four Gurus, see Yadav, *Glimpses of Greatness*, 33–55; Sivananda, *Hindu Fasts and Festivals*, 65–70; Keshavadas, *Sadguru Dattatreya*, 8–16; "The 24 Gurus." For a Saṃnyāsin's interpretation of some of Datta's teachers, see Oman, *The Mystics, Ascetics, and Saints of India*, 157–60. In a dialogue between the Vedāntic master Ramaṇa Maharṣi (1879–1950) and the musician Dilip Kumar Roy we read:

> Dilip: Śrī Aurobindo often refers to you as someone who has never had a Guru.
>
> Bhagavan: This depends on what you call a Guru. He doesn't necessarily need to adopt a human form. Dattātreya had twenty-four Gurus: the elements, etc. This means that all existing forms in this world were his Guru. The Guru is absolutely necessary. The Upanishads say that only a Guru can rescue a man from the jungle of mental and sensory perceptions; therefore there must be a Guru. (Osborne, *The Teachings of Ramana Maharshi*, 84)

54. See *Bhāgavata Purāṇa* 5.5.32–34, where several ascetic vows that imitate the behavior of animals are described. See also the legend of Ādi-Bharata recorded in *Viṣṇu Purāṇa* 2.13.

55. *Bhāgavata Purāṇa* 1.3.26 states:

Even as a perennial lake has canals by the thousands, even so there are innumerable Avatāras of Hari, the receptacle of goodness (*sattva-guṇa*).

56. The *locus classicus* of the Avatāra doctrine is *Bhagavad-gītā* 4.7–8.

57. The first *khaṇḍa* of the *Mudgala Purāṇa* reports such an instance in which, though it is Gaṇeśa who acts as "Avatāric savior," Dattātreya plays an important role. The story goes that once the gods went to Dattātreya in order to seek help from the demon Mātsaryāsura who had conquered the three worlds. Dattātreya then advised them to invoke the grace of Gaṇeśa as Vakratuṇḍa (literally "the one with the twisted trunk") by chanting the *mantra gaṃ*. Having done this, they obtained Vakratuṇḍa's grace and he subdued the demon.

58. Prādurbhāva, literally "becoming visible," "appearance." On the shorter and possibly earlier Prādurbhāva lists—where Dattātreya never appears—see Brinkhaus, "Early Developmental Stages of the Viṣṇuprādurbhāva Lists."

Vibhava, literally "development." In *Vaiṣṇavism*, it connotes the evolution of the Supreme Being into secondary forms.

59. On the systematization of the *daśa-avatāra* list, see Handiqui, *The Naishadhacarita of Śrīharsha*, 520; Basham, *The Wonder That Was India*, 304. On the earlier inscription at Mahābalipuram, see H. Krishna Shastri, "Two Statues of Pallava Kings and Five Pallava Inscriptions in a Rock Temple at Mahābalipuram," 5.

60. See Jaiswal, *The Origin and Development of Vaiṣṇavism: Vaiṣṇavism from 200 BC to AD 500*, 144.

61. The other Avatāras listed are Dharma Nārāyaṇa, Narasiṁha, Vāmana, Māndhātṛ, Jāmadagnya, Rāma, Vyāsa, Buddha, and Kalkin. The *Brahmāṇḍa Purāṇa* and the *Vāyu Purāṇa* also list Dattātreya as the fourth Avatāra and the first human one in a list of ten, immediately after the three celestial Avatāras Nārāyaṇa, Narasiṁha, and Vāmana. Here Dattātreya—who is said to have had Mārkaṇḍeya as his precursor (*puraḥsara*)—takes Kūrma's place in the classic list of the *daśa-avatāras*.

62. *Pāñcarātra* texts are traditionally classified into three groups: (1) of divine origin (*divya*); (2) given by sages (*muni-prokta*) and occuring in three subdivisions, that is, *sāttvika*, *rājasa*, and *tāmasa*; (3) of human origin (*pauruṣa*). The *Sāttvata Saṃhitā*, together with the *Pauṣkara Saṃhitā* and the *Jayākhyā Saṃhitā*, belongs to the first group and is thought to have come directly from Vasudeva. There also exists a *Dattātreya Saṃhitā*, which the fourteenth-century *Siddhānta-ratnākara* of Śrīśaila Veṅkaṭasudhi lists among the *muni-prokta*, *tāmasa* texts. These latter texts are believed to have been composed by sages after studying the *divya* and *sāttvika muni-prokta Saṃhitās*. Being viewed as independent, original compositions, the *tāmasa* texts are thought to be not entirely authoritative.

63. Schrader, *Introduction to the Pāñcarātra and the Ahirbudhnya Saṃhitā,* 43–46. Schrader erroneously enumerated thirty-nine instead of thirty-eight Vibhava forms. On the *Sāttvata Saṃhitā,* see S. K. Ramachandra Rao, *Āgama-Kosha,* 4: 113–23.

64. For a critical assessment of Schrader's study, see Jitendra Nath Banerjea, *The Development of Hindu Iconography,* 391–93.

65. See S. K. Ramachandra Rao, *Āgama-Kosha,* 4: 125.

66. Ibid., 112–13.

67. *Naiṣadha-carita* 21.94 reads:

> I bow to thee incarnate as Dattātreya, who followed the path of absolute monism. He gave Arjuna his fame. His appellation "Sinless" [*anagha*] was occasioned by his Yoga meditations. He acted like the sun on the darkness of worldly delusion, to which king Alarka was subject.

For this translation, as well as for a fine discussion on the Dattātreya Avatāra, see Handiqui, *The Naishadhacarita of Śrīharsha,* 309, 520–22.

68. See Hazra, *Studies in the Upapurāṇas* 2: 416.

69. This English rendering is taken from H. S. Joshi, *Origin and Development,* 56. On the purpose of Dattātreya's Avatāra, see Asoke Chatterjee Shastri, "The Deities and Deification in the Brahmapurāṇa."

70. See Dhere, *Datta Sampradāyācā Itihāsa.*

71. Mokashi-Punekar, "An Introduction to Shri Purohit Swami and the Avadhoota Gita," 14.

72. Ibid., 18–19.

73. On the *Brahma Purāṇa,* see Söhnen and Schreiner, *Brahmapurāṇa: Summary of Contents, with Index of Names and Motifs,* vol. 2.

74. See Rocher, *The Purāṇas,* 154–56 (on the *Brahma Purāṇa*), 191–96 (on the *Mārkaṇḍeya Purāṇa*). P. V. Kane dated the *Mārkaṇḍeya Purāṇa* even earlier, between the fourth and sixth century; see his *History of Dharmaśāstra,* vol. 5, pt. 2, 903. Pargiter placed the *Mārkaṇḍeya Purāṇa* in western India, near the Narmadā river; see Pargiter, *The Mārkaṇḍeya Purāṇa,* viii–xiii.

75. Ibid., xx. See also Hazra, *Studies in the Purāṇic Records on Hindu Rites and Customs,* 8–13.

76. F. E. Pargiter, *The Mārkaṇḍeya Purāṇa,* xxi. For more observations on Dattātreya by the same author, see Pargiter, *Ancient Indian Historical Tradition,* 7, 27, 178, 228–30.

77. On Dattātreya's names and epithets in the *Mārkaṇḍeya Purāṇa*, see Desai, *Ancient Indian Society, Religion, and Mythology as Depicted in the Mārkaṇḍeya-Purāṇa*, 169.

78. See Dattātreya's teaching to the Sādhyas in *Mahābhārata* 5.36.5. On the Pāśupatas' practice of courting dishonor, see David N. Lorenzen, *The Kāpālikas and Kālāmukhas: Two Lost Śaivite Sects*, 185–92. See also Daniel H. H. Ingalls, "Cynics and Pāśupatas: The Seeking of Dishonor"; Minoru Hara, "A Note on the Pāśupata Concept of Purity (saucha)." Especially in the "unmarked stage" (*avyakta avasthā*, the second of the five stages in the spiritual path of the sect), the Pāśupata adept actively encourages censure from the people by means of peculiar practices, notably the six so-called doors (*dvāras*): *krāthana* (snoring or pretending to be asleep), *spandana* (shaking one's limbs as if afflicted by "wind disease"), *mandana* (walking as if crippled), *śṛṅgāraṇa* (making amorous gestures in the presence of women), *avitat-karaṇa* (acting as if devoid of judgement), and *avitad-bhāṣaṇa* (uttering senseless or contradictory words). The rationale for such behavior is the transfer of good and bad *karman*. On this issue, as well as for an up-to-date bibliography on the Pāśupatas, see Alberto Pelissero, "The Soul as a Grain of Rice: The Way Out of Karman in Abhinavagupta's Paramārthasāra," 267-69.

79. S. Jaiswal suggests that Dattātreya "may have been a god of some local semi-civilized tribe which was brahmanized through Vaiṣṇavism;" see Jaiswal, *The Origin and Development of Vaiṣṇavism*, 145.

3

Dattātreya in Minor *Upaniṣads*

This chapter deals with the presence and role of Dattātreya within some of the minor *Upaniṣads*, mainly technical manuals for the use of disciples of either Advaita Vedānta or Yoga: (1) the *Yoga Upaniṣads*, (2) the *Saṃnyāsa Upaniṣads*, and (3) the *Viṣṇu Upaniṣads*. It was the German scholar Paul Deussen who grouped these *Upaniṣads* according to the tendency predominant in each of them.[1] Dattātreya—either in his role of Yoga teacher or in that of Avadhūta or Paramahaṃsa—is mentioned in the *Darśana* and *Śāṇḍilya* within the corpus of the twenty-one *Yoga Upaniṣads*; in the *Bṛhad-avadhūta, Jābāla, Nārada-parivrājaka, Bhikṣuka,* and *Yājñavalkya* within the corpus of the twenty *Saṃnyāsa Upaniṣads*; and, of course, in the *Dattātreya* within the corpus of the *Vaiṣṇava Upaniṣads*. In the following pages, I will offer an outline of these texts, highlighting Dattātreya's place within them.

As seen in chapter 2, Dattātreya's portrayal and teachings within the *Mārkaṇḍeya Purāṇa* are essentially those of a *jñāna-yogin*. This emphasis on *jñāna* within a nondual framework characterizes Dattātreya throughout his unfolding. This doesn't mean, however, that the deity was impermeable to other influences. On the contrary, the *Yoga Upaniṣads* mirror the synthetic and complex assimilation of assorted teachings on Yoga. The crux of my argument is that Dattātreya offers a case through which to examine the textual and cultic development of Yoga as an inclusive body of ideologies and practices. Scholars usually differentiate Patañjali's Yoga from its later manifestations and commentaries,[2] and these from the further developments within the varied traditions of *Kuṇḍalinī-Yoga* (Kashmiri *Śaivism*, *Śākta* traditions such as *Śrī-vidyā, Krama, Mantra-śāstras,* etc.) and subsequent medieval ramifications.[3] However, important strands also exist within Hindu tradition that assimilate, incorporate, and revise with selective exclusion.[4] From early days within Yogic and Tantric circles, there was the tendency to acquire multiple initiations in different traditions. The story of Dattātreya's twenty-four Gurus is emblematic. This inevitably led to the cross-fertilization of concepts and the formulation of Yogic and Tantric homologies. For these assimilative circles including ideas, teachings, and practices from across the ocean of traditions, Dattātreya is truly a paradigm. He is an icon whose character speaks of this complex assimilation of Yoga-rooted traditions. Thus, if Dattātreya's core identity is that of a *jñāna-yogin*, for the historian of religions he exemplifies the concept of a "honeybee" Yogin, whose character and *upadeśa* are developed by gathering from across varieties and types of traditional "flowers of Yoga." Dattātreya appears with different nuances in each context, and it is precisely this composite or mix that is most appealing. Rather than confusing us, it enriches our understanding of how Yogic adepts and religious writers saw and still see Dattātreya's figure. In this perspective, these minor *Upaniṣads* are important crossover texts bridging the Yoga traditions as well as making the *Vaidika/Tāntrika* connection.

The *Yoga Upaniṣads* were composed later than Patañjali's *Yoga-sūtra* and mainly expound Vedānta-based Yogic teachings—particularly within the Tantric framework of *Haṭha-Yoga* and *Kuṇḍalinī-Yoga*[5]—betraying the influence of the pan-Indian Nātha schools.[6] The origins of Nāthism are obscure. Though scholars date its development between the seventh and twelfth centuries, its Yogic cult is based on very ancient esoteric doctrines and practices, perhaps anterior to both Buddhism and what we nowadays call Hinduism. Bearing an unmistakeable *Śaiva* character, the movement of Nātha Yogins probably developed from Nepal, Tibet, and the Himalayan regions of India from whence it gradually spread to the whole subcontinent. It has been described as a particular phase of the Siddha cult, whose members aspired to bodily immortality (*kāya-siddhi, divya-śarīra*) and to the condition of living liberation (*jīvanmukti*)[7] through the purification, rejuvenation, and alchemical "transubstantiation" of the body (*rasāyana, kāya-sādhana*). *Haṭha-Yoga* was developed within Nāthism. Its two most outstanding adepts—possibly legendary figures—were Matsyendra and his disciple Gorakṣa, also known as Matsyendranāth and Gorakhnāth, to whom various Yogic treatises and mythological narratives and poems, both in Sanskrit and vernacular languages, are ascribed. Northern India and western India have a tradition of nine Nāthas (*nav-nāth*). In the Marāṭhī list, Shashibhusan Dasgupta includes Matsyendra, Gorakṣa, Gahinī, Jyālendra, Kārina-pā, Carpaṭa, Revaṇa, Bhartṛ, and Gopicandra.[8] This, however, is just one of various, conflicting lists of the Marāṭhī *nav-nāth*.[9] Due to the integration of *Śaiva* and *Vaiṣṇava* elements in Marāṭhī spirituality, the nine Nāthas came also to be known as the nine Nārāyaṇas.[10]

Most of the *Yoga Upaniṣads* are late compositions written in verse form, ascribed to the fourteenth and fifteenth centuries. Possibly, how-

The Nātha Yogin Matsyendranāth.

ever, some of them or sections of them are as old as some of the classical *Upaniṣads*. In fact, these minor *Upaniṣads* may well reflect ideas, beliefs, and practices which were operative before the epic and medieval period.[11] One of the themes particularly relevant in the *Yoga Upaniṣads* is that of sound (*nāda*), of phonic emanation and mystical audition—among them the quintessential *praṇava oṃ*, the *bīja mantras* or "seed" phonemes, and so on—which accompanies certain Yogic exercises and is viewed as a means of attaining *Brahman*. For instance, *Darśana Upaniṣad* 6.36–38 describes the perception of sounds in the highest *cakra* at the crown of the head, the *brahma-randhra* or "cavern of *Brahman*":

> When air [*prāṇa*] enters the *brahma-randhra*, *nāda* (sound) is also produced there, resembling at first the sound of a conch-blast [*śaṅkha-dhvani*] and like the thunder-clap [*megha-dhvani*] in the middle; and when the air has reached the middle of the head, like the roaring of a mountain cataract [*giri-prasravaṇa*]. Thereafter, O great wise one! the *ātman*, mightily pleased, will actually

> appear in front of thee. Then there will be the ripeness of the knowledge of *ātman* from Yoga and the disowning by the Yogin of worldly existence.[12]

The soteriological dimension of *Nāda-Brahman*—leading to a kind of sonorous theophany—pervades the entire spectrum of the *Upaniṣads*. The link of these texts with Patañjali's Yoga is fairly clear, their Tantric characterization notwithstanding. As Guy L. Beck observes: "Most of them expound and dilate upon the practice of Praṇava-Japa, the repetition of AUM, and employ terminology from the classical system."[13]

The *Darśana Upaniṣad*,[14] the ninetieth *Upaniṣad* within the *Sāma Veda* corpus, consists of 224 stanzas distributed over ten *khaṇḍas*, in the form of a dialogue between the Yogin Dattātreya and his pupil Sāṃkṛti.[15] The text presents an exposition of the eightfold path of Yoga, leading to liberating knowledge and the experience of *Brahman*. In the fourth *khaṇḍa*, Dattātreya directs his disciple to focus on the "internal places of pilgrimage," such as Śrī Parvata as the crest, Kedāra as the forehead, Benares as the junction of the brows, Kurukṣetra as the region of the breasts, Prayāg as the lotus of the heart, and so on. In particular, *manas* is said to be the best of *tīrthas*, the purification of which is essential. The aim is the experience of the nondual *Brahman*, which is one with the soul. As in the *Mārkaṇḍeya Purāṇa* account, Dattātreya recommends the practices of *prāṇāyāma* and *dhyāna* particularly on the *oṃ* syllable.[16] Drawing in *prāṇa* through the *piṅgalā* channel and expelling it through the *iḍā*, is said to result in lightness of body, glowing of the digestive fire, clear manifestation of sound and vision.[17] The adept is instructed to practice such *prāṇāyāma* exercise six times during the three divisions of the day, namely, in the morning, at noon, and in the evening. Meditation is related to the various elements and parts of the body. The earth is associated with Aniruddha, water with Nārāyaṇa, fire with Pradyumna, air with Saṃkarṣaṇa, and ether with the *paramātman*. The self is associated with Vāsudeva. It is said that the mind of the Yogin is annihilated once he meditates on the clear ether of the heart: liberation is then in the palm of the Yogin's hand. Georg Feuerstein notes:

> The fundamental practices of Dattātreya's Yoga are identical with those introduced in the *Yoga-sūtra*. . . . The text is fairly orthodox in style and contents. Much attention is given to the psychoenergetic currents [*nāḍī*] and their purification, whereas the higher Yogic practices are only sketchily described.[18]

The *Śāṇḍilya Upaniṣad*,[19] the fifty-eighth *Upaniṣad* within the *Atharva Veda* corpus, elucidates *Haṭha-Yoga* and Vedāntic metaphysics. The text is divided into three chapters in which Śāṇḍilya figures as the disciple of Atharvan. The first chapter, defining the limbs of the eightfold path, mentions ten components for moral observance *(yama)* and self-discipline *(niyama)*. It describes the principal postures *(āsana)* and the ten main channels *(nāḍī)* of the life force and devotes special attention to the practice of breath retention *(kumbhaka)*, through which the awakening of the *kuṇḍalinī* is said to be produced. The second and third chapters offer an exposition of Vedānta metaphysics, forming the philosophical basis of its teachings. The *Upaniṣad* appears as a composite work with numerous interpolations; many of its stanzas are found in the *Yoga-yājñavalkya-gītā*.[20]

References to Dattātreya are found in the last portion of the third chapter. To the question of Śāṇḍilya on how this universe came into being, how it subsists, and how it will finally be absorbed into the imperishable *Brahman*, Atharvan replies that three "aspects" arose from the formless *Brahman*: *niṣkala* (the indivisible), *sakala* (the divisible), and *sakala-niṣkala* (the divisible and indivisible). The *Upaniṣad* defines the *niṣkala* aspect as truth, wisdom, and bliss; actionless and non-attached. The *sakala* aspect co-exists with the ignorance of the *ātman*, primordial matter, illusion, the three *guṇas*, and so on. The *sakala-niṣkala* aspect of *Brahman* is identified with Śiva Maheśvara who, after having performed severe *tapas*, proclaimed, "May I bring forth progeny." Everything originated from him: the syllable *oṃ*; the three utterances (*bhūr, bhuvas, svar*); the three-footed *gāyatrī*; the three *Vedas*; the triad of Brahmā, Viṣṇu, and Rudra; the castes; and the three sacrificial fires. Maheśvara alone is said to pervade reality and to be enshrined in the hearts of all beings. He alone is in front, behind, to the left, to the right, below, above, everywhere. Finally, Maheśvara is identified with Dattātreya, depicting the latter as an Avatāra of Śiva. This is an important exception, given the overall *Vaiṣṇava* identity of Dattātreya within the *Purāṇas*. Even within a *Śaiva* perspective, some attributes of Dattātreya in *Śāṇḍilya Upaniṣad* 3.1.6 call to mind the *Mārkaṇḍeya Purāṇa* account:

> Then, of this Lord, who is playing with his Ātmic power [*ātma-śakti*], who is full of compassion towards his devotees, whose form is of Dattātreya, whose beautiful body is without clothing of any kind; who has four arms resembling the petals of the lotus; and whose form is not fearful and reveals his sinlessness. This then is the partly divisible and partly indivisible form (of the Brahman).[21]

After answering the question on why Maheśvara is called Dattātreya, Atharvan thus closes the *Upaniṣad* (3.2.7–15):

> He, who, after knowing this, meditates on the transcendent Brahman in the attitude "I am He," becomes the knower of the Brahman. Here occur the following verses: He who would meditate, always in this manner, on the eternal Lord of Lords, Dattātreya, the auspicious and the tranquil, the lord who resembles the Indranīla gem (in complexion), who is intent on the unravelling of the Māyā (illusion) investing the Ātman, the god, nude in form [*avadhūta*] and having the cardinal directions as his garments [*digambara*], whose entire body is smeared with holy ashes, who wears the crown of matted hair, the glorious lord, with four arms and charming limbs, with eyes resembling full-blown lotus flowers, who is the treasure-mine of Jñāna and Yoga, the preceptor of the Universe, who is the object of affection of all classes of Yogins, compassionate towards his devotees, the all-witness, who is served by Siddhas (accomplished adepts)—such a one, released from all sins, will attain beatific bliss.[22]

Mention should also be made of a *Yoga-śāstra* treatise, a medieval Tantric work in 334 *ślokas* in which Dattātreya expounds the principles of *Mantra-Yoga, Haṭha-Yoga, Laya-Yoga,* and *Rāja-Yoga* to Sāṃkṛti.[23] Of these 334 *ślokas*, as many as 136 are found almost verbatim in the *Yoga-tattva Upaniṣad*.[24] Although the *Yoga-śāstra* speaks of the tradition of 840,000 postures, it describes only the lotus posture in detail. Besides *prāṇāyāma*, we find the description of important aspects of *Laya-Yoga* and of three *bandhas* of *Haṭha-Yoga*: the *mahā-mudrā*, the *khecarī-mudrā*, and the *vajrolī-mudrā*.[25] Another noteworthy Yoga text, known as "The Book of God Dattātreya," is the *Yoga-rāja-ṭiḷaka* of the Marāṭhī Amṛtānanda, written around 1540.[26]

The *Saṃnyāsa Upaniṣads*, the earliest known works on renunciation, are short texts of strong Advaita Vedānta leaning.[27] F. O. Schrader attempted a chronology of these *Upaniṣads* by identifying an older and a later group. The earlier group comprises the *Āruṇi, Brahma, Jābāla, Kaṭha-śruti, Kuṇḍikā, Laghu-saṃnyāsa,* and *Paramahaṃsa Upaniṣads*, while the later group includes the *Bhikṣuka, Bṛhad-avadhūta, Bṛhat-saṃnyāsa, Laghu-avadhūta, Maitreya, Nārada-parivrājaka, Nirvāṇa, Parabrahma, Paramahaṃsa-parivrājaka, Śāṭyāyanīya, Turīyātīta-avadhūta,* and *Yājñavalkya Upaniṣads*. Between these two groups is the *Āśrama Upaniṣad*.[28] Detailed studies by J. F. Sprockhoff, a student of Schrader, have, overall, confirmed Schrader's subdivision: Sprockhoff assigns the earlier group to the last few centuries before the common era, the *Āśrama Upaniṣad* to approximately 300 C.E., and the texts of the later group—with the exceptions of the *Nārada-parivrājaka,* which he dates to about 1150 C.E., and the *Śāṭyāyanīya,* which he dates around 1200 C.E.—to the fourteenth and fifteenth centuries.[29] Some of the late *Saṃnyāsa Upaniṣads* evidence the properties of medieval legal compendia (*nibandha*) and are composed of collections of passages taken from older *smṛtis* and other sources. The Advaita Vedānta characterization of the major monasteries of early medieval India explains the Advaita leaning of most of these texts. The *Saṃnyāsa Upaniṣads* are part of a broader literary tradition concerning renunciation and related topics. Besides providing significant data for the history of Hindu asceticism, these texts trace the development of Brahminical theology concerning *saṃnyāsa.*[30]

In these *Upaniṣads,* renunciation is viewed not as an end in itself but as a path leading to union with *Brahman* or *mokṣa.*[31] An enlightning definition of *saṃnyāsa* is given by Vāsudevāśrama at the beginning of his *Yati-dharma-prakāśa,* an important treatise on world renunciation probably composed between 1675 and 1800:

> (1.2) Renunciation is the abandonment of rites known through injunctions—the *śrauta* and *smārta,* the permanent, occasional and optional—after reciting the *praiṣa* formula.[32]

Patrick Olivelle comments:

> Renunciation essentially is a negative state: one is a renouncer not because one performs certain distinctive actions . . . but because one does not perform actions and does not conform to customs that characterize life-in-society. Renunciation . . . consists of an abandonment of one life-style, not the adoption of another. . . . Any positive element in the life of renouncers . . . is only incidental to renunciation.[33]

Hindu tradition offers three basic views regarding the renouncer's *āśrama.* The *vikalpa* or option view, perhaps the earliest, asserts that a person in any of the first three *āśramas* (*brahmacarya, gṛhastha, vānaprastha*) may renounce directly if he is totally detached from the pleasures of this world and the next; hence he is free to choose and not obliged to pass gradually through all the *āśramas.* The *samuccaya* view maintains the opposite, that is, that a man should pass through all four *āśramas* sequentially. This is the classical view as taught by Manu.

An interpretation of this view is that a man's life span, taken to be one hundred years, should be divided into four equal parts: a student during the first twenty-five years, a householder during the second, a forest hermit during the third, and a renouncer during the fourth. The third view, called *bādha*, considers the householder's to be the only true *āśrama*, leaving no room for *saṃnyāsa*.[34]

Qualifications for *saṃnyāsa* fall into two categories: internal dispositions and external circumstances. The main internal disposition required is that of *vairāgya*, which Vāsudevāśrama in *Yati-dharma-prakāśa* 4.1 calls "the cause of renunciation."[35] With regard to external circumstances, two prevailing views exist: the first and more restrictive view is that only Brahmins are entitled to take up *saṃnyāsa*, while the second (possibly the more widely followed, since ancient sacred texts record numerous instances of non-Brahmins becoming renouncers) extends such qualification to all twice-born men, thus including Kṣatriyas and Vaiśyas. On this issue, the Muni Dattātreya is mentioned in *Yati-dharma-prakāśa* 3.8–13 as the upholder of the narrower Brahminical point of view:

> Likewise, a *smṛti* also states: "To carry the emblem of Viṣṇu is the *dharma* of those born from the mouth, not of the Kṣatriyas or the Vaiśyas," said the sage Dattātreya.
>
> The emblem is the bamboo staff. Carrying it is the special insignium of a renouncer, who is a form of Viṣṇu. That (i.e. carrying a staff) is the *dharma*, viz. the duty, only of those born from the mouth, viz. those of Brāhmaṇic birth. That is the meaning of the *smṛti*.[36]

If in this unspecified *smṛti* passage Dattātreya appears in the role of a *Vaiṣṇava* sage upholding the sectarian Brahminical point of view concerning renunciation,[37] Vāsudevāśrama, on the contrary, subscribes to the more liberal view that all twice-born men are entitled to renounce. The unanimous opinion of Brahminical authorities is that Śūdras are not entitled to renounce, while the position of women is somewhat controversial. The Brahminical domain is rigidly male oriented, although the *smṛtis* and other ancient texts offer examples of female renouncers.[38] In any case, within the *Saṃnyāsa Upaniṣads* women and their bodies are depicted very negatively, said to excite lust in men and to pull men away from the path of virtue.[39] We find a veritable hatred of women and sexuality in many of the authors of these texts, evidencing a male, Brahminical, Vedāntic milieu.

The late *Bṛhad-avadhūta Upaniṣad* is the seventy-ninth within the *Kṛṣṇa Yajur Veda* corpus. This short text comprises a total of thirty-six *ślokas.* Of them, twenty-six are taken from Vidyāraṇya's *Pañcadaśī,*[40] and reflect the thoughts of a man who has gained insight into his identity with *Brahman.* The *Upaniṣad* describes the nature of the Avadhūta, his conduct, and the absence of obligation on his part to study scriptures of any kind, concluding with the glorification of the blessed state of self-realization. Like the *Darśana Upaniṣad,* it takes the form of a dialogue between Dattātreya, herein the exemplary model of the Avadhūta, and his pupil Sāṃkṛti. Raeside, noting the sectarian character of this *Upaniṣad,* thinks that it must postdate Dattātreya's establishment as the center of a cult.[41] However, Dattātreya's characterization as an Avadhūta might well have originated at an early date. At the beginning, the *Upaniṣad* offers a noteworthy and popular explanation of the Avadhūta. The four syllables *a, va, dhū, ta* are taken separately as standing for *akṣara, vareṇya, dhūta-saṃsāra-bandhana,* and *tat-tvam-asyādi-lakṣya:*

> (1) Once Sāṃkṛti went up to the Blessed Avadhūta, Dattātreya, and asked: Lord, who is an Avadhūta? What is his state? What is his emblem? What is his conduct? The most compassionate Lord Dattātreya said to him:
>
> (2) Because he is imperishable [*akṣara*], because he is the most excellent [*vareṇya*], because he has shaken off the bonds of *saṃsāra* [*dhūta-saṃsāra-bandhana*], and because he is denoted by the phrase "You are that" [*tat-tvam-asyādi-lakṣya*], he is called "Avadhūta."[42]

The *Jābāla Upaniṣad,* part of the *Śukla Yajur Veda* and 13th among the 108 *Upaniṣads,* is a short text divided into six sections, in the form of a dialogue between the pupils Bṛhaspati, Atri, Janaka, and their teacher Yājñavalkya. The text discusses: (1) the worship of the *Avimukta,* variously identified with Śiva, the infinite and unmanifest *ātman,* and the Avadhūta who knows the *ātman;* (2) the prayer leading to immortality and identified with the *Śatarudrīya* hymn; (3) the renunciation of worldly life by those keeping or not keeping a sacred fire; and (4) the high position accorded to the class of ascetics called Paramahaṃsas. The *Jābāla Upaniṣad* ends with a description of the austere way of life led by the unclad Paramahaṃsas. At the beginning of the last section, Dattātreya—together with other sages including Durvāsas—is mentioned as one of the Paramahaṃsas:

> Paramahaṃsas are men such as Saṃvartaka, Āruṇi, Śvetaketu, Durvāsas, Ṛbhu, Nidāgha, Jaḍabharata, Dattātreya, and Raivataka, who have no visible emblem [*avyakta-liṅgā*], who keep their

conduct concealed [*avyakta-ācārā*], and who, although they are sane [*anunmattā*], behave like madmen [*unmattavad-ācarantaḥ*].[43]

If not a later addition or interpolation to the *Jābāla Upaniṣad*—an early text possibly prior to the common era—this passage mentioning Dattātreya as one of the great Paramahaṃsas would be an indication of the antiquity of his renown as the highest type of renouncer. The same list of Paramahaṃsas is found in the third section of the late *Yājñavalkya Upaniṣad*. In fact, the first three sections of this composite *Upaniṣad* are identical with sections 4, 5, and 6 of the *Jābāla Upaniṣad*. Moreover, *Bṛhaj-jābāla Upaniṣad* 7.6, contained within the *Śaiva Upaniṣads*, reports the same list of Paramahaṃsas, and *Rudrākṣa-jābāla Upaniṣad* 46 mentions Dattātreya in yet another list of sages surrounding Rudra-Śiva.[44] Paramahaṃsas live without any outward symbol of their state and thus abandon the emblems of ordinary renouncers, emblems such as the staff, begging bowl, garment, sacrificial thread, topknot, and so on.[45] Renunciation being a negative state, advancement in *saṃnyāsa* is always marked by abandonment of emblems associated with lower levels, and thus the higher types of renouncers are expected to be totally naked. A description of the Paramahaṃsa closes the *Jābāla Upaniṣad*:

> Triple staff, water pot, sling, bowl, water strainer, topknot, sacrificial string: abandoning all these in water with the words: "Earth *svāhā*," let him seek after the self. He is clad as he was at birth. He is indifferent to the pairs of opposites. He has no possessions. He is firmly established in the path of Brahman. His mind is pure. Merely to sustain his life, he begs food randomly at the prescribed time, using his stomach as a begging bowl [*udara-pātreṇa*] and remaining the same both when he receives and when he does not. In deserted houses, in temples, on haystacks, by anthills, at the foot of trees, in potter's sheds, in sheds for fire sacrifices, on sandy banks of rivers, in mountain caves, in glens, in the hollows of trees, in lonely spots, or in open fields, he lives without a home. He does not strive. He is selfless. He devotes himself completely to meditating on the pure Brahman. He is grounded in the Supreme Self. He is dedicated to the uprooting of impure acts. Such a man who abandons his body through renunciation is called a Paramahaṃsa.[46]

The most common and perhaps the oldest classification of renouncers, from the lowest to the highest, is the fourfold division of Kuṭīcaka, Bahūdaka, Haṃsa, and Paramahaṃsa.[47] The *Āśrama Upaniṣad* is the earliest document in the *Saṃnyāsa Upaniṣads* to provide such a classification. However, the *Nārada-parivrājaka Upaniṣad* and other late texts offer a sixfold classification, adding the Turīyātīta[48] as the fifth and the Avadhūta as the sixth, supreme class. The difference between the Turīyātīta and the Avadhūta adept is not clear, and, in fact, some texts such as the *Turīyātīta-avadhūta Upaniṣad* combine them into a single class. It is important to stress that Dattātreya is usually presented as either a Paramahaṃsa or an Avadhūta. The Avadhūta is regarded as one possessing perfect *jñāna* or liberating knowledge and, therefore, is not subject to any rule or prohibition whatsoever. He thus becomes the veritable emblem of freedom and antinomian behavior.[49] The six classes are also distinguished by the goals to which they aspire. Whereas the *Āruṇi Upaniṣad* states that Kuṭīcakas aspire to the atmospheric world, Bahūdakas to the heavenly world, Haṃsas to the Penance-world, and Paramahaṃsas to the Truth-world, *Nārada-parivrājaka Upaniṣad* 177–78 states that both Turīyātītas and Avadhūtas attain liberation in this life.[50]

Theoretically, each class has different lifestyles based on the gradation of their detachment. The classic account of the Paramahaṃsa is Vidyāraṇya's *Jīvanmukti-viveka*, the final chapter being a commentary on the *Paramahaṃsa Upaniṣad* (4.4–19).[51] The *Jīvanmukti-viveka* distinguishes three levels of detachment; dull, intense, and extremely intense. At the intense level two types of renunciation are possible: one who is too weak to undertake a life of wandering becomes a Kuṭīcaka, while one who is stronger becomes a Bahūdaka. At the extremely intense level there are also two types: one who wishes to attain the world of Brahmā becomes a Haṃsa, while one who is intent on liberation in this very life becomes a Paramahaṃsa. The implicit assumption is that these classes of renouncers represent a hierarchy, from the lowest Kuṭīcakas to the highest Paramahaṃsas. The criterion, again, is a negative one: the more one is removed from life in society and is independent of the rules of *dharma*, the more elevated his renunciatory status will be. Thus each of the four types of *saṃnyāsa* is defined by the abandonment of practices peculiar to the preceding type. For instance, Vāsudevāśrama says that it is the abandonment of the staff and so forth that constitutes the essential state of a Paramahaṃsa—not any positive feature characteristic of that state. The use of specific ritual formulae is another case in point. Paramahaṃsas use only the mystic syllable *oṃ* as their *mantra*. Consequently, whenever a rite is prescribed other than the *oṃ*, the rule is interpreted as applying only to "Kuṭīcakas and the rest."

The enlightened Paramahaṃsas stand at the highest point of the hierarchical division, completely outside the normal working of *saṃsāra*: like the Avadhūta, they are believed to be beyond good and evil, free from all social and religious obligations. Nevertheless, it must be emphasized that the strict, most orthodox representatives of Advaita Vedānta uphold that such transcendence of the social and dharmic domain should not jeopardize caste rules and regulations. In other words, Brahminical theology tended to "neutralize" the possible consequences of the disrupting of all social norms which is implied in the Paramahaṃsa or Avadhūta ideal as well as in the notion of *jīvanmukti*. The fourth section of the *Paramahaṃsa Upaniṣad*[52] describes the way of life of the Paramahaṃsa:

> A mendicant shall be naked. He shall neither pay homage nor utter *svadhā*, neither give praise nor utter *vaṣaṭ*. For him there is neither invitation nor dismissal, neither *mantras* nor meditation nor even worship, neither the perceptible nor the imperceptible, neither the separate nor the non-separate, neither day nor night, nor anything at all! His is a homeless state.
>
> A mendicant thus should neither accept nor even look at such things as gold . . .
>
> He does not fear pain. He longs not for pleasure. He forsakes love. He is not attached anywhere either to the pleasant or to the unpleasant. He does not hate. He does not rejoice. The activities of all his senses have come to rest. Firmly fixed in knowledge, the self ever abides in the self alone. He is called an ascetic. He alone is a Yogin; and he alone is a knower. "I am that *Brahman* who is consummate bliss and pure consciousness:" realizing this, he becomes one who has done all there is to do.[53]

The *Nārada-parivrājaka Upaniṣad*, probably composed about 1150 C.E., is the 43d among the 108 *Upaniṣads* and is part of the *Atharva Veda*. The longest of all *Saṃnyāsa Upaniṣads*—evidencing the properties of medieval legal compendia—it is divided into nine chapters dealing with the means to reach *mokṣa*, the orders of ascetics and their qualifications to renounce the world, the cases of "emergency *saṃnyāsa*" to be resorted to by the afflicted, the duties of renunciants, the total renunciation of motivated action, and the liberating *mantra* (*tāraka-mantra*) enabling to cross the ocean of existence. Finally, the *Upaniṣad* ends with a description of the real form of *Brahman* and the means of realizing that ultimate bliss. Dattātreya is mentioned in verse 154, toward the end of chapter 3, describing the adoption by a Brahmin of the state of Paramahaṃsa or Avadhūta:

> Like Śvetaketu, Ṛbhu, Nidāgha Vṛṣabha, Durvāsas, Saṃvartaka, Dattātreya and Raivataka, he has no visible emblem; he keeps his conduct concealed; he acts as if he were a fool, a lunatic, or a goblin [*bāla-unmatta-piśācavad*]; and, although he is sane, he behaves like a madman.[54]

Besides the seeking of dishonor and the imitation of animals—wandering about like worms, unnoticed and despised—the "vow of madness" taken by these supreme renunciants is theologically associated to the transcendence of rationality.[55] Madness becomes a proof of divinity in the eyes of believers. The expression *bāla-unmatta-piśācavad* is not uncommon in the *Saṃnyāsa Upaniṣads*, and it especially designates the Avadhūta. The term *bāla* can mean both a madman and a child, indicating in either case irrational behavior. *Unmatta* can designate both a lunatic and a man who is intoxicated. *Piśāca* is a class of demonic beings believed to eat raw flesh; dwelling around cremation grounds, they produce feelings of fear and disgust in those who behold them. The Avadhūta's behavior has its exemplary model in the figure of Śiva himself, the lord of Yoga. The thirty-sixth of Śiva's thousand names praises the deity as "the one concealed in the guise of madness."[56]

Bhikṣuka Upaniṣad 235 also mentions Dattātreya among the Paramahaṃsa ascetics:

> Paramahaṃsas are men such as Saṃvartaka, Āruṇi, Śvetaketu, Jaḍabharata, Dattātreya, Śuka, Vāmadeva, and Hārītaka, who, eating eight mouthfuls, seek only liberation by the Yogic path.[57]

Before analyzing the *Dattātreya Upaniṣad*, it seems appropriate to highlight the salvific value which the medieval *Muktikā Upaniṣad* attributes to the Upaniṣadic corpus as a whole, and to the *Dattātreya Upaniṣad* in particular. The *Muktikā Upaniṣad*, in the form of a dialogue between Rāma and his exemplar devotee Hanumān, is a Vedānta treatise possibly dating from the late fourteenth century. It consists of two sections, the second dealing with various Yogic processes. It is said to be part of the *Śukla Yajur Veda* and is usually listed among the so-called *Vedānta Upaniṣads*.[58]

In the first *adhyāya*, Rāma explains to Hanumān how, in order to attain *videha-mukti* or disembodied liberation, one must study the 108 *Upaniṣads*. Rāma then lists the names of these various *Upaniṣads*, among which he cites the *Dattātreya Upaniṣad*, together with their respective purificatory *mantras* or *śāntis*.[59] The *Dattātreya Upaniṣad*, together with thirty other *Upaniṣads* belonging to the *Atharva Veda*, is said to have as its *śānti* the words *bhadraṃ karṇebhiḥ*, meaning "what is good [let us hear] with our ears."[60] Rāma explains how these sacred texts are able to do away with the three *bhāvanas* of doubt, vain thought, and false thought, and confer *jñāna* and *vairāgya* by destroying the three *vāsanās* of book-lore, world, and body.

The *Dattātreya Upaniṣad*, number 101 within the *Atharva Veda* corpus, is included among the *Vaiṣṇava Upaniṣads*.[61] A Tantric sectarian work, clearly evidencing a *Śākta* leaning, it is divided into three short sections specifically dealing with the salvific power of Dattātreya *mantras*. Raeside's argument that this *Upaniṣad* presumably postdates Dattātreya's establishment as the center of a cult is convincing.[62] The first *khaṇḍa* opens with Brahmā the creator questioning lord Viṣṇu-Nārāyaṇa about who can help cross the ocean of *saṃsāra*. Viṣṇu replies:

> Meditate on my essence which is pure and which is the same as truth, bliss, and knowledge, as "I am in all circumstances Datta himself" . . . If you meditate on Nārāyaṇa as Dattātreya . . . the same becomes the boat. This truth alone ought to be understood. It is the boat that takes one across the ocean of birth and death, womb, etc.[63]

Accordingly, after meditating on Viṣṇu-Dattātreya, Brahmā realizes that the infinite and peerless *Brahman* alone remains as the "residuum" after negation of all else. What follows is the exposition of a collection of *tāraka-mantras* of Dattātreya: from the monosyllabic *daṃ* up to a sixteen-syllabled one, followed by the enunciation of a *mantra* in the *anuṣṭubh* meter, and closing with the all-important *mālā-mantra* of Dattātreya.[64] In Tantric practice, the fundamental *mantra* of a deity is often formed by taking the first syllable or letter of the name, as in this case *da* for Dattātreya, and adding the nasal sound (*anunāsika*) to it. *Daṃ* thus stands for Dattātreya[65] and it is said to be the *haṃsa*, the *ātman* established in all *jīvas*. In its lengthened form, *dāṃ* symbolizes the impersonal *paramātman*. Within the Dattātreya *sampradāya*, even more important than *daṃ* or *dāṃ*, is the phoneme *draṃ* or *drāṃ* (*daṃ*/*dāṃ* plus *r*), the supreme *mantra* of the deity. This is possibly derived from the fact that the syllable *da* is contained in the lotus of the *maṇipūra-cakra*—one of the six Yogic psychoenergetic centers located at the navel—whose *mantra* is *raṃ*, a phoneme representing fire or Agni. The repetition of this sonic vibration (*spanda*) is believed to make the deity present and alive (*jāgṛt*). The *mantra* of a *devatā* is that *devatā*. Although semantics has no place in the understanding of these sounds—believed to embody the subtle potency (*śakti*) of a deity—it is nevertheless worthwhile to notice that the meaning of the verbal root *dram* is "to roam," "to wander." Even semantically *draṃ* fits well with Dattātreya's persona: as an eternal Avatāra and Avadhūta he is believed to be omnipresent, incessantly roaming across the Indian subcontinent!

The six-syllabled salvific *mantra* is: *oṃ śrīṃ hrīṃ klīṃ glauṃ drāṃ*. This is a *bīja mantra*, a collection of meaningless "seed" (*bīja*) sounds in a meta-Sanskrit transcending ordinary speech. These *bījas* are believed to be sonic manifestations of the fundamental constituents of the cosmos, not mere symbols of the elements, but the cosmic elements in their essential form. *Bīja-mantras* are a middle level (*madhyamā*) stage of *Śabda-Brahman*, linking ordinary speech (*vaikharī*) to the higher levels of speech (*vāc*). As simple phonemes with no lexical meaning, they require interpretation, since each *bīja* is usually identified with a specific deity. Of course, *oṃ* is the fundamental *bīja-mantra* representing the very first vibration in the process of manifestation. It is the physical reproduction of a subtle sound which only the Yogin can perceive in his heart. From the *oṃ*, all other *bīja-mantras* originate. The first eight (*aiṃ, hrīṃ, śrīṃ, krīṃ, klīṃ, strīṃ, hlīṃ, trīṃ*) are said to represent the eightfold nature of *Brahman*. This six-syllabled *mantra*—asymmetrical and heteromorphemic as the following ones—begins with the *praṇava oṃ* and closes with the *bīja drāṃ* identifying Dattātreya. *Śrīṃ* is the seed of pleasure or *rāma-bīja*. It is also called *lakṣmī-bīja* and identifies the goddess of fortune and abundance Śrī-Lakṣmī, Viṣṇu's consort, also revered as Dattātreya's consort in the *Mārkaṇḍeya Purāṇa* account. *Hrīṃ* is the seed of energy or *śakti-bīja*. It is also known as *māyā-bīja* and is the seed *mantra* of the goddess Tripurā or Tripurasundarī, denoting the unity of the male and female principles. It is also revered as the primal vibration of the goddess Bhuvaneśvarī, the Devī of the three worlds and one of the ten forms (*mahā-vidyās*) of Śiva's consort Satī.[66] *Klīṃ* is the seed of love or *kāma-bīja*, and identifies the procreative desire of Śiva as the god of love Kāma. It represents joy, bliss, and the pleasure of sexual union. It is not clear who or what the *bīja glauṃ* identifies: it may denote another form of Devī or perhaps even Gaṇeśa, the remover of obstacles.[67] Nevertheless, it is fairly clear that this *mantra* bears a *Śākta* flavor. It appears to celebrate Dattātreya as united to the various forms of his Śakti—Lakṣmī, Māyā-Bhuvaneśvarī—through Kāma exemplifying Tantric blissful union.

The eight-syllable *mantra* reported in the *Dattātreya Upaniṣad* is a mixed *mantra,* in the sense that it is partly in *bīja* form and partly semantically meaningful: *draṃ* (*drāṃ*) *dattātreyāya namaḥ,* meaning "*draṃ* (*drāṃ*) let there be prostration to Dattātreya." The portion *dattātreyāya* is said to express *sat-cit-ānanda,* while that of *namaḥ* full-blown bliss. No reference is made to Dattātreya's Śakti or female counterpart. According to various authorities, *mantras* may be divided into male, female, and neuter. Masculine *mantras* end in *huṃ* and *phaṭ,* female in *svāhā,* neuter in *namaḥ,* as in our case.

The twelve-syllable formula is another mixed *mantra*: *oṃ āṃ hrīṃ kroṃ ehi dattātreyāya svāhā.* It opens with the *praṇava oṃ,* and it ends with a powerful ". . . come [*ehi*]! Hail [*svāhā*] to Dattātreya." *Ehi* is not a *bīja-mantra* but the imperative form of the verbal root *i* + *ā*.[68] The term *svāhā,* believed to bear a magical, strengthening power since Atharva Vedic times,[69] is an exclamation used in making oblations to the gods as well as an utterance of consecration. *Svāhā* is also believed to be the esoteric name of Agni's consort. The *āṃ* should be understood as the letter *ā* (a + a)—Śiva-Śakti in inseparable union (*yāmala*)—with the addition of the *anunāsika.* Any true *bīja-akṣara* or seed syllable should end with the continuous nasal sound of the "unpronounceable vibration" of the *candra-bindu. Hrīṃ* again identifies a Śakti, while the sacred sound *kroṃ* possibly identifies another form of Devī. The *mantra* might be understood as a universal call to partake in Dattātreya's worship: the whole manifest universe—symbolized by *āṃ*—and the god's Śakti or Śaktis—*hrīṃ, kroṃ*—are invoked to come and duly honor him. Again, the overall *Śākta* characterization of this *tāraka-mantra* evidences Dattātreya's link to a *Śākta* milieu.

The sixteen-syllable formula is another example of a mixed *Śākta mantra*: *oṃ aiṃ kroṃ klīṃ klūṃ hrāṃ hrīṃ hrūṃ sauḥ dattātreyāya svāhā.* The *bīja-mantra aiṃ* is the seed of the teacher or *guru-bīja.* It is also known as *vahni-jāyā,* identifying Agni's consort, and as *vāgbhava,* identifying the goddess of speech Sarasvatī. If *klīṃ* identifies Kāma and *hrīṃ* identifies a Śakti, *kroṃ, klūṃ, hrāṃ* and *hrūṃ* may possibly denote various other forms of Devī and of Śiva. The *bīja-mantra sauḥ*—understood to be made up of the three *mātṛkās s, au,* and *ḥ*—is also known as the heart-*mantra* and bears great symbolical relevance, especially in the *Kaula* Tantrism of Abhinavagupta. As L. Silburn observes:

> SAUḤ is the heart *mantra,* the supreme I-ness, and it should not be considered as a formula meant for recitation, but as an energy

> to be activated in order to obtain the comprehension full of potency [*mantra-vīrya*] through which one goes back to the source—the universal Heart and its rhythm.[70]

In our context, the *bīja sauḥ* could even be interpreted as another "name" of Dattātreya, the source and heart of all beings, eternally united to his Śakti in an embrace of love. Thus, also this *mantra* points to the Tantric blissful union of Śiva and Śakti, alias Dattātreya and Lakṣmī, or one of the Devī's innumerable forms.

In each of the above *mantras* the meter is said to be the *gāyatrī*, the Ṛṣi Sadāśiva, and the presiding *devatā*, of course, Dattātreya. Apart from the *Dattātreya Upaniṣad*, the seer of all sacred *mantras* pertaining to Dattātreya is said to be Sadāśiva, that is, the eternal Śiva.[71] Finally and most importantly, the function of the *mantra* is explained, which is liberation from the painful wheel of *saṃsāra*. The *bījas* of the Tantric *mantra* are thought to communicate an exact knowledge of the *devatā* and of the universe, so as to enable the adept to acquire the knowledge of reality, saving himself from transmigration. According to Indian authors, the salvific force of *mantra* is manifest in the etymology of the word itself. As *Kulārṇava-tantra* 17.54 states: "By meditation on the deity of boundless glow in the form of the highest principle, he is saved from all danger; therefore it is called *mantra*." The recitation of these *tāraka-mantras* is part of the *pūjā* program of the Tantric adept. The various *mantras* are believed to magically purify the worshiper's body and mystical centers (*cakras*), to the point of making one's form a fit receptacle for the deity itself (*aṅga-nyāsa*). This may bring about the identification of the worshiper with the *devatā* worshipped. As Mircea Eliade observes:

> *Nyāsa*, the "ritual projection" of divinities into various parts of the body, [is] a practice of considerable antiquity but one that Tantrism revalorized and enriched. The disciple "projects" the divinities, at the same time touching various areas of the body; in other words, he homologizes his body with the Tantric pantheon. . . . Several kinds of *nyāsa* are distinguished according to their degree of interiorization, for in some cases the divinities and their symbols are "put" into the various organs of the body by a pure act of meditation.[72]

Dattātreya's meaningful *mantra* in the *anuṣṭubh* meter, of which all portions are in the vocative, closes the first part of the *Upaniṣad*:

dattātreya hare kṛṣṇa unmatta-ānanda-dāyaka;
digambara mune bāla piśāca jñāna-sāgara.

Oh Dattātreya [who are] Hari, Kṛṣṇa and the crazy bliss-bestower![73]
Oh you [who are] the naked ascetic, the hermit [having made the vow of silence], the child, the demon, the ocean of knowledge!

This is perhaps the most popular and well known of all Dattātreya *mantras*. No *Śākta* element is recognizable in it. It certainly developed out of a sectarian ascetic milieu, possibly linked to that which produced the *Saṃnyāsa Upaniṣads*. Three features of Dattātreya in this *mantra* need to be noted: (1) his *Vaiṣṇava* identity, since Dattātreya is none other than Hari and Kṛṣṇa (and Nārāyaṇa; see the very beginning of the *Dattātreya Upaniṣad*); (2) his characterization as an antinomian ascetic (*unmatta, bāla, piśāca*) of the highest class (*digambara, muni*); (3) his celebration as supreme *jñānin* (*jñāna-sāgara*). Although these features are found in the *Mārkaṇḍeya Purāṇa* account, as well as separately in other Purāṇic accounts, it is only in the *Saṃnyāsa Upaniṣads* that the second feature is especially encountered: the naked ascetic, Paramahaṃsa or Avadhūta, is there described with precisely the same terms *bāla, unmatta,* and *piśāca* (*bāla-unmatta-piśācavad*). The first feature is clearly derived from Dattātreya's overall Purāṇic characterization as an Avatāra of Viṣṇu, while the third feature is a constant of Dattātreya throughout the literature. It may be concluded that this most popular *anuṣṭubh mantra* of Dattātreya brings together the deity's three fundamental natures: that of a Guru or teacher of liberating knowledge, that of a supreme ascetic or Yogin, and that of an Avatāra of Viṣṇu.

The second *khaṇḍa* of the *Dattātreya Upaniṣad* offers the important *mālā-mantra* of Dattātreya. This is a text or spell written in the form of a wreath. The Tantric adept is instructed to practice the mental repetition or vocal muttering (*japa*) of the deity's *mantra*. The correct practice of *japa* is one of the most important elements of Tantric *pūjā*. By means of its proper performance, the power of the *mālā-mantra* is believed to be discharged, granting the adept the desired boon.[74] The repetition of Dattātreya's *mālā-mantra* is naturally intended for the attainment of *mokṣa*. The text runs as follows:

Here one should utter *oṃ*. *Oṃ*! Prostrations to lord Dattātreya, propitiated through remembrance [of his name], dispeller of great fears, bestower of the highest knowledge, of the nature of consciousness and bliss, appearing in the guise of a child, a madman, a demon, the great Yogin, the Avadhūta, the enhancer of Anasūyā's bliss, the son of Atri, the bestower of the fruits of all desires!

Here one should utter *oṃ*.

Prostrations to the redeemer from the bonds of worldly existence!

Here one should utter *hrīṃ*.

Prostrations to the giver of all kinds of powers!

Here one should utter *kroṃ*.

Prostrations to He who attracts all kinds of accomplishments!

Here one should utter *sauḥ*.

Prostrations to the shaker of all minds!

Here one should utter *śrīṃ*. Here one should [also] utter *mahoṃ*.

Prostrations to the long-lived!

Here one should utter *vaṣaṭ*.

Subdue, subdue!

Here one should utter *vauṣaṭ*.

Attract, attract!

Here one should utter *huṃ*.

Be averse, be averse!

Here one should utter *phaṭ*.

Drive away, drive away!

Here one should utter *ṭha, ṭha*.

Paralyse, paralyse!

Here one should utter *kha, kha*.

Slay, slay!

Prostrations to the excellent one, prostrations to the excellent one!

Svāhā, nourish, nourish [my body]!

Destroy, destroy the highest *mantras*, the highest *yantras* and the highest *tantras* [of my adversaries]!

Ward off, ward off the [malignant influences of the] planets!

Ward off, ward off ailments!

Destroy, destroy anguish!

Drive away, drive away poverty!

Nourish, nourish the body!

Fill, fill the mind with joy!

Prostrations unto Thee, the real form of all *mantras, yantras, tantras* and *pallavas*!

Oṃ! Prostrations to Śiva!

Thus the *Upaniṣad*.

The *mālā-mantra* can be divided into two parts. The first part, the utterance of *bīja-mantras* from *oṃ* through *mahoṃ*, praises Dattātreya by enumerating his wonderful attributes and qualities. The text presents him as a bestower of both *mukti* (through *jñāna*) and *bhukti*, worldly enjoyments—a typical characteristic of Tantric deities. The second part, which comprises the utterance of *mantras* from *vaṣaṭ* to *svāhā* and extends to the end of the *Upaniṣad*, is an invocation to the deity so that it may, on one hand, protect, support, and nourish his adept, and, on the other hand, drive away, slay, destroy, and so forth, all enemies and evil influences. The function of these exclamations is clearly that of magically averting all adverse circumstances standing in the way of spiritual realization. In particular, *vaṣaṭ* and *vauṣaṭ* have the function of enticing or assuaging power, the phonetic complex *v-s* being associated from Vedic liturgy with superhuman speed. The *bīja huṃ*, also known as *varman*, the warrior, has the function of fighting against any evil force. In Vedic liturgy, *huṃ* was recited by the *udgātṛ* to connect portions of the *Sāma Veda* used in *soma* sacrifices. The exclamation *phaṭ* is called *astra*, meaning "weapon," and is generally used as an aggressive *mantra*. From the times of the *Yajur* and *Atharva Vedas*, *phaṭ* was thought to have the power of driving away demons and evil influences. The sound *phaṭ* bears in itself the idea of explosion. A similar function is attributed to the sound *ṭha*, said to be an imitative sound of a particularly loud noise, as of a golden pitcher rolling down steps. *Kha*, bearing the same function of warding off evil influences, may designate one of the nine orifices of the human body as well as space, air, and ether. L. Silburn, within the context of Kashmiri *Śaivism*, notes that the *mantra kha* relates to resorption and is associated with the rising of *kuṇḍalinī*.[75]

The *mālā-mantra* ends with *oṃ namaḥ śivāya*, identifying Dattātreya with Śiva. The *Upaniṣad*, which opens proclaiming Dattātreya's *Vaiṣṇava* identity—*nārāyaṇaṃ dattātreyam*—in the end acknowledges his *Śaiva* character. This integration of *Vaiṣṇava* and *Śaiva* elements, so typical of Maharashtrian spirituality, represents the leitmotif of Dattātreya's modern typology, which is legitimized and rooted precisely in Dattātreya's eclectic religious background. From the very beginning, we are faced with a coexistence of both elements in Dattātreya's icon: although his identification with Viṣṇu-Nārāyaṇa appears as his core Purāṇic identity, important *Śaiva* traits are present, given Dattātreya's early portrayal as a Yogin as well as the exemplary Avadhūta. Dattātreya's mythical origins facilitated his religious and ritual acceptability by both *Vaiṣṇavas* and *Śaivas*, establishing the premises for his later characterization as a manifestation of the holy triad.

Finally, in its third *khaṇḍa*, the *Upaniṣad* mentions the reward promised to its reader (*dattātreya-vidyā-phala*): he who masters this mantric knowledge and practices it properly is said to become holy; to attain the merit of having muttered the sacred *gāyatrī*, the *mahā-rudra*, and the *praṇava* innumerable times; and to be absolved from all sins (*pāpa*). To sum up, the overall Tantric framework of the *Dattātreya Upaniṣad* is evident. The text concerns itself with the efficacy of the deity's *mantras*. Dattātreya is the *devatā* on which the adept is called to meditate upon, with the support of devices such as *yantras*, in order to attain fusion (*sāyujya*) with the deity, transmuting his body into the very form of the god.[76] Dattātreya is traditionally viewed as one of the many authors of the sixty-four *Tantras*,[77] and of specific Tantric works such as the *Gandharva-tantra*, the *Tantra-kaumudī*, the *Śakti-saṅgama*, the *Rudra-yāmala*, the *Kālikā*, the *Kulārṇava*, the *Tantra-tattva* and the *Mahā-nirvāṇa*.[78] On the subject of *mantra* as well as *stotra*, dozens of sectarian Tantric works attributed to Dattātreya exist, such as the *Dattātreya-mantra*, the *Dattātreya-mālā-mantra*, the *Dattātreya-kavaca*, the *Dattātreya-vajra-kavaca*, the *Dattātreya-bodha*, the *Dattātreya-cakra*, the *Dattātreya-gāyatrī*, the *Dattātreya-kalpa*, the *Dattātreya-tantra*, and so on.[79] Dattātreya's worship as it is described in the *Dattātreya Upaniṣad* may be compared to the worship of female deities within *Śākta* Hinduism: the *Śākta Upaniṣads*, with their meditative techniques of absorption, are cases in point.[80] In particular, Dattātreya's connection with Śāktism is accounted for within the *Tripurā-rahasya*, "The Secret [Doctrine] of [the Goddess] Tripurā."[81]

This study of Dattātreya's presence within eight of the so-called minor *Upaniṣads*, brings me now to a few concluding remarks. Chronologically speaking, the oldest of these documents mentioning Dattātreya would appear to be the *Jābāla Upaniṣad*, possibly composed prior to the common era. The other *Saṃnyāsa Upaniṣads*, the two *Yoga Upaniṣads* and the *Dattātreya Upaniṣad*, are late compositions ascribed to the medieval period, perhaps the fourteenth or fifteenth century. Despite this chronological uncertainty and the gap in time, all *Saṃnyāsa Upaniṣads* appear extremely coherent in their portrayal of the supreme renunciant. Even the *Yoga Upaniṣads*, in their presentation of Dattātreya as teacher of an integrative type of Yoga, contain elements and themes which are surely much older than their date of composition. In other words, Dattātreya seems to have been appropriated across the centuries by a variety of Yogic and renunciatory circles, continuing to the point at which his sectarian characterization is mirrored in the *Dattātreya Upaniṣad*. Rather than envisioning a plurality of separate Dattātreyas molded one at a time in each single environment or *sampradāya*, it seems more reasonable to argue for an ongoing cross-fertilization taking place among a variety of religious circles: Tantric and Nātha adepts, Brahmin renouncers, *Vaiṣṇavas* and *Śaivas*, *Śāktas*, and so forth. All of them, perhaps unknowingly, participated in the molding of what ultimately becomes a remarkable integrative figure. This development was made possible by the composite portrayal qualifying the deity from its very first emergence.

Notes

1. See Deussen, *Sechzig Upanishad's des Veda.* Paul Deussen was expanding on a classification first proposed in 1878 by Weber, *History of Indian Literature,* 156. Deussen's division—also including the group of the *Śiva Upaniṣads*—does not reflect an indigenous classification. This fivefold division, with the addition of the *Śākta Upaniṣads,* was followed by the Adyar Library when, under the direction of F. Otto Schrader, it drew up a plan to publish critical editions of all minor *Upaniṣads.*

2. See Chapple and Viraj, *The Yoga Sūtras of Patañjali.*

3. This unfolding of the Yoga tradition in stages has been noticed by various scholars. See Varenne, *Yoga and the Hindu Tradition;* Beck, *Sonic Theology: Hinduism and Sacred Sound.*

4. As in Kṣemarāja, the *Krama* commentaries, later *Śrī-vidyā* writers such as Śrīvidyānandanāth of the *Saubhāgya-ratnākara,* Amṛtānanda, and Bhāskararāya. This tendency to revision by selective exclusion is also found among the contemporary *Śaṅkarācāryas* of Kāñcīpuram or Śṛṅgeri, as well as in the teachings of personalities such as the late Svāmin Muktānanda of Ganeshpuri in Maharashtra.

5. *Haṭha-Yoga,* literally "forceful discipline," comprises a vast Tantric collection of doctrines and practices aimed at self-realization by means of perfecting the body. *Kuṇḍalinī-Yoga* is the Tantric discipline involving the deliberate arousal of the *kuṇḍalinī-śakti.* For an introduction to *Haṭha-Yoga* and *Kuṇḍalinī-Yoga,* see Gupta, Hoens, and Goudriaan, *Hindu Tantrism,* 163–85. On *kuṇḍalinī,* see Silburn, *Kuṇḍalinī: Energy of the Depths.*

6. On the connection between Nātha literature and the *Yoga Upaniṣads,* see Bouy, *Les Nātha-yogin et les Upaniṣads.*

7. On the crucial notion of *jīvanmukti* and its Upaniṣadic roots, see Sprockhoff, "Die Idee der Jīvanmukti in den Spaten Upaniṣads"; Fort, "Going or Knowing? The Development of the Idea of Living Liberation in the Upaniṣads"; Oberhammer, *La délivrance, dès cette vie (jīvanmuktiḥ);* Fort and Mumme, *Living Liberation in Hindu Thought.*

8. See Shashibhusan Dasgupta, *Obscure Religious Cults*, 208. There, Dasgupta offers a fine presentation of Nāthism; see 191–255, 367–98. On the Nāthas, see also Tessitori, "Yogīs (Kānphaṭā)"; Weston Briggs, *Gorakhnāth and the Kānphaṭa Yogīs*; Dvivedi, *Nāth Sampradāy*. On the Nāthas in Nepal, see Lienhard, "Problèmes du syncretisme religieux au Népal"; N. J. Allen, "The Coming of Macchendranāth to Nepāl: Comments from a Comparative Point of View." See also two articles by Véronique Bouillier: "La caste sectaire des Kānphaṭā Jogī dans le royaume du Népal: l'exemple de Gorkha" and "Une caste de Yogī Newar: Les Kusle-Kāpāli." On the Nātha sect in southern India, see Dhere, *Śrīguru Gorakṣanātha: Caritra āṇi Paramparā*. For a presentation of some of the most important Nātha works, see Kalyani Mallik, *Siddha-siddhānta-paddhati and Other Works of the Nātha Yogīs*; Akshaya Kumar Banerjea, *Philosophy of Gorakhnath: With* Goraksha-vacana-sangraha. A collection of Nātha poems is offered in Dvivedi, *Nāth Siddhon kī Bāniyān*.

9. For other lists, see Śarmā, *Hindī ko Marāṭhī Santon kī Den*, 58–65.

10. See Vaudeville, "The Shaiva-Vaishnava Synthesis in Maharashtrian Santism," 220.

11. See Varenne, *Yoga and the Hindu Tradition*, 182. On the *Yoga Upaniṣads*, see the Sanskrit edition of Pandit A. Mahadeva Sastri (Adyar, 1920); it includes the commentary of Śrī Upaniṣad-Brahma-Yogin. For a survey of the main *Yoga Upaniṣads*, see Eliade, *Yoga: Immortality and Freedom*, 128–35.

12. Ayyangar, *The Yoga Upanishads*, 141.

13. Beck, *Sonic Theology*, 97. For an overview of the esteem accorded to *nāda* or *Nāda-Brahman* in the *Yoga Upaniṣads*, see ibid., 92–97.

14. For an English translation of this *Upaniṣad*, see Ayyangar, *The Yoga Upanishads*, 116–47. For a summary, see N. S. Subrahmanian, *Encyclopaedia of the Upaniṣads*, 406–8.

15. According to Hindu mythology, he was the son of Viśvāmitra and the founder of the Vaiyāghrapadya family.

16. On the importance of practising *dhyāna* on the *oṃ* syllable, Jan A. Schoterman—in his analysis of the eighth chapter of the *Kubjikā Upaniṣad*—notes how at least two so-called *Praṇava Upaniṣads* existed, one consisting of the literal text of *Gopatha Brāhmaṇa* 1.1.16–30, and another one identical to the *Brahma-vidyā Upaniṣad*:

> From a rather early time, there must have circulated more than one Upaniṣadic text that dealt with the nature of OM (among them also the *Māṇḍūkya Upaniṣad*) and that therefore could be designated by the title *Praṇava Upaniṣad*. (Schoterman, "The Kubjikā Upaniṣad and Its Atharvavedic Character," 323)

17. *Piṅgalā,* literally "yellow," "gold-colored." One of the three primary channels of the life force. It is situated to the right of the central conduit (*suṣumnā-nāḍī*) and terminates in the right nostril. The *piṅgalā* channel is associated with *sūrya* and is responsible for heating the body.

Iḍā, literally "refreshment," "comfort." It is situated to the left of the *suṣumnā-nāḍī.* The *iḍā-nāḍī* is generally thought to commence in the "bulb" (*kanda*) and to extend to the left nostril. It coils around the central channel and is associated with the cooling energy of the moon.

18. Feuerstein, *Encyclopedic Dictionary,* 88.

19. For an English translation of this *Upaniṣad,* see Ayyangar, *The Yoga Upanishads,* 448–91; K. Narayanasvami Aiyar, *Thirty Minor Upanishads,* 173–91. For a summary, see Subrahmanian, *Encyclopaedia of the Upaniṣads,* 451–55.

Śāṇḍilya is the name of several teachers, including a famous authority of the *Pāñcarātra* tradition.

20. A work on *Haṭha-Yoga,* consisting of 506 stanzas written in the form of a dialogue between Yājñavalkya and his wife Gargī. P. C. Divanji, who edited this text in 1954, dated it to around the second century C.E. An analysis of the contents and terminology, however, suggests a much later date, perhaps the thirteenth or fourteenth century.

21. This English translation is taken from Ayyangar, *The Yoga Upanishads,* 488–89. See also K. N. Aiyar, *Thirty Minor Upanishads,* 190.

22. Ayyangar, *The Yoga Upanishads,* 490–91. For an analysis of Dattātreya's various attributes, see Bahadur, *Dattātreya: The Way and the Goal,* 21-55.

23. On the *Yoga-śāstra* treatise, see Awasthi, *Yoga Shastra of Dattātreya.*

A relatively late development, *Yoga-tattva Upaniṣad* 21f. defines *Mantra-Yoga* as the recitation of various *mantras* made up of the *mātṛkās,* the primary sounds of the Sanskrit alphabet. A ritualistic discipline, this kind of Yoga is said to be especially suitable for the beginner. If diligently pursued, it is believed to gradually lead to salvific knowledge and the attainment of supernormal powers. For an introduction to *Mantra-Yoga,* see Gupta, Hoens, and Goudriaan, *Hindu Tantrism,* 90–117.

Laya-Yoga or "the discipline of [meditative] absorption"—analogous to *Kuṇḍalinī-Yoga*—describes various Tantric meditative exercises aimed at dissolving the conditional mind, often through such means as *prāṇāyāma* and *mudrā.* The term *laya* refers to the dissolution of one's *vāsanās,* leading to a state of *samādhi.*

Rāja-Yoga or "royal discipline" generally designates the classical Yoga of Patañjali's *Yoga-sūtras.* Though traditionally opposed to *Haṭha-Yoga*—often thought of as a mere preparatory discipline to *Rāja-Yoga*—important texts such as the *Haṭha-yoga-pradīpikā* seek to bridge these two approaches.

24. For a translation of this *Upaniṣad* of the *Kṛṣṇa Yajur Veda,* also belonging to the medieval period, see K. N. Aiyar, *Thirty Minor Upanishads,* 192–201.

25. *Mahā-mudrā,* literally "great seal." Both the *Gheraṇḍa Saṃhitā* (3.6f.) and the *Haṭha-yoga-pradīpikā* (3.10–18) explain it as follows: one presses the left heel against the buttocks, while stretching the right leg and catching hold of one's toes. Then one contracts the throat and gazes at the spot between the eyebrows. The practice is repeated with the left leg extended. According to *Haṭha-yoga-pradīpikā* 3.11–12, this practice awakens one's *kuṇḍalinī-śakti,* since the *prāṇa* is now directed through one's *suṣumnā.*

Khecarī-mudrā, literally "space-moving seal," the *mudrā* of the elongated tongue, freely moving within the space of the cranium, in the region of the nasal cavities. This technique has great importance in *Haṭha-Yoga,* where it is used in conjunction with breath control. The *amṛta* nectar is believed to flow abundantly from the "skull cavity" (*kapāla-kuhara*) and to be absorbed by the adept through his tongue. Through this *mudrā,* the semen is said to be prevented from falling.

Vajrolī-mudrā, literally "seal of the thunder." *Gheraṇḍa Saṃhitā* 3.45f. describes this technique as follows: the adept places one's palms on the ground and raises one's legs without letting the head touch the ground. This practice is praised as the best of Yoga exercises leading to all kinds of powers, notably control over one's semen. *Haṭha-yoga-pradīpikā* 3.87–91, however, defines the *vajrolī-mudrā* as the sexual technique of directing one's semen upwards as well as sucking up the female ejaculate (*rajas*) with the penis. By preserving one's sperm and sucking up the female's *rajas,* the Yogin is believed to acquire longevity, and eventually bodily immortality.

26. See Priyolkar, *Yoga-rāja-ṭiḷaka.*

27. In 1912, twenty of these *Saṃnyāsa Upaniṣads* were critically edited with a commentary by F. O. Schrader. In 1929, T. R. C. Dikshit published seventeen of them with a commentary by Śrī Upaniṣad-Brahma-Yogin. In 1992, Patrick Olivelle produced a new translation of this Upaniṣadic corpus.

The only *Saṃnyāsa Upaniṣad* with a non-Advaita orientation is the *Śāṭyāyanīya,* composed within a *Śrī-Vaiṣṇava* milieu.

28. See Schrader, *Saṃnyāsa Upaniṣads,* xxvi–xxxiv.

29. See Sprockhoff, *Saṃnyāsa: Quellenstudien zur Askese im Hinduismus—I Untersuchungen über die Saṃnyāsa-Upaniṣads.* Olivelle, on the other hand, dates the earlier group to the first centuries of, rather than before, the common era; see Olivelle, *Saṃnyāsa Upaniṣads,* 8–11.

30. For an overview of the Brahminical literature on *saṃnyāsa,* see ibid., 11–18. See also *Rules and Regulations of Brahmanical Asceticism: Yatidharmasamuccaya of Yādava Prakāśa,* edited and translated by Patrick Olivelle.

31. On renunciation and liberation, see Olivelle, *Saṃnyāsa Upaniṣads,* 78–81.

32. Rites are divided into *śrauta,* commanded by Vedic revelation, and *smārta,* commanded by authoritative tradition. Both fall into three categories:

the *nitya* or permanently obligatory such as daily fire sacrifice; the *naimittika*, to be performed on particular occasions such as sacramental rites; and the *kāmya*, enacted to procure a desired end. *Praiṣa* is the technical term for the formula "I have renounced" (*saṃnyastaṃ mayā*). It constitutes the essential element of the ceremony of *saṃnyāsa*. Even at the point of death one can renounce merely by proclaiming the *praiṣa*, either orally or mentally. On *saṃnyāsa* as a nonritual state or as the perfection of ritual from within a Brahminical perspective, see ibid., 60–71, 82–97.

33. Olivelle, *Vāsudevāśrama Yatidharmaprakāśa*: *A Treatise on World Renunciation*, 30.

34. On the development of the Brahminical *āśrama* ideology, see Olivelle, *The Āśrama System: The History and Hermeneutics of a Religious Institution*.

35. On renunciation and detachment, see Olivelle, *Saṃnyāsa Upaniṣads*, 75–78.

36. Olivelle, *Vāsudevāśrama Yatidharmaprakāśa*, 61–62. See also Yādava Prakāśa's *Yati-dharma-samuccaya* 2.65. "Those born from the mouth" refers to the cosmogonic myth of *Ṛg Veda* 10.90, where it is said that Brahmins were born from the mouth of the Puruṣa who was offered in sacrifice. The other three classes of Kṣatriyas, Vaiśyas, and Śūdras were born from the Puruṣa's arms, thighs, and feet respectively.

37. In Yādava Prakāśa's *Yati-dharma-samuccaya*, a twelfth-century *Vaiṣṇava* text on the rules and regulations of Brahminical asceticism, Dattātreya is quoted as an authority recommending Viṣṇu's worship and also as describing the way a Yogin should envision Viṣṇu's bodily form; see *Yati-dharma-samuccaya* 5.136–42.

38. See Olivelle, "Renouncer and Renunciation in the Dharmaśāstras." On contemporary women renouncers, see Catherine Ojha, "Condition féminine et renoncement au monde dans l'hindouisme: Les communautés monastiques de femmes à Benares"; Rigopoulos, "Women and Ritual: The Experience of a Contemporary Marāṭhī Āśram"; Johnsen, *Daughters of the Goddess*.

39. See *Nārada-parivrājaka Upaniṣad* 156, 160, 196–97; *Yājñavalkya Upaniṣad* 315–16 (where 315 is borrowed from *Yoga-vāsiṣṭha* 1.21.1–6); *Bṛhat-saṃnyāsa Upaniṣad* 270.

40. The *Pañcadaśī*, so named because it consists of fifteen chapters, is perhaps the greatest among the post-Śaṅkara Advaita Vedānta treatises. Vidyāraṇya, whose original name was Mādhava, was a learned Vedānta scholar probably born around 1314 C.E. He was the famous minister of the kings Harihara and Bukka, founders of Vijayanagar, the last autochthonous monarchy in Indian history. Brother of the Vedic commentator Sāyaṇa and conqueror of Goa, Vidyāraṇya apparently retired to ascetic life around 1368. He was head of the Śṛṅgeri *maṭha* from 1377 to 1386 and author of numerous

works, notably of the *Sarva-darśana-saṃgraha*, a compendium of all philosophical views.

41. Raeside, *Dattātreya*, 490.

42. This English translation, as the following, is taken from Olivelle, *Saṃnyāsa Upaniṣads*, 273.

43. Ibid., 145–46.

44. See A. Mahadeva Sastri, *The Śaiva Upanishads*, 121, 163.

45. On the renouncers' possessions and emblems, see Olivelle, *Saṃnyāsa Upaniṣads*, 105–7.

46. Ibid., 146.

"Triple staff": A renouncer carrying three staffs tied together (*tri-daṇḍin*) is identified as a *Vaiṣṇava*. The three *daṇḍas* represent forms of restraint: *vāg-daṇḍa* or restraint in speech, *kāya-daṇḍa* or restraint of the bodily senses, and *mano-daṇḍa* or restraint of mind (*Manu-smṛti* 11.10). In the *Yati-dharma-samuccaya* of Yādava Prakāśa, Dattātreya is quoted as an authority praising the Brahmin who carries the emblem of the triple staff. Such a Brahmin is to be revered as Nārāyaṇa himself. The triple staff is said to be the means of liberation for twice-born people and to signal the cessation of all rules; see *Yati-dharma-samuccaya* 2.51, 3.41, 6.299, 7.108. Those carrying a single staff (*eka-daṇḍīs*), identified as *Śaiva* renouncers, belong to one of the ten orders founded by Śaṅkara.

"Sacrificial string": In Yādava Prakāśa's *Yati-dharma-samuccaya*, Dattātreya is twice quoted as extolling the characteristics and the importance of the Brahminical string. Wearing the ninefold string is said to be the means of liberation for twice-born people; see *Yati-dharma-samuccaya* 3.34–37, 8.65.

"Earth *svāhā*": Literally "the earth, hail!" The ritual formula used when discarding the sacrificial thread in water. *Bhūr*, the first of the three great utterances (together with *bhuvas*, air/atmosphere and *svar*, heaven), designates the first of the three worlds. *Svāhā* is an exclamation used in making oblations to the gods. It is regarded as a blessing and magical spell. The renunciant discards all exterior insigna by relinquishing them to the earth.

"Begging bowl": The Paramahaṃsa is an *udara-pātrin*, a renouncer who uses his stomach as a begging-bowl. While the renouncer known as *pāṇi-pātrin* uses his hand as a begging-bowl, the *udara-pātrin* eats "like a cow," meaning that the donor throws the food on the ground and the renouncer eats it directly from there. See Vāsudevāśrama's *Yati-dharma-prakāśa* 57.56–57: "Like a cow, the sage always seeks food with his mouth." See also *Mahābhārata* 1.86.17; *Āruṇi Upaniṣad* 11; *Nārada-parivrājaka Upaniṣad* 182; and *Bṛhat-saṃnyāsa Upaniṣad* 268.

"He lives without a home": A characteristic of all *saṃnyāsins* is that they are homeless wanderers, not expected to spend two nights in the same village. The renouncer must dwell only in solitary and secluded spots. On the wandering behavior of renunciants, see Olivelle, *Saṃnyāsa Upaniṣads*, 101–3.

"Such a man who abandons his body": The Paramahaṃsa may be buried on land or in water, or he may be cut into pieces and scattered. A Kuṭīcaka is cremated, and a Bahūdaka is buried in the earth or in water, while a Haṃsa is to be buried in water only. The *ekoddiṣṭa-śrāddha* and the *sapiṇḍī-karaṇa* are not performed on behalf of a dead renouncer, and the period of impurity following death need not be observed by his relatives.

47. There are several unrelated and conflicting classifications of renouncers in Brahminical literature. Some authors distinguish four categories of *saṃnyāsa*: *vairāgya-saṃnyāsa*, *jñāna-saṃnyāsa*, *jñāna-vairāgya-saṃnyāsa*, and *karma-saṃnyāsa*. The Kuṭīcaka, literally "hut-dweller," is a religious mendicant living at his son's expense. The Bahūdaka, literally "one having much water," is a mendicant who begs his food at bathing places. The Haṃsa, usually translated "swan," refers to the wild goose (*Anser indicus*), whose high flight inspired the ancient Indians to make it the symbol of the sun and, later, of the *ātman* as well as of a certain kind of *saṃnyāsin*. The Paramahaṃsa or "supreme swan," designates the ascetic of the highest order.

48. The term literally means "one who is beyond the fourth." The "fourth" may refer both to the fourth class of renouncers, namely the Paramahaṃsa, and to the fourth state of consciousness beyond which is *Brahman*; see *Nārada-parivrājaka Upaniṣad* 178–79, 189–91.

49. Within Beṅgalī Tantrism, Avadhūtas are divided into two broad classes: Gṛhastha and Sadāśiva. Thus even a householder having attained *brahma-jñāna* may be classed as an Avadhūta; see Banerji, *Tantra in Bengal: A Study in Its Origin, Development and Influence*, 192–94.

50. On the classification of renouncers, see Olivelle, *Saṃnyāsa Upaniṣads*, 98–100.

51. For a fine edition and translation of the *Jīvanmukti-viveka*, see Vidyāraṇya, *La liberazione in vita: Jīvanmuktiviveka*.

52. The 19th among the 108 *Upaniṣads*, it is part of the *Śukla Yajur Veda*. The description of the path and way of life of the Paramahaṃsa is thoroughly inscribed within the framework of Advaita Vedānta metaphysics.

53. Olivelle, *Saṃnyāsa Upaniṣads*, 139–40.

"Nor utter *svadhā* . . . nor utter *vaṣaṭ*": Forbidding *svadhā* and *vaṣaṭ* is an indirect prohibition of ritual activity.

"There is neither invitation nor dismissal": The ceremonial invitation of deities at the beginning of a sacrifice. The deities are dismissed at its conclusion.

54. Ibid., 184. This list of sages is similar to that of *Jābāla Upaniṣad* 69: Āruṇi and Jaḍabharata are omitted, whereas Vṛṣabha, who is omitted in the *Jābāla*, is herein listed.

55. On these issues, see ibid., 107–12.

56. See Chidbhavananda, *Śiva Sahasranāma Stotram*, 25. On the behavior of saints as if mad, see Kinsley, "'Through the Looking Glass': Divine Madness in the Hindu Religious Tradition." See also Feldhaus, *The Deeds of God in Ṛddhipur*; June McDaniel, *The Madness of the Saints: Ecstatic Religion in Bengal*; Georg Feuerstein, *Holy Madness: The Shock Tactics and Radical Teachings of Crazy-Wise Adepts, Holy Fools, and Rascal Gurus.*

57. Olivelle, *Saṃnyāsa Upaniṣads*, 237.

The 60th among the 108 *Upaniṣads*, the *Bhikṣuka Upaniṣad* is part of the *Śukla Yajur Veda*. It classifies renunciants into the four categories of Kuṭīcaka, Bahūdaka, Haṃsa, and Paramahaṃsa and explains their distinctive characteristics.

The last three ascetics, Śuka, Vāmadeva, and Hārītaka, were not mentioned in the two lists previously quoted of *Jābāla Upaniṣad* 69 and *Nārada-parivrājaka Upaniṣad* 154.

58. For an English rendition, see K. N. Aiyar, *Thirty Minor Upanishads*, 1–12.

59. On the Vedic affiliation of the *Upaniṣads* according to the *Muktikā Upaniṣad*, see Bouy, "Matériaux pour servir aux études upaniṣadiques. (1) Un manuscrit sanskrit de Tanjore," 105–7. The term *śānti* designates any expiatory or propitiatory rite for averting evil or calamity.

60. Compare with *Ṛg Veda* 1.89.8.

61. See A. Mahadeva Sastri, *The Vaiṣṇava Upaniṣads*, 159.

62. See Raeside, *Dattātreya*, 490.

63. With few changes, I have followed the translation of Bahadur, *Dattātreya*, 24, 53–54. See also Subrahmanian, *Encyclopaedia of the Upaniṣads*, 325–27.

64. On the understanding of word within Tantrism as well as on Tantric *mantras*, see Padoux, *Vāc: The Concept of the Word in Selected Hindu Tantras*; Bharati, *The Tantric Tradition*, 101–63; Mookerjee and Khanna, *The Tantric Way: Art, Science, Ritual*, 132f.; Gupta, Hoens, and Goudriaan, *Hindu Tantrism*, 90–117. See also Wade T. Weelock, "The Mantra in Vedic and Tantric Ritual."

65. On *daṃ* as Dattātreya's specific *mantra*, see also S. K. Ramachandra Rao, *Āgama-Kosha*, 4:134.

66. On the sacred syllable *hrīṃ*, see Mahadevan, *Śaṅkara and Lalitādvaita*. Bhuvaneśvarī is said to nourish the three worlds and is described as holding fruit in one of her four hands. Her breasts are large and ooze milk. Of bright complexion, she holds a goad and a noose; see Kinsley, *Hindu Goddesses*, 162.

On the ten *mahā-vidyās*, a late *Śākta* counterpart to the *Vaiṣṇava daśa-avatāras*, see ibid., 161–65. See also Chintaharan Chakravarti, *Tantras: Studies on Their Religion and Literature*, 85–86.

67. The *mūla-mantra* of Gaṇeśa reads: "aum aiṃ hrīṃ śrīṃ glīṃ glauṃ gaṃ gaṇapataye varavarada sarva janāṇ me vasamanāya svāhā" [*aum aiṃ hrīṃ śrīṃ glīṃ glauṃ gaṃ* O Gaṇapati, O Best of Protectors, allow me to control all people, *svāhā*].

68. For a Vedic example, see *Taittirīya Saṃhitā* 1.2.7.1.f.: "mitro na ehi sumitradhā . . . " [Come to us as a friend, making good friends . . .].

69. See *Atharva Veda* 5.9.1–6.

70. See Silburn, *Kuṇḍalinī*, 55. On the *sauḥ mantra*, see the work of Muller-Ortega, *The Triadic Heart of Śiva. Kaula Tantricism of Abhinavagupta in the Non-Dual Shaivism of Kashmir*; see also Padoux, *Vāc*, 416–26.

71. See Bahadur, *Dattātreya*, 24.

72. Eliade, *Yoga: Immortality and Freedom*, 210–11. Bharati gives two other definitions of the term *nyāsa*: the process of charging a part of the body with a specified power through touch, and the process of placing one meditational entity into another; see Bharati, *The Tantric Tradition*, 91, 273. On *nyāsa*, see Padoux, "Contributions à l'étude du mantraśāstra."

73. On the concept of *ānanda*, see Olivelle, "Orgasmic Rapture and Divine Ecstasy: The Semantic History of *Ānanda*."

74. On the place of *japa* in Tantric ritual, see Gupta, Hoens, and Goudriaan, *Hindu Tantrism*, 153–54. On the practice of *japa* or *nāmasmaraṇa*, see Tulpule, *Mysticism in Medieval India*, 127–45. See also *Kalyāṇa Kalpataru* 5, no. 1 (January 1938), which contains more than seventy articles on the divine name.

75. See Silburn, *Kuṇḍalinī*, 153–55.

76. On *yantras*, see Madhu Khanna, *Yantra: The Tantric Symbol of Cosmic Unity*.

77. See Geden, "Tantras." See also Briggs, *Gorakhnāth and the Kānphaṭa Yogīs*, 281. Alain Daniélou reiterates Dattātreya's role as "originator of the *Tantras* and the Tantric rites," though he immediately adds that "he also restored Vedic hymns (*Mahābhārata* 2.48.2–4)." Daniélou further notes:

> [Dattātreya] created the plant from which the sacrificial liquor, the *soma*, can be prepared . . . His love for songs and musical instruments as well as his association with people of low birth made him ritually impure. Yet he was greatly praised by the gods whom he saved from the demons. (Daniélou, *Hindu Polytheism*, 183)

78. The *Gandharva-tantra*, revealed by Dattātreya to Viśvāmitra, is a work in forty-two *paṭalas* describing a variety of *vidyās* and various aspects of Tantric *pūjā*. Dattātreya is often mentioned in all these texts; see *Rudra-yāmala* 17.85.

79. For an overview of the works attributed to Dattātreya, see K. Kunjunni Raja, *New Catalogus Catalogorum: An Alphabetical Register of Sanskrit and Allied Works and Authors,* vol. 8, 313–19. See also S. Kuppuswami Sastri and P. P. Subrahmanya Sastri, *An Alphabetical Index of Sanskrit Manuscripts in the Government Oriental Manuscripts Library,* pt. 1, 319–21. The famous scholar Gopīnāth Kavirāj wrote a brief summary of the twenty-two *paṭalas* (about 700 *ślokas*) of the *Dattātreya-tantra* in his work *Tantrik Sahity,* 293. For the Sanskrit text of the *Dattātreya-tantra* (ca. twelfth century), in which Śiva instructs Dattātreya on various alchemical and magical practices including the six acts for inflicting various kinds of injury on enemies (*śānti, vaśya, stambhana, vidveṣa, uccāṭana* and *māraṇa*), see Bhaṭṭa, *Indrajāla-vidyā-saṃgraha,* 132–79. See also Dīkṣit, *Dattātreyatantram.*

80. On *Śākta* Tantrism, see Brooks, *The Secret of the Three Cities: An Introduction to Hindu Śākta Tantrism.* By the same author, *Auspicious Wisdom: The Texts and Traditions of Śrīvidyā Śākta Tantrism in South India.* For an overview of the *Śākta Upaniṣads,* see A. Mahadeva Sastri, *The Śākta Upanishads.*

81. See chap. 7.

4

Dattātreya in the Literature of the Mahānubhāvas

After the Purāṇic period, the first datable testimony to the next stage of Dattātreya's cult is found in the early Mahānubhāva texts, as Raeside notes.[1] This is a cardinal phase in the deity's development—a valuable piece in the puzzle of his unfolding—since Dattātreya's appropriation by the Mahānubhāvas introduces him to the Marāṭhī religious and cultural milieu. Though Dattātreya was most probably brought to the Marāṭhī area through the medium of the Nātha movement—with whom the Mahānubhāvas were certainly linked—it must be stressed that the earliest literary documents mentioning Dattātreya are those of the Mahānubhāva sect. It is precisely in the Marāṭhī area that Dattātreya emerges as one of the leading deities within the Hindu pantheon.

In this chapter, Dattātreya's role and his presence within Mahānubhāva texts and theology are delineated. Dattātreya's connections with *śakti-pīṭhas*, Śaṅkara and the Daśanāmī order, the Aghora *sampradāya*, Nāthism, and even Jainism are also reviewed. A few remarks on a theological aspect of Mahānubhāva doctrine will conclude the discussion.

The religious movement of the Mahānubhāvas or "Those of the Great Experience," flourished in Maharashtra around the thirteenth century. It was founded by Guru Cakradhar, who, according to legend, was born into the family of a royal minister of Broach, Gujarat, as Haripāḷadeva. He was dissolute and given to gambling, and he died young. However, before his body could be cremated, it was reanimated by the spirit of Cāṅgadeva Rāuḷ,[2] who, at the very time of Haripāḷadeva's death, breathed his last in Dvārakā. The reborn Haripāḷa carried on his secular life for some time, but one day, after losing heavily at gambling, he felt a sudden disgust for worldly life and left on a pilgrimage to Rāmṭek, near Nāgpur. He met his Guru Guṇḍam Rāuḷ[3] in Ṛddhipur and was initiated into the *para-mārga*. Renamed Cakradhar, he spent twelve years wandering in the wilderness as a naked ascetic, settling down at Paiṭhaṇ on the banks of the Godāvarī. This marked the end of his period of solitude (*ekāka*). The last seven years of Cakradhar's life were spent wandering up and down the Godāvarī. During this time he was joined by Nāgadeva, alias Bhaṭobāsa, who was to become the preceptor of the sect after his death. According to tradition, Cakradhar died in 1272. Many of his followers, however, believe him to be an immortal dwelling somewhere in the Himalayas.

The Mahānubhāva sect was highly influential in the development of Marāṭhī literature.[4] Charlotte Vaudeville notes that, besides the medieval *Vaiṣṇava Sahajiyā* sect of Bengal, the most ancient "*Vaiṣṇava*" sect north of the Godāvarī was that of the Mahānubhāvas. In fact, following Hajariprasad Dvivedi, she views Cakradhar and Guṇḍam Rāuḷ—the founders of the Mahānubhāvas—as originally Nāthas, possibly low-caste Bhairava worshipers who in time shifted from Tantric, Nātha *Śaivism* to "nominal" *Vaiṣṇavism*.[5] If this is true, Dattātreya's eclectic *mūrti* would have been perfect for effecting the *Śaiva-Vaiṣṇava* connection. Vaudeville defines the sect as essentially a Yogic cult with Dattātreya as its divinized Guru. In an earlier work, she linked Dattātreya to the synthetic movement of Nātha Yogins, "since Dattātreya appears in the Tantra-mahārṇava as the 'Nāth' of the southwest region."[6] Eleanor Zelliot and Maxine Berntsen offer the following portrait of the Mahānubhāvas:

> Considered heterodox at best, the Mahanubhavs rejected caste and the worship of idols, refused to acknowledge the ritual and scriptural authority of Brahmans . . . created an order of women *sannyasis* as well as one of men, and acknowledged the reality of only one god, Parmeshwar, who has five major incarnations: Krishna, Dattatreya, and three sect figures. Although the Mahanubhavs seem to have been popular at first, spreading chiefly north of the Godavari River even as the Varkari sect[7] spread south, they came to be considered suspect sometime in the next two centuries. They adopted a secret script in which to preserve their sacred texts, and slipped into an inconspicuous position outside the mainstream of Maharashtrian society.[8]

Besides Kṛṣṇa and Dattātreya, the other three sect figures are Cāṅgadeva Rāuḷ of Dvārakā, Guṇḍam Rāuḷ of Ṛddhipur, and, of course, the founder Cakradhar of Paiṭhaṇ, the fifth and last manifestation of Parameśvara.[9] The five "descents" of the Mahānubhāvas are best known as Pañca-Kṛṣṇas. The first references to Dattātreya are found in the *Līḷā-caritra* and the *Sūtra-pāṭha*. The *Līḷā-caritra*, an anecdotal biography of Cakradhar, was written in prose by his disciple Mhāibhaṭa between

1272 and 1278. The *Sūtra-pāṭha* is a collection of Cakradhar's teachings, in the form of aphorisms, selected from the *Līḷā-caritra* by Keśirāja around 1290.[10] The most relevant data taken from the *Līḷā-caritra* are the following:

1. At Mātāpur, the modern Mahur on the Devagiri hill, Śrī Dattātreya Prabhu passed on his *śakti* or Avatāra to "the Gosāvī" Śrī Cāṅgadeva Rāuḷ, under the guise of a tiger which laid its paw on Cāṅgadeva's head.[11] (*ekānka* 1)
2. Cakradhar advised visiting the sacred Ātma-tīrtha at Pañcāḷeśvara[12] because it is connected with Dattātreya and "is not like other places." (*pūrvārdha* 43)
3. When Cakradhar celebrated Dattātreya's excellence, two pupils expressed the desire to have Datta's *darśana*. Cakradhar taught them how to achieve "that supreme *darśana*." Then the disciples left for Devagiri at Mātāpur. However, not having followed Cakradhar's orders with care, later they had to return. (*pūrvārdha* 62)
4. Cakradhar visited Pañcāḷeśvara and indicated the place of Dattātreya's hut. (*pūrvārdha* 312)
5. Among the Avatāras of Īśvara through which an individual soul may be freed from *saṃsāra*, Cakradhar mentioned "Śrī Dattātreya Prabhu in Mātāpur." Mhāibhaṭa, however, protested that Dattātreya doesn't bestow any *darśana* and Cakradhar then pointed to himself as the only means of release in the present age. (*uttarārdha* 113)
6. When Vāmadeva, a competing Yogin, was asked to conjure up demons and was unable to do it, he justified himself by saying that some demons had gone to Kolhāpur[13] and others to Mātāpur. (*uttarārdha* 284)

Within the *Sūtra-pāṭha*, besides the mention of Dattātreya as one of the five manifestations of Parameśvara, only four *sūtras* at the end of the *vicāra* section refer to him:

7. "Śrī Dattātreya Prabhu's Avatāra [is] in all four *yugas*." (282)
8. "The three afflictions of Alarka were eliminated at the very first sight [of Dattātreya] when he said: '*Śambali, śambali*!' That speech is a very shower of nectar." (283)

9. "That supreme *darśana*!" (284)

10. "Śrī Dattātreya Prabhu is the first cause (*ādi-kāraṇa*) of this path." (285)

As Raeside points out, the only link with the Purāṇic Dattātreya is the reference to Alarka in *Sūtra-pāṭha, vicāra* 283. However, other early fourteenth-century Mahānubhāva works exist which refer to three Purāṇic stories of Dattātreya. The *Gadya-rāja*[14] of Hayagrīva, written around 1320, contains five *ślokas* on Dattātreya (232–36). Besides the first and fifth generic verses, the other three *ślokas* highlight the following:

> Dattātreya gave sovereignty over the whole world to Sahasrārjuna, who had made an incense burner of his hands. (233)
>
> Dattātreya put an end to the hardships of Madālasā's son [Alarka] through the arrows of triple utterance (*vāk-traya*). He manifested as an outcaste, bearing a meat load upon a carrying pole (*kāvaḍī*). (234)
>
> Dattātreya acted as a priest at Reṇukā's cremation when Paraśurāma, urged by his mother, asked him to do so. (235)

The *Sahyādri-varṇana* of Ravaḷobāsa, a poem in 517 verses which Raeside dates to approximately 1330,[15] is concerned with Dattātreya for more than a third of its length. The poem is not a description of the Sahyādri mountains[16] but rather an account of some of the episodes in the life of Dattātreya. Said to have appeared and to have lived in an offshoot of the Sahyādri's range, Dattātreya is again presented as the *ādi-kāraṇa* or primeval cause of the Mahānubhāva sect. In addition to discussing Dattātreya's birth in Atri's line, the text mentions the Alarka story, the Sahasrārjuna-Kārtavīrya story, and the Paraśurāma story, offering some extra details.

A more articulate presentation of these three tales is found in the *Sahyādra-līḷā*, a text which Raeside dates between 1330 and 1400 and which has been published by V. B. Kolte as an appendix to the *Sahyādri-varṇana*. These accounts are the most developed stage in the Mahānubhāva legends concerning Dattātreya. In the first story, Cakradhar tells Mahādāisā—one of his first female pupils—how Śrī Dattātreya Prabhu encountered Alarka in the Sahyādri mountains. Dattātreya appeared as an outcaste Māṅg[17] dressed in a *dhotī* and wearing a turban, a necklace of *bora* beads, and sandals at his feet. A meat-cutting knife thrust into his waist-cloth, Dattātreya is depicted bent under the weight of a *kāvaḍī* of meat carried on his shoulder. Upon seeing Alarka, he shouted: "*Semboli! Semboli!*" an expression analogous to the one found in the *Sūtra-pāṭha* (*śambali*) and probably derived from Sanskrit *śambala*, "provisions for a journey," referring to his load of meat. Thanks to this *darśana* of Dattātreya, Alarka was instantly at peace and offered obeisance to him.

The second story tells how Dattātreya granted boons to King Sahasrārjuna. Being armless[18] and thus unfit to govern, the king consigned his kingdom to his minister's care and departed. After visiting the hermitages of many great Ṛṣis, he came to that of Śrī Dattātreya Prabhu in the Sahyādris. Seeing that spirits were not hostile there, he decided to stay, though performing no service at all. One day Sahasrārjuna obtained Dattātreya's *darśana*. Wishing to worship him by scenting his hair, he placed a burning ember with incense on his arm stumps. Smelling Sahasrārjuna's burning flesh, Dattātreya ordered him to drop the ember at once and, satisfied with such proof of devotion, bestowed upon him the three boons: a thousand arms, unmatched strength, sovereignty over the world, all on condition that he not anger a woman, a Brahmin, or a cow. The story ends by telling how Sahasrārjuna, having committed just these sins, fell into disgrace. As we know, Sahasrārjuna-Kārtavīrya ultimately harmed Reṇukā, Jamadagni, and the Kāmadhenu.

The third story is that of Dattātreya's officiation for Paraśurama. While being instructed by Mahādeva in Kailāsa, Paraśurāma was summoned by his dying mother, Ekavīrā, who told him that Śrī Dattātreya Prabhu should act as priest at her funeral ceremony. Ekavīrā told her son how he would recognize Dattātreya: at his sight shoots would spring out from dry wood. Ekavīrā soon died[19] and Paraśurāma set out, carrying both her corpse and that of his father on his shoulder in a *kāvaḍī*. After a period of wandering, Paraśurāma came to the Sahyādris, where he met Dattātreya disguised as a hunter and wearing a *dhotī* in the style of a wrestler. In his left hand Dattātreya held a pair of dogs and under his arm, a pitcher; in his right hand he held meat and a coconut shell full of liquor; he wore thick sandals. With him was a Devī with braided hair, also wearing sandals. Upon seeing Dattātreya, Paraśurāma's carrying pole began sprouting shoots. He prostrated before Dattātreya and asked him to officiate at his mother's funeral rites. At first Dattātreya refused but, when requested by his Devī, he finally relented. Dattātreya then had Paraśurāma shoot an arrow and, placing his toe on the spot where the arrow fell, created there all the *tīrthas*. This was Sarva-tīrtha, mentioned in all accounts of

Mātāpur. At this place, Dattātreya performed the final rites for Ekavīrā in the *mūḷa-darī*:[20] he took a stone, set it up in the *mūḷa-pīṭha*, sprinkled it with liquor, offered it meat, and then invited everyone to enjoy partaking in the consecrated food.

In this last story, Dattātreya's link with Ekavīrā-Reṇukā is evidence of an association with *Śākta* worship. Two other tales in the *Sahyādra-līḷā* relate Dattātreya to Ekavīrā. In the first, known as the establishment of Ekavīrā, devotees questioned Cakradhar on why meat and wine were pleasing to Ekavīrā, a Ṛṣi's wife. The Gosāvī replied that since it was Dattātreya himself who had offered both to Ekavīrā, she was thus gratified and accepted the offer. In the second story, that of the enjoyment of Ekavīrā, Cakradhar—who was staying in Pratiṣṭhāna—told Mahādāisā and his pupils how a large crowd had come to the Ekavīrā festival because Dattātreya had once consecrated her and had invited everyone to partake in the celebration. Clearly, these tales signal the licentious atmosphere prevalent at Devī festivals, where meat and liquor were freely distributed as *prasāda*.

Another short story in the *Sahyādra-līḷā* relates how Śrī Dattātreya Prabhu sported in Merubāḷā, a sacred pool in Mātāpur near the Devadeveśvara temple.[21] The Mahānubhāva testimonies indicate that by the thirteenth century, and possibly even earlier, Dattātreya had a shrine at Mātāpur, evidence of a link with Śāktism.[22] Even today, Mahur, with its temple of Ekavīrā-Reṇukā, and Kolhāpur, with its Mahālakṣmī temple, are the two main *śakti-pīṭhas* of Maharashtra.[23] Various Devī shrines are found in other locales associated with Dattātreya's worship, such as on Mount Abu (Guru Shikhar) and in the Girnār area. Dattātreya's connection with Śāktism is surely archaic and a constant throughout the deity's unfolding. Within the literature, the *Śākta* element appears from Dattātreya's first portrayal in the *Mārkaṇḍeya Purāṇa*, in Mahānubhāva texts, and in the sectarian *Dattātreya Upaniṣad*; and it finds its crowning in the *Tripurā-rahasya*. Dattātreya's link to Śāktism via Nāthism and other Yogic and Tantric circles is also apparent.

By locating Dattātreya's *āśrama* at Mātāpur or in the Sahyādri, the Mahānubhāva accounts transfer the Alarka and Sahasrārjuna episodes there as well. Within an overall heterodox atmosphere, interesting details are added here: in the Alarka story, Dattātreya's appearance as an outcaste Māṅg carrying a load of meat and the mantric cry *"semboli"* with which he heals Alarka; in the Sahasrārjuna story, the burning stumps of King Sahasrārjuna. From the Mahānubhāva tales one also gathers the idea that Dattātreya's manifestations had a tendency to appear suddenly and unexpectedly. As the Marāṭhī saying goes: *datta mhaṇūna ubhā rahāṇeṃ*, "To appear all of a sudden like Datta."

One last Mahānubhāva tale from the *Sahyādra-līḷā* is noteworthy, since it indicates a link of Dattātreya with Śaṅkara (b. seventh century C.E.), the great founder of Advaita Vedānta. Cakradhar, who was staying at Belopur,[24] was asked by Mahādāisā why a Saṃnyāsin—who does not follow any common duty or norm of conduct—is nevertheless generally accepted. Cakradhar answered that one time Śaṅkara had asked Śrī Dattātreya Prabhu the boon that the order of Saṃnyāsins he had founded be well received by the world, and Dattātreya, pleased with him and his request, granted the wish.

Śaṅkara is traditionally credited with the authorship of various hymns in Dattātreya's praise, such as the *Dattātreya-bhujaṃga-stotra*.[25] The *Guruvaṃśa-kāvya*, a versified chronicle of Śaṅkara's life inspired by the Jagadguru of Śṛṅgeri Saccidānanda Bhāratī (d. 1814), narrates how, at the end of his life, Śaṅkara traveled from Siddheśvarī in Nepal to Dattātreya's *āśrama* at Mahur. There he abandoned his stick, which turned into a tree, and his alms bowl, which turned into a sacred *tīrtha*. From then on he remained in the company of the immortal Dattātreya,[26] in perennial conversation on Vedānta. The biographies inspired by the Śṛṅgeri *maṭha*, such as the *Śaṅkara-vijaya-vilāsa*, specifically connect Dattātreya to Śaṅkara with regard to the latter's "final disappearance." Thus, Dattātreya is said to have manifested himself to Śaṅkara at Badarīnātha. The immortal Yogin took him by the hand to a nearby cave, from which they were never seen to emerge. This version is probably related to a preexisting tradition, since Śaṅkara's entrance into a cave is employed as a metaphor to indicate the end of his life. Even before the cave episode, Śaṅkara is said to have had a vision of the divine Yogin Dattātreya, who blessed him and recognized his omniscience. In another late biography, the *Śaṅkara-dig-vijaya* of Mādhava,[27] Kapila, Dattātreya, Vyāsa and Śaṅkara are mentioned together as the teachers of the *satya*, *tretā*, *dvāpara*, and *kali* age respectively (9.22).

Dattātreya's connection with Śaṅkara's Daśanāmī order is also well established. In the *Dabistān* of Moshan Fani (d. 1670), the Daśanāmī renunciants are said to "follow the dictates of 'Datāteri,' whom they . . . venerate as a deity . . . an incarnation of Narayan, and [who] in the retaining of the breath attained to such a degree that he is exempted from death."[28] George Weston Briggs also mentions the Atīts, identified as degraded Daśanāmīs, as a class of ascetics revering Dattātreya.[29] The ten branches of the Daśanāmī order (Āraṇya, Āśrama, Bhāratī, Giri, Parvata, Purī, Sarasvatī, Sāgara, Tīrtha, and Vaṇa) are

The *trimukhī mūrti* of Dattātreya at the Jūnā Akhāḍā at Haridvār, carved out of a marble rock.

associated with the four principal *maṭhas* of Advaita Vedānta in the four corners of India: the Āraṇya and Vaṇa with the Govardhana *maṭha* in Purī on the east coast (*mantra*: *prajñānaṃ brahma*); the Giri, Parvata, and Sāgara with the Jyotis *maṭha* near Badarīnātha in the Himalayas (*mantra*: *ayam ātma brahma*); the Tīrtha and Āśrama with the Śāradā *maṭha* in Dvārakā on the west coast (*mantra*: *tat tvam asi*); and the Sarasvatī, Bhāratī, and Purī with the Śṛṅgeri *maṭha* in south India (*mantra*: *ahaṃ brahmāsmi*).[30] It should also be noted that the Jūnā Akhāḍā—one of the seven Akhāḍās founded by Daśanāmī Nāga Saṃnyāsins supposedly organized by Śaṅkara—has Dattātreya as its tutelary deity, identified as Rudra-Śiva.[31] This Akhāḍā was apparently founded in Śṛṅgeri in 1113 C.E. and its original *devatā* was Bhairava. Both Bhairava and Dattātreya are connected with dogs, and there are evident similarities between the Nāgas of the Jūnā Akhāḍā and the Nāthas, for instance, in the Girnār area.[32] Dattātreya's link to Śaṅkara and the Daśanāmī order was certainly inspired by the former's characterization as a divine *jñāna-yogin*. Dattātreya was thus appropriated by the Vedāntin milieu in order to sanction the truth of Advaita, as well as to emphasize the excellence of the Daśanāmī order of renunciants.

Dattātreya's typology as a honeybee Yogin, shared by a *koiné* of various Tantric and Yogic groups,[33] finds another notable illustration in his appropriation by the Aghora *sampradāya*,[34] of which Śiva is the mythical initiator and Dattātreya the first teacher (*ādi-guru*) and Śiva incarnate.[35] As in the Mahānubhāva story when he granted a boon to Śaṅkara, Dattātreya is also here presented as granting a boon of omniscience to Bābā Kīnārām, the seventeenth-century reformer of the modern Aghora *sampradāya*.[36] The story runs as follows:

> From Junagadh Bābā Kīnārām reached Girnār, the pious seat of Ādiguru Dattātreya. There was Siddheśvar Dattātreya sitting on "Kuṇḍ Aghorī Śila" with his *kamaṇḍalu* odiously with a big piece of flesh. The Ādi Guru Dattātreya cut out a piece of the same flesh by his teeth and made over the same to Mahārāj Śrī [Bābā Kīnārām] to eat. No sooner than he ate it, he found that he was blessed with far sight [*divya-dṛṣṭi*]. [For this he had to pass a test]. Guru Dattātreya said: "The emperor of Delhi." Mahārāj Śrī added: "Going on a black horse with a white shawl that is slipping down." Guru Dattātreya commended him to go and preach the society.[37]

Witnessing the incident taking place in Delhi from Girnār was the result of Kīnārām's *divya-dṛṣṭi*. The sacred hill of Girnār consists of five principal peaks and is still today an important center of Dattātreya worship. The five peaks are those of Ambā Mātā, crowned by the temple of that Devī; of Gorakhnāth, the highest of all (3,666 feet above sea level); Oghad Shikhar; Guru Dattātreya; and Kalka's peak, which until recently was the resort of Aghorīs. Thus at Girnār Dattātreya, besides being connected with the Aghorīs, is linked to Devī worship and particularly to western Nāthism, the Gorakhnāth peak being one of the Nāthas most important centers.[38] Indeed, Gorakhnāth as well as Dattātreya were probably originally worshipped *as* sacred mountains.

But the principal group of temples at Girnār is that of the Jainas, sixteen temples in all. The most notable is that of Neminātha, the twenty-second Jaina Tīrthaṅkara, built in about the twelfth century.[39] In the last century, the archaeologist J. Burgess was told that "King Dattātri" had been the first convert of Neminātha, and around 1930 Śrī Purohit Svāmin reported that the Jainas actually worship Dattātreya *as* Neminātha.[40] This connection may be due to two reasons. The first is that in Jaina tradition Neminātha is regarded as a cousin of Balarāma and Kṛṣṇa, thus establishing a link with the Hindu *Vaiṣṇava* tradition. The second and most important reason is that in Jaina *Mahā-purāṇas* Datta figures seventh in the list of nine Vāsudevas: Jaina heroes (half-Cakravartins) who engage in war and kill their enemies, the Prati-vāsudevas. Having gone against the precept of *ahiṃsā* the Vāsudevas are said to be reborn in hell. However, befitting their status as illustrious beings or *śalākā-puruṣas* the Jaina scriptures say that they will be reborn in the next time cycle as Tīrthaṅkaras.[41] Dattātreya's link with Jaina asceticism is further proven by his presence at Mount Abu. Originally an important *Śaiva* center, Mount Abu became one of the holy places of Jainism in the eleventh century. Here, on the highest peak of Guru Shikhar, among the Jaina temples, is a small cell where the footprints (*pādukās*) of Guru Dattātreya are worshipped: every year pilgrims flock to this spot for Dattātreya's *pūjā*. To the northwest is another peak with a shrine dedicated to the worship of Dattātreya's mother, Anasūyā.[42] The area of Mount Abu and Girnār has been the crossroad of a wide variety of Yogic and Tantric circles, a fertile environment where the honeybee Yogin Dattātreya was linked and amalgamated to a complex network of religious teachings and practices.

The early Mahānubhāvas appear to have had strong ties with the Nātha Yogins. Scholars such as Dhere, H. Dvivedi, and Vaudeville have all pointed out the connections between the Nāthas and the Mahānubhāvas, suggesting that both Cakradhar (alias Cāṅgadeva Rāuḷ) and Guṇḍam Rāuḷ may have been Nātha Yogins.[43] Both the *Līḷā-caritra* and the stories of Guṇḍam Rāuḷ are full of miracles performed through

Yogic powers. There is also the curious episode of *ekānka* 10, where Cakradhar "received" the power to arrest the aging process from a *rāja-guru* called Udhalināth.

With reference to the earliest influence of Nāthism upon Marāṭhī religion and literature, mention must be made of the great saint-poet Jñāndev (d. 1296). Author in 1290 of the *Jñāneśvarī*,[44] a Vedāntic commentary on the *Bhagavad-gītā* that inspired subsequent religious literature, Jñāndev was the fountainhead of the Vārkarī movement in the Marāṭhī region. Vārkarīs are also referred to as Sants[45] or Bhāgavatas, *Vaiṣṇava bhaktas*. Although Dattātreya is never mentioned in Jñāndev's major works—the focus of devotion being Viṭṭhala of Paṇḍharpur—there is one *abhaṅg* or short devotional poem attributed to him concerning Dattātreya.[46] It celebrates Dattātreya as the one formless Yogin—*ek yogī nirākārī*—the term *nirākārī* bringing to mind the *nirguṇa-bhakti* ideal of the northern Sant tradition.[47] Dattātreya is said to be the repository of *Brahman*'s bliss, to which one must resort with full faith. The *abhaṅg* mentions the value of a bath (*snāna*) at Pañcāḷeśvara, certainly one of the oldest *tīrthas* sacred to Dattātreya. Moreover, the *Yogisampradāyāviṣkṛti*—whose attribution to Jñāndev is however dubious—presents Dattātreya as the originator of the lineage of the nine Nāthas, identified with the "nine Nārāyaṇas" of the Avadhūta *sampradāya* apparently founded by Dattātreya himself. According to tradition, Jñāndev was initiated into the Nātha sect by his elder brother Nivṛtti, a disciple of Gahinīnāth, said to be the third or fourth in the Marāṭhī *nav-nāth* lineage. Gahinīnāth and Gorakhnāth—to whom the *Viveka-darpaṇa* and the *Gorakha-gītā*[48] are attributed—are considered to be the founders of mystical literature in Marāṭhī that was subsequently taken up by Jñāndev. Tulpule remarks:

> Scholars are divided on the question of locating these early Nāthas, the northerners, the Bengālīs and the Maharashtrians claiming that they belong to their respective regions. It seems truer that, like the early Ṣūfīs, they were itinerant mystics and the three provinces concerned must have been their temporary habitats.[49]

Apparently countering Dhere's opinion of a connection of Dattātreya with Nāthism from an early period, Charles Pain and Eleanor Zelliot have observed:

> At some point Datta became connected with the traditions of the Natha yogis and Dasnamis, both pan-Indian Shaiva ascetic orders. Datta has only minor importance in the Natha tradition of

northern India, and his connection with the Maharashtrian Natha tradition appears to come rather late. However, he attains prominence in the eighteenth-century Marathi Natha work *Nav-nāth-bhakti-sār*, where he is regarded as the founder of the Natha *sampradāy* (tradition) and guru of Gorakhnath and Matsyendranath. The connection between the Datta cult and Natha tradition continues to be very strong.[50]

Nevertheless, if many popular Nātha texts celebrating Dattātreya are late, this doesn't mean that the deity achieved prominence within Nāthism only as of the eighteenth century.[51] Despite the opinions of Pain and Zelliot, I agree with Dhere, H. Dvivedi, and Vaudeville. In other words, I'm persuaded that Dattātreya's appropriation by the Mahānubhāva sect came via the pan-Indian schools of Nātha Yogins.[52] The Mahānubhāva Datta did not originate in a vacuum or come out of thin air. Apart from the possible identification of Cakradhar and Guṇḍam Rāuḷ as Nātha Yogins, from about the tenth century relevant Nātha themes were originating around *śakti-pīṭhas* and in Tantric contexts: the same milieux with which the honeybee Yogin Dattātreya is connected from early times. These relevant themes include their *sādhana* of drinking the "*soma* nectar," linking the Nāthas to alchemy (*rasāyana*),[53] avadhūtahood, and bodily immortality. Concerning the ritual drinking of *soma*—which traces its roots in the Vedic rite of *soma* sacrifice—Dattātreya is traditionally celebrated as the veritable creator of the plant from which the juice (*rasa*) of *soma* is extracted.[54] It seems reasonable to suggest that Dattātreya found a place in the mythology of western Nātha groups at an early date and that he was received by the Mahānubhāvas chiefly through their medium. Dattātreya's characterization as supreme Guru and Yogin, coupled with his hybrid *Śaiva-Vaiṣṇava* identity, must have captivated the founders of the Mahānubhāva sect, leading them to select him as one of the five "descents" of Parameśvara.

I bring this chapter to a close by signaling a theological problem posed by Mahānubhāva adepts: the attainment of liberation.[55] The *Sūtra-pāṭha* teaches that the presence of one of the five Avatāras of Parameśvara is indispensable in order to achieve *mokṣa*. Unfortunately, despite Cakradhar's supposed immortality and the *Līḷā-caritra* saying—where Cakradhar indicates himself as the only means of release in the present age (*uttarārdha* 113)—Mahānubhāvas note that neither Cakradhar nor any other Avatāra has yet manifested since the end of the thirteenth century. How then can anyone be saved from rebirth? Indeed, this problem was strongly felt since the fourteenth century.

The *Smṛti-sthaḷa*, an anecdotal biography of Nāgadeva who was the first *ācārya* of the Mahānubhāvas after Cakradhar's death, was precisely intended to offer guidance as to how to cope "in the absence of God." The predominant theme of the narrative is the remembrance of Cakradhar's life and sayings, revered as "God verbalized" (*vacanarūpa parameśvara*). The painful mood of abandonment and separation (*viraha*) runs through the text, although hope for salvation is never lost.[56] In this connection, it must be remembered that the one Pañca-Kṛṣṇa popularly revered as eternal is precisely Dattātreya. This belief, linked to the Nātha perception of Dattātreya as an immortal Yogin, seems to find confirmation in the Mahānubhāvas' conviction that Dattātreya's Avatāra takes place in all four *yugas* (*Sūtra-pāṭha, vicāra* 282) and that he is the *ādi-kāraṇa* or primeval cause of the Mahānubhāva path, constantly operating in the world (*Sūtra-pāṭha, vicāra* 285). Unlike other Avatāras whose stay on earth is limited to a fixed period of time, Dattātreya is believed to constantly dwell on earth in an invisible form, appearing only to a few. Thus, Mahānubhāva adepts may still hope to experience the liberating presence of an Avatāra of Parameśvara, either through Dattātreya's intrinsic power of giving *darśana* (though admittedly a rare boon to obtain!), or, perhaps more "easily," by accepting the possibility that he may manifest himself under disguise or as an authoritative Guru, to be revered as a veritable manifestation of Datta.

In conclusion, Dattātreya's emergence in the Mahānubhāva texts appears as the first evidence of his presence in the Marāṭhī speaking area. It testifies to a crucial phase in the deity's unfolding, witnessing his appropriation by a variety of religious groups: Śāktas, Nāthas, Śaṅkara's Daśanāmīs, Aghorīs, and possibly even Jaina ascetic circles. The eclectic, integrative spirituality of Dattātreya's icon finds its privileged abode in the Marāṭhī region, always receptive to religious and cultural influences from both the north and south of the subcontinent. The Mahānubhāva Datta preceded the next fundamental period: the ascent to the top of the Marāṭhī pantheon at the time of the *Guru-caritra* of Sarasvatī Gaṅgādhar, truly the "Bible" of all Dattātreya devotees.

Notes

1. Raeside, *Dattātreya*, 490. The presentation of Dattātreya's place in Mahānubhāva literature is based on Raeside's contribution.

2. Also known by the Sanskrit name of Cakrapāṇi. In the Marāṭhī region, Rāuḷ is the name of a very low caste of Bhairava worshipers.

3. Also known by the Sanskrit name of Govindaprabhu.

4. On the role of Mahānubhāvas in the development of Marāṭhī literature, see Tulpule, *Classical Marāṭhī Literature: From the Beginning to A.D. 1818:* chap. 4 ("The Rise of the Mahānubhāva Sect"), 315–17; chap. 11 ("The Mahānubhāva Septette"), 338–42; chap. 14 ("The Contribution of the Mahānubhāvas"), 348–52; and chap. 21 ("Later Mahānubhāvas and Vīraśaivas"), 371–73.

5. See Vaudeville, "The Shaiva-Vaishnava Synthesis in Maharashtrian Santism," 221.

6. See Vaudeville, *Kabīr,* 1:101 n. 3. On Dattātreya being the Nātha presiding over the western region, see Shashibhusan Dasgupta, *Obscure Religious Cults,* 206.

7. The Vārkarī or Vārakarī movement, founded by Jñāndev, is constituted of Maharashtrian *Vaiṣṇavas* devoted to the god Viṭṭhala or Viṭhobā of Paṇḍharpur. The term *vārakarī* means "makers of a *vāra,*" that is, of a regular trip to a holy spot. For a collection of the Vārkarī's devotional poems, see Dandekar, *Vārkarī Bhajan-mālā Saṃgraha.*

8. Feldhaus, "The Orthodoxy of the Mahanubhavs," from Eleanor Zelliot and Maxine Berntsen's editors' introduction to the essay, 264–65. On the Mahānubhāvas, see Raeside, "The Mahānubhāvas"; Feldhaus, *The Religious System of the Mahānubhāva Sect: The Mahānubhāva Sūtrapāṭha.* See also Crooke, "Berar"; Russell and Lal, *The Tribes and Castes of the Central Provinces of India,* 4:176–83.

9. On Guṇḍam Rāuḷ's biography, see Feldhaus, *The Deeds of God in Ṛddhipur.* Cakradhar, also known as Cāṅgadeva Rāuḷ of Paiṭhaṇ, has a complicated prehistory. Some scholars think that he might be identified with the first of the Pañca-Kṛṣṇas, Cāṅgadeva Rāuḷ of Dvārakā. Y. K. Deshpande and R. C. Dhere have identified Cakradhar with a famous Nātha adept, Harināth, the grand-teacher of Mukundarāj.

10. Divided into three parts—the *ekānka,* the *pūrvārdha,* and the *uttarārdha*—the *Līḷā-caritra* contains about twelve hundred anecdotes (*līḷās*) of Cakradhar. To the *Sūtra-pāṭha,* originally classified under fourteen heads by Keśirāja, two more chapters by Paraśurāma and Rāmeśvara were later added. All in all, the *Sūtra-pāṭha* contains about 1,250 utterances expressing the principles of Cakradhar's philosophy. Both texts were lost with the fall of the Yādava kingdom of Devgiri, and reconstructed in the early fourteenth century.

11. Mahur is listed in a 1957 monograph on *tīrthas* of the *Kalyāṇa Kalpataru Series,* p. 238. The sacred sites mentioned are the temples of Anasūyā-Datta and Reṇukā, the *samādhi* of Jamadagni, and the sacred pool (*kuṇḍ*) of Paraśurāma. It is said that Dattātreya's *āśrama* was once located here and that Dattātreya was Jamadagni's Guru.

Prabhu, literally "mighty," "powerful," means master, lord, and expresses the notion of universal authority.

In Maharashtra, the Gosāvīs are identified as *Śaiva* Yogins or renunciants. In the case of Cāṅgadeva, the epithet simply identifies him as an ascetic.

12. On the south bank of the Godāvarī, east of Paiṭhaṇ. The Datta temple there was rebuilt in 1963 and reconsecrated by a group of Mahānubhāvas.

13. On Kolhāpur, see Dave, *Immortal India*, 2:137–43. See also Mate, *Temples and Legends of Maharashtra*, 26–52.

14. This text, comprising 279 *ślokas* based on the tenth chapter of the *Bhāgavata Purāṇa*, narrates a few *līlās* of the Pañca-Kṛṣṇas. For an English translation, see Raeside, *Gadyarāja: A Fourteenth Century Marāṭhī Version of the Kṛṣṇa Legend.*

15. The *Sahyādri-varṇana* has been edited by V. B. Kolte under the title *Ravaḷobāsa-kṛta Sahyādri-varṇana.*

To keep Mahānubhāva literature secret, Ravaḷobāsa invented a cipher known as the *sakaḷa-lipī*. Other Mahānubhāva authors created other ciphers such as the *sundarī, aṅka, vajra*, and so forth, but the *sakaḷa* was the most common. It was first deciphered by Rajavade and later by V. L. Bhave. More recently it was clarified by V. B. Kolte, in his introduction to the *Sahyādri-varṇana*, and expounded in English by Raeside; see *Bulletin of the School of Oriental and African Studies* 33, ii, 328.

Tulpule dates the *Sahyādri-varṇana* to 1353; see Tulpule, *Classical Marāṭhī Literature*, 338.

16. On this locale, see Dave, *Immortal India*, 4:156–60.

17. One of the lowest of the old untouchable castes of Maharashtra. Its traditional occupation was rope-making.

18. The legend that Kārtavīrya was born armless, or as having only fingerless stumps in place of hands, is found in *Gaṇeśa Purāṇa* 1.72–73 and *Reṇukā-māhātmya* 27.

19. Ekavīrā-Reṇukā, however, is not usually said to die on such occasion; see Gail, *Paraśurāma Brahmane und Krieger*, 211.

20. Perhaps a gorge or chasm between hills; see *Sthāna-pothī* 77. The *Śrī-dattātreya-jñān-koś* by P. N. Joshi mentions a *mūla-jharī* in a list of minor holy places at Mahur (p. 374).

21. See Dhere, *Datta Sampradāyācā Itihāsa*, 212–13; Prabhudesai, *Devī-kośa*, 2:457.

22. Dattātreya may also be possibly linked to the outcaste Devī Mātāṅgī, who has a *sthāna* at the main temple of Mahur. Devī Mātāṅgī's shrines are found at most other Devī temples in Maharashtra. For instance, at Tuḷjāpūr (*Devī-kośa* 2.467). According to the *Nārada Purāṇa*, Mātāṅgī is black, with hairy legs, and often drunk.

23. On the identity of Reṇukā and Ekavīrā, see *Devī-kośa*, 2.443, 2.461ff.; Dhere, *Śākti-pīṭhāncā Śodha*, 33. Nowadays the name of the Devī at Mahur is Ekavīrā, also known as Reṇukā, Jogāī, and Yallāmmā. Her form is not on view.

Traditionally, Maharashtra is said to have three-and-a-half *śakti-pīṭhas*: Mahur, Kolhāpur, Jogeśvarī at Ambā Jogāī and Saptaśṛṅgī near Nāsik (*Devī-kośa*, 2.472). Although there is a controversy over which is the half, Mahur is always referred to as a full *śakti-pīṭha*. The origin of *śakti-pīṭhas* is related to Satī's postmortem. When Śiva discovers Satī's body, he picks her up and, sobbing and grieving, carries her about the universe causing cosmic disruptions. Viṣṇu is summoned to end Śiva's grief and follows him, slicing bits and pieces from Satī's body until nothing remains. The various pieces of Satī's corpse fall to the earth, and wherever a bit of her body lands, a sacred place of the goddess, that is a *pīṭha*, is established. Realizing that Satī's corpse has disappeared, Śiva ends his grief and retires to his mountain abode. On *śakti-pīṭhas*, see Sirkar, *Śākta Pīṭhas*. See also Pratapaditya Pal, "The Fifty-one Śākta Pīṭhas," 1039–60.

24. Belopur is on the Pravarā, north of Rahuri in the Ahmednagar district. It was Cakradhar's last residence; see *uttarārdha* 458.

25. See Sastri and Sastri, *An Alphabetical Index*, pt. 1, 320.

26. Dattātreya's portrayal as an immortal suggests Nātha influence.

27. Although tradition ascribes the composition of this work to Mādhava or Vidyāraṇya in the fourteenth century, Yoshitsugu Sawai has come to the conclusion that the *Śaṅkara-dig-vijaya* was probably compiled in the eighteenth century, the terminus ad quem being 1799; see Sawai, *The Faith of Ascetics and Lay Smārtas. A Study of the Śaṅkaran Tradition of Śṛṅgeri*. For an edition of Mādhava's text, see *Śaṅkara-dig-vijaya*.

28. See Shea and Troyer, *The Dabistān or School of Manners: The Religious Beliefs, Observances, Philosophic Opinions, and Social Customs of the Nations of the East*, 244.

29. Briggs, *Gorakhnāth and the Kānphaṭa Yogīs*, 24 n. 5.

The Atīts are addressed as Siddha Nāgas and the highest among them, the Mahātīts, are revered as the most respected members of their Akhāḍās; see Sinha and Saraswati, *Ascetics of Kashi: An Anthropological Exploration*, 125–26. The term *atīt* also designates the seventh and highest stage of a *Vaiṣṇava* Nāga ascetic.

30. Naturally, all the *ācāryas* at the four *maṭhas*—the *Śaṅkarācāryas*—trace their *guru-paramparā* back through a number of illustrious Vedāntins up to "Ādi Śaṅkara." On the Daśanāmī tradition, see Cenkner, *A Tradition of Teachers: Śaṅkara and the Jagadgurus Today*. See also Bedi and Bedi, *Sadhus: The Holy Men of India*, 78–86.

31. The *akhāḍās*, literally "gymnasium," were founded as centers of military training for Nāga ascetics. The Jūnā, literally "old," has its head office at Benares, with branches at Prayāg, Haridvār, Oṃkār, Ujjāin, and Nāsik.

Nowadays, the Jūnā Akhāḍā has the largest number of Nāga followers, with about one thousand Avadhūtanīs or women Nāga ascetics. The tutelary deity of the Āvāhan Akhāḍā, affiliated to the Jūnā Akhāḍā and founded in 650 C.E., is Dattātreya Gajānan.

The Daśanāmīs are divided into two groups: the *śāstra-dhārīs*, those who "hold" the Scriptures, and the *astra-dhārīs*, those who "hold" weapons. Apparently, the order of warrior-renouncers was to protect the monastic institutions from Muslim attack. The *Śaiva* Nāgas are thus *astra-dhārīs* and follow their own mores of life. As militant ascetics, they fought in the armies whose chieftains offered the best compensation for their services. As a result, the Nāgas became powerful landowners (*zamīndārs*), and the Akhāḍās ammassed extensive tracts of land. The area of the Girnār hills was a land estate (*jāgīr*) under the control of the Nāga *mahant* of the Jūnā Akhāḍā until recently. On the order of warrior-renouncers, see Lorenzen, "Warrior Ascetics in Indian History"; Orr, "Armed Religious Ascetics in Northern India." See also Sarkar, *A History of Dasnami Naga Sanyasis*.

32. The vehicle of Bhairava—Śiva's terrifying aspect—is the dog with whom he is identified.

Nāgas and Nāthas are often indistinguishable; see Visuvalingam, "Bhairava's Royal Brahmanicide: The Problem of the Mahābrāhmaṇa," 159, 213 n. 15. On the spread of Bhairava's cult by "Nāth Siddhas, Dattātreyins, and Aghorīs," see White, *Myths of the Dog-Man*, 105.

33. A class of Yogins known as Lāl Pādrīs, "the wearers of yellow robes," are listed as followers of Dattātreya "who was eminent in the practice of Yoga and who is held in high esteem by Yogīs"; see Briggs, *Gorakhnāth and the Kānphaṭa Yogīs*, 74.

34. Possibly deriving from the Kāpālika sect, the Aghora *sampradāya* was supposedly founded by Brahma Giri, a *śiṣya* of Gorakhnāth. A *Śaiva* sect defying any *dharma* rule, its adepts are said to live in cremation grounds and to eat the flesh of dead animals (except horses) as well as of humans for ritual purposes. On the Aghorīs, see Barrow, "On Aghorīs and Aghorapanthis"; Balfour, "Life History of an Aghori Fakir"; Russell and Lal, *The Tribes and Castes of the Central Provinces of India*, 2:13–17; Parry, "Sacrificial Death and the Necrophagous Ascetic"; Parry, "The Aghori Ascetics of Benares"; Svoboda, *Aghora: At the Left Hand of God*; Marchetto, "Aghora-mārga: analisi delle dottrine e del metodo." On Aghora texts, see Ram Dular Singh, *Aghora Granthāvali: Collected Works of Aghora Manuscripts*.

35. According to a popular tradition, Dattātreya is the eternal Guru of all Nāthas and Śiva is the first Nātha. In this way, Śiva himself is made into a disciple of Dattātreya! Datta is also said to have been the first Aghorī. Briggs thus portrays Dattātreya:

> Dattātreya was probably a deified Brahmin of the tenth century, to whom the famous story of the testing of the virtue of the wife of Atri has been attached. His shrines are scattered here and there in the districts about Poona, and in one place his image has three heads to represent the Hindu Triad. He was an Aghorī. (Briggs, *Gorakhnāth and the Kānphaṭa Yogīs*, 74–75)

This identification of Dattātreya as both a Brahmin and an Aghorī is another indirect testimony of Datta's integrative force.

36. According to tradition, Kīnārām was born near Benares in 1658 and died in 1771. Though his parents were Kṣatriyas, the name of his father, Śrī Akbar Singh, betrays a Muslim descent. On Kīnārām's life and teachings, see Amar Singh, *Aghor Peetha and Baba Kina Ram*. See also Gupta, "The Kīnā Rāmī: Augharṣ and Kings in the Age of Cultural Contact."

37. This account is taken from a brochure of the modern Aghora *sampradāya*; see also Singh, *Aghor Peetha and Baba Kina Ram*, 19. According to legend, the teacher of Kīnārām was one Kālūrām, believed to be Dattātreya himself. A curious story narrates that when Kīnārām reached the Hariścandra Ghāṭ in Benares, he was put to test by Kālūrām, whom he saw feeding gram to the skulls of the dead! Then Kīnārām realized that Kālūrām was none other than Dattātreya. At this, Kīnārām ordered the skulls to stop eating. Kālūrām then expressed his desire for food. Kīnārām prayed to the Gaṅgā, and suddenly fish jumped out of the river and were baked in the fire of a nearby funeral pyre; see ibid., 20.

38. On Girnār, see *The Imperial Gazetteer of India*, 12:247–48; Dave, *Immortal India*, 2:115–22. See also Briggs, *Gorakhnāth and the Kānphaṭa Yogīs*, 119.

39. See H. G. Sastri, *A Historical and Cultural Study of the Inscriptions of Gujarat from Earliest Times to the End of the Caulukya Period* (circa 1300 A.D.), 160ff.

40. Burgess, *Report on the Antiquities of Kathiawad and Kacch*, 175–76; Purohit Swami, *An Indian Monk: His Life and Adventures*, 75.

According to Nātha mythology, Nemināth (Nīmnāth) and Pārasnāth, sons of Matsyendranāth, were born in Ceylon. They were slain, but Gorakhnāth restored them to life. Initiated by their father, they became the founders of the two Jaina sects of the Nīmnāthīs and Pārasnāthīs; see Briggs, *Gorakhnāth and the Kānphaṭa Yogīs*, 72–73. See also Eliade, *Yoga: Immortality and Freedom*, 309–11.

41. Among the Digambaras the most important *Mahā-purāṇa* is the one begun by Jinasena in the Rāṣṭrakūṭa court in Karnataka and completed by his disciple Guṇabhadra (late ninth century). For the Śvetāmbaras the most important *Mahā-purāṇa* is the *Triṣaṣṭi-śalākā-puruṣa-caritra* composed by Hemacandra in the Cāḷukya court in Gujarat between 1160 and 1172 C.E. In Jaina tradition figure sixty-three *śalākā-puruṣas*: the twenty-four Tīrthaṅkaras,

twelve Cakravartins, nine Baladevas, nine Vāsudevas, and nine Prati-vāsudevas. Datta's Prati-vāsudeva is Bali or even Prahlāda, whereas his corresponding Baladeva or righteous half-brother is Nandimitra. In Hindu mythology it was the dwarf Avatāra Vāmana—not Dattātreya—who manifested for the purpose of restraining Bali. For an English translation of Datta's episode in Hemacandra's work, see Johnson, *Triṣaṣṭiśalākāpuruṣacaritra; or, The Lives of Sixty-Three Illustrious Persons by Ācārya Śrī Hemacandra*, 4:49–51.

42. On Mount Abu, at the south end of the Arawalli Hills on the borders between Gujarat and Rajasthan, see Jayantavijayaji, *Holy Abu: A Tourist's Guide to Mount Abu and Its Jaina Shrines*, 169. See also Dave, *Immortal India*, 3:60–66.

43. See Dhere, *Datta Sampradāyācā Itihāsa*, 62. He sees the Nātha sect as a movement of reform against Tantric excesses, using the name of Dattātreya as its Satguru, rejecting any connection with wine and women and crediting Dattātreya with the authorship of the *Avadhūta-gītā*. Raeside notes that Cāṅgadeva Rāuḷ is shared by both Mahānubhāvas and Nāthas; see Raeside, "Dattātreya," 489.

44. For a fine English rendering, see Swami Kripananda, *Jnaneshwar's Gita: A Rendering of the Jnaneshwari.*

45. Historically, the term *sant* refers to the early nonsectarian poet-saints of northern India and Maharashtra, considered "liberal" *Vaiṣṇavas*. On Santism, see Schomer and McLeod, *The Sants: Studies in a Devotional Tradition of India.*

46. On Viṭṭhala, see the classic monograph by Deleury, *The Cult of Viṭhobā*. On the pilgrimage to Paṇḍharpur participate the *pālkhīs* of the Nāthas (Gorakhnāth, Macchindranāth) as well as the *pālkhī* of the devotees of Nṛsiṃha Sarasvatī, founder of the Datta *sampradāya*; see ibid., plate 4. The *abhaṅg*, literally "unbroken," is the more common form of Marāṭhī *bhakti* poetry, generally composed of four lines in an ABBC rhyme; see Tulpule, *Classical Marāṭhī Literature*, 451–52.

For the poem concerning Dattātreya, see *Śrī Jñāneśvara Mahārājāñcī Gāthā, abhaṅg* 403, n.123. Quoted in Dhere, *Datta Sampradāyācā Itihāsa*, 66.

47. See Vaudeville, "Sant Mat: Santism as the Universal Path to Sanctity," 26–29.

48. The *Viveka-darpaṇa*, a philosophical treatise written in rhythmic prose, narrates the theory and practice of Yoga as propounded by the Nāthas. The *Gorakha-gītā*, a commentary on the *Bhagavad-gītā*, is ascribed to Gorakhnāth. His disciple Gahinī gave it a literary form.

49. Tulpule, *Classical Marāṭhī Literature*, 315.

50. Charles Pain with Eleanor Zelliot, "The God Dattatreya and the Datta Temples of Pune," 97.

51. On Dattātreya's link to Nātha texts, see Dhere, *Datta Sampradāyācā Itihāsa*, 53–58.

52. For an appreciation of Nātha poems dedicated to Dattātreya, see Dvivedi, *Nāth Siddhon kī Bāniyān*, 5–7, 55–62.

53. See Shashibhusan Dasgupta, *Obscure Religious Cults*, 250ff. Nātha textual traditions concerning *rasāyana* date from about the tenth century onward. On *rasāyana* within Nāthism, see also White, "Why Gurus are Heavy," 46. By the same author, see "The Ocean of Mercury: An Eleventh Century Alchemical Text" and especially his comprehensive study *The Alchemical Body: Siddha Traditions in Medieval India.*

54. See Daniélou, *Hindu Polytheism*, 183. See also Gupta, *From Daityas to Devatas in Hindu Mythology*, 24.

55. On this issue see Feldhaus, "The Orthodoxy of the Mahanubhavs," 277ff.

56. On the *Smṛti-sthaḷa*, see Feldhaus and Tulpule, *In the Absence of God: The Early Years of an Indian Sect. A Translation of Smṛtisthaḷ with an Introduction.*

5

The *Guru-caritra* and the Rise of the Dattātreya Cult

With the *Guru-caritra* and its presentation of the two first historical Avatāras of the Datta *sampradāya*, we reach the core of Dattātreya's cult. This Marāṭhī work, revered as the most authoritative sacred text by all Datta devotees, is familiar to all the people of Maharashtra. In this chapter, I sketch the lives of the two Dattātreya Avatāras whose biographies—or, rather, hagiographies—are given in the *Guru-caritra*. Their miraculous lives show how Dattātreya and his cult were largely sanitized from within a Brahminical perspective, stressing the values of ritual observances and of *varṇāśrama-dharma*. At the same time, the influence and "contamination" with Islam could not be avoided and is clearly perceptible within the Datta *sampradāya*.

An outline of Dattātreya's worship in the three pilgrimage places connected with the two Avatāras—Audumbar, Narsobāvāḍī, and Gāṇagāpūr—still today the most important *sthānas* for all devotees, follows. I conclude the chapter by presenting Dattātreya's special link with possession phenomena: these *sthānas* are especially resorted to by the seemingly possessed, as Dattātreya is regarded as a most powerful healing deity.

The *Guru-caritra* (The Life of the Guru),[1] the basic religious text of the modern Dattātreya cult, was written in Marāṭhī around 1538 (according to Tulpule) or 1550 (according to Raeside) by Sarasvatī Gaṅgādhar, whose mother tongue was probably Kannaḍa.[2] Divided into fifty-one chapters containing more than seven thousand *ovīs* (with an addendum giving chapter contents and instructions, *avataraṇikā*, regarding its reading), it is a dialogue between two religious adepts, namely the Siddha and the Nāmadhāraka. Tradition divides this hagiographic text into three *kāṇḍas*: *jñāna-kāṇḍa* (chaps. 1–24), *karma-kāṇḍa* (chaps. 25–37), and *bhakti-kāṇḍa* (chaps. 38–51). Tulpule observes:

> Although the *Guru-caritra* does not excel as a work of literature, it occupies an important place in the religious life of Mahārāṣṭra, even today, and is almost held in awe and read devoutly by the

common man, in the faith that it is a great healer of ailments, both physical and spiritual. It enjoys the same popularity with the theistic masses as a work like the *Jñāneśvarī* among the followers of the cult of Paṇḍharpur.[3]

Contrary to the Vārkarī *sampradāya*, which was liberal in its outlook, the Datta *sampradāya* was a revivalistic cult attempting to preserve Brahminical orthodoxy, the system of castes, and overall emphasis on ritualistic religion. Many of the *Guru-caritra*'s chapters are concerned with caste duties, rules of conduct, appropriate ritual performances, *karma-vipāka*, and so forth.

The subject of the *Guru-caritra* is the life of two holy men, revered as the first historical Avatāras of Dattātreya within the Datta *sampradāya*: Śrīpāda Śrīvallabha (c. 1323–53), born in Pīṭhāpur in present-day Andhra Pradesh, east Godāvarī district, and Nṛsiṃha Sarasvatī (c. 1378–1458), born in Karañjā, Akolā district. Dattātreya, though in essence an Avatāra of Viṣṇu, was commonly regarded as a deity in his own terms. In any case, the belief in the existence of "Avatāras of an Avatāra" is a special feature of Dattātreya or Dattobā.[4] Viewed as an eternal, ubiquitous Avatāra, Dattātreya "appears" under various guises, though his *darśana* is said to be very difficult to attain: within the Datta *sampradāya* and even outside of it, many are the Gurus, Yogins, and renunciants who have been elevated to the status of Avatāras of Dattātreya.[5] The belief in the existence of Avatāras of Datta is also testimonied in Purāṇic literature. *Skanda Purāṇa* 1.2.46.163–64 mentions a Yogin, Vallinātha by name, said to be a partial manifestation (*aṃśa*) of Dattātreya. This Vallinātha, most probably a Nātha Yogin, established himself at the Bahūdaka *tīrtha* of the *Mahī-sāgara-saṅgam*, where the river Mahī joins the sea at the Bay of Cambay in Gujarat.[6] It is believed that if a person worships Dattātreya as Vallinātha, he will attain perfection in Yoga as well as prosperity in cattle.

Śrīpāda Śrīvallabha's life is narrated in the fifth and ninth chapters of the *Guru-caritra*. Around the beginning of the fourteenth century in the village of Pīṭhāpur, near Rajahmundry, lived a pious Brahmin couple. The man's name was Apaḷarāja, and he belonged to the Āpastamba branch of the *Vedas*. His wife's name was Sumatī. One day, Dattātreya, under disguise as a beggar, came to their house requesting alms as a *mādhūkarin*.[7] The couple was always hospitable to guests and, though they were busy with a *śrāddha* ceremony,[8] Dattātreya was served with such honor that he offered a boon to the pious couple, after he revealed his true identity. Sumatī asked that she might become the mother of a son as worthy as the deity.[9] Dattātreya, uttering the words *tathāstu*,[10] granted the woman's wish, and on the fourth day of the bright half of the month of *Bhādrapada* she bore a son who was named Śrīpāda. As he grew up, he attracted people due to his rare qualities and extraordinary features. He was invested with the sacred thread at the age of seven, at which time he could recite all the four *Vedas*.[11] At the age of sixteen he refused marriage, telling his parents that he was already married to Yoga and renunciation. He then announced his intention to leave the village on a pilgrimage.[12] Old Sumatī complained that her other children were lame or otherwise disabled and nobody would be left to care for her.[13] Śrīpāda merely cast a glance at his brothers, and all were rid of their deformities, becoming strong and healthy. He then received permission from his parents to leave, promising to return in the future.[14]

Śrīpāda embarked on a pilgrimage across the subcontinent, initiating and instructing religious adepts, particularly in the Himalayas. The *Guru-caritra* relates of his sojourn in Kāśī, Badarīnātha, Gokarṇa, and Kuravapur, on the banks of the Kṛṣṇā river.[15] Two episodes regarding his final stay in Kuravapur deserve mention. The first tells of a village widow, Ambikā, who lived with her only son. Both were on the point of suicide, because, Śrīpāda was told, the boy was foolish and unable to work to support his mother. Śrīpāda took pity upon them, instructing them to observe the vow of *śani-pradoṣa* and to practice the constant worship of Śiva.[16] As a result, the foolish boy was transformed into a wise and learned man. Śrīpāda promised the mother Ambikā that, in her next life, she would have a son like himself, foretelling his future birth as Nṛsiṃha Sarasvatī.

In a second episode Śrīpāda granted a boon to a poor village washerman who always bowed down to Śrīpāda when he went to the Kṛṣṇā river for his daily bathing. The two never spoke to each other. Once the washerman saw a king passing by, full of glory and riches, and he realized how miserable and worthless his life was compared to that of the king. At that moment, Śrīpāda appeared there for his bathing. Śrīpāda promised the washerman that, in his next life, he would be a king in a Muslim family and that he would meet him again under a different name (Nṛsiṃha Sarasvatī).[17] The village of Kuravapur gradually became famous as a center of Dattātreya worship, the benevolent and powerful Śrīpāda showering his grace on a great number of people through *camatkāras*[18] of various sorts. Finally, on the twelfth day of the second fortnight of the month of *Āśvina*, Śrīpāda disappeared into the waters of the holy Kṛṣṇā.[19]

Nṛsiṃha Sarasvatī, the second Avatāra of Dattātreya and the central figure in the history of the cult, is among the most revered saints within the *sampradāya* up to the present.[20] Tulpule views him as the veritable founder of the Dattātreya cult, which "arose probably as a reaction against the activity of the Sufis who were systematically encroaching upon the traditional religion of Mahārāṣṭra."[21] Much of the *Guru-caritra* (chaps. 11–51) is devoted to the narration of Nṛsiṃha's life, forming a kind of sacred *mantra*. Nṛsiṃha Sarasvatī was born within a Brahmin family. Mādhav, his father, belonged to the Vājasaneyī branch of the *Vedas*,[22] whereas Ambā, his mother, was the recipient (in her previous birth as the widow Ambikā) of Śrīvallabha's boon that he would be reborn as her son. Soon after Nṛsiṃha's birth on the fourteenth day of the bright half of *Vaiśākha*, the child, who was named Narahari,[23] was found to be mute. He performed various miracles for his distressed parents, but not until he turned an iron hammer into a golden one were Mādhav and his wife convinced of his extraordinary powers.[24] The child made them understand that he would be able to speak only after his thread ceremony (*mauñjī-bandhana*) took place. The only sound that emanated from his mouth was the sacred syllable *oṃ*.[25]

The main phases of Nṛsiṃha's life imitate, in almost all respects, those of Śrīpāda's. At the time of the thread ceremony, which took place in his eighth year as the tradition, the boy could recite all the four *Vedas* and six *Śāstras*.[26] After the rite, he asked permission to leave on pilgrimage. He comforted his mother, telling her of the impermanent nature of the material world.[27] He assured her that she and her husband would have other sons and daughters, and finally promised to stay with them until the birth of another son. Accordingly, he remained with them for another year and then left the village at the age of nine.[28]

Narahari embarked upon an itinerant life for about thirty years, visiting various *tīrthas* in the north.[29] Thus he gave sanctity to places like Gāyā, Prayāg, Badrīkedar, and so on. The first stopover of this long *yātrā*, in Kāśī, deserves special mention. Chapter 12 of the *Guru-caritra* informs us that here, at the age of ten, he practiced severe penance and received *dīkṣā* within Śaṅkara's Daśanāmī order from one Kṛṣṇa Sarasvatī, by whom he was renamed Nṛsiṃha Sarasvatī. According to Daśanāmī rules, only the Tīrtha, Āśrama, and Sarasvatī renunciants can aspire to become "holders of the staff" (*daṇḍa-dhārin*) and Daṇḍin Svāmins. In particular, only those belonging to the Brahmin caste can become ascetics in the Daṇḍin subsect, claiming a superior status.[30] Daṇḍins hold Dattātreya in great esteem. As H. H. Wilson observes: "Besides Śaṅkara, the different orders of Daṇḍins hold in high veneration the Muni Dattātreya."[31] Nṛsiṃha Sarasvatī started initiating many adepts along the path of *saṃnyāsa*, and the *Guru-caritra* emphasizes his contribution to the revitalization of the fourth *āśrama*, which was then in decline. This regeneration of the Saṃnyāsin ideal, was mainly centered on the revalorization of Brahminical codes of conduct and the performance of ritual sacrifices. Śaṅkara's characterization of *saṃnyāsa* in terms of intellectual realization, study, and self-consciousness did not constitute Nṛsiṃha Sarasvatī's prior concern. The emphasis of his teaching was based more on notions of *dharma* and *karman*, that is, on the performance of the correct ritual acts, rather than on *jñāna*.

After his period of itinerant life, Nṛsiṃha Sarasvatī returned to Karañjā to meet his aged parents.[32] Everyone in the village was overjoyed, and Nṛsiṃha, to please them, is said to have assumed as many forms as the number of villagers worshiping him. He then blessed his parents by giving them instant *mokṣa*.[33] After a few days' stay at Karañjā he proceeded south, returning to the Deccan area and staying for some time at Audumbar and Narsobāvāḍī,[34] both on the banks of the Kṛṣṇā. Finally, he settled at Gāṇagāpūr (Gulbarga district) for the last twenty-three years of his life, on the confluence of the Bhīmā and the Amarajā, where he died on the first day of the month of *Māgha* in *śaka* 1380, that is, in 1458 C.E.

Among the many miraculous deeds attributed to Nṛsiṃha Sarasvatī, one is particularly noteworthy. A poor Brahmin who had a small house with a bean vine earned a living by officiating as *pujārī* and by begging.[35] When he was given no alms he would go pick the beans. The small vine was important for him and his family. One day Nṛsiṃha came to his house to beg and the Brahmin, having nothing else to offer, cooked the beans and served them to the guest. The latter was greatly pleased. While departing, however, he cut off the trunk of the vine. The Brahmin and his family were shocked, but didn't dare complain. Later, the Brahmin decided to dig out the roots of the plant and, lo and behold, found a jar full of gold coins beneath it! He then realized the meaning of the Saṃnyāsin's action and became his great *bhakta*. The man's pious response to Nṛsiṃha's test emphasizes the exemplary conduct that should characterize a Brahmin. The gift of gold, dramatically changing the life of the Brahmin and his family, is a typical instance of Dattātreya's readiness to bestow material welfare (*bhukti*) on his devotees.

Many other miraculous episodes are reported throughout the *Guru-caritra*: a barren buffalo giving milk, a member of the Mahār caste able to recite the *Vedas*, a devotee performing extraordinary acts such as feeding nearly three thousand people from a small pot, curing

A modern image from Gāṇagāpūr of *trimukhī* Dattātreya with the *trimūrti*. At the center, the two Datta Avatāras: Nṛsiṃha Sarasvatī with the *Guru-caritra* and, above him, Śrīpāda Śrīvallabha.

the Bahāmanī king Allāuddīn by a mere blessing, bringing a man back to life,[36] being simultaneously present at eight different places, and so on.

In his *Bhakta-vijaya*, Mahīpati (1715–90)[37] offers a portrait of Nṛsiṃha Sarasvatī. He identifies him as a Paramahaṃsa and an Avadhūta who soon gave up "his staff and gourd," that is, his regular *saṃnyāsa* in the Daśanāmī order. Not agreeing that Nṛsiṃha got the name Sarasvatī from his connection with the homonymous Daśanāmī order in Kāśī, Mahīpati says that he was given that name at a tender age since "no Brahmin could be compared to him, for on the tip of his tongue Sarasvatī presided." Mahīpati's sketch of Nṛsiṃha's life is wholly dependent on the *Guru-caritra*, though the hagiographer mixes together the *Guru-caritra* accounts of Śrīpāda Śrīvallabha and Nṛsiṃha Sarasvatī. To be sure, the biographies of the two saints bear strong affinities in the *Guru-caritra* itself, and thus it is highly probable that Mahīpati, following the tradition of the sacred text, envisioned Nṛsiṃha Sarasvatī as none other than Śrīpāda Śrīvallabha reincarnated. In this perspective, the "coalescence" of the biographical traits of the two saints is to a certain extent justified by the effort to uphold the theological truth of the sameness of the two Datta Avatāras. Also in Mahīpati's account the emphasis is placed on the saint's Vedic knowledge and Brahminical orthodoxy (though he is identified as an Avadhūta), as well as on his performance of miracles through his *siddhis* (granting material welfare to his devotees in accordance with the prominence of the *bhukti* ideal in the Datta typology).[38]

The life of Nṛsiṃha Sarasvatī is said to have been spent primarily in the preaching of *varṇāśrama-dharma*, with the aim of purifying and reviving the traditional Vedic religion. As Narayan H. Kulkarnee points out:

> Nṛsiṃha Sarasvatī was a strict believer in the *varṇāśrama-dharma* and enjoined upon his followers, particularly the Brahmins, even more strict regulations. If we are to believe the *Guru-caritra*, the Bahāmanīs, the Adilshahs, the Qutubshahs were won over by Nṛsiṃha Sarasvatī with his miraculous powers. In a broader perspective his efforts can be regarded as an attempt to reconcile the Muslim rule to the Hindu way of life. But the effort cannot be said to have succeeded.[39]

During all his itinerant life, "the Guru," as he is called even today, encouraged the practice of *yajñas*. The presence near Gāṇagāpūr of a hill of ashes, of which handfuls are still taken away as *prasāda* by devotees, has led many to hypothesize that this site must have been one of intense ritual activity (*yajña-bhūmi*). Unfortunately, no writings of Nṛsiṃha Sarasvatī have come down to us. His mission may be described as that of awakening the Hindus, particularly the Brahmin caste, to the disastrous conditions into which they had fallen under Muslim rule, and making them conscious of their duties toward society. He was the first to propound the idea of a *Mahārāṣṭra-dharma*, later to be repeated by Rāmdās (1608–1681), the great religious "activist" of the following century.[40]

Two contradictory motifs animated the Dattātreya *sampradāya* from its very outset. On one hand, the call for a regeneration of Vedic ritual and Brahminical religion, then in decline due to Muslim rule, emphasized Dattātreya's portrayal as a Brahminical deity.[41] The theme of orthodoxy and ritual purity is the focus of the entire *Guru-caritra*. Besides the Purāṇic and *Pāñcarātra* literature upholding this characterization (as in the *Brahma Purāṇa* account and *Sāttvata Saṃhitā* 12.109–114) Dattātreya is linked to Brahminical orthodoxy through his adoption as Yogin-God by groups such as the Daśanāmī order. On the other hand, the political situation and the cultural atmosphere of medieval Maharashtra favored an interreligious exchange, which in some cases brought a blending of Hinduism and Islam. The eclecticism of Marāṭhī spirituality is evidenced not only by the symbiosis of *Śaiva* and *Vaiṣṇava* elements but also by the encounter on a popular level of Hindu *bhakti* with Sufism: within the broader Datta movement, there are Gurus venerated as Avatāras of Dattātreya who are clearly Faqīrs.[42] To be sure, this blending of Hinduism with Islam did not affect all religious groups uniformly. One might wonder why the Datta *sampradāya*—a revivalistic, Brahminical cult—got so "friendly with the enemy," to an even greater extent than the liberal Vārkarī *sampradāya*. I think the reason lies in Dattātreya's antinomian roots, which could not be simply cancelled or obliterated: at a popular level, the deity's link to Islam was favored by the assimilation to the impure Muslims of nonconformist Nāthas[43] and socially disreputable groups, such as the Aghorīs. In other words, Dattātreya's appeal to Yogic, extremist, and unorthodox groups—such as the Mahānubhāvas—favored the contact with Islam, making it almost natural. Even the Marāṭhī Ānanda *sampradāya*,[44] including many Muslim converts to Hinduism, may be regarded "either as an Islamic version of Datta *sampradāya* or at least as a sub-cult of that sect," as Narayan H. Kulkarnee states.[45] Pūrṇānanda, one of the four prominent figures within the Ānanda *sampradāya* with Sahajānanda, Nijānanda, and Raṅganāth,[46] was the author in 1610 of the *Avadhūta-ṭīkā*, extolling Dattātreya as the supreme Avadhūta.

Given this inextricable amalgam of unorthodox and orthodox elements in Dattātreya's icon, the question remains why a revivalistic, Brahminical milieu stressing *karman* and *dharma* would choose him, a *jñāna-mūrti*, as its *iṣṭa-devatā*. Certainly the eclectic character and multisymbolic force of Dattātreya as Guru, Yogin, and Avatāra, made him popular in practically all social strata, a kind of religious magnet appealing to the masses. Although the original characterization of Datta as a *jñāna-yogin* was surely not lost within the *sampradāya*, stress was laid on *dharma* rules and ritual. In time, the elitist, ascetic *jñāna-mārga* of Yogins and renunciants came to be flanked by the more popular *bhakti-mārga*. In the end, all three fundamental paths of *jñāna*, *karman*, and *bhakti* were assimilated within the deity's cult. For these reasons, the Dattātreya icon stands as the most impressive paradigm of Marāṭhī integrative spirituality.

The three main residences of Nṛsiṃha Sarasvatī were Audumbar, Narsobāvāḍī, and Gāṇagāpūr. Today Audumbar, a tiny village, is situated near the railway station of Bhīlavāḍī, on the southern track of the Puṇe-Bangalore railway. A visitor crosses the Kṛṣṇā river by ferry, since the Audumbar *kṣetra* is itself on the Kṛṣṇā. The place acquired its name from the *uḍumbara* trees that are found in the area.[47] The chief object of worship here, as at all Dattātreya shrines, is a set of two *pādukās* of Nṛsiṃha Sarasvatī. The *pādukās* are wooden sandals consisting of a wooden sole and a wooden peg. Since no leather is used, it is the footgear of many ascetics, especially *Vaiṣṇava* adepts. More specifically, the term *pādukā* refers to the raised impression of the feet or the sandals of a saint or deity. The feet have always been an object of devotion in the Indian subcontinent. *Śakti* is believed to be stored in abundance in the feet, and the grace of massaging or touching the feet of a reputed saint is one of the blessings most yearned for by devotees. The sandals, being an emblem of royal dignity, are a symbol of spiritual authority and power. They are also a symbol of wandering, of being constantly on pilgrimage, a characteristic of all ascetics and, of course, of Dattātreya. The so-called *mantra* of the sandals (*pādukā-mantra*)—supposedly revealed by Śiva to the goddess—is *pādukāṃ pūjayāmi*, "I worship the sandals [of the Guru]."[48] A common practice among both Nātha adepts and Datta devotees is the placing of the *pādukās* of a deceased saint on his own *samādhi*.[49] Worship at the Audumbar *sthāna* includes *pālkhī* procession of the *pādukās* and the celebration of festivals such as *Datta-jayantī* and Śrīpāda Śrīvallabha and Nṛsiṃha Sarasvatī death anniversaries. Here and at Narsobāvāḍī the day sacred to Dattātreya is not Thursday, as tradition, but Saturday. During the last century, the princes of Sāṅglī, with the economic support of other devotees, erected a temple over the *pādukās*. Besides the hospitality of the local *pujārīs*, there are a few *dharma-śālās* to accomodate modern visitors.

Narsobāvāḍī is located close to the Jayasingpur station on the Miraj-Kolhāpur railway. Legend reports that even before Nṛsiṃha's time this place was sanctified by the austerities of various saints, including one Rāmacandra Yogin. It was considered a *sarva-tīrtha*, since all the gods had once stayed in this locale, on the banks of the Kṛṣṇā, for one whole year. The *Guru-caritra* states that the deity Amareśvara,[50] attended by sixty-four Yoginīs, resided here. The Dattātreya temple, on the bank of the river under an *uḍumbara* tree, was supposedly built by a Muslim king of Bījāpur,[51] and contains the *pādukās* of Nṛsiṃha Sarasvatī. There is a story about the sacred area of this temple: one Bahirāmbhaṭṭa,[52] a Brahmin from the nearby village of Ālāsa, having no offspring, came daily to Narsobāvāḍī to take *darśana* of Nṛsiṃha.[53] One day Nṛsiṃha, on his way to Gāṇagāpūr, asked the Brahmin to worship his *pādukās*, named *mano-hara*,[54] under an *uḍumbara* tree, and he foretold how that place would enjoy great importance in the future. The regular routine of worship is centered on the *pādukās* taken in procession and on the celebration of the Avatāras of Dattātreya. Besides Nṛsiṃha Sarasvatī, mention must be made of the eighteenth-century saint Vāsudevānanda Sarasvatī, also believed to be a Datta incarnation. In his lifetime he visited Narsobāvāḍī frequently and is said to have had the vision of Dattātreya there, wherein he gave new rules for the better management of the *sthāna*.

The village of Gāṇagāpūr in northern Mysore—today part of Karnataka—is located fifty miles to the south-east of Solāpur, on the main line of the Bombay-Madras route. The Gāṇagāpūr *kṣetra*, which Nṛsiṃha Sarasvatī selected as his final abode, lies fourteen miles south of Gāṇagāpūr station near the *saṅgama*, the confluence of the Bhīmā and Amarajā rivers.[55] The small Amarajā river is considered by devotees as the "remnant of *amṛta*." The story goes that once the gods were engaged in a fierce battle against the demon Jālandhara.[56] So many of the Devas died during this cosmic struggle that it was necessary to carry the nectar of immortality to that place in order to revive them. Some of the *amṛta* was spilled where the Amarajā originates, and from then onward the course of the small river began to flow. To Indian eyes the water of all rivers is for humans what the *amṛta* is for the gods.[57] Thus, on the confluence of the Bhīmā and the Amarajā, about two miles from the *sthāna*, is the most sacred *tīrtha*, known as *Satkula*.[58] Bathing at this place is thought to be equivalent to bathing at Prayāg. Not far from this ford is the so-called *viśrānti-kaṭṭā*, or resting

The welcome sign at the Gāṇagāpūr railway station.

platform, where Nṛsiṃha Sarasvatī used to lie when going to and from the confluence.

The old blocks making up the *maṭha* of Nṛsiṃha Sarasvatī today form the most sacred part of the small but elegant Dattātreya *mandir*, recently rebuilt in the Cāḷukyan style. On a raised platform on the southern side of the *mandap* is the holy *garbha-gṛha*: a small room divided by a wall. The outer part has two doors and the visitor is only admitted up to this point. In the inner portion is "the holy of holies," the *nirguṇa-pādukās*,[59] today covered by silver busts of Brahmā, Viṣṇu, and Śiva. These *pādukās*, a concrete sign of the eternal presence of Dattātreya in his form as Nṛsiṃha Sarasvatī, have represented the most sacred object of worship within the Dattātreya cult for centuries.[60] The small opening in the wall gives the pilgrim a glimpse of a *mūrti* of Datta.[61] Facing the *pādukās* in a niche in the western wall is a small Gaṇeśa image known as Śrī Vighnahar Cintāmaṇi,[62] a *mūrti* made of sand, said to have been erected there by Nṛsiṃha Sarasvatī himself at the request of the ruler of Gāṇagāpūr. After the establishment of this icon, Nṛsiṃha founded the *maṭha* and took up residence there. Around the shrine are various items connected with the life of "Śrī Guru"; the chief object of interest being an *aśvattha* tree standing outside the *maṭha*.[63] According to legend, a *brahma-rākṣasa*[64] had made

Modern *trimukhī* Dattātreya at Gāṇagāpūr, on the confluence of the Bhīmā and Amarajā.

Shrine honoring Nṛsiṃha Sarasvatī in Gāṇagāpūr. Its *pujārī* proudly poses in front of it.

this tree his abode and the people were afraid of going near it. Nṛsiṃha Sarasvatī took pity upon them and gave *mokṣa* to the *brahma-rākṣasa*. These days, images of Nāganāth and Hanumān are on the platform surrounding the tree.[65] M. S. Mate's description of present-day ritual activity at Gāṇagāpūr helps us appreciate the importance of *pādukā* worship,[66] which dates back to the very beginnings of the Dattātreya cult:

> Early morning at three o'clock is the Kakad-arati. After this, the puja of the previous day is removed and the maha-puja begins. The other rituals, the sixteen upacharas, are offered without touching the padukas. Vighnahar Cintamani is then worshipped, and the puja of the other deities in the vicinity of the math is also performed. On this being completed, the prath or morning arati is sung, bringing to an end the puja. The whole ceremony takes around three hours . . . The padukas are placed during the course of this puja in front of the door of the innermost chamber of the garbha-grha. From this time to the presentation

> of the maha-naivedya, that is, approximately till one o'clock, the padukas are on view—darshan for any one. Similarly, all offerings including various types of pujas are to be done during this period. After the mahā-naivedya is presented, the padukas are removed from the door and placed in front of the image so that they can be viewed only through the small window in the wall.[67]

During the year, more than fifteen festivals, most of them including *pālkhī* procession, take place at Gāṇagāpūr. The most popular of them celebrates the *puṇya-smaraṇa*, Nṛsiṃha Sarasvatī's death anniversary, and takes place during the first four days of the bright half of the month of *Māgha*. Important aspects of this festival are the worship of Saṃnyāsins and a collective *snāna* in the waters of the Bhīmā. This occasion attracts the largest number of pilgrims to Gāṇagāpūr. Other important *utsavas* are Nṛsiṃha's and Śrīpāda's birthdays along with *Datta-jayantī*, celebrated on the fourteenth day of the full moon of the month of *Mārga-śīrṣa*.[68] During this festival, Dattātreya is worshipped through a mask of Viṣṇu (*mukhavat*),[69] icon of the infant deity. Such sobriety and the absence of any *trimūrti* symbolism could be interpreted as a vestige of antiquity, when devotees worshipped an *ekmukhī mūrti* of Datta.[70] Gāṇagāpūr is certainly the most sacred *sthāna* for all Dattātreya devotees. I was told that, about sixteen years ago, the local glory of Gāṇagāpūr was a youth living on the outskirts of the village; he was revered as an Avatāra of Datta.[71] During my visit to Gāṇagāpūr in 1991, I could find no trace of this "contemporary manifestation." In any case, the periodic emergence of supposed Avatāras of Dattātreya is a distinctive feature within the Datta cult.

A special characteristic of Audumbar, Narsobāvāḍī, Gāṇagāpūr, and in general all Dattātreya temples is their reputation as healing centers. These *tīrthas* are nowadays more well known for their alleged supernatural powers than as religious locales. People who believe to be possessed by evil spirits (*bhūt-bādhā*) such as *pretas*[72] and *piśācas*,[73] or to be victims of black magic (*karṇī*) come to these *sthānas* in great numbers, in hopes of being set free by the powerful, wakeful (*jāgṛt*) deity. As Mate explains:

> The victim is to be taken to the shrine and made to attend the worship and more especially the prayer or aratis. Due to the influence of the god, the spirits gradually become uneasy and ultimately leave their captive alone. At the time of the prayers one often sees in the shrine victims dancing, constantly bending

> backwards and forwards, and the entire atmosphere is filled with their wailings and shrieks. Although most of the deities are objects of *sakāma-bhakti*, none except Dattatreya is as prominent in the field of evil spirits and black magic.[74]

It is not clear why these *sthānas* have become popular as healing centers. The *Guru-caritra* narrates two or three episodes of Śrīpāda Śrīvallabha and Nṛsiṃha Sarasvatī saving people from the clutches of evil spirits, but this doesn't seem sufficient to explain the healing force attributed to these shrines. While in Gāṇagāpūr, I myself witnessed various scenes of *bhūt* possession and exorcism at the main Dattātreya temple. In particular, I remember a woman who started trembling and screaming while still circumambulating the sacred tree near the *saṅgama*. At the beginning of the music and singing of *āratī*, nearly all *bhūt* victims begin shaking and moaning, appearing to be in terrible pain. Some faint and fall to the ground, while others may move and swing at an incredible speed, even beating their heads on the ground. The belief, however, is that who is really being hurt is only the *bhūt*, who feels Dattātreya's presence and power. All informants assured me that they could feel no pain at all. As soon as the *āratī* ends, most of the screaming and writhing stops and the *bhūt* victims regain normal consciousness. The idea is that at this time Dattātreya relaxes the punishment and the *bhūt*, exhausted, withdraws into his victim allowing the person to regain consciousness. In any case, it is not believed that the *bhūt* leaves the victim when the *āratī* ceases. Most exorcisms and cures require at least a few weeks of participation in regular *āratī* sessions. Difficult cases may require a year or even a longer period of proximity to the *jāgṛt-sthāna*.

Bhūt victims usually speak of experiencing a general feeling of what they define as "wrongness." Everything in their lives and in themselves seems to get spoiled and go bad. Thus, for many the experience of "becoming right" again, or restoring harmony, results in a lasting bond of devotion to Dattātreya. The treatment, cleansing, and cure functions as an initiation into a new faith, a discovery or rediscovery of a spiritual dimension.

Besides Dattātreya's and also Kāḷ Bhairav's temples, there are two other kinds of healing centers in Maharashtra. These are the temples of the Mahānubhāva sect[75] and the burial places *(dargāhs)* or memorials *(chillas)* of Muslim holy men *(pīrs)* as well as the tombs *(samādhis)* of certain Hindu saints. Exorcism as well as possession appear always to be a prerogative of "unclean," Tantric, non-Brahminical or anti-Brahminical groups. Keeping in mind Dattātreya's

Devotees circumambulating a sacred tree near the confluence of the Bhīmā and Amarajā in Gāṇagāpūr. People thought to be possessed by evil spirits come here in hopes of being freed by Dattātreya.

old "impure," antinomian characterization as well as his integrative force, I would argue that an explanation for the god's "healing nature" is precisely his link—from the thirteenth century onward—with the unorthodox Mahānubhāva sect coupled with the deity's association with important *śakti-pīṭhas* such as Mahur. Moreover, Dattātreya's function as a healer can also be related to his "contamination" with Sufism: from at least the sixteenth century onward, various Muslim Pīrs have come to be recognized as Avatāras of Dattātreya.[76]

It is useful to distinguish between deities who do possess and deities who don't, since indeed not all Maharashtrian deities possess their devotees.[77] For example, among male gods, Śiva, Gaṇeśa, Rāma, Hanumān, Viṣṇu, Viṭhobā and Kṛṣṇa never possess, whereas Khaṇḍobā, Mhasobā, Mhaskobā, Vetāḷ, Jyotibā along with Dattātreya and Kāḷ Bhairav possess. Among female goddesses, Pārvatī, Sarasvatī, Sītā and Gaurī don't possess, whereas Mahālakṣmī, Ekavīrā, Bhavānī, Jānubāī, Kāḷubāī, Ambābāī, Jogābāī, Bāṇabāī, Yamāī do.[78] Following D. D. Kosambi, John M. Stanley has argued that the gods who do possess people correspond to those "ancient non-Aryan Maharashtrian gods who are gradually being assimilated into the great tradition as avatars of Śiva and Pārvatī."[79] Dattātreya's non-Brahminical elements have led even other scholars to identify him as a preceptor of non-Aryan tribes.[80]

This schematic distinction, however—almost a kind of dual opposition between Aryan and non-Aryan gods—does not seem to fit the case. What we call Hinduism has been since Vedic times a complex amalgam and interaction of a variety of components. The late Günther D. Sontheimer, for example, distinguished five: the Brahminical works and teachings, asceticism and renunciation, tribal religion, folk religion, and *bhakti* currents.[81] A religious phenomenon, always to be contextualized in time and space, may partake of some or even all of these components, though what determines its core character is which component is emphasized. Now, to be sure possession and exorcism are typical of a non-Brahminical, tribal and folk milieu. But even here, where the non-Brahminical component is prevalent, the dynamic interplay between all components is ongoing and should be recognized. What is often talked about as the process of "Sanskritization" or "Brahminization" of tribals, requires by the same token the consideration of the influences exercised by tribals on the so called "great tradition": cultural influences never work one way only.

The case of Dattātreya, with its eclectic background, is exemplary in this regard. The deity has been appropriated by both Brahminical and non-Brahminical groups depending on which component was prevalent at a particular time in a particular religious environment. These different appropriations contributed to the making of Dattātreya's plural identities, or, perhaps better, contributed to the molding of a unique *mūrti* accommodating a variety of apparently contradictory facets. If the main objective of Nṛsiṃha Sarasvatī's appropriation of Dattātreya was the awakening of Brahminical orthodoxy and the reinforcement of Vedic ritual, so as to counter Islamic dominance as well as Tantric excesses, the Datta *sampradāya* came in fact to tolerate a syncretistic blending between Hinduism and Islam. And even though Dattātreya is nowadays commonly identified as a Brahmin and his temples are viewed as centers of Brahmin worship, all this coexists with his main sanctuary—Gāṇagāpūr—being considered one of the most important healing centers of the seemingly possessed.

In conclusion, Śrīpāda Śrīvallabha and especially Nṛsiṃha Sarasvatī are to be regarded as the actual founders of the "religion" of Dattātreya in the Marāṭhī area. The Datta cult was and still is very popular, attracting masses of people through the assimilative nature of Dattātreya's icon. This integrative force will be mirrored in the subsequent unfolding of the Datta movement, even beyond the boundaries of the Datta *sampradāya* per se. The *Guru-caritra* remains the most sacred repository of Dattātreya's *līlās*, nurturing feelings of awe and devotion. For centuries, it has inspired the heart of ascetics and *bhaktas* and the creativity of *kīrtankārs*, becoming the source for the elaboration of more stories on Dattātreya and his Avatāras, and contributing to the ongoing vitality of the Datta movement.

Notes

1. See Kāmat, *Guru-caritra*. For a useful summary of the text, see D. D. Joshi, *Śrī Guru-caritra Kathā-sār*. See also Shenoy, *Sri Guru Charitra*.

2. See Tulpule, *Classical Marāṭhī Literature*, 352.

3. Ibid., 353.

4. In Maharashtra, Dattātreya is popularly known as Dattobā, just as Viṭṭhala is often referred to as Viṭhobā.

5. On the *guru-paramparā* of the Datta *sampradāya*, see chap. 6.

6. The Mahī, about 350 miles in length, is a river in western India. Its source is the Mehad lake near the town of Amjhera in Madhya Pradesh, on the west side of the Vindhya mountains. On the Mahī river, see Dave, *Immortal India*, 4:99–103.

7. A deity disguised as a beggar is a classic theme throughout Purāṇic literature. *Mādhūkara*, literally "similar to a bee," is the ideal type of begged food. As a bee neither selects flowers beforehand nor harms them in the process of extracting the nectar, so the ideal renouncer should neither preselect the houses at which he will beg nor become a burden on the householders. A renouncer begs just a few morsels at each house, approaching after people have had their meals. On *saṃnyāsa* begging rules as well as on the renunciant's lifestyle, see Kane, *History of Dharmaśāstra*, vol. 2, pt. 2, 934ff.

8. Hospitality to guests (*atithi*) is one of the duties of Brahmins. According to the *Śāstras* only a Brahmin can be a guest, and hospitality is restricted to one meal and one overnight stay if the guest arrives late in the evening and cannot return home. When a Saṃnyāsin turns up, the host considers himself fortunate since he is given the opportunity of earning merit through serving a renouncer. The theme of the pious and hospitable couple welcoming a guest is recurrent, the guest being God himself.

The *śrāddha* rites, which are performed for departed ancestors, are believed to supply them with nourishment after the funeral rites have endowed them with ethereal bodies. Until funeral rites have been performed and the first *śrāddha* ceremony has been celebrated, the deceased is thought to be a wandering ghost. Only afterward does the deceased "ascend" to the position of a *pitṛ* in the abode of the *pitṛ-loka*. *Śrāddha* ceremonies are observed at fixed periods by surviving relatives. These rites are marked by the offering of *piṇḍas* or balls of rice and meal to three paternal and three maternal forefathers. Traditionally, the first to be fed are Brahmins. But Sumatī, moved by compassion, ignored this custom and gave alms to the unexpected *atithi*.

9. The request of such a boon—as well as the granting of it by a deity—is another exemplary theme attested to throughout Purāṇic literature.

10. Literally "So let it be." The solemn assurance of a Guru or deity granting the desired boon.

11. According to the *Śāstras*, however, the *upanayana* ceremony is to take place in the eighth year for a Brahmin, in the eleventh for a Kṣatriya, and in the twelfth for a Vaiśya. The presentation of Śrīpāda's thread ceremony in the boy's seventh year is an apologetic device, highlighting his precocious nature. Śaṅkara's biographies report that the sacred thread was conferred upon him by his mother, Āryāmbā, when he was just five years old.

A typical characterization of extraordinary beings, Śrīpāda's precocious knowledge of all the four *Vedas* stresses the Brahminical orthodoxy of Dattātreya's first Avatāra.

12. Sixteen is a crucial age according to Indian symbology. Often at this age epic heroes as well as saints are said to manifest themselves. Śrīpāda's "marriage with Yoga and renunciation" marks his conversion to the lifestyle of the Saṃnyāsin. On the number sixteen, see Gonda, *Change and Continuity in Indian Religion*, 115–30.

Pilgrimage is another motif within Indian spirituality. All great religious figures, both of the past (e.g., Śaṅkara) and the present (e.g., Gandhi), feel the necessity—especially at the beginning of their mission—to embark on pilgrimages across the subcontinent. Dattātreya, emblem of the wandering ascetic constantly traveling to holy sites, represents a paradigm for the holy *homo viator*. On pilgrimage, see Bhardwaj, *Hindu Places of Pilgrimage in India: A Study in Cultural Geography*. See also Agehananda Bharati, "Pilgrimage Sites and Indian Civilization," 1:85–126. On major and secondary *tīrthas*, see the *tīrthāṅka* monograph in the *Kalyāṇa Kalpataru Series*.

13. The parents' and especially the mother's despair when learning of their son's decision to leave the village on a religious quest—as well as their efforts to avert his choice—is another leitmotif within Indian spirituality. An example is Śaṅkara's departure from his mother Āryāmbā and his native village of Kālaṭi: consent for the eight-year-old Śaṅkara to become a Saṃnyāsin was given by Āryāmbā only when, his foot in the mouth of a crocodile, he was in danger of drowning in a nearby river.

14. The son must be present at the deathbed and perform the funeral rites for his parents. As a Saṃnyāsin, he is expected to bestow his purifying blessings upon them. Many are the instances in devotional literature in which a "divine son" is said to grant *mokṣa* to his beloved and pious parents.

15. For a brief presentation of the Kṛṣṇā river, see Dave, *Immortal India,* 4:42–46.

16. The lack of economic sustenance is a realistic element within the overall hagiographic scheme of the episode. *Śani-pradoṣa,* literally "Saturn evening," is the name of a *pūjā* in Śiva's honor.

17. Granting wealth is a typical boon of Dattātreya and his Avatāras, said to be bestowers of both *bhukti* and *mukti.* This Tantric feature evidenced in the *Mārkaṇḍeya Purāṇa*'s presentation of Datta, relates the deity to *Śaivism;* see O'Flaherty, *Śiva: The Erotic Ascetic,* 258–59. See also Kamalakar Mishra, *Significance of the Tantric Tradition,* 47–51.

18. Literally "astonishment," "surprise"; in popular parlance, any miraculous or magical feat. The technical meaning of *camatkāra* in late texts of Kashmiri *Śaivism* is a form of aesthetic rapture of realization; see Dyczkowski, *The Doctrine of Vibration,* 147f.

19. The mysterious disappearance of holy figures in rivers is a hagiographic motif aimed at immortalizing the person.

20. On Nṛsiṃha Sarasvatī's life and works, also including his *guru-paramparā,* see Dhere, *Datta Sampradāyācā Itihāsa,* 78–134.

21. Tulpule, *Classical Marāṭhī Literature,* 352.

22. Name of the hymns of the white *Yajur Veda* ascribed to Ṛṣi Yājñavalkya.

23. Name of Viṣṇu as man-lion, thus the same as Narasiṁha. According to *Viṣṇu Purāṇa* 3.10, the ceremony of name giving is performed by the father on the tenth day after birth. In any case, the child gets a "secret name" known only to the parents immediately after birth.

24. Another *camatkāra* emphasizing the role of Dattātreya as wealth-bestower.

25. Through this apologetic device, the text emphasizes the boy's "*Brahman* nature."

26. An expression emphasizing Nṛsiṃha's omniscience. The six *Śāstras* are none other than the six *darśanas.*

27. The *upadeśa* relative to the world's impermanence and the urgency of *ātma-vicāra* is a leitmotif within religious literature.

28. The Indian son regards his parents as incarnate deities and must be obedient to them. Though the call to ascetic life vanquishes all customary duties, the son must guarantee the future welfare of his parents.

29. The hypothesis of a Tantric or Nātha influence upon Narahari should be kept in mind.

30. On the material and symbolic relevance of the staff or *daṇḍa*, see Olivelle, *Renunciation in Hinduism: A Medieval Debate*, 1:35–54; A. Glucklich, "The Royal Scepter (Daṇḍa) as Legal Punishment and Sacred Symbol."

31. H. H. Wilson, *A Sketch of the Religious Sects of the Hindus*, 205.

32. Again the motif of the pious Hindu son, who, in his role as a renunciant, returns to his dying parents to bestow his blessing on them, promise of liberation from *saṃsāra*.

33. The power inherent in an Avatāra or saint is thought capable of bestowing instant *mokṣa*, even if the recipient is not qualified to receive it.

34. The *Guru-caritra* reports that he remained at Audumbar for nearly four months, during which he blessed sixty-four Yogins. H. S. Joshi, however, reports that Nṛsiṃha Sarasvatī remained there for years practicing penance, and only after being disturbed by an ignorant Brahmin—whom the goddess Bhuvaneśvarī had asked to surrender to Nṛsiṃha—did he stop his *tapas*. The dull Brahmin was later blessed with knowledge and many boons from Nṛsiṃha.

In the *Guru-caritra*, Narsobāvāḍī figures as the offshoot of the village of Āmrapur. H. S. Joshi reports that Nṛsiṃha Sarasvatī lived there for more than twelve years.

35. The indigence of many Brahmins who serve as *pujārīs* in village India is a realistic element.

36. To his widowed wife, Nṛsiṃha had inadvertently given the customary blessing *aṣṭa-putra saubhāgyavatī bhava*, "may the married woman be blessed with eight sons." Nṛsiṃha's powerful blessing, though inadvertently given, could not but realize itself.

37. The most prominent among Marāṭhī hagiographers, Mahīpati lived at Taharabad, Ahmednagar district. As a devout Bhāgavata, he spent his life in the performance of *kīrtanas* and writing biographies of saints. Among his most important collections are the *Bhakta-vijaya* (1762), the *Santa-līlāmṛta* (1767), the *Bhakta-līlāmṛta* (1774), and the *Santa-vijaya*, left incomplete at his death in 1790. He is also credited as being the author of a *Dattātreya-janman* in 112 verses. On Mahīpati, see Tulpule, *Classical Marāṭhī Literature*, 429–32.

38. See Abbott and Godbole, *Stories of Indian Saints: An English Translation of Mahipati's Marathi* Bhakta-vijaya, 2:366–76.

39. Narayan H. Kulkarnee, "Medieval Maharashtra and Muslim Saint-Poets," 203.

40. See Tulpule, *Classical Marāṭhī Literature*, 352.

41. On the Datta Brahminical cult, see Sardar, *The Saint-Poets of Maharashtra (Their Impact on Society)*, 143–49.

42. In the Deccan, the dominant Sufi order was that of the Chishtī. The Sufi first established themselves around Devgiri, renamed Daulatabad by the Muslim rulers, around the beginning of the fourteenth century. Indianizing themselves, these Sufis seemed particularly tolerant toward non-Muslims, sometimes evidencing liberal and even pro-Hindu tendencies. On Sufism in the Deccan, see Nizami, "Sufi Movement in the Deccan"; Aziz, "Glimpses of Muslim Culture in the Deccan." On the fascinating phenomenon of Muslim poet-saints, see Dhere, *Musalmān Marāṭhī Santa-Kavī*.

43. G. S. Ghurye notes:

> The chief of the Mahanta of a Nathapanthi "akhada" or "dalica" is always known as the Pir . . . The most important centres of the Nathapanthis are situated in predominantly Muslim localities . . . The daily course of life that is lived at Nathapanthi centres, typically in the past, approximates the life of a Muslim Pir. (Ghurye, *Gods and Men*, 138–39)

On the cross-fertilization of Hindu and Muslim religiosity in Nāthism, see White, "The Wonders of Śrī Mastnāth."

44. This *sampradāya* is an example of Hindu-Muslim cross-fertilization. A case of such "fusion of horizons" is represented by the story of Mṛtyuñjaya (1575–1650), also known as Muntojī. He came from a royal Muslim family of the Bahāmanī dynasty of Bedar, connected to the Kādrī branch of the Sufis. Under the influence of Sahajānanda of Kalyāṇī, who initiated him into the Ānanda *sampradāya*, he converted to Hinduism. For the *guru-paramparā* of the Ānanda *sampradāya*, see Bhave, *Mahārāṣṭra Sārasvata*, 338. See also Dhere, *Datta Sampradāyācā Itihāsa*, 70–72.

45. Kulkarnee, "Medieval Maharashtra and Muslim Saint-Poets," 203.

46. The catchphrase of this school, *sahaja pūrṇa nijānandī raṅgalā*, mentions its four prominent authors.

47. Within the *sampradāya*, the *uḍumbara* tree *(Ficus glomerata)* is viewed as particularly sacred to Datta; see Enthoven, *Folkore of the Konkan*, 36, 71–72. It is a large tree without aerial roots and its wood is greyish-white or reddish-grey, soft, and very light. The leaves are ovate-oblong to lanceolate, three to eight inches long, thin, glabrous and shining on both surfaces. The *uḍumbara's* leaves, bark, fruit, and juice are used in local medicine. In Vedic times its wood—said to concentrate in itself the essence of all other trees—was used to make sacrificial tools as well as the most sacred sacrificial post *(yūpa)*.

For a narrative concerning the presence of "god's fish" (*devāce māse*) in the "water hole" in the Kṛṣṇā at Audumbar, see Feldhaus, *Water and Womanhood: Religious Meanings of Rivers in Maharashtra*, 94–96.

48. *Kulārṇava-tantra* 12.12 states that it is the highest *mantra* of all.

49. See Enthoven, *The Folklore of Bombay*, 150.

50. Literally "lord of the immortals." A title often attributed to Indra, Viṣṇu and Śiva. Amareśvara is also the name of one of the twelve great *liṅgas*.

51. On the kingdom of Bījāpur and the prominent role played by the Sufi, see Eaton, *Sufis of Bijapur (1300–1700): Social Roles of Sufis in Medieval India.*

52. Literally "the lord Bahirā." *Bhaṭṭa* is a title of respect often affixed to the names of learned men, especially Brahmins. The proper name Bahirā might be connected to Bahirobā, a Maharashtrian deity said to prevent disease.

53. The unfortunate destiny of sterility, leading people from time immemorial to temples and holy men in the hope of being blessed with offspring, is a recurrent theme throughout religious literature. Living saints as well as tombs of Sādhus and Faqīrs often become famous for their reputation of granting offspring; see Sharif, *Islam in India or the Qanūn-I-Islām*, 18. On the theme of childlessness and its relation to disease goddesses, such as Śītalā and Māriammai, see Kolenda, "Pox and the Terror of Childlessness: Images and Ideas of the Smallpox Goddess in a North Indian Village."

54. Literally "heart-stealing," meaning fascinating, charming.

55. *Saṅgama* is the confluence of two rivers or of a river with the ocean. The most sacred of all *saṅgamas* is that of the Gaṅgā and Yamunā at Prayāg. The site is called *triveṇī*, "a confluence of three," the third river being the mythical Sarasvatī, believed to join the two through a subterranean channel.

The Bhīmā, literally "the fearful or tremendous one," is the main tributary of the upper Kṛṣṇā river. On the banks of the Bhīmā are situated numerous *tīrthas* and pilgrimage places, foremost of which is Paṇḍharpur. Here the river curves in the shape of a crescent moon facing east and thus is also called Candra-bhāgā, "moon-portion." In Gāṇagāpūr, the first ten days of the month of *Jyeṣṭha* are devoted to the worship of the Bhīmā. On this river, see Dave, *Immortal India*, 4:71–73.

The Amarajā literally means "the one born from the immortal."

On the Gāṇagāpūr *kṣetra*—besides Mate, *Temples and Legends of Maharashtra*, 79–101—see Kulkarṇī, *Śrī Kṣetra Gāṅgāpūr Māhātmya*; Raṇpise, *Tripurā Śrīkṣetra Māhātmya: Gāṅgāpūr, Paṇḍharpur, Tuḷjāpūr*; Pain, "Gangapur: The Center of the Dattatreya Cult"; Pujārī, *Śrīkṣetra Gāṇagāpūr-varṇan*.

56. Literally "water-bearer." Name of an Asura produced by the contact of a flash from Śiva's eye with the ocean and adopted by the god of the waters. He was called Jālandhara for having captured the waters flowing from Brahmā's eye; see *Padma Purāṇa* 5.141ff.

57. See *Mahābhārata* 15.32.4ff.

58. Literally "good or noble family."

59. Literally "footprints devoid of attributes." The *nirguṇa* adjective emphasizes the inherent transcendent value of this sacred object of worship. From a spiritual point of view, these *pādukās* signify the deity's omnipresence.

60. It is said that Nṛsiṃha, before dying, addressed his disciples with these words: "My permanent presence henceforward shall be in these *nirguṇa-pādukās*."

61. When in Gāṇagāpūr in November 1991, I had *darśana* of a peculiar *mūrti* of Dattātreya: *bāla-datta* or baby Datta. The festival of *Datta-jayantī*, usually falling in December, was approaching.

62. Gaṇeśa, literally "lord of the *gaṇas*," remover of obstacles and fulfiller of all desires. On this popular god see Courtright, *Gaṇeśa: Lord of Obstacles, Lord of Beginnings*. See also Brown, *Ganesh: Studies of an Asian God;* Grimes, *Gaṇapati: Song of the Self*. For a presentation of the god's various forms, see Bühnemann, *Forms of Gaṇeśa: A Study Based on the* Vidyārṇavatantra.

63. The original tree died some years ago and a new one was planted in its place.

64. A demon, the ghost of a Brahmin who led an unholy life. *Manu-smṛti* 12.60 defines a *brahma-rākṣasa* as a Brahmin who, having had relations with outcasts or with the woman of others, is condemned to be reborn in a demonic being, feeding himself on human flesh.

65. Nāganāth, literally "serpent-chief," is probably an epithet of Śiva, ruler of the chtonic forces. The *nāga-naṭeśa liṅga* is a *liṅga* sacred to Śiva. Association of a *mūrti* of Nāganāth with a tree is quite common.

In the *Rāmāyaṇa* Hanumān, literally "having [large] jaws," headed a monkey-army and assisted Rāma in his war against Rāvaṇa. His form as monkey-god is popular all over India, incarnating the ideal of the exemplary *bhakta* rendering selfless service. In Maharashtra he is best known as Māruti, the son of Marut, the wind-god, and in most villages in the Deccan he is the chief deity. Māruti is supposed to guard the village against evils of all kind. Therefore, care is taken to build his temple at the outskirts of a village, preventing evil forces from crossing its boundaries. On Māruti, see Enthoven, *The Folklore of Bombay*, 188–92.

66. Today, individual worship of the *pādukās* includes the seven-day reading of the *Guru-caritra*, known as *saptāha-parāyaṇa*, and the performance of other *pūjās*.

67. Mate, *Temples and Legends of Maharashtra*, 91–92.

The *kākaḍ-āratī* is named after the lamp used in the *āratī* consisting of a *kākaḍā*, a coarse wick of cloth. This rite of the awakening of the god is of great antiquity; Nāmdev mentions it in one of his *abhaṅgs*.

Upacāras, literally "service," "worship," are various ritual acts involving specific articles of worship, such as presenting flowers to the deity. These *upacāras* are variously numbered: five, ten, sixteen, eighteen, up to sixty-four.

The *mahā-naivedya* is a great food offering presented to a god.

68. Śrīpāda Śrīvallabha's birth anniversary coincides with the most popular Marāṭhī festival of *Gaṇeśa-caturthī*, the birthday of Gaṇeśa.

The day of Dattātreya's birth is traditionally believed to be Wednesday (even though the anonymous *Dāsopant-caritra*, in verse 588, states it was Monday); see Shakti M. Gupta, *Vishnu and His Incarnations*, 42. G. S. Ghurye notes that Datta's birthday is listed in a curious way in the Punjabi almanac as *Dattātreya-utpatti*, "the production or outcoming of Dattātreya"; see Ghurye, *Gods and Men*, 212.

69. Literally "possessing a mouth." Here, *mukha* denotes the head of the deity seen from the front.

70. See Mate, *Temples and Legends*, 94.

71. Prof. E. Fasana of the University of Trieste, Italy, who visited Gāṇagāpūr around 1982, gave me this information.

72. Literally "departed," "dead." The term *preta* identifies a ghost, an evil spirit animating a carcass and haunting places such as crossroads, cremation grounds, and cemeteries.

73. The most malignant order of beings, placed by the *Vedas* as lower than the *rākṣasas*. This class of demons is termed *piśāca* because of their fondness for flesh or even because of their yellowish appearance.

74. Mate, *Temples and Legends*, 96–97. *Sakāma-bhakti*, literally "wish-granting devotion."

75. For instance, G. S. Ghurye notes that nowadays the Mahānubhāva monastery at Saṅgvī Havelī, a village seven miles to the west of Puṇe, is especially known for its efficacy as a spirit-exorcising center:

> Quite a number of people who are "possessed"—more often they are women as anyone having intimate knowledge of Maharashtrian society should be able to tell, and their number in the total may not have decreased during the last four centuries of the exorcist efficiency of Datta—they are asked to attend the daily prayer and worship at the monastery and are promised relief by that performance. It is reported, too, that patients do get better and leave for their homes! (Ghurye, *Gods and Men*, 214)

On possession within the Mahānubhāva sect, see Skultans, "Gender and Experience of Affliction: Family Relations, Beliefs and Attitudes Towards Mental Illness in Maharashtra."

76. It should be noted that even the Mahānubhāva sect has come to assimilate a number of Muslim views and practices.

77. On possession in Maharashtra, see Stanley, "Gods, Ghosts, and Possession." See also Assayag, "Sacrifice et violence. Les genres de la possession daus le sud de l'Inde," and, by the same author, *La colère de la déesse décapitée. Traditions, cultes et pouvoir dans le sud de l'Inde.* On the general phenomenology

of possession in the Indian subcontinent, see Rahmann, "Shamanistic and Related Phenomena in Northern and Middle India"; Jones, "Shamanism in South Asia: A Preliminary Survey"; Kakar, *Shamans, Mystics and Doctors;* Schoembucher, "Gods, Ghosts and Demons: Possession in South Asia."

78. Moreover, female folk deities connected with water and rivers, the Sātī Āsarās, often possess their devotees; see Feldhaus, *Water and Womanhood: Religious Meanings of Rivers in Maharashtra,* 13, 70, 90 n. 45, 128–30, 132, 134, 167. Dattātreya is sometimes related to these Sātī Āsarās, for example through the *uḍumbara* tree which is particularly sacred to him; see ibid., 144 n. 48. For an introduction to Devī possession outside the Marāṭhī milieu, see Erndl, "Śerāṅvālī. The Mother Who Possesses."

79. Stanley, "Gods, Ghosts, and Possession," 58 n. 6.

80. See Jaiswal, *The Origin and Development of Vaiṣṇavism,* 145. Also, Hartsuiker, *Sādhus: Holy Men of India,* 34.

81. See Sontheimer, "Hinduism: The Five Components and Their Interaction."

6

Eknāth, Dāsopant, and the Unfolding of the Dattātreya Movement

Dattātreya's cult did not confine itself to the orthodox Datta *sampradāya*, the *guru-paramparā* of Nṛsiṃha Sarasvatī's successors. Within the Marāṭhī region, Dattātreya rapidly became one of the most popular deities, second only to Gaṇeśa. What might be called the Dattātreya movement, cutting across caste divisions and religious barriers, grew rapidly. The Datta icon functioned as a magnet, attracting and synthesizing teachings across traditions and canons. For this reason, the Datta movement is to be thought of not as antagonistic to the Datta *sampradāya* but rather as encompassing and widening its scope. Once again, and perhaps in its fullest form, Dattātreya sets the paradigm for the assimilation of Siddha, Yoga, and Sant environments. True to his nature as honeybee Guru, Yogin, and Avatāra, he was easily "appropriated" across the ocean of traditions. In this chapter, Dattātreya's place among some of the great poet-saints of Maharashtra, included in the Sant lineage of the Vārkarī *sampradāya*, will be presented.

In devotional literature, the god Dattātreya is extolled as the Guru of Janārdan, Eknāth's teacher. Therefore, I'll examine Datta's place within the hagiographic materials concerning both Janārdan and his *śiṣya* Eknāth, Maharashtra's third great Sant after Jñāndev and Nāmdev. Despite the fact that we find no traces of Dattātreya in Eknāth's own writings, the link of the latter with the deity is evidenced by religious, cultural, and even familial ties. After briefly examining Datta's tangential presence in the writings of two great poet-saints of later times, Tukārām and Rāmdās, I shall focus on the poet-saint Dāsopant, a prolific writer, contemporary of Eknāth, and outstanding Datta devotee. Lastly, I'll sketch the unfolding of the Datta movement up to recent times, review the main personalities revered as devotees or Avatāras of Datta and conclude with some comments concerning their role and function in Maharashtra's religious life.

Despite the fundamental opposition between the Vārkarī *sampradāya*, fostering a liberal, egalitarian religion, and the Datta *sampradāya*, aiming to enforce ritual orthodoxy through a revival of

Brahminical religion, Dattātreya found a place also within the Vārkarī movement, known as the Marāṭhī Sant tradition. Typically, the Sant is a layman of low caste, a Śūdra, an untouchable, or even a Muslim *mleccha*, who supports himself and his family on his traditional trade. Whereas northern Santism propounds a *nirguṇa* kind of *bhakti*, the Sants of Maharashtra or Vārkarīs are *saguṇa bhaktas*, devoted to the *mūrti* of Viṭṭhala of Paṇḍharpur, considered a spontaneous manifestation (*svarūpa*) of the Godhead. Central to the devotion of all Vārkarīs, however, is not the Viṭṭhala *mūrti* per se but devotion to the name of the deity, symbol of the pure (*nirañjana*), invisible, all-pervading Godhead. This spiritual attitude tended to blur not only the distinction between *nirguṇa* and *saguṇa* but also the distinction between *Śaivism* and *Vaiṣṇavism*. In the Marāṭhī region, we witness a merging of *Śaivism* and *Vaiṣṇavism*, or what Vaudeville has called "the gradual merging of the *Śaiva* faith into the nonsectarian *Vaiṣṇava bhakti* of the Sants." Originally, *Śaivism* appears to have been the basic faith in the Marāṭhī speaking area. Cakradhar, founder of the Mahānubhāvas; Jñāndev, originator of the Vārkarīs and author of the Vedāntic *Jñāneśvarī*; and Mukundarāj, author of the first Old Marāṭhī work *Viveka-sindhu*, were all in some way or other linked to the Nātha tradition. The interpenetration of Nātha and Vedāntic traditions resulted in a form of nominal *Vaiṣṇavism* or Kṛṣṇaism, in other words, in a tendency to transfer the role of Śiva as supreme lord to Viṣṇu or Viṭṭhala-Kṛṣṇa. This pattern is traceable in the Mahānubhāva sect and also seems to be evidenced in the *Śaiva* origins of the god Viṭṭhala of Paṇḍharpur.[1] Precisely because of Dattātreya's eclectic character, his inextricable mix of *Śaiva* and *Vaiṣṇava* motifs, he also came to be included in the devotional synthesis of the Vārkarīs. Although no trace of Dattātreya is found in the major writings of Jñāndev and Nāmdev (1270–1350), beginning with the sixteenth century—with the third great Sant Eknāth (1533–1599) and Dāsopant (1551–1615)—Dattātreya becomes connected with the *bhakti* tradition of the Sants.

Both Eknāth and Dāsopant flourished at the time of the *Gurucaritra* and were probably influenced by the Datta *sampradāya* as well as by the old centers of Datta worship, such as Pañcāḷeśvara along the Godāvarī. They are both considered as devotees of Dattātreya. Eknāth is possibly connected to Nṛsiṃha Sarasvatī's devotional milieu through his Guru Janārdan although, as Raeside notes, for both Eknāth and Dāsopant there exists no sure connection with the author of the *Gurucaritra* Sarasvatī Gaṅgādhar. Eknāth's link to Dattātreya is explained by his devotion to his Guru Janārdan. The syncretistic quality of Dattātreya's cult is evidenced by the blending of Hinduism and Islam within Janārdan's persona. He belonged to the Sufi tradition according to recent research. Tulpule explains:

> Refuting the . . . popular notion that Janārdan was initiated directly by god Dattātreya, Bendre has, on the evidence of the Yoga-saṅgrāma of Sheikh Muhammad, convincingly shown that he was a disciple of Cānda Bodhale, who belonged to the Ṣūfīs and whose traditional name was Said Cāndasāheb Kādrī. The story of god Dattātreya appearing before Eknāth in the form of a Muslim mendicant [*malaṅg*] is a clear twist of the historical truth about the Guru of Eknāth being the disciple of a Ṣūfī in the line of Sijrā-i-kādrī. Eknāth himself concealed this fact in order not to invite the displeasure of the orthodoxy and traced his spiritual lineage to god Dattātreya through his Guru Janārdan. Modern research has . . . laid bare this connecting link between the tradition of later Marāṭhī poet-saints and the Ṣūfīs.[2]

The intriguing hypothesis that even Eknāth's writings were directly influenced by Sufi mystics of the Kādrī or Qādiri school has also been advanced.[3]

Whatever the truth of the identification of Said Cāndasāheb Kādrī (Cānda Bodhale) with the legendary Dattātreya, what interests us is that devotion to Datta reveals an experience of "spiritual unity" amid religious diversity. In this regard, it is important to mention Kabīr,[4] the veritable paradigm of Hindu-Muslim unity. The fifteenth-century Muslim Sant of Benares was the vanquisher of religious divisions in the name of *nirguṇa-bhakti*. Within the vast corpus of sayings attributed to Kabīr, Dattātreya is mentioned in two *ramainīs* within the *Bījak*. In *ramainī* 8, telling how the nondual teaching of the *Upaniṣads* (*tat tvam asi*) gave happiness to various sages, Kabīr names Dattātreya who "feasted of the same relish."[5] In *ramainī* 69, Kabīr mentions Dattātreya along with other sages, dishonoring the violence of certain "Yogins" of his times: "Tell me, when did Dattātreya ever attack a fort?"[6] In the Marāṭhī region, Kabīr was viewed as the paradigm of a "spiritual faith" beyond the barriers of institutionalized religions. Certainly, Nāmdev's permanence in the north of the subcontinent and in Punjab for about twenty years, contributed to the development of the *bhakti* movement in the north and inspired poet-saints like Kabīr as well as Guru Nānak through their mainspring, Rāmānanda. The popularity of Kabīr in the Marāṭhī area, however, stems from about the eighteenth century, thanks to the work of hagiographers like Mahīpati and the proliferation of cheap editions of so-called Kabīr verses.[7] Kabīr is considered as an exemplary figure both within the Vārkarī Sant tradition and the Datta movement.[8]

Janārdan[9] is another example of a holy man attempting an integration of the two warring elements of Hinduism and Islam. Our knowledge about him is scant, the historical data being inextricably fused within a hagiographic horizon. The principal "sources" available are Janārdan's own *abhaṅgs*. His fame is primarily due to having been Eknāth's teacher. According to tradition Janārdan was born in 1504 (*śaka* 1426) in the village of Caḷisgāon, Kandesh district, as a Deśastha Brahmin belonging to the Āśvalāyana branch of the *Vedas*.[10] In his youth he is said to have led an amoral life, much as young Tulsīdās did. Later, he converted to a spiritual life by the grace of a saint whom he met under an *uḍumbara* tree at Aṅkalakop, Satārā district, on the Kṛṣṇā. Though untenable on the grounds of chronology, this saint is identified by tradition—as well as by scholars such as R. D. Ranade—as none other than Nṛsiṃha Sarasvatī, thus making Janārdan an adept of the Datta *sampradāya*.[11] The description Janārdan makes in his first *abhaṅgs* "points to that Saint as being his Guru."[12] Apart from the problem of chronology, however, Eknāth never mentions the name of Nṛsiṃha Sarasvatī in his writings, saying in his *abhaṅgs* that Janārdan received Dattātreya's *upadeśa* and blessings directly from the deity. Eknāth, in his *Bhāgavata*, invokes Dattātreya as his Guru's Guru, who directed him to write his *magnum opus*. If Nṛsiṃha Sarasvatī was truly Janārdan's Guru, it seems strange that Eknāth did not list his name as well as that of Śrīpāda Śrīvallabha in Janārdan's spiritual lineage: this Dattātreya lineage comprehends only Sahasrārjuna and Yadu in the *satya-yuga*, and Janārdan as the third *śiṣya* in the *kali-yuga* (*Eknāthī Bhāgavata* 9.430). In general, devotees tend to dismiss these problems by pointing out the unreliability of chronologies coupled with the fact that Nṛsiṃha Sarasvatī, being an Avatāra of Datta, could not be placed by Eknāth within the *śiṣya-paramparā* of the deity. Although directly relating Janārdan to Nṛsiṃha Sarasvatī is a historical impossibility—the mysterious figure who initiated him being identified with Cānda Bodhale—some kind of connection between Janārdan and the milieu of the devotees of the *Guru-caritra* cannot be ruled out a priori.[13]

What is certain is that Janārdan was in the service of the Muslim rulers as military commander in the army of Daulatabad or Devgiri, a town and fort within the sultanate of Ahmednagar. He acquired fame by performing both his secular obligations and religious duties with equanimity. Janārdan is said to have died in 1575. He has left a few *abhaṅgs*, and his *samādhi* is located in the fort of Daulatabad.

Hagiographic accounts emphasize his piousness toward his *iṣṭa-devatā*. Eknāth notes that Janārdan alone, in virtue of his devotion, had the fortune of being accepted as disciple by Dattātreya in this *kali-yuga*. Janārdan is described sitting in a solitary place in his fort, worshipping and meditating upon Dattātreya until noon. Only after completing this long *pūjā*, would he do his routine work. Mahīpati, in his *Bhakta-līlāmṛta*, gives the following account of Janārdan's worship of Dattātreya:

> Janārdan's royal patron, the king, issued an order to his secretaries, that none need come to visit him on Fridays. In accordance with this order of the king . . . Janārdan made it his habit to devote the day to his own most important private duties. There was a very extensive lake on the plateau of the nearby mountain, the water of which was very pure. There was no passing by of people there. There was also a dense forest, beautiful with flowers and fruit. Simply viewing the scene brought rest to the mind . . . Śrī Dattātreya was accustomed to come to that spot, and any good man who performed *anuṣṭhāna* here could see a visible manifestation of him. So Janārdan every Friday used to climb the mountain, take his bath in the lake and perform his accustomed rites. He would then make a thousand *liṅgas* of clay, and worship them with proper ceremony. At the completion of his worship, Śrī Datta would give him a visible manifestation of himself. As each met the other, each was filled with joy. They would converse together on the happiness of the soul. They experienced a shower of joy.[14]

Dattātreya is said to have given *darśana* to Janārdan whenever needed. R. D. Ranade furnishes an illuminating account of *Eknāthī Bhāgavata* 9.430–39, 454, in which Eknāth describes the first *darśana* of Dattātreya to Janārdan:

> The divine discontent that Janārdan felt was so great, that in thinking of his Guru, he lost all outward sense. Seeing the divinely discontented state of Janārdan's heart, God Dattātreya . . . approached him and favoured him by placing his hand on his head. Miraculous was the effect of this touch! Janārdan became the master of all spiritual illumination. He clearly felt the emptiness of this transitory world, and realised within himself the true nature of *ātman*. Dattātreya taught him that faith which preaches inaction through action. Janārdan now understood the secret of living free, though embodied. The faith that was generated in Janārdan's heart through the grace of God Dattātreya was so

> determinate and fearless, that he never thought himself polluted even when he accepted the house-holder's life, and continued to perform the duties of that station . . . Janārdan could not control the oncoming of this rapturous ecstasy, and lay on the ground motionless like a corpse. Dattātreya brought his mind down to the world of phenomena, and gently admonished him that even that kind of emotional surging was after all the work of the sāttvic quality, and that the highest state consisted in suppressing the emotional swelling, and living a quiet life with the conviction of the realised Self. Having finished his worship, Janārdan wanted to prostrate himself before his Guru. But when he lifted his eyes, to his utter amazement he found that Dattātreya had vanished away.[15]

It has been noted that Eknāth's description of Janārdan's swoon upon experiencing the sāttvic state and of Dattātreya's intervention to bring him back to consciousness might betray a Sufi influence. The episode could be interpreted as the suppression of an ecstatic condition (*ḥāl*) and the attainment of sobriety (*ṣaḥw*) as recommended by Sufis of the Chishtī or Kādrī schools. Nevertheless, Dattātreya's *upadeśa* of maintaining lucidity and self-control and of cultivating "inaction through action" is a time-honored *sādhana* from the time of the *Bhagavad-gītā*.[16] Janārdan's spiritual accomplishments while remaining immersed in worldly duties is not an uncommon achievement: in fact, this is a characteristic feature of many of the poet-saints of Maharashtra, fulfilling both the worldly as well as the spiritual aims of life. This is in harmony with Dattātreya's promise of both *bhukti* and *mukti*.

Eknāth, born as a Brahmin in 1533 in the orthodox center of Paiṭhaṇ (Pratiṣṭhāna)—the "Benares" of the Marāṭhī speaking area—is a link figure in many ways. He revitalized the *bhakti* tradition that began with Jñāndev and prepared the way for the greatest of poet-saints, the seventeenth century Tukārām.[17] He included northern Sants like Kabīr and Raidās in his listing as if they were part of the Marāṭhī tradition, ideally envisioning all Sants as one homogeneous whole.[18] He bridged the Sanskritic tradition through his Marāṭhī works and translations (his *magnum opus* being the *Eknāthī Bhāgavata*) and wrote songs and drama poems like the *bhārūḍs*,[19] in which he connected himself to untouchables, Faqīrs, Mahānubhāvas, prostitutes, and so forth. In fact, Eknāth was the Marāṭhī Sant who more than anyone absorbed a variety of religious influences. Tulpule noted: "Eknāth . . . stands on the confluence of three different currents, namely those of Datta, Viṭṭhala and the Sufis, all merging in his mystical writings."[20]

His very name, Eknāth, seems to indicate a link with Nāthism,[21] a connection also suggested by the subjects and form of his *bhārūḍs*. In one of these drama poems, we find the identification of Eknāth and Janārdan with the Mahānubhāvas.[22] This capacity to integrate these multifarious influences made Eknāth attuned to Dattātreya's inclusive typology. In this regard, R. D. Ranade's definition of Eknāth's age as a time of "synthetic mysticism," could not be more apt.[23]

Apparently, Eknāth lost his parents—Sūryanārāyaṇ and Rukmiṇībāī—in his infancy. The name Eknāth, besides pointing to Nātha influence, suggests that he was the only child left to carry on the family lineage. Raised by his grandfather Cakrapāṇi, son of Bhānudās (1448–1513), he was inspired with great devotion for Viṭṭhala.[24] Eknāth's initiation to spiritual life by Janārdan,[25] traditionally ascribed to the year 1545 when he was just twelve years old, certainly prompted his religious eclecticism. Eknāth was in the unusual position of being exposed to the highly orthodox Brahminical world, through his family ties, and also to Islam, through the dominating Ahmednagar sultanate.[26] According to tradition, Eknāth lived with Janārdan only six years.[27] He followed Janārdan's will in all respects, setting the ideal of the pious *guru-bhakta*.[28] We are told that after a prolonged practice of spiritual exercises at Janārdan's feet, coupled with the study of texts such as Jñāndev's *Jñāneśvarī* and *Amṛtānubhava*,[29] Eknāth attained God's vision.[30] He then married at his Guru's wish and led the life of a householder,[31] though with his mind always fixed on God.[32]

A prolific writer and perhaps the foremost popularizer of nondual doctrines through the medium of his mother tongue, Marāṭhī, Eknāth always wrote his compositions under the joint pen name Eka-Janārdan, "the Eka(nātha) of Janārdan." Even his literary vocation was apparently inspired by his Guru: while on a pilgrimage with Janārdan, Eknāth listened to a discourse on the *Bhāgavata Purāṇa* and, at his master's direction, wrote a Marāṭhī commentary on the subject. This work bears the title *Catuḥślokī Bhāgavata*, as it only deals with four verses from the ninth chapter of the second *skandha* of the original text.[33] This proved to be the nucleus of his major work, for he soon turned to the *Bhāgavata Purāṇa* again and, between 1570 and 1573, wrote his commentary on its eleventh *skandha*, popularly known as the *Eknāthī Bhāgavata*, containing more than 18,000 *ovīs*.[34] If Eknāth is to be considered the reviver of the thirteenth-fourteenth century *bhakti* movement, his eclectic spirituality also caused him to challenge Brahminical notions of purity and codes of conduct. Besides his translations of sacred texts like the *Bhāgavata Purāṇa* into Marāṭhī—for which he had to face accusations and defend himself before the Brahmins of Benares[35]—his *abhaṅgs* and

Eknāth in meditation surrounded by snakes.

bhārūḍs carry the message of love and God's oneness with creatures such as dogs, birds, untouchable Mahārs, Muslims, prostitutes, beggars, and a host of lowly characters. Zelliot points out: "After Eknāth's death, no one continued his open-handed, open-hearted acceptance of all *bhaktas*. Paiṭhaṇ saw no more radical saints."[36]

Eknāth's main aim was to find practices and beliefs, in both Hinduism and Islam, that could be incorporated into a higher, mystical truth of oneness (*ekatva*). He envisioned religious conversion as a manifestation of ignorance, to be avoided. Modern Marāṭhī hagiography often casts Eknāth in the role of saving Hinduism from the hated Muslim tide. However, as both Hindu and Muslim historians point out, this medieval period was one of tolerance, participation of Hindus in the Islamic government and, perhaps most important of all, cultural exchange.[37] An example of Hindu and Muslim encounter, may be found precisely in one of Eknāth's *bhārūḍs*: the *Hindu-Turk Saṃvād*. The first and last verses of this poem are illuminating:

Eknāth:

(1) The goal is one; the ways of worship are different.
Listen to the dialogue between these two!

(2) The Turk calls the Hindu "Kafir!"
The Hindu answers: "I will be polluted—get away!"
A quarrel broke out between the two;
A great controversy began.

Muslim:

(3) O Brahmin, listen to what I have to say:
Your scripture is a mystery to everyone.
God has hands and feet, you say.
This is really impossible!

Hindu:

(4) Listen, you great fool of a Turk!
See God in all living things.
You haven't grasped this point
And so you have become a nihilist.

. . . .

(63) At that moment, they saluted each other.
With great respect, they embraced.
Both became content, happy,
Quiet, calm.

(64) "You and I quarreled
to open up the knowledge of the high truth,
in order to enlighten the very ignorant.
In place of karma-awakening!"

(65) "In place of words we have established the word's meaning."
The highest truth pierced them both.
Enlightenment was the purpose of this quarrel
Both have been satisfied.

(66) The argument was about oneness.
The argument became agreement.
Ekā-Janārdan says: "Self-knowledge
And great bliss came to both."[38]

Eknāth's link with Dattātreya is known only through minor works, such as *padas* and *stotras* attributed to him, and later hagiographies.[39] Besides his *Bhāvārtha-rāmāyaṇa*, a Marāṭhī version of the *Rāmāyaṇa* of Vālmīki, Eknāth is known principally for devotional poems addressed not to Dattātreya but to Viṭṭhala of Paṇḍharpur. Nevertheless—apart from Eknāth's link with Janārdan[40] it should be noted that Godubāī, the last of Eknāth's three children,[41] was the mother of Mukteśvar, "the best representative of the literary talent of the sixteenth century"[42] and a great devotee of Dattātreya, whom he regarded as both his deity and Guru. His original name was Mudgala, which he later changed into the more poetical pen name Mukteśvar, suggestive of his devotion to Dattātreya whom he called Līlā-viśvambhara.[43] According to tradition, it was Eknāth himself who initiated Mukteśvar into spiritual life.[44]

Mahīpati gives two versions of the *darśana* which Dattātreya granted to Eknāth through Janārdan. In the *Bhakta-vijaya* collection (45.82–85), composed in 1762, Dattātreya appears as a Muslim soldier on horseback, red-eyed, bristling with weapons, and "speaking the language of Muhammadans." Doubting that this can be his Guru's *devatā* and unwilling to partake food with a Muslim, Eknāth, fearing pollution, causes the vision to disappear. Nevertheless, soon after Dattātreya appears again (45.105ff.) as a Muslim Faqīr accompanied by a woman who is none other than Māyā, and a dog that is really the Kāmadhenu. This time, despite his hesitation, Eknāth is blessed by Dattātreya:

> In the Muhammadan language the son of Anasūyā said to Janārdan, "I am very hungry, let us eat together at once." On producing an earthen vessel with His own hands He himself milked the she-dog. Crumbling the bread in the milk, the two sat together to eat. The Sadguru said to Janārdan: "Who is that whom

I see over there? Invite him and bring him here to sit and eat with us." Hearing these words Eknāth felt hesitation. "Why, he seems clearly to be a Fakir. How shall I do that which is not lawful?" . . . He came near to the Fakir with fear. He said: "I will not stay close to you, but give me at once your favour." Then Janārdan in his love gave him a mouthful of what was left . . . Janārdan then called Eknāth and placed him at his Swami's feet. He gave him His blessing and spoke to him in words of promise . . . Then without a moment's delay He became invisible. Janārdan said to Eknāth: "You will now be satisfied with what has occurred today. Tell me where you have placed the favour which He gave you?" Eknāth said in reply: "I threw away that morsel." Janārdan then took the *pānsupārī* out of his mouth and with his own hand put it into Eknāth's mouth.[45]

In the *Bhakta-līlāmṛta,* composed by Mahīpati some years later in 1774, there is only one *darśana* of Dattātreya (13.164–205). Again, he appears as a Muslim, dressed in leather and with bloodshot eyes. Eknāth overcomes his doubts and is blessed by Dattātreya who "casting aside his Muhammadan guise . . . assumed the beautiful *saguṇa* form, six armed, of elongated eyes, his face the ornament of the universe."[46] In chapter 52 of the recent *Datta-prabodha,* which Dhere dates to 1860,[47] Eknāth encounters Dattātreya three times: the god appears as a Muslim huntsman, as a Pathan, and as a Malaṅg,[48] proving the persistence in oral tradition[49] of the fourteenth-century Mahānubhāva stories reviewed in chapter 4.[50] Eknāth had apparently no knowledge of any story connecting Dattātreya with Paraśurāma and Reṇukā, for in his *Bhāvārtha-rāmāyaṇa* the funeral ceremonies of Jamadagni and Reṇukā are dismissed in half a verse: "Then in the Sahyādri Paraśurāma performed the last rites for the two of them."[51]

The link between Dattātreya and the Vārkarī tradition continues after Eknāth. Tukārām's Guru, Śrī Rāghava Caitanya, is said to have received initiation by Datta in a vision he had at Girnār. Tukārām himself (1598–1649), the most beloved Sant in the Vārkarī *sampradāya,* has celebrated Dattātreya in a few of his *abhaṅgs.*[52] Here is one, showing that the image of Datta with three heads and six arms was a familiar one from the sixteenth century:

I fall prostrate before the one with three heads and six hands.
A bag of alms hanging from his shoulder;
Dogs in front of him.
He bathes in the Gaṅgā daily.

A staff and water-pot are in his hands;
On his feet are clanking wooden sandals;
On his head a splendrous coil of hair;
On his body beautiful ashes.
Tukā says, I bow to him who is clad in space.[53]

To Samarth Rāmdās (1608–81), the great religious and political activist establisher of the *Mahārāṣṭra-dharma* (first propounded by Sarasvatī Gaṅgādhar in the *Guru-caritra*) is ascribed an *āratī* of three stanzas in Datta's praise. In the first stanza he extols the birth of the deity, narrating how Brahmā, Viṣṇu, and Śiva tried to ruin the *tapas* of Anasūyā and Atri, and how they were finally converted into infants by Anasūyā. In the second stanza, the wives of the three gods come to visit Anasūyā, begging her to return their husbands to them. Anasūyā asks them to recognize their respective husbands in the three babes, but they fail to do so. Anasūyā then explains to the goddesses the logic of the various manifestations of the Godhead, after which they return satisfied to their abodes. The third stanza presents the belief that Dattātreya is constantly present in the world, moving to three different places during the course of the day: at Kāśī in the morning for his bath, at Karvīr for his meal,[54] and then at Mātāpur or Mahur where he rests for the night. The author finally offers his respects to the deity whose life and deeds are so wonderful.[55] In his *Dāsa-bodha*, Rāmdās mentions the school based on the chanting of Datta's name as one of the "salvation schools" current in Maharashtra, alongside those of Rāma, Viṭṭhala, Śiva, Kṛṣṇa, Hari, and so forth.[56]

With the encyclopedic writer Dāsopant we come to one of the greatest devotees of Dattātreya. Dāsopant, who used to refer to himself as the follower or servant of Datta, is believed to have been born in 1551 and to have died in 1615.[57] He was a contemporary of Eknāth, and Mahīpati, in his *Bhakta-līlāmṛta*, records their meeting. Most scholars are of the opinion that Dāsopant lived under the rule of Ali Barid Shāh (d. 1582), the Muslim king of Bedar. At Ambā Jogāī, also known as Mominabad, is the *samādhi* or tomb of Dāsopant. Two families living there claim descent from Dāsopant: one called the major branch (*thorlen devghar*), the other the minor branch (*dhākṭen devghar*). Other branches of the family are said to be at Bāvagi near Bedar and at Candrapur near Nāgpur and all claim to possess manuscript copies of Dāsopant's works.[58] A member of the so-called *Eknāth-pañcaka*,[59] Dāsopant was an incredibly prolific writer.

The anonymous and incomplete seventeenth- or eighteenth-century *Dāsopant-caritra* is our only available source on Dāsopant, there presented as an Avatāra of Datta.[60] We are told that he was born in a Brahmin family in the village of Nārāyaṇpeṭh, then under the rule of the Bahāmanī dynasty of Bedar. His father, *deśpāṇḍya* of Nārāyaṇpeṭh, was named Digambarpant or Digambarrāya, and his mother was named Pārvatī.[61] Dāsopant's legendary life may be usefully summarized. His birth is described thus:

> This Mahārāj Dāsopant, having the very form of Shri Datta, descended verily for the saving of the world into the home of the householder Digambar. He, whose face was full of smiles, long eyed, straight-nosed, of fair complexion, his hands reaching to his knees, possessed of every noble quality, and beyond all comparison, descended as an Avatār into this world.[62]

When Dāsopant was twelve years old[63] he was taken hostage by the Bahāmanī king, due to a debt of 200,000 rupees that Digambarrāya had contracted with the Muslim monarch. If in one month's time Digambarrāya did not repay his debt, the boy would remain with the king and be converted to Islam. However, in response to Dāsopant's innate purity and devotion, Dattātreya himself, disguised as an untouchable Mahār,[64] appeared at the king's palace just before the lapsing of the alloted time:

> Becoming a Mahār (Paḍewār), a staff in his hand, a blanket on his shoulder, and with cash and bills of exchange in his hand, he suddenly appeared in their midst. He greeted them with "Salām! Salām!" Looking all around He saw extreme bewilderment. He was the Supreme-God directly before them, but all were dull of wit, and did not recognize Him.[65]

Saying he had been sent by Digambarrāya, he gave the king all the money he had requested and more, instantly vanishing from sight. Saved from the humiliation of losing his Brahminical state, Dāsopant returned to his parents in great pomp, the king having realized the divine intervention and the boy's greatness. After narrating the events to his astonished parents, who knew nothing of the Mahār and had no money to repay the debt, Dāsopant realized Dattātreya's grace. At the age of sixteen,[66] he decided to consecrate his life to his beloved deity by becoming an Avadhūta, wholly identifying himself with Datta. In secret, Dāsopant set out for Mātāpur, the privileged abode of Dattātreya and believed to be his original seat of manifestation as well as his sleeping place. Following the course of the Godāvarī, during his journey he stopped at Hilālpur and made a visit to one Kṛṣṇājīpant, said to be the best of *bhaktas*, assuring him that Datta would grant him *mokṣa*. He visited Prempur, where he worshipped Mārtaṇḍa with great devotion, then proceeding to Nāndeḍ. Here he was questioned about his parents by the local people, who realized Dāsopant's spiritual excellence. He replied that Avadhūta was both his mother and father in every place, and that he had no one but him. Finally, Dāsopant arrived at Mātāpur, said to be the original place for gaining the fourth state (*turīya*), where the lord of Yogins rests. After climbing to the top of the sacred mountain of Mātāpur, he entered the temple of Tripurasundarī,[67] where he worshipped the goddess with sixteenfold rites, asking her the boon of meeting Dattātreya. He said, "Aside from Thee, O Ambā, there is no door to the attaining of Datta." The goddess granted him a vision of Dattātreya. Dāsopant then climbed to the summit of the Sahyādri range, to the abode of Datta, stopping on his way at Anasūyā's shrine.

At this point, the *Dāsopant-caritra* (verses 414 to 636) furnishes an account of the Purāṇic story of Anasūyā. The text thus describes Dattātreya's birth:

> It was on the second day of the dark half of the month of *Kārttika*, on a Monday, under the constellation of *Kṛttikā*, that Śrī Dattātreya descended as Avatāra in the home of Anasūyā. Beautiful was he with his feet placed together. He obscured the light of a million suns. Around his beautiful waist was the yellow silk garment. Around his neck a garland of flowers displayed its beauty. He was of a complexion purely dark, tender-limbed, a face with a soft smile, extraordinarily beautiful. A crown on his head, and alligator shaped earrings glistened in his lordly ears. His six arms bristled with weapons, of various kinds in each hand. Such was the fair form in which the giver of blessing to Atri manifested himself. In his two lower hands were a rosary and water-jar. In his middle hands a musical instrument and trident. In his glorious upper lotus hands the divine conch-shell and disk displayed their beauty.[68]

After the long parenthesis, beginning at verse 636, Dāsopant is described climbing the mountain toward Datta's shrine. His appearance along the way excited the curiosity of the local people, who recognized him as a great soul, a *yoga-bhraṣṭa*.[69] They questioned him about his Guru. Dāsopant answered that he saw only Datta every-

Trimukhī **Dattātreya as Rāja Yogin.**

where and always. Dāsopant then retired in solitude and began his austerities and meditations, concentrating his whole being on Dattātreya for twelve full years. After this period, the deity appeared to him in a dream, telling him:

> Go from here to Rākṣasa-bhuvana on the bank of the Gaṅgā (Godāvarī). On the sand bed of the river you will find without fail my *pādukās*. While performing your austere rites there you will easily gain a direct manifestation of Myself. I, Avadhūta, will meet you there without effort on your part.[70]

Dāsopant obeyed and, under the riverbed of the Godāvarī, found Datta's *pādukās* and worshipped them. Sitting on the riverbed, totally absorbed in meditation on Dattātreya, he finally attained his *darśana*.[71] Dāsopant proceeded to worship him and sang his praise.[72] Datta comforted Dāsopant, embracing him and saying sweet words. He invited him to ask for whatever boon his heart desired. Dāsopant asked that he might take refuge at his feet, thus making him his *pādukās*.[73] Mightily pleased, Dattātreya blessed Dāsopant by giving him the highest *upadeśa*: the explanation of the great *mahā-vākya ahaṃ brahmāsmi*.[74] After this, Dāsopant lost himself in contemplation, the whole world within and without having become the very form of Datta. Having been returned to consciousness by his Sadguru, Dāsopant again praised his lord and confessed his unwillingness to reenter the world and its sensuous trappings. Datta assured him by saying that he, Dāsopant, was verily the perfect *sat-cit-ānanda*. Dāsopant again bowed to his Sadguru and asked the final, supreme question: why did Dattātreya, unchangeable and qualityless (*nirguṇa*), appear with the three *guṇas*.[75] To this, Datta answered thus:

> While Brahma was existing in its own joy, the sentence "I am Brahman" arose spontaneously from it suddenly. Just as when a person is fast asleep, and then awakes of his own accord, so in Its true nature this sound arose. And this sound in Its true nature is called the Great Māyā, the Mine-of-knowledge. And whatever forms there are, they belong to it altogether. From this Supreme Being there developed the law of cause and effect, and to this is given the name of Primal material cause [mūla-prakṛti], generally spoken of simply as Prakṛti.[76]

At this point, the manuscript abruptly ends (verse 778). Apparently Dāsopant, after living at various sites along the Godāvarī, finally settled at Ambā Jogāī where he died in 1615.

Among the fifty-two works ascribed to Dāsopant,[77] both in Marāṭhī and Sanskrit, the most outstanding is the *Gītārṇava* (The Ocean of the *Gītā*), a versified commentary on the *Bhagavad-gītā* often ramifying into long digressions, containing more than 100,000 *ovīs*.[78]

Tulpule notes:

> Dāsopant is like an iceberg, only one-tenth part of which is visible and the remainder is submerged. A sample study has shown that where Jñāndev writes five *ovīs* by way of commentary on the Gītā, Dāsopant writes about 1,300. The anecdote that he required ink worth a penny every day and that it took twenty years to complete this work may be true.[79]

Dāsopant was a master for his delineations of characters and fluid style. Apart from the *Gītārṇava*, certainly known to Moropant (1729–94) and probably to Rāmdās,[80] copies of Dāsopant's works have been found only among his descendants and at Yekhehal at the Āpcand *maṭha* of the poet Ātmarām, author in c. 1800 of an encyclopedic biography of Rāmdās, the *Dāsa-viśrāma-dhāma*.[81] Among Dāsopant's works are the *Gītārtha-candrikā*, a much smaller exposition of the *Gītā*; the *Grantha-rāja*, an independent philosophical treatise; the *Padārṇava* (The Ocean of Devotional Songs); and the *Pañcī-karaṇa*, a work on metaphysics written on a long piece of cloth popularly known as *Pāsoḍī*.[82] Among other works attributed to Dāsopant (often referred to as Digambara-anucara),[83] are the *Datta-māhātmya*[84] and various collections of devotional hymns dedicated to Dattātreya: the *Dattātreya-nāma-valī*, the *Dattātreya-daśa-nāma-stotra*, the *Dattātreya-dvādaśa-nāma-stotra*, the *Dattātreya-ṣoḍaśa-nāma-stotra*,[85] the *Dattātreya-śata-nāma-stotra*, the *Dattātreya-sahasra-nāma-stotra*, and the *Siddha-dattātreya-stotra*.

The earliest references to Dāsopant are to be found in Mahīpati's hagiographic works. Apart from a mention of Dāsopant in a list of saints in *Bhakta-vijaya* 57.178 and an invocation in chapter 1 of the *Bhakta-līlāmṛta* (in which he is described as having received Datta's blessings), there are two relevant loci in the *Bhakta-līlāmṛta* both of which relate him to Eknāth. The first, narrated in *Bhakta-līlāmṛta* 22.48–65, records Dāsopant's forest meeting with Eknāth, who was returning from Benares. The second, in *Bhakta-līlāmṛta* 22.79–101, furnishes an account of a visit paid by Dāsopant to Eknāth at Paiṭhaṇ. Both episodes are worth quoting:

> From childhood Dāsopant had cherished the desire for a visible manifestation of Śrī Dattātreya. He had therefore undertaken severe austerities . . . He abandoned all his friends and went alone into the forest. He lived on fallen leaves. He took not the least care of his body. He slept on the bare rock, enduring cold and heat. If any human being unexpectedly appeared, he would run

away from him. Without ceasing he kept Śrī Dattātreya in his mind. From these austerities . . . he finally lost all bodily consciousness, and because he slept on rocks, his body was covered with sores. For twenty years he carried on austerities . . . then finally Dattātreya gave him a visible manifestation of Himself.[86] As Dattātreya embraced him, his body became divine, and through the blessing bestowed upon him he became a prolific poet. And through the grace of the Sadguru . . . there came to him great wealth[87] and the respect of great men . . .

Dāsopant had placed his abode in Ambā Jogāī. He had heard of Śrī Eknāth's good fame from everyone's lips. As Eknāth was returning from the supreme pilgrimage (Benares), the two unexpectedly met. They embraced one another with great joy in their hearts . . . After much solicitation, Dāsopant took Eknāth to his home. Waves of joy and happiness arose in his soul . . . They dined on daintily cooked food. Then they listened to the reading of the *Bhāgavata*, and at night Hari *kīrtanas* took place, attracting all and sundry.

A month thus passed, and then Eknāth asked leave . . . Dāsopant pleaded with him to accept horses and money for the journey . . . Śrī Eknāth, however, had a mind indifferent to worldly things, and would take none of Dāsopant's wealth. Nor would he even take a horse, "Because," he said, "the way is difficult."[88] In leaving, Eknāth said to Dāsopant: "I am to celebrate at my home the festival of the birthday of Kṛṣṇa.[89] If it is convenient, come to the sacred city of Pratiṣṭhāna." "I certainly will come," he replied.[90]

Two months passed in this way, and then came the festival of Kṛṣṇa's birth. Uddhava,[91] according to his custom, began to make all the necessary preparations . . . Suddenly, on the day of full moon Dāsopant arrived . . . Eknāth had not heard that he had arrived, when unexpectedly he appeared at the main door. A strange sight was now seen. Śrī Datta, with his trident in his hand, stood watching at the entrance, as a doorkeeper. Dāsopant saw him, and was supremely amazed. He leaped from his palanquin and made a *sāṣṭāṅga-namaskāra*.[92] He embraced Datta and exclaimed: "Why have you come here?" The Son of Anasūyā . . . replied: "Eknāth is not a human *bhakta*, but a visible Avatāra of Śrī Pāṇḍuraṅga.[93] For the salvation of the world he has become an Avatāra in this *kali-yuga*. Only if by good fortune there exists the richness of a *puṇya,* performed in a former birth, can one have the opportunity of serving him. Know this fact for a truth. I hold this trident in my hand, and guard securely the door. I will go in and inform Eknāth of your presence. Until then, do not enter in." As Avadhūta thus spoke, Dāsopant was overcome with astonishment, and extolling Śrī Nātha's glory said: "I did not recognize his extraordinary greatness." Śrī Datta informed Eknāth that Dāsopant had come to see him, and Eknāth with Uddhava came out to welcome him . . . They fell at each other's feet and embraced one another. Eknāth then took Dāsopant by the hand, and led him into the house. Uddhava made the proper arrangements for all the palanquins and carriages. He gave the men the materials and the necessities for cooking. Nothing was lacking . . . Dāsopant performed his bath, and finished his meal with Eknāth. All night he sat listening to the Hari *kīrtanas* . . . He then perfumed the image of Pāṇḍuraṅga, anointed him and worshipped him with various ceremonies . . . The Brahmins recited aloud from the *Vedas,* and finally handfuls of flowers were offered. The days were spent in feeding Brahmins, the nights in Hari *kīrtanas.* From the first day of the fortnight to the ninth, the festival was at its full. On the tenth, the *Gopāl-kālā*[94] was excellently dramatized. Dāsopant . . . exclaimed: "I have seen with my own eyes the unprecedented, gracious voice of Śrī Eknāth, his make-up, his dramatic power, and his mine of philosophic knowledge. I thought myself to be a worshiper of Datta in visible form, but since seeing the glory of Eknāth with my own eyes, I have become one-who-recognizes-no-duality." The great festival ended, there was feasting on the twelfth day. Dāsopant then took leave, and returned to his own home.[95]

In this last account Mahīpati, to emphasize Eknāth's greatness, has Dattātreya serve him as his doorkeeper. That a god may act as the servant of a saint is not exceptional in hagiographic literature. *Bhaktavijaya* 46.1–44 narrates how Śrī Kṛṣṇa himself, disguised as a menial Brahmin (Śrī Khaṇḍya), served Eknāth and his wife in their house. This narration precedes the famous episode of Eknāth freely eating with untouchables. The story goes that he once invited untouchables to a feast prepared for Brahmins only. In this way he attracted the wrath of the orthodox circles of Paiṭhaṇ which outcasted him. Then, however, Kṛṣṇa as the menial Brahmin intervened telling Eknāth to serve a feast to all his ancestors. The ancestors came, and all the Brahmins of Paiṭhaṇ saw the splendid heavenly Brahmins eating at Eknāth's table. This divine approbation of the saint's behavior led the Brahminical authorities to reintegrate him into the Brahmin caste.

Coming back to our story of Dāsopant's visit to Eknāth, it is clear that Mahīpati—a staunch Bhāgavata and a devotee of Viṭṭhala—envisioned Eknāth as superior to Dāsopant. In the end, Dāsopant is said to have passed from a dualistic type of devotion to the supreme nondual vision, thanks to Eknāth's influence and teachings.

After Janārdan, Eknāth, Dāsopant, and Mukteśvar, R. C. Dhere presents a list of nine other prominent figures in the Sādhu-Sant Datta *paramparā*: Nirañjan Raghunāth, Nārāyaṇ Mahārāj Jalvankar, Māṇikprabhu, Akkaḷkoṭ Mahārāj, Vāsudevānanda Sarasvatī, Mahārāj Bāḷekuṇḍrikar, Viṣṇudās, Rāmānanda Bīḍkar, and Dīkṣit Svāmin. A longer list is offered by H. S. Joshi, who, though excluding the last three, adds eight more names: Bhairav Avadhūta Jñānsāgar, Dattanāth Ujjayinīkar, Yogānanda Sarasvatī alias Gaṇḍ Mahārāj, Sāī Bābā of Śirḍī, Nūri Mahārāj, Śrī Datta Mahārāj of Aste, Nārāyaṇ Mahārāj Keḍgāokar, and finally Raṅga Avadhūta, born in 1898.[96] N. S. Karandikar comes up with an even longer list, comprising forty personalities: herein, Gorakhnāth stands as the originator of the lineage and is followed by the three Mahānubhāva sect-figures Cakrapāṇi, Govindaprabhu, and Cakradhar.[97] G. S. Ghurye also mentions one Ātmarām Paramahaṃsa (d. 1731), who, though not listed by Dhere, Joshi, and Karandikar, was a significant figure within the Marāṭhī Datta movement:

> Ātmarām Paramahaṃsa was a unique personality. He represents the Maharashtrian counterpart of Kabīr. He believed in a synthesis of Hinduism and Islām . . . He named his tutelary deity Shāhā Datta. The date of his birth is not known. He was well-known in Khandesh by A.D. 1678 and relinquished his body in A.D. 1731. It speaks volumes for the work of Nṛsiṃha Sarasvatī . . . that this *Śaiva* ascetic as a Paramahaṃsa not only adopted Datta as his tutelary deity, but tended to live after the pattern of Dattātreya's description as a Paramahaṃsa . . . in the state of an infatuated child.
>
> The ascetics who adopted Datta . . . whether they were formally of a new school or of the older *Śaiva* school, may be said to have belonged to a distinctive Maharashtrian school of asceticism.[98]

This "distinctive Maharashtrian school of asceticism," is the Datta *sampradāya* founded by Nṛsiṃha Sarasvatī. But not all ascetics who adopted Datta as their *iṣṭa-devatā* necessarily belonged to it. As seen, a larger *koiné* of ascetics who chose Datta as their *iṣṭa-devatā* comprised

Nāthas, Mahānubhāvas, Aghorīs, Śāktas, Sufis, and so forth. This is what has been more generally termed the Dattātreya movement, to whom the ascetics comprised in the above lists belonged. These Gurus, Yogins, and Faqīrs are viewed by their devotees as Avatāras of Dattātreya. They are all celebrated for their superhuman powers and charisma—often of a bizarre, *unmatta* character—as well as for their wisdom and devotion. Most of them are connected with the main centers of Datta worship, both old and new, such as Girnār (Nirañjan Raghunāth, Nārāyaṇ Mahārāj Jalvankar) and Gāṇagāpūr (Vāsudevānanda Sarasvatī, Mahārāj Bāḷekuṇḍrikar, Śrī Datta Mahārāj of Aste, Nārāyaṇ Mahārāj Keḍgāokar, Raṅga Avadhūta). In these sanctified places, they are believed to have obtained inspiration and *sākṣātkāra* from the deity. Some, however, are totally detached from any pilgrimage place or *sampradāya*, as is the case with Sāī Bābā of Śirḍī (d. 1918), while others, such as Dattanāth Ujjayinīkar (1718–1849), are connected with the Nātha tradition of northern India. Significantly, at least one of these saints, Nūri Mahārāj (1869–1923),[99] can be identified as a Muslim and three others, namely, Māṇikprabhu (1817–65), Akkaḷkoṭ Mahārāj (d. 1878), and Sāī Bābā—believed to be intimately linked with one another—are eclectic figures, Sāī Bābā evidencing a Sufi background.[100]

From a literary standpoint, Vāsudevāṇanda Sarasvatī (1854–1914)[101] stands out as a prominent figure within the *paramparā*, being as he is the only one to have written about Dattātreya both in Sanskrit and Marāṭhī and to have collected most of the previous materials written on the deity's worship. Apart from his many *stotras* in Dattātreya's praise (see the *Datta-māhātmya*),[102] among Vāsudevānanda's major works are the *Guru Saṃhitā* and the two-thousand verse *Dvisahasrī*, both based on the *Guru-caritra*. His *Datta Purāṇa*, in sixty-four chapters, presents all the main stories, both Purāṇic and sectarian, regarding Dattātreya and his worship.[103]

The already mentioned *Datta-prabodha*, a Marāṭhī composition attributed to Kāvaḍībovā dating around 1860, is another popular text within the contemporary Datta movement, describing the *līlās* of the deity as drawn from the *Purāṇas* and other sources. Most of the devotional, sectarian literature on Dattātreya, however, is unpublished and lies scattered in Indian libraries. Gonda summarizes the situation thus:

> A good many of these writings belong to the usual genres produced and handed down in various religious communities, such as *stotras* (hymns of praise), *sahasranāma-stotras* (thousand names), *mantras*, *kavacas* ("armours," that is, preservative charms). There is

> a *Dattātreya-gāyatrī*, a *Dattātreya-gītā*, a *Dattātreya-campū*, a *Dattātreya-tantra*, etc. The *Datta-māhātmya*, dealing with the life of the deity, contains in the form of a dialogue between Maitreya and Vidura the story of Atri observing penance to obtain a boon from the . . . trinity who wished to be born as his sons, and other mythological themes as well as Dattātreya's attachment to wine and women. Other works deal with ritual: the *Dattātreya-kalpa*, the *Dattātreya-pūjā-paddhati* (a ritual manual of Dattātreya worship).[104]

Within a nondual[105] philosophical framework, the modern saints in the *paramparā* evidence common traits. In the first place, a high degree of tolerance and eclecticism both inter-religious (interaction and amalgamation with Sufism) as well as intra-religious (Nāthism mingling with Brahmanism, the Mahānubhāvas, *Śaiva* Tantrism, etc.). In the second place, a teaching stressing *bhakti* toward the deity and the Guru, exemplified by the topicality of *pādukā* worship within the cult, culminating in an attitude of surrender.[106] The *upadeśa* is linked to the most important feature of the Guru, Yogin, or Faqīr: his personal charisma, which typically identifies him as a miracle worker having great *siddhis*. Finally, the value of asceticism and *saṃnyāsa*—though again not necessarily within a *śuddha* Brahminical context—as exemplified by lord Dattātreya himself, paradigm of the assimilative Yogin and supreme Avadhūta. Today the Dattātreya movement maintains an important place in the religious life of Maharashtra, fostering the ideal of a synthetic spirituality. On one level, through the vitality of the Datta *sampradāya* and the alleged sanctity of pilgrimage sites such as Gāṇagāpūr, renown as a powerful healing center. On an even broader level, through the activities of the living saints and their *sthānas*. These holy men, by acquiring fame as miracle workers and healers, continue even after their death to keep devotion to Datta alive.[107] In conclusion, it can be said that the legacy of Dattātreya's assimilative force successfully spread and was received even within part of the Vārkarī tradition as well as in a variety of Marāṭhī religious circles. In the course of centuries, this ongoing network of relations brought to the fore an always richer, integrative spirituality, which is the distinctive mark of the Dattātreya movement to the present day.

Notes

1. See Vaudeville, "The Shaiva-Vaishnava Synthesis in Maharashtrian Santism," 223–24.

2. Tulpule, *Classical Marāṭhī Literature*, 353. On Cānda Bodhale being Janārdan's Guru, see also Dhere, *Musalmān Marāṭhī Santa-Kavī*, 87–89.

Written in 1645 and containing 2,319 *ovīs*, the *Yoga-saṅgrāma* is the most outstanding of Sheikh Muhammad's three philosophical compositions.

Sheikh Muhammad (1560–1650) of Śrīgonde, Ahmednagar district, is thought to be an Avatāra of Kabīr. He was the son of Rāje Muhammad, a Kādrī Sufi. In chapter 15 of his *Yoga-saṅgrāma*, Sheikh Muhammad states that Cānda Bodhale was the Guru of both Janārdan and himself. On Sheikh Muhammad, see Kulkarnee, "Medieval Maharashtra and Muslim Saint-Poets," 217–19; Wagle, "Hindu-Muslim Interactions in Medieval Maharashtra," 56–58.

Also known as Candrabhat, Cānda Bodhale was a *Vaiṣṇava* and yet, being a follower of the Sufi path, dressed like a Malaṅg or a Faqīr. His shrine, situated east of the fort of Daulatabad, was built like a Muslim tomb in order not to displease the Muslim rulers; see *Bhakta-līlāmṛta* 14.173–76. These days, a fair in Cānda Bodhale's honor is held every year on the fifth day of the lunar half of the month of *Caitra*.

The Kādrī or Qādiriyya order was brought to India by Muhammad Ghawth (d. 1482 or 1517). It was imported from Iraq by the Bahāmanī sultans and has been present on Deccani soil from 1422; see Schimmel, *Islām in the Indian Subcontinent*, 59. On Hindu-Muslim syncretism in the Deccan, see van Skyhawk, "Nasīruddīn and Ādināth, Nizāmuddīn and Kāniphnāth: Hindu-Muslim Religious Syncretism in the Folk Literature of the Deccan."

3. See van Skyhawk, *Bhakti und Bhakta: Religionsgeschichtliche Untersuchungen zum Heilsbegriff und zur religiosen Umwelt des Śrī Sant Eknāth*. By the same author, see "Sufi Influence in the *Ekanāthī-bhāgavat*: Some Observations on the Text and Its Historical Context."

4. A Muslim weaver (*julāhā*) of Benares, Kabīr was the greatest poet-singer of the north Indian Sant tradition. Considered a Sufi by the Muslims and a *bhakta* of the Rāmānanda school by the Hindus, he represented a peculiar blending of traditional Hinduism, the *Vaiṣṇava bhakti* of the great reformers, and the Yogic Nātha schools. His iconoclastic nondualism might be classified as *nirguṇa-bhakti*, of which he was the initiator. Though Kabīr did not adhere to Nātha beliefs, he appears to have been more conversant with the Nātha tradition than with the Islamic orthodox tradition; on the connections of northern Santism with Nāthism, see Barthwal, *The Nirguṇa School of Hindi Poetry*. On Kabīr, see Vaudeville's two-volume study, entitled *Kabīr*; see also Vaudeville's *A Weaver Named Kabīr: Selected Verses with a Detailed Biographical and Historical Introduction*. On the *nirguṇī* tradition, see Lorenzen, "The Lives of *Nirguṇī* Saints." By the same author, see *Praises to a Formless God: Nirguṇī Texts from North India*. In a poem by a disciple of Dādū, Sundaradās the younger (1596–1689), Dattātreya is thus described among other *nirguṇī* saints of the *kali-yuga*: "The hero Dattātrey roams at will. Independent, not dependent, he wiped out all distinctions"; see ibid., 162.

5. See Barthwal, *Traditions of Indian Mysticism. Based upon Nirguṇa School of Hindi Poetry*, 62. This *ramainī* is taken from the Benares edition of the *Bījak*. With reference to Kabīr's denial that God may specially manifest in the *daśa-avatāras*, a Kabīr-panthī motto says: "Dattātreya, Gorakhnāth, Hanumān, and Prahlāda neither read scriptures nor got instruction and yet obtained immortal bodies, but Kṛṣṇa died by a single arrow"; see ibid., 290. What appears a variant to this saying, however, says: "Brahmā is dead with Śiva . . . the immortals are dead. In Mathurā, Krishna, the cowherd, died. The ten incarnations . . . are dead. Machhandranāth, Gorakhnāth, Dattātreya and Vyās are no longer living. Kabīr cries with a loud voice: all these have fallen into the slip-knot of death"; see Russell and Lal, *The Tribes and Castes of the Central Provinces of India*, 1:236.

6. See Vaudeville, *Kabīr: Au cabaret de l'amour*, 77. See also H. H. Wilson, *A Sketch of the Religious Sects of the Hindus*, 240 n. 1.

7. For the popular Marāṭhī perception of Kabīr, see Abbott and Godbole, *Stories of Indian Saints*, vol. 1, chaps. 5–7, 11, 24. On the major legends concerning Kabīr, see Lorenzen, *Kabīr Legends and Ananta-Das's Kabīr Parachai*.

8. Noteworthy in this regard is the case of the Sāī Bābā of Śirḍī (d. 1918) from the Ahmednagar district, believed by his devotees to be an Avatāra of Dattātreya. When he was once asked to which religion he belonged, he tersely answered: "Kabīr." He often identified himself with Kabīr, saying he had been his disciple in one of his previous lives. For a presentation of Sāī Bābā's life and teachings, as well as for an overview of his connection with Kabīr, see Rigopoulos, *The Life and Teachings of Sai Baba of Shirdi*.

9. One of Viṣṇu's names, meaning "exciting or agitating men" (*janān ardati iti janārdana*). The 126th name in the list of the 1,000 names of the god; see *Mahābhārata* 13.149.27b.

10. Āśvalāyana was a pupil of Śaunaka, author of *sūtras* relating to the *Ṛg Veda* and founder of a Vedic school.

11. An *āratī* on Nṛsiṃha Sarasvatī, still sung at Gāṇagāpur, is traditionally ascribed to Janārdan.

12. Ranade, *Mysticism in Maharashtra*, 218–19.

13. According to Kṛṣṇadās Jagadānanda, author in 1698 of the *Pratiṣṭhāna-caritra*, the name of Janārdan's Guru was Candraśekhar, called an incarnation of Dattātreya (1.28). This Candraśekhar, however, is probably Cānda Bodhale whom Mahīpati calls Candrabhat in his *Bhakta-līlāmṛta*.

14. Abbott, *The Life of Eknāth: Śrī Eknāth Charita*, 17–18.
Anuṣṭhāna is a religious ceremony.
"With proper ceremony": This ritual, previously mentioned as customary for Nṛsiṃha Sarasvatī, is a common practice among *Śaiva* adepts. Sand *liṅgas* are found on the banks of rivers, near temples or holy fords. On the phallus, emblem of Śiva's potency and creative power, see Mahadev Chakravarti, *The Concept of Rudra-Śiva through the Ages*, 106–42.

15. Ranade, *Mysticism in Maharashtra*, 229–30.

"Continued to perform the duties of that station": When one has mentally renounced all fruits of actions and is firmly established in *Brahman*, worldly duties are believed to represent no hindrance, just as writing on water leaves no traces whatsoever.

The concrete sign of Datta's grace, Janārdan's experiences of ecstasy signal mystical initiation.

16. On the alleged Sufi influence, see van Skyhawk, "Sufi Influence in the *Ekanāthī-bhāgavat*: Some Observations on the Text and Its Historical Context," 72–73. The lesson of performing actions without leaving any contaminating traces (*naiṣkarmya*) finds its *locus classicus* in chapter 5 of the *Bhagavad-gītā*.

17. A famous *abhaṅg* credited to Tukārām says:

By the grace of the Sant the building is complete.
Jñāndev laid the foundation and raised the temple frame.
His servant Nāma filled out the temple structure.
Janārdan's Eknāth put up the column of the *Bhāgavata*.
Sing *bhajan* at peace: Tukā has become the pinnacle!
(Panshikar, *Viśvavandh Śrī Tukārām Mahārāj Yāñchi Sampūrṇa Abhaṅg*, *abhaṅg* 4488)

18. Though Eknāth probably never met with followers of Kabīr and Raidās during his pilgrimage to Benares and the north in 1573, he was certainly aware of a living tradition: he mentions about fifty Sants in his works.

19. The term has no clear etymology. *Bhārūḍs* have no standard form and are more often acted out rather than being sung as *bhakti* songs.

20. Tulpule, *Classical Marāṭhī Literature*, 354.

21. The Nāthas—though relatively dormant from the fourteenth to the eighteenth century—produced some notable works even during Muslim rule: Mukundarāj's *Yoga-mārtaṇḍa* and *Mūḷa-stambha*, Satyāmalanāth's *Siddhānta-rahasya* and *Nava-ratna-mālā*, and the rare palm-leaf manuscript *Vaijanātha-kalā-nidhi*. Another manuscript with the title *Mūḷa-stambha*, but attributed to "Dattātreya Avadhūta," is found as n. 671 in the catalogue of the Marāṭhī manuscripts in the Charles D'Ochoa Collection.

22. See Zelliot, "Eknāth's Bhārūḍs: The Sant as Link Between Cultures," 102–3.

23. See Ranade, *Mysticism in Maharashtra*, 256–58.

24. The name Bhānudās, "slave of the sun," was apparently attached to him because of a *pūjā* honoring the sun, which the ten-year-old saint performed for seven days in a temple outside Paiṭhaṇ. Bhānudās brought back the image of god Viṭṭhala to Paṇḍharpur from Hampi. On Bhānudās, see Ranade, *Mysticism in Maharashtra*, 213–14, 218. Also, Abbott, *Bhānudās: A Translation from the* Bhakta-vijaya *of Mahīpati*.

25. According to Jagadānanda, earliest biographer of Eknāth, it was Cakrapāṇi who entrusted young Eknāth to his friend Janārdan. At the time, Janārdan was living in "Amadavati," perhaps the modern Ahmednagar, and not in Devgiri or Daulatabad as Mahīpati—relying on Keśava's *Life of Eknāth* written at Devagad in 1720—claims in his *Bhakta-līlāmṛta*. Jagadānanda states that Janārdan moved to Daulatabad around 1547, after bringing Eknāth's education to completion. For Mahīpati's version of Eknāth's meeting with Janārdan, see Abbott, *The Life of Eknāth*, 7–9.

26. The Islamic influence on Eknāth is highlighted by the number of Persian and Arabic words found in his works, as well as by the presence of Muslim holy men in his *bhārūḍs*; on the five instances in which Eknāth met with some facets of Islam, see Zelliot, "A Medieval Encounter between Hindu and Muslim: Eknāth's Drama-Poem *Hindu-Turk Saṃvād*," 174–75.

27. The *Pratiṣṭhāna-caritra* claims that Eknāth completed his education with Janārdan at the age of fourteen.

28. A famous episode highlights Eknāth's identification with Janārdan. When Janārdan was meditating on a distant hill, enemies suddenly attacked the fort of Daulatabad. Eknāth, who had remained at the fort, assumed the form of Janārdan, that is, disguised himself as his Guru, fought bravely, and defeated the enemies. Afterwards, he put aside the robes of his teacher and began his usual work. Janārdan came to know of the incident and his joy knew no bounds. Eknāth's absorption into the personality of his Guru is similar to the discipline known as *fanā-fi-sh-Shaykh* among Sufis: the personality of the pupil (*murīd*) is absorbed into the personality of the master (*shaykh*). An account of Eknāth's *upāsana* toward Janārdan, including miraculous feats performed by Eknāth, is found in Abbot, *The Life of Eknāth*, 9–14, 17.

29. The ascendancy of Jñāndev on Eknāth is shown not only from the latter's major work, the *Eknāthī Bhāgavata*, but also from Eknāth's critical edition of the *Jñāneśvarī*, today regarded as the standard text. This work is believed to have been divinely inspired by Jñāndev himself.

30. This mystical experience, related to an episode of diligent accounting work of Eknāth, is expressed in one of his *abhaṅgs*:

> Janārdan is the Lord of the three worlds. He opened an account with me. The account was for large amounts. And always in the name of Rām. He gave me "I am He" as his bond. I reverently accepted it. He gave me garments of love. I received from him the leaves of Salvation. I quickly built the city of Absorption into *Brahman*. I went and sat in the bastion of *Caitanya*. I will collect the revenue of Self-knowledge and I will send it to my Swami. By the hands of the saints will I send the balance of accounts. *Bhakti* will be the beautiful receipt. Such are the business relations I acquired through *puṇya* in a former birth. I am fully satisfied in Janārdan. (Abbott, *The Life of Eknāth*, 16)

31. According to the *Pratiṣṭhāna-caritra*, Janārdan chose the daughter of Trivikrama Śāstri of Daulatabad as Eknāth's wife. It was only after Eknāth's departure to Paiṭhaṇ with his wife and his Guru's *pādukās* that Janārdan moved to Daulatabad. According to Mahīpati and more current legends, however, things went differently: Eknāth went to Janārdan at Daulatabad and later performed a pilgrimage across the subcontinent for about two-and-a-half years, during which time he stopped at Paiṭhaṇ and received his Guru's letter to end the pilgrimage and prepare for marriage. It is believed that Eknāth's bride was one Girijābāī from Bījāpur.

32. Ranade points out that Eknāth surpassed all saints of Maharashtra in accomplishing reconciliation between worldly and spiritual life; see *Mysticism in Maharashtra*, 216.

33. At this stage, Eknāth is aware of being a novice in the field of letters: he says that he has woven a rustic blanket in Marāṭhī as against the fine shawl of Sanskrit.

34. See Maharashtra, *Śrī Ekanāthī Bhāgavata*. See also van Skyhawk, *Bhakti und Bhakta*. In addition to biographies of saints, philosophical monographs, translations of Sanskrit texts into Marāṭhī and various poems, the other major works of Eknāth are the *Rukmiṇī-svayaṃvara* (1571) and the *Bhāvārtha-rāmāyaṇa*, unfinished in the forty-fifth chapter of the sixth *kāṇḍa* at his death in 1599.

35. In his introduction to J. E. Abbot's *The Life of Eknāth*, G. V. Tagare observes:

> Though Eknāth is silent about the reasons of his migration to Varanasi to write the remaining 26 chapters there, the legend goes that while a Brahmin disciple of Eknāth's was reading [the first five] preliminary chapters on the bank of the Gaṅgā at Varanasi, the Pandits there became infuriated that the holy teaching of Vyāsa was being "polluted in the vernacular spoken by Śūdras." Eknāth was summoned to Varanasi where he convinced the Pandits that his was the correct interpretation and that translation of a holy work in a modern language does not pollute it. And when the work was completed . . . the presiding deity of Varanasi vouchsafed for the correctness of translation after which it was led in a procession—a sort of victory-parade on behalf of the upholders of the cause of modern Indo-Aryan languages. (See Abbott, *The Life of Eknāth*, xx)

36. Zelliot, "Four Radical Saints in Maharashtra," 138.

37. On the history of medieval Deccan, see Sherwani and Joshi, *History of Medieval Deccan (1295–1724)*.

38. See Zelliot, "A Medieval Encounter," 177–78, 188.

39. See H. S. Joshi, *Origin and Development*, 104–5.

40. According to Pangarkar, this link naturally led Eknāth to Dattātreya worship, as his family tradition led him to Viṭṭhala worship; see ibid., 105.

41. The other two were Haripaṇḍit and Gaṅgābāī.

42. See Tulpule, *Classical Marāṭhī Literature*, 367. Tulpule notes that Mukteśvar probably lived during the first half of the sixteenth century. This, however, cannot be true given the fact that Eknāth, Mukteśvar's grandfather, was born in 1533. Mukteśvar's probable birth-date must then be assigned to the late part of the sixteenth century.

43. Literally "the all-sustaining out of his own divine play." On Mukteśvar, see ibid., 367–71. See also Dhere, *Datta Sampradāyācā Itihāsa*, 151–53.

44. See H. S. Joshi, *Origin and Development*, 109.

45. Abbott and Godbole, *Stories of Indian Saints*, 1:163–64. *Pānsupārī*, a roll of betel leaf with areca nut, is believed to be a powerful mouth-digestive.

46. Abbott, *The Life of Eknāth*, 21.

47. See Dhere, *Datta Sampradāyācā Itihāsa*, 209. The *Śrī-dattātreya-jñān-koś* says that the *Datta-prabodha* was published in Baroda in 1900, and quotes excerpts from it; see 479–99.

48. Possibly a misprint for Mātāṅg.

49. According to Raeside, there is no literary influence since none of the Mahānubhāva works were known outside the sect until after 1900; see Raeside, "Dattātreya," 499 n. 78.

50. On these three appearances of Dattātreya to Eknāth, see H. S. Joshi, *Origin and Development*, 107.

51. *Bhāvārtha-rāmāyaṇa, bāla-kāṇḍa* 16.168. Eknāth's account of the death of Reṇukā and Jamadagni resembles the version given in the *Reṇukā-māhātmya*.

52. See Dhere, *Datta Sampradāyācā Itihāsa*, 72–75. Tukārām's *abhaṅgs* amount to more than 4,600. G. A. Deleury edited an anthology of Tukārām's poems; see Toukaram, *Psaumes du pèlerin*.

53. See Pain and Zelliot, "The God Dattātreya," 96. This *abhaṅg* of Tukārām is found in most Marāṭhī pamphlets on Datta worship and in P. N. Joshi, *Śrī-dattātreya-jñān-koś*, 15.

54. According to another tradition, Dattātreya takes his morning bath at Haridvār on the Gaṅgā or at Pañcāḷeśvara on the Godāvarī. The deity is believed to meditate at Girnār.

Karvīr is a name of the modern Kolhāpur, the abode of goddess Mahālakṣmī and one of the most popular *śakti-pīṭhas* of Maharashtra (together with Mahur, Saptaśṛṅgī, and Tuḷjāpūr, abodes of Reṇukā, Jagadambā, and Bhavānī, respectively). Dattātreya is believed to beg for alms at midday in the courtyard of the Mahālakṣmī temple. For a recent study on the goddess Bhavānī of Tuḷjāpūr, see Jansen, *Die Bhavani von Tuljapur: Religionsgeschichtliche Studie des Kultes einer Göttin der indischen Volksreligion.*

55. See Mate, *Temples and Legends*, 100.

56. Ghurye, *Gods and Men*, 218. Emphasizing the influence of Nāthism in the molding of Dattātreya's *mūrti*, Ghurye quotes Rāmdās, who said that Datta, Gorakṣa, and other Siddhas always lived on alms; see ibid., 216. On Dattātreya's place in Rāmdās's *Dāsa-bodha* and the Samarth *sampradāya*, see Dhere, *Datta Sampradāyācā Itihāsa*, 68–70.

57. This information was gathered from Dāsopant's descendants by Viśvanāth Kāśīnāth Rājvāḍe at Ambā Jogāī (Hyderabad State) in 1902. In 1615, Tukārām at Dehu was seventeen years old, whereas Rāmdās at Jamb was only seven.

58. The family line of Dāsopant, as given by his descendants, is the following: Digambarpant (Dāsopant's father), Dāsopant, Dattajīpant, Viśvambhara, Dāsobā, Dattajī, Devajī, Viśvambhara, Gurubovā, Avadhūta, Atrivārada, Viśvambhara.

59. A pentad of contemporary writers comprising Eknāth, Dāsopant, Janī Janārdan, Rām Janārdan, and Viṭhā Reṇukānandana.

60. Paradoxically, though Dāsopant is presented as an Avatāra of Datta, he is said to seek and finally attain the *darśana* of the deity of whom he is a manifestation! Only the first 778 verses of the *Dāsopant-caritra* have come down to us. The text was supplied in 1902 to Viśvanāth Kāśīnāth Rājvāḍe by a branch of Dāsopant's descendants living in Ambā Jogāī. It was translated in 1927 by J. E. Abbott; see his *Dāsopant Digambar*. Both Dhere and Joshi are diffident regarding the text's authenticity.

61. A *deśpāṇḍya* is a government official, hereditary accountant, and record keeper of a province *(parganā)*. The name of Dāsopant's mother evidences a *Śaiva* background. The name of the father, if not a hagiographic input, proves his devotion to Dattātreya and explains the son's identification with the deity. The anonymous author of the *Dāsopant-caritra*, by his own admission, is a *Śaiva*, his family and caste deity being Mārtaṇḍa, other name for Khaṇḍobā.

62. See Abbott, *Dāsopant Digambar*, 3. On the special bodily features of a divine person, see Burnouf, "Sur les trente-deux signes caractéristiques d'un grand homme."

63. Dāsopant's age must be understood as symbolic. Toward the end of the *Dāsopant-caritra*, he is again described as "seeming about twelve years old." Number twelve is synonymous of totality, fullness, spiritual maturity, the completion of a cycle and the beginning of a new one.

64. The most numerous among the untouchable castes of Maharashtra. Their hereditary work is to remove dead cattle from the village, sweep the streets, run errands for the village officers, and guard village properties. On the Mahār caste, see Russell and Lal, *The Tribes and Castes of the Central Provinces of India*, 4:129–46.

65. Abbott, *Dāsopant Digambar*, 13.

66. Joshi reports that his father "being learned, god-fearing and wealthy, got him married at a young age"; see H. S. Joshi, *Origin and Development*, 113. The *Dāsopant-caritra*, however, does not mention Dāsopant's marriage. It simply states that, at the age of sixteen, he adopted the life of an Avadhūta. The number sixteen is almost certainly symbolic, representing the time of spiritual awakening.

67. Datta's association with the *śakti-pīṭhas* of Mahur—the main one being that of Reṇukā—has already been mentioned. His connection with Nāthism and Devī worship is an old and important piece of the puzzle of Datta's icon. Nāthism and Śāktism are related. The Nāthas of Gorakhpur worship, besides Bhairava, a goddess called Bālāsundarī, which is probably but another form of Tripurasundarī; see Bhandarkar, *Vaiṣṇavism, Śaivism and Minor Religious Systems*, 146.

68. Abbott, *Dāsopant Digambar*, 58–59.

"With his feet placed together": The paramount importance of the Guru's or deity's feet, and similarly of the *pādukās*, is evoked once again.

"The yellow silk garment": An ochre-colored garment, such as that worn by Kṛṣṇa-Gopāla. The *pītāmbara* identifies a religious mendicant.

The description of Dattātreya's face calls to mind the features of a manifestation of Viṣṇu. *Śyāma-sundara*, dark and beautiful, is an epithet of Kṛṣṇa.

"Alligator shaped earrings": The *makara* is a kind of sea monster, often an ornament on headdresses. It represents the astrological sign Capricorn and is depicted with the head and forelegs of an antelope and the body and tail of a fish. Earrings shaped in the form of a *makara* are an emblem of Viṣṇu.

69. The term designates one who has left the practice of Yoga or meditation. Dāsopant was recognized as one who, in his previous birth, had been interrupted during his performance of Yoga and had thus come back to complete his *sādhana.*

70. Abbott, *Dāsopant Digambar*, 67. The locale described is about forty miles southeast of Aurangabad.

71. According to Joshi, Dāsopant attained Dattātreya's vision after a twelve year period of *tapas* and worship of the *pādukās*; see H. S. Joshi, *Origin and Development*, 113.

72. Joshi reports that Dāsopant was initiated into the Nātha sect soon after having attained Dattātreya's *darśana*; see ibid., 111, 113. However, there is no textual evidence supporting this claim.

73. Apparently, Dāsopant worshipped Dattātreya only in his *pādukā* form, never as an idol. Although he never described an icon of Dattātreya in his writings, at the end of his *Pāsoḍī* Datta is said to bear the six traditional items; see ibid., 113.

74. The Upaniṣadic saying *ahaṃ brahmāsmi*, "I am *Brahman*," is found in *Bṛhadāraṇyaka Upaniṣad* 1.4.10. The Śṛṅgeri *maṭha* and the orders depending

from it—Sarasvatī, Bhāratī, Purī—have this formula as their *mantra*. A connection of the unknown author of the *Dāsopant-caritra* and of part of the Datta *sampradāya* with the *maṭha* of Śṛṅgeri—and with its Sarasvatī order to which Nṛsiṃha Sarasvatī belonged—is not improbable.

75. Perhaps the most crucial theological question. Even at the beginning of the *Mārkaṇḍeya Purāṇa* (4.31), the first of the four questions that Jaimini poses to the birds is why Vāsudeva, though devoid of qualities (*nirguṇa*), assumed human shape with its qualities (*guṇa*). The Sāṃkhyan category of *guṇa*, as Gerald J. Larson notes:

> Comes to encompass . . . the entire range of subjective and objective reality, whether manifest (*vyakta*) or unmanifest (*avyakta*). It becomes the "thread" that runs through all of ordinary experience and throughout the natural world, tying together, as it were, the *tattva* realm, the *bhāva* realm, and the *bhūta* realm. (Larson and Bhattacharya, *Sāṃkhya: A Dualist Tradition*, 66)

In a Sāṃkhyan context, the *traiguṇya* issue is resolved by considering it an emanation or transformation (*pariṇāma*) from primordial materiality (*mūla-prakṛti*), radically separated and different from the principle of pure transcendental consciousness (*puruṣa*). Within a nondual perspective, the problem arises of how the absolute *nirguṇa-brahman* could possibly appear as *saguṇa*: it is precisely this theological crux which leads to the elaboration of the various theories concerning the nature and function of the illusory power of *māyā*.

76. Abbott, *Dāsopant Digambar*, 77.

" 'I am Brahman' arose": The affirmation of the "I" principle or the awareness brought about by the realization of one's own identity disrupts the pristine state of undifferentiated, nonreflective unity, leading toward a subject-object opposition, a dualistic universe of discourse.

"This sound arose": Creation takes place through the divine vibration or word (*śabda*, *vāc*), expression of *Brahman*'s will. All things are manifested in their concrete shape as the expression of the subtle divine potency or *śakti* of *Brahman*.

"The great Māyā": *Mahā-māyā* may be interpreted as both the beginningless illusory power and the great goddess hypostatizing that power, assimilated to the *śakti* of *Brahman*.

77. See ibid., 5–6.

78. The work is so vast that only the first three chapters and a part of the fourth have been published; see Bhave, *Gītārṇava*.

79. Tulpule, *Classical Marāṭhī Literature*, 360.

80. In the *Samartha-pratāpa* of Giridhara, a biography of Rāmdās written about half a century after his death, the author imagines a banquet given by Rāmdās to authors past and present. The plates are their literary works. Dāsopant is a guest, and the *Gītārṇava* is his contribution to the banquet.

81. See Dev, *Dāsa-viśrāma-dhāma* (1–4).

82. For more on these works by Dāsopant, see Deshmukh, *Gītārtha-candrikā;* Dev, *Grantha-rāja;* on the *Padārṇava,* Lele, *Dāsopantācī Padē;* and on the *Pañcīkaraṇa,* Pohnerkar, *Dāsopantāncī Pāsoḍī. Pāsoḍī* means "doubled cloth." It is preserved in its tattered form at Ambā Jogāī.

83. Literally "the servant or follower of Dattātreya."

84. See Katre, *Datta-māhātmya.*

85. This hymn celebrates the sixteen manifestations of Dattātreya, seemingly proving Dāsopant's belief in at least sixteen Avatāras of the deity; see H. S. Joshi, *Origin and Development,* 114.

86. Again, the motif of the difficulty of obtaining Dattātreya's *darśana*: the lord of Yoga manifests himself only to one striving to follow his exemplary *saṃnyāsa.*

87. Material prosperity is a traditional and greatly desired consequence of Dattātreya's blessings which encompass both *bhukti* and *mukti.*

88. This episode of Eknāth's refusal of Dāsopant's gifts—apparently aiming at highlighting Eknāth's ascetic superiority over Dāsopant—is significant: whereas the *Vaiṣṇava* Eknāth envisions wealth as dangerous and polluting (the traditional view), the Avatāra of Datta, emblem of *vairāgya* who practiced the most severe penance for twenty years, seems to view wealth without fear of contamination and as a divine blessing, pointing to a higher model of dispassion.

89. *Kṛṣṇa-janmaṣṭamī.* This festival falls on the eighth day of the second half of the month of *Śrāvaṇa;* see Sivananda, *Hindu Fasts and Festivals,* 91–99.

90. Abbott, *The Life of Eknāth,* 194–96.

91. Name of a Yādava nephew of Vāsudeva, friend and counsellor of Kṛṣṇa. In our story, Eknāth takes the place of Kṛṣṇa, whom Uddhava (now in his next incarnation) eagerly serves: a hagiographic device to stress Eknāth's oneness with Viṭṭhala-Kṛṣṇa.

92. The offering of one's whole self to a Guru or deity, with the eight limbs of the body touching the ground.

93. Other name for Viṭṭhala.

94. A play in honor of Kṛṣṇa-Gopāla.

95. Abbott, *The Life of Eknāth,* 197–99.

96. See H. S. Joshi, *Origin and Development,* 115–82.

97. Here is the complete list: Gorakhnāth, Cakrapāṇi, Govindaprabhu, Cakradhar, Janārdan, Eknāth, Dāsopant, Mukteśvar, Mahīpatidās Yogin, Kinārām Aghorī, Siddheśvar Mahārāj, Nipāt Nirañjan, Virūpākṣabuvā Nāgnāth, Nārāyaṇ

Svāmin, Sādhu Mahārāj Kandharkar, Cidambar Dīkṣit, Bhairav Avadhūta Jñānsāgar, Dattanāth Ujjayinīkar, Raghunāth Bhātajī of Nāsik, Nirañjan Raghunāth, Kṛṣṇendra Guru, Anantasūta Kāvaḍībovā, Māṇikprabhu, Nārāyaṇ Mahārāj Jalvankar, Viṣṇubavā Brahmacārin, Bālmukunda, Akkalkoṭ Mahārāj, Vāsudev Balvant Phadke, Nṛsiṃha Sarasvatī of Āḷandī, Nārāyaṇ Gurudatta Mahārāj, Kṛṣṇa Sarasvatī, Vāmanrav Vaidya Vāmorikar, Mahārāj Bāḷekuṇḍrikar, Vāsudevānanda Sarasvatī, Viṣṇudās Mahurkar, Sāī Bābā of Śirḍī, Śrī Datta Mahārāj of Aste, Nārāyaṇ Mahārāj Keḍgāokar, Raṅga Avadhūta, Gulavani Mahārāj. For a presentation of all forty personalities, see P. N. Joshi, *Śrī-dattātreya-jñān-koś*, 266–357.

It should be noted that one of these saints, namely, Vāsudev Balvant Phadke (1845–83), was a popular political figure founder of an anti-British movement. His plan was to restore Hindu *dharma* to its pristine purity and to set up Hindu rule. He envisioned himself as the "savior" of Hindu India and many of his followers revered him as an Avatāra of the great Śivājī. Sought by the British police for a series of crimes including robberies and acts of terrorism, he was often able to find refuge in Gāṇagāpur. He was arrested on July 20, 1879 and died in prison on February 17, 1883. On V. B. Phadke, see Fuchs, *Godmen on the Warpath: A Study of Messianic Movements in India*, 165–74. For a recent biography on Mahārāj Bāḷekuṇḍrikar (1855–1905), see Kher, *Avadhuta Yogi Pant Mahārāj of Balekundri*.

98. Ghurye, *Indian Sādhus*, 217–18. For some general remarks on the Datta movement, see Pai, *Religious Sects in Ancient India (Ancient & Medieval)*, 87.

99. Initiated by one Abdul Husein Nūri of Marehra (Etvah district, Uttar Pradesh)—a Faqīr laying emphasis on the perception of divine light (*nūr*) hidden in one's heart—Nūri Mahārāj's mysticism focused on the visualization of Allāh's transcendental effulgence. Light plays a crucial function in Sufi cosmology and mysticism, often in relation to the effects of *dhikr* practice. On Nūri Mahārāj, see H. S. Joshi, *Origin and Development*, 160–61.

100. On Māṇikprabhu, see ibid., 130–35.

On Akkaḷkoṭ Mahārāj, see ibid., 136–42. One of the most famous Avatāras of Dattātreya in recent times, he is believed by his followers to be the third historical Datta Avatāra after Śrīpāda Śrīvallabha and Nṛsiṃha Sarasvatī. Akkaḷkoṭ Mahārāj is especially revered for his miraculous powers and child-like (*bāla*) and mad (*unmatta*) aspects. See Karandikar, *Biography of Sri Swami Samarth Akkalkot Mahārāj*.

On Sāī Bābā, see H. S. Joshi, *Origin and Development*, 158–59; Rigopoulos, *The Life and Teachings of Sai Baba of Shirdi*.

101. See H. S. Joshi, *Origin and Development*, 143–53.

102. Portions of this *Datta-māhātmya*, not to be confused with the homonymous work of Dāsopant, have been published in the *Śrī-dattātreya-jñān-koś*, 463–78.

103. See Vāsudevānanda Sarasvatī, *Datta-Purāṇa and Other Works, together with his Biography Gurudeva-Caritra*.

104. Gonda, *Medieval Religious Literature in Sanskrit*, 224. For an overview of the texts connected with the Datta movement, see Keshavadas, *Sadguru Dattātreya*.

Dattātreya-gītā: Probably to be identified with the *Avadhūta-gītā*, also known as *Datta-gītā*.

Maitreya, literally "friendly," "benevolent," is a Ṛṣi, son of Kuśarava and disciple of Parāśara.

Vidura, literally "intelligent," "wise," is a son of Vyāsa and younger brother of Dhṛtarāṣṭra and Pāṇḍu. In the *Mahābhārata*, he is depicted as "the wisest of the wise," giving advice to both Kauravas and Pāṇḍavas.

105. The Indian Sufi ideal is *waḥdat al-wujūd*, the unity of all beings, divine and human. In verse 11 of Eknāth's *Hindu-Turk Saṃvād*, the Turk says: "Allāh, you exist everywhere . . . you are the seeing and the seen . . . the knower and the known . . . you are life and the giver of life . . . you are the alms that fill the stomach and take away sin"; see Zelliot, "A Medieval Encounter," 179–80.

106. This attitude of complete surrender recalls the practice of *prapatti* within the Rāmānujīya schools and that of *tawakkul* within Sufism.

107. These days, the *samādhis* of saints like Akkaḷkoṭ Mahārāj and Sāī Bābā attract thousands of pilgrims and devotees. The same can be said of the *dargāhs*, tombs of Muslim holy men; see Saiyed, "Saints and Dargāhs in the Indian Subcontinent: A Review."

7

The *Tripurā-rahasya*

Nothing elucidates Dattātreya's link to Śāktism and goddess worship better than an analysis of the *Tripurā-rahasya* (The Secret [Doctrine] of [the Goddess] Tripurā).[1] Tripurā, also known as Lalitā[2] or Lalitā Tripurasundarī, is acknowledged as the most important form of Śrī-Lakṣmī: the benign manifestation, maternal, ever beautiful and young, of the supreme Śakti. The meaning of the name Tripurā, though often rendered as "the one of the three cities" (see the Tripura myth of *Mahābhārata* 8.24), is usually interpreted by *Śākta* authorities as well as by our text as "the one who is anterior (*purā*) to the three (*tri*)." The goddess is understood to be prior to all triads such as the three *Vedas*, the three gods (Brahmā, Viṣṇu, and Śiva), the three worlds, the three times (past, present, and future), the three states of consciousness and so forth. She is thus variously identified with pure consciousness (the supreme *Puruṣa*), the "fourth state" (*turīya*), and the impersonal *Brahman*. The name Tripurā extols her radical transcendence beyond time, eternal, prior to all manifestation. Within the *Tripurā-rahasya*, our Guru-God teaches *Śākta* nondualism to his disciple Paraśurāma. The stories told by Dattātreya provide the best explanation of the content of his *upadeśa*, as we shall presently see.

The *Tripurā-rahasya* is a medieval *Śākta* work composed between the eleventh and seventeenth centuries.[3] Apparently, it was confined to the boundaries of south India, exercising only regional influence. The text has left no trace, in terms of textual reference or quotation, in any literary composition that we know of. Its isolation contrasts with its contemporary renown, proven by different editions and translations in languages of the subcontinent and the degree of concordance among them. The *Tripurā-rahasya*'s recent fame is largely due to the noted Tamiḷ saint of Tiruvaṇṇāmalai, Ramaṇa Maharṣi (i.e., Veṅkaṭaramaṇa Ayyār, 1879–1950). As Douglas Renfrew Brooks notes, the *Tripurā-rahasya* seems to have gained repute only in recent times:

> Such texts appear to follow the spheres of influence established by popular gurus. There is no evidence . . . that the *Tripurā-rahasya*

exercised an influence on Bhāskararāya or his eighteenth- and nineteenth-century disciples.[4]

The *Tripurā-rahasya* is believed to be the abbreviated version of an original *Datta Saṃhitā* or *Dakṣiṇāmūrti Saṃhitā* in eighteen thousand verses ascribed to Dattātreya. This work was summarized in six thousand *sūtras* divided into fifty *khaṇḍas* by Dattātreya's disciple Paraśurāma. Finally, Sumedha Hāritāyana, a disciple of Paraśurāma, produced the text that has come down to us.[5]

The *Tripurā-rahasya* is divided into three parts. The *māhātmya-khaṇḍa*, or section dedicated to the celebration of the goddess, comprises 6,687 *ślokas*, divided into eighty *adhyāyas*. This portion is concerned with the myths relative to the origin of Tripurā, the description of Devī *mantra* and *yantra* rituals, the various Śaktis and feats of the goddess, and the cosmic struggle between Tripurā and the Asura demons. The *jñāna-khaṇḍa*, or section concerning salvific knowledge, comprises 2,163 *ślokas*, divided into twenty-two *adhyāyas*. Couched within a nondual perspective, this portion presents esoteric philosophical issues illustrated through poignant parables and allegories. Among the main themes treated are the reality of pure consciousness, the nature of the manifest world, and the necessary qualifications of the aspirant seeking *mokṣa*. The third section or *caryā-khaṇḍa*, dedicated to the proper rules of ritual conduct, has been lost and must have comprised about 3,000 *ślokas*. Its content may have been similar to that of the *Paraśurāma-kalpa-sūtras*, which describe the secrets of the cult of Tripurā based on the *Śrī-vidyā*[6] ritual.

The *āśrama* of Paraśurāma is traditionally located on mount Malaya in south India (several times mentioned in the *Mahābhārata* and other works), and the beginning of the *māhātmya-khaṇḍa* states that Sumedha wrote his work in the town of Hālāsya (Madurai). The text is in the form of a conversation between the sage Nārada and Hāritāyana, not between Śiva and Devī as is usually the case with Tantric works. This exchange is further the context for presenting a dialogue between Dattātreya and Paraśurāma, background for the narration of a series of subordinate stories, following a typically Purāṇic scheme. In accordance with tradition, the *guru-paramparā* of those detaining secret knowledge of Tripurā is said to have had a divine origin: Śiva first revealed it to Viṣṇu who in turn revealed it to Brahmā. In the world of humans, the sage Saṃvarta[7] is said to have transmitted it to Dattātreya, here presented as lord of Avadhūtas. Other important figures mentioned within the *paramparā* are Durvāsas, Agastya, and Lopāmudrā.[8] Two texts that the author uses and reelaborates are the

Devī-māhātmya of the *Mārkaṇḍeya Purāṇa* and the *Lalitā-māhātmya* or *Lalitopākhyāna* of the *Brahmāṇḍa Purāṇa*.[9]

The *Tripurā-rahasya*'s technical language, which could be identified as Kashmiri *Śaivite*, is common to both *Āgamas* and *Tantras*. There are even dualist and *Śaiva Siddhānta* interpretations of these texts using the same idiom. In south India, this sort of technical language seems to have preceded the crystallization of *Spanda* and *Pratyabhijñā* theologies. *Śrī-vidyā Śākta* cults were present in southern regions from at least the seventh century, even though their emergence as a written Sanskrit tradition dates from about the ninth century.[10] On the other hand, the link of southern Śāktism to the nondual Śaṅkara tradition and their reciprocal influence was especially important. The Vedāntization of Śāktism within a *Śaiva* idiom was achieved through texts such as the *Saundarya-laharī*, the *Prapañca-sāra*, and the *Lalitā-triśatī-bhāṣya*.[11] The corpus of works concerning the cult of Tripurā-Lalitā, though not particularly vast if compared with that of other forms of Devī such as Durgā and Kālī, is still remarkable.[12] Texts such as the *Tripurā-rahasya* are important not only because they focus on a popular goddess but also because they reveal some of the history of *Śākta* cults, which attempted to legitimize themselves even within the more conservative milieux of the orthodox *smārta* communities. As Brooks notes:

> Between the ninth and twelfth centuries, southerners distance themselves from Kashmiri *Kaulism* in order to distinguish Śrīvidyā from morally suspect Tantrism. Śākta non-dualism is broadly construed to be compatible with Śaṅkara's *advaita* Vedānta.[13]

A connection was certainly established between the *Śrī-vidyā* tradition and the southern orthodox Śaṅkara *pīṭhas*. One way through which Dattātreya was possibly appropriated within southern Śāktism was via Śaṅkara's Daśanāmī *sampradāya*. Perhaps through its Sarasvatī order centered in the Śṛṅgeri *maṭha*, to which Nṛsiṃha Sarasvatī—founder of the Datta *sampradāya*—apparently belonged. Although the *māhātmya-khaṇḍa* portrays Dattātreya in a way that reminds us of the *Mārkaṇḍeya Purāṇa* account, he is sanitized and kept out of explicit left-hand *Kaula-Vāma* contexts. The *Tripurā-rahasya*'s core presentation of Dattātreya is that of its *jñāna-khaṇḍa*, where the Guru-God is truly a *jñāna-mūrti*, the prime teacher of nondualism. In any case, Dattātreya's connection to Devī worship is a constant throughout the deity's unfolding. The *Śākta* element appears in Datta's first characterization in the *Mārkaṇḍeya*

Purāṇa and is clearly evidenced in Mahānubhāva literature and in his connection with *śakti-pīṭhas* such as Mahur. It is further testimonied by the sectarian *Dattātreya Upaniṣad.* Dattātreya's link to Tripurā is certainly of southern origin: Bhāskararāya, in his commentary to the eighth verse of the *Tripurā Upaniṣad,* mentions Dattātreya as one of the twelve sages and demigods associated with the meaning of the *Śrī-vidyā mantra.*[14] Dattātreya also appears to have a place in the *mantras* of Tirumūlar's *Tiru-mantiram,* the greatest treatment of Yoga in Tamiḷ literature and the source of *Śaiva Siddhānta* philosophy.[15]

Tripurā's cult is based on the double doctrine of the *Śrī-vidyā* and *Śrī-cakra,* the *mantra* and *yantra* constituting the sounding body and the graphic symbol of Devī.[16] The *Śrī-vidyā mantra,* of fifteen (*pañcadaśākṣarī*) or sixteen (*ṣoḍaśākṣarī*) syllables, is thought to represent the subtle form of the goddess. Two important versions of the *Śrī-vidyā* exist. The first, characterizing south Indian Śāktism from the sixth century, is attributed to Śiva as Kāmeśvara and thus called the Kāmarāja *vidyā.* The second is called the Lopāmudrā *vidyā,* from the name of the wife of sage Agastya, who—like Dattātreya—is also one of the *vidyā*'s lords (*vidyeśvara*). Important to *Śrī-vidyā* texts closely related to Kashmiri traditions, the Lopāmudrā *vidyā* has apparently fallen out of use in south India. The Kāmarāja and Lopāmudrā *vidyās* are known as *kādi-vidyā* and *hādi-vidyā,* respectively. The most widely used *kādi-vidyā* occurs in three separate portions called "peaks" (*kūṭas*): the peak of the nature of speech (*vāg-bhava-kūṭa; ka e ī la hrīṃ*), the peak of Kāmarāja (*kāmarāja-kūṭa; ha sa ka ha la hrīṃ*), and the supreme peak of Śakti (*śakti-kūṭa; sa ka la hrīṃ*). The triadic, hierarchical configuration of the *mantra* is reflected in the adept's *japa* practice which can be vocal, mental, or silent. To again quote Brooks:

> The universe of triadic signs is said to reflect the supreme deity's own intentionality. At the moment of creation the cosmos emerges from the Absolute's pure illumination (*prakāśa*) which propels (*sphurat*) itself into a state of reflective consciousness (*vimarśa*) . . . Śakti is the active, manifest, and creative component of the universe . . . inasmuch as . . . Śiva is the Śākta's reference for the unmoving eternal . . . The true identity of the inner Self (*ātman*) with Brahman occurs as a dynamic process of reflective cognition (*vimarśa*) in which there is a simultaneous recognition of the source of its being, the pure consciousness (*cit*) of the illuminative (*prakāśa*) Brahman.[17]

Associated with the *mantra* of Tripurā, the *Śrī-cakra* ritual and practice are essential components of the *Śākta* cult. Although the *mantra* and *yantra* are two distinct principles operating on separate levels, they are mutually influential and complementary. The theological claim that they constitute an indissoluble whole is often made by *Śākta* adepts. It is argued that *mantra* and *yantra* are not two different aspects of the cult but, rather, one complex of sound and form, in which it is possible to "visualize" the *mantra* sound as form and to "hear" the graphic body of the *yantra* as sound. Regarding the nature of a *yantra* Stella Kramrisch notes:

> A *yantra* is a geometrical contrivance by which any aspect of the Supreme Principle may be bound (*yantr*, to bind; from the root "*yam*") to any spot for the purpose of worship. It is an artifice in which the ground (*bhūmi*) is converted into the extent of the manifest universe.[18]

There are a series of correspondences between each syllable of the *mantra* and each geometrical structure of the *yantra*. These correspondences are graphically expressed by assigning each phoneme of the *mantra* to particular areas of the diagram. Since each of the fifteen or sixteen syllables making up Devī's *mantra* indicates an aspect of the goddess, in some cases the phonemes are substituted with representations of the sixteen Nityās—the eternal goddesses identified with the moon's phases (*kalās*)—or sometimes even with the minor deities of the *Śrī-cakra*.[19] In the *Śrī-vidyā* tradition, the *Śrī-cakra* is revered as the source of all *yantras*, being the very form (*svarūpa*) of the Absolute. In actuality, the *yantra* functions as an instrument (*-tra*) to gain control ($\sqrt{yam}$) and channel the psychic energies of the *sādhaka*, as a support for meditation. The geometrical figures become "animated," acting as pulsating models through the movements of expansion and contraction from the center to the periphery and back, reproducing the cyclical process of manifestation and reabsorption of the Absolute. The *Śrī-cakra* symbolizes the spiritual itinerary of the *sādhaka*, the passage from ignorance to the moment of the realization of one's identity with *Brahman* represented by the *cakra*'s center or "drop" (*bindu*), symbol of the original undifferentiated totality of Śiva-Śakti. Perhaps most important of all is the adept's experience of the *yantra* as the veritable body of Devī.

Now for an overview of those passages in the *māhātmya-khaṇḍa* which concern Dattātreya.[20] Chapter 4 closes with the narration of how Paraśurāma, not grasping Saṃvarta's teachings relative to the *ātman* and Tripurā's nature, is advised by Saṃvarta to seek the help of the great Yogin Dattātreya.[21] Chapter 5 narrates how Paraśurāma, pained by his identification with the body, directs himself toward the Gandhamādana mountain,[22] where Dattātreya's *āśrama* is located. In chapter 6, Dattātreya appears to Paraśurāma in the effulgence of his Tantric aspect: surrounded by Yogins and resplendent in his youth, he embraces a young woman and has a jar of liquor in front of him. Paraśurāma, considering that good and bad are but the products of one's imagination, refuses to be led astray by appearances. Dattātreya gives a talk on the necessity of subduing one's senses and on the value of renunciation, and expresses marvel over Paraśurāma's equanimity with respect to his contradictory aspect. Paraśurāma answers that the teacher must be viewed as Śiva himself and that Dattātreya's way, good or bad as it may appear, would also be his own. Paraśurāma explains the reasons that have brought him there: tired with *saṃsāra*, he wishes to take refuge at Datta's feet so as to attain *ātma-jñāna*, like an elephant plunging into the cool waters of the Gaṅgā while surrounded by a burning forest.[23] Dattātreya tells him that the noble quality of his desire is Devī's grace and invites him to listen to his *upadeśa*. Dattātreya explains that the supreme Śiva (Paraśiva) is none other than the *ātman* residing in all beings. It is through the power of his own *māyā* that he withdraws himself. In this world nothing exists or can be known apart from that which manifestly appears: that *ātman* which shines forth throughout the world is Paraśiva. The *ātman*, appearing in infinite forms, is nonetheless one and the same, eternally shining of its own splendor. Only through the recognition of *ātman* (*pratyabhijñāna*) can one attain knowledge, which is ultimately the grace of the supreme Śakti, Tripurā. Precisely in order to honor her with devotion one must carefully listen to the celebration of her greatness.

At the beginning of chapter 7, Dattātreya states that not even the gods know who the goddess is or where she dwells. She is beyond the *Vedas*, the *Śāstras*, and the *Tantras*. She cannot be apprehended through the usual means of knowledge or reasoning. She may be understood only through the experience of being, the "I am" experience. It is impossible to measure the ocean of her greatness and beauty. Dattātreya then narrates some of the great deeds accomplished by Tripurā and her Śaktis.

In the last two chapters, 79 and 80, Paraśurāma asks Dattātreya some final questions. He inquires why Agastya, a great knower of both *Vedas* and *Śāstras*, did not attain Tripurā's vision. Dattātreya replies that only the *dīkṣā* given by an authoritative Guru leads to that perfect devotion necessary to practise Tripurā's cult and attain *mokṣa*. He who limits himself to the study of Vedic texts, ignoring the *Śākta* tradition, does not deserve access to the goddess. Dattātreya refers to the *Tantras* as that essence which sages reaped from the churning of the ocean of all scriptures, produced by Parameśvara himself to offer salvation to all beings. Both the twice-born ones as well as Śūdras may have access to these texts. Agastya, who had solely followed the Vedic path, was able to attain a place in the city of the goddess only after receiving *dīkṣā* from his bride.

Dattātreya further explains some rituals relative to Tripurā's cult: the making and consecration of Devī's image, the auspicious time for worship, the festivals dedicated to her, and so on. Dattātreya teaches how to attain Devī's favor, listing the fruits which will be achieved, juxtaposing them with the sins accumulated by those neglecting her cult. The Guru illustrates the ceremony of the offering of the *Śrī-cakra* (*śrī-cakra-dāna-vidhi*), its efficacy, and the benefits acquired by those handing down the Tripurā tradition. The *māhātmya-khaṇḍa* ends with the traditional *phala-śruti*, Dattātreya solemnly declaring that all those who learn of the myths celebrating the goddess will feel a sentiment of pure devotion, leading them to salvation.

In the twenty-two *adhyāyas* of the *Tripurā-rahasya*'s *jñāna-khaṇḍa*, the dialogue between Hāritāyana and Nārada constitutes the external frame: Hāritāyana, the disciple of Paraśurāma, narrates how he had received *upadeśa* from his teacher. He evokes the spiritual *mārga* of Paraśurāma himself, depicting the relationship between the latter and his Guru Dattātreya. Within the body of the *jñāna-khaṇḍa*, Nārada remains silent and Hāritāyana has the role of storyteller. The text puts all new dialogue entries into his mouth, such as: "Paraśurāma, greatly surprised, asked . . . " or: "Dattātreya, full of compassion, answered . . . "

Hāritāyana narrates how Paraśurāma, unable to fully understand the teachings he had received from Saṃvarta, is initiated by Dattātreya into advancing stages of *sādhana*: eventually, he receives initiation to the worship of Tripurā, mastering the secrets of ritual practice. Paraśurāma is then said to leave Dattātreya and to retire on mount Mahendra, dedicating himself to Tripurā's worship for twelve years in complete solitude. Realizing the limits of ritual worship devoid of liberating knowledge, he returns to Dattātreya who was residing on the Gandhamādana mountain, hoping that the Guru will give him insight into that esoteric *upadeśa* originally imparted to him by Saṃvarta. This introductory section covers the first *adhyāya* and half of the second. From here on, Dattātreya conducts the dialogue, having accepted Paraśurāma as disciple.

In the following *adhyāyas*, Dattātreya avoids abstract theory: the captivating quality of these chapters is that the teaching is conveyed through the behavior of various characters, acting in a number of different plots. The main stories that Dattātreya tells are five: from *adhyāya* 3 to 10, the story of prince Hemacūḍa and his wife Hemalekhā; from *adhyāya* 12 to 14, the story of Taṅgaṇa's son and prince Mahāsena; from *adhyāya* 15 to 17, the story of Aṣṭāvakra and King Janaka;[24] in *adhyāya* 20, the story of the consultation of the goddess; and finally in *adhyāya* 21 the story of Vasumān, the Brahmin demon. In these tales, the principal spokesmen for Dattātreya are Hemalekhā, Taṅgaṇa's son, the female ascetic with Janaka, and Hemāṅgada. To each of these enlightened characters corresponds an alter ego of Paraśurāma in the figures of Hemacūḍa, Mahāsena, Aṣṭāvakra, and Vasumān. From the outset, Dattātreya tells Paraśurāma that the primal obnubilating factor within man is lack of discrimination (*vicāra*). He explains that the company of the good (*satsaṅga*) is the most important factor in the achieving of *mokṣa*; a fundamental theme already found in Dattātreya's teachings to the Sādhyas in *Mahābhārata* 5.36.1–21. Dattātreya then narrates the first tale to Paraśurāma.

Once upon a time, after a terrible storm during a hunting expedition, Prince Hemacūḍa (one of the two sons of Muktācūḍa, king of the Daśārṇa people)[25] finds himself alone in the wilderness. Wandering across the jungle, he comes to the *āśrama* of sage Vyāghrapāda, where he is greeted by his beautiful daughter Hemalekhā. The two fall in love and, after having obtained Vyāghrapāda's blessings and permission to marry, leave the *āśrama*. Hemacūḍa takes Hemalekhā to the capital of his father's kingdom, where their marriage is performed with great pomp.

Soon, however, Hemacūḍa sees that Hemalekhā is not at all interested in sensual gratification, indifferent to the pleasures of worldly enjoyment which he values so dearly. Asked the reason, Hemalekhā says that she has come to realize the momentariness and subjectivity of sensual pleasures, which depend on one's mind and are subject to pain. Sensual attraction is said to be caused by the idea one has of beauty: Hemalekhā recognizes it as a mental projection, conditioned by cultural and social identifications. After listening to his wife's words, Hemacūḍa loses his interest in sensual gratification and feels depressed, since out of habit and subtle tendencies he is still attracted to sense objects.

Hemalekhā, realizing that her husband's dejection reveals a potential for spiritual growth, offers him an *upadeśa* on the ultimate basis of the means of valid knowledge (*pramāṇas*). This she identifies in faith or *śraddhā*, fundamental presupposition of one's life and spiritual quest. The mind is said to be the root cause of all miseries and yet, if properly trained, can be viewed as the best means of attaining *mokṣa.* Since mind is like a monkey jumping incessantly, one must control its modifications, making it one-pointed, sharp, and inward. Hemalekhā invites her husband to practice systematic meditation: through such *dhyāna*, coupled with *vicāra*, he will attain the highest goal. This attainment requires the grace of the great goddess Tripurā, the acme of pure, absolute consciousness, within whom Hemacūḍa is to take refuge.

Hemalekhā tells her husband that the karmic order is both created and maintained by Devī. If the compassionate goddess is pleased with one who has devoted himself to her, the process of *karman* can be abolished. One who surrenders the fruits of actions is said to easily realize the truth. In this case, the deity will not wait for that aspirant's karmic residues to be exhausted: the laws of *karman* are no longer operative in such an enlightened person.

With the help of Hemalekhā, Hemacūḍa begins the practice of meditation, experiencing inner joy. However, at this stage, he is not yet able to live in the two worlds, inner and outer, simultaneously. For his advancement, Hemalekhā asks him to retire in solitude and realize the *ātman* which he is, through a process of elimination of what he is not. The prince retires to his royal garden dedicating himself to *dhyāna.* Asking the fundamental question "Who am I?" (*ko'ham*) he realizes that he cannot be his body, his *prāṇa*, his senses, his mind, or even his intellect. Controlling all his thought constructions, he attains a state of emptiness and is suddenly plunged into darkness. Transcending even that darkness, he experiences a flash of light. After slipping into deep sleep, the dream state, and returning to consciousness, he thinks that the experiences of darkness and light might have been the phases of a dream. Thus, he tries once more to control his mind one-pointedly. This time he crosses the stupified state and finds himself absorbed into a blissful state of awareness he had never experienced before.

Hemalekhā explains that the Self is not to be confused with something to be attained, since "It" *is* always: only the knowledge of the Self can be attained, not the Self. This is similar to something hidden by the dark: when darkness is removed by the light of a lamp, the object is revealed. Turning on the light does not mean creating the object. This is the case with the Self as well. By concentrating on the *ātman*, one is brought to "remember" the *ātman*, his true identity, removing ignorance, which is a kind of forgetfulness. Unfamiliar images appearing in the mind after having removed some thought constructions, must not be identified with the *ātman*. Hemalekhā explains that an aspirant must gain some idea of the *ātman* from the scriptures and from those sages who have realized it, so as not to mistake the projections of his mind for the true Self. Such indirect knowledge will help to attain direct experience later on.

The prince undertakes an intense *sādhana* for several months, finally establishing himself in a blissful state. As the princess approaches, Hemacūḍa opens his eyes, and Hemalekhā asks him to please share his experiences with her. Hemacūḍa begs Hemalekhā not to bother him and wonders how she, though having realized that highest state, is still entangled in the world. Hemalekhā then reveals to her husband that he has not yet experienced the *ātman*: experience of the Self can never be affected by the opening or closing of one's eyes. The *ātman* is independent and free of all conditions. Unless this knot of delusion is loosened, realization will never be attained. Millions of these knots of delusion exist. One must untie these knots, transcend all dualities, and let the awareness of the *ātman* permeate one's waking, dreaming, and deep sleep states. There must not be a wall between any of the aspects of life. Hemalekhā advises Hemacūḍa to probe further in his contemplation, practicing more and more. He continues his *sādhana* and gradually attains maturity in his realization, becoming firm in that *ātman* awareness. From then onward, he lives as a great *jīvanmukta* while at the same time enjoying worldly objects, ruling his subjects, amassing wealth, and administering the kingdom. Therefore—concluded Dattātreya—the company of sages is the first step and the guiding force throughout one's *sādhana*.

On a subsequent occasion, Paraśurāma tells Dattātreya that he cannot understand how this universe can be a mere appearance: his own experience tells him the contrary. The Guru pinpoints how the cause of this misunderstanding lies in *avidyā*: through one's identification with the body, materiality is perceived as the only reality. As a person believes the world to be, so it appears to him. In fact, this whole universe depends on supreme consciousness just as an unstable reflection seen in a stable mirror. Yogins, through the practice of concentration and meditation, see the truth and experience unity with the divine. After this premise, Dattātreya narrates the story of the universe within the mountain.

Long ago in the holy city of Sundara in Bengal there lived a king, Suṣeṇa by name, who decided to perform the ritual of *aśva-medha* in Śiva's homage. According to tradition, a horse was allowed to roam freely, yet closely guarded by the king's princes and soldiers. If the horse entered a neighboring king's territory, that ruler would have to either pay a tribute or try to capture the horse. The king's army, however, easily conquered all the challengers, until it reached the banks of the Airāvatī river where it found the sage Taṅgaṇa, famous for his great austerities. The arrogant soldiers, filled with pride, passed by without duly honoring him. The sage was not disturbed by their irreverent behavior, but his son became furious and, through his supernatural powers, conquered the entire army. The few warriors who managed to escape were astonished to see that young man lead his captives and the horse directly into a hillside, walking through the solid rock as if it were air.[26] The distraught king, having learned what had happened, sent his brother Mahāsena to appease the sage, who then ordered his son to release the captives. Mahāsena, after witnessing the phenomenon of the horse and princes coming out of the rock, humbly asked Taṅgaṇa how this was done. The sage answered that since his son wished to become king, he had instructed him in some special techniques to attain the highest powers: through his *saṅkalpa-śakti* he had created a universe inside a hill, where he ruled a continent surrounded by an ocean.[27] Mahāsena asked if he could visit that universe. At this request the sage instructed his son to show him everything and then plunged back into *samādhi*.

The young ascetic took Mahāsena to the hill and easily entered it, but the prince, unable to follow him, cried out for help. Taṅgaṇa's son instructed him to leave his physical body in a hole and cover it with leaves, and to enter the hill with his subtle body. Unable to do this by himself, the young ascetic entered Mahāsena's body, "pulling" the subtle body out of his physical body and leaving the latter in a pit.[28] He then entered the solid rock with his guest. Shocked by this separation from his physical body, Mahāsena's subtle body lost consciousness. The young sage then "united" Mahāsena's subtle body to a gross body that he instantly materialized in the hill world. Regaining consciousness, Mahāsena realized that the sage was transporting him across a vast abyss. Above, below, and all around, he saw infinite space. He saw remote planets, the sun, moon, and the entire world as if reflected in the sky. Finally, they landed on the golden Meru and began their journey across the seven circular continents and their oceans. Here, amidst all the gods and creatures, Mahāsena saw the young ascetic as Brahmā, Viṣṇu, and Śiva and also as ruling over the earth as a universal monarch. At last, the sage said it was time for them to return to the outside world.[29] They both stepped out of the hill. Taṅgaṇa's son made Mahāsena's subtle body unconscious, drew it out of the gross body he had materialized for him, and "united" it once again with his original body. Returning to his normal state, Mahāsena looked at the world around him and was greatly surprised to see it appear entirely different. The young sage told him that it was the same country he had lived in before, but 1,200 million years had passed, though they had spent only one day in the world inside the hill. Customs, languages, and land formations had gone through tremendous changes. Taṅgaṇa was still in *samādhi*, though several thousands of generations had passed. Where Mahāsena's capital city had been, there was now a forest full of wild animals.[30]

On hearing this Mahāsena was plunged in despair, grieving for the loss of his brother, wife, sons, friends, etc. The sage told him to have patience and exercise his power of discrimination in order to overcome his identification with the body and discover the Self. Mahāsena, declaring himself to be his disciple, asked his help to overcome grief. The sage noted that people deluded by ignorance do not realize their true nature and grieve uselessly. Only after realizing the *ātman* a person overcomes sorrow, just as a dreamer overcomes his dream identity and concerns upon awakening.

Mahāsena objected that the comparison of the waking state with the dream state did not seem appropriate: objects created in a dream or through magic are illusory and do not serve any purpose. But the objects of the waking state are real and useful. Taṅgaṇa's son explained that the objects of the waking and dreaming states are all alike, constantly changing. The "reality" of the external world is maintained by one's thoughts. If one thinks it is unreal, then the universe becomes unreal. The waking and dreaming states are like two different kinds of dream, since our world is also the result of Tripurā's creative imagination. Therefore, pure consciousness is like the canvas on which this picturelike universe is painted.

Thanks to the sage's words, Mahāsena was freed from grief. The young ascetic taught that willful *saṅkalpa* is of two kinds: perfect and imperfect. *Saṅkalpa* untouched by doubt, holding one thought and that only in mind, is said to be perfect. Thus, this external world is projected through the willful thinking of the Creator. Because of the Creator's affirmation, people believe it to be real. Imperfect *saṅkalpa* is due to one's doubt; in such case one's volitions are not taken seriously or even perceived by others. Therefore, all aims projected by a doubtful or wavering mind cannot be materialized. A perfect *saṅkalpa*, said the sage, can be attained through various means, such as birth, gems, herbs, Yoga, austerities, *mantras*, and grace.[31] When one is exercising his power of volition, he should become so absorbed that he should not be aware of the fact that he is doing it. He should maintain this nondual state until the intended result appears. The power of volition of one's ātmic consciousness is veiled by ignorance. When that veil is lifted, one realizes the perfection of *saṅkalpa*.

Taṅgaṇa's son then taught how it is always the divine *saṅkalpa* which is responsible for the appearances of proximity and distance in space, as well as for the perception of shorter and longer time spans. Everything is to be understood as the free play or *līlā* of Tripurā, as everything is grounded in that reflecting mirror constituted by pure consciousness: if one understands this he is liberated. The sage presented the unfolding of the act of manifestation from the one pure consciousness by listing the thirty-six "principles of reality" (*tattvas*) taken from Kashmiri *Śaivism* albeit with some modifications. These comprise the twenty-five Sāṃkhya *tattvas*, five "pure" principles (*śiva, śakti, sadā-śiva, īśvara, śuddha-vidyā*), five "impure" principles enveloping the Self (*kalā, aśuddha-vidyā, rāga, kāla, niyati*), and the *citta* (viewed in isolation, i.e. not subsumed under the Sāṃkhyan triad of *buddhi, ahaṃkāra* and *manas*). Having received this *upadeśa*, Mahāsena was entirely freed from error, cutting his identification with the body and abiding in pure consciousness.

All in all, the sage's teaching seems to come closer to Abhinavagupta's *ābhāsa-vāda* ("appearance doctrine"), representing the most "orthodox" *Śākta* position, rather than to Śaṅkara's *kevalādvaita-vāda*. If the world is to be regarded as the manifestation or unfolding of pure consciousness it cannot be viewed as thoroughly unreal or nonexistent. In fact, it is to be revered as the veritable wondrous body of the supreme goddess.

The third story is prompted by Paraśurāma's questions: If the *ātman* is unknowable, then how can one realize it? If the highest goal is the realization of *ātman*, then what is it like? And after realizing this truth, how should one behave and live? Moreover, why does one perceive so many differences in the practices and behavior of those who are said to possess liberating knowledge? Dattātreya then narrates the following tale.

The learned and pious Janaka, King of Videha, once held a great sacrifice in homage to the goddess in the presence of innumerable great Brahmins and leading scholars.

At the same time, the god Varuṇa had begun a sacrifice in his kingdom below the sea. He had invited all priests and Brahmins but only a few had come since most of them had gone to Janaka's sacrifice. Then one of Varuṇa's sons, wanting to bring the Brahmins who had assembled in Videha to his father, dressed himself as a Brahmin and came to Janaka's residence. He was a very astute fellow, and immediately started insulting all the Brahmins that had convened there, saying that he could not identify even one wise person among them. All the Brahmins, greatly insulted, challenged him to a public debate. The son of Varuṇa accepted and the Brahmins all agreed to his proposal that whoever lost the contest would be drowned in the sea. Through the use of cavils *(vitaṇḍā)* and destructive dialectics (*jalpa*),

Varuṇa's son was able to win against thousands of Brahmins who, once drowned, were taken to the site of Varuṇa's sacrifice where they were received with full honors.

But when the son of the Brahmin Kahola, Aṣṭāvakra, learned that his father had been drowned he went to Videha. He was also skilled in the art of argumentation and captious criticism and succeeded in defeating Varuṇa's son, ordering that he be drowned. Then the son of Varuṇa manifested his true identity and had all the Brahmins who had been drowned come back to Videha safe and sound. Having freed all these great sages, Aṣṭāvakra's pride grew immensely; so much so that he started treating all of them with contempt.

At this time a woman ascetic appeared.[32] She was young and beautiful and wore an ochre robe. Fleeing from Aṣṭāvakra, the Brahmins took refuge in her. She asked Aṣṭāvakra to answer the following question, without having recourse to captious tricks: what is that condition which once known one attains perfect immortality, all doubts vanish, and nothing remains to be known or desired? Aṣṭāvakra was not able to give a convincing answer since he only knew the truth from book-knowledge and not from personal experience, as if contemplating all the reflections of the mirror of pure consciousness but not the mirror itself. Having been put to shame by the woman sage, he declared himself to be her disciple and asked her to answer that question.

She responded that nothing can be achieved through mere polemics. The supreme goddess is the foundation of all reality; without her nothing would be manifested. The secret of reality safeguarded in the scriptures is revealed only to sincere seekers through Tripurā's grace. One knowing that secret, however, must experience it in order to realize it: intellectual knowledge, though a necessary condition, is not a sufficient condition. To contemplate pure consciousness, a seeker must turn his mind inward, disciplining its roaming tendencies and cultivating desirelessness. This should be done naturally and not through will power. The female ascetic then took leave, advising Aṣṭāvakra to eventually clear his remaining doubts by asking King Janaka himself, the wisest among the wise.[33]

King Janaka told Aṣṭāvakra that consciousness or the highest reality is neither completely known nor entirely unknown. If it cannot be known, then how can a teacher explain it? All spiritual practices are for the purpose of mind purification. Consciousness—which is omnipresent—manifests itself only when the mind has withdrawn from all objects and has thus been purified. Aṣṭāvakra inquired why realization cannot be achieved in deep sleep, when the mind is naturally withdrawn from all objects. King Janaka answered that once the mind is covered with the coating of deep sleep, it spontaneously abandons the reflection of all objects. In deep sleep, however, the mind is "dissolved" and can reflect only its own slumber. Utilizing two fundamental categories of Kashmiri *Śaivism*, Janaka explained the twofold condition of the mind: "pure light" (*prakāśa*) or the state devoid of mental constructions, and "reflection" (*vimarśa*) or the state characterized by mental fabrication. The state of "pure light" is said to manifest itself at the time of meditative concentration (*samādhi*), in deep sleep, and in the very instant of perception prior to its mental elaboration. Ordinary people, though constantly experiencing pure instants of perception during their lives, are unaware of them. The state of deep sleep represents the "undifferentiated": this was the first entity to arise in the process of manifestation and coincides with pure non-being or darkness. In *samādhi*, on the other hand, it is pure consciousness which manifests itself: this is the goddess Tripurā, whose nature is pure being. This is the reason why, concluded Janaka, deep sleep is not in itself sufficient to attain realization.

Aṣṭāvakra further inquired as to when these instants of perception devoid of *vimarśa* or mental constructions occur in ordinary experience. Janaka gave various examples, such as when a man makes love to his lover for the first time or when a sudden emotion such as joy or fear overcomes one. He also mentioned those intermediate moments occurring between the wake, dream, and dreamless states. Heretics and dialecticians teach that the Self does not exist and that it can be divided up into a succession of instants. But Janaka argued to the contrary: the "pure light" of the Self devoid of mental constructions exists precisely within such instantaneous flux, between one instant and the following one, though it is usually not perceived. Even between two thoughts there is an instant of pure objectlessness which disappears the next moment, when the mind contacts another object.[34] A mundane person is not conscious of such nondual states, but a Yogin learns how to stop his mind before it reaches the next object, extending the nondual awareness.

Next, Aṣṭāvakra asked why, if such instants of perception manifesting pure consciousness concern everybody in ordinary experience, people continue living their illusory lives in the world. King Janaka replied that *avidyā* is the cause of bondage and its removal is the true cause of *mokṣa*. Knowledge of the *ātman* is twofold: direct and indirect. Indirect knowledge is received through a Guru or the scriptures and is grasped by a purified intellect. Indirect knowledge is indispensable to progress along the path and predisposes one to gain direct, liberating knowledge later. In fact, direct knowledge alone is capable of dispelling the darkness of ignorance and of granting *mokṣa*. The "description" of reality received from a teacher bears a pedagogical value: an ordinary person lacking such preparatory intellectual understanding has no opportunity to attain self-realization, even if he or she were to experience a spontaneous kind of *samādhi*. Those who are intellectually aware of the nature of *samādhi* but do not practice inward contemplation or are incapable of focussing their attention, do not benefit from it in the least. If a flash of the *ātman* is better than no flash at all, it is nonetheless useless for gaining freedom from *avidyā*. After the king concluded his discussion, Aṣṭāvakra attained the condition of a *jīvanmukta*.

It should be noted that Janaka, an alterego of Dattātreya, in narrating how he himself attained enlightenment (17.79–81) presents an antinomian picture: while embracing a woman and drinking inebriating beverages he listens to the celestial voices of Siddhas who proclaim the principle of nonduality. On the other hand, perhaps in an effort to seek approval, Janaka's *upadeśa* insists on the three stages of orthodox Advaita Vedānta instruction, namely *śravaṇa* (listening to the teaching), *manana* (deeply pondering over it), and *nididhyāsana* (practicing meditation).

In chapter 18 Dattātreya further teaches to Paraśurāma how the realization of the Self is not the result of an activity but simply the disclosure of what alone *is* through the removal of all mental constructions: this is the effulgence of consciousness in its immaculate form. Everything is pervaded (*vyāpti*) or immersed in the light of pure consciousness, manifesting itself in limited and multiple objects through the power of its freedom. Nothing can exist or be produced independently from it. Even the mind is nothing but the "product" of the illusory, dynamic play of consciousness. Therefore, there are actually no bounds from which to free oneself: one simply needs to recognize the only reality of pure consciousness, without a second. Ignorance (*avidyā*) is to be understood as an epistemological error or distortion. Dattātreya closes the discussion distinguishing three types of enlightened beings (excellent, medium, low). In answering a previous question of Paraśurāma (15.9–19), he notes that their different behavior in the world is due to the specific past actions (*prārabdha-karman*) of each individual.

In chapter 19 Dattātreya explains how pure consciousness is like a gem treasured in the immaculate casket of the mind. Unfortunately, it cannot be seen since the casket is plunged into the mud of infinite mental blemishes. To remove all taints and see the gem of pure consciousness one must cultivate a spiritual discipline and discriminative knowledge. Impurities, though innumerable, fall into three categories. They may be born out of transgressions (*aparādha-vāsanās*), bad actions performed in the past (*karma-vāsanās*), and all the infinite range of a person's desires (*kāma-vāsanās*). The worst transgression which leads a person to disaster is lack of faith. Linked to it is the ruinous transgression of doubt. *Karma-vāsanās* can be eliminated only through divine grace and *kāma-vāsanās* through detachment (*vairāgya*). But the principal instrument for attaining enlightenment is the very desire for liberation (*mumukṣā*) which must be as strong as possible and accompanied by dispassion toward all worldly objects.

Describing the different characteristics of those who have attained liberating knowledge—which depend upon individual qualities—Dattātreya refers to himself and his brothers Durvāsas and Candramas (19.74–75). He notes how Durvāsas is prone to wrath and Candramas to sensual pleasures, while he is the emblem of dispassion having detached himself from social obligations and all possessions. Despite these differences they are all perfectly enlightened just as Brahmā, Viṣṇu, and Śiva.

Dattātreya lists three types of Jñānins: the lowest level have glimpsed the ultimate truth, but they are not established in it. The second type, through long and arduous discipline, have control over their minds, to the point that their *vāsanās* have been eradicated and their minds purified. They maintain their physical existence to discharge accumulated *karman*, which now exhausts itself naturally. Their stability in the *ātman* still requires practice and a conscious effort. The highest Jñānins are those who remain completely unaffected by external objects, without any effort. These have attained such a degree of mastery over their minds that they may be fully focused on several objects at the same time. Dattātreya gives the example of the Haihaya king Arjuna Kārtavīrya, whom he had gifted with one thousand arms and who was defeated in battle by Paraśurāma. Arjuna could simultaneously handle all sorts of weapons through each of his thousand arms, masterly coordinating all his actions (19.100–101). Though to an average person these Jñānins might seem scatterbrained, their daily activities flow naturally and spontaneously. They experience pleasure and pain, are aware of good and evil, but are above all dualities. Wholly disengaged from worldly processes, they act out their roles till the end. These Jñānins remain absorbed in pure consciousness as they walk, eat or work, seeing no difference between *samādhi* and daily activities.

In the twentieth *adhyāya*, Dattātreya tells the story in which Tripurā explains the nature of pure consciousness and of how to attain it. At the court of the god Brahmā, in the *satya-loka*,[35] a debate was held on what constitutes true knowledge. The Ṛṣis who were assembled there—Atri among them—embarked upon the exegesis of a Vedic passage, each of them producing arguments in favor of his own interpretation. They were unable to agree on the royal path leading to perfect knowledge. Some recommended the path of austerities, others the path of intellectual debate, others the path of devotion, and still others the practice of rituals. Finally, they all came to Brahmā, asking him to eliminate their confusion. But Brahmā, knowing that these arrogant sages did not really trust him, replied that he himself did not know the answer, and he suggested they go ask the omniscient Śiva. They found Śiva in the company of Viṣṇu. Brahmā himself posed the question. Śiva realized the Ṛṣis' lack of faith and, declaring that he had no clear answer on the subject, suggested they all meditate on the goddess of knowledge.

Brahmā, Viṣṇu, Śiva, and all the sages began meditating on Tripurā. The goddess graciously abandoned her transcendent form and became word: from the skies above she spoke to them, declaring that all who worship her are never frustrated in their search for truth. The gods and seers then addressed various hymns of praise to Tripurā. They asked Devī to tell them of her transcendent and immanent form, to describe her majesty, the knowledge one may attain of her, the fruit of such knowledge, and the best means of realizing it. They also asked her who the true *sādhaka* is, what the highest of all realizations is, and who the best of all Siddhas is.

The compassionate Tripurā answered all questions, saying that this very universe is a manifestation of herself as pure consciousness. She is the omnipresent one: the universe is her body and she is the indweller in all. Without her, nothing could ever exist. Beyond the multiple universes, in the center of the ocean of nectar, is the Island of Jewels. Here, under the shade of the *kadamba* trees,[36] is a temple composed of jewels that grant all desires. Inside, on a throne the four angles of which are formed by Brahmā, Śiva, Viṣṇu, and Īśvara, and the top of which is formed by Sadāśiva, is the icon of Tripurasundarī. The omnipotent Śakti in her immanent form is engaged in an eternal embrace with her Beloved.[37] All other deities are none other than her secondary manifestations. Blinded by *māyā*, humans do not recognize Tripurā. She is the support of all things and at the same time absolutely removed (*kevala*) from all things. The "drama" of losing herself in the world and rediscovering herself in her pure transcendence is part of the ongoing play.

The knowledge one may have of Tripurā is multiple: dual or nondual, superior or inferior. Dualistic knowledge is similar to a dream state; only nondual knowledge is true wisdom. Still, the realization of Advaita cannot dawn if one has not practiced the worship of the goddess, obtaining her grace. Once this knowledge is attained, all doubts and fears disappear, all desires vanish. The fruit of Devī's knowledge is the cessation of sorrow and pain. Distinction among the knower, the known, and the act of knowing fades away. The qualification to achieve deliverance is the cultivation of a burning desire to reach it. One endowed with such a passion for *mokṣa* is already virtually free; it is only a question of "time" within the field of his karmic trajectory.

The three major obstacles to liberation are lack of faith, desire, and lethargy. Lack of faith expresses itself as doubts and erroneous thinking. Cultivating opposite thoughts through scriptural authority and sound logic can neutralize them.[38] Desires breed traces (*vāsanās*), and these in turn breed new desires in an ongoing spiral. The *vāsanās*, staining the mind, prevent understanding: a training in detachment reveals the flaws inherent in limited objects. Lethargy, the third major obstacle, is the product of *tamas*. The only cure for this affliction is dedicated worship of the goddess: she frees her devotees from their mental and spiritual dullness in proportion to the intensity of their *bhakti*. Renouncing one's identification with the body is, in and of itself, the mark of realization. *Siddhis*, powers which the adept or Siddha may attain along the path, are of minimum importance and often hinder realization. One is recommended not to lose time in the search of magic powers.[39]

Finally, three levels of realization may be distinguished: superior, medium, and inferior. Tripurā employs the analogy of Vedic recitation: when a well-trained Brahmin easily recites a text without mispronouncing a single syllable although engaged in other occupations, this is said to be the superior kind of recitation. The medium level is when a Brahmin correctly recites a text while engaged in other occupations, although subjecting himself to a constant effort of attention. The inferior kind is the correct recitation which demands such a concentrated effort that all other occupations are excluded. The same can be said for the three levels of realization: at the highest, one's enlightenment experience is compatible with the most intense engagement in social life. At an intermediate level, realization is still compatible with social life, though requiring a degree of effort in one's attention. At the inferior level, one's intuition of the *ātman* requires constant concentration, at the expense of all other occupations. He who has achieved the supreme nondual condition constantly abides in it, in sleep as well as when engaged in deep thought or social life. Such an enlightened one is the best of Siddhas. All distinctions between such a person and the goddess are obliterated; one realizes that there never was a time in which they were separated.

Having answered all the seers' questions, Tripurā became silent. The seers, satisfied and freed of all doubts, returned to their abodes. Dattātreya ended his narration by assuring Paraśurāma that, through constant meditation on these sacred words of the goddess, he would attain the key to the unveiling of *ātman*.

The fifth and last story is that of the Brahmin demon (*brahma-rākṣasa*). Ratnāṅgada, a king of the Parvatas, lived in the city of Amṛtā, along the Vipāśā river.[40] He had two brave and intelligent sons: Rukmāṅgada and Hemāṅgada. The first was well versed in scriptures, the second was already considered a sage. During a hunting expedition, they found themselves in a thick forest. After having killed various animals, they halted near a pond. Here, in a banyan tree, they found a *brahma-rākṣasa* who had great knowledge of sacred texts. He had philosophical debates with learned men who occasionally passed by, and, after defeating them, devoured them. Rukmāṅgada decided to challenge the *brahma-rākṣasa*: unfortunately, he was soon defeated and captured by the demon. Hemāṅgada intervened, begging him not to devour his brother and to let him go free. The demon agreed on condition that Hemāṅgada solve the questions he put to him. If Hemāṅgada failed to answer even one of these, he would be devoured. Hemāṅgada accepted the challenge and succeeded in answering all questions. The dialogue between Hemāṅgada and the Brahmin demon is the substance of the story, repeating all the main points concerning the nature and realization of pure consciousness which have already been presented above. Due to his brother's success, Rukmāṅgada was freed and the *brahma-rākṣasa* was instantly restored to his original human condition as the Brahmin Vasumān. He had been cursed to become a demon by Kāśyapa, a disciple of the sage Aṣṭaka,[41] whom Vasumān had defeated on the subject of the *ātman* by using malicious arguments and sophistry. After narrating this last tale, Dattātreya gave Paraśurāma a final review of all the teachings and the proper means of attaining *mokṣa*. The *jñāna-khaṇḍa*, as the *māhātmya-khaṇḍa*, ends with the sacred invocation of Tripurā's *bīja-mantra hrīṃ*.

In conclusion: Dattātreya's role as authoritative expounder of *Śākta* nondualism in south India—so nicely conveyed in these stories of the *Tripurā-rahasya*—shows the deity's assimilative force across *sampradāyas* and canons. Dattātreya is himself a *saṅgama*, the privileged confluence of different streams of Indian religious and philosophical traditions. From the public *bhakti*-centered religion of the Vārkarīs up to the more private *mantra*-based ritualism of southern

Śāktism, Dattātreya's icon exhibits the capacity of absorbing new traits, of transforming and renovating itself. Understanding Datta as the supreme Guru, Yogin, and Avatāra constantly present across the subcontinent is not simply a potent religious metaphor. It is a fact, concretely mirrored in his appropriation by different religious movements all over India and even beyond its borders: in Nepal as well as in Tamilnadu, in Gujarat and Maharashtra as well as in Kerala and Andhra Pradesh. Following Dattātreya's triumphant *vijaya* across the subcontinent, one is brought to appreciate the deity's ubiquitous presence and integrative nature, indeed his distinctive mark across the centuries.

Notes

1. The expression "the goddess," used in previous chapters to translate Devī, can be misleading. In English when we speak of God, we omit the article. If we want to make the same statement about ultimate reality as feminine, it sounds odd to say, "praise be to Goddess." Language requires us to say "praise be to the Goddess," or "to a Goddess." On *Śākta* theological grounds, however, Tripurā is not one goddess among many but Goddess Supreme. For a survey of Śāktism and its textual tradition, see Gopīnāth Kavirāj's chapter "Śākta Philosophy," in his *Aspects of Indian Thought*, 175–215.

On the *Tripurā-rahasya*, see Goudriaan and Gupta, *Hindu Tantric and Śākta Literature*, 166ff. For an introduction to the study of the *Tripurā-rahasya*, see Kavirāj, "The Philosophy of Tripurā Tantra," in *Aspects of Indian Thought*, 216–28. Only a few excerpts from the *māhātmya-khaṇḍa* have ever been translated into Western languages. For the Sanskrit text, accompanied by a Hindī introduction and commentary, see Mukund Lāl Śāstrī, *The Tripurārahasya (Māhātmyakhaṇḍa)*. For an Italian translation of a selection of *stotras* of the *māhātmya-khaṇḍa*, see Schwarz, "La Grande Dea nell'Innologia del Māhātmyakhaṇḍa del Tripurārahasya." There have been various editions and translations of the *jñāna-khaṇḍa*. Often quoted is an edition published in Belgaum (Mysore) in 1894. Gopīnāth Kavirāj and Nārāyaṇ Śāstrī Khiste have furnished a critical edition, published in Benares between 1925 and 1928. An edition by Kavirāj was published in Benares in 1965 by the Varanaseya Sanskrit Vishvavidyalaya, bound with a commentary to the text known as *Tātparya-dīpikā* completed in 1831 by Śrīnivāsa. Swāmī Sanātanadevaji Mahārāja has also contributed another edition of the *jñāna-khaṇḍa* together with the *Jñāna-prabhā* Hindī commentary. This was published in Benares in 1967. The first English translation of the *jñāna-khaṇḍa* was offered by Swami Sri Ramanananda Saraswathi (Sri Munagala S. Venkataramaiah) in the pages of the *Bangalore Mythic Society's Journal* (January 1938—April 1940) and was later published in a volume by the Sri Ramanasramam of Tiruvaṇṇāmalai, with the title *Tripurā Rahasya; or, The Mystery Beyond the Trinity*. An English translation by A. U.

Vasavada, published in Benares in 1965 by the Chowkhambha Sanskrit Series Office, is based on a Marāṭhī translation from the original Sanskrit by B. B. Joshi. Mention must also be made of the French translation by Michel Hulin, published in Paris in 1979 by Fayard, with the title *La doctrine secrète de la Déesse Tripurā (Section de la connaissance)*. Finally, an excellent Italian translation, with introduction and notes, has been written by Alberto Pelissero. Published in Turin in 1995 by Ananke, its title is *Il segreto della Dea Tripurā.*

2. Lalitā means "graceful," "lovely." For a fine treatment on the great goddess and the *Śrī-vidyā Śākta* tradition in south India, see the work of Brooks, *Auspicious Wisdom.*

3. See Hulin, *La doctrine secrète,* 13.

4. Brooks, *Auspicious Wisdom,* 57.

Born in the town of Bhāgā in Maharashtra, Bhāskararāya Bhārati was initiated by his father, Gambhīrarāya, to the cult of Sarasvatī, receiving his *upanayana* in Benares, where he completed his studies. Initiated into Tripurā's cult by his teacher Nṛsiṃhānandanāth, he was given the name Bhāsurānandanāth. After traveling extensively, Bhāskararāya returned to south India settling in Tamilnadu, Thañjavūr district, around 1841. He died in Madhyārjunakṣetra, the modern Tiruvidyai Marudur. Among his important works are the *Setu-bandha,* including a commentary on the *Yoginī-hṛdaya,* the independent treatise *Varivasyā-rahasya,* and commentaries on the *Lalitā-sahasra-nāma* and the *Bhāvana* and *Tripurā Upaniṣads.* Though a follower of Advaita Vedānta, he expoused a kind of synthetic doctrine. His advocacy of the most controversial Tantric practices and his encyclopedic knowledge of the *Śrī-vidyā* canon make Bhāskararāya one of the greatest exponents of southern Śāktism.

Besides Ramaṇa Maharṣi, another important figure who contributed to popularize the *Tripurā-rahasya* in northern India was the Svāmin Karpātrī (1907–82), a Brahmin-born leader of the Śaṅkarācārya order of Daṇḍins; see Ramasso, "Il Tripurā Rahasya nell'ottica dottrinale e ideologica di Svāmī Karpātrī."

5. Lakṣmaṇ Rāṇaḍe, author of a commentary on the *Paraśurāma-kalpa-sūtra* known as *Sūtra-tattva-vimarśinī* (1888), identifies Hāritāyana's synthesis of the dialogue between Dattātreya and Paraśurāma not with the *Tripurā-rahasya* but with the *Paraśurāma-kalpa-sūtra.* This is improbable, since the *Paraśurāma-kalpa-sūtra* is not a dialogue between Dattātreya and Paraśurāma. On the *Paraśurāma-kalpa-sūtra,* see A. M. Sastri and S. Y. Dave, *Paraśurāmakalpasūtra with the Commentary by Rāmeśvara Sūri Entitled Saubhāgyodaya.*

6. Literally "the knowledge of [the goddess] Śrī," or "auspicious wisdom."

7. Literally "rolling up," "destruction." Śaṅkara mentions one Saṃvarta in his commentary on *Brahma-sūtra* 3.4.37. Our text honors him as an Avadhūta, recalling the antinomian behavior of Pāśupatas, especially in their *avyakta* stage of spiritual development. On the Pāśupatas, see Lorenzen, *The Kāpālikas and Kālāmukhas.*

8. Agastya, a famous Ṛṣi, is the author of several Vedic hymns (*Ṛg Veda* 1.166–191). As Vasiṣṭha, Agastya is said to have been the son of both Mitra and Varuṇa from Urvaśī: their seed "fell" at the sight of the beautiful goddess of dawn, impregnating her.

Lopāmudrā is a girl the Ṛṣi Agastya formed from the most graceful parts of different animals. Chapter 53 of the *māhātmya-khaṇḍa* celebrates Lopāmudrā, endowed by Tripurā with the knowledge known as *Traipurī-vidyā.*

9. The *Devī-māhātmya* has inspired the *Tripurā-rahasya*'s *māhātmya-khaṇḍa* particularly in its narration of the cosmic struggle between the goddess and the demon Mahiṣa. On the *Devī-māhātmya,* see Coburn, *Encountering the Goddess: A Translation of the Devī-Māhātmya and a Study of Its Interpretation.*

The *Lalitā-māhātmya* is probably an independent work added to the *Brahmāṇḍa Purāṇa* by *Śākta* devotees, eager to place it within the corpus of an authoritative collection.

10. On the genesis of the *Śrī-vidyā* textual tradition, see Brooks, *Auspicious Wisdom,* 29ff.

11. See ibid., 44–50. Brooks discusses the importance of two works attributed to Śaṅkara's teacher's teacher Gauḍapāda: the *Śrī-vidyā-ratna-sūtra* and the *Subhagodaya,* prominent in the contemporary self-understanding of *Śrī-vidyā.*

12. Mention must be made of the *Lalitā-sahasra-nāma,* a hymn of the thousand names of the goddess Lalitā, divided into three chapters comprising 320 *ślokas.* Another text reporting a list of the thousand names of the goddess is the *Devī-nāma-vilāsa* (1666) of the Kashmiri Sahib Kaula. Hymns of the thousand names of the goddess are recurrent within Purāṇic, Āgamic, and Tantric literature and largely employed in *Śākta* worship.

13. Brooks, *Auspicious Wisdom,* 48.

14. See Brooks, *The Secret of the Three Cities,* 170.

15. For an English rendering of this seventh century work, see Natarajan, *Tirumular Tirumantiram Holy Hymns.* On Tamiḷ Siddhas, see Zvelebil, *The Poets of the Powers.* See also Ganapathy, *The Philosophy of the Tamil Siddhas.*

16. On the *Śrī-vidyā* and *Śrī-cakra,* see Brooks, *Auspicious Wisdom,* 81–146.

17. Ibid., 91.

18. Kramrisch, *The Hindu Temple,* 1:11. On *yantras,* see Khanna, *Yantra: The Tantric Symbol of Cosmic Unity.*

19. Rare instances of *Śrī-yantras* with both *mantra* and divine figures attached to them are found in Rawson, *The Art of Tantra,* figs. 50 and 65.

20. Chapters 1 and 2 of the *māhātmya-khaṇḍa* present the "author" of the work, the seer Sumedha Hāritāyana. Chapter 3 introduces Paraśurāma, and chapter 4 his meeting with sage Saṃvarta. Chapters 5 and 6 present the Guru

Dattātreya. Chapters 7 to 9 narrate the story of Tripurā Ambikā, mother of the worlds and supreme goddess. Chapters 10 to 46 follow the presentation of the principal forms or Śaktis of Tripurā and their deeds. Chapters 47 to 78 present the narration of the *Lalitā-māhātmya*. In chapters 79 and 80, Dattātreya answers Paraśurāma, clearing his doubts.

21. There had already been a meeting between Paraśurāma and Dattātreya, during Jamadagni's funeral rites. Reṇukā had advised Paraśurāma to seek Dattātreya's help if he should ever be in difficulty.

22. Literally "intoxicating with fragrance." Situated to the south of the Kailāsa, it is said to be one of the four mountains enclosing the world's central region.

23. A well-known image, symbolizing the condition of freedom and safety attained by the soul. Compare with *Bhāgavata Purāṇa* 11.7.29, praising the Avadhūta identified as Dattātreya: "In the midst of people who are burnt by the wild fire of desire and greed, you remain like an elephant, standing in the cool waters of the holy river Gaṅgā, without being scorched by fire."

24. Aṣṭāvakra was a Muni renown for his asceticism. At birth, due to the curse of his father Kahoḍa, eight limbs of his body were deformed. The sage is linked to the *Aṣṭāvakra-gītā*, an important nondual text in twenty *adhyāyas*.
Janaka, "progenitor," "father," is the name of various kings. The one here referred to is the king of Videha, father of Sītā, renown for his knowledge and sanctity.

25. Daśārṇa is the name of a people from central India, already mentioned in the *Mahābhārata*. The capital of the Daśārṇas seems to have been Mṛttikāvatī near Gwalior.

26. This *siddhi* is known as *prākāmya*: the irresistible will by which one can pass through solid earth or cannot be soaked in water; see Vyāsa's commentary to Patañjali's *Yoga-sūtra* 3.45.

27. This continent reflects the classic cosmology of insular continents. Our text as well as all Purāṇic accounts narrate of seven *dvīpas* stretching out from the *axis mundi* of mount Meru.

28. The separation or "pulling out" of one's subtle body from the gross, physical body—a process occuring naturally at death—is a shamanic feat attested to within Yogic literature. For a Nātha episode, see Eliade, *Yoga: Immortality and Freedom*, 316–17. On the art of entering another's body, see ibid., 393–94.

29. The idea that the earth, a cavern, a tree, or a mountain may contain mysterious realms is a recurrent theme within Indian mythology. According to a Yogic understanding of human physiology, every *cakra*, especially that of the heart, is believed to be the seat of latent energy: the Yogin's entry into the

"cavern" of his heart symbolizes the unearthing of his nature, disclosing a new world. In the story, however, Taṅgaṇa's son materializes a world through his *saṅkalpa-śakti*. The power to create, rearrange, or even destroy the material elements (*bhūta*) through one's *saṅkalpa* is known as *īśitṛtva*; see Vyāsa's commentary to Patañjali's *Yoga-sūtra* 3.45. The claim is that each *jīvātman* can create or dismantle whatever world it wishes. A significant parallel to such narrative is found in the *Yoga-vāsiṣṭha* (6.2.56–94), a work dated between the sixth and twelfth centuries. On this episode, see O'Flaherty, *Dreams, Illusion and Other Realities*, 234–45, 293–96. On the *Yoga-vāsiṣṭha*, see Venkatesananda, *The Concise Yoga Vāsiṣṭha*.

30. To a spatial displacement, consequence of Mahāsena's access into a different world, a temporal displacement follows, inevitable consequence of Mahāsena's reentrance into his world. This relativity of time and space is intended to show how all the worlds are but the creation of one's imagination.

31. A list of powerful objects and forces often reported in Tantric and Yogic texts; see *Yoga-sūtra* 4.1.

32. The presence of a female ascetic ridiculing Aṣṭāvakra's wriggling argumentation is not surprising in a *Śākta* text. Although rare, the presence of women sages is attested to from the time of the *Upaniṣads*. The story of Gargī Vācaknavī, Yājñavalkya's questioner in a philosophical debate at Janaka's court, offers a case in point; see *Bṛhadāraṇyaka Upaniṣad* 3.8.1–12.

33. This fifteenth chapter of the *Tripurā-rahasya*'s *jñāna-khaṇḍa* appears to have the *Mahābhārata* as its source. The episode of Aṣṭāvakra is found in *Mahābhārata* 3.132–34, whereas that of the female ascetic finds a parallel in *Mahābhārata* 12.308 (here, however, it is Janaka and not Aṣṭāvakra who is instructed by the woman sage).

34. In the course of a conversation on how the pure "I" may be realized, Ramaṇa Maharṣi once observed:

> *Tripurā-rahasya* and other works point out that the interval between two consecutive *saṅkalpas* (ideas or thoughts) represents the pure *aham* ("I"). Therefore holding on to the pure "I" one should have the *prajñāna-ghana* for aim, and there is the *vṛtti* present in the attempt. (Ramana Maharshi, *Talks with Sri Ramana Maharshi*, 276)

35. Literally "world of truth." Also known as world of Brahmā, it is the highest of the seven upper worlds.

36. *Nauclea Cadamba*. These trees produce orange-colored blossoms.

37. The best representation of the oneness of the female and male principles is what is known as Śiva *ardha-nārī*, Śiva "half-female." Within a *Śākta* context, however, we would say Devī *ardha-nara*, goddess "half male."

38. On the practice of cultivating opposite thoughts, see *Yoga-sūtra* 2.33.

39. Tripurā's warning concerning *siddhis* constitutes a refrain throughout Yogic literature; see Vyāsa's commentary to *Yoga-sūtra* 3.37. For the presentation of a specific tradition of *Siddha-Yoga,* namely, the one of the ascetic Nityānanda (d. 1961) and of his disciple the Svāmin Muktānanda (1908–82), see Brooks et al., *Meditation Revolution: A History and Theology of the Siddha Yoga Lineage.* In particular, Muktānanda is said to have resided in a place in Vajreśvarī which had a small Dattātreya temple close to it. Nowadays, there is a large image of Dattātreya in the *āśrama* of Ganeshpuri.

40. The Vipāśā corresponds to the modern river Beas crossing the state of Himachal Pradesh.

41. Literally "consisting of eight parts." It may indicate one who is acquainted with the eight books of Pāṇini's grammar. Aṣṭaka is also the name of a son of Viśvāmitra, author of a Ṛg Vedic hymn (10.104).

8

The *Avadhūta-gītā*

As evidenced in the course of this study, the movement of the Nātha Yogins played a substantial role in the expansion of Dattātreya's cult. It was primarily through Nāthism that Datta was introduced to the Marāṭhī speaking area and was adopted by the Mahānubhāvas and a variety of other religious groups. In this chapter, I will analyze the content of the most important work of Nātha inspiration attributed to Dattātreya, the *Avadhūta-gītā* or "Song of the Free."[1] It was probably written between the fourteenth and eighteenth centuries[2] and Shankar Mokashi-Punekar, accepting the hypothesis of the text's western Nātha origin,[3] has suggested the Sahyādri region as its place of composition. The *Avadhūta-gītā* is still popular today, and even the Svāmin Vivekānanda (1863–1902), the Vedāntin reformer of modern India, held it in high esteem. Capturing the ascetic quality of both Nāthism and the Avadhūta ideal, he observed:

> Men like the one who wrote this Song keep religion alive. They have actually realized; they care for nothing, feel nothing done to the body, care not for heat, cold, danger, or anything. They sit still, enjoying the bliss of Ātman, and though red-hot coals burn the body, they feel them not.[4]

The *Avadhūta-gītā* comprises 289 *ślokas* divided into eight chapters, though originally it seems to have had only seven.[5] The eighth chapter, for its content and language—especially from the eleventh verse onward—appears to be a later interpolation. In 1972, Mokashi-Punekar found in the Trivandrum Library what he has identified as the introductory chapter to certain south Indian editions of the *Avadhūta-gītā*. He defines this introductory chapter as "predominantly Nathist," philosophically "post-Advaitic," and linguistically "Maharashtrian in origin, emerging out of a basically oral tradition of Sanskrit discourse." He argues:

> The text is based in the *original* forms of western India Natha cult; but, soon, in this very area, a Vedicized Dattism was to be

> revived; and another plebian Bhakti evangelicism was to overwhelm and absorb Nathism . . . The original Avadhoota Gita had this chapter plus the first seven cantos of the printed Nirnaya Sagar Press edition; the 8th misogynic chapter is a later attempt to induct sexual morality into Nathism by the so-inclined Nathists of a later date, probably Brahminical, who could not stomach the laxity of Avadhoots.[6]

Opposed to the balanced tone of the preceding seven chapters—possibly the work of a single person—the eighth *adhyāya* may be viewed as the later product of a conservative branch of Nātha ascetics, perhaps under the influence of the Brahminical orthodox milieu of the revivalistic Datta *sampradāya*. Dattātreya is attributed with the authorship of the *Avadhūta-gītā* at the very beginning and end of the text. Like the problematic eighth chapter, however, even these parts containing Datta's name are most probably later interpolations.

The *Avadhūta-gītā* is but one among many extant *Gītās*. Indeed, the "*Gita* label" is associated with hundreds of specimens.[7] One could be induced to hypothesize the existence of a literary genre, inaugurated by the popularity of the *Bhagavad-gītā*.[8] This would not be an isolated occurrence: the poetic genre of the *Dūta-kāvyas*, for instance, was initiated by Kālidāsa's celebrated poem *Megha-dūta*. However, in the case of *Gītās* only a few of these texts, such as the *Īśvara-gītā*, follow the exemplary structure of the *Bhagavad-gītā*. The vast majority are detached or entirely different in their scope and content,[9] and the *Gītā* titling refers mainly to their metrical structure. Even isolated collections of teachings, usually anonymous, often bear the *Gītā* appellation. The *Avadhūta-gītā*, as well as a few other *Gītās*, have been considered rare instances of independent compositions,[10] although a manuscript exists which attributes our text to the *siṃhādri-khaṇḍa* of the *Padma Purāṇa*.[11] Among the hundreds of *Gītās*, the *Jīvanmukta-gītā*[12] or "The Song of the Liberated-in-Life" rates special mention. A late Vedāntic *Śaiva* composition attributed to Dattātreya, possibly dating to the eighteenth century, it consists of only twenty-four *ślokas* in the *anuṣṭubh* meter. Within a Yogic framework, the text is a celebration of the Liberated-in-Life, each verse describing the *jīvanmukta*'s realization.

A typical *Gītā* is a dialogue between a sage or deity and a disciple; in it, an *upadeśa* said to reveal liberating truth is expounded. Broadly speaking, *Gītās* may be divided into two groups: (1) those in which various teachings are expounded by divine masters or Ṛṣis, such as the *Īśvara-gītā*, the *Vyāsa-gītā*, the two *Kapila-gītās*, the *Aṣṭāvakra-gītā*, the *Jīvanmukta-gītā* and, of course, the *Avadhūta-gītā* and (2) those in which the central figure is a deity, such as the *Śiva-gītā*, the *Uddhava-gītā*, the *Devī-gītā*, the *Sūrya-gītā*, the *Gaṇeśa-gītā*, and the two *Rāma-gītās*.[13] Although the popularity of these *Gītās* cannot match the *Bhagavad-gītā*'s fame, a certain number—including our text—continue playing a considerable role within sectarian circles.

Originally, the *Avadhūta-gītā* is believed to have been a dialogue between Dattātreya and Gorakhnāth, though in most printed versions no mention is made of an encounter between the two.[14] Mohan Singh includes the *Avadhūta-gītā* in a list of twenty-five works he ascribes to Gorakhnāth, and Hajariprasad Dvivedi states that the *Gorakṣa-siddhānta-saṃgraha* mentions the *Avadhūta-gītā* as a work of Gorakhnāth.[15] Jan Gonda observes that, in some versions, the *Avadhūta-gītā* appears as the last chapter of the *Gorakṣa Saṃhitā*, a manual on *Haṭha-Yoga*.[16] Though Gonda thinks it doubtful that this last chapter belonged to the original version of the *Gorakṣa Saṃhitā*, the fact that the *Avadhūta-gītā* is attached to a text attributed to Gorakhnāth is in itself evidence of its connection to a Nātha milieu.

Concerning Dattātreya's link to Nāthism, the *Gorakṣa-siddhānta-saṃgraha*—quoting the *Tantra-mahārṇava*—mentions him as one of the twelve "great Nāthas" or Mahā-nāthas: seventh in rank, Dattātreya is said to wield spiritual influence over a region nine *krośas* wide in the western direction and on the western banks of the Sarasvatī river.[17] Dvivedi identified one of the later Nāthas named "Dattajī" with Dattātreya himself, evidently viewing him as a historical figure subsequently deified, though he does not attribute the authorship of the *Avadhūta-gītā* to him.[18] The *Dabistān* of Moshan Fani (d. 1670)—after noting how the ten orders of the Daśanāmī renunciants follow the dictates of "Datāteri" or Dattātreya—relates the following tale of how Gorakhnāth lost in a magical bout with him. Gorakhnāth disappeared under water in the shape of a frog, but "Datāteri" was able to find him and bring him forth. Then "Datāteri" concealed himself under water, and Gorakhnāth, in spite of all his searching, could not find him "because he was mixed with water, and water cannot be distinguished from water."[19]

In another legend, Dattātreya humbled Gorakhnāth by stopping his sack (*jholī*) from moving in the air. Gorakhnāth had attained vast *siddhis* and, feeling it to be below his dignity to go from house to house with his begging *jholī*, decided to use his powers to have the *jholī* itself go beg his food. Dattātreya, to punish his pride, had his *jholī* fall down from midair. A psychic battle followed, in the course of which Gorakhnāth was defeated. Having learned his lesson, Gorakhnāth surrendered to Dattātreya, and humbly asked spiritual instruction of him.

Apart from these episodes, narratives exist, both in Hindī and vernacular languages such as Marāṭhī, in which Dattātreya is teacher of Gorakhnāth or, in any case, superior to him.[20] If, according to legend, it was Śiva who initiated all Nāthas in the practice of *Haṭha-Yoga*, in the *Śrī-nav-nāth-bhakti-kathā-sār*[21] it is Dattātreya who takes Śiva's place as *ādi-guru*.

Before analyzing the *Avadhūta-gītā*, a critical evaluation of Gonda's following remarks on the text is in order:

> This work . . . is held to incorporate information on the teachings of Dattātreya, a union of Brahmā, Viṣṇu and Śiva. It is a short and well-written philosophical treatise setting forth the absolute identity of the individual soul with the All which is described as the Void (Śūnya), Nirvāṇa, etc. Part of its ideas are however common to other mystical schools, among them Śivaite and Buddhist Tantras.[22]

Besides the fact that the *Avadhūta-gītā* can hardly be defined a "well-written philosophical treatise,"[23] Gonda's comments on the philosophical content of the text are vague. The *Avadhūta-gītā* is generally classified as a minor work (*prakaraṇa*) of Advaita Vedānta.[24] Nonetheless, the heart of the *Avadhūta-gītā* lies in its Nāthist inspiration and core philosophy of *sama-rasya* (even essence, sameness, equalness). Though this Nātha ideal is analogous to that of many nondual Āgamic systems of ancient and medieval India, the *Avadhūta-gītā*'s nondual orientation appears subordinate to the ecstatic spirituality of the Avadhūta, who wishes to transcend all philosophical and theological constructions. As *Avadhūta-gītā* 1.36 states, echoing the *Gorakṣa-siddhānta-saṃgraha*, its "philosophy" is beyond both dualism and nondualism (*dvaita-advaita-vivarjita*).[25] Similar statements are found in other Tantric texts—for example in the *Kulārṇava-tantra*—and are intended to proclaim the religious superiority of Yogic and Tantric doctrine. The ultimate goal of Nāthism is to surpass and abandon even the Nātha and Siddha theoretical frameworks, and our text freely satirizes Yoga postures and practices, breath-control techniques, the attainment of powers, and so on. It thus seems reasonable to argue that the *Avadhūta-gītā* was the product of a Nātha milieu, aimed at its own transcendence through the presentation of the exemplary type of the Avadhūta, identified in Dattātreya. To again quote Mokashi-Punekar:

> The Avadhoota Gita sounds like one huge sarcastic protest—against several previous philosophical systems; Advaita, Dvaita,

> Patanjala Yoga, Nyaya, Sankhya and certain kinds of Tantrism. . . It is also an ecstatic song: "I am Kevala." It is written in rudimentary Sanskrit so that any man who knows anything about Hindu mysticism can understand it. Yet it is considered an essential text, primarily by Nathists, but also by Vedantins in general (though it makes fun of Vedantins of the Shankara Advaita school).
>
> It is strange that many previous editors of the Avadhoota Gita have described it as a work upholding the Advaita Vedanta school as propounded by Shankaracharya.[26]

The first, introductory *adhyāya* of the *Avadhūta-gītā* is the longest, comprising seventy-six *ślokas*. The central topic is the perfection of the self and its real nature, its oneness with *Brahman*. The nondual orientation is explicit from the outset:

> (1.1) Through the grace of Īśvara alone, the desire for nonduality arises in wise men to save them from great fear.
>
> (1.2) How shall I salute the formless Being, indivisible, auspicious, and immutable, who fills all this with His Self and also fills the self with His Self?
>
> (1.3) The universe composed of the five elements is like water in a mirage. Oh, to whom shall I make obeisance; I who am one and taintless (*eko nirañjanaḥ*)?[27]

The core of the *Avadhūta-gītā*'s *upadeśa* is the attainment of natural equanimity (*samatva*), the true mark of the liberated one. There is no need to search for the Self if one realizes he already is that very Self. The freedom of the Avadhūta brings him to the denial of all external authorities, such as the *Vedas*, the caste system, or the worlds of gods and men (1.34). *Śloka* 36, in its rejection of both *dvaita* and *advaita* and in its presentation of supreme reality as *sama*—beyond the reach of mind and speech (*manovācam agocaram*)[28]—represents the "manifesto" of the *Avadhūta-gītā*'s teaching:

> (1.36) Some seek nonduality, others duality. They do not know the truth, which is the same (*sama*) [at all times and everywhere], devoid of both duality and nonduality (*dvaita-advaita-vivarjita*).

Sama, literally "same," "equal," is the goal of the Nātha adept striving toward perfection. The noun *samatā* or *samatva* means equanimity, evenness, or even indifference. *Sama* is a key concept from the time of the *Bhagavad-gītā*, where it is used alone and in compounds, especially as *sama-darśana* ("equal vision," a synonym of *sama-dṛṣṭi*). In *Bhagavad-gītā* 2.48d Yoga is defined as *samatva* (*samatvaṃ yoga ucyate*) and in 9.29a Kṛṣṇa declares himself to be the same (*samo'ham*) toward all beings. The Nātha striving toward *samatā* or *sama-rasya* is explained by Gopīnāth Kavirāj:

> This ideal is described in one word as *samarasya*, which implies obliteration of traces of all kinds of existing differences . . . by a positive process of what may be described as mutual interpenetration. This ideal underlies the principle of unification between *Purusha* and *Prakriti* . . . *Śiva* and *Śakti* . . . It stands for the *samatā* of the Avadhūta Yogīs, which is really a unification . . . of . . . the One and the Beyond.[29]

In Yogic and Tantric literature,[30] we find a strong insistence on the ideal of *sama-rasya*, also frequently evoked within Kashmiri *Śaivism*.[31] Within Nāthism, the realization of *samatva* is deemed the highest spiritual fulfillment. *Sama-rasya* is said to be achieved through a gradual process, beginning when the Sadguru's grace brings about a condition of mental quietness (*citta-viśrānti*) in the Yogin. Then the realization of *śuddha-caitanya* or pure consciousness may "flash" into the awareness of the adept's purified *buddhi* as a vision of supreme reality, *parama-pada*. As a consequence, the physical body of the Yogin is said to be illumined and "transmuted," achieving immortality (*piṇḍa-siddhi*). He then becomes a Siddha. The next step is to "unite" the luminous body of the Siddha with the universal uncreated light of *parama-pada*, already revealed to the adept at the time of his first ātmic awareness. In Nātha texts, the progressive experience of *sama-rasya*—culminating in a condition with no relapse (*vyutthāna*)—is described in four successive stages. To again quote Gopīnāth Kavirāj:

> (1) The Transcendental Reality is revealed as the Universe. In other words, the difference between what is Formless and what has Form disappears for ever and it is co-eternal with the vision of the Universe *in ātman*.
>
> (2) In the transitional stage there is a tendency in the Powers to move out. This has to be restrained and the Powers contained within the *ātman*.
>
> (3) The *ātman* is realized as a continuum of unbroken *prakāśa* with Supreme Dynamism.

(4) As a result of all this, there is a unique Vision of Being which is unborn. This is the Supreme Integral Vision which marks the stage of *nirutthāna*. It is a Vision of Eternity, when infinite varieties are seen as an expression of the One and when the One reveals Itself in every point of the Infinite.

The Nātha ideal is first to realise *jīvanmukti* through *piṇḍa-siddhi* which secures an Immaculate Body of Light free from the influence of Time ... and then to realise *parā-mukti* or the Highest Perfection through the process of mutual integration (*samarasīkaraṇa*).[32]

Siddha-siddhānta-paddhati 5.7 states that only the ineffable grace of one's Guru enables the adept to "shake off" the *siddhis* he has attained, realizing the permanent state (*nirutthāna*) and uniting his body with *parama-pada*. It is difficult to overemphasize the importance of the deified Guru within Nāthism and the Datta movement, whether physically present in his "human form," or spiritually manifest through his *pādukās-caraṇas* or stone *mūrtis*.[33] By the Guru's grace, everything in the world is perceived as a manifestation of the incorruptible light (*parama-pada*). The material world, as well as one's own body, is viewed not as illusory or as something to be transcended but rather as a perfect hierophany of the Godhead: the value accorded to bodily immortality is, in this regard, exemplary. The realized person is free to act as he pleases, with nothing to accept or reject. He is beyond rules, microcosmic epiphany of the freedom of the divine. From the Avadhūta standpoint, all pretenses at "sealing" reality into thought constructions, philosophical schemes, dualism and nondualism, and so forth are but insane and worthless attempts: *parama-pada* is *anyad eva*, wholly other. *Avadhūta-gītā* 1.48–49 proclaims:

> (1.48) The Self certainly does not become pure through the practice of six-limbed Yoga.[34] It certainly is not purified by the destruction of the mind. It certainly is not made pure by the instructions of the teacher. It is itself the truth, it is itself the illumined one.
>
> (1.49) There is no body made up of five elements; nor is there anyone who is disembodied. All is verily the Self alone. How can there be the three states and the fourth?[35]

The Avadhūta recognizes that he is part and parcel of that same, all-inclusive reality; nothing is deemed wrong or imperfect, everything being accepted as the play of *parama-pada*.

Śloka 1.58 presents another important technical term often utilized in the text: *sahaja*, "natural," "innate," "original." *Sahaja* is a complex notion, interpreted in a variety of ways by Tantric and Yogic schools, both Hindu and Buddhist.[36] It literally means "together born" or "coemergent," indicating that realization is not external to the Yogin but his very condition. Vaudeville notes:

> *Sahaja* is . . . a kind of Absolute, or transcendent Reality . . . equated with the Void, *śūnya*. The Yogic "Sahaja" is often spoken of as a mysterious, totally inaccessible "place" or "land," a kind of unlocated Paradise . . . In the Nāth-panthī form of Tantric Yoga . . . Sahaja is identified with the all-pervading ultimate Reality . . . which in turn is equated with Paramaśiva or Sadāśiva (conceived as "Ādināth") and with the perfect, interior Guru, the Sadguru.[37]

In the *Avadhūta-gītā*, *sahaja* expresses an inherent characteristic of both the *ātman* and supreme reality.[38] The Avadhūta seeks the "nectar of naturalness" (*sahaja-amṛtam*, 2.17), a state of spontaneous existence coinciding with the experience of divine identity. Once the adept has realized that supreme *tattva*, he is "filled with the innate joy of his own mind," (*manasā kalpita-sahaja-anandam*, 7.9). The Avadhūta obliterates all distinctions between *saguṇa* and *nirguṇa*: everything manifests its own nature, his *sahaja* attitude being but a reflection of *parama-pada*, the supreme *sahaja*.

The second *adhyāya* of the *Avadhūta-gītā* comprises forty *ślokas*. In the paradoxical spirit of the text, this chapter begins by praising the Guru as a veritable gem, whatever his intellectual knowledge or social status—"even if he be young, illiterate, or addicted to the enjoyment of sense objects, even if he be a servant or a householder"—and closes by reminding us that "where mind and speech can utter nothing, there can be no instruction by a teacher." What really counts is the Guru's capacity to impart spiritual insight beyond words and speech, simply through his presence and example. The mystical experience of the Avadhūta is effectively conveyed in *śloka* 11:

> (2.11) Where there is such a natural Being, how can there be "I," how can there be even "you," how can there be the world?

Echoing *Bhagavad-gītā* 2.23–24, where Kṛṣṇa declares that the imperishable *ātman* is unaffected by fire, water, and wind, *Avadhūta-gītā* 2.13–14 speaks of supreme consciousness:

(2.13) It does not move about on the earth nor is It carried by air. It is not submerged in water nor does It dwell in fire.

(2.14) Space is pervaded by It, but It is not pervaded by anything. It is existing within and without. It is undivided and continuous.

Ślokas 15 and 16 deal with the Yogic practice of concentration, leading to the attainment of a condition of contentless awareness:

(2.15) One should successively take recourse to the objects of concentration, as mentioned by the Yogins, in accordance with their subtlety, invisibility, and attributelessness.

(2.16) When through constant practice one's concentration becomes objectless, then, being divested of merits and demerits, one attains the state of complete dissolution in the Absolute through the dissolution of the object of concentration, but not before then.

This state of contentless awareness leads to the understanding of the subtlest of the subtle, as the water within the kernel of the coconut (2.19cd, 2.20cd). At the same time, this experience of the ground of Being brings the aspirant to the intuitive understanding of its "fullness" (*pūrṇatā*) reflected through the infinite variety of its manifestations. Thus, the Avadhūta relinquishes the "poison" of a dualistic vision, attaining a balanced all-embracing vision, since *caitanya* itself coincides with the "nectar of naturalness":

(2.17) For the destruction of the terrible, poisonous universe, which produces the unconsciousness of delusion, there is but one infallible remedy, the nectar of naturalness (*sahaja-amṛtam*).

On man's destiny in the afterlife, *Avadhūta-gītā* 2.26 may be usefully compared to *Bhagavad-gītā* 8.5, where Kṛṣṇa declares:

And at the hour of death, on Me alone
Meditating, leaving the body
Whoso dies, to My estate he
Goes; there is no doubt of that.

Ecstatic Avadhūta teased by village boys.

The Avadhūta, on the other hand, remarks:

> It has been said that the destiny of those devoted to action is the same as their thought at the end, but it has *not* been said that the destiny of those established in Yoga is the same as their thought at the end.

The Avadhūta, established in his Yogic realization, is beyond all disciplines. Having realized the truth of *sama-rasya*, he has gone beyond the illusory wheel of *saṃsāra*, whatever his thought at the moment of death: nothing can affect the supremely free one. As a consequence, the Avadhūta's afterlife destiny is unimaginable in its transcendence (2.27): there are no paths, such as the "path of the fathers" (*pitṛ-yāna*) or the "path of the gods" (*deva-yāna*) along which he travels. Having attained the highest, he has transcended the cosmic net of time and space (2.28). Whether the Avadhūta dies at a holy spot or in the house of an untouchable is irrelevant to one who has "dissolved" in *Brahman* (2.29).

The wholly otherness of the *ātman*, in which all Yogic rules and religious conventions are obliterated, is the subject of *ślokas* 2.31 through 2.40:

> (2.32) He attains to the supreme, eternal Self, in whom exists no *Veda*, no initiation, no tonsure, no teacher, no disciple, no perfection of symbolic figures, no hand-posture or anything else.

The reality of *ātman* has nothing to do with exercises such as *āsana*, *prāṇāyāma*, *dṛṣṭi*, nor with the whole complex of *nāḍī* physiology (2.35). Moreover:

> (2.39) When injunctions cease and the Yogin attains the supreme Self, his mind being void of differentiations, he has neither purity nor impurity; his contemplation is without distinguishing attributes; and even what is usually prohibited is permissible to him.

The third *adhyāya* of the *Avadhūta-gītā*, comprising forty-six *ślokas*, begins with praise to lord Śiva,[39] tutelary deity of all Nātha adepts, identified with the *ātman* and with the Avadhūta himself:

> (3.2cd) I am thus the pure Śiva, devoid of all doubt. O beloved friend, how shall I bow to my own Self in my Self?

This chapter is, in essence, a reiteration of the two motifs delineated in the preceding *adhyāya*: the indescribability of *caitanya* or *ātman*—beyond intellectual grasp—and the ecstatic joy of the Avadhūta who, having experienced the *ātman*, is free and beyond all regulations and conventions. *Ślokas* 3 to 42 repeat these two themes through various images and metaphors, as well as through the refrain of the last portion of each verse, in which the Avadhūta sings:

> I am the nectar of knowledge, having equal feelings, like the sky (*jñāna-amṛtaṃ sama-rasaṃ gaganopamo'ham*).

The Avadhūta is compared with the vast expanse of the sky (*gagana*) throughout the poem.[40] *Avadhūta-gītā* 3.3 proclaims:

> I am devoid of root and rootlessness and am ever manifest. I am devoid of smoke and absence of smoke and am ever manifest. I am devoid of light and absence of light and am ever manifest. I am the nectar of knowledge, having equal feelings, like the sky.[41]

The noun *gagana* conveys two characteristics of *ātman* or *caitanya* in the spirit of *sama-rasya*: (1) its paramount freedom (*svātantrya*) beyond all constrictions and (2) its radical transcendence preventing an identification with anything whatsoever. Though appearing to have color and form, the sky is formless: a distinctive feature, coupled with its all-pervasive quality. As a technical term, *gagana* is often found in Tantric literature. Here, one is reminded of the *Cid-gagana-candrikā*,[42] revolving on the adept's freedom to roam at will in the "sky" of the heart of consciousness. Within Yoga and Nātha circles, the thousand-petalled *cakra* located at the head's top (*sahasrāra-cakra*) is also known as *gagana-maṇḍala*, "the circle of the sky," designating the experience of liberating bliss, believed to culminate in bodily immortality.

Ślokas 3.41 and 3.42 solemnly declare:

> (3.41) In thy mind there is neither the meditator, meditation, nor the object of meditation. Thou hast no *samādhi*. There is no region outside thee, nor is there any substance or time. I am the nectar of knowledge, having equal feelings, like the sky.
>
> (3.42) I have told thee all that is essential. There is neither thou, nor anything for me or for a great one; nor is there any teacher or disciple. The supreme reality is natural and exists in its own way. I am the nectar of knowledge, having equal feelings, like the sky.

The last two verses of the third chapter convey the balanced *rasa* of the Avadhūta's freedom:

> (3.45) I am neither of the nature of the void (*śūnya*) nor of the nature of the non-void. I am neither of pure nature nor of impure nature. I am neither form nor formlessness. I am the supreme reality of the form of its own nature.
>
> (3.46) Renounce the world in every way. Renounce renunciation in every way. Renounce the poison of renunciation and non-renunciation. The Self is pure, immortal, natural, and immutable.

The *Avadhūta-gītā*'s fourth *adhyāya*, comprising twenty-five *ślokas*, is also centered on the unknowability and otherness of both the *ātman* and the Avadhūta. *Ślokas* 4.3 to 4.24 repeat a constant refrain:

> I am free from disease, my form has been
> extinguished (*svarūpa-nirvāṇam anāmayo'ham*).

This phrase is often preceded by the rejection of pairs of opposites: "And how shall I say that I have both ignorance and knowledge?" (4.5c); "And how shall I speak of good and evil?" (4.7c); "And how shall I speak of emptiness and non-emptiness?" (4.9c). The term *anāmaya*, "free from disease," is a name of Śiva. This double meaning is not casual, given the *Śaiva* orientation of Nāthism. This *āmaya* or "dis-ease"—also "rawness"—corresponds to one's identification with the *nāma-rūpa* complex. This spiritual immaturity haunts the adept as long as he clutches to a discipline, a religious belief, a Guru, or a *sādhana*: only the letting go of everyone and everything is thought to prepare the aspirant for the experience of the unveiling of *caitanya*. The compound *svarūpa-nirvāṇa* is also noteworthy. Though the presence of the noun *nirvāṇa* may be interpreted as evidence of Buddhist influence, the *Bhagavad-gītā* itself uses it, especially in the compound form *brahma-nirvāṇa*, "extinction in *Brahman*" or "extinction which is *Brahman*."[43] Both *svarūpa-nirvāṇa* and *brahma-nirvāṇa* are positive expressions, designating the *mukta*'s bliss and freedom. As *Avadhūta-gītā* 4.8 states, the extinction of one's form coincides with the discovery of consciousness (*saṃvid*) as one's true nature:

> (4.8) I am not the worshiper or of the form of the worshipped. I have neither instruction nor practice. How shall I speak of myself

who am of the nature of consciousness (*saṃvit-svarūpam*)? I am free from disease, my form has been extinguished.

The supreme *ātman*, beyond mind and speech and thus beyond reasoning (*tarka*), cannot be grasped through the categories of identity or difference:

(4.13cd) Friend, how can I speak of it [the Self] as identical or different (*sama-asamam*)? I am free from disease, my form has been extinguished.

The Avadhūta's absolute is *anirvacanīya*, inexpressible. Even the *Avadhūta-gītā*'s "neither . . . nor . . . " formulations are not propositions pointing at something which is indefinable. There is never an attempt to solve the mystery of the *ātman*'s ineffability, at reducing the absolute in terms of an "it" or object. All expressions are simply linguistic means (*upāya*) to indicate, in a poetic fashion, the radical otherness of the absolute and of the Avadhūta's enlightenment. The text aims at elevating inexpressibility as a third truth value, through the rejection of all views (*dṛṣṭis*). All pairs of opposites (*dvandvas*) do not apply to the mystery of *caitanya* and *sama-rasya* and are therefore rejected.

Avadhūta-gītā 4.14 highlights another typical trait of the Avadhūta, namely, his freedom from all forms of discipline:

(4.14) Neither have I conquered the senses nor have I not conquered them. Self-restraint or discipline never occurred to me. Friend, how shall I speak of victory and defeat? I am free from disease, my form has been extinguished.

He is also free from rituals such as morning and evening devotions (4.18, 4.22), from relative or ultimate aims, from both Yoga and Viyoga (4.19), as well as from reasoning and argumentation:

(4.20) I am neither ignorant nor learned, I observe neither silence nor absence of silence. How shall I speak of argument and counter-argument? I am free from disease, my form has been extinguished.

The fourth chapter ends with the praising of the nectar of renunciation (*tyāga-amṛtam*) and the recognition of the transcendent reality of *sama-rasya*, beyond speech and versification:

(4.24) The wise, my child, give up all meditations; they give up all good and evil deeds and drink the nectar of renunciation. I am free from disease, my form has been extinguished.

(4.25) There is verily no versification where one knows nothing. The supreme Avadhūta, plunged in equanimity and pure of thought, prattles (*pralapati*) about the truth.

This last verse is also the closing *śloka* of the following fifth, sixth, and seventh *adhyāyas* of the poem. It is also found, in a slightly modified form, in *Avadhūta-gītā* 1.75.

The fifth *adhyāya*, comprising thirty-two *ślokas*, presents the otherness of supreme consciousness while at the same time emphasizing the lesson of *sama-rasya*: everything has the same taste for the Avadhūta, who has realized *caitanya* as both beyond all and in all. After equating the syllable *oṃ* with the sky—symbol of transcendental freedom—the refrain found throughout chapter 5, repeated from *ślokas* 2 to 31, is the following:

Why dost thou, who art the same in all, grieve in thy mind? (*kimu rodiṣi mānasi sarva-samam*)

The expression *sarva-sama*, "identical with (or: in) all things," "equal toward everything," designates both the enlightened Avadhūta as well as the supreme *ātman*. Once this recognition has been achieved, no room is left for grief. *Avadhūta-gītā* 5.4c includes language itself in its flamboyant rejection of all philosophies and doctrines, so explicitly advocated throughout *adhyāya* 1:

(5.4c) That which is the same in all is free from the euphonic combination of words.

The letters of the Sanskrit alphabet and their sounds are not to be construed as the corresponding aspects of the absolute: the supreme has no "parts." Even the *oṃ* syllable indicates the absolute only insofar as it points, through its *bindu*, to the domain of silence and to the mystery of *caitanya*. As Nātha texts say, all sounds or *nādas* will ultimately be reabsorbed into the essential *nāda*, the "unstruck sound" of silence (*anāhata*). *Śloka* 5.12 proclaims:

(5.12) There is no bondage due to the snare of good and evil qualities. How shall I perform the actions related to life and death? There is only the pure, stainless [*ātman*], the same in all (*śuddha-nirañjana-sarva-samam*). Why dost thou, who art the same in all, grieve in thy mind?

The noun *nirañjana*, "stainless," "spotless," is an important technical term within Nāthism.[44] It frequently appears in Nātha and Yoga literature as a synonym of *nirguṇa-brahman* or of Śiva.[45] In Yogic circles, *nirañjana* is often construed as a state of perfect purity in which one's mind is unlimited.[46] Within Nāthism, *jñāna* or *gyān nirañjana* is the *siddhi* all Yogins strive to attain. Once this condition is achieved, the Yogin is free of impurities and *guṇas*. *Nirañjana* is equivalent to *parama-pada*, also known as *nātha-pada*, and to *sahaja*. The *nirañjana-siddhi* is thought of as a "place" within the map of *Haṭha-Yoga* physiology: it is identified with the *brahma-randhra* cavity. The tendency to signify a metaphysical reality with a peculiar Yogic state or place within the body is characteristic of Nātha and Tantric circles as well as of Santism (Kabīr). Vaudeville has pointed out that in Rajasthan and Orissa a Nirañjanī sect exists that is apparently older than the Nātha movement itself.[47] *Netra-tantra*[48] 7.37–39 gives a definition of the *nirañjana* state:

> The Yogins, O fair one, who attain this state, become one with Him [Śiva], the spotless (*nirañjana*), who is subtle, who holds within himself all the modalities, who is changeless, supreme, free of all objectivity, all-pervading, the perfect and peerless condition of the supreme Lord.

The highest consciousness is identical with freedom, as *Avadhūta-gītā* 5.13 declares. From this standpoint, the Avadhūta cannot but reject all dichotomies, including the *dvandva* of *mokṣa* and *bandha*:

> (5.19) There is no state of liberation (*mokṣa-padam*), no state of bondage (*bandha-padam*), no state of virtue, no state of vice. There is no state of perfection, and no state of destitution. Why dost thou, who art the same in all, grieve in thy mind?

The oneness of the *jīvātman* with *cit* is expressed in *śloka* 5.21:

> (5.21) The Self is here in the universal consciousness which is the all and undivided. It is here in the universal consciousness which is absolute and immovable. It is here in the universal consciousness which is devoid of men and other beings. Why dost thou, who art the same in all, grieve in thy mind?

The penultimate *śloka* solemnly proclaims:

> (5.31) Since the *śrutis* have variously declared that this [universe] made of ether . . . is like the water of a mirage, and since the Self is one, indivisible, and the same in all, why dost thou, who art the same in all, grieve in thy mind?

The sixth *adhyāya* of the *Avadhūta-gītā* comprises twenty-seven *ślokas*. Its first verse is almost identical, except for its last portion, to the above mentioned *śloka*. In their last portion verses 1 through 21, with the exception of verse 3, state:

> If there is only one, indivisible, all-comprehensive bliss, how can there be . . . ? (*yadi ca eka-nirantara-sarva-śivam . . . katham*)

The missing part is filled in by utilizing pairs of opposites, which are all rejected as unfitting to designate such ineffable reality. The chapter celebrates supreme reality as all-pervading and, at the same time, unknowable. Thus, *śloka* 6.1 rejects the pair of "comparable and comparison," *śloka* 6.2 the pair of "worship and austerity," *śloka* 6.5 the pair of "notion differentiated by exterior and interior," *śloka* 6.6 the pair of "first and last," *śloka* 6.9 the pair of "cloud and water" (standing for the original cause and the manifold phenomena), *śloka* 6.9 the pair of "good and evil," *śloka* 6.11 the pair of "coming and going," and so forth. The aim is not to objectify the transcendent absolute by identifying it with some given "thing" or notion, but to highlight its otherness, silencing all answers as well as all questions,[49] all pretenses at unveiling the mystery of Being. *Śloka* 6.12 cogently sings the oneness, beyond thought and speech, of the ultimate:

> (6.12) No such distinctions exist as *Prakṛti* and *Puruṣa*. There is no difference between cause and effect. If there is only one indivisible, all-comprehensive bliss, how can one speak of *Puruṣa* and non-*Puruṣa*?

The born or perishable and the unborn or imperishable are both said to be false and to have no place in the supreme (6.15), as the masculine and the non-masculine, the feminine and the non-feminine (6.16). *Śloka* 6.21 declares:

> (6.21) No such change as delusion and freedom from delusion exists. No such change as greed and freedom from greed exists. If

there is only one indivisible, all-comprehensive bliss, how can there be the concept of discrimination and lack of discrimination?

Ślokas 6.22 through 6.26 repeat, in the last portion, the solemn refrain:

> I am indeed Śiva, the supreme truth. In such case, how can I make any salutation?

Salutation implies dualism. Indeed:

> (6.22) There is never any "you" and "I."

In the Self, the distinction of teacher and disciple, as well as the consideration of instruction (6.23), is shattered. In the Self there is no division of bodies—such as gross, subtle, and causal—nor is there any division of worlds (6.24). *Śloka* 6.25 declares that the Self is verily spotless, immovable, and pure. Finally, *śloka* 6.26 notes that there is no distinction such as body and bodyless in the Self, nor is there false perception or illusion, which only occur within the realm of *avidyā*.

The *Avadhūta-gītā*'s seventh *adhyāya*, comprising only fifteen *ślokas*, is a description and glorification of the Avadhūta, who is presented in a memorable way:

> (7.1) Clad in a patched garment made of rags gathered on the road, he follows the path which is devoid of merit and demerit and stays in an empty abode, he, the pure and stainless one, plunged in equanimity.
>
> (7.2) His goal is neither to aim nor not to aim at an object. He is skillful, being devoid of right and wrong. He is the absolute truth, stainless and pure. How can the Avadhūta engage in discussion and disputation?
>
> (7.3) Free from the obstructing snare of desire, absorbed in meditation and devoid of purificatory rites, he is thus at peace, devoid of everything. He is the truth, pure and stainless.

Ślokas 7.4, 7.5, 7.6, 7.8 and 7.11 again utilize the noun *gagana* in the compound *gagana-ākāra*, "having the form of the sky," metaphorically expressing the transcendence of the absolute. *Śloka* 7.9ab highlights the Avadhūta's freedom, leading him to the attainment of perfect, natural bliss (*sahaja-ānanda*):

(7.9ab) He is a Yogin free from union (*yoga*) and separation (*viyoga*); he is an enjoyer (*bhogī*) free from enjoyment and lack of enjoyment.

Finally, in an "anarchic" impulse, the Avadhūta bursts out:

(7.13) All this [universe] is like Indra's net, that is, illusion, like a mirage in the desert. Śiva alone exists (*kevalaḥ śivaḥ*), undivided and formless.

(7.14) To all things, from the performance of religious duties to liberation (*dharmādau mokṣa-paryantam*), we are completely indifferent (*nirīhāḥ*). How can the wise imagine attachment and detachment?

The *Avadhūta-gītā*'s eighth and last *adhyāya* comprises twenty-eight *ślokas*. The first verse is a confession of three major sins that the adept, still enveloped in *avidyā*, commits by positing a subject-object dualism:

(8.1) By making pilgrimage to Thee, Thy all-pervasiveness is destroyed. By the act of meditation, Thy transcendence of consciousness is destroyed. By my singing Thy praise, Thy transcendence of speech is destroyed. Ever forgive these three sins.

Similar confessions of sin are found in Kabīrian *nirguṇī* literature as well as in many *abhaṅgs* of the Marāṭhī poet-saints. *Ślokas* 8.2–4 reproduce *Bhāgavata Purāṇa* 11.11.29–31. They are a description of the true Muni taking refuge (*maccharaṇo*) in the supreme Avadhūta—Śiva or Dattātreya himself—rather than in Kṛṣṇa. The Muni is depicted as possessing nothing (*akiñcana*). *Akiñcanya* is the culmination of one's surrender to the deity, characterized by a condition of vulnerability. One then belongs to the deity, having renounced all individual rights. The presentation of the ideal Muni as *anīho* echoes the variant *nirīha* of *Avadhūta-gītā* 7.14. The sage is indifferent, not because of apathy, but because everything now bears the same taste for him. Such a qualification brings us back to the core experience of *sama-rasya*.

Ślokas 8.6–9 offer a definition of the Avadhūta through a symbolic interpretation of each of the *bīja-mantras* composing the noun, a typical Tantric device:

(8.6) The significance of the letter "*a*" is that the Avadhūta is free from the snare of desire (*āśā-pāśa-vinirmuktaḥ*), is pure in the beginning, middle, and end, and lives ever in bliss.

(8.7) The syllable *"va"* is indicative of him by whom all tendencies have been renounced (*vāsanā varjitā*), whose speech is wholesome, and who lives in (all) living things (*vartamāneṣu varteta*).

(8.8) The syllable *"dhū"* is indicative of him whose limbs are grey with dust (*dhūli-dhūsara-gātrāṇi*), whose mind is destroyed, who is pure, and who is free from the practices of concentration and meditation (*dhāraṇā-dhyāna-nirmukto*).

(8.9) The syllable *"ta"* is indicative of him who firmly bears the thought of the real (*tattva-cintā*), who is devoid of [all other] thoughts and efforts (*cintā-ceṣṭā-vivarjitaḥ*), and who is free from dullness and egoism.

The text may be compared with *Bṛhad-avadhūta Upaniṣad* 1.2:

The Avadhūta is so called because he is immortal (*akṣara*); he is the greatest (*vareṇya*); he has discarded worldly ties (*dhūta-saṃsāra-bandhana*); and he is indicated in the meaning of the sentence "Thou art That," etc. (*tat-tvam-asyādi-lakṣya*).

In keeping with all texts dealing with *saṃnyāsa*, the *Avadhūta-gītā* designates the Avadhūta in terms of what he is not anymore, in terms of what he has renounced: the bondage of desire—already mentioned in 7.3—the *vāsanās*, the practices of concentration and meditation, all thoughts and efforts.

In *ślokas* 8.11 through 8.26 we come to the *Avadhūta-gītā*'s virulently anti-female hymn. This is almost certainly a later addition by a conservative male-renunciatory milieu, possibly a branch of the Nāthas themselves. These *ślokas* portray a group of ascetics unwilling to compromise with any kind of Śāktism or positive evaluation of woman. The Avadhūta becomes through his *tapas* the veritable incarnation of his tutelary male deity. As in the *Saṃnyāsa Upaniṣads*, woman (*nārī*) is discussed in terms of her physical form, envisaged as simultaneously tempting and disgusting. Woman is reduced to dangerous, unclean, destructive sexuality; she is wicked, impure, a veritable hell. Her power to seduce men as well as gods and demons is the force responsible for enslaving all beings in the dreadful net of *saṃsāra*, of which her sexual organ (*bhagā*) is both the symbol and the vehicle or matrix. Woman is thus the concrete emblem of bondage. Through her alluring and deceitful (*kauṭilya*) force she is said to "melt" all men:

(8.24) Woman is like a furnace, man like a jar of ghee; through contact [with her] he may melt. Therefore, she should be given up.[50]

Women are believed to annihilate men, "sucking up" man's seed through the insatiable black hole of their *yoni*. The only way to escape a woman's snare is to avoid her company: only chastity creates the premises for the ascetic life and the exiting from the painful wheel of life and death.[51] *Śloka* 8.27 is an epilogue to the anti-female hymn, warning the adept to preserve his heart-mind or awareness (*citta*):

> The body, bound to the elements [composing it], is overcome with thoughts. With the destruction of the mind, [even] the elements are destroyed. Thus, the mind must be preserved at all costs. With the well-being of the mind, the intellectual faculties can develop.

The *Avadhūta-gītā* ends with the traditional *phala-śruti*:

> (8.28) [This song was] composed by the Avadhūta Dattātreya, having the form of bliss. Whoever reads or hears it has never any rebirth.

In conclusion, this Nātha text presenting Dattātreya as the paramount Avadhūta, paradigm of *sama-rasya* and *sahaja*, recapitulates and magnifies the deity's core identity as mirrored in the *Mārkaṇḍeya Purāṇa* and the *Yoga* and *Saṃnyāsa Upaniṣads*. The *Avadhūta-gītā*, whatever its date of composition, may be said to capture the heart of Datta's ascetic nature. Dattātreya—for whom all paths and teachings ultimately bear equal taste—came to be perceived as at the same time all-embracing in his serene equanimity, and above and beyond all philosophies and theologies in his transcendent aspect as *jñāna-mūrti*.

Notes

1. For a study on the *Avadhūta-gītā*—also known as *Avadhūta-grantha*, *Dattātreya-gītā*, *Datta-gītā-yoga-śāstra*, and *Vedānta-sāra*—see Mokashi-Punekar, "An Introduction to Shri Purohit Swami and the Avadhoota Gita." In Mokashi-Punekar, *Avadhoota Gita*, 3–73. See also Pellegrini, "L'*Avadhūtagītā* di Dattātreya." The earliest published edition of the *Avadhūta-gītā* was printed in Puṇe, at the Bhandarkar Oriental Research Institute, in 1912. Among the many editions, besides the Nirnaya Sagar Press standard text (Bombay, n.d.), mention must be made of the *Śri-dattātreya-gītā* (*Avadhūta-gītā*) with Sanskrit commentary of Vivecana (Ahmedabad, 1923), and of the *Śrī Avadhūta Gītā* with Hindī commentary, printed at the Agra University Press (Agra, 1960). For an overview of the principal English translations based on the Bombay edition,

see Nakulabadhut, *A English Translation to the Avadhūtagītā;* Mal, *Awadhoota Gītā;* Ashokananda, *Avadhūta Gītā of Dattātreya* (first published in 1946 in *The Voice of India,* magazine of the Vedānta Society); Hari Prasad Shastri, *Avadhut Gita by Mahatma Dattatreya;* Bahadur, *Dattātreya: The Way and the Goal,* 151–237; Mokashi-Punekar, *Avadhoota Gita;* Chetanananda, *Avadhuta Gita of Dattatreya;* Keshavadas, "The Avadhuta Gita of Lord Dattatreya" (Song of the Highest Master of Realization), in Keshavadas, *Sadguru Dattatreya,* 130–200. For a partial translation into English, see Sivananda, *Sarvagita Sara,* 51–81. Noteworthy are the French renderings of Dupont and of David-Neel, *L'Avadhūta Gītā de Dattatraya.* For an Italian translation of selected passages, see Pellegrini, "Dall'*Avadhūtagītā* di Dattātreya: Passi scelti."

An *Avadhūta-gītā* on Advaita Vedānta tenets, with initial verses identical to those of Śaṅkara's *Vākya-vṛtti,* is attributed to Govinda Bhagavatpāda, traditionally believed to be Śaṅkara's Guru. This *Avadhūta-gītā* comprises only forty-eight verses, however, and it is not to be confused with our text. On Govinda Bhagavatpāda's *Avadhūta-gītā,* see T. Narayana Sastri, *The Age of Śaṅkara,* 55.

2. Mokashi-Punekar's hypothesis of the *Avadhūta-gītā* being earlier than the *Siddha-siddhānta-paddhati*—a work possibly dating to about the eleventh or twelfth century and traditionally ascribed to Gorakhnāth himself—seems frankly unlikely; see Mokashi-Punekar, *Avadhoota Gita,* 68 n. 1. A. Sannino Pellegrini, basing her argument on a comparison with the *Aṣṭāvakra-gītā,* suggests that the original nucleus of the text may be dated to about the fourteenth century, whereas the interpolations containing Dattātreya's name are dated to the beginning of the fifteenth century, with the rise of the Datta *sampradāya* of Nṛsiṃha Sarasvatī; see Pellegrini, "Dall'*Avadhūtagītā* di Dattātreya," 5–6. Though highly improbable, a sixteenth-century attribution could also be advanced on the basis of Dāsopant being credited with the authorship of an *Avadhūta-gītā.* We know that even Pūrṇānanda—one of the four prominent figures within the Ānanda *sampradāya*—was the author in 1610 of an *Avadhūta-ṭīkā.* All in all, a late chronology is supported by Gopīnāth Kavirāj's studies on the language of most Nātha texts.

3. See Mokashi-Punekar, *Avadhoota Gita,* 174–75 (appendix 1).

4. Quoted in Ashokananda, *Avadhūta Gītā of Dattātreya,* vi.

5. The *Descriptive Catalogue* in the Adyar Library (9:254–57) notes that in most southern editions there are only seven chapters. Even the Trivandrum Library lists only seven. The *Catalogue of Sanskrit and Prakrit MSS.* in the Rajasthan Oriental Research Institute (pt. 1, 32), knows of a *Datta-gītā*—identical with the *Avadhūta-gītā*—which also has only seven chapters.

6. Mokashi-Punekar, *Avadhoota Gita,* 174–75 (appendix 1).

7. An important phenomenon within the literature of both *Itihāsas* and *Purāṇas,* the *Gītās* developed as an attempt to ideally "reproduce" or "imitate" the *Bhagavad-gītā.* In the *Mahābhārata,* the *Bhagavad-gītā* is flanked by

the *Anu-gītā* and fourteen other *Gītās* of various content. In Purāṇic texts, special sections, either devotional or doctrinal in content, receive the appellation of *Gītās*, even though independent treatises or portions of larger scriptural frameworks.

8. This is the opinion of C. Mackenzie Brown; see his work *The Triumph of the Goddess: The Canonical Models and Theological Visions of the Devī-Bhāgavata Purāṇa*. He contrasts *Gītās* and *Māhātmyas*, admitting that there is no absolute demarcation between the two. Some of his arguments, such as that *Māhātmyas* emphasize *bhakti* and the mythic deeds of the deity, while *Gītās* (bearing a revelatory nature) tend to balance *bhakti* and *jñāna* and minimize the mythic dimension, are valid. On a whole, however, his definition of "genre" for the hundreds of different extant *Gītās* appears improper.

9. On this issue, see chapter 15 ("Gītās, Māhātmyas, and Other Religious Literature") of Gonda's *Medieval Religious Literature in Sanskrit*, 271–86.

10. The *Avadhūta-gītā*, the *Aṣṭāvakra-gītā*, the *Uttara-gītā*, and the *Pāṇḍava-gītā* are grouped together as independent works. See Aiyar, "Imitations of the Bhagavad-gītā and Later Gītā Literature"; Raghavan, "Greater Gītā."

11. Ibid., 109.

12. See Dhere, *Datta Sampradāyācā Itihāsa*, 249–53. To my knowledge there have been only two English translations of this short text. The most reliable one is that of Bahadur in *Dattātreya: The Way and the Goal*, 56–74. His translation was reprinted by Coombe Springs Press in 1982, with the title *Jīvanmukta Gītā: The Liberated in Life*. A second inaccurate rendering is by Keshavadas in his anthology *Sadguru Dattatreya*, 1–5. On the *Jīvanmukta-gītā* see Rigopoulos, "Notes on the *Jīvanmuktagītā* and the Concept of Living Liberation."

13. *Īśvara-gītā:* For a fine treatment on this *Śaiva Gītā*, included in *Kūrma Purāṇa* 2.1–11, see Piantelli, *Īśvaragītā o 'Poema del Signore'*.

The *Vyāsa-gītā*, included in *Kūrma Purāṇa* 2.12–24, is the immediate continuation of the *Īśvara-gītā*.

The more popular *Kapila-gītā* is contained in *Bhāgavata Purāṇa* 3.25–33. The other is part of the *Padma Purāṇa*.

On the *Aṣṭāvakra-gītā*, see Nityaswarupananda, *Aṣṭāvakra Saṃhitā*. See also Pellegrini, "Il canto di Aṣṭāvakra (*Aṣṭāvakragītā*)."

On the *Śiva-gītā*, which is said to be part of the *Padma Purāṇa*, see Rocher, *The Purāṇas*, 212–13; Vallauri, "La *Śivagītā*." There is also an edition of the *Śiva-gītā* with the commentary of Śrī Abhinava Nṛsiṃha Bhāratī, *Śrī Śiva-gītā-bhāṣyam*.

The *Uddhava-gītā*, also known as the *Hari-gītā*, is found in the eleventh book of the *Bhāgavata Purāṇa*, *adhyāyas* 6-29. For an English translation, see Madhavananda, *Uddhava Gītā*.

On the *Devī-gītā* and a comparison with the *Bhagavad-gītā*, see C. M. Brown, *The Triumph of the Goddess*, 177ff.

The *Sūrya-gītā* was first translated into English by L. Charmier in 1904.

The *Gaṇeśa-gītā* comprises *adhyāyas* 138–48 of the *Gaṇeśa Purāṇa's krīḍā-khaṇḍa* or *uttara-khaṇḍa;* see Kiyoshi Yoroi, *Gaṇeśa Gītā: A Study, Translation with Notes, and a Condensed Rendering of the Commentary of Nīlakaṇṭha.* For an evaluation of the *Gaṇeśa-gītā,* see Courtright, *Gaṇeśa,* 220–21.

Both *Rāma-gītās* are based on *Adhyātma Rāmāyaṇa* 7.5. For more details on *Gītā* collections, see Aiyar, "Imitations of the Bhagavad-gītā and Later Gītā Literature"; and Raghavan, "Greater Gītā." See also Piano, *Bhagavad-gītā: Il canto del glorioso Signore,* 52–54.

14. See, however, the introductory chapter of certain south Indian editions of the *Avadhūta-gītā* as reported in Mokashi-Punekar, *Avadhoota Gita,* 173–87. In the introductory chapter, the Brahmin Dattātreya initiates the cowherd Gorakṣa into *ātma-jñāna* and unbroken bliss through a series of questions and answers. Mokashi-Punekar, identifying the language of these texts as "Maharashtra-based Sanskrit," concludes that Nāsik is the birth-place of Gorakhnāth; see ibid., 184 n. 1.

15. See Mohan Singh, *Gorakhnāth and Medieval Hindu Mysticism,* 9.

The *Gorakṣa-siddhānta-saṃgraha,* literally "The Compendium of Gorakṣa's Doctrine," is a seventeenth- or eighteenth-century text expounding the doctrine of *samatva,* drawing on earlier scriptures on *Haṭha-Yoga.* See Kavirāj, *Gorakṣa-siddhānta-saṃgraha.*

Mokashi-Punekar, unable to locate this reference to the *Avadhūta-gītā* as a work of Gorakhnāth in the *Gorakṣa-siddhānta-saṃgraha,* has argued that Dvivedi obtained this information from another source; see Mokashi-Punekar, *Avadhoota Gita,* 37.

16. See Gonda, *Medieval Religious Literature in Sanskrit,* 222.

Better known as *Gorakṣa-paddhati,* the *Gorakṣa Saṃhitā* consists of 202 stanzas, many of which are found in other texts of *Haṭha-Yoga.* Ascribed to Gorakhnāth, the work was probably composed during the thirteenth century. It expounds a "six-limbed" Yoga, focusing on the recitation of the *oṃkāra* and the arousal of *kuṇḍalinī-śakti.*

17. See Shashibhusan Dasgupta, *Obscure Religious Cults,* 206.

18. See Dvivedi, *Nāth Sampradāy,* 178. One Dattajī is listed in the family line of Dāsopant; see chap. 6.

19. See Shea and Troyer, *The Dabistān or School of Manners,* 244–45. The episode is also reported by Briggs, *Gorakhnāth and the Kānphaṭa Yogīs,* 191. This legend is linked to *Avadhūta-gītā* 1.51: "As water, when water has been poured into water, has no distinctions, so *Puruṣa* and *Prakṛti* appear nondifferent to me." See also *Kaṭha Upaniṣad* 2.4.15.

20. See Mokashi-Punekar, *Avadhoota Gita,* 37 n. 1, 65–66.

21. Synthesized in the *Śrī-nav-nāth-kathā-sār,* it is a modern devotional text of the Marāṭhī branch of the Nātha *sampradāya* and narrates the biogra-

phies of the mythical nine Nāthas. A fine edition of the *Śrī-nav-nāth-kathā-sār* has been edited by the Jaya Hind Prakashan of Bombay.

22. Gonda, *Medieval Religious Literature in Sanskrit*, 222–23.

23. As Mokashi-Punekar puts it:

> There is a reckless stylistic spontaneity and solecism which marks the work from the beginning to the end. In fact, the Avadhoota Gita itself counsels that no novitiate should be disrespectful to a Guru merely on the ground that he uses unsound grammar or metre. (Mokashi-Punekar, *Avadhoota Gita*, 36)

24. A. Sannino Pellegrini has noted the affinities in terms of language, style, and content between the *Avadhūta-gītā* and the apparently earlier *Aṣṭāvakra-gītā*. It is suggested that the unknown author of the *Avadhūta-gītā* was directly inspired by the *Aṣṭāvakra-gītā*, although developing his own conceptions in an original way; see Pellegrini, "Dall'*Avadhūtagītā* di Dattātreya," 4–6.

25. See Kavirāj, *Gorakṣa-siddhānta-saṃgraha*, 16. See also Mallik, *Siddha-siddhānta-paddhati*, 24–25.

26. Mokashi-Punekar, *Avadhoota Gita*, 42. All editors and translators of the *Avadhūta-gītā*—with the exception of Mokashi-Punekar—say it is an Advaita Vedānta work. Even the *Descriptive Catalogue* issued by the Adyar Library, includes the *Avadhūta-gītā* in the volume devoted to Advaita Vedānta.

27. In the main, I followed Swami Ashokananda's translation. Nevertheless, I've intervened where I thought the translation could be improved.

28. A typical characterization of supreme reality; see *Taittirīya Upaniṣad* 2.4.1. For a Nātha parallel, see *Gorakh-bodh* 50–51.

29. From Gopīnāth Kavirāj's prefatory note to Banerjea, *Philosophy of Gorakhnath*, xiii–xiv.

30. The *Svacchanda-tantra*, one of the earliest Āgamas, describes the seven stages in the process of attaining *mukti*, culminating in the experience of *samarasya*. Kavirāj mentions the Tantric Buddhism of the Kāla-cakra school and its ideal of *Vajra-Yoga*, the Vīra-śaivas of the Jaṅgam school, adepts of the Siddha school such as Svatantrānandanāth, author of the *Mātṛkā-cakra-viveka*, and the *sādhana* of certain other Tantric schools—especially the ones affiliated to the *ardha-kālī* line—and their conception of the *guru-pādukā-mantra*; see ibid., xiv–xv.

31. In commenting on the second verse of Kṣemarāja's *Spanda-saṃdoha*, Mark S. G. Dyczkowski remarks:

> When all the trammels of phenomenal existence have been overcome, the supernal "nectar" of the paramount bliss of one's own nature flows uninterrupted "from the ocean of consciousness" . . . consisting of the harmonious unity (*sāmarasya*) of Light and Bliss. Free of the strictures imposed

by the practice of meditation (*dhyāna*) and worship (*pūjā*) . . . it unfolds spontaneously within (consciousness). (Dyczkowski, *The Stanzas on Vibration*, 61–62)

32. From Gopīnāth Kavirāj's prefatory note to Banerjea, *Philosophy of Gorakhnath*, xvi–xvii.

33. Vaudeville notes:

Like the Vajrayānas and Sahajiyās, the Nāth-panthīs are fervent adepts of *guru-vāda*. But, in the popular form of "Nāthism" prevalent in northern and central India from the middle ages to modern times, Guru worship tends to take the coarser form of the "Guru Gorakhnāth" cult. The stone image of Guru Gorakhnāth is worshipped in Nāth-panthīs' shrines like that of Macchendra (Matsyendranāth) in Nepāl and that of Guru Dattātreya in Mahārāshtra. (Vaudeville, *Kabīr*, 136–37)

34. The six limbs are: *āsana*, *prāṇāyāma*, *pratyāhāra*, *dhāraṇā*, *dhyāna*, and *samādhi*. The first two limbs of the classical *aṣṭāṅga-yoga*, *yama* and *niyama*, are omitted.

35. The four states of consciousness are: waking (*jagrat*), dreaming (*svapna*), sleep (*suṣupti*), and the "fourth" (*turīya*), the condition of self-realization.

36. The term *sahaja*, in its compound form *sahaja-ātmā*, first appears in *Avadhūta-gītā* 1.39. On the concept of *sahaja* in Tantric Buddhism, see Kvaerne, "On the Concept of Sahaja in Indian Buddhist Tantric Literature."

37. Vaudeville, *Kabīr*, 125–26.

38. See *Avadhūta-gītā* 1.58, 2.11, 2.17, 2.30, 3.42, 3.46, 7.4, 7.9, 7.10.

39. On *Śaivism* as the basic faith in Maharashtra, see Vaudeville, "The Shaivaite Background of Santism in Maharashtra."

40. See, in addition to the *Avadhūta-gītā*'s third chapter, 1.6, 1.27, 2.3, 2.12, 4.2, 5.1, 5.26, 7.4–6, 7.8, 7.11. In one case, *Avadhūta-gītā* 6.9, *gagana* is merely one of the four elements.

41. The Avadhūta is without origin or cause as well as without any "non origin" or "non cause": he is neither "born" nor "unborn." Pairs of opposites do not apply to the transcendent one.

Smoke and absence of smoke, light and absence of light, are the two paths—*dhūma-mārga* and *dīpti-mārga*—along which the subtle body of the departed travels. *Dhūma-mārga* is the "southern path" or "way of the fathers," leading through smoke to the moon. *Dīpti-mārga* is the "northern path" or "way of the gods," leading through fire or light to the sun. The Avadhūta is beyond karmic trajectories as well as beyond that knowledge which leads to the heavenly realm of the sun. On karmic paths, see Potter, "The Karma Theory and Its Interpretation in Some Indian Philosophical Systems."

42. See Miśra, *Cidgaganacandrikā: With the Commentary by Raghunātha Miśra Entitled* Kramaprakāśika. Although ascribed to Kālidāsa, Rastogi thinks that the *Cid-gagana-candrikā* was written by Śrīvatsa as a commentary on a *Krama stotra*; see Rastogi, *Krama Tantricism of Kashmir: Historical and General Sources*, 1:180ff., 195ff., 257. The *Cid-gagana-candrikā* has also been edited by Trivikrama Tirtha.

43. See *Bhagavad-gītā* 2.72d and 5.24d.

44. On *nirañjana*, see Vaudeville, *Kabīr Granthāvalī* (*Dohā*), xv–xvi. In the Tantric Buddhist tradition, *nirañjana* is said to be of the nature and form of the void, like the sky; see Dasgupta, *Obscure Religious Cults*, 283. The term is found in *Avadhūta-gītā* 1.3 referring to the "stainless" Avadhūta, in 1.43 referring to the one reality, in 4.4 as a quality (coupled with *sāñjana* or "stained") not pertaining to the supremely free Avadhūta, and in 4.23 referring to the immaculate nature of the Avadhūta. It is used another six times in the *Avadhūta-gītā*'s seventh *adhyāya* to describe the Avadhūta's and the absolute's innate purity.

45. See *Śiva-svarodaya* 141. *Nirañjana* also denotes the full moon, symbolizing the fullness of Śiva's energy.

46. *Haṭha-yoga-pradīpikā* 4.3–4 lists *nirañjana* as a synonym of *Rāja-Yoga*, *samādhi*, *unmanī* (beyond *manas*), *manonmanī* (extinction or surpassing of *manas*), *amaratva* (immortality), *laya*, *tattva*, *śūnya-aśūnya*, *para-pada*, *amanaska* (lack of mental activity), *advaita*, *nirālamba* (lack of support), *jīvanmukti*, *sahaja*, and *turya*.

47. Vaudeville, *Kabīr Granthāvalī* (*Dohā*), xv.

48. On this *Tantra*, see Brunner, "Un Tantra du Nord: Le Netra Tantra."

49. On apophatism, see Panikkar, *Myth, Faith and Hermeneutics: Cross-Cultural Studies*, 257–76.

50. A similar verse is found in the *Subhāṣitārṇava* collection of sayings; see Böhtlingk, *Indische Sprüche*, 1:12 n. 62.

51. On the male-female dynamics within Indian asceticism, see O'Flaherty, *Śiva: The Erotic Ascetic*. By the same author, see also *Sexual Metaphors*.

9

The Development of Dattātreya's Iconography

This last chapter traces the development of Dattātreya's iconography from its one-headed form through its more complex, three-headed portrayal, which has been popular since the sixteenth century. The oldest carvings of Dattātreya represent the deity in a standing posture with one head (*ekmukhī*), two or four arms, often bearing the common emblems of Viṣṇu coupled with the *pādukās*, usually placed in front of the *mūrti*. In the Marāṭhī area, the iconographic representation of Datta as *ekmukhī* and *caturbhujo*—Viṣṇu's standard depiction—is attributed to the influence of the thirteenth-century Mahānubhāva sect. Although there are texts such as the *Sahyādri-varṇana* in which Dattātreya is described as having one head and two hands only, traditionally the sect supports the idea of Dattātreya as a four-armed manifestation, on the basis of two Upaniṣadic references. *Darśana Upaniṣad* 1.1 states:

> Dattātreya, the great Yogin, Bhagavat, the high-souled intent on the welfare of all beings, *the four-armed* Mahāviṣṇu holds sway over the dominion of Yoga, as its crowned king.[1]

Śāṇḍilya Upaniṣad 3.2.10f., celebrating Dattātreya as a manifestation of Śiva Maheśvara, proclaims:

> He who would meditate . . . on the eternal Lord of Lords, Dattātreya, the auspicious and the tranquil . . . *with four arms* and charming limbs . . . the treasure-mine of Jñāna and Yoga . . . such a one, released from all sins, will attain beatific bliss.[2]

Besides describing Dattātreya as four armed, these passages implicitly assume that the deity was thought of as *ekmukhī*, not *trimukhī*. In old places of Mahānubhāva worship such as Mahur (today believed to be the sleeping place of Datta), he is worshipped in the one-headed form. Also, in Paṇḍharpur, in the Dattātreya temple, there is a fine one-headed icon carved out of a single stone. Though texts do not offer much details on how to shape an image of Datta, both *Matsya*

Purāṇa 99.14 and *Agni Purāṇa* 49.27 refer to idols of the deity. In particular, the *Agni Purāṇa* states that Dattātreya should be represented as having two arms (*dvi-bāhu*), with the goddess Śrī-Lakṣmī seated on his left lap. *Viṣṇu-dharmottara Purāṇa* 3.85.65a says that Dattātreya should be sculptured exactly like Vālmīki (*vālmīki-rūpaṃ sakalaṃ dattātreyasya kārayet*), who is described thus (3.85.64):

> Vālmīki should be represented as white in color and with matted coils of hair making the face invisible. He is serene and ascetic, and neither fat nor emaciated.[3]

Vālmīki[4] is the celebrated Ṛṣi believed to have collected songs and tales of the Avatāra Rāma, organizing them into the *Rāmāyaṇa*. He is also believed to have invented the *śloka* meter.[5] According to tradition, while immersed in austerities and the recitation of a *mantra* in perfect immobility, he was overrun with ants (*valmī*) to the point that an anthill or termite mound (*vālmīka*) grew up over him. *Skanda Purāṇa* 5.1.24.7–36, narrates that this *mantra* had been given to him by Ṛṣi Atri. A popular legend reports that he was a robber-hunter who repented and retired to a hermitage on the Citrakūṭa mountain.

The idea that Dattātreya should be sculptured like Vālmīki highlights the affinity between the two. Vālmīki, like Dattātreya, was a great Ṛṣi and a master of Yoga, capable of performing extraordinary ascetic feats. Through the *Rāmāyaṇa* stories, Vālmīki manifests a *Vaiṣṇava* identity even while evidencing *Śaiva* traits. The episode of Vālmīki receiving Sītā at his *āśrama* on the Citrakūṭa mountain when she was banished by Rāma (*Rāmāyaṇa* 7.49) finds a parallel with the episode in which Rāma, together with Sītā and Lakṣmaṇa, is received at the *āśrama* of Dattātreya's parents, Atri and Anasūyā, also located on the Citrakūṭa mountain (*Rāmāyaṇa* 2.117.5ff.).

In the Marāṭhī area, *ekmukhī mūrtis*—both old and new, bearing six arms—are found in temples in Bombay, Nāsik, Ahmednagar, and Puṇe; at the *āśrama* of Upāsanī Mahārāj[6] (1870–1941) in Sākurī; and at many other sites. Although Dattātreya is usually clean shaven in iconographic representations, sometimes he is wearing a beard: this represents an effort to characterize him as an Avadhūta or a Yogin.[7] Due to the influence of Nātha brotherhoods and Tantric circles, old and modern *ekmukhī* representations of Dattātreya are also found in northern India (Benares), in sub-Himalayan regions, and even in Nepal,[8] as in the *Vaiṣṇava* temple of Bhatgāon, the modern Bhaktapur.[9]

The Dattātreya temple at Bhatgāon, eight miles from the Paśupatināth *mandir*—the most sacred *Śaiva* temple in Nepal—deserves special

The Dattātreya temple in Bhaktapur, Nepal. Statues of the Malla wrestlers, Jayamalla and Phatta, serve as guardians of the temple.

mention.[10] Located in what today is known as Dattātreya square, it is one of the older if not the oldest temple of the town, exhibiting an *ekmukhī, dvi-bāhu mūrti* of Datta. Built around the middle of the fifteenth century by the Malla ruler Jayayakṣa (1428–82), grandson of the illustrious Jayasthiti, the temple later underwent change and restoration. The foundation is square and it is three stories high; local tradition says it was carved out of the wood of a single tree, as was the famous *kāṣṭha-maṇḍap* of Kathmandu.[11] Erotic scenes are depicted around the base of the temple, and the facade is adorned with beautiful arcades on the ground floor. The classic four emblems of Viṣṇu are placed two on each of the front columns: the *śaṅkha* and the *cakra* to the left and the *gadā* and the *padma* to the right.[12] At the main entrance near the two columns, statues of the temple's guardians, the Malla wrestlers Jayamalla and Phatta, stand three meters high.[13] Facing the Dattātreya temple is a tall column with a bronze sculpture of Viṣṇu's vehicle Garuḍa on top. The Datta *mūrti* venerated in the temple is said to have been the object of worship for Dalādana Muni, to whom is ascribed the beautiful *Datta-laharī*, a Sanskrit poem in 102 *ślokas* in the *śikhariṇī* meter.[14] Traditionally regarded as one of the oldest devotees of Dattātreya, Dalādana Muni in his poem glorifies the deity, saying that it incorporates the *trimūrti* of Brahmā, Viṣṇu, and Śiva.

Both Jayasthiti Malla and Jayayakṣa Malla were staunch devotees of Viṣṇu; the latter described himself as an Avatāra of Śrī Lakṣmī-Nārāyaṇa.[15] Though the history of religion in Nepal after the tenth century was one of growing ascendancy of *Śaivism*,[16] Jayasthiti Malla was perhaps the first king to claim to be a manifestation of Viṣṇu.[17] The presence of a Dattātreya temple stressing the deity's *Vaiṣṇava* identity in the eclectic environment of medieval Nepal,[18] proves the integrative spirituality of our *mūrti*. The syncretistic evidence is further confirmed by the popular belief that Dattātreya was the teacher of Śiva and that he was Buddha's cousin Devadatta,[19] perhaps due to the similarity between the two names.[20] At the *Mahā-śiva-rātri* festival, large crowds gather at the Dattātreya temple to pay homage to "Śiva's Guru" as well as to seek cures from evil possession and sickness, as Dattātreya is regarded as a healing deity even in Nepal.[21] A pilgrimage to all the sacred places of Nepal is not considered complete unless homage is paid to this Datta temple.[22]

The first appearance of *ekmukhī mūrtis* of Dattātreya—either represented as the prototype of the Yogin and the Avadhūta or with *Vaiṣṇava* emblems as an Avatāra of Viṣṇu—is the product, on the one hand, of the pan-Indian Nātha movement in northern as well as western India, and, on the other hand, of the Marāṭhī Mahānubhāva sect.

In the Marāṭhī area in particular, the encounter and reciprocal influence of the Mahānubhāvas and the Nāthas proved fruitful. If the oldest iconic representations of Dattātreya are *ekmukhī* with two or four hands, the deity was later identified with more syncretic icons including the *trimūrti*, up to its modern trifacial representation. T. A. Gopinatha Rao distinguishes three modes of representing Dattātreya:

1. Brahmā, Viṣṇu, and Śiva standing side by side. This icon is usually referred to as Hari-Hara-Pitāmaha.[23] Whereas Viṣṇu and Śiva are each associated with a Devī, Brahmā has no goddess by his side. The three gods are also shown seated on a *padmāsana*, below which are carved the swan, the eagle Garuḍa, and the bull Nandin, their respective vehicles.
2. Viṣṇu sculptured in the Yogic posture of *padmāsana*. His triple nature is evidenced by the presence of the characteristic emblems—the swan, the Garuḍa, and the bull—carved on a *padmāsana* pedestal. Viṣṇu is shown with a *jaṭā-mukuṭa*[24] on his head. In two of his hands he holds the *cakra* and *śaṅkha*; his other two hands exhibit Yogic *mudrās*.
3. Dattātreya sculptured as a human being with three heads and six arms bearing the emblems of Brahmā, Viṣṇu, and Śiva. He is attended by dogs of different colors, traditionally four in number, and by a white cow. Modern iconography sometimes depicts only three dogs. As Dhere has observed, one can find no certain reference to this modern three-headed Dattātreya prior to the *Guru-caritra* (c. 1550) and the hymns attributed to Eknāth (1523–99).

According to Gopinatha Rao, an example of Dattātreya as Hari-Hara-Pitāmaha is found at Haḷebīḍ in Mysore, on the wall of a Hoyṣaḷeśvara temple dedicated to Śiva and Pārvatī.[25] Here, however, the figures of Brahmā, Viṣṇu, and Śiva are similar—if not identical—to their ordinary images. This is why scholars of Indian art have called this identification of Hari-Hara-Pitāmaha with Dattātreya into question, some of them rejecting it altogether.[26] Indeed, we have no proof that the carving of Hari-Hara-Pitāmaha was originally meant as a representation of Dattātreya. It seems more reasonable to suggest that Dattātreya came to be identified with this syncretic icon at a subsequent stage. If Bahadur Singh is correct in assigning what he takes to be two Hari-Hara-Pitāmahas from Uttar Pradesh to the tenth and eleventh centuries,[27] it might be hypothesized that Dattātreya was identified with this icon no earlier than the sixteenth century, with the flourishing of the modern Dattātreya cult.

The second manner of carving Dattātreya's image is thus described by Gopinatha Rao, who takes a stone sculpture in Bādāmi—northern Mysore—as an example. It was possibly executed between the tenth and twelfth centuries.

> Dattātreya is sculptured . . . as Viṣṇu in the Yoga posture, and his triple nature is indicated by the . . . characteristic emblems, the swan, the Garuḍa and the bull of the three gods Brahmā, Viṣṇu and Śiva, being carved on the pedestal, which is a *padmāsana*. The figure of Viṣṇu may be seen to have a *jaṭā-mukuṭa* on the head, and a few *jaṭās* or ropes of matted hair . . . hanging down from it. The *cakra* and the *śaṅkha* are in two of the hands, while his other two hands rest upon the crossed legs in the *yoga-mudrā* pose . . . In the right ear Dattātreya wears a *sarpa-kuṇḍala*, characteristic of Śiva, and in the left ear, the *makara-kuṇḍala*, characteristic of Viṣṇu. This piece of sculpture . . . may well be assigned to the later Chālukya period. It is a remarkably well finished piece of sculpture.[28]

Despite Khare's doubts,[29] this second kind of *ekmukhī* sculpture may well represent Dattātreya. Ascetic marks such as the earrings and the Yogic posture of the deity are significant elements which fit in with Datta's synthetic persona. Viṣṇu seated in *padmāsana* bearing Yogic *mudrās* offers a delightful example of the blending of *Vaiṣṇava* and *Śaiva* motifs: on one hand, Dattātreya's Purāṇic identity as a manifestation of Viṣṇu; on the other hand, the deity taking Śiva's role as the supreme lord of asceticism and Yoga (*yogīśvara, yoga-nātha*).

The third way of representing Dattātreya is with three heads and six arms, surrounded by four dogs of different colors, said to represent the four *Vedas*, and by a cow, said to represent Mother Earth.[30] This image is extremely popular throughout the Marāṭhī area as well as all over India.[31] The astrological interpretations of this iconographic representation, mentioned in chapter 1, eloquently prove its renown. Datta came now to be represented as *trimukhī*, the three heads on the single trunk representing the triad of Brahmā, Viṣṇu, and Śiva. Although the earliest specimens of such *mūrti* date not prior to the sixteenth century, the belief in Dattātreya as incorporating the triad must have developed at a relatively early stage in the "imaginative laboratory" of Datta's *bhaktas*. At a popular level even the "sonic correspondence" between the ending of the deity's name, *-treya*, and the numeral adjective *traya* or *tri* ("three")—though etymologically wrong—played a role in establishing Datta's triadic characterization. In the *Dāsopant-caritra* (609) it is explicitly stated that "the promised blessing of the gods was 'Datta traya' [Three are given you] and hence his name Dattātreya." Indeed, his mythic background particularly favored such a solution. For example, a modern interpretation of Datta's origins narrates that when Atri embraced the three newborn babies these were instantly combined in one single form, with three heads and six arms.[32]

The *trimūrti* as such is a relatively "recent" product in Indian religious history, even though the tendency to distinguish triads of divine powers has its origins in the *Vedas*.[33] Gonda assigns the value of the triadic division as lying essentially in the number three, "which can often be described as the higher synthesizing unity of which the other two . . . are parts or individual aspects."[34] Gonda has highlighted the variety of groups of three gods in Vedic texts. He notes that the triad of Varuṇa-Mitra, Indra, and the Aśvins—prominent in the works of Georges Dumézil[35]—is but one of many groups of three.[36] The ascendancy of Brahmā, Viṣṇu, and Śiva to the highest rank of the Hindu pantheon was gradual. It was only in the Epic and Purāṇic period that the *trimūrti* came to be accepted as incarnating the three functions of the Godhead. Especially in the *Purāṇas*, the triad of Brahmā, Viṣṇu, and Śiva is often depicted as a single entity, the three gods appearing as one indivisible whole.[37] Thus, sectarian *Vaiṣṇava* and *Śaiva* rivalry for superiority coexisted with a more tolerant attitude aimed at reconciling the deities. This was achieved either by distinguishing their functions while highlighting their unity—as in the case of *trimūrti* representations—or by emphasizing their fundamental oneness through syncretistic icons such as Hari-Hara.[38] It is a fact that in a vast mass of rituals and customs the two gods Viṣṇu and Śiva figure conjointly. To quote Gonda:

> On the mythological plane the Śivaite Purāṇas, which were generally speaking inclined to what has been called "a tendency to compromise," could in this way regard Viṣṇu and Brahmā as Śiva's servants and allow their cults.
>
> This remarkable tendency has no doubt been promoted by the essentially kindred and congenial doctrine of the Trimūrti, the triune unity of Brahmā, Viṣṇu and Śiva as aspects and manifestations of the Highest Being which, of course, in Viṣṇuite eyes was Viṣṇu, in Śivaite opinion Śiva. Thus dominant Śaivism was already at an early date able to cover, include and adopt, not to reconcile and syncretize, Vaiṣṇavism by accepting Viṣṇu as one

of the components of the Trinity and putting him on a par with the other members Brahmā and Rudra-Śiva.[39]

Though the *trimūrti* ideology per se is not especially significant in *Śaivism, Vaiṣṇavism,* or Advaita Vedānta, it became important within the Datta movement as the emblem of the deity's assimilative nature. Dattātreya was regarded as the *pūrṇa-devatā* or *pūrṇa-avatāra,* typifying the fullness of divinity and the supreme descent, storehouse of infinite bliss. In this perspective, the *trimūrti* is the highest of all characterizations, expressing at the same time the oneness and the threefold nature and function of the divine. In the *trimukhī* portrayal Dattātreya's *Vaiṣṇava* identity is the most prominent, the central face being that of Viṣṇu. In his six hands he holds the emblems of the three gods, and his physical appearance is that of a wandering ascetic.[40] I recall Tukārām's eloquent description:

> I fall prostrate before the one with three heads
> and six hands.
> A bag of alms hanging from his shoulder;
> Dogs in front of him.
> He bathes in the Gaṅgā daily.
> A staff and water-pot are in his hands;
> On his feet are clanking wooden sandals;
> On his head a splendrous coil of hair;
> On his body beautiful ashes.
> Tukā says, I bow to him who is clad in space.[41]

The poet-saint's portrait of Dattātreya highlights the deity's ascetic identity. As a renunciant, Datta carries a bag of alms, a staff, and a water-pot and wears wooden sandals. Accompanied by dogs, he bathes in the Gaṅgā daily and has a splendrous coil of hair—like Vālmīki—and ashes besmeared all over his body: traits which point to his *Śaiva* nature. Tukārām's bowing to the one who is clad in space (*digambara*) represents Dattātreya as an Avadhūta.

Datta, especially in the older pictures and carvings, is usually depicted naked, with the exception of a small loincloth (*langoṭī*). While Tukārām mentions the dogs,[42] he omits mention of the cow. The cow was a later addition to Datta's modern iconography; even today it is not always present in Datta's pictures, whereas dogs—either four or three—are always present. Although Nātha Yogins are often accompanied by cows and, indeed, Gorakh means "protector of cows," the cow's presence in Datta's portrayals is to be ascribed to a post-sixteenth-century influence of the western Brahminical Datta movement. Contrasting the presence of the "impure" dogs,[43] the cow highlights the deity's Brahminical orthodoxy and strengthens its *Vaiṣṇava* identity. A form of Devī and a symbol of Mother Earth, Dattātreya's cow is none other than Kāmadhenu, the mythical wish-fulfilling cow belonging to sage Vasiṣṭha.[44] She who grants all desires was produced at the churning of the ocean (*samudra-mathana;* see *Mahābhārata* 1.23.50 and *Rāmāyaṇa* 7.23.21). The belief in the cow's sanctity increased in the Epic and Purāṇic period, especially in the *Vaiṣṇava Purāṇas,* where it gained the stature it retains even today.[45] The sacredness of the cow—mirrored in all Indo-European cultures—is related to its purity and nonerotic fertility, to its sacrificing and motherly nature, sustenance of human life.[46]

In the Marāṭhī area, no other Hindu deity, besides Kāḷ Bhairav and Khaṇḍobā, is so closely associated with dogs as is Dattātreya.[47] This connection goes back to the thirteenth century. It is due to Datta's link with *Śaiva* heterodox groups and Nāthas—who used to surround themselves with dogs—as well as to the influence of the Mahānubhāva sect.[48] In Mahānubhāva sources, Dattātreya is said to be fond of hunting and hence of dogs. In the *Līḷā-caritra, uttarārdha* 146, Paraśurāma has a *darśana* of Dattātreya, who appears with a pair of dogs in his hands.[49]

The four different-colored dogs surrounding Dattātreya are said to represent the four *Vedas* or even the four human appetites, both of which Datta mastered. In Mādhava's *Śaṅkara-dig-vijaya* 6.24–35, Śiva is portrayed in the same fashion as Dattātreya and we witness the same paradoxical identification of dogs with the *Vedas.* The story goes that once Śaṅkara was in Benares and, after having bathed at dawn at the sacred *maṇi-karṇikā ghāṭ,* directed himself with his disciples to the Viśvanāth temple.[50] On a narrow path, he met with a Śvapaca, an outcaste, who had a pot of liquor in his hand and was attended by four barking dogs. Śaṅkara, fearing pollution, asked the outcaste to move out of his way. But the man did not move and, launching into a philosophical discourse on identity and difference, declared the oneness of all *jīvātmas.* The great master of nondualism repented and prostrated at the outcaste's feet, worshipping him with the verses of the *Manīṣā-pañcaka* hymn.[51] Then the outcaste revealed himself as none other than lord Śiva, and the four dogs assumed the form of the four sacred *Vedas.*[52]

The equation dogs = *Vedas,* clearly aiming at scandalizing and infringing Brahminical norms, also has the function of exorcizing the uncleanliness and sexual licentiousness traditionally attributed to these animals. The presence of dogs is part and parcel of Dattātreya's antinomian identity;[53] in many of his temples dogs are supported, fed, and even regularly worshipped.[54] Datta's connection with the two opposite poles of cow and dog—indicating the spectrum of purity and pollution—portrays the full, all-embracing sanctity of the *trimukhī* deity.

Another important aspect of Dattātreya's iconography is the sacred footprints or wooden sandals (*pādukās*).[55] From time immemorial, the feet or footwear of a god or holy man have been, for both Hindus and non-Hindus, an object of devotion, the concrete symbol of the active presence of the divine.[56] Within a Hindu context, Dattātreya's worship under *pādukā* form is a characteristic *Vaiṣṇava* feature, rooted in Viṣṇu Trivikrama's striding through the universe in three steps (*Ṛg Veda* 1.22.17–18).[57] An inscription marking the dedication of Dattātreya's *pādukās* by Jayasiṃha, a Kashmiri king, is found at the famous Viṣṇupada temple in old Gāyā.[58] The original footprints of Datta are believed to be located on the lonely peak at Mount Girnār.[59] As pointed out in chapter 5, it was Nṛsiṃha Sarasvatī who gave impulse to footprint worship by installing his *pādukās* in both Narsobāvāḍī and Gāṇagāpūr. At Narsobāvāḍī, Dattātreya is worshipped through the aniconic symbol of his *pādukās* rather than as an idol. In fact, he is often venerated in the form of his *pādukās* only: this impersonal identification and *pūjā* is thought to be the highest of all adorations. The deity's *śakti* is believed to be stored chiefly in its feet. In Dattātreya's case, the value and relevance of the *pādukās* is even more accentuated than in other *Vaiṣṇava* circles: as the eternal Yogin, he is believed to be constantly roaming across the subcontinent, never in one place for long.

At shrines, temples, and *sthānas*, Dattātreya is worshipped in other forms as well. One finds, in addition to the *mandirs* erected in honor of holy men revered as Avatāras of the deity, small shrines containing simple brass masks of Datta, usually in the *trimukhī* form. Perhaps the most vivid representation of Dattātreya is that known as *bāla-datta*, that is, of Datta as a three-headed infant, often lying in a cradle, bearing the divine attributes of the three gods. This icon, which I saw at Gāṇagāpūr, imitates the popular depictions of Kṛṣṇa as the divine infant (*bāla-kṛṣṇa*), thus implicitly reiterating Dattātreya's *Vaiṣṇava* identity. Still other *mūrtis* depict him as *bāla-avadhūta*, as a very young Avadhūta, being linked to the *Bhāgavata Purāṇa* story of the twenty-four Gurus of twelve-year-old Dattātreya. Finally, mention must be made of those icons showing Dattātreya being worshipped with folded palms by Gorakhnāth and/or Matsyendranāth, or even collectively by all nine Nāthas.[60]

Among *trimukhī* Dattātreyas deserving notice is a fine sculpture of a standing Datta in Lepakṣi, Andhra Pradesh, on a column of the sixteenth-century Vīrabhadra temple.[61] H. S. Joshi indicates the presence of another interesting and apparently old *trimukhī* Dattātreya in a temple-cave on the river Narmadā at Broach, Gujarat:

> The idol having three heads and six hands is peculiar and unique in the sense that one of the hands is on the phallus. The hands on the left have Cakra, Śaṅkha, and Vyākhyāna Mudrā, while the two right ones hold Kamaṇḍalu and phallus, and the last one has Varada pose . . . [In] an inscription . . . written on the gate-wall surrounding the compound of the temple . . . the idol is stated to be that of Dattātreya, which was found in the ancient cave in the temple of Dattātreya, built in 1807 A.D. The idol from its style, stone etc. can very well be assigned to a period between the twelfth and thirteenth century.[62]

The inscription seems to prove without doubt the Dattātreya identity of this icon. The date of its composition, however, is most probably later than the twelfth or thirteenth century: the earliest specimens of *trimukhī* Dattas have been dated to the sixteenth century. The deity holding the phallus or *liṅga* with one of its six hands is an interesting *mudrā*. Various icons of Śiva exist where the phallus is held in one of the deity's hands,[63] bearing an unmistakable Tantric character. This *mudrā* may well symbolize the ascetic practice of *coitus reservatus*.

In a Rāma temple in Pāṭaṇ, Gujarat, there is a recent *trimukhī* Datta with eight arms. Joshi describes it thus:

> The idol, though a modern imitation . . . is peculiar in the sense that it has eight hands. The . . . right hands hold Ḍamaru, Śaṅkha, Padma, and Kamaṇḍalu . . . the left ones hold Cakra, Pustaka, Gadā, and Kāmadhenu. The last emblem is rather peculiar . . . The idol has . . . four hands resting on four small figures standing with folded hands called Veda-Puruṣas . . . They . . . represent the four Vedas . . . It is worth noting that though prominence is given to Viṣṇu by giving him all the four hands with characteristic emblems, the Ruṇḍa Mālā and the serpent on the neck [of the icon] favour Śiva.[64]

The modernity of this Datta image is testimonied by the symbolism of the four *Vedas* and of Kāmadhenu. The *mūrti* holding the *Vaiṣṇava* symbol of Kāmadhenu in one of its hands is certainly peculiar.

Sculpture of *trimukhī* Dattātreya in Lepakṣi, Andhra Pradesh, on a column of the sixteenth century Vīrabhadra temple.

The presence of Dattātreya icons in Gujarat, Andhra Pradesh, as well as Tamilnadu and Kerala, is not surprising. In Gujarat, this is due mainly to the presence of Nātha groups (Girnār).[65] In Andhra Pradesh, one must take into account the cultural homogeneity of some of its areas with Maharashtra and Mysore.[66] Further south, in Tamilnadu[67] and Kerala, there is Dattātreya's link with Śāktism. In Kerala, Datta's connection with Epic heros such as Paraśurāma must also have played a role in his renown. In 1956, G. S. Ghurye synthesized the presence of Datta shrines in Maharashtra, confirming that new Dattātreya temples continue to be built:

> The progress of the cult and worship of Datta can be gauged from the fact that in Poona at the beginning of the nineteenth century there was only one shrine of Datta . . . In contemporary Poona, Datta with eleven temples is firmly established.
>
> The most famous temple . . . is the one at Vadi-Narasimha . . . in Kolhapur district . . . well-known as an exorcising centre . . .
>
> In Pandharpur . . . Datta has three out of about fifty-four temples dedicated to him.
>
> In Kolaba district there is a well-known temple of Datta on a hill near Cheul . . . but even that temple is not older than A.D. 1848.[68]

In 1969, Charles Pain located seven Dattātreya temples in Puṇe, plus another one dedicated to the nineteenth-century Svāmin of Akkaḷkoṭ.[69] Pain writes:

> New temples continue to be built . . . If one observes the pictures of the god in homes, tea shops, storefronts, and motor rickshaws, it would seem that in this city Datta is a deity almost more important than any other, except for the ubiquitous Ganpati. The three-headed image of Datta is found in most of the Datta temples in Pune, though one-headed (*ekmukhī*) images are found at the Math of Ganganath Mahārāj and the Kala Datta (Black Datta) Mandir in Kasba Peth, which seems to be a particularly old temple. The six-armed *ekmukhī* images of Datta are found at several important Datta temples in Maharashtra.[70]

The Dagadu Halvāī Datta Mandir,[71] consecrated in 1904, is perhaps the most popular of all Datta temples in Puṇe, due to the belief that the deity is particularly "awake" (*jāgṛt*) here. Among those who worship at this temple one finds middle-class Brahmins, ascetics, and even prostitutes. It is reported that Dagadu Halvāī had this *mandir* built on the edge of Puṇe's red-light district, so that the prostitutes would have a place to worship: Dattātreya, the supreme Avadhūta, untouched by purity and impurity, is the patron lord of prostitutes.[72]

Pain's reference to a Dattātreya temple connected with Nātha adepts again proves the link existing between this Yogic movement and the deity:

> The Datta temple in the courtyard of a Someshwar (Shiva) temple in Ravivar Peth has a connection with the Nath ascetic order. Across from the temple is a Nath ashram . . . In this temple, Datta is depicted as the guru of the nine legendary Naths . . . and their pictures are hung along the walls of the *sabhā-maṇḍap*. Inside the ashram is a sacred fire . . . and pictures of Shiva, Dattatreya, Hanuman, and Gorakhnath.[73]

Apart from a few inscriptions that H. S. Joshi interprets as possibly referring to Dattātreya,[74] two from the Belur *tālukā* in Mysore explicitly refer to our deity. These inscriptions are dated 1261 and 1270, during a period when Datta's worship in central India was being fostered by the Mahānubhāva sect. One incription states:

> From the lotus navel of Viṣṇu was born Brahmā. From the mind of Brahmā were born nine sons among whom was Atri, whose fame was greater than that of Pitāmaha in the three worlds. That son of Sarasijasambhava's mind once worshipped Kañjāsana, Viṣṇu and Rudra. Those three, having been pleased, appeared before him. On this occasion he besought them to become his sons, and those resplendent ones famed in the highest throughout the three worlds were born accordingly. Hari as Dattātreya, Agajāvara as Durvāsas, and Abja as Candra were born from his mind, body and eyes as sons to Atri.[75]

Here we find a new variant of the myth according to which the *trimūrti*, pleased with Atri's devotion and *tapas*, consented to be born as the Ṛṣi's sons. Atri is presented as the greatest of the nine (and not seven) sons of Brahmā, even greater than Brahmā himself. The fact that Viṣṇu as Dattātreya is born from Atri's mind seems to indicate his superiority over Śiva as Durvāsas, born from Atri's body, and over Brahmā as Candra, born from Atri's eyes.[76]

A seal-inscription dated 1235 from Shimoga, in Mysore, refers to Dattātreya along with Gauḍapāda and Govinda. One side of the seal contains the impression of a boar, while the reverse shows the impression of Śrī Vidyāśaṅkara. The inscription seems to confirm Dattātreya's link to Advaita Vedānta and its lineage of teachers.[77]

As evidenced by these sources and the temples and sculptures found in Haḷebīḍ, Bādāmi, Kaḷagi, and other places, Datta's presence in Mysore—today's Karnataka—is impressive.[78] Even here the orthodox, Brahminical framing of Dattātreya did not prevent an Islamic appropriation of the deity: as seen in the symbiosis of a Datta shrine with the Sufi saint Bābā Qālandār Shāh in the Chikmagalur district.[79] Besides the fundamental influence of the Datta *sampradāya* centered in Gāṇagāpūr in northern Mysore, a role in the diffusion of the deity's cult and renown was certainly played by the Advaita Vedānta establishment of Śṛṅgeri. More recently, the deity was adopted by the Wadiyar dynasty of the Mahārājas of Mysore (1799–1947), as shown by the fine monograph on the deity by His Highness Sri Jaya Chamarajendra Wadiyar Bahadur.

I bring this chapter to a close by quoting a hymn of Śrī Raṅga Avadhūta that nicely synthesizes Dattātreya's manifold facets:[80]

> My hearty solicitations to Thee! Oh merciful Lord! Gurudeva Datta! May all our distractions be removed and our mind be firmly fixed on Thee!
>
> Unborn art Thou, yet Thou hast manifested Thyself for the sake of Thy devotees and hast incarnated Thyself as the true essence of Brahmā, Viṣṇu, and Maheśa, all in one.
>
> Thou art one-faced in one place and three-faced in another; [thus] Thou art endowed with forms though really attributeless! Verily, the sacred penance of the sage Atri is seen incarnate in Thee!
>
> Thou art seen having two, four or even six hands and Thy form, Oh Avadhūta!, pours out the essence of intelligence through the various emblems in Thy hands.
>
> Who can grasp Thy sport when even the *Vedas* are dumbfounded, staggering in bewilderment at Thee, standing perpetually by Thy side in the form of dogs?
>
> To outer appearance Thou standeth on wooden sandals (*pādukās*), signifying spiritual indifference, for in reality they are nothing but activity and renunciation, bestowing enjoyment and emancipation on the devotees.[81]
>
> Thou hast seated Thyself all naked in the penance-grove, which is nothing but the heart of Thy devotees—the cremation ground where dead bodies in the form of passion and anger are ever burning!

The Scriptures in the form of birds sing Thy essence and the *Purāṇas* hum in the form of bees Thy attributeless form.

Free from even an iota of longing, Thou standeth under the Udumbara, the wish-fulfilling tree of contentment on the banks of the sacred Gaṅgā—the spiritual discipline (*sādhana*).

The auspicious matted hair (*jaṭā*) on Thy head shines forth as flames of Jñāna-Agni, and thus the whole face consisting of Existence, Consciousness, and Bliss (*saccidānanda*)—all joy, joy and joy incarnate!

Thou hast clad Thyself in *geruā*[82] cloth drenched in self-control, and the well-known six supernatural powers grace Thy hands, O Formless One, in the form of Thy six hands![83]

Do not the beads of the *rudrākṣa* rosary on Thy neck signify the series of universes?[84] Indeed, Thou hast remained aloof though pervading everywhere. No space is devoid of Thee!

Thou hast burnt Thy ego, and besmearing Thyself with sacred ashes Thou art wandering around the whole world somewhere in a covert form, elsewhere all open, with unmanifest signs Thou playeth everywhere.[85]

All homeless and self-sportive art Thou. Only a few rare Jñānins know Thee,[86] and once eyeing Thee remain firm in their goal, meditating and pondering over Thy blessed Self.

The world-nourishing bag on Thy shoulder[87] is verily the goddess Annapūrṇā,[88] the goddess Padmā[89] dwells in the *padma* resting in Thy hand, and the Gāyatrī[90] is standing by Thy side in the form of a cow.

Oh Dātār [Datta] of Girnār, the annihilator of the ego of Gorakhnāth,[91] Thou Thyself art Nṛsiṃha Sarasvatī, the Saviour in the iron age,[92] the joy in the minds of Thy devotees.

Oh Śrīpāda Vallabha incarnate, shall I find Thee in Kuravapur? Or shall I go to Vāḍī, Audumbar or Gāṇagāpūr to find Thee in Nṛsiṃha Sarasvatī's form?

Shall I visit Akkaḷkoṭ? Will Svāmīrāja[93] be there? Or shall I hasten my feet to Māṇiknagar to see Thee in Māṇikprabhu incarnate? Or should I go to Mahurgadh [Mahur]? Say, say, where can I behold Thee?[94]

Or should I speed to Garuḍeśvar to see Thy ascetic form as the incarnation of Vāsudevānanda Sarasvatī? Instruct me, oh silence incarnate,[95] if Thou art moving in some new garb!

What nonsense am I speaking? Where not art Thou? Thou art shining in every nook and corner. What can I do if the faithless blind do not see that formless form?[96]

Oh Datta, Thine be the eternal victory, Thine be the eternal victory, Thine be the eternal victory for my outward speech is waning in silence! Seeing Thee pervading everywhere I remain all exultant!!

Notes

1. This translation is taken from Ayyangar, *The Yoga Upanishads*, 116.

2. Ibid., 490–91.

3. See Bhattacharyya, *Pratimālakṣaṇa of the Viṣṇudharmottara*, 256.

4. On Vālmīki's legends, see Dange, *Encyclopaedia of Purāṇic Beliefs and Practices*, 1247–48. In Maharashtra, Vālmīki is sometimes said to be a Koḷī, a member of a tribe of fishermen, hunters, and robbers; see Feldhaus, *Water and Womanhood*, 103.

5. See Vitsaxis, *Hindu Epics, Myths, and Legends in Popular Illustrations*, 23–25.

6. The most prominent figure among Sāī Bābā's disciples. On Upāsanī's life and teachings, see Narasimhaswami and Subbarao, *Sage of Sakuri: Life Story of Shree Upasani Mahārāj*; Godamasuta, *The Talks of Sadguru Upasani-Baba Mahārāja*.

7. For a bearded Datta, see S. K. Ramachandra Rao, *Indian Iconography*, 123.

8. See Pal, *Vaiṣṇava Iconology in Nepal: A Study in Art and Religion with 110 Illustrations*, 11–12 (fig. 97).

9. Fifteen kilometers east of Kathmandu, Bhatgāon is believed to be the oldest town in the Kathmandu valley. In 1768, the Brahmin majority of the population welcomed the Gurkhas, who thereupon spared the town. Only one of its four temples is Buddhist. Cassiano da Macerata, an Italian Capuchin missionary who traveled to Tibet and Nepal (1738–56), describes Bhatgāon (as of about 1740) in his travel journal; see Petech, *Il nuovo ramusio: I missionari italiani nel Tibet e nel Nepal: I missionari cappuccini*, vol. 2, pt. 4, 24–26. On Bhatgāon's religious life, see the report by Costantino da Loro; ibid., vol. 2, pt. 2, 18–20. For a recent study on Bhaktapur, see Levy, *Mesocosm: Hinduism and the Organization of a Traditional Newar City in Nepal*. By the same author, see also "The Power of Space in a Traditional Hindu City."

10. On this Datta temple, see Auer and Gutschow, *Bhaktapur: Gestalt, Funktionen, und religiöse Symbolik einer nepalischen Stadt im vorindustriellen Entwicklungsstadium*, 7–8, 56–57, 86, 100–11, 128.

11. Literally "wooden house," from which the name of Kathmandu is thought to be derived. This pagoda-like temple, dedicated to Gorakhnāth, was erected in 1596.

12. The conch (*śaṅkha*) symbolizes the constant renewal of the process of manifestation while the discus (*cakra*) is an emblem of royalty; the mace (*gadā*) symbolizes the power of knowledge while the lotus (*padma*) represents the universe. On *Vaiṣṇava* symbolism, see Liebert, *Iconographic Dictionary of the Indian Religions,* 138. See also Smith, *A Sourcebook of Vaiṣṇava Iconography According to Pāñcarātrāgama Texts. Sanskrit Texts Compiled and Arranged with Commentary in English.*

13. The presence of these guardian deities brings to mind the famed five-storied Nyatapole temple. Its staircase is guarded by the king's two champions, Jayamalla and Phatta, each said to be as strong as ten Nepalese. The largest temple of Nepal, it was built to appease the terrible wrath of Śiva Bhairava, believed to cause floods and epidemics. Construction began in 1708.

14. See H. S. Joshi, *Origin and Development,* 185 n. 1. The date of the *Datta-laharī* is unknown. For an edition of this poem, see Ācārya, *Bṛhat-stotra-ratnākara,* 2:589–600. The *Dattātreya-vajra-kavaca,* revered as a portion of the *himavat-khaṇḍa* of the *Rudra-yāmala-tantra,* places Dalādana Muni's *āśrama* on the Vindhya mountains. The text narrates that Dalādana Muni once invoked Dattātreya in order to verify if the latter was really a *smartṛ-gāmin,* that is, one who immediately manifests himself to whoever remembers him with full concentration. Then Dattātreya instantly appeared to Dalādana blessing him with an "impenetrable armor" (*vajra-kavaca*), meaning an immortal body. On the *Dattātreya-vajra-kavaca,* see ibid., 624–30.

15. See Pal, *Vaiṣṇava Iconology in Nepal,* 10.

16. A description of popular Nepali *Śaivism* at the beginning of the eighteenth century is found in a letter written by the Italian Capuchin missionary Giuseppe Felice da Morro to his *Procuratore Generale* on July 29, 1717; see Petech, *Il nuovo ramusio: I missionari italiani nel Tibet e nel Nepal,* vol. 2, pt. 1, 96–106.

17. This claim was subsequently adopted by all the Gurkha kings, the present monarch still being considered an Avatāra of Viṣṇu. Jayasthiti Malla's devotion to Viṣṇu is indicated by the laudatory appellations (*virudas*) with which he called himself: Daitya-nārāyaṇa, Asura-nārāyaṇa, and Daitya-nārāyaṇa-avatāra; see Pal, *Vaiṣṇava Iconology in Nepal,* 10. Jayayakṣa Malla had *Vaiṣṇava* temples built in addition to the Dattātreya temple, and others must have emulated the king for a large number of epigraphs of his reign record the consecration of images and temples of Viṣṇu. On this period of Nepali history, see Petech, *Mediaeval History of Nepal (c. 750–1480)*; Regmi, *Medieval Nepal,* Pt. 1, *Early Medieval Period 750–1530 A.D.* On the Malla dynasty, see Brinkhaus, "The Descent of the Nepalese Malla Dynasty as Reflected by Local Chroniclers."

18. On Nepali syncretism, see Lienhard, "Problèmes du syncrétisme religieux au Népal."

19. Literally "god-given." A cousin and opponent of the Buddha, friend of the malevolent king Ajātaśatru. Devadatta tried to kill the Buddha and took a number of disciples away, thus creating the first schism. On Devadatta, see Bareau, "Les agissements de Devadatta selon les chapitres relatifs au schisme dans les divers *vinayapiṭaka*."

20. The identity Dattātreya = Devadatta might have been supported by Brahminical circles, given Devadatta's fame as "bitter foe of the Buddha, the Judas Iscariot of the Buddhist story;" Rhys Davids, *Buddhist India*, 13. While in Nepal Dattātreya is identified with Devadatta, in a southern Indian legend from Sucindram, Devadatta is said to oppose Atri, Dattātreya's father. The legend highlights the opposition between Brahminical religion and Buddhism, opposition typical of southern Indian orthodoxy. The southern legend, which offers a new version of the Purāṇic myth of the *trimūrti*'s birth to chaste Anasūyā, maintains that Atri, in order to stop a draught, once asked the divine triad to grant him rain. Brahmā, Viṣṇu, and Śiva told the Ṛṣi that the draught might be the whim of Devadatta, or the curse of the Buddha, and advised him to go to the Himalayas and pray to Devendra, that is, Indra, for redress. After various tests of Atri's *tapas* by the *trimūrti* through Nārada, the Ṛṣi was granted the boon; see Das, *Temples of Tamilnad*, 7.

21. In the section on Nepal's geography of a Tibetan text of 1820, the *'Dzam-gling-rgyas-bshad* written by Bla-ma Btsan-po, we read:

> In Kho-khom (Bhatgaon) . . . there are many temples and symbols, which are known to both Buddhists and non-Buddhists in common as being great in conferring benediction, such as Tsa-ra-ṇa-pa-ta, called Bla-ma Dha-ta-tri [Dattātreya] by the Gau-sān [Gosains]. (Wylie, *A Tibetan Religious Geography of Nepal*, 18)

22. See H. S. Joshi, *Origin and Development*, 185 n. 1.

23. Another name for the *trimūrti* of Viṣṇu, Śiva, and Brahmā. Hari, from a lost root *hṛ* "to be yellow or green," is a name of Viṣṇu-Kṛṣṇa. Some interpret the root *hṛ* to mean "to remove evil or sin." Hara, literally "seizer," "destroyer," is a common name of Śiva. Pitāmaha is the name of a paternal grandfather, and thus becomes another name of Brahmā, the father of all.

24. A diadem or crown (*mukuṭa*) of twisted locks of hair (*jaṭā*) is often worn by Śiva as well as by *Śaiva* ascetics.

25. See T. A. Gopinatha Rao, *Elements of Hindu Iconography*, vol. 1, pt. 1, 253. Both Gopinatha Rao and Sheo Bahadur Singh view a damaged sculpture preserved at the Rājputānā Museum at Ajmer as a variant to this Hari-Hara-Pitāmaha of Haḷebīḍ; see ibid., 253–54; Singh, *Brahmanical Icons in Northern India: A Study of Images of Five Principal Deities from Earliest Times to circa 1200 A.D.*, 189. For an assessment of syncretic *Vaiṣṇava* images from Rājputānā, see Agrawāla, "Some Important Mediaeval Images of Viṣṇu from Rājaputānā."

26. G. H. Khare and G. S. Ghurye have both rejected such identification; see Ghurye, *Gods and Men*, 213.

27. See Singh, *Brahmanical Icons in Northern India*, 189–90.

28. Gopinatha Rao, *Elements*, 1:254–55.

Sarpa-kuṇḍala: also known as *nāga-kuṇḍala*, literally "snake earring." Śiva is often represented as having snakes twined around his neck.

The early dynasty of the Cāḷukyas of Bādāmi (c. 556–757), formerly called Vātāpī, included the area of western and central Deccan. Vātāpī, the second capital of the Cāḷukyas, was founded by Pulakeśin I about 550. The later Cāḷukya dynasty, ruling the same area, had Kalyāṇa as its capital and lasted from c. 973 to 1189.

29. Quoted in Ghurye, *Gods and Men*, 213.

30. Gopinatha Rao makes two mistakes in presenting the modern *mūrti* of Datta: he says it has four arms (instead of six) and that it is attended by a bull (instead of a cow). See Gopinatha Rao, *Elements*, 1:255. Rao also quotes two *dhyāna-ślokas* taken from the *Dattātreya-kalpa*. The first one mentions Dattātreya surrounded by the nine Nāthas; see ibid., 47.

31. Modern *trimukhī* images of Datta are found all across the subcontinent. A nice specimen is found in the Śrī Lakṣmī-Nārāyaṇa temple in New Delhi: it appears with verses from the *Ṛg Veda* and the *Kaivalya Upaniṣad* below the *mūrti*.

32. As Raeside observes:

> One can see how suitable Dattātreya is for this role with the Purāṇic support of the Atri-Anasūyā legend—itself a device to bring the trinity within a single womb—and possibly also by his associations with a Shakta Tripura-sundarī cult. This three-headed Dattātreya is the productive form of modern Hinduism. (Raeside, "Dattātreya," 498)

33. On the *trimūrti*, see Gonda, "The Hindu Trinity"; Bailey, "Trifunctional Elements in the Mythology of the Hindu Trimūrti"; Long, "Trimūrti." Also, H. S. Joshi, *Origin and Development*, 3–50; Bhattacharji, *The Indian Theogony: A Comparative Study of Indian Mythology from the Vedas to the Purāṇas*, 351–63; Handiqui, *Yaśastilaka and Indian Culture or Somadeva's Yaśastilaka and Aspects of Jainism and Indian Thought and Culture in the Tenth Century*, 363–71; Mathothu, *The Development of the Concept of Trimūrti in Hinduism*.

34. Gonda, *Triads in the Veda*, 8.

35. For an overview of Dumézil's tripartite model, see Dumézil, *Les dieux souverains des Indo-Européens*.

36. See Gonda, *Triads in the Veda*, 65–68. For a critical evaluation of Dumézil's studies, see Belier, *Decayed Gods: Origin and Development of Georges Dumézil's "Idéologie Tripartie."*

37. The joint feats of the Purāṇic *trimūrti* are numerous. Apart from the accounts relative to Dattātreya, see *Agni Purāṇa* 61.27; 66.12; 78.31; 92.45. See also *Matsya Purāṇa* 265.4.

38. For an overview of these icons, see Banerjea, *The Development of Hindu Iconography*, 540–63.

39. Gonda, *Viṣṇuism and Śivaism: A Comparison*, 95–96.

40. In a symbolic interpretation of *trimukhī* Datta, the three heads of the deity represent the three *guṇas*, *sattva*, *rajas*, and *tamas*, and the six hands the pairs of *yama-niyama*, *śama-dama*, and *dayā-śānti*. The Kāmadhenu represents the *pañca-bhūtas*, and the four dogs the forces of *icchā*, *vāsanā*, *āśā*, and *tṛṣṇā*. Dattātreya, as the Guru-God, is beyond the *guṇas*, although he is the ruler of all their functions and activities. This symbolic interpretation calls to mind the later personification of *sattva*, *rajas*, and *tamas* with Viṣṇu, Brahmā, and Śiva. In Maharashtra, a fine specimen of *trimukhī* Datta with six hands is found in a temple near Gokarṇa in the Konkan district. A visit to this shrine is believed to secure answers to one's prayers; see *Bombay Gazetteer: District Konkan: Kanara*, 296.

41. The translation is by Charles Pain; see Pain and Zelliot, "The God Dattātreya," 96.

42. Like Eknāth, who composed a *bhārūḍ* celebrating the dog as a great *bhakta*, Tukārām is also associated with dogs, which he praised in various *gāthās*; see Tulpule, "The Dog as a Symbol of Bhakti," 280–82.

43. For the Indian perception of the dog, see Crooke, *Things Indian: Being Discursive Notes on Various Subjects Connected with India*, 142–48. See also White, *Myths of the Dog-Man*, 87–113.

44. On the wish-fulfilling cow, see Biardeau, "Kāmadhenu."

45. All that comes forth from the cow is held sacred, especially the so-called *pañca-gavya* or the cow's five products: milk, clarified butter, curds, dung, and urine. Nowadays, the most sacred "cow holiday" is *gopāṣṭamī*, when the cow is treated as Devī in the hopes that it may continue showering its blessings. On the contemporary relevance of cow worship, see Magul, "Present-Day Worship of the Cow in India."

46. On these issues, see O'Flaherty, *Sexual Metaphors and Animal Symbols in Indian Mythology*, 249–52. The cow's sanctity was favored by five factors: its importance for Vedic sacrifice, its figurative use in Vedic literature, the law against the killing of a Brahmin's cow, the doctrine of nonviolence, and its association with Devī worship; see W. N. Brown, "The Sanctity of the Cow in Hinduism." On the cow's sacredness, see also Heston et al. "An Approach to the Sacred Cow of India"; Minor, "Cow, Symbolism and Veneration." On the material relevance of cows on Indian soil, see Batra, *Cows and Cow-Slaughter in India: Religious, Political, and Social Aspects*.

47. Kāḷ Bhairav, like Dattātreya, is often accompanied by a black dog, or even rides on a dog. Black dogs are especially associated with Śiva and his cult, and Rudra is known as the lord of dogs (*śva-pati*). When Kāḷ Bhairav uses a dog as his vehicle he is called Śvāśva, "he whom the dog serves as a horse." As noted in chapter 4, the Nāgas of the Dattātreya Jūnā Akhāḍā originally worshipped Bhairava as their *iṣṭa-devatā*.

Dogs are associated with Khaṇḍobā's cult, whose abode is the temple at Jejuri in Puṇe district. According to the *Mallāri-māhātmya*, Śiva assumed the Khaṇḍobā Avatāra in ancient times to destroy the two demons Maṇi and Malla. The dog played a fundamental role in the deity's battle with the demons, catching the drops of blood of the wounded demon Maṇi in his mouth (due to Maṇi's youth and demonic force, these drops created more demons as soon as they touched the ground). Dogs are worshipped in Khaṇḍobā's cult and *bhaktas* eagerly take their *darśana*, viewing them as a manifestation of their *iṣṭa-devatā*. Devotees begging in Khaṇḍobā's name are called Vāghyās (from Sanskrit *vyāghra*, "tiger") and occasionally act like dogs, "barking" their devotion to Khaṇḍobā; on the dog and the Vāghyās in Khaṇḍobā's mythology and ritual, see Sontheimer, "The Mallāri/Khaṇḍobā Myth as Reflected in Folk Art and Ritual," 163–66. On the Vāghyās, see also Russell and Lal, *The Tribes and Castes of the Central Provinces of India*, 4:603–6.

48. For instance, a dog called Ḍāṅgarā appears as a *bhakta* in the life of Cakradhar, the founder of the Mahānubhāva sect; see *Līḷā-caritra, uttarārdha* 305, 341.

49. In one undated manuscript of the *Kālikā Purāṇa*, Dattātreya is said to be attended by dogs; see H. S. Joshi, *Origin and Development*, 188.

50. On the Viśvanāth temple, housing the "primeval *jyotir-liṅga*," see Eck, *Banaras, City of Light*. See also Dave, *Immortal India*, 1:1–8.

51. For an edition with English translation of the *Manīṣā-pañcaka*, see Mahadevan, *Manīṣāpañcaka*.

52. The episode is reminiscent of Kṛṣṇa's teaching in *Bhagavad-gītā* 5.18:

> In a knowledge-and-cultivation-perfected
> Brahmin, a cow, an elephant,
> And in a mere dog, and an outcaste,
> The wise see the same thing. (Edgerton, *The Bhagavad Gītā*, 30)

Śaṅkara-dig-vijaya 11.1–42, turns this encounter into an armed sectarian confrontation between Ugrabhairava, a Kāpālika, and Śaṅkara's disciple Padmapāda, manifesting as Narasiṃha. A later Nātha version of this same legend is found in the *Gorakṣa-siddhānta-saṃgraha*. Translations of these texts are found in Lorenzen, *The Kāpālikas and Kālāmukhas*, 32–36.

53. A curious story tells of a Brahmin named Viṣṇudatta, a great *bhakta* of Dattātreya, who saw his *iṣṭa-devatā* in the form of a madman distributing the flesh of a dead ass to dogs; see H. S. Joshi, *Origin and Development*, 189.

54. See Enthoven, *The Folklore of Bombay*, 216.

55. See H. S. Joshi, *Origin and Development*, 189–90.

56. The footprints of Jaina Tīrthaṅkaras as well as those of the Buddha are among the major objects of veneration for the followers of Jainism and Buddhism, especially in the early representations of these religions. In Buddhist iconography, footprints were used in place of the founder's actual figure, which came into general use only after 100 C.E.

57. See Bakker, "The Footprints of the Lord."

58. See Buchanan, *Patna-Gaya Report: An Account of the Districts of Bihar and Patna in 1811–1812*, 1:112.

59. On the sacredness of Girnār, see Purohit Swami, *An Indian Monk*, 66ff. See also Svoboda, *Aghora: At the Left Hand of God*, 297–322.

60. See the plates in P. N. Joshi, *Śrī-dattātreya-jñān-koś*, 24–25. See also the covers and plates of Nātha texts such as the *Śrī-nav-nāth-kathā-sār* and the *Nav-nāth-caritra va Kathā*.

61. See Ramesan, *Temples and Legends of Andhra Pradesh*, 41.

62. H. S. Joshi, *Origin and Development*, 49–50.
In the *vyākhyāna-mudrā*, literally "the gesture of explanation [of the scriptures]," typical of Śiva Dakṣiṇāmūrti, the tips of the thumb and forefinger are touching with the palm of the hand facing front.
The *varada* or *abhaya-mudrā* is the gesture believed to confer tranquillity and absence of fear to all beings. It is formed in the following way: the right hand exposes the palm; the five fingers, stretched and joined vertically at the level of the shoulder, face toward the outside. When the palm of the hand is slightly curved, this gesture is said to symbolize Dattātreya himself and it is known as *Dattātreya-mudrā*; see Shukla, *Semiotica Indica: Encyclopaedic Dictionary of Body-Language in Indian Art and Culture*, 1:205.

63. See M. Chakravarti, *The Concept of Rudra-Śiva through the Ages*, 167. It should be recalled that *Bhaviṣya Purāṇa* 3.4.17.67–78 attributes the origin of *liṅga* worship to the time when Śiva—holding his *liṅga* in his hand—approached Anasūyā overcome by lust, together with Brahmā and Viṣṇu. Anasūyā, in order to ridicule the three gods, cursed Śiva to be worshipped as a *liṅga*, Brahmā to be worshipped in the form of a head, and Viṣṇu to be worshipped as feet.

64. H. S. Joshi, *Origin and Development*, 50.

65. On the popularity of Dattātreya's Avatāra in Gujarat, see Rangarajan, *Spread of Vaiṣṇavism in Gujarat Up to 1600 A.D.: A Study with Special Reference to the Iconic Forms of Viṣṇu*, 152.

66. In the Andhra region the existence of a locale known as Dattātreya Hills is reported.

67. An interesting image of Dattātreya is signaled in Vaḷḷi's Cave in Tiruchendur; see J. Ayyar, *Southern Indian Shrines*, 215; Das, *Temples of Tamilnad*, 22.

68. Ghurye, *Gods and Men*, 218–19. Testimony of a Dattātreya temple being built in the twentieth century comes from Nāsik; see Eidlitz, *Unknown India: A Pilgrimage into a Forgotten World*, 58–59.

On Datta's presence in Paṇḍharpur, see Deleury, *The Cult of Viṭhobā*, 54 and plates 2, 3. To the right of a chamber of Viṭhobā's temple—facing a *mūrti* of the goddess Mahālakṣmī—there is a Dattātreya shrine and on its left a shrine of the goddess Annapūrṇā. The coupling of Datta with Devī *mūrtis* is another indication of the former's connection with Śāktism.

On the Datta temple near Cheul and on how a pious Brahmin succeeded in obtaining the deity's *darśana* there, see Enthoven, *Folklore of the Konkan*, 16.

69. Akkaḷkoṭ Mahārāj's fame is widespread throughout Maharashtra and Karnataka. It is noteworthy that many devotees of Datta recognize Gajānan Mahārāj of Śegāon and Sāī Bābā of Śirḍī to be his Avatāric successors. All saintly figures within the Datta movement are believed to be intimately linked with one another.

70. Pain and Zelliot, "The God Dattatreya," 102. On another Dattātreya temple in Wāī, south of Puṇe, see Feldhaus, *Water and Womanhood*, 170 n. 25.

71. Named after a famous Puṇe sweet-merchant who built it. The *pūjā* is performed by five Deśastha Brahmin householders. Unlike other Datta temples in Puṇe, it has a complete *mahā-pūjā* service consisting of sixteen acts of *sevā* to the god.

72. On the day I arrived in Gāṇagāpūr in November 1991, the first person I met was a prostitute. She told me she had come on pilgrimage to Gāṇagāpūr to honor her beloved *iṣṭa-devatā*.

73. Pain and Zelliot, "The God Dattatreya," 103.

74. Joshi mentions three inscriptions dedicated to the *trimūrti*; these, however, make no explicit reference to Dattātreya's name, genealogy, or deeds. The first is found in a "very old temple" in the village of Lakhamundul in the Sirmor district on the right bank of the Jumnā river; the second (dated 973) is located at Kurda in the Deccan, while the third is a copperplate inscription found in the Gorakhpur district near the river Gandhak; see H. S. Joshi, *Origin and Development*, 78–79.

75. Ibid., 79–80. The remaining portion of the inscription deals with the lunar race and the genealogy of the donor.

Sarasijasambhava: literally "lotus born," a name of Brahmā.

Kañjāsana: literally "having a lotus as his seat," another name of Brahmā.

Agajāvara: literally "the husband of the mountain-born," a name of Śiva.

Abja: literally "born in water," lotus, another epithet of Brahmā.

76. Joshi, quoting the work of T. A. Gopinatha Rao, notes how Candra is referred to as the eye-born son of Atri in inscriptions dated 914 and 1122 and even after; see ibid., 80.

77. See ibid. The seal-inscription is documented in *Epigraphia Carnatica* 80, vol. 7, 1, 30. On Gauḍapāda, Govinda and the relation between the two, see Potter, *Encyclopedia of Indian Philosophies*, vol. 3, *Advaita Vedānta up to Śaṃkara and His Pupils*, 12–15. See also Piantelli, *Śaṅkara e la rinascita del Brāhmanesimo*, 24–32. The boar identifies Viṣṇu as Varāha.

78. On the *ekmukhī* Dattātreya temple in Kaḷagi, Bijāpūr district, of the later Cāḷukya period, see Hardy, *Indian Temple Architecture: Form and Transformation. The Karṇāṭa Drāviḍa Tradition 7th to 13th Centuries*, 176, 211 n. 33, 334. The Phalahāradeva *maṭha*, situated in the Bābā Buḍan hills northwest of Mysore, is believed to have been Dattātreya's hermitage; see H. S. Joshi, *Origin and Development*, 80–81. Ghurye signals the existence of two other shrines dedicated to Dattātreya at Hubli; see Ghurye, *Gods and Men*, 213.

79. See Bharati, *Hindu Views and Ways and the Hindu-Muslim Interface: An Anthropological Assessment*, 78–79. On the devotion of Faqīrs toward Dattātreya in the region of Mysore, see Mokashi-Punekar, *Avadhoota Gita*, 10.

80. See H. S. Joshi, *Origin and Development*, 185–87.

81. Again the ideal pair of *bhukti* and *mukti*, both said to be generously bestowed by Datta. The comparison of the two graces—worldly enjoyment ("activity") and spiritual freedom ("renunciation")—with the deity's *pādukās* evokes an original image.

82. Literally "of the color of red ochre." The dress of the renunciant.

83. However, the traditional *siddhis* or supernatural powers of classical Yoga number eight, not six.

84. Each of the 108 beads of the standard *rudrākṣa* rosary (though there also exist *mālās* of 16, 32, or 64 beads, as well as ones including up to 1,000 beads) is believed to represent a world or a universe in miniature: Śiva "plays" with the worlds he has created, wearing them as an ornament of his inconceivable splendor. The *Rudrākṣa-jābāla Upaniṣad* summarizes the benefits of wearing *rudrākṣa* rosaries; see Sivananda, *Lord Śiva and His Worship*, 160–65.

85. Devotional texts insist on the difficulty of obtaining Dattātreya's *darśana* as well as on the god's unforeseeable ways: he may appear to a Yogin, a thief, or a prostitute and not to a devotee or respected Brahmin. Paradoxically, though Datta is said to constantly roam everywhere, he passes unnoticed. Only his *kṛpā*, devotees believe, can "open the eyes" allowing recognition and granting the beatific vision.

86. The difficulty of knowing Datta is again stressed. Only "few rare Jñānins" may see the deity. Once they achieve this, their only goal is to remain

absorbed in that vision. The act of knowing is inseparably linked with seeing. Knowledge depends on vision, that is, experience; and the goal of knowledge is supreme vision.

87. The ascetic's sack, usually known as *jholī* or *cūpadarī*, a rectangular piece of cloth in which the renouncer keeps his begged food.

88. Literally "filled with or possessed of food." A form of Durgā, worshipped for her power of providing food. The *mūrtis* of Annapūrṇā usually depict her as holding a cooking pot and a spoon.

89. A name of Śrī-Lakṣmī, referring to the deity's qualities of fertility and purity; see Kinsley, *Hindu Goddesses*, 21.

90. Personification of the most sacred Ṛg Vedic *mantra* honoring the sun, Gāyatrī, also known as Sāvitrī, is Brahmā's wife, mother of the four *Vedas* and of the three higher castes of the "twice-born."

91. Śrī Raṅga Avadhūta alludes to popular tales telling how Dattātreya humbled Gorakhnāth; see chap. 8.

92. Śrī Raṅga Avadhūta views Nṛsiṃha Sarasvatī as the savior available to us in this *kali-yuga*. A natural viewpoint for any adept of the Datta movement.

93. Literally "the king of masters," an epithet of Dattātreya as well as of Nṛsiṃha Sarasvatī.

94. In this and the next *śloka*, Śrī Raṅga Avadhūta enumerates places where Avatāras of Dattātreya have flourished: Akkaḷkoṭ, Māṇiknagar, Mahur, and Garuḍeśvar.

95. Śrī Raṅga Avadhūta's portrayal of Dattātreya as "silence incarnate" may allude to an identification of the deity with Śiva Dakṣiṇāmūrti.

96. The paradoxical, dual motif of Dattātreya's omnipresence and invisibility is again highlighted. The poet urges the reader to realize the formless nature of Dattātreya rather than search for his visible manifestation. Within a nondual perspective, the realization of Datta's *nirguṇa* aspect represents the crowning of one's spiritual *sādhana*.

Conclusion

Dattātreya's distinctive feature of constantly being attributed new roles and functions over the course of centuries, making him a veritable Protean figure, evidences his power of attraction over that complex, pluralistic network of religions which is called Hinduism. Through the study of the main phases of Dattātreya's appropriation and re-creation in a variety of religious communities, I hope I have succeeded in offering an adequate picture of the deity's mythical unfolding and composite identities.

First emerging as a semidivine Ṛṣi, Dattātreya displays an integrative force mirrored in the *Mārkaṇḍeya Purāṇa,* where he appears as a great Guru, a master of Yoga, and an Avatāra. His core identity as a *jñāna-yogin* and an ascetic—Paramahaṃsa or Avadhūta—is evidenced both within *Śaiva Tantras* and sectarian *Upaniṣads* as well as within Brahminical sources.

Worshipped as one of Parameśvara's five manifestations in Mahānubhāva theology, the deity's popularity culminates around the sixteenth century with the orthodox Datta *sampradāya* of Nṛsiṃha Sarasvatī. Dattātreya was recognized as an immortal *pūrṇa-avatāra,* encompassing the *trimūrti* of Brahmā, Viṣṇu, and Śiva: a natural solution, given the deity's mythical background. The richness of Datta's icon was further enhanced with its appropriation by southern Indian Śāktism. Striking evidence of Dattātreya's plural makeups can be gauged by confronting the texts of the *Tripurā-rahasya* and the *Avadhūta-gītā.* In the former, Datta, as supreme Guru, expounds the supremacy of Devī to Paraśurāma, that is, of the female as the highest manifestation of the divine. In the latter, Datta, as Avadhūta, is linked to a rigidly male renunciatory environment despising women and affirming the supremacy of the male as the only fitting receptacle for the divine. Due to his manifold, even antagonistic identities, Dattātreya may be compared to a multifaceted prism, each facet representing a different aspect. Taken together, these facets reflect the dyadic oppositions of male-female, pure-impure, sacred-profane, and so forth.

The Dattātreya of the Yoga and Nātha tradition, coexisted and intermingled—via western Nāthism and the heterodox Mahānubhāvas—with the Purāṇic, Brahminical tradition of the Datta *sampradāya*. These religious currents, through a process of cross-fertilization, contributed to the rise of a broad, eclectic Datta movement, confirmed by traces of Dattātreya's presence found in other religions.[1] Datta's mingling with popular Islam through Sufi saints and Faqīrs,[2] is attested to from the medieval period. Besides being tangentially present in Buddhism through his identification with Buddha's cousin Devadatta (in the syncretistic milieu of Nepal and in southern Indian legends), Dattātreya's link with Jainism is noteworthy. As mentioned in chapter 4, "King Dattātri" is said to have been the first convert of the twenty-second Jaina Tīrthaṅkara Neminātha, and Śrī Purohit Svāmin reported that the Jainas worship Dattātreya as Neminātha. The Datta shrines of Nātha adepts amid Jaina sanctuaries in the areas of Mount Abu and Girnār, as well as Dattātreya's characterization as a "clad-in-space" (*digambara*), must have favored his identification as a Jaina ascetic.[3]

It could be argued that Dattātreya's integrative icon aims at its own transcendence. The episode of *Bhāgavata Purāṇa* 11.7.24–11.9.33, enumerating Datta's twenty-four Gurus from the natural world, highlights the *homo religiosus* constant search for meaning and freedom. The whole universe, of which Dattātreya is a divinized anthropomorfic symbol, becomes the treasure-house of learning, the true *karma-bhūmi*. Thus, the belief is instilled that the devotee finds Dattātreya in everyone—animal or human—as well as everywhere: on earth, in the sky, in the bottom of the ocean, in a fire blaze, in a sea wave. He is said to be ever present around us and within each of us as the inner ruler (*antaryāmin*). As the immortal Guru, Yogin, and Avatāra, Dattātreya affirms his omnipresent, ubiquitous nature. In this perspective, most *bhaktas* of the Datta movement feel that the deity belongs to humanity as a whole and is beyond religious and theological constructions. The belief in Dattātreya's immortality—an idea most probably derived from the Nātha milieu—along with the belief that he is always roaming throughout the subcontinent under different guises, is precisely what determines his ongoing, fresh mythical relevance. As the perpetual wanderer or Avadhūta, he is the symbol of constant change and renewal.

A significant example of Dattātreya's interreligious eclecticism is represented by the Sāī Bābā movement.[4] Sāī Bābā of Śirḍī (d. 1918), who certainly had Muslim origins, was and still is identified as an Avatāra of Datta by many of his devotees.[5] One of his closest disciples was Upāsanī Bābā (1870–1941), a Hindu and a popular Guru who founded an *āśrama* at Sākurī, a few miles from Śirḍī. Upāsanī's connection with Datta is evident from the temple he had built in the deity's honor. In turn, one of Upāsanī's closest disciples was Meher Bābā from Puṇe (1894–1969), a Parsi who was to become one of the most popular Indian Gurus in the West, especially in the sixties.[6] Finally, the Hindu saint Satya Sāī Bābā of Puttaparthi (b. 1926) in Andhra Pradesh presents himself as an Avatāra of Dattātreya.[7] In 1940, he declared himself the reincarnation of Śirḍī Sāī Bābā. His late biographer N. Kasturi (1897–1987)[8] recalled:

> He has revealed that His Reality is Datta Deva or Dattātreya or the Trinity in One as conceived in Hindu mythology. Once when cameras were clicking all around Him, He told one of the photographers: "Here! Click now. I shall give you my Real Form!" And the picture was of the Trinity. So, the Feet are of Datta Deva.[9]

From the theological perspective of Satya Sāī Bābā's *bhaktas* and the saint's own declarations, the Sāī Bābā Avatāra is triple, appearing in three manifestations over 250 years: Śirḍī Sāī Bābā, the present Puttaparthi Satya Sāī Bābā, and the future Preman Sāī Bābā, who, according to Satya Sāī Bābā's own prediction, will be born in the Mandya district of Karnataka eight years after his death, in 2028 or 2029. The Sāī Bābā triple manifestation would thus mirror Dattātreya's triadic typology.[10]

The Avadhūta Gajānan Mahārāj[11] (d. 1910), a popular figure from the Vidarbha region of Maharashtra, is also thought to be a manifestation of the supreme Avadhūta Dattātreya. He first appeared in the village of Śegāon on February 23, 1878. Like his contemporary Sāī Bābā of Śirḍī, with whom he was supposedly connected, Gajānan Mahārāj is believed to be the successor of Akkaḷkoṭ Mahārāj.[12] Gajānan's charming and well kept *āśrama* in Śegāon is an important center of Datta worship even today.

The connection of Dattātreya with Nāthism, particularly with its western branch, continues to be strong. Such solidarity is evidenced not only by the many pamphlets of sectarian literature relating the mythical nine Nāthas to their tutelary deity Dattātreya,[13] but by the presence of Nātha adepts and sanctuaries at all major Datta pilgrimage sites, as I had the opportunity to see during my visit to Gāṇagāpūr. I encountered Nātha ascetics and shrines throughout Maharashtra: in Bombay, Nāsik, Śirḍī, Sākurī, Khamgāon, and Śegāon as well as in Puṇe, Solāpur, Akkaḷkoṭ, Paṇḍharpur, Tuḷjāpūr, and so forth.[14]

The famed Vedāntic mystic Māruti Kampli of Bombay, better known as Śrī Nisargadatta Mahārāj (1897–1981),[15] belonged to the Navnāth *sampradāya*. His Guru was Śrī Siddharāmeśvar Mahārāj, connected to the Nātha subsect said to have been founded by Revaṇanāth, the seventh mythical Nātha in the Navnāth lineage. Śrī Nisargadatta met his teacher at the age of thirty-four, was given the *mantra ahaṃ brahmāsmi*, and is said to have attained realization after three years of intense *sādhana*. He often observed that his enlightened state was the consequence of placing complete faith in the Guru. A dialogue took place between Śrī Nisargadatta and a visitor on April 1, 1972.

> QUESTIONER: I see here pictures of several saints and I am told that they are your spiritual ancestors. Who are they and how did it all begin?
>
> MAHARAJ: We are called collectively the "Nine Masters." The legend says that our first teacher was Rishi Dattatreya, the great incarnation of the Trinity of Brahma, Vishnu and Shiva. Even the "Nine Masters" (Navnath) are mythological.
>
> Q: What is the peculiarity of their teaching?
>
> M: Its simplicity, both in theory and practice.
>
> Q: How does one become a Navnath? By initiation or by succession?
>
> M: Neither. The Nine Masters' tradition, Navnath Parampara, is like a river—it flows into the ocean of reality and whoever enters it is carried along.
>
> Q: Does it imply acceptance by a living master belonging to the same tradition?
>
> M: Those who practise the sadhana of focussing their minds on "I am" may feel related to others who have followed the same sadhana and succeeded. They may decide to verbalize their sense of kinship by calling themselves Navnaths. It gives them the pleasure of belonging to an established tradition . . .

Q: If I like your teaching and accept your guidance, can I call myself a Navnath?

M: Please your word-addicted mind! The name will not change you . . . It is like a family name, but here the family is spiritual.

Q: Do you have to realize to join the Sampradaya?

M: The Navnath Sampradaya is only a tradition, a way of teaching and practice. It does not denote a level of consciousness. If you accept a Navnath Sampradaya teacher as your Guru, you join his Sampradaya. Usually you receive a token of his grace—a look, a touch, or a word, sometimes a vivid dream or a strong remembrance. Sometimes the only sign of grace is a significant and rapid change in character and behaviour. . .

Q: Since you count your spiritual ancestry from Rishi Dattatreya, are we right in believing that you and all your predecessors are reincarnations of the Rishi?

M: You may believe in whatever you like and if you act on your belief, you will get the fruits of it; but to me it has no importance. I am what I am and this is enough for me. I have no desire to identify myself with anybody, however illustrious. Nor do I feel the need to take myths for reality. I am only interested in ignorance and the freedom from ignorance. The proper role of a Guru is to dispel ignorance in the hearts and minds of his disciples . . .[16]

The contemporary relevance of Dattātreya within the ascetic community of the Mahānubhāvas—currently estimated to be of 100,000 to 200,000 adepts—is on a par with the other four manifestations of Parameśvara. All pilgrimage places, festivals, and ritual activities are related to the five human Avatāras of the supreme Parameśvara. Mahānubhāvas view their shrines, relics, and stones (*saṃbandhī pāśāṇs, oṭās*)—sometimes carved in the shape of Dattātreya or one of the other Avatāras—not as divine objects or *mūrtis*, but simply as memorials of Parameśvara's action and presence among humans.[17]

Even though in today's Maharashtra most Dattātreya temples are regarded as centers of Brahmin worship (due to the influence of the *Guru-caritra* and the Datta *sampradāya*),[18] it is a fact that devotion to Datta cuts across religious and social barriers. Among the deity's *bhaktas* are prostitutes,[19] untouchables, *Vaiṣṇava* Brahmins, Muslims, common householders, *Śaiva* ascetics, *Śāktas*, thieves, scholars, illiterates, the sane and the insane, the seemingly possessed, artists and musicians, and so on. The deity has inspired a number of disciplines, particularly in the arts. Music is said to be very pleasing to Dattātreya and is part and parcel of his identity.[20] In the *Mārkaṇḍeya Purāṇa*, Datta is hymned by Gandharvas (18.23) and he himself declares (19.11–12):

> And who shall worship me and Lakshmi with songs . . . and with lute, flute, conchs and other gladsome musical instruments, to them I will give supreme gratification.[21]

A chapter of the *Guru-caritra* is devoted to a classification of *rāgas* and their presiding *devatās*. The importance of music in the Datta cult has also been favored by the influence of Sufi mysticism—notably of the Chishtī variety—[22]which accords a prominent place to *samā'*, musical sessions held with the object of inducing a state of spiritual ecstasy.[23]

Sadashiv Krishna Phadke, a modern writer, has listed some of Dattātreya's salient characteristics. The following outline of Phadke's account offers a few of Mokashi-Punekar's observations:

1. Datta's work is primarily to transform and salvage (*uddhāra*) by guiding; he does not kill the impious. Datta is primarily a teacher god (Guru). He was born in the *sattva* sphere: there is no room for tragedy here; everything is austere beauty, love, and serenity.
2. Datta is Brahminical.
3. Rāma, Kṛṣṇa, and Buddha were married. Datta is an Avadhūta.
4. As such, Datta is unbound by Vedic injunctions (*vidhi-niṣedha*). The Avadhūta is above all these.
5. The passing or termination of other Avatāras has been mentioned by the *Purāṇas*; not so of Datta.
6. Images of Datta are obtained according to the temperments of the devotees. Images of Rāma and Kṛṣṇa are fairly fixed.
7. Many Datta worshipers have been deified into Avatāras of Datta, and these Avatāras continue till the present day. There are still actual manifestations of Datta.
8. Datta grants a vision of himself in such diverse forms as a shepherd,[24] a Saṃnyāsin, a Yati,[25] a Brahmin, or a Faqīr. He comes in dreams to fulfil the desire of his devotees. Whatever the form, it rounds off with a vision of a six-handed figure,[26] and the face is heavenly bright (*divya*).

9. Datta's *pādukās* or wooden sandals are worshiped. He loves the *uḍumbara* tree, has Kāmadhenu and dogs with him. Thursday, being teacher's day (*guruvar*), is a special day for him.
10. Datta was a worshiper of Śiva and Śiva gave him knowledge and liberation.[27] Some *Purāṇas*, on the other hand, consider him a manifestation of Viṣṇu.
11. He taught *ātma-vidyā* and the path of Yoga.
12. His behavior was like the non-intoxicated behaving like the intoxicated.
13. His grace is harder to obtain than that of Śiva or Viṣṇu. This can be known from the lives of his devotees.[28]

The Occident's first significant encounter with Dattātreya was through the missionary activity of Śrī Purohit Svāmin. A short biographical sketch of this ascetic who brought Hinduism and Dattātreya to the West is in order. Born in the Berār area in 1882 as Śaṅkar Gajānan Purohit—his name possibly betraying his father's devotion to Gajānan Mahārāj—he met his Guru Bhagavan Śrī Haṃsa (b. 1878) between 1903 and 1906. After having gone on pilgrimage to various holy sites, he is said to have experienced the *turīya* state on Mount Girnār and, later, to have had *sākṣātkāra* of his *iṣṭa-devatā* Dattātreya at Mahur. Soon after these transformative experiences, Purohit married on condition that, with the birth of a son, he would be allowed to become a renunciant. After two daughters he finally had a son, who unfortunately died within a few months. With his wife's and mother's consent he then took orders and organized the *āśrama* of his Guru Śrī Haṃsa at Lavāsā in Gujarat.

During the period 1931–36 he went to England as a Hindu missionary and there associated with the Irish poet William Butler Yeats (1865–1939). When Yeats' health was declining in 1936, Śrī Purohit Svāmin took him to the island of Majorca for a few months' rest; there they jointly translated some *Upaniṣads* and Patañjali's *Yoga-sūtras*. That same year the prospect of World War II and the declining health of Śrī Haṃsa brought Śrī Purohit Svāmin back to India. Śrī Haṃsa died shortly after his return. Subsequently, Śrī Purohit Svāmin went on lecture tours while also translating Indian holy texts into English. He died in 1941 after surgery in a Bombay clinic.[29]

Although Yeats knew and studied with Śrī Purohit Svāmin, it does not necessarily follow that the poet accepted the latter's religious faith or that he used his theology to articulate poetic notions regarding divinity. Nevertheless, Yeats' later essays—such as his *Supernatural Songs* (1935) and his play *The Herne's Egg* (1938)—betray the influence of Hindu ideas. Mokashi-Punekar maintains that Yeats absorbed the mystery of worship-centered polytheism from Śrī Purohit Svāmin:

> Yeats' later essay on *Prometheus Unbound* is written in the light of this mystery and emphasizes the need for what it describes as dedicating all other images of worship to one initiatory image. This is how polytheism keeps its passionate devotion alive.[30]

Yeats's fascination with India and the Orient preceded his meeting with Śrī Purohit Svāmin,[31] and is linked with his lifelong passion for occultism and esoterism.[32] He was connected with the Theosophical Society, founded in the late nineteenth century by Madame Helena Petrovna Blavatsky (1831–91) and Colonel W. S. Olcott (1832–1907). Yeats joined London's Blavatsky Lodge in 1887, at the age of twenty-two. Three years later, he was initiated into the Hermetic Order of the Golden Dawn.

In *Crossways* (1889), Yeats's first poetical collection, his three lyrics *Anashuya and Vijaya*, *The Indian upon God*, and *The Indian to His Love* indicate that he romantically envisioned India as the treasure trove of wisdom and beauty. It is a curious coincidence that Yeats chose the name of Dattātreya's mother, Anasūyā, for the enamored young priestess of his first poem set in India.

Yeats wrote in his introduction to Śrī Purohit Svāmin's autobiography:

> The book lies before me complete; it seems to me something I have waited for since I was seventeen years old. About that age, bored by an Irish Protestant point of view that suggested by its blank abstraction chlorate of lime, I began to question the country-people about apparitions . . . When Shri Purohit Swami described his journey up those seven thousand steps at Mount Girnar, that creaking bed, that sound of pattens in the little old half-forgotten temple, and fitted everything into an ancient discipline, a philosophy that satisfied the intellect, I found all I wanted.[33]

In *Meru*, the twelfth and last of his *Supernatural Songs* collection (1934), the poet honors the superior wisdom of Indian asceticism over the great civilizations of Egypt, Greece, and Rome. Yeats's description of naked ascetics in the Meru caves celebrates those who have relinquished all ties, the perfect Avadhūtas:

Civilisation is hooped together, brought
Under a rule, under the semblance of peace
By manifold illusion; but man's life is thought,
And he, despite his terror, cannot cease
Ravening through century after century,
Ravening, raging, and uprooting that he may come
Into the desolation of reality:
Egypt and Greece, good-bye, and good-bye, Rome!
Hermits upon Mount Meru or Everest,
Caverned in night under the drifted snow,
Or where that snow and winter's dreadful blast
Beat down upon their naked bodies, know
That day brings round the night, that before dawn
His glory and his monuments are gone.[34]

Finally, as in a game of sonic resonances, Dattātreya's "hidden presence" may be fathomed in T. S. Eliot's[35] (1888–1965) fifth and last section of *The Waste Land—What the Thunder Said* (395–433)—composed in 1922:[36]

Ganga was sunken, and the limp leaves
Waited for rain, while the black clouds
Gathered far distant, over Himavant.
The jungle crouched, humped in silence.
Then spoke the thunder
DA
Datta: what have we given?
My friend, blood shaking my heart
The awful daring of a moment's surrender
Which an age of prudence can never retract
By this, and this only, we have existed
Which is not to be found in our obituaries
Or in memories draped by the beneficent spider
Or under seals broken by the lean solicitor
In our empty rooms
DA
Dayadhvam: I have heard the key
Turn in the door once and turn once only
We think of the key, each in his prison
Thinking of the key, each confirms a prison
Only at nightfall, aethereal rumours
Revive for a moment a broken Coriolanus

DA
Damyata: The boat responded
Gaily, to the hand expert with sail and oar
The sea was calm, your heart would have responded
Gaily, when invited, beating obedient
To controlling hands

I sat upon the shore
Fishing, with the arid plain behind me
Shall I at least set my lands in order?
London Bridge is falling down falling down falling down
Poi s'ascose nel foco che gli affina
Quando fiam uti chelidon—O swallow swallow
Le Prince d'Aquitaine à la tour abolie
These fragments I have shored against my ruins
Why then Ile fit you. Hieronymo's mad againe.
Datta. Dayadhvam. Damyata.
Shantih shantih shantih[37]

The Sanskrit expression used, *datta dayadhvam dāmyata*—"give, be compassionate, restrain yourself"—is from *Bṛhadāraṇyaka Upaniṣad* 5.2,[38] in which Prajāpati teaches the meaning of the thunder's voice calling for cultivation of the virtues of charity, compassion, and self-control.[39] Though the thunder's voice was not intended to denote Dattātreya, I would like to close my study with a brief commentary on this lyric, eliciting—through its "*bīja-mantra*" *da*—the subtle presence of the deity. The mantric phoneme, even if unconsciously produced, is always believed to embody the deity itself, or to possess the power of "attracting" its corresponding divine force: the sound calls for the form and vice versa.[40]

The first *da* or thunderbolt is allegorically interpreted as *Datta*. The poet bitterly meditates upon the fundamental act of giving in the passion of sexual love. His bitterness lies in the impossibility of really communicating and transmitting the most profound sense of one's existence. "Datta," as Dattātreya, is potentially linked with such a poetical theme: On one level, through the Tantric sensuousness of his nature, in which human intercourse is sacralized as one of the most potent cyphers of divine power; on another level, in the impenetrable mystery which abides in this very act and which points to Datta's inconceivable nature.

The second *da* is *Dayadhvam*. Here the poet highlights human solitude and the impossibility of communicating with others. Men are caged within the prison of their own ego, with no effective chance of escaping their subjectivism. No real encounter with "the other" can take place, no sympathetic "com-passion" is possible, and once again the thunder's invitation is disclaimed.

The third *da* is *Damyata*. The poet's answer to the thunder's call is positive at first, yet the option of control, or self-control, is denied through the expression "your heart *would have* responded," the conditional implying the failure of a prospect, its non-realization. Nevertheless, in Eliot's following verses, there is a search for individual purification and meaning: "These fragments I have shored against my ruins" (430). The concluding invocation—*shantih, shantih, shantih*—points to the Peace which surpasses all understanding, indicating a metaphysical solution to existential misery.

The final section of *The Waste Land* frees the poem from the desolation and radical pessimism of its preceding sections. The poet delineates an apocalypse of sorts; every individual is advised to embark on an interior journey to find a meaning to one's life, a salvific message. *What the Thunder Said* is charged with a purificatory force, pointing to a metaphysical dimension: the only *telos* in which to "anchor" the waste land of the world and its desolated history. Hope in a spiritual renewal, in a "non-cruel April,"—couched in *Upaniṣadic* language—will find its solution with the poet's conversion to Anglicanism in 1927. It might be argued that Eliot's redemptive search in *The Waste Land* was Christian from the outset, dominated as it is by an apocalyptic or eschatological tension: a desperate call for a moral regeneration of history and the human condition.

From a nondual viewpoint—Dattātreya's—the only liberating redemption lies in the removal of *avidyā*. If recognition (*pratyabhijñā*) of one's identity with *Brahman* does not take place, one's destiny will be tragically tied to this dream world of *saṃsāra*. The salvific presence in our midst of a "māyic appearance" of the Absolute—in the form of Datta, the immortal Guru, Yogin, and Avatāra—is believed to be a constant reminder of our true ātmic nature. The deity's benevolent guidance, ferrying us across this worldly ocean of illusion, is always thought to be at hand: wherever we look, there we shall find him, in the external world as well as in our subjective internal realm. I like to think of Dattātreya's "sonic reflection" in the clear waters of Eliot's poetry as but another indication of the deity's ubiquitous and elusive nature.

Notes

1. Śrī Purohit Svāmin writes:

Thousands of people have visions of Him [Dattātreya]. He every now and then incarnates in new forms. The followers of Shiva and Vishnu worship Him as incarnations of them. The Yogis worship Him as the Master Yogi; the Jains worship Him as Neminath, and even the Moslems worship Him as the great Fakir. I have come across many a

Mohammedan Fakir who had a special devotion for Him. He is above all caste and creed and religion, for His is the mission of Love and Peace and divine union. (Purohit Swami, *An Indian Monk*, 75)

2. See Mokashi-Punekar, *Avadhoota Gita*, 10-11.

3. On the two main sects of Jainism, the Śvetāmbaras and Digambaras, see Surendranath Dasgupta, *A History of Indian Philosophy*, 1:170–71.

4. The expression "Sāī Bābā movement" was first adopted by Charles S. J. White in his article "The Sāī Bābā Movement: Approaches to the Study of Indian Saints." By the same author, see also "Structure and the History of Religions: Some Bhakti Examples" and "The Sāī Bābā Movement."

5. The identification of Sāī Bābā of Śirḍī with Dattātreya is such that the *Śrī Sāī Satcarita*—the most "authoritative" hagiography on the saint's life—is often called "the modern *Guru-caritra*"; see *Shri Sai Satcharita; or, The Wonderful Life and Teachings of Shri Sai Baba*, xvii. On Sāī Bābā of Śirḍī as Dattātreya, see also Babu, *Dattātreya: Glory of the Divine in Man.*

6. On Meher Bābā's life, see Anzar, *The Beloved: The Life and Work of Meher Baba*; Hopkinson and Hopkinson, *Much Silence: Meher Baba, His Life and Work.* On Meher Bābā's teachings, see Meher Baba, *Discourses*; Meher Baba, *God Speaks*; Purdom, *God to Man and Man to God: The Discourses of Meher Baba.*

7. On Satya Sāī Bābā's life, see Kasturi, *Sathyam Sivam Sundaram: The Life of Bhagavan Sri Sathya Sai Baba.* On the living saint's teachings, see the collection of his discourses in Satya Sai Baba, *Sathya Sai Speaks: Discourses Given by Bhagavan Sri Sathya Sai Baba.*

8. In 1981 Kasturi, a noted poet and humorist, won the State Sahitya Academy Award for his contributions to Kannaḍa literature.

9. Kasturi, *Loving God*, 312. This episode took place in the forest of the Wild Life Sanctuary, near the Nilgiri mountains, in the late seventies. For more details, see Murphet, *Sai Baba: Invitation to Glory*, 80–85. For other instances of Satya Sāī Bābā's identification with Dattātreya, see Kasturi, *Sathyam Sivam Sundaram*, 1:85, 198–201. Satya Sāī Bābā is often identified with Dattātreya in his role as supreme Guru; see the article "National Conference of Bal Vikas Gurus" in *Sanathana Sarathi* 37, no. 8 (August 1994): 208. Among the many *bhajans* sung in Satya Sāī Bābā's praise, one finds the following:

> Datta Guru, Datta Guru, Dattātreya Guru;
> Sāī Nātha, Dīna Nātha, Brahma Rūpa Guru;
> Alakha Nirañjana Bhava Bhaya Bhañjana Dattātreya Guru;
> Dattātreya Guru, Sāī Nātha Guru, Dīna Nātha Guru.

10. The first public announcement of his future manifestation as Preman Sāī was made on July 6, 1963, day of *Guru-pūrṇimā*. Satya Sāī referred the

Sāī Bābā lineage to Śiva's mythology, that is, to a boon Śiva and Śakti granted to Ṛṣi Bharadvāja, due to the latter's piousness in the preparation of a sacrifice taught to him by Indra:

> After the Yaga was over, They (Shiva and Shakti) were so pleased that they conferred even more boons on the sage. Shiva said that they would take Human Form and be born in the Bharadvaja lineage or Gothra thrice: Shiva alone as Shirdi Sai Baba, Shiva and Shakti together at Puttaparthi as Sathya Sai Baba, and Shakti alone as Prema Sai later. (Sathya Sai Baba, *Sathya Sai Speaks*, 3:23–24)

For an analysis of this claim and of the Bharadvāja myth, see Swallow, "Ashes and Powers: Myth, Rite and Miracle in an Indian God-Man's Cult."

11. On Gajānan Mahārāj, see K. R. Kulkarni, *The Saint of Shegaon: A Book of Poems on the Life of Shri Gajanan Mahārāj*. See also Dāsgaṇū, *Shree Gajanan Vijay*. Dāsgaṇū was a Citpāvan Brahmin whose original name was Gaṇeś Daṭtātreya Sahasrabuddhe (1868–1962). A devotee of Śiva who became a Vārkarī and a follower of the Sāī Bābā of Śirḍī, Dāsgaṇū was a great performer of song-sermons (*kīrtanas*) and a prolific writer. His Marāṭhī version of the *Godāvarī-māhātmya* deserves special mention. He was a staunch Hindu nationalist, a firm advocate of the caste system, and a Brahmin and Maharashtrian chauvinist.

12. On the connection between Gajānan Mahārāj and Sāī Bābā, see Rigopoulos, *The Life and Teachings of Sai Baba of Shirdi*, 137–39.

On Gajānan Mahārāj and Akkaḷkoṭ Mahārāj, see Pain and Zelliot, "The God Dattatreya," 104. Śrī Purohit Svāmin mentions a visit he paid to Gajānan Mahārāj:

> I . . . took the train for Akola. I wanted to pay my respects to Shri Gajanan Mahārāj, who was lodged there. I entered into the ashram . . . hundreds were coming in and going out, but the Swami was lying on a mattress covered . . . with a beautiful Kashmere shawl. That morning he had never once looked at anybody. Folk came in, touched his feet with their foreheads, and went away. Nobody dared to ask him to open his eyes. I entered to salute him, and whom should I see but my father Dadasahib, come to ask the Swami about my whereabouts. He had had no news of me and . . . was extremely anxious . . . I saluted him, and then the Swami . . . I sat at the feet of the Swami, silently praying that he might let us see him . . . The Swami all of a sudden took off his shawl, looked at us, and asked my father to go to the station and catch the train, and not to worry about me. He gave me his blessings and covered himself up as before. Everybody regarded us as unusually lucky. (Purohit Swami, *An Indian Monk*, 80–81)

13. See devotional texts such as the previously mentioned *Nav-nāth-caritra va Kathā* and the *Śrī-nav-nāth-kathā-sār*.

14. Locales I visited during two sojourns in Maharashtra. The first itinerary refers to October-November 1985, the second itinerary to November-December 1991. On the presence of Nātha ascetics in contemporary Maharashtra, see Pain and Zelliot, "The God Dattatreya," 103.

15. On Nisargadatta Mahārāj's teachings, see Nisargadatta Mahārāj, *I Am That: Talks with Sri Nisargadatta Mahārāj*. See also Powell, *The Nectar of the Lord's Feet: Final Teachings of Sri Nisargadatta Mahārāj.*

16. Nisargadatta Mahārāj, *I Am That*, 500–502, 505.

17. On Mahānubhāva practice, see Feldhaus, "The Orthodoxy of the Mahanubhavs," 270–76.

18. Episodes of Brahmin intolerance toward outcasts are sometimes reported. For a recent case of untouchables not being admitted inside a Datta temple in Śedgāo (famous as a healing center) by the local Brahmin "healer," see Saptarshi, "Orthodoxy and Human Rights: The Story of a Clash."

19. In his introduction to Śrī Purohit Svāmin's autobiography, Yeats noted:

> There are Indian courtesans that meditate many hours a day awaiting without sense of sin their moment, perhaps many lives hence, to leave man for God. For the present they are efficient courtesans. Ascetics, as this book tells, have lived in their houses and received pilgrims there. Kings, princes, beggars, soldiers, courtesans, and the fool by the wayside are equal to the eye of sanctity, for everybody's road is different, everybody awaits his moment. (Purohit Swami, *An Indian Monk*, xxv)

20. The relevance of music in the Datta cult has been signaled by R. C. Dhere, G. S. Ghurye, and S. Mokashi-Punekar. Charles Pain and Eleanor Zelliot mention the following episode:

> A noted classical singer and Datta devotee, Hirabai Barodekar, had a dream in which Dattatreya appeared as a bearded man. She searched for a temple with this image and, finding it, returned there once a year to sing a concert to Dattatreya. (Pain and Zelliot, "The God Dattatreya," 103)

21. Pargiter, *The Mārkaṇḍeya Purāṇa*, 107.

22. The Chishtī order is the most widely disseminated Sufi brotherhood in India. Tradition claims that it was founded by Khwadja Ahmad Abdal of Chisht (d. 965–66) and brought to India by Mu ᶜīn al-Dīn Chishti of Sistān (b. 1142). In 1193 he went to Delhi, but almost immediately moved to Ajmer where he died in 1236. The order lays special stress on the words *illa'llāh* and uses vocal music in religious services. The neophyte must observe poverty, contentment, remembrance of Allah, and austerity. On the Chishtī order, see Rizvi, *A History of Sufism in India*, 2:264–318.

23. See Lawrence, "The Early Chishtī Approach to Samā'." For a general presentation of *samā'*, see Molé, *La danse extatique en Islam*. Among the saints worshipped as Datta Avatāras, the Sāī Bābā of Śirḍī was renown for his love of music and dance; see Rigopoulos, *The Life and Teachings of Sai Baba of Shirdi*, 64–65, 105–6, 183. Charles Pain and Eleanor Zelliot interpret Dattātreya's connection to music as due to the influence of Nātha brotherhoods; see Pain and Zelliot, "The God Dattatreya," 107 n. 12.

24. That Dattātreya may grant *darśana* as a shepherd, that is, as a member of the Dhangar shepherd caste of Maharashtra, whose tutelary deity is Khaṇḍobā, is valuable information. This attests to devotion to Datta even within the tribal, pastoral environment of the region and offers another clear indication of the deity's connection with a non-Brahminical social milieu. On the Dhangar caste, see Karve, *Maharashtra State Gazetteer, Maharashtra: Land and Its People*, 20–21.

25. Literally "a striver," anyone who has restrained his passions and has abandoned the world.

26. An implicit reference to Dattātreya as manifestation of the *trimūrti* of Brahmā, Viṣṇu, and Śiva.

27. Belief that Datta was a worshiper of Śiva and attained liberating knowledge from him is a modern interpretation derived from a *Śaiva* sectarian milieu. With this turn, the circle is complete: from a mythical identification of Dattātreya with Śiva, and his subsequent presentation as Śiva's Guru in Aghorī and Nepali religiosity, we now find him identified as Śiva's *śiṣya*. Dattātreya appears as Śiva's disciple, Śiva's teacher, or Śiva himself depending on the major or minor relevance of certain mythical strands. Once again we are faced with a *Śaiva* characterization of the deity.

28. Quoted in Mokashi-Punekar, *Avadhoota Gita*, 31–34.

29. The works of Śrī Purohit Svāmin, besides his autobiography, *An Indian Monk*, include: *The Holy Mountain*, *The Geeta*, *The Ten Principal Upanishads*, and *Aphorisms of Yoga, by Bhagwan Shree Patanjali*. All published by Faber and Faber during the 1930s, their translations were influenced by Yeats's poetical and linguistic suggestions. All except *The Geeta* contain either an introduction or a preface by Yeats. The Svāmin published an English translation of his Marāṭhī poems under the title *The Song of Silence*. Yeats included some of these poems in *The Oxford Book of Modern Verse*.

30. Mokashi-Punekar, *Avadhoota Gita*, 35. On polytheism, see Yeats's comments in his introduction to Śrī Purohit Svāmin's autobiography, *An Indian Monk*, xxii–xxiii. On the reciprocal influence and interaction between Śrī Purohit Svāmin and Yeats, see Mokashi-Punekar, "W. B. Yeats and Sri Purohit Swami." See also Zolla, *Lo stupore infantile*, 211-12.

31. Mention must be made of Yeats's 1912 introduction to the English translation of Rabindranath Tagore's *Gītāñjali* collection, for which the Beṅgalī poet won the Nobel Prize in 1913.

32. See Harper, *Yeats and the Occult*; Flannery, *Yeats and Magic*; and Kinahan, *Yeats, Folklore, and Occultism*. On Yeats's connection with the philosophy of neo-Platonism, see F. A. C. Wilson, *Yeats and Iconography*, and, by the same author, *W. B. Yeats and Tradition*. See also Hough, *The Mystery Religion of W. B. Yeats*.

33. Purohit Swami, *An Indian Monk*, xvii–xviii.

34. Yeats, *Collected Poems*, 333–34. For a commentary on this sonnet, see Smith, *W. B. Yeats: A Critical Introduction*, 153–58.

35. Twenty-three years younger than Yeats, Eliot knew of his fascination for Indian religion and philosophy. In 1925, two years before his conversion to Anglicanism, Eliot became a member of the executive board of the Faber and Gwyer (subsequently Faber and Faber) publishing house, later becoming director of its literary section. Since Śrī Purohit Svāmin—via Yeats—published his translations of Hindu texts for Faber and Faber from 1934 onward, Eliot must have known the works of the Indian renunciant.

36. In a letter to Bertrand Russell, dated August 15, 1923, the poet noted that *What the Thunder Said* was not just the better part of the poem but actually the only part justifying the whole.

37. Eliot, *Collected Poems 1909–1962*, 78–79.

38. The *Upaniṣad* lists the three "*da*" in different order: first *dāmyata*, then *datta*, and third *dayadhvam*. Eliot studied Sanskrit at Harvard from 1911 to 1913.

39. For an examination of this passage of the *Bṛhadāraṇyaka Upaniṣad*, see Della Casa, *Upaniṣad*, 141–42. On this "riddle text" of the thunder's voice, see the observations of Oldenberg, *The Doctrine of the Upaniṣads and the Early Buddhism*, 82, 108–9.

40. S. K. Phadke has drawn attention to the thunder story of *Bṛhadāraṇyaka Upaniṣad* 5.2, symbolically relating it to Dattātreya's nature. See Mokashi-Punekar, *Avadhoota Gita*, 34–35.

General Bibliography

Abbott, Justin E. *Bhānudās: A Translation from the* Bhakta-vijaya of Mahīpati. The Poet-Saints of Maharashtra Series, no. 1. Puṇe: Scottish Mission Industries, 1926.

Abhinava Nṛsiṃha Bhāratī. *Śrī Śiva-gītā-bhāṣyam.* Bangalore, 1962.

Agrawāla, Ratna Chandra. "Some Important Mediaeval Images of Viṣṇu from Rājaputānā." *The Adyar Library Bulletin* 18, pt. 3–4 (December 1954): 257–63.

Aiyar, P. "Imitations of the Bhagavad-gītā and Later Gītā Literature." In *The Cultural Heritage of India,* 2d ed., edited by H. Bhattacharya, 2:204f. Calcutta: Ramakrishna Mission Institute of Culture, 1957–62.

Allen, N. J. "The Coming of Macchendranāth to Nepāl: Comments from a Comparative Point of View." In *Oxford University Papers on India,* edited by N. J. Allen et al., vol. 1, pt. 1. Delhi: Oxford University Press, 1986.

Assayag, Jackie. "Sacrifice et violence: Les genres de la possession dans le sud de l'Inde." *Nouvelle Revue d'Ethnopsychiatrie* 13 (1989): 151–83.

———. *La colère de la déesse décapitée: Traditions, cultes et pouvoir dans le sud de l'Inde.* Paris: CNRS, 1992.

Aziz, K. K. "Glimpses of Muslim Culture in the Deccan." In *Vijayanagara, City and Empire: New Currents of Research,* edited by Anna Libera Dallapiccola, in collaboration with Stephanie Zingel-Avé Lallemant, 1:159–76. Stuttgart: Steiner Verlag, 1985.

Balfour, Henry. "Life History of an Aghori Fakir." *Journal of the Anthropological Institute of Great Britain and Ireland* 26 (1897): 340ff.

Banerjea, Akshaya Kumar. *Philosophy of Gorakhnath: With* Goraksha-vacana-sangraha. Prefatory note by Mahamahopadhyaya Gopinath Kaviraj.

Foreword by C. P. Ramaswami Aiyar. Gorakhpur, 1962. Reprint, Delhi: Motilal Banarsidass, 1988.

Banerjea, Jitendra Nath. *The Development of Hindu Iconography*. Calcutta: University of Calcutta, 1956.

Banerji, S. C. *Tantra in Bengal: A Study in Its Origin, Development and Influence.* New Delhi: Manohar, 1992.

Bareau, André. "Les agissements de Devadatta selon les chapitres relatifs au schisme dans les divers *vinayapiṭaka*." *Bulletin de l'École Française d'Extrême-Orient* 78 (1991): 87–132.

Barrow, H. W. "On Aghoris and Aghorapanthis." *Journal of the Anthropological Society of Bombay* 3 (1893): 197–251.

Barthwal, P. D. *The Nirguṇa School of Hindi Poetry*. Benares, 1936.

Basham, A. L. *The Wonder That Was India*. New York, 1959. Reprint, New Delhi: Rupa & Co., 1989.

Beck, Guy L. *Sonic Theology: Hinduism and Sacred Sound*. Columbia: University of South Carolina Press, 1993.

Bedi, Rajesh, and Ramesh Bedi. *Sadhus: The Holy Men of India*. New Delhi: Brijbasi Printers, 1991.

Belier, Wouter W. *Decayed Gods: Origin and Development of Georges Dumézil's "Idéologie Tripartie."* Leiden: E. J. Brill, 1991.

Bharati, Agehananda. *The Tantric Tradition*. London: Rider & Company, 1965.

———. "Pilgrimage Sites and Indian Civilization." In *Chapters in Indian Civilization*, edited by J. W. Elder, 1:85–126. Dubuque: Kendall/Hunt Publishing Company, 1970.

Bhardwaj, Surinder Mohan. *Hindu Places of Pilgrimage in India: A Study in Cultural Geography*. Berkeley and Los Angeles: University of California Press, 1973.

Bhave, V. L. *Mahārāṣṭra Sārasvata*. 5th ed., containing a supplement by Shankar Gopal Tulpule. Bombay, 1963.

———, ed. *Gītārṇava*. The Mahārāṣṭra Kavi Series, 1905–6.

Biardeau, Madeleine. *La décapitation de Reṇukā dans le mythe de Paraśurāma*. Pratidānam (Kuiper Festschrift), The Hague, 1968.

———. "The Story of Arjuna Kārtavīrya without Reconstruction." *Purāṇa* 12, no. 2 (July 1970): 286–303.

———. "Études de mythologie Hindoue (4)." *Bulletin de l'École Française d'Extrême-Orient* 63 (1976): 175–82.

Böhtlingk, O. *Indische Sprüche*. 2d ed. Vol. 1. Wiesbaden, 1966.

Bouillier, Véronique. "La caste sectaire des Kānphaṭā Jogī dans le royaume du Népal: L'exemple de Gorkha." *Bulletin de l'École Française d'Extrême-Orient* 75 (1986): 105–47.

———. "Une caste de Yogī Newar: Les Kusle-Kāpāli." *Bulletin de l'École Française d'Extrême-Orient* 80, no. 1 (1993): 75–106.

Bouy, Christian. "Matériaux pour servir aux études upaniṣadiques. (1) Un manuscrit sanskrit de Tanjore." *Journal Asiatique* 278, no. 1–2 (1990): 71–134.

———. *Les Nātha-yogin et les Upaniṣads*. Publications de l'Institut de Civilisation Indienne, fasc. 62. Paris: Diffusion de Boccard, 1994.

Brinkhaus, Horst. "The Descent of the Nepalese Malla Dynasty as Reflected by Local Chroniclers." *Journal of the American Oriental Society* 111, no. 1 (January–March 1991): 118–22.

———. "Early Developmental Stages of the Viṣṇuprādurbhāva Lists." *Wiener Zeitschrift für die Kunde Südasiens* 1993 Supplementband: 101–10.

Brooks, Douglas Renfrew. *The Secret of the Three Cities: An Introduction to Hindu Śākta Tantrism*. Chicago: University of Chicago Press, 1990.

———. *Auspicious Wisdom: The Texts and Traditions of Śrīvidyā Śākta Tantrism in South India*. Albany, N.Y.: SUNY Press, 1992.

Brough, John. *The Early Brahmanical System of Gotra and Pravara: A Translation of the* Gotra-pravara-mañjarī *of Puruṣottama-paṇḍita*. Cambridge: Cambridge University Press, 1953.

Brown, C. Mackenzie. *The Triumph of the Goddess: The Canonical Models and Theological Visions of the Devī-Bhāgavata Purāṇa*. Albany, N.Y.: SUNY Press, 1990.

Brown, Robert L., ed. *Ganesh: Studies of an Asian God*. Albany, N.Y.: SUNY Press, 1991.

Brunner, Helene. "Un Tantra du Nord: Le Netra Tantra." *Bulletin de l'École Française d'Extrême-Orient* 61 (1974): 125–97.

Bühnemann, Gudrun. *Forms of Gaṇeśa: A Study Based on the* Vidyārṇavatantra. Wichtrach: Institut für Indologie, 1989.

Burgess, J. *Report on the Antiquities of Kathiawad and Kacch. Archaeological Survey of Western India*, vol. 2. London, 1876.

Burnouf, M. E. "Sur les trente-deux signes caractéristiques d'un grand homme." In *Le Lotus de la Bonne Loi*: Traduit du Sanscrit, accompagné d'un commentaire et de vingt et un mémoires relatifs au Buddhisme, 553–647. 1852. Reprint, Paris: Adrien Maisonneuve, 1989.

Cenkner, William. *A Tradition of Teachers: Śaṅkara and the Jagadgurus Today.* Delhi: Motilal Banarsidass, 1983.

Chakravarti, Chintaharan. *Tantras: Studies on Their Religion and Literature.* Calcutta: Punthi Pustak, 1963.

Chakravarti, Mahadev. *The Concept of Rudra-Śiva through the Ages.* Delhi: Motilal Banarsidass, 1986.

Chapple, Cristopher, and Yogi Ananda Viraj. *The Yoga Sūtras of Patañjali: An Analysis of the Sanskrit with Accompanying English Translation.* Delhi: Sri Satguru Publications, 1990.

Charmier, L., trans. *Sūrya-gītā.* Madras, 1904.

Chatterjee, J. C. *Kashmir Shaivaism.* 1914. Reprint, Srinagar: Research and Publications Department, 1962.

Chidbhavananda, Swami. *Śiva Sahasranāma Stotram: With Namavali, Introduction, and English Rendering.* Tirupparaitturai: Sri Ramakrishna Tapovanam, 1985.

Coburn, Thomas B. *Encountering the Goddess: A Translation of the Devī-Māhātmya and a Study of Its Interpretation.* Albany, N.Y.: SUNY Press, 1991.

Courtright, Paul B. *Gaṇeśa: Lord of Obstacles, Lord of Beginnings.* New York: Oxford University Press, 1985.

Crooke, William. "Aghori." In *Encyclopaedia of Religion and Ethics,* edited by James Hastings. New York: Charles Scribner's Sons, 1928.

———. "Berar." In *Encyclopaedia of Religion and Ethics,* edited by James Hastings. New York: Charles Scribner's Sons, 1928.

da Cunha, Jerson H. *The Sahyādri Khaṇḍa of the Skanda-purāṇa.* Bombay, 1877.

Dandekar, Mamasaheb. *Vārkarī Bhajan-mālā Saṃgraha.* Nāgpur: Vārkarī Prakāśan Maṇḍal, 1990.

Dasgupta, Shashibhusan. *Obscure Religious Cults.* 2d ed. Calcutta: Firma K. L. Mukhopadhyay, 1962.

Dasgupta, Surendranath. *A History of Indian Philosophy.* 5 vols. Cambridge, 1922. Reprint, Delhi: Motilal Banarsidass, 1975.

Dave, J. H. *Immortal India.* 4 vols. Bombay: Bharatiya Vidya Bhavan, 1991.

Della Casa, Carlo. *Upaniṣad.* Torino: Unione Tipografico-Editrice Torinese, 1976.

Deshmukh, Bhagavantha, ed. *Gītārtha-candrikā.* Aurangabad, 1962.

Deussen, Paul. *Sechzig Upanishad's des Veda.* Leipzig: F. A. Brockhaus, 1905.

Dev, S. S., ed. *Dāsa-viśrāma-dhāma* (1–4). Dhule, 1912–23.

———. *Grantha-rāja*. Puṇe, 1914.

Dhere, R. C. *Śrīguru Gorakṣanātha: Caritra āṇi Paramparā*. Bombay, 1959.

———. *Musalmān Marāṭhī Santa-Kavī*. Puṇe: Jñānrāj Prakashan, 1967.

———. *Śākti-pīṭhāncā Śodha*. Kolhapur, 1973.

Dikshit, T. R. C., ed. *Saṃnyāsa Upaniṣads*. With the Commentary of Śrī Upaniṣad-Brahma-Yogin. Madras: Adyar Library, 1929.

Dimmitt, Cornelia, and J. A. B. van Buitenen, eds. and trans. *Classical Hindu Mythology: A Reader in the Sanskrit Purāṇas*. Philadelphia: Temple University Press, 1978.

Dowson, John. *A Classical Dictionary of Hindu Mythology and Religion, Geography, History and Literature*. London: Routledge & Kegan Paul, 1961.

Dumézil, Georges. *Les dieux souverains des Indo-Européens*. Paris: Editions Gallimard, 1977.

Dunuwila, Rohan A. *Śaiva Siddhānta Theology: A Context for Hindu-Christian Dialogue*. Delhi: Motilal Banarsidass, 1985.

Dvivedi, Hajariprasad. *Nāth Sampradāy*. Allahabad: Hindustani Academy, 1950.

———. *Nāth Siddhon kī Bāniyān*. Benares: Nagaripracarini Sabha, 1957.

Dyczkowski, Mark S. G. *The Doctrine of Vibration: An Analysis of the Doctrines and Practices of Kashmir Shaivism*. Albany, N.Y.: SUNY Press, 1987.

———. *The Canon of the Śaivāgama and the Kubjikā Tantras of the Western Kaula Tradition*. Albany, N.Y.: SUNY Press, 1988.

———. *The Stanzas on Vibration: The* Spandakārikā *with Four Commentaries: The* Spandasaṃdoha *by Kṣemarāja, the* Spandavṛtti *by Kallaṭabhaṭṭa, the* Spandavivṛti *by Rājānaka Rāma, the* Spandapradīpikā *by Bhagavadutpala*. Albany, N.Y.: SUNY Press, 1992.

Eaton, Richard Maxwell. *Sufis of Bijapur (1300–1700): Social Roles of Sufis in Medieval India*. Princeton: Princeton University Press, 1978.

Eck, Diana L. *Banaras, City of Light*. New York: Alfred A. Knopf, 1982.

Edgerton, Franklin, trans. *The Bhagavad Gītā*. Cambridge: Harvard University Press, 1944. Reprint, New York: Harper and Row, Harper Torchbook, 1964.

Eliade, Mircea. *Yoga: Immortality and Freedom*. Translated from the French by Willard R. Trask. 3d ed. Bollingen Series 56. Princeton: Princeton University Press, 1973.

Eliot, T. S. *Collected Poems 1909–1962*. 1963. Reprint, London: Faber and Faber, 1990.

Elizarenkova, Tatyana J. *Language and Style of the Vedic Rsis.* Edited with a Foreword by Wendy Doniger. Albany, N.Y.: SUNY Press, 1995.

Erndl, Kathleen M. "Śerāṅvālī: The Mother Who Possesses." In *Devī: Goddesses of India*, edited by John Stratton Hawley and Donna Marie Wulff, 173–94. Berkeley and Los Angeles: University of California Press, 1996.

Feldhaus, Anne. *The Religious System of the Mahānubhāva Sect: The Mahānubhāva Sūtrapāṭha.* New Delhi: Manohar, and Columbia, Mo.: South Asia Books, 1983.

———. *The Deeds of God in Ṛddhipur.* New York: Oxford University Press, 1984.

———. "The Orthodoxy of the Mahanubhavs." In *The Experience of Hinduism: Essays on Religion in Maharashtra*, edited by Eleanor Zelliot and Maxine Berntsen, 264–79. Albany, N.Y.: SUNY Press, 1988.

Feldhaus, Anne, and Shankar Gopal Tulpule. *In the Absence of God: The Early Years of an Indian Sect. A Translation of Smṛtisthaḷ with an Introduction.* Honolulu: University of Hawaii Press, 1992.

Feuerstein, Georg. *Encyclopedic Dictionary of Yoga.* New York: Paragon Press, 1990.

———. *Holy Madness: The Shock Tactics and Radical Teachings of Crazy-Wise Adepts, Holy Fools, and Rascal Gurus.* New York: Arkana Books, 1992.

Flannery, M. C. *Yeats and Magic.* Colin Smythe, 1977.

Fort, Andrew O. "Going or Knowing? The Development of the Idea of Living Liberation in the Upaniṣads." *Journal of Indian Philosophy* 22 (1994): 379–90.

Fort, Andrew, and Patricia Mumme, eds. *Living Liberation in Hindu Thought.* Albany, N.Y.: SUNY Press, 1996.

Gail, A. *Paraśurāma Brahmane und Krieger.* Wiesbaden, 1977.

Ganapathy, T. N. *The Philosophy of the Tamil Siddhas.* New Delhi: Indian Council of Philosophical Research, 1993.

Geden, A. S. "Tantras." In *Encyclopaedia of Religion and Ethics*, edited by James Hastings. New York: Charles Scribner's Sons, 1928.

Glucklich, A. "The Royal Scepter (Daṇḍa) as Legal Punishment and Sacred Symbol." *History of Religions* 28, no. 2 (November 1988): 97–122.

Gonda, Jan. *Change and Continuity in Indian Religion.* Disputationes Rheno-Trajectinae 9. The Hague: Mouton, 1965.

———. *Vedic Literature.* Wiesbaden: Otto Harrassowitz, 1975.

———. *Viṣṇuism and Śivaism: A Comparison*. New Delhi: Munshiram Manoharlal, 1976.

Graves, Robert. *Greek Myths* (1955).

Grimes, John A. *Gaṇapati: Song of the Self.* Albany, N.Y.: SUNY Press, 1995.

Gupta, Roxanne Poormon. "The Kīnā Rāmī: Augharṣ and Kings in the Age of Cultural Contact." In *Bhakti Religion in North India: Community Identity and Political Action*, edited by David N. Lorenzen, 133–42. Albany, N.Y.: SUNY Press, 1995.

Gupta, Sanjukta, Dirk Jan Hoens, and Teun Goudriaan. *Hindu Tantrism*. Leiden: E. J. Brill, 1979.

Hacker, Paul. "Ānvīkṣikī." *Wiener Zeitschrift für die Kunde Süd-und Ostasiens* 2 (1958): 54–83.

Halbfass, Wilhelm. *India and Europe: An Essay in Understanding*. Albany, N.Y.: SUNY Press, 1988.

Handiqui, Krishna Kanta. *Yaśastilaka and Indian Culture or Somadeva's Yaśastilaka and Aspects of Jainism and Indian Thought and Culture in the Tenth Century*. Sholapur: Jaina Saṁskṛti Saṁrakshaka Sangha, 1949.

Hara, Minoru. "A Note on the Pāśupata Concept of Purity (saucha)." In *Svasti Sri: Dr. B. Ch. Chhabra Felicitation Volume*, edited by K. V. Ramesh et al., 237–44. Delhi: Agam Kala Prakashan, 1984.

Harper, George Mills, ed. *Yeats and the Occult*. London: Macmillan, 1975.

Hazra, R. C. *Studies in the Upapurāṇas*. 2 vols. Calcutta: Sanskrit College, 1963.

———. *Studies in the Purāṇic Records on Hindu Rites and Customs*. Dacca, 1940. Reprint, Delhi: Motilal Banarsidass, 1987.

Hopkins, E. Washburn. *Epic Mythology*. Strassburg, 1915. Reprint, Delhi: Motilal Banarsidass, 1974.

Hough, Graham. *The Mystery Religion of W. B. Yeats*. Harvester Press, 1984.

The Imperial Gazetteer of India. Vol. 12. Oxford: Clarendon Press, 1908.

Ingalls, Daniel H. H. "Cynics and Pāśupatas: The Seeking of Dishonor." *Harvard Theological Review* 55 (1962): 281–98.

Jamison, Stephanie W. *The Ravenous Hyenas and the Wounded Sun: Myth and Ritual in Ancient India*. Ithaca and London: Cornell University Press, 1991.

Jansen, Roland. *Die Bhavani von Tuljapur: Religionsgeschichtliche Studie des Kultes einer Göttin der indischen Volksreligion*. Stuttgart: Steiner Verlag, 1995.

Jayantavijayaji, Shrī. *Holy Abu: A Tourist's Guide to Mount Ābu and Its Jaina Shrines*. Translated from Gujarātī with an introduction by Umākānt Premānand Shāh. Foreword by V. S. Agrawāla. Bhāvnagar: Shrī Yashovijaya Jaina Granthamālā, 1954.

Johnsen, Linda. *Daughters of the Goddess: The Women Saints of India*. St. Paul: Yes International Publishers, 1994.

Jones, Rex L. "Shamanism in South Asia: A Preliminary Survey." *History of Religions* 7, no. 4 (1968): 330–47.

Kakar, Sudhir. *Shamans, Mystics, and Doctors*. New York: Knopf, 1982.

Kalyāṇa Kalpataru Series. Gorakhpur: Gita Press.

Kane, Pandurang Vaman. *History of Dharmaśāstra*. 5 vols. (7 pts.). Poona: Bhandarkar Oriental Research Institute, 1930–62.

Karve, Iravati. *Maharashtra State Gazetteer, Maharashtra: Land and Its People*. Bombay: Directorate of Government Printing, Stationery and Publications, Maharashtra State, 1968.

Kaviraj, Gopinath. *Aspects of Indian Thought*. Burdwan: University of Burdwan, 1966.

———, ed. *Gorakṣa-siddhānta-saṃgraha*. Princess of Wales Sarasvati Bhavan Texts, no. 18. Benares: Vidya Vilas Press, 1925.

Kerényi, Károly. *Die Mythologie der Griechen*. Zurich: Rhein-Verlag, 1951.

Khanna, Madhu. *Yantra: The Tantric Symbol of Cosmic Unity*. London: Thames and Hudson, 1979.

Kinahan, Frank. *Yeats, Folklore, and Occultism*. Unwin Hyman, 1988.

Kinsley, David. "'Through the Looking Glass': Divine Madness in the Hindu Religious Tradition." *History of Religions* 13, no. 4 (May 1974): 270–305.

———. *Hindu Goddesses: Visions of the Divine Feminine in the Hindu Religious Tradition*. Berkeley and Los Angeles: University of California Press, 1986.

Kolenda, Pauline. "Pox and the Terror of Childlessness: Images and Ideas of the Smallpox Goddess in a North Indian Village." In *Caste, Cult and Hierarchy: Essays on the Culture of India*, edited by Pauline Kolenda, 198–221. New Delhi: Folklore Institute, 1983.

Kolte, V. B., ed. *Sthāna-pothī*. Malkapur, 1950.

———. *Śrī-cakradhar-caritra*. Malkapur, 1952.

———. *Ravaḷobāsa-kṛta Sahyādri-varṇana*. Puṇe, 1964.

Kramrisch, Stella. *The Hindu Temple*. 2 vols. Calcutta, 1946. Reprint, Delhi: Motilal Banarsidass, 1981.

Kripananda, Swami, trans. *Jnaneshwar's Gita: A Rendering of the Jnaneshwari*. Foreword by Ian M. P. Raeside. Introduction by Shankar Gopal Tulpule. Albany, N.Y.: SUNY Press, 1989.

Kulkarnee, Narayan H. "Medieval Maharashtra and Muslim Saint-Poets." In *Medieval Bhakti Movements in India: Śrī Caitanya Quincentenary Commemoration Volume*, edited by N. N. Bhattacharyya, 198–231. New Delhi: Munshiram Manoharlal, 1989.

Kvaerne, Per. "On the Concept of Sahaja in Indian Buddhist Tantric Literature." *Temenos* 11 (1975): 88–135.

Larson, Gerald James, and Ram Shankar Bhattacharya, eds. *Encyclopedia of Indian Philosophies*. Vol. 4, *Sāṃkhya: A Dualist Tradition in Indian Philosophy*. Princeton: Princeton University Press, 1987.

Lawrence, B. B. "The Early Chishtī Approach to Samā'." In *Islamic Society and Culture: Essays in Honour of Professor Aziz Ahmad*, edited by Milton Israel and N. K. Wagle, 69–93. New Delhi: Manohar, 1983.

Lele, K. V., ed. *Dāsopantācī Padē*. Wai, n.d.

Levitt, S. H. "The Sahyādri-khaṇḍa: Some Problems . . ." *Purāṇa* 19, no. 1 (1977): 8–40.

Levy, Robert I. *Mesocosm: Hinduism and the Organization of a Traditional Newar City in Nepal*. With the collaboration of Kedar Raj Rajopadhyaya. Berkeley and Los Angeles: University of California Press, 1990.

———. "The Power of Space in a Traditional Hindu City." *International Journal of Hindu Studies* 1, no. 1 (1997).

Lewis, I. M. *Ecstatic Religion: An Anthropological Study of Spirit Possession and Shamanism*. Harmondsworth: Pelican Books, 1971.

Liebert, G. *Iconographic Dictionary of the Indian Religions*. Leiden: E. J. Brill, 1976.

Lienhard, Siegfried. "Problèmes du syncrétisme religieux au Népal." *Bulletin de l'École Française d'Extrême-Orient* 65, fasc. 1 (1978): 239–70.

Lorenzen, David N. *The Kāpālikas and Kālāmukhas: Two Lost Śaivite Sects*. Berkeley and Los Angeles: University of California Press, 1972.

———. "Warrior Ascetics in Indian History." *Journal of the American Oriental Society* 98 (1978): 61–75.

———. *Kabir Legends and Ananta-Das's Kabir Parachai*. With a Translation of the *Kabir Parachai* prepared in collaboration with Jagdish Kumar and Uma Thukral and with an edition of the Niranjani Panthi recension of this work. Albany, N.Y.: SUNY Press, 1991.

———. "The Lives of *Nirguṇī* Saints." In *Bhakti Religion in North India: Community Identity and Political Action,* edited by David N. Lorenzen, 181–211. Albany, N.Y.: SUNY Press, 1995.

Macdonell, A. A. *Vedic Mythology*. Strassburg, 1898. Reprint, Delhi: Motilal Banarsidass, 1974.

Madhavananda, Swami, trans. *Uddhava Gītā*. Reprint, Calcutta: Advaita Ashrama, 1978.

Mahadevan, T. M. P. *Manīṣāpañcaka*. Madras, 1967.

———. *Śaṅkara and Lalitādvaita*. Madras: The South Indian Sanskrit Association, 1974.

Maharashtra. *Śrī Ekanāthī Bhāgavata*. Bombay: Government of Maharashtra, 1971.

Mallik, Kalyani. *Siddha-siddhānta-paddhati and Other Works of the Nātha Yogīs*. Foreword by Rao Bahadur P. C. Divanji. Puṇe: Puṇe Oriental Book House, 1954.

Mani, Vettam. *Purāṇic Encyclopaedia: A Comprehensive Dictionary with Special Reference to the Epic and Purāṇic Literature*. Delhi: Motilal Banarsidass, 1975.

Marchetto, Monia. "Aghora-mārga: Analisi delle dottrine e del metodo." Thesis, *Cà Foscari* Venice University, 1996.

Mate, M. S. *Temples and Legends of Maharashtra*. 3d ed. Bombay: Bharatiya Vidya Bhavan, 1988.

McDaniel, June. *The Madness of the Saints: Ecstatic Religion in Bengal*. Chicago: University of Chicago Press, 1989.

Meyer, Johann Jakob. *Sexual Life in Ancient India: A Study in the Comparative History of Indian Culture*. Reprint, Delhi: Motilal Banarsidass, 1989.

Mishra, Kamalakar. *Significance of the Tantric Tradition*. Varanasi: Ardhanarisvara Publications, 1981.

Miśra, Raghunātha, ed. *Cidgaganacandrikā: With the Commentary by Raghunātha Miśra Entitled* Kramaprakāśika. Varanāsī: Sampurnānand Sanskrit Vishvavidyālaya, 1980.

Mitchiner, John E. *Traditions of the Seven Ṛṣis*. Delhi: Motilal Banarsidass, 1982.

Molé, M. *La danse extatique en Islam*. Sources Orientales 6. Paris, 1963.

Mookerjee, Ajit, and Madhu Khanna. *The Tantric Way: Art, Science, Ritual*. London: Thames and Hudson, 1977.

Muir, J. *Original Sanskrit Texts on the Origin and History of the People of India, Their Religion and Institutions*. 2d ed. Vol. 1. Amsterdam: Oriental Press, 1967.

Muller-Ortega, Paul Eduardo. *The Triadic Heart of Śiva: Kaula Tantricism of Abhinavagupta in the Non-Dual Shaivism of Kashmir*. Albany, N.Y.: SUNY Press, 1989.

Natarajan, B., trans. *Tirumular Tirumantiram Holy Hymns*. 10 vols. with introduction, synopsis, and notes. Madras: ITES Publications, 1979.

Nityaswarupananda, Swami, trans. *Aṣṭāvakra Saṃhitā*. Text with English rendering, comments and index. 5th ed. Calcutta: Advaita Ashrama, 1981.

Nizami, K. A. "Sufi Movement in the Deccan." In *History of Medieval Deccan (1295–1724)*, edited by H. K. Sherwani and P. M. Joshi, 2:175–99. Hyderabad: Government of Andhra Pradesh, 1973.

Oberhammer, Gerhard. *La délivrance, dès cette vie (jīvanmuktiḥ)*. Publications de l'Institut de Civilisation Indienne, fasc. 61. Paris: Diffusion de Boccard, 1994.

O'Flaherty, Wendy Doniger. *Hindu Myths: A Sourcebook Translated from the Sanskrit*. Harmondsworth: Penguin, 1975.

———. *Sexual Metaphors and Animal Symbols in Indian Mythology*. Delhi: Motilal Banarsidass, 1980.

———. *Śiva: The Erotic Ascetic*. London: Oxford University Press, 1981.

———. *Dreams, Illusion and Other Realities*. Chicago: University of Chicago Press, 1984.

Ojha, Catherine. "Condition féminine et renoncement au monde dans l'hindouisme: Les communautés monastiques de femmes à Benares." *Bulletin de l'École Française d'Extrême-Orient* 73 (1984): 197–222.

Oldenberg, Hermann. *The Doctrine of the Upaniṣads and the Early Buddhism*. Translated by Shridhar B. Shrotri. 1908. Reprint, Delhi: Motilal Banarsidass, 1991.

Olivelle, Patrick. "Renouncer and Renunciation in the Dharmaśāstras." In *Studies in Dharmaśāstra*, edited by R. Lariviere, 81–152. Calcutta: Firma KLM, 1984.

———. *Renunciation in Hinduism: A Medieval Debate*. 2 vols. Vienna: Publications of the De Nobili Research Library, 1986.

———. *The Āśrama System: The History and Hermeneutics of a Religious Institution*. New York: Oxford University Press, 1993.

———. "Orgasmic Rapture and Divine Ecstasy: The Semantic History of *Ānanda*." *Journal of Indian Philosophy* 25, no. 2 (1997): 153–80.

Orr, W. G. "Armed Religious Ascetics in Northern India." *Bulletin of the John Rylands Library* 24 (1940): 81–100.

Osborne, Arthur. *The Teachings of Ramana Maharshi*. Tiruvannamalai: Sri Ramanasramam, 1962.

Padoux, André. "Contributions a l'étude du mantraśāstra." *Bulletin de l'École Française d'Extrême-Orient* 67 (1980): 59–102.

———. *Vāc. The Concept of the Word in Selected Hindu Tantras*. Albany, N.Y.: SUNY Press, 1990.

Pal, Pratapaditya. "The Fifty-one Śākta Pīṭhas." In *Orientalia Iosephi Tucci Memoriae Dicata*, edited by G. Gnoli and L. Lanciotti, 1039–1060. Serie Orientale Roma 56, 3. Roma: Istituto Italiano per il Medio ed Estremo Oriente, 1988.

Pandey, K. C. *Abhinavagupta: An Historical and Philosophical Study*. Varanasi: Chowkhamba, 1963.

———. *An Outline of History of Śaiva Philosophy*. Reprint, Delhi: Motilal Banarsidass, 1986.

Panikkar, Raimundo. *Myth, Faith and Hermeneutics: Cross-Cultural Studies*. New York: Paulist Press, 1979.

Panshikar, N. V., ed. *Viśvavandh Śrī Tukārām Mahārāj Yāñchi Sampūrṇa Abhaṅg*. Puṇe: Panshikar Prakashan, 1968.

Parry, Jonathan P. "Sacrificial Death and the Necrophagous Ascetic." In *Death and the Regeneration of Life*, edited by M. Bloch and J. P. Parry, 74–110. Cambridge: Cambridge University Press, 1982.

———. "The Aghori Ascetics of Benares." In *Indian Religion*, edited by Richard Burghart and Audrey Cantlie, 51–78. London: Curzon Press; New York: St. Martin's Press, 1985.

Pelissero, Alberto. "The Soul as a Grain of Rice: The Way Out of Karman in Abhinavagupta's Paramārthasāra." *East and West* 42, nos. 2–4 (December 1992): 261–80.

Pellegrini, Agata Sannino. "Il canto di Aṣṭāvakra (*Aṣṭāvakragītā*)." *La Memoria*. Annali della Facoltà di Lettere e Filosofia dell'Università di Palermo 3 (1984): 307–28.

Petech, Luciano. *Mediaeval History of Nepal (c. 750–1480)*. Roma: Istituto Italiano per il Medio ed Estremo Oriente, 1958.

———, ed. *Il nuovo ramusio: I missionari italiani nel Tibet e nel Nepal: I missionari cappuccini*. Vol. 2, pts. 1–4. Roma: La Libreria dello Stato, 1952.

Piano, Stefano, trans. *Il mito del Gange: Gaṅgā-Māhātmya*. Torino: Promolibri, 1990.

———. *Bhagavad-gītā: Il canto del glorioso Signore*. Milano: San Paolo, 1994.

Piantelli, Mario. *Śaṅkara e la rinascita del Brāhmanesimo*. Fossano: Editrice Esperienze, 1974.

———, trans. *Īśvaragītā o 'Poema del Signore.'* Parma: Luigi Battei, 1980.

Pingree, David. "Representation of the Planets in Indian Astrology." *Indo-Iranian Journal* 8, no. 4 (1965): 249–67.

———. *Jyotishastra: Astral and Mathematical Literature*. Wiesbaden: Otto Harrassowitz, 1981.

Pohnerkar, N. S., ed. *Dāsopantāncī Pāsoḍī*. Aurangabad, n.d.

Potter, Karl H. "The Karma Theory and Its Interpretation in Some Indian Philosophical Systems." In *Karma and Rebirth in Classical Indian Traditions*, edited by Wendy Doniger O'Flaherty, 241–67. Albany, N.Y.: SUNY Press, 1980.

———. ed. *Encyclopedia of Indian Philosophies*. Vol. 3, *Advaita Vedānta up to Śaṃkara and His Pupils*. Princeton: Princeton University Press, 1981.

Prabhudesai, P. K., ed. *Devī-kośa*. 4 vols. Puṇe, 1967–72.

Priyolkar, A. K., ed. *Yoga-rāja-ṭiḷaka*. Bombay, 1956.

Raeside, I. M. P. "The Mahānubhāvas." *Bulletin of the School of Oriental and African Studies* 39 (1976): 585–600.

———, ed. and trans. *Gadyarāja: A Fourteenth Century Marāṭhī Version of the Kṛṣṇa Legend*. Translated from the Marāṭhī with Annotations. Bombay: Popular Prakashan; School of Oriental and African Studies, 1989.

Raghavan, V. "Greater Gītā." *The Journal of Oriental Research* 12 (1940): 107–21.

Rahmann, Rudolf. "Shamanistic and Related Phenomena in Northern and Middle India." *Anthropos* 54 (1959): 681–760.

Rao, S. K. Ramachandra. *Āgama-Kosha* (*Āgama* Encyclopaedia). 5 vols. Bangalore: Kalpatharu Research Academy, 1992.

Rastogi, N. *Krama Tantricism of Kashmir: Historical and General Sources*. Vol. 1. Delhi: Motilal Banarsidass, 1981.

Rawson, P. *The Art of Tantra*. London, 1973.

Regmi, D. R. *Medieval Nepal*. Pt. 1, *Early Medieval Period 750–1530* A.D. Calcutta: K. L. Mukhopadhyay, 1965.

Rhys Davids, T. W. *Buddhist India*. 1971. Reprint, Delhi: Motilal Banarsidass, 1981.

Rigopoulos, Antonio. "Women and Ritual: The Experience of a Contemporary Marāṭhī Āśram." *Annali* (Napoli, Istituto Universitario Orientale) 53, fasc. 3 (1993): 279–302.

Rizvi, S. A. A. *A History of Sufism in India.* 2 vols. New Delhi: Munshiram Manoharlal, 1983.

Rocher, Ludo. *The Purāṇas.* Wiesbaden: Otto Harrassowitz, 1986.

Russell, R. V., and Rai Bahadur Hira Lal. *The Tribes and Castes of the Central Provinces of India.* 4 vols. London: Macmillan and Co., 1916.

Saiyed, A. R. "Saints and Dargāhs in the Indian Subcontinent: A Review." In *Muslim Shrines in India: Their Character, History, and Significance,* edited by Christian W. Troll, 240–56. Delhi: Oxford University Press, 1989.

Śaṅkara-dig-vijaya. Śrīrangam: Vilasa, 1972.

Sarkar, Jadunath. *A History of Dasnami Naga Sanyasis.* Foreword by Sri K. M. Munshi. Allahabad: Sri Panchayati Akhara Mahanirvani, 1959.

Śarmā, Vinayamohan. *Hindī ko Marāṭhī Santon kī Den.* Patnā: Bihār Rāstrabhāṣā Pariṣad, 1957.

Sarmah, Thaneswar. *The Bhāradvājas in Ancient India.* Delhi: Motilal Banarsidass, 1991.

Sastri, A. Mahadeva, ed. *The Yoga Upaniṣads.* With the Commentary of Śrī Upaniṣad-Brahma-Yogin. Adyar, 1920.

———. *The Śaiva-Upanishads.* With the Commentary of Śrī Upaniṣad-Brahma-Yogin. Madras: Adyar Library, 1925.

———. *The Śākta Upanishads.* With the Commentary of Śrī Upaniṣad-Brahma-Yogin. Madras: Adyar Library, 1925.

———. *The Vaiṣṇava Upaniṣads.* With the Commentary of Śrī Upaniṣad-Brahma-Yogin. Adyar: Adyar Library, 1953.

Sastri, A. M., and S. Y. Dave, ed. *Paraśurāmakalpasūtra with the Commentary by Rāmeśvara Sūri Entitled Saubhāgyodaya.* 2d ed. Baroda: Oriental Institute, 1950.

Sastri, H. G. *A Historical and Cultural Study of the Inscriptions of Gujarat from Earliest Times to the End of the Caulukya Period (circa 1300 A.D.).* Ahmedabad: B. J. Institute of Learning & Research, 1989.

Sastri, R. Anantakrishna. *Śiva Sahasranāma Stotra (Sanskrit Text): With an English Translation of Śrī Nīlakaṇṭha's Commentary.* Madras: V. Ramaswami Sastrulu & Sons, 1955.

Sastri, T. Narayana. *The Age of Śaṅkara.* Madras, 1916–17.

Sawai, Yoshitsugu. *The Faith of Ascetics and Lay Smārtas: A Study of the Śaṅkaran Tradition of Śṛṅgeri.* Vienna: Publications of the De Nobili Research Library, 1992.

Schimmel, Annemarie. *Islām in the Indian Subcontinent.* Leiden: E. J. Brill, 1980.

———. *The Mystery of Numbers.* New York: Oxford University Press, 1993.

Schoembucher, Elisabeth. "Gods, Ghosts and Demons: Possession in South Asia." In *Flags of Fame: Studies in South Asian Folk Culture,* edited by Heidrun Brückner, Lothar Lutze, and Aditya Malik, 239–67. New Delhi: Manohar, 1993.

Schomer, Karine, and W. H. McLeod, eds. *The Sants: Studies in a Devotional Tradition of India.* Berkeley: Berkeley Religious Studies Series; Delhi: Motilal Banarsidass, 1987.

Schoterman, Jan A. "The Kubjikā Upaniṣad and Its Atharvavedic Character." In *Ritual and Speculation in Early Tantrism: Studies in Honor of André Padoux,* edited by Teun Goudriaan, 313–26. Albany, N.Y.: SUNY Press, 1992.

Schrader, F. O. *Introduction to the Pāñcarātra and the Ahirbudhnya Saṃhitā.* Adyar: Adyar Library and Research Centre, 1916.

———, ed. *Saṃnyāsa Upaniṣads.* Madras: Adyar Library, 1912.

Sharif, Ja'far. *Islam in India or the Qanūn-I-Islām.* Composed under the Direction of and Translated by G. A. Herklots. 1921. Reprint, London: Curzon Press, 1972.

Shastri, Dakshina Ranjan. *Origin and Development of the Rituals of Ancestor Worship in India.* Calcutta: Bookland Private, 1963.

Shastri, H. Krishna. "Two Statues of Pallava Kings and Five Pallava Inscriptions in a Rock Temple at Mahābalipuram." *Archaeological Survey of India Memoir* 26 (1926).

Sherwani, H. K., and P. M. Joshi, ed. *History of Medieval Deccan (1295–1724).* 2 vols. Hyderabad: Government of Andhra Pradesh, 1973.

Shulman, David Dean. *The King and the Clown in South Indian Myth and Poetry.* Princeton: Princeton University Press, 1985.

Silburn, Lilian. *Kuṇḍalinī: Energy of the Depths.* Albany, N.Y.: SUNY Press, 1988.

Singh, Amar. *Aghor Peetha and Baba Kina Ram.* Varanasi: Kalpana Press, 1988.

Singh, Mohan. *Gorakhnāth and Medieval Hindu Mysticism.* Lahore, 1937.

Singh, Ram Dular. *Aghora Granthāvali: Collected Works of Aghora Manuscripts.* Varanasi: Bibliographical Society of India, 1986.

Sinha, Surajit, and Baidyanath Saraswati. *Ascetics of Kashi: An Anthropological Exploration.* Varanasi: N. K. Bose Memorial Foundation, 1978.

Sirkar, D. C. *Śākta Pīṭhas.* Delhi: Motilal Banarsidass, n.d.

Sivananda, Swami. *Lord Siva and His Worship*. Shivanandanagar: Yoga-Vedanta Forest Academy Press, 1989.

Skultans, Vieda. "Gender and Experience of Affliction: Family Relations, Beliefs and Attitudes towards Mental Illness in Maharashtra." In *Gender, Caste, and Power in South Asia: Social Status and Mobility in a Transitional Society*, edited by John P. Neelsen, 139–71. New Delhi: Manohar, 1991.

van Skyhawk, Hugh. *Bhakti und Bhakta: Religionsgeschichtliche Untersuchungen zum Heilsbegriff und zur religiosen Umwelt des Śrī Sant Eknāth*. Stuttgart: Steiner Verlag, 1990.

———. "Nasīruddīn and Ādināth, Nizāmuddīn and Kāniphnāth: Hindu-Muslim Religious Syncretism in the Folk Literature of the Deccan." In *Flags of Fame: Studies in South Asian Folk Culture*, edited by Heidrun Brückner, Lothar Lutze, and Aditya Malik, 445–67. New Delhi: Manohar, 1993.

Smith, Daniel H. *A Sourcebook of Vaiṣṇava Iconography According to Pāñcarātrāgama Texts. Sanskrit Texts Compiled and Arranged with Commentary in English*. Madras: Pāñcarātra Pariśodhana Pariṣad, 1969.

Smith, Stan. *W. B. Yeats: A Critical Introduction*. London: Macmillan, 1990.

Sontheimer, Günther D. "The Mallāri/Khaṇḍobā Myth as Reflected in Folk Art and Ritual." *Anthropos* 79 (1984): 155–70.

———. "Hinduism: The Five Components and Their Interaction." In *Hinduism Reconsidered*, edited by Günther D. Sontheimer and Hermann Kulke, 197–212. New Delhi: Manohar, 1989.

Sörensen, S. *An Index to the Names in the Mahābhārata. With Short Explanations and a Concordance to the Bombay and Calcutta Editions and P. C. Roy's Translation*. 1904. Reprint, Delhi: Motilal Banarsidass, 1978.

Sprockhoff, J. F. "Die Idee der Jīvanmukti in den Spaten Upaniṣads." *Wiener Zeitschrift für die Kunde Süd-und Ostasiens* 7 (1963): 190–208.

———. *Saṃnyāsa: Quellenstudien zur Askese im Hinduismus—I Untersuchungen über die Saṃnyāsa-Upaniṣads*. Abhandlungen für die Kunde des Morgenlandes 42, no. 1. Wiesbaden: Kommissionverlag Franz Steiner, 1976.

Stanley, John M. "Gods, Ghosts, and Possession." In *The Experience of Hinduism: Essays on Religion in Maharashtra*, edited by Eleanor Zelliot and Maxine Berntsen, 26–59. Albany, N.Y.: SUNY Press, 1988.

Subrahmanian, N. S. *Encyclopaedia of the Upaniṣads*. London: Oriental University Press, 1986.

Tagore, Rabindranath. *Gitanjali.* With an introduction by W. B. Yeats. London: Printed at Chiswick Press for the India Society, 1912.

Tessitori, L. P. "Yogīs (Kānphaṭā)." In *Encyclopaedia of Religion and Ethics*, edited by James Hastings. New York: Charles Scribner's Sons, 1928.

Tirtha, Trivikrama, ed. *Cid-gagana-candrikā.* Calcutta: University Press, 1936.

Toukaram, *Psaumes du pèlerin.* Translation, introduction, and commentaries by G. A. Deleury. Paris: Gallimard, 1956.

Tulpule, Shankar Gopal. *Classical Marāṭhī Literature: From the Beginning to A.D. 1818.* Wiesbaden: Otto Harrassowitz, 1979.

———. *Mysticism in Medieval India.* Wiesbaden: Otto Harrassowitz, 1984.

———, ed. *Dṛṣṭānta-pāṭha.* Puṇe, 1966.

Utgikar, N. B. "The Story of Ṛṣi Aṇī-māṇḍavya in Its Sanskrit and Buddhist Sources." *All-India Oriental Conference* 2 (1922): 221–38.

Vallauri, M. "La *Śivagītā.*" *Memorie della Regia Accademia di Scienze di Torino.* Ser. 2, vol. 70, pt. 2 (1942): 299–316.

Varenne, Jean. *Yoga and the Hindu Tradition.* Chicago: University of Chicago Press, 1976.

Vaudeville, Charlotte. *Kabīr Granthāvalī (Dohā).* Pondichéry: Publications de l'Institut Français d'Indologie, 1957.

———. "Sant Mat: Santism as the Universal Path to Sanctity." In *The Sants: Studies in a Devotional Tradition of India*, edited by Karine Schomer and W. H. McLeod, 21–40. Berkeley: Berkeley Religious Studies Series; Delhi: Motilal Banarsidass, 1987.

———. "The Shaivaite Background of Santism in Maharashtra." In *Religion and Society in Maharashtra*, edited by Milton Israel and N. K. Wagle, 32–50. Toronto: Centre for South Asian Studies, University of Toronto, 1987.

———. "The Shaiva-Vaishnava Synthesis in Maharashtrian Santism." In *The Sants: Studies in a Devotional Tradition of India*, edited by Karine Schomer and W. H. McLeod, 215–28. Berkeley: Berkeley Religious Studies Series; Delhi: Motilal Banarsidass, 1987.

———. *A Weaver Named Kabir: Selected Verses with a Detailed Biographical and Historical Introduction.* New Delhi: Oxford University Press, 1993.

Venkatesananda, Swami. *The Concise Yoga Vāsiṣṭha.* With an Introduction and Bibliography by Christopher Chapple. Albany, N.Y.: SUNY Press, 1984.

Vidyāraṇya. *La liberazione in vita: Jīvanmukti-viveka*. Edited and translated by Roberto Donatoni. Milano: Adelphi, 1995.

Visuvalingam, Elizabeth-Chalier. "Bhairava's Royal Brahmanicide: The Problem of the Mahābrāhmaṇa." In *Criminal Gods and Demon Devotees: Essays on the Guardians of Popular Hinduism*, edited by Alf Hiltebeitel, 157–229. Albany, N.Y.: SUNY Press, 1989.

Vitsaxis, V. G. *Hindu Epics, Myths, and Legends in Popular Illustrations*. With a Foreword by A. L. Basham. New York, 1977.

Vora, Dhairyabala P. *Evolution of Morals in the Epics (Mahābhārata and Rāmāyaṇa)*. Bombay: Popular Book Depot, 1959.

Wagle, N. K. "Hindu-Muslim Interactions in Medieval Maharashtra." In *Hinduism Reconsidered*, edited by Günther D. Sontheimer and Hermann Kulke, 51–66. New Delhi: Manohar, 1989.

Wasson, R. Gordon. "The Soma of the Rig Veda: What Was It?" *Journal of the American Oriental Society* 91, no. 2 (1971): 169–91.

Weber, A. *History of Indian Literature*. London, 1878.

Weelock, Wade T. "The Mantra in Vedic and Tantric Ritual." In *Mantra*, edited by Harvey P. Alper, 96–122. Albany, N.Y.: SUNY Press, 1989.

White, David Gordon. "Why Gurus are Heavy." *Numen* 31, fasc. 1 (July 1984): 40–73.

———. *Myths of the Dog-Man*. Chicago: University of Chicago Press, 1991.

———. "The Ocean of Mercury: An Eleventh-Century Alchemical Text." In *Religions of India in Practice*, edited by Donald S. Lopez, Jr., 281–87. Princeton: Princeton University Press, 1995.

———. "The Wonders of Śrī Mastnāth." In *Religions of India in Practice*, edited by Donald S. Lopez, Jr., 399–411. Princeton: Princeton University Press, 1995.

———. *The Alchemical Body: Siddha Traditions in Medieval India*. Chicago: University of Chicago Press, 1996.

Wilson, F. A. C. *Yeats and Iconography*. London: Gollancz, 1960.

———. *W. B. Yeats and Tradition*. London: Methuen, 1968.

Yeats, William Butler. *The Oxford Book of Modern Verse*. Oxford: Clarendon Press, 1936.

———. *Collected Poems*. London: Picador Classics, 1990.

Yoroi, Kiyoshi. *Gaṇeśa Gītā: A Study, Translation with Notes, and a Condensed Rendering of the Commentary of Nīlakaṇṭha*. Disputationes Rheno-Trajectinae 12. The Hague: Mouton, 1968.

Zelliot, Eleanor. "A Medieval Encounter between Hindu and Muslim: Eknāth's Drama-Poem *Hindu-Turk Saṃvād*." In *Images of Man: Religion and Historical Process in South Asia*, edited by Fred W. Clothey, 171–95. Madras: New Era Publications, 1982.

———. "Eknath's Bhāruḍs: The Sant as Link Between Cultures." In *The Sants: Studies in a Devotional Tradition of India*, edited by Karine Schomer and W. H. McLeod, 91–109. Berkeley: Berkeley Religious Studies Series; Delhi: Motilal Banarsidass, 1987.

———. "Four Radical Saints in Maharashtra." In *Religion and Society in Maharashtra*, edited by Milton Israel and N. K. Wagle, 131–44. Toronto: Centre for South Asian Studies, University of Toronto, 1987.

Zvelebil, K. V. *The Poets of the Powers*. London, 1973.

Zysk, Kenneth G. "The Science of Respiration and the Doctrine of the Bodily Winds in Ancient India." *Journal of the American Oriental Society* 113, no. 2 (April–June 1993): 198–213.

Selected Bibliography on Dattātreya and His Movement

Abbott, Justin E., trans. *Dāsopant Digambar: Translation of the* Dasopant Charitra. Poet-Saints of Maharashtra Series, no. 4. Puṇe: Scottish Mission Industries, 1927.

Abbott, Justin E., trans. *The Life of Eknāth. Śrī Eknāth Charita.* Translated from the *Bhaktalīlāmṛta.* Puṇe, 1927. Reprint, Delhi: Motilal Banarsidass, 1981.

Abbott, Justin E., and N. R. Godbole, trans. *Stories of Indian Saints: An English Translation of Mahipati's Marathi* Bhakta-vijaya. 2 vols. in 1. Puṇe, 1933. Reprint, Delhi: Motilal Banarsidass, 1982.

Ācārya, Nārāyaṇ Rām, ed. *Bṛhat-stotra-ratnākara.* 4th ed. Vol. 2. Bombay: Nirnaya Sagar Press, 1953.

Aiyar, K. Narayanasvami. *Thirty Minor Upanishads.* Adyar, 1914.

Anzar, Naoshervan. *The Beloved: The Life and Work of Meher Baba.* North Myrtle Beach, S.C.: Sheriar Press, 1974.

Ashokananda, Swami, trans. *Avadhūta Gītā of Dattātreya.* 3d ed. Madras: Sri Ramakrishna Math, 1988.

Auer Gerhard, and Niels Gutschow. *Bhaktapur: Gestalt, Funktionen, und religiöse Symbolik einer nepalischen Stadt im vorindustriellen Entwicklungsstadium.* Darmstadt, 1974.

Śrī Avadhūta Gītā. With Hindī Commentary. Agra: Agra University Press, 1960.

Avadhūta-gītā. Bombay: Nirnaya Sagar Press, n.d.

Avadhūta-gītā. Puṇe: Bhandarkar Oriental Research Institute, 1912.

Awasthi, Brahma Mitra, ed. *Yoga Shastra of Dattātreya*. New Delhi: Swami Keshawananda Yoga Institute, 1985.

Ayyangar, T. R. Srinivasa, trans. *The Yoga Upanishads*. Adyar: Adyar Library, 1938.

Ayyar, J. *Southern Indian Shrines*. Madras: Madras Times Printing & Publishing Co., 1920.

Babu, Sarath R., ed. *Dattātreya: Glory of the Divine in Man*. Ongole, 1981.

Bahadur, Sri Jaya Chamarajendra Wadiyar. *Dattātreya: The Way and the Goal*. London: George Allen & Unwin, 1957. Reprint, Delhi: Motilal Banarsidass, 1982.

———. *Jīvanmukta Gītā: The Liberated in Life*. Reprint, Coombe Springs Press, 1982.

Bailey, G. M. "Trifunctional Elements in the Mythology of the Hindu Trimūrti." *Numen* 26, fasc. 2 (1979): 152–63.

Bakker, Hans. "The Footprints of the Lord." In *Devotion Divine: Bhakti Traditions from the Regions of India: Studies in Honour of Charlotte Vaudeville*, edited by Diana L. Eck and Françoise Mallison, 19–37. Groningen: Egbert Forsten; Paris: École Française d'Extrême-Orient, 1991.

Barthwal, P. D. *Traditions of Indian Mysticism: Based upon Nirguṇa School of Hindi Poetry*. With a Foreword by Prof. Syam Sunder Das. New Delhi: Heritage Publishers, 1978.

Batra, S. M. *Cows and Cow-Slaughter in India: Religious, Political, and Social Aspects*. The Hague: Institute of Social Studies, 1981.

Bhandarkar, R. G. *Vaiṣṇavism, Śaivism, and Minor Religious Systems*. Varanasi: Indological Book House, 1965.

Bharati, Agehananda. *Hindu Views and Ways and the Hindu-Muslim Interface: An Anthropological Assessment*. Santa Barbara: Ross-Erikson, 1982.

Bhaṭṭa, Jīvānanda. *Indrajāla-vidyā-saṃgraha*. 3d ed. Calcutta, 1915.

Bhattacharji, Sukumari. *The Indian Theogony: A Comparative Study of Indian Mythology from the Vedas to the Purāṇas*. Chambersburg: Anima Publications, 1988.

Bhattacharyya, D. C. *Pratimālakṣaṇa of the Viṣṇudharmottara*. New Delhi: Harman Publishing House, 1991.

Biardeau, Madeleine. "Kāmadhenu." In *Dictionnaire des mythologies*, edited by Y. Bonnefoy. Paris: Flammarion, 1981.

Bombay Gazetteer. District Konkan: Kanara, chap. 14.

Briggs, George Weston. *Gorakhnāth and the Kānphaṭa Yogīs*. Calcutta: Motilal Banarsidass, 1938.

Brooks, Douglas Renfrew, Swami Durgananda, Paul E. Muller-Ortega, William K. Mahony, Constantina Rhodes Bailly, and S. P. Sabharathnam. *Meditation Revolution: A History and Theology of the Siddha Yoga Lineage*. South Fallsburg, New York: Agama Press, 1997.

Brown, W. N. "The Sanctity of the Cow in Hinduism." *The Economic Weekly* (Bombay) 16 (February 1964): 244–55.

Buchanan, Francis. *Patna-Gaya Report: An Account of the Districts of Bihar and Patna in 1811–1812*. Vol. 1. Patna, n.d.

Chetanananda, Swami, trans. *Avadhuta Gita of Dattatreya*. Calcutta: Advaita Ashrama, 1984.

Crooke, William. *Things Indian: Being Discursive Notes on Various Subjects Connected with India*. London: John Murray, 1906.

Dange, Sadashiv Ambadas. *Encyclopaedia of Purāṇic Beliefs and Practices*. Vol. 2. New Delhi: Navrang, 1987–1990.

Daniélou, Alain. *Hindu Polytheism*. Bollingen Series 73. New York: Bollingen Foundation, 1964.

Das, R. K. *Temples of Tamilnad*. Bombay: Bharatiya Vidya Bhavan, 1991.

Dāsgaṇū. *Shree Gajanan Vijay*. An English Adaptation by N. B. Patil. Shegaon: Shree Gajanan Mahārāj Sansthan, 1980.

Śrī-dattātreya-gītā (Avadhūta-gītā). With Sanskrit Commentary of Vivecana. Ahmedabad, 1923.

David-Neel, Alexandra, trans. *L'Avadhūta Gītā de Dattatraya*. Paris: Adyar, 1958.

Deleury, G. A. *The Cult of Viṭhobā*. Puṇe: Deccan College Post-Graduate and Research Institute, 1960.

Desai, Nileshvari Y. *Ancient Indian Society, Religion, and Mythology as Depicted in the Mārkaṇḍeya-Purāṇa (A Critical Study)*. Baroda: Mahārāja Sayajirao University of Baroda Press, 1968.

Dhere, R. C. *Datta Sampradāyācā Itihāsa*. 2d ed. Puṇe: Nilakanth Prakashan, 1964.

Dīkṣit, Rājeś, ed. *Dattātreyatantram: Bhāṣāṭīkayā Sametam*. Delhi: Dehātī Pustak Bhaṇḍār, 1975.

Dupont, trans. *L'Avadhūta Gītā*. Paris, 1933.

Eidlitz, Walther. *Unknown India: A Pilgrimage into a Forgotten World*. New York: Roy Publishers, 1952.

Enthoven, R. E. *The Folklore of Bombay*. Oxford: Clarendon Press, 1924.

———. *Folklore of the Konkan*. Compiled from materials collected by the late A. M. T. Jackson, Indian Civil Service. Delhi, 1915. Reprint, Delhi: Cosmo Publications, 1976.

Feldhaus, Anne. *Water and Womanhood: Religious Meanings of Rivers in Maharashtra*. New York: Oxford University Press, 1995.

Fuchs, Stephen. *Godmen on the Warpath: A Study of Messianic Movements in India*. New Delhi: Munshiram Manoharlal, 1992.

Ghurye, G. S. *Gods and Men*. Bombay: Popular Book Depot, 1962.

———. *Indian Sādhus*. 2d ed. Bombay: Popular Prakashan, 1964.

Godamasuta, ed. *The Talks of Sadguru Upasani-Baba Mahārāja*. 4 vols. 1957. Reprint, Sakuri: Shri Upasani Kanya Kumari Sthan, 1978.

Gonda, Jan. "The Hindu Trinity." *Anthropos* 63 (1968): 212–26.

———. *Triads in the Veda*. Amsterdam: North-Holland Publishing Company, 1976.

———. *Medieval Religious Literature in Sanskrit*. Vol. 2, fasc. 1 of *A History of Indian Literature*. Wiesbaden: Otto Harrassowitz, 1977.

Goudriaan, Teun, and Sanjukta Gupta. *Hindu Tantric and Śākta Literature*. Vol. 2, fasc. 2 of *A History of Indian Literature*. Wiesbaden: Otto Harrassowitz, 1981.

Gunaji, Nagesh Vasudev. *Shri Sai Saṭcharita; or, The Wonderful Life and Teachings of Shri Sai Baba*. Adapted from the Original Marathi of Hemadpant. 10th ed. Bombay: Sri Sai Baba Sansthan, 1982.

Gupta, Shakti M. *From Daityas to Devatas in Hindu Mythology*. Bombay: Somaiya Publications, 1973.

———. *Vishnu and His Incarnations*. Bombay: Somaiya Publications, 1974.

Handiqui, Krishna Kanta, ed. and trans. *The Naishadhacarita of Śrīharsha* (Cantos 1–22). *For the First Time Translated into English with Critical Notes and Extracts from Unpublished Commentaries, Appendices and a Vocabulary*. Lahore: Punjab Sanskrit Book Depot, 1934.

Hardy, Adam. *Indian Temple Architecture: Form and Transformation. The Karṇāṭa Drāviḍa Tradition 7th to 13th Centuries*. New Delhi: Indira Gandhi National Centre for the Arts, 1995.

Hartsuiker, Dolf. *Sādhus: Holy Men of India*. Thames and Hudson, 1993.

Heston, A., et al. "An Approach to the Sacred Cow of India." *Current Anthropology* 12 (1971): 191–201.

Hopkinson, Tom, and Dorothy Hopkinson. *Much Silence: Meher Baba, His Life and Work*. New York: Dodd, Mead, 1974.

Hulin, Michel, trans. *La doctrine secrète de la Déesse Tripurā (Section de la connaissance)*. Paris: Fayard, 1979.

Jaiswal, Suvira. *The Origin and Development of Vaiṣṇavism: Vaiṣṇavism from 200 BC to AD 500*. New Delhi: Munshiram Manoharlal, 1981.

Johnson, Helen M., trans. *Triṣaṣṭiśalākāpuruṣacaritra; or, The Lives of Sixty-Three Illustrious Persons by Ācārya Śrī Hemacandra*. 6 vols. Gaekwad's Oriental Series. Baroda: Oriental Institute, 1931–62.

Joshi, D. D. *Śrī Guru-caritra Kathā-sār*. Puṇe: Ādarś Vidyārthī Prakāśan, 1986.

Joshi, Hariprasad Shivprasad. *Origin and Development of Dattātreya Worship in India*. Baroda: Mahārāja Sayajirao University of Baroda Press, 1965.

Joshi, P. N. *Śrī-dattātreya-jñān-koś*. Bombay: Surekha Prakashan, 1974.

Kāmat, Rāmacandra Kṛṣṇa, ed. *Guru-caritra*. Bombay, 1990.

Karandikar, N. S. *Biography of Sri Swami Samarth Akkalkot Mahārāj*. Bombay: Akkalkot Swami Math, 1978.

Kasturi, N. *Sathyam Sivam Sundaram: The Life of Bhagavan Sri Sathya Sai Baba*. 4 vols. Prasanthi Nilayam: Sri Sathya Sai Books and Publications, 1981.

———. *Loving God*. Prasanthi Nilayam: Sri Sathya Sai Books and Publications, 1982.

Katre, S. L., ed. *Datta-māhātmya*. Bombay, 1974.

Kavirāj, Gopīnāth. *Tantrik Sahity*. Lakhnau: Hindi Samiti, 1972.

———, ed. *Tripurārahasya (Jñānakhaṇḍa): With the Commentary Tātparyadīpikā by Śrīnivāsa*. Varanasi: Varanaseya Sanskrit Vishvavidyalaya, 1965.

Kavirāj, Gopīnāth, and Nārāyaṇ Śāstrī Khiste, eds. *Tripurārahasya (Jñānakhaṇḍa)*. Varanasi, 1925–1928.

Keshavadas, Sadguru Sant. *Sadguru Dattatreya*. Oakland: Vishwa Dharma Publications, 1988.

Kher, Indira. *Avadhuta Yogi Pant Mahārāj of Balekundri*. Bombay: Bharatiya Vidya Bhavan, 1994.

Kulkarṇī, Cidambar Śrīpādrāv. *Śrī Kṣetra Gāṅgāpūr Māhātmya*. Revised 21st printing. Beḷgāṃv: Sarasvatī Pustak Bhāṇḍār, 1988.

Kulkarni, K. R. *The Saint of Shegaon: A Book of Poems on the Life of Shri Gajanan Mahārāj*. Nagpur, 1969.

Kunjunni Raja, K. *New Catalogus Catalogorum: An Alphabetical Register of Sanskrit and Allied Works and Authors.* Vol. 8. Madras: University of Madras, 1974.

Long, J. B. "Trimūrti." In *Abingdon Dictionary of Living Religions*, edited by Keith Crim. Nashville: Abingdon Press, 1981.

Lorenzen, David N. *Praises to a Formless God: Nirguṇī Texts from North India.* Albany, N.Y.: SUNY Press, 1996.

Magul, T. "Present-Day Worship of the Cow in India." *Numen* 15 (1968): 63–80.

Mal, Kanoo, trans. *Awadhoota Gita.* With a Foreword by K. S. Ramaswami Sastri of Bellari. Madras: S. R. Murthi & Co., 1920.

Mate, M. S. "Ganagapur—Dattatreya." In *Temples and Legends of Maharashtra.* 3d ed. Bombay: Bharatiya Vidya Bhavan, 1988.

Mathothu, Kurian. *The Development of the Concept of Trimūrti in Hinduism.* Bangalore: Saint Paul's Press, 1974.

Meher Baba. *Discourses.* 6th ed. 3 vols. San Francisco: Sufism Reoriented, 1967.

———. *God Speaks.* New York: Dodd, Mead, 1973.

Minor, R. N. "Cow, Symbolism and Veneration." In *Abingdon Dictionary of Living Religions*, edited by Keith Crim. Nashville: Abingdon Press, 1981.

Mishra, Ram Ugra. "Yoga in Mārkaṇḍeya Purāṇa." *Journal of the Yoga Institute* (Bombay). 13, no. 6 (1968): 85–87.

Mokashi-Punekar, Shankar. "W. B. Yeats and Sri Purohit Swami." In *The Image of India in Western Creative Writing*, edited by M. K. Naik et al. Dharwar: Karnataka University; Madras: Macmillan, 1972.

———, ed. *Avadhoota Gita.* With English Translation by Shree Purohit Swami. New Delhi: Munshiram Manoharlal, 1979.

Murphet, Howard. *Sai Baba: Invitation to Glory.* Delhi: Macmillan India, 1982.

Nakulabadhut, Sanjomi Ram Ram. *A English Translation to the Avadhūtagītā.* Calcutta, 1908.

Narasimhaswami, B. V., and S. Subbarao. *Sage of Sakuri: Life Story of Shree Upasani Mahārāj.* 4th ed. Sakuri: Shri Upasani Kanya Kumari Sthan, 1966.

"National Conference of Bal Vikas Gurus." *Sanathana Sarathi* 37, no. 8 (August 1994): 206–209.

Navnāth-caritra va Kathā. Puṇe: Sarathi Prakāśan, 1987.

Śrī-navnāth-kathā-sār. Bombay: Jaya Hind Prakashan, n.d.

Nisargadatta Mahārāj. *I Am That: Talks with Sri Nisargadatta Mahārāj*. Translated from the Marathi tape-recordings by Maurice Frydman and revised and edited by Sudhakar S. Dikshit. Bombay: Chetana, 1973.

Olivelle, Patrick. *Vāsudevāśrama Yatidharmaprakāśa: A Treatise on World Renunciation*. Critically edited with introduction, annotated translation and appendices. Pt. 1: Text; Pt. 2: Translation. Vienna: Publications of the De Nobili Research Library, 1976–77.

———. *Saṃnyāsa Upaniṣads: Hindu Scriptures on Asceticism and Renunciation*. Translated with introduction and notes. New York: Oxford University Press, 1992.

———, ed. and trans. *Rules and Regulations of Brahmanical Asceticism: Yatidharmasamuccaya of Yādava Prakāśa*. Albany, N.Y.: SUNY Press, 1995.

Oman, John Campbell. *The Mystics, Ascetics, and Saints of India: A Study of Sadhuism, with an Account of the Yogis, Sanyasis, Bairagis, and Other Strange Hindu Sectarians*. London: T. Fisher Unwin, 1905.

Pai, D. A. *Religious Sects in Ancient India (Ancient and Medieval)*. 1928. Reprint, Delhi: Eastern Book Linkers, 1981.

Pain, Charles. "Gangapur: The Center of the Dattatreya Cult." Unpublished typescript, n.d.

Pain, Charles with Eleanor Zelliot. "The God Dattatreya and the Datta Temples of Pune." In *The Experience of Hinduism: Essays on Religion in Maharashtra*, edited by Eleanor Zelliot and Maxine Berntsen, 95–108. Albany, N.Y.: SUNY Press, 1988.

Pal, Pratapaditya. *Vaiṣṇava Iconology in Nepal: A Study in Art and Religion with 110 Illustrations*. Calcutta: Asiatic Society, 1970.

Pargiter, F. Eden. *Ancient Indian Historical Tradition*. Reprint, Delhi: Motilal Banarsidass, 1962.

———, trans. *The Mārkaṇḍeya Purāṇa*. *Bibliotheca Indica* 125. Calcutta, 1904. Reprint, Varanasi-Delhi: Indological Book House, 1981.

Pelissero, Alberto, trans. *Il segreto della Dea Tripurā. Sezione sulla gnosi*. Torino: Ananke, 1995.

Pellegrini, Agata Sannino. "Dall'*Avadhūtagītā* di Dattātreya: Passi scelti." *La Memoria*. Annali della Facoltà di Lettere e Filosofia dell'Università di Palermo 6 (1990): 3–24.

———. "L'*Avadhūtagītā* di Dattātreya." In *Atti del IV e del V convegno nazionale di studi sanscriti*, edited by O. Botto, 249–62. Torino: Associazione italiana di studi sanscriti, 1991.

Powell, Robert, ed. *The Nectar of the Lord's Feet: Final Teachings of Sri Nisargadatta Mahārāj.* Longmead Shaftesbury Dorset: Element Books, 1987.

Pujārī, Kṛṣṇaṃbhaṭ Narharbhaṭ. *Śrīkṣetra Gāṇagāpūr-varṇan.* Gāṇagāpūr, 1935.

Purdom, Charles B. *God to Man and Man to God: The Discourses of Meher Baba.* North Myrtle Beach, S.C.: Sheriar Press, 1975.

Purohit Swami, Shri. *An Indian Monk: His Life and Adventures.* With introduction by W. B. Yeats. London: Macmillan and Co., 1932.

———, trans. *The Holy Mountain: Being the Story of a Pilgrimage to Lake Manas and of Initiation on Mount Kailas in Tibet, by Bhagwan Shri Hamsa.* London: Faber and Faber, 1934.

———, trans. *The Geeta.* London: Faber and Faber, 1935.

———, trans. *The Ten Principal Upanishads.* London: Faber and Faber, 1937.

———, trans. *Aphorisms of Yoga, by Bhagwan Shree Patanjali.* London: Faber and Faber, 1938.

Raeside, I. M. P. "Dattātreya." *School of Oriental and African Studies* 45 (1982): 489–500.

Ramana Maharshi. *Talks with Sri Ramana Maharshi.* 3 vols. in 1. 7th ed. Tiruvannamalai: Sri Ramanasramam, 1984.

Ramasso, Claudia. "Il Tripurā Rahasya nell'ottica dottrinale e ideologica di Svāmī Karpātrī." Thesis, *Cà Foscari* Venice University, 1996.

Ramesan, N. *Temples and Legends of Andhra Pradesh.* Bombay: Bharatiya Vidya Bhavan, 1988.

Ranade, R. D. *Mysticism in Maharashtra (Indian Mysticism).* Puṇe, 1933. Reprint, Delhi: Motilal Banarsidass, 1982.

Rangarajan, Haripriya. *Spread of Vaiṣṇavism in Gujarat Up to 1600 A.D.: A Study with Special Reference to the Iconic Forms of Viṣṇu.* Bombay: Somaiya Publications, 1990.

Raṇpise, Vasanta. *Tripurā Śrīkṣetra Māhātmya: Gāṅgāpūr, Paṇḍharpūr, Tuḷjāpūr.* Gāṇagāpūr, 1982.

Rao, S. K. Ramachandra. *Indian Iconography.* Bangalore, 1981.

Rao, T. A. Gopinatha. *Elements of Hindu Iconography.* Vol. 1, Pt. 1. Reprint, New York: Paragon Book, 1968.

Rigopoulos, Antonio. *The Life and Teachings of Sai Baba of Shirdi.* Albany, N.Y.: SUNY Press, 1993.

———. "Notes on the *Jīvanmuktagītā* and the Concept of Living Liberation." *Asiatica Venetiana* 1 (1996): 129–40.

Russell, R. V., and Rai Bahadur Hira Lal. *The Tribes and Castes of the Central Provinces of India.* 4 vols. London: Macmillan and Co., 1916.

Sanātanadevaji Mahārāja, Swāmī, trans. *Tripurārahasya: Jñānakhaṇḍa.* With the *Jñānaprabhā* Hindī Commentary. Varanasi, 1967.

Sand, Erik Reenberg. "*Mātāpitṛbhakti*: Some Aspects of the Development of the Puṇḍalīka Legend in Marathi Literature." In *Devotional Literature in South Asia: Current Research, 1985–1988,* edited by R. S. McGregor, 138–47. Cambridge: Cambridge University Press, 1992.

Saptarshi, Kumar. "Orthodoxy and Human Rights: The Story of a Clash." In *The Experience of Hinduism: Essays on Religion in Maharashtra,* edited by Eleanor Zelliot and Maxine Berntsen, 251–63. Albany, N.Y.: SUNY Press, 1988.

Saraswathi, Swami Sri Ramanananda (Sri Munagala S. Venkataramaiah), trans. *Tripura Rahasya; or, The Mystery Beyond the Trinity.* Tiruvannamalai: Sri Ramanasramam, 1959.

Sardar, G. B. *The Saint-Poets of Maharashtra (Their Impact on Society).* Bombay: Orient Longmans, 1969.

Sastri, S. Kuppuswami, and P. P. Subrahmanya Sastri. *An Alphabetical Index of Sanskrit Manuscripts in the Government Oriental Manuscripts Library.* Pt. 1. Madras: Government Press, 1938.

Śāstrī Mukund Lāl, ed. *Kathābodha: Sajanikṛtaṭīkopetaḥ.* On Dattātreya System of Thought: With the Commentary of Sajani. Varanasi, 1926.

———, ed. *The Tripurārahasya (Māhātmyakhaṇḍa).* Introduction and Commentary by Pandit Śrī Nārāyaṇ Śāstrī Khiste. Varanasi: Chowkhambha Sanskrit Series Office, 1932.

Satya Sai Baba. *Sathya Sai Speaks: Discourses Given by Bhagavan Sri Sathya Sai Baba.* Compiled by N. Kasturi. 12 vols. Prasanthi Nilayam: Sri Sathya Sai Books and Publications.

Schwarz, Silvia. "La Grande Dea nell'Innologia del Māhātmyakhaṇḍa del Tripurārahasya." Thesis, Università degli Studi di Torino, 1986.

Shastri, Asoke Chatterjee. "The Deities and Deification in the Brahmapurāṇa." *Purāṇa* 30, no. 1 (February 1989): 19–20.

Shastri, Hari Prasad, trans. *Avadhut Gita by Mahatma Dattatreya.* 1934. Reprint, London: Shanti Sadan, 1948.

Shea, David, and Anthony Troyer, trans. *The Dabistān or School of Manners: The Religious Beliefs, Observances, Philosophic Opinions and Social Customs of the Nations of the East.* With an introduction by A. V. Williams Jackson. Washington: M. Walter Dunne, 1901.

Shenoy, B. Ramabai, trans. *Sri Guru Charitra.* Bombay: Bharatiya Vidya Bhavan, 1994.

Shukla, H. L. *Semiotica Indica: Encyclopaedic Dictionary of Body-Language in Indian Art and Culture*. Vol. 1. New Delhi: Aryan Books International, 1994.

Singh, Sheo Bahadur. *Brahmanical Icons in Northern India: A Study of Images of Five Principal Deities from Earliest Times to circa 1200 A.D.* New Delhi: Sagar Publications, 1977.

Sivananda, Swami. *Sarvagita Sara*. Shivanandanagar: Yoga-Vedanta Forest Academy Press, 1986.

———. *Hindu Fasts and Festivals*. Shivanandanagar: Yoga-Vedanta Forest Academy Press, 1987.

van Skyhawk, Hugh. "Sufi Influence in the *Ekanāthī-bhāgavat*: Some Observations on the Text and Its Historical Context." In *Devotional Literature in South Asia: Current Research, 1985–1988*, edited by R. S. McGregor, 67–79. Cambridge: Cambridge University Press, 1992.

Söhnen, Renate, and Peter Schreiner, eds. and trans. *Brahmapurāṇa: Summary of Contents, with Index of Names and Motifs*. 2 vols. Wiesbaden: Otto Harrassowitz, 1989.

Subrahmanian, N. S. *Encyclopaedia of the Upaniṣads*. London: Oriental University Press, 1986.

Svoboda, Robert E. *Aghora: At the Left Hand of God*. New Delhi: Rupa & Co., 1986.

Swallow, D. A. "Ashes and Powers: Myth, Rite, and Miracle in an Indian God-Man's Cult." *Modern Asian Studies* 16, no. 1 (1982): 136–45.

Tagare, Ganesh Vasudeo, trans. *The Bhāgavata-Purāṇa*. Delhi: Motilal Banarsidass, 1976–78.

Tilak, Lokamanya Bal Gangadhar. *The Orion; or, Researches into the Antiquity of the Vedas*. Puṇe, 1893. Reprint, New Delhi: Munshiram Manoharlal, 1972.

The Tripurā-rahasya (Jñāna-khaṇḍa). Belgaum, 1894.

"The 24 Gurus." *Yoga International* 1, no. 4 (January-February 1992): 21–25.

Tulpule, S. G. "The Dog as a Symbol of Bhakti." In *Devotion Divine: Bhakti Traditions from the Regions of India: Studies in Honour of Charlotte Vaudeville*, edited by Diana L. Eck and Françoise Mallison, 273–85. Groningen: Egbert Forsten; Paris: École Française d'Extrême-Orient, 1991.

Vaidyanathan, K. R. *Temples and Legends of Kerala*. Bombay: Bharatiya Vidya Bhavan, 1988.

Vasavada, A. U., trans. *Tripurā-rahasya (Jñānakhaṇḍa)*. With a comparative study of the process of individuation. Varanasi: Chowkhambha Sanskrit Series Office, 1965.

Vāsudevānanda Sarasvatī. *Datta-Purāṇa and Other Works, Together with His Biography Gurudeva-Caritra*. Puṇe, 1954.

Vaudeville, Charlotte. *Kabir: Au cabaret de l'amour*. Paris: Gallimard, 1959.

———. *Kabīr*. 2 vols. Oxford: Oxford University Press, 1974.

White, Charles S. J. "The Sai Baba Movement: Approaches to the Study of Indian Saints." *Journal of Asian Studies* 31, no. 4 (1972): 863–78.

———. "Structure and the History of Religions: Some Bhakti Examples." *History of Religions* 18, no. 1 (August 1978): 77–94.

———. "The Sai Baba Movement." In *The Sai Baba Movement: Study of a Unique Contemporary Moral and Spiritual Movement*. New Delhi: Arnold-Heinemann, 1985.

Wilson, H. H. *A Sketch of the Religious Sects of the Hindus*. 1861. Reprint, New Delhi: Cosmo Publications, 1977.

Wylie, Turrell. *A Tibetan Religious Geography of Nepal*. Serie Orientale Roma 42. Roma: Istituto Italiano per il Medio ed Estremo Oriente, 1970.

Yadav, Yogacharya Hansraj. *Glimpses of Greatness*. 3d ed. Bombay: Bharatiya Vidya Bhavan, 1991.

Zolla, Elémire. *Lo stupore infantile*. Milano: Adelphi, 1994.

Index

Abbott, J. E., 163 n. 60
Abdal, Ahmad Khwadja, 262 n. 22
abhaṅg, 107 n. 46; Eknāth's, 138, 141, 160 n. 30; Janārdan's, 138; Jñāndev's, 99; Nāmdev's, 132 n. 67; of poet-saints, 213; Tukārām's, 145, 159 n. 17, 162 n. 52, 162 n. 53
ābhāsa-vāda, 181
abhaya-mudrā, 245 n. 62
Abhinavagupta, 25 n. 88, 72, 181
Abja. *See* Brahmā
Abu. *See* Mount Abu
Adhara (star), 10
adharma, 46
Adhyātma Rāmāyaṇa, 218 n. 13
Ādi-Bharata, 52 n. 54
ādi-guru, 198
Adilshahs, 115
Aditi, 16 n. 4, 22 n. 64
advaita, 221 n. 46
Advaita Vedānta (*kevalādvaita-vāda*), 37, 49 n. 26, 57, 62, 63, 68, 82 n. 40, 84 n. 52, 95, 97, 171, 181, 184, 187, 190 n. 4, 195, 198, 199, 216 n. 1, 219 n. 26, 230, 237
Adyar Library, 216 n. 5, 219 n. 26
Agajāvara. *See* Śiva
Āgamas, 14, 171, 191 n. 12, 198, 219 n. 30
Agastya, 170, 172, 174, 175, 191 n. 8
Aghora *sampradāya*, 89, 97, 105 n. 34, 106 n. 37
Aghorīs, 46, 98, 101, 105 n. 32, 105 n. 34, 155, 263 n. 27; assimilation to Muslims, 116; Dattātreya as first Aghorī, 105 n. 35
Agni, 2, 3, 10, 16 n. 9, 17 n. 11, 19 n. 36, 21 n. 59, 70, 72, 238
Agni Purāṇa: characteristic features of Dattātreya's image, 43, 224; connection of Dattātreya with Arjuna Kārtavīrya, 48 n. 12; *trimūrti*'s joint feats, 243 n. 37
aham, 193 n. 34
ahaṃ brahmāsmi, 97, 150, 164 n. 74, 252
ahaṃkāra, 181
ahiṃsā, 98
Ahirbudhnya Saṃhitā, 43
Ahmednagar, 160 n. 25, 224; district of, 104 n. 24, 129 n. 37, 157 n. 2, 158 n. 8; sultanate of, 138, 141
aiṃ, 71, 72, 86 n. 67
Airāvatī, 4, 178
ajagara, 38, 51 n. 48
Ajātaśatru, 241 n. 19
Ajmer, 241 n. 25, 262 n. 22

Akbar Singh, Śrī, 106 n. 36
akhāḍās, 105 n. 31
akiñcanya, 213
Akkaḷkoṭ, 252
Akkaḷkoṭ Mahārāj, 154, 155, 167 n. 97, 167 n. 100, 168 n. 107, 235, 238, 246 n. 69, 248 n. 94, 251, 261 n. 12
Akola, 261 n. 12; district of, 110
akṣara, 65, 214
Alarka: appears as a worm drawing blood, 49 n. 23; attained perfection in Yoga, 49 n. 23; blessed by Dattātreya in Mahānubhāva story, 91, 92–93, 94; etymology, 49 n. 23; received Yoga instruction from Dattātreya, 33–38, 50 n. 28, 54 n. 67
Ālāsa, 118
Aldebaran, 22 n. 65
Ali Barid Shāh, 146
Alioth (star), 2
Alkaid (star), 2
Allāh, 167 n. 99, 168 n. 105, 262 n. 22
Allāuddīn, 115
Alnilam (star), 8
Alnitak (star), 8
āṃ, 72
"Amadavati," 160 n. 25
amanaska, 221 n. 46
Amarajā, 113, 118, 131 n. 55
amaratva, 221 n. 46
Āmardaka, 14, 24–25 n. 86
Amareśvara, 118, 131 n. 50
āmaya, 207
Ambā, 112
Ambā Jogāī (Mominabad), 104 n. 23, 146, 150, 152, 163 n. 57, 163 n. 60, 166 n. 82
Ambā Mātā, 98
Ambarīṣa, 23 n. 76
Ambikā, 111, 112
Amjhera, 126 n. 6
Āmrapur, 129 n. 34
Amṛtā, 188
amṛta (immortality), 10
amṛta (nectar), 81 n. 25, 118
Amṛtānanda, 62
Amṛtānanda (*Śrī-vidyā* writer), 78 n. 4
Amṛtānubhava, 141
aṁśa, 44, 110
anāhata, 209
anāmaya, 207
ānanda, 86 n. 73
Ānanda *sampradāya*, 116, 130 n. 44, 216 n. 2
Anantasūta Kāvaḍībovā, 167 n. 97
Anashuya and Vijaya, 256
Anasūyā, 1, 11, 12, 19 n. 41, 27, 28, 75, 144, 152, 241 n. 20, 242 n. 32, 256; allegorical interpretation of her giving birth to the *trimūrti*, 20 n. 44; astrological identifications, 9, 10; cursed Brahmā, Viṣṇu, and Śiva, 245 n. 63; *Dāsopant-caritra*'s story, 148; mythical origins and feats, 4, 5–8; offered hospitality to Rāma, Sītā, and Lakṣmaṇa at her *āśrama* on the Citrakūṭa mountain, 4, 39, 224; rebelled against her husband, 5, 19 n. 33; representation in Rāmdās's *āratī*, 146; shrine in the Sahyādri range, 148; shrine on Mount Abu, 98; teacher of *mātā-pitṛ-bhakti*, 18 n. 31; temple of Anasūyā-Datta, 102 n. 11; worship of her at the temple of Sucindram, 20 n. 49
anasūya, 18 n. 31
Andhra Pradesh, 110, 189, 233, 235, 245 n. 66, 251
Āndhras. *See* Sātavāhanas
aṅga-nyāsa, 73
Aṅgiras, 1, 2, 15 n. 4, 16 n. 8, 17 n. 11

Aṅgirases, 2, 17 n. 11
Anglicanism, 259, 264 n. 35
anīho, 213
animals: imitation of them by renouncers, 40–41, 52 n. 50, 52 n. 54
Aṇīmāṇḍavya. *See* Māṇḍavya
Aniruddha, 24 n. 83, 60
anirvacanīya, 208
aṅka (secret script), 103 n. 15
Aṅkalakop, 138
Annapūrṇā, 238, 246 n. 68, 248 n. 88
Anser indicus, 84 n. 47
ant: one of Dattātreya's Gurus, 52 n. 50
antaryāmin, 250
anthills, 28, 66
aṇu, 25 n. 89
Anu-gītā, 217 n. 7
anunāsika, 70, 72
anunmatta, 66
anuṣṭhāna, 139, 158 n. 14
ānvīkṣikī, 33, 49 n. 24, 49 n. 25
Apaḷarāja, 110
apāna, 50 n. 37
aparādha-vāsanās, 185
Āpastamba branch, 110
Āpcand *maṭha*, 151
Apollodorus Mythographus, 8
āratī, 122, 123, 132 n. 67, 158 n. 11; by Rāmdās in Datta's praise, 146
Arawalli Hills, 107 n. 42
ardha-kālī line, 219 n. 30
Ārdrā (constellation), 9
Arjuna, 18 n. 31, 23 n. 77, 51 n. 45
Arjuna Kārtavīrya (Kārtavīrya, Kārtavīryārjuna, Sahasrārjuna), 20 n. 45, 28, 42; austerities, 47 n. 7; battle against Rāvaṇa and victory over him, 32, 49 n. 21; blessed with four boons (among which one thousand arms) by Dattātreya, 29, 54 n. 67; blocked the Narmadā with his thousand arms, 32; born armless, 93, 94, 103 n. 18; celebrated for his qualities in the *Viṣṇu Purāṇa*, 32; "golden aerial chariot" received from Dattātreya, 29; highest Jñānin, fully focused on several objects at the same time, 185; his sons kill Jamadagni, 32; invaded Laṅkā, 32; *Mahābhārata* myth relative to him, 29; Mahānubhāva story of Dattātreya granting him boons, 92, 93, 94; major myths, 47 n. 7; *Mārkaṇḍeya Purāṇa* account of his receiving boons from Dattātreya, 29–31; mentioned in later texts of Tantric ritual, 32; Paraśurāma kills him and all his sons, 32, 47 n. 7; Purāṇic connections with Dattātreya, 48 n. 12; Tantric texts praising him, 49 n. 20; thousand arms identified with the thousand rays of Sudarśana, 49 n. 19; universal monarch through Dattātreya's favor, 31; visit to the *āśrama* of Jamadagni where he takes away the Kāmadhenu, 32; within Dattātreya's lineage, 138; worship he rendered to Dattātreya without resorting to any kind of austerity, 32
Arneb (star), 10
arrow maker (= blacksmith): one of Dattātreya's twenty-four Gurus, 41
Ārtha-śāstra, 33
Āruṇi, 65, 69, 84 n. 54
Āruṇi Upaniṣad, 62, 67, 83 n. 46
Arvarīvat, 16 n. 8
Āryāmbā, 127 n. 11, 127 n. 13
Aryan gods, 125
āśā, 243 n. 40
āsana, 61, 205, 220 n. 34

Ashokananda, Swami, 219 n. 27
āśrama: ideology, 82 n. 34; rules, 34, 63
Āśrama Upaniṣad, 62, 63, 66
Aṣṭaka, 188, 194 n. 41
aṣṭāṅga-yoga, 33, 36, 60, 61, 220 n. 34
asta-putra saubhāgyavatī bhava, 129 n. 36
Aṣṭāvakra, 176, 182, 183, 184, 192 n. 24, 193 n. 32, 193 n. 33
Aṣṭavakra-gītā, 192 n. 24, 196, 216 n. 2, 217 n. 10, 217 n. 13, 219 n. 24
astra, 76
astra-dhārīs, 105 n. 31
astrology, 21 n. 50
aśuddha-vidyā (as a *tattva*), 181
Asura-nārāyaṇa: as Jayasthiti Malla, 240 n. 17
Asuras, 22 n. 67, 23 n. 74, 25 n. 93, 48 n. 14, 131 n. 56, 170
asūyā, 20 n. 44
Āśvalāyana, 158 n. 10; branch, 138
Aśvamedha, 4
aśva-medha, 178
aśvattha tree, 119
Aśvins, 2, 3, 16 n. 9, 229
Atharva Veda, 16 n. 5, 17 n. 14, 61, 68, 70, 72, 76, 86 n. 69
Atharvan, 61, 62
atīt, 104 n. 29
atithi, 126–27 n. 8
Atīts (degraded Daśanāmīs), 95, 104 n. 29
ātma-jñāna, 174, 218 n. 14
ātman, 40, 59, 60, 61, 62, 65, 70, 84 n. 47, 139, 172, 174, 177, 178, 180, 181, 183, 184, 185, 187, 188, 195, 200, 202, 205, 206, 207, 208, 209, 210
Ātmarām, 151
Ātmarām Paramahaṃsa, 154
ātma-śakti, 61
Ātma-tīrtha, 91
ātma-vicāra, 128 n. 27
ātma-vidyā, 33, 34, 255
Ātreyas, 3, 5, 17 n. 24, 18 n. 29
Atri, 6, 7, 11, 15 n. 2, 17 n. 12, 17 n. 15, 17 n. 16, 17 n. 24, 18 n. 31, 19 n. 33, 19 n. 41, 27, 28, 30, 65, 75, 92, 106 n. 35, 146, 148, 156, 186, 237, 242 n. 32, 247 n. 76; astrological identifications, 9, 10, 21 n. 57; besought the *trimūrti* to become his sons (inscription), 236; embraced the three newborn babies who were instantly combined in a single form, 229; gave *mantra* to Vālmīki, 224; instructed Nimi in the performance of the *śrāddha* ritual, 4, 47 n. 6; name etymology, mythical origins and feats, 1–5; offered hospitality to Rāma, Sītā, and Lakṣmaṇa at his *āśrama* on the Citrakūṭa mountain, 4, 39, 224; popular meaning of his name, 20 n. 48; Soma is born from his tears, 10–11; Sucindram legend, 241 n. 20
Atrivārada, 163 n. 58
Audumbar, 109, 113, 117–18, 122, 129 n. 34, 130 n. 47, 238
AUM. *See oṃ*
Aurangabad, 164 n. 70
Aurobindo, Śrī, 52 n. 53
Aurva, 23 n. 74
Avadhūta, 37, 65, 236, 256; as "stainless" (*nirañjana*), 221 n. 44; compared to the sky (*gagana*), 206; connection with animals and the wilderness, 40, 69; definition according to the *bīja-mantras* making up the term, 213–14; divided into two classes in Beṅgalī Tantrism, 84 n. 49; Dāsopant, 147; Dattātreya, 51 n. 48, 57, 62, 65, 67, 69, 71, 75, 76, 116, 148, 150, 153, 156, 159 n. 21,

170, 192 n. 23, 198, 213, 215, 224, 226, 230, 232, 237, 251; etymology and portrayal, 51 n. 48; freedom and transcendence of all notions and disciplines, 198, 199, 201, 205–14, 220 n. 41, 221 n. 44; Gajānan Mahārāj, 251; identified with Śiva, 212; nature and behavior, 65, 67, 69, 74, 196, 212; Nṛsiṃha Sarasvatī, 115; perfect Yogin, 51 n. 48; *sahaja* as goal, 202–3; *samatā* (*sama-rasya*, equanimity), 198, 199, 200, 206, 208–13; Saṃvarta, 190 n. 7; seeking of dishonor, 69; Śiva as exemplary model, 69; supreme class of renouncers, 67, 68, 195; symbolic explanation of the term, 65; "vow of madness," 69

Avadhūta (member of Dāsopant's family line), 163 n. 58

Avadhūta (twelve-year-old Dattātreya), 40, 42, 51 n. 48, 51–52 n. 49, 232

Avadhūta *sampradāya*, 99

Avadhūta-gītā (*Avadhūta-grantha, Datta-gītā, Datta-gītā-yoga-śāstra, Dattātreya-gītā, Vedānta-sāra*), 156, 168 n. 104, 195–221, 249; anti-female conviction, 41, 214–15

Avadhūta-gītā (of Dāsopant), 216 n. 2

Avadhūta-gītā (of Govinda Bhagavatpāda), 216 n. 1

Avadhūta-grantha. See Avadhūta-gītā

Avadhūtanīs, 105 n. 31

Avadhūta-ṭīkā, 116, 216 n. 2

Āvāhan Akhāḍā, 105 n. 31

Avatāra: descents of Viṣṇu are innumerable, 53 n. 55; doctrine, 53 n. 56; Mahānubhāva doctrine (Pañca-Kṛṣṇas), 90, 91, 100; of Dattātreya, 101, 110; of Śiva, 61; role and function, 42, 44; systematization of the *daśa-avatāra* list, 53 n. 59

avataraṇikā, 109

Āveśa Avatāra (= Guṇa Avatāra), 43

avidyā, 178, 183, 184, 212, 213, 259

Avimukta, 65

avitad-bhāṣaṇa, 55 n. 78

avitat-karaṇa, 55 n. 78

avyakta, 165 n. 75, 190 n. 7

avyakta avasthā, 55 n. 78

avyakta-ācāra, 66

avyakta-liṅga, 65

axis mundi, 192 n. 27

ayam ātma brahma, 97

Ayodhyā, 4

Āyu, 10, 22 n. 61,

Āyu (king), 39

āyus, 10

Bābā Buḍan hills, 247 n. 78

Bādāmi (Vātāpī), 228, 237, 242 n. 28

Badarīnātha, 95, 97, 111

bādha, 64

Badrīkedar, 112

Bahadur, Sri Jaya Chamarajendra Wadiyar, 237

Bahāmanī: dynasty, 130 n. 44, 147; king, 115, 147; sultans, 157 n. 2

Bahirā, 131 n. 52

Bahirāmbhaṭṭa, 118, 131 n. 52

Bahirobā, 131 n. 52

Bahūdaka, 66, 67, 84 n. 46, 84 n. 47, 85 n. 57

Bahūdaka *tīrtha*, 110

bāla, 69, 74, 167 n. 100

bāla-avadhūta, 40, 232

bāla-datta, 232

Baladevas, 107 n. 41

bāla-kṛṣṇa, 232

Balāraka (*gotra*), 28

Balarāma, 14, 24 n. 83, 98

Bālāsundarī, 164 n. 67

bāla-unmatta-piśācavad, 69, 74

Bāḷekuṇḍrikar, Mahārāj, 154, 155, 167 n. 97

Bali, 50 n. 39; Datta's Prati-vāsudeva, 107 n. 41
Bālmukunda, 167 n. 97
bandha, 210
bandhas (of *Haṭha-Yoga*), 62
Baroda, 162 n. 47
Barodekar, Hirabai, 262 n. 20
Bāvagi, 146
Bay of Cambay, 110
Beas. *See* Vipāśā river
Beck, Guy L., 60
Bedar, 130 n. 44, 146, 147
bee: offering a lesson in renunciation, 38, 52 n. 51, 126 n. 7; one of Dattātreya's Gurus, 41
begging: *mādhūkara* type, 52 n. 51
Belopur, 95, 104 n. 24
Belur *tālukā*, 236
Benares (Kāśī, Vārāṇasī), 18 n. 31, 34, 38, 60, 105 n. 31, 106 n. 36, 106 n. 37, 111, 112, 115, 137, 141, 151, 152, 157 n. 4, 158 n. 5, 159 n. 18, 161 n. 35, 190 n. 4, 224, 231; Dattātreya takes his morning bath here, 146
Bendre, 137
Bengal, 90, 99, 178
Berār area, 255
Berntsen, Maxine, 90
Betelgeuse, 9, 10
Bhadrā, 15 n. 2
bhadraṃ karṇebhiḥ, 70
Bhadrāśva (Raudrāśva), 28
Bhāgā, 190 n. 4
bhagā, 214
Bhagavad-gītā, 18 n. 31, 19 n. 39, 53 n. 56, 99, 107 n. 48, 140, 150, 151, 159 n. 16, 196, 197, 200, 202, 203, 207, 216 n. 7, 217 n. 13, 221 n. 43, 244 n. 52
Bhāgavata, 99, 129 n. 37, 154
Bhāgavata Purāṇa, 23 n. 76, 27, 33, 38, 40, 42, 45, 50 n. 33, 50 n. 40, 51 n. 48, 52 n. 53, 52 n. 54, 53 n. 55, 103 n. 14, 141, 152, 192 n. 23, 213, 217 n. 13, 232, 250
Bhagīratha, 18 n. 25
Bhagnātma. *See* Soma
Bhairav Avadhūta Jñānsāgar, 154, 167 n. 97
Bhairava, 24 n. 84, 90, 97, 101 n. 2, 164 n. 67, 240 n. 13; connection with dogs, 97, 105 n. 32, 244 n. 47
Bhairava-tantra, 24 n. 84
bhajan, 159 n. 17, 260 n. 9
Bhakta-līlāmṛta, 129 n. 37, 139, 145, 146, 151, 157 n. 2, 158 n. 13, 160 n. 25
Bhaktapur. *See* Bhatgāon
Bhakta-vijaya, 115, 129 n. 37, 144, 151, 153
bhakti, 44, 46, 116, 117, 125, 156, 160 n. 30, 187, 188, 196, 217 n. 8; movement, 136, 137, 140, 141; *nirguṇa*, 99, 136, 137, 157 n. 4; poetry, 107 n. 46; *saguṇa*, 136; songs, 159 n. 19; *Vaiṣṇava*, 136, 157 n. 4
bhakti-mārga, 117
Bhānudās, 141, 159 n. 24
Bharadvāja, 2, 15 n. 4, 261 n. 10
Bharata, 23 n. 75
Bharati, Agehananda, 86 n. 72
Bhartṛ, 58
bhārūḍs, 140, 141, 142, 143, 159 n. 19, 160 n. 26, 243 n. 42
Bhāskararāya (Bhāskararāya Bhārati, Bhāsurānandanāth), 78 n. 4, 170, 172, 190 n. 4
Bhatgāon (Bhaktapur, Kho-khom), 224, 239 n. 9, 241 n. 21
Bhaṭobāsa (Nāgadeva), 90, 101
bhaṭṭa, 131 n. 52
Bhava, 5, 18 n. 28
Bhāvana Upaniṣad, 190 n. 4
bhāvanas, 70
Bhavānī, 162 n. 54
Bhāvārtha-rāmāyaṇa, 144, 145, 161 n. 34, 162 n. 51

bhāvas, 33, 165 n. 75
Bhave, V. L., 103 n. 15
Bhaviṣya Purāṇa, 20 n. 49, 245 n. 63
Bhaviṣyottara Purāṇa, 48 n. 11, 50 n. 33
bhedābheda, 14, 25 n. 88
Bhikṣuka Upaniṣad, 57, 62, 69, 85 n. 57
Bhīlavāḍī, 117
Bhīma, 23 n. 77
Bhīmā (Candra-bhāgā), 113, 118, 122, 131 n. 55
Bhīṣmaka, 23 n. 79
bhoga, 32
Bhosa, 49 n. 21
Bhṛgu, 1, 15 n. 4, 47 n. 9
bhukti, 76, 113, 115, 128 n. 17, 140, 166 n. 87, 247 n. 81
bhūmi, 173
bhūr, 61, 83 n. 46
Bhūridatta (also known as Datta), 28
Bhūridatta-jātaka, 28
bhūt possession, 123
bhūt-bādhā, 122
bhūta, 165 n. 75, 193 n. 29
Bhuvaneśvarī, 71, 85 n. 66, 129 n. 34
bhuvas, 61, 83 n. 46
Biardeau, Madeleine, 47 n. 7
Bījak, 137, 158 n. 5
bīja-mantras, 59, 71; *aiṃ*, 71, 72; *āṃ*, 72; composing the term Avadhūta, 213–14; *da*, 258, 259, 264 n. 38; *daṃ*, 70; *dāṃ*, 70; *draṃ*, 70, 71, 72; *drāṃ*, 70, 71, 72; *gaṃ*, 53 n. 57; *hlīṃ*, 71; *hrāṃ*, 72; *hrīṃ*, 71, 72, 75, 188; *hrūṃ*, 72; *huṃ*, 72, 75, 76; *klīṃ*, 71, 72; *klūṃ*, 72; *krīṃ*, 71; *kroṃ*, 72, 75; "peaks" (*kūṭas*) of the *kādi-vidyā*, 172–73; *raṃ*, 70; *sauḥ*, 72–73, 75; *śrīṃ*, 71, 75; *strīṃ*, 71; *trīṃ*, 71
Bījāpur, 118, 131 n. 51, 161 n. 31; district of, 247 n. 78
bindu, 173, 209
birds: in Eknāth's works, 142
Bla-ma Btsan-po, 241 n. 21
Blavatsky, Helena Petrovna, 256
Blavatsky Lodge, 256
boa constrictor, 40
Bodhisatta (= Buddha), 28
Bombay, 224, 252, 255
bora beads, 92
Brahmā (Abja, Kañjāsana, Pitāmaha, Sarasijasambhava), 1, 6, 7, 8, 10, 11, 12, 16 n. 8, 17 n. 10, 19 n. 32, 19 n. 41, 20 n. 44, 24 n. 85, 40, 61, 67, 70, 131 n. 56, 146, 158 n. 5, 169, 170, 179, 185, 186, 193 n. 35, 198, 226, 227, 228, 229, 230, 236, 237, 241 n. 20, 241 n. 23, 243 n. 40, 245 n. 63, 246 n. 75, 248 n. 90, 249, 252, 263 n. 26; emblems, 227, 228; vehicle, 227, 228
Brahma Giri, 105 n. 34
Brahma Purāṇa, 17 n. 17, 33, 42, 44, 45, 48 n. 12, 54 n. 73, 54 n. 74, 116
Brahma Upaniṣad, 62
brahmacarya, 63
brahma-jñāna, 84 n. 49
Brahman, 15 n. 2, 36, 37, 38, 59, 60, 62, 63, 64, 66, 68, 70, 71, 84 n. 48, 99, 128 n. 25, 150, 159 n. 15, 160 n. 30, 164 n. 74, 165 n. 76, 169, 172, 173, 199, 205, 207, 259; aspects of, 61
Brāhmaṇas, 10
Brahmāṇḍa Purāṇa, 12, 15 n. 3, 19 n. 35, 49 n. 19, 53 n. 61, 171, 191 n. 9
brahma-nirvāṇa, 207
brahma-rākṣasa, 119, 121, 132 n. 64, 188
brahma-randhra, 59, 210
Brahma-sūtra, 190 n. 7
Brahma-vaivarta Purāṇa, 23 n. 74

Brahma-vidyā Upaniṣad, 79 n. 16
Brahmin: Citpāvan, 261 n. 11; Deśastha, 138, 246 n. 71
"Brahminization," 125
Bṛhadāraṇyaka Upaniṣad, 16 n. 6, 164 n. 74, 193 n. 32, 258, 264 n. 38, 264 n. 39, 264 n. 40
Bṛhad-avadhūta Upaniṣad, 57, 62, 64–65, 214
Bṛhaddevatā, 1, 4
Bṛhaddharma Purāṇa, 43
Bṛhaj-jābāla Upaniṣad, 66
Bṛhaspati, 11, 15 n. 4, 16 n. 8, 22 n. 66, 30
Bṛhaspati (Yājñavalkya's pupil), 65
Bṛhat-saṃnyāsa Upaniṣad, 62, 82 n. 39, 83 n. 46
Briggs, George Weston, 95, 105 n. 35
Broach, 89, 233
Brooks, Douglas Renfrew, 169, 171, 172, 191 n. 11
Brown, C. Mackenzie, 217 n. 8
Buddha, 42, 53 n. 61, 226, 241 n. 19, 241 n. 20, 245 n. 56, 250, 254
buddhi, 181, 200
Buddhism, 58, 198, 207, 241 n. 19, 241 n. 20, 241 n. 21, 245 n. 56, 250; Tantric, 202, 219 n. 30, 220 n. 36, 221 n. 44; temple in Bhatgāon, 239 n. 9
Budha, 10, 11, 22 n. 61
Bukka, 82 n. 40
Burgess, J., 98

caitanya, 160 n. 30, 203, 206, 207, 208, 209
cakra, 59, 73, 192 n. 29, 206
cakra (Viṣṇu's emblem), 226, 227, 228, 233, 240 n. 12
Cakradhar (Gosāvī, Haripāḷa, Haripāḷadeva), 89, 90, 91, 92, 94, 95, 98, 99, 100, 101, 102 n. 10, 104 n. 24, 154, 166 n. 97, 244 n. 48; also known as Cāṅgadeva Rāuḷ, 98, 102 n. 9; identified with Harināth, 102 n. 9; linked to Nāthism, 136
Cakrapāṇi. *See* Cāṅgadeva Rāuḷ
Cakrapāṇi (Eknāth's grandfather), 141, 160 n. 25
Cakravartins, 98, 107 n. 41
Caḷisgāon, 138
Cāḷukya (Chālukya) court, 106 n. 41; dynasty, 242 n. 28; period, 228, 247 n. 78
camatkāras, 111, 128 n. 18, 128 n. 24
Cānda Bodhale (Candrabhat, Said Cāndasāheb Kādrī), 137, 138, 157 n. 2, 158 n. 13
Candra. *See* Soma
Candra-bhāgā. *See* Bhīmā
Candrabhat. *See* Cānda Bodhale
candra-bindu, 72
Candragupta Maurya, 33
Candramas. *See* Soma
Candrapur, 146
Candraśekhar, 158 n. 13
Cāṅgadeva Rāuḷ ("Gosāvī," Cakrapāṇi), 89, 90, 91, 98, 101 n. 2, 102 n. 9, 103 n. 11, 107 n. 43, 154, 166 n. 97
Canis Major (constellation), 8, 9, 10
Capricorn, 164 n. 68
Carpaṭa, 58
Cassiano da Macerata, 239 n. 9
caste system: decline of, 44; defense of in Datta *sampradāya*, 110, 262 n. 18; Eknāth's unorthodox behavior, 141–42, 153–54, 161 n. 35; not to be jeopardized by renouncers' antinomian tendency, 68; origin, 61; rejected by the Avadhūta, 199; rejected by the Mahānubhāvas, 90
Castor (star), 9
Catalogue of Sanskrit and Prakrit MSS., 216 n. 5
Catuḥślokī Bhāgavata, 141
caturbhujo, 223
Ceylon, 106 n. 40
Chāndogya Upaniṣad, 10

Charles D'Ochoa Collection, 159 n. 21
Cheul, 235, 246 n. 68
Chidbhavananda, Swami, 5, 12
Chikmagalur district, 237
child: one of Dattātreya's twenty-four Gurus, 41
childlessness, 131 n. 53
chillas, 123
Chisht, 262 n. 22
Chishti, Mu ʿīn al-Dīn, 262 n. 22
Chishtī order, 130 n. 42, 140, 254, 262 n. 22
Cidambar Dīkṣit, 167 n. 97
Cid-gagana-candrikā, 206, 221 n. 42
cit, 172, 210
Citrakūṭa mountain, 4, 5, 17 n. 25, 39, 224
citta, 215
citta (as a *tattva*), 181
citta-viśrānti, 200
coitus reservatus, 233
Costantino da Loro, 239 n. 9
cow: not among Dattātreya's twenty-four Gurus, 41; not in Tukārām's portrayal of Dattātreya, 230; sacredness, 243 n. 45, 243 n. 46. *See* also Kāmadhenu
Crossways, 256
Cucīntira Sthala Purāṇa, 20 n. 49
cūpadarī, 248 n. 87

DA, 257, 258
da, 258, 259, 264 n. 38
Dabistān, 95, 197
Dādū, 157 n. 4
Dagadu Halvāī Datta Mandir, 235
Daitya-nārāyaṇa: as Jayasthiti Malla, 240 n. 17
Daitya-nārāyaṇa-avatāra: as Jayasthiti Malla, 240 n. 17
Daityas, 7, 11, 20 n. 47, 30, 48 n. 11, 50 n. 39
Dakṣa, 5, 11, 16 n. 4, 19 n. 32, 22 n. 69
Dakṣiṇāmūrti, 245 n. 62, 248 n. 95
Dakṣiṇāmūrti Saṃhitā. See Datta Saṃhitā
Dalādana Muni, 226, 240 n. 14
daṃ, 70, 85 n. 65
dāṃ, 70
Ḍamaru, 233
Damyata, 258, 259, 264 n. 38
Dānavas, 11, 20 n. 47, 22 n. 67, 30
daṇḍa, 83 n. 46, 129 n. 30
daṇḍa-dhārin, 112
Daṇḍins, 112, 190 n. 4
Ḍāṅgarā, 244 n. 48
Daniélou, Alain, 86 n. 77
Danu, 22 n. 67
dargāhs, 123, 168 n. 107
darśana, 91, 92, 93, 101, 110, 118, 122, 132 n. 61, 144, 145, 150, 163 n. 60, 164 n. 72, 166 n. 86, 231, 244 n. 47, 246 n. 68, 247 n. 85, 263 n. 24
Darśana Upaniṣad, 57, 59, 60, 65, 223
darśanas, 128 n. 26
daśa-avatāra, 42, 43, 53 n. 59, 53 n. 61, 85 n. 66, 158 n. 5
Dāsa-bodha, 146, 163 n. 56
Daśanāmī (Dasnami) order, 89, 99, 101, 115, 116, 171; follows the dictates of "Datāteri," 95, 197; ten branches, 95–97, 104 n. 30, 105 n. 31, 112
Daśārṇa people, 176, 192 n. 25
Dāsa-viśrāma-dhāma, 151
Dāsgaṇū (Gaṇeś Dattātreya Sahasrabuddhe), 261 n. 11
Dasgupta, Shashibhusan, 58, 79 n. 8
Dāsobā, 163 n. 58
Dāsopant (Digambara-anucara), 135, 136, 146–54, 163 n. 57, 163 n. 58, 163 n. 59, 163 n. 60, 163 n. 61, 163 n. 63, 164 n. 66, 164 n. 69, 164 n. 71, 164 n. 73, 165 n. 80, 166 n. 82, 166 n. 85, 166 n. 88, 166 n. 97, 167 n. 102, 216 n. 2, 218 n. 18; initiated into the Nātha sect, 164 n. 72

Dāsopant Digambar, 163 n. 60
Dāsopant-caritra, 133 n. 68, 146–50, 163 n. 60, 163 n. 61, 163 n. 63, 164 n. 66, 165 n. 74, 229
Datāteri. *See* Dattātreya
Datta. *See* Dattātreya
Datta, 257, 258, 264 n. 38
Datta (received by gift), 28
Datta Ātreya (= Dattātreya), 28
datta dayadhvam dāmyata, 258
Datta Mahārāj of Aste, Śrī, 154, 155, 167 n. 97
Datta Purāṇa, 155
Datta Saṃhitā (*Dakṣiṇāmūrti Saṃhitā*), 170
Datta *sampradāya*, 107 n. 46, 109, 110, 112, 116, 117, 125, 126, 126 n. 5, 130 n. 47, 135, 136, 138, 140, 154, 156, 165 n. 74, 171, 196, 216 n. 2, 237, 249, 250, 253
Datta-gītā. *See Avadhūta-gītā*
Datta-gītā-yoga-śāstra. *See Avadhūta-gītā*
Datta-jayantī, 117, 122, 132 n. 61
Dattajī, 163 n. 58, 218 n. 18
Dattajī (later Nātha), 197
Dattajīpant, 163 n. 58
Datta-laharī, 226, 240 n. 14
Datta-māhātmya (of Dāsopant), 151, 156
Datta-māhātmya (of Vāsudevānanda Sarasvatī), 155, 167 n. 102
Dattanāth Ujjayinīkar, 154, 155, 167 n. 97
Datta-prabodha, 145, 155, 162 n. 47
Dattātreya (Datāteri, Datta, Dattātri, Dattobā): *abhaṅg* on him by Jñāndev, 99; *abhaṅg* on him by Tukārām, 145–46; above all caste, creed, and religion, 260 n. 1; acted as priest at Reṇukā's funeral, 92, 93–94; addicted to meat (*māṅsa*), 31, 39, 45, 93, 94, 97; addicted to sensual pleasure though not affected by it, 29, 30; addicted to singing and music, 29, 31, 45, 86 n. 77, 254, 262 n. 20, 263 n. 23; advised gods to invoke the grace of Gaṇeśa in order to subdue the demon Mātsaryāsura, 53 n. 57; advised King Janamejaya to worship an image of Kṛṣṇa at Guruvāyur so as to rid himself of leprosy, 39–40; Aghorī and first teacher (*ādi-guru*) of the Aghora *sampradāya*, 97, 105–106 n. 35; antinomian character, 31, 39, 40, 45–46, 74, 75, 92, 93, 94, 116, 123–25, 137, 144, 232, 244 n. 53; appearance as beggar (*mādhukarin*), 110, 163 n. 56; appearance as child (*bāla*), 74, 75, 132 n. 61, 154; appearance as demon (*piśāca*), 74, 75; appearance as Faqīr (Fakir), 144–45, 254, 259 n. 1; appearance as hunter holding dogs, 93, 231; appearance as madman (*unmatta*), 31, 40, 74, 75, 244 n. 53; appearance as Mahār, 147; appearance as Malaṅg, 145; appearance as Muslim huntsman, 145; appearance as Muslim mendicant, 137; appearance as Muslim soldier, 144; appearance as naked ascetic (*digambara*), 28, 62, 74, 146, 230, 237, 250; appearance as outcaste Māṅg, 92, 94; appearance as Pathan, 145; appearance as Saṃnyāsin and Yati, 254; appearance as shepherd, 254, 263 n. 24; *āratī* in his praise by Rāmdās, 146; *āśrama* at Mātāpur, 94, 95; *āśrama* in Gandhamādana mountain, 174, 175; assimilative force, 188–89; association with people of low birth, 86 n. 77; astrological interpretations of

modern iconography, 8–10; author of *Avadhūta-gītā*, 107 n. 43, 195–221; author of *Datta Saṃhitā*, 170; author of *Jīvanmukta-gītā*, 196; author of *Mūḷa-stambha*, 159 n. 21; author of *Tantras*, 77, 86 n. 77, 86 n. 78, 87 n. 79; Avadhūta, 51 n. 48, 57, 62, 65, 67, 69, 71, 75, 76, 116, 148, 150, 153, 156, 159 n. 21, 170, 192 n. 23, 198, 213, 215, 224, 226, 230, 232, 237, 249, 250, 251, 254; Avatāra (as eternal Pañca-Kṛṣṇa), 90, 91, 101, 249; Avatāra of Śiva, 61, 223, 259 n. 1; Avatāra of Viṣṇu, 27, 28, 30, 42–44, 45, 46, 47 n. 3, 53 n. 61, 54 n. 67, 54 n. 69, 74, 95, 110, 116, 122, 148, 164 n. 68, 226, 228, 236, 245 n. 65, 249, 250, 255, 259 n. 1; Avatāras of, 110 (as Vallinātha), 110–11, 115, 118, 238 (as Śrīpāda Śrīvallabha), 111–16, 118, 138, 238 (as Nṛsiṃha Sarasvatī), 116, 122, 155 (Gurus, Yogins, and Faqīrs in the Datta movement), 118, 238 (as Vāsudevānanda Sarasvatī), 147, 163 n. 60 (as Dāsopant), 158 n. 8, 251, 260 n. 5, 263 n. 23 (as Sāī Bābā of Śirḍī), 166 n. 85 (sixteen manifestations), 167 n. 100, 238 (as Akkaḷkoṭ Mahārāj), 238 (as Māṇikprabhu), 251, 260 n. 9 (as Satya Sāī Bābā), 251 (as Gajānan Mahārāj), 254; Āveśa Avatāra, 43; *bāla-avadhūta*, 40, 42, 51 n. 48, 51–52 n. 49, 232; *bāla-datta*, 232; begs at midday in the courtyard of the Mahālakṣmī temple, 162 n. 54; bestower of *bhukti* as well as *mukti*, 76, 113, 115, 128 n. 17, 128 n. 24, 140, 152, 166 n. 87, 237, 247 n. 81; bestower of highest knowledge, 75; beyond *guṇas* (*nirguṇa*), 237, 238, 243 n. 40, 248 n. 96; birthday, 122, 133 n. 68, 148; born in the *sattva* sphere, 254; born to Atri and Anasūyā, 1, 5, 7, 20 n. 44, 75, 148; Brahmin deity, 116, 125; bright-faced (*divya*), 254; called Līlā-viśvambhara by Mukteśvar, 144; *caturbhujo*, 223, 237; comes in dreams, 254; compassion, 62; connection with cow, 227, 228, 230–31, 232, 233, 238 (as Gāyatrī), 242 n. 30, 243 n. 40, 255; connection with dogs, 8, 9, 10, 93, 97, 144, 145, 227, 230, 231–32, 243 n. 40, 244 n. 49, 244 n. 53, 255; connection with Islam, 116, 125, 237, 247 n. 79, 250, 253, 259–60 n. 1; connection with Jainism, 98, 250; connection with Nāthism, 89, 90, 99–100, 101, 102 n. 6, 104 n. 26, 105 n. 35, 107 n. 51, 108 n. 52, 163 n. 56, 164 n. 67, 197–99, 220 n. 33, 224, 226, 232, 235, 236, 238, 242 n. 30, 250, 251–53, 263 n. 23; connection with Śāktism and Devī worship (Tripurā), 37, 94, 124, 162 n. 54, 164 n. 67, 169–94, 235, 242 n. 32, 246 n. 68, 249, 253; connection with Śaṅkara, to whom he granted the boon that his order of Saṃnyāsins be accepted in the world, 95–97; connection with tribals, 263 n. 24; constant wandering, 117, 127 n. 12, 146, 162 n. 54, 189, 230, 232, 238, 247 n. 85, 248 n. 96, 250; creator of all *tīrthas*, 93; creator of *soma* plant, 86 n. 77, 100; cult, 44–46, 112, 117, 119, 121, 125, 130 n. 41, 135, 136, 195, 228, 235, 237, 254, 262 n. 20; cursed Rāvaṇa, 49 n. 21; *darśana*

Dattātreya *(continued)*
difficult to obtain, 166 n. 86, 247 n. 85, 247–48 n. 86, 248 n. 96; *darśanas* to Dāsopant, 147, 148, 149–50, 151–52, 152–53, 164 n. 72; *darśanas* to Eknāth, 137, 144–45, 162 n. 50; *darśanas* to Janārdan, 139–40, 144–45; Daśanāmīs follow his dictates, 197; Dattātreya Gajānan tutelary deity of the Āvāhan Akhāḍā, 105 n. 31; declared Eknāth to be an Avatāra of Śrī Pāṇḍuraṅga, 152; declared to be sinless (*anagha*), 30, 31, 32, 48 n. 15, 54 n. 67; deified Brahmin, 106 n. 35; deified Guru (Sadguru), 28, 62, 74, 90, 100, 101, 105 n. 35, 117, 144, 150, 152, 220 n. 33, 243 n. 40, 248 n. 93, 249, 250, 254, 259, 260 n. 9; description by Sundaradās the younger, 157 n. 4; disguising saintliness and actively courting dishonor, 46, 255; dissimulating his dispassion, 29, 31, 46; *dvi-bāhu*, 224, 226, 237; *ekmukhī*, 122, 223, 224, 226, 227, 228, 235, 237, 247 n. 78; equanimity (*sama-rasya*), 30, 38–39, 51 n. 48, 185, 215; eternal Avatāra, 71, 110, 119, 254, 259; eternal Guru and Satguru of all Nāthas, 105 n. 35, 107 n. 43; explained the *mahā-vākya ahaṃ brahmāsmi* to Dāsopant, 150; extols the Brahminical string, 83 n. 46; father of Nimi, 29; feet bestow purity and excellence in Yoga, 50 n. 33; first convert of Neminath, 98; followed path of absolute monism, 54 n. 67; founder of the Avadhūta *sampradāya*, 99; founder of the Nātha *sampradāya*, 99, 100; Girnār as his seat, 97–98, 162 n. 54, 232; god of local semi-civilized tribe, 55 n. 79, 125; Gorakhnāth's Guru, 100, 197„ 198, 218 n. 14, 220 n. 33; grace hard to obtain, 255; granted boon of omniscience to Bābā Kīnārām, 97; granted offspring to childless kings, 39; Hari-Hara-Pitāmaha, 227–28; healer from possession by evil spirits and link with possession phenomena, 109, 122–25, 134 n. 78, 226, 235, 253, 262 n. 18; historical descent according to F. E. Pargiter, 28–29, 54 n. 76; holds phallus (*liṅga*) in iconography, 233; iconography, 43, 223–48, 254; identified as a Brahmin, 34, 37, 38, 40, 45, 254; identified as a Muni, 46, 112; identified as Dakṣiṇāmūrti, 248 n. 95; identified as Devadatta (Buddha's cousin), 226, 241 n. 20, 250; identified as Hari, 74; identified as Janārdan's Guru, 135, 137, 138, 139, 158 n. 13, 159 n. 15; identified as Kālūrām, 106 n. 37; identified as Kṛṣṇa, 74; identified as Neminath, 98, 250, 259 n. 1; identified as Śiva, 61–62, 76, 97, 174, 263 n. 27; identified as Viṣṇu (Nārāyaṇa), 70, 74, 76, 223, 224, 227, 228, 229, 230, 233; identified with the *trimūrti*, 76, 106 n. 35, 226–30, 263 n. 26; image according to *Agni Purāṇa*, 43, 224; image according to *Viṣṇu-dharmottara Purāṇa* (Dattātreya as Vālmīki), 224; immortal Yogin, 95, 101, 104 n. 26, 158 n. 5, 250, 259; indulgence in liquor (*mada*), 29, 30, 31, 39, 45, 48 n. 14, 93, 94, 156, 174; initiated Śrī Rāghava Caitanya (Tukārām's Guru), 145; inscrip-

tions, 233, 236–37, 246 n. 74, 246 n. 75, 247 n. 77; instructed by Śiva in the *Dattātreya-tantra,* 87 n. 79; integrative spirituality, 76, 90, 136, 226, 228, 249, 250, 253; interpretations of his name, 27–28, 228–29; Jamadagni's Guru, 102 n. 11; Janārdan's worship of, 139–40, 158 n. 14, 159 n. 15; Jñānin supreme, 36–37, 57, 58, 62, 74, 97, 117, 171, 172, 215, 223, 238, 249; Kabīr-panthī motto, 158 n. 5; *līlās,* 126; lineage, 138; loves the *uḍumbara* tree, 255; made love with a beautiful woman identified as his consort (Lakṣmī), 29, 30, 45, 71, 73, 156, 174; *Mahābhārata* account of his granting four boons (among which one thousand arms) to Arjuna Kārtavīrya, 29, 54 n. 67; Mahānubhāva accounts and link with Mahānubhāvas, 90–95, 124, 223, 226, 236, 249, 250, 253; *mantras,* 70–77; Mārkaṇḍeya as his precursor, 53 n. 61; *Mārkaṇḍeya Pūraṇa* account of his granting boons to Arjuna Kārtavīrya, 29–31, 54 n. 67, 249; master of the *Vedas,* 231; Mātāpur as his original seat of manifestation, privileged abode and sleeping place, 146, 147, 148, 223; Matsyendranāth's Guru, 100; mentions of in Kabīr's *ramainīs,* 137; mentions of in the *Mahābhārata,* 47 n. 8; morning bath at Haridvār or Pañcāḷeśvara, 162 n. 54; movement, 126, 135–56, 166–67 n. 97, 167 n. 98, 167 n. 99, 167 n. 100, 168 n. 104, 201, 246 n. 69, 248 n. 92, 250; names and epithets in the *Mārkaṇḍeya Purāṇa,* 55 n. 77; names *Datta* and *Dattātreya* as identifying different figures, 28; observed the *ajagara* "mode of life," 38; oldest *tīrtha* at Pañcāḷeśvara, 99, 103 n. 12, 136; omnipresence, 249, 250, 259; paradigm of *sahaja,* 215; Paramahaṃsa, 57, 65–69, 249; patron lord of prostitutes, 236; performed austerities, 29; pilgrimage places and main temples, 117–22, 130 n. 47; plunged into a lake for innumerable years, 20 n. 47, 29; plural identities, 125; practiced Yoga on the Vindhyas, 50 n. 33; Prādurbhāva, 43; Prādurbhāvāntara, 43; praises the Brahmin who carries the triple staff, 83 n. 46; priest at Paraśurāma's *śrāddha* ceremony, 49 n. 22; primeval cause (*ādi-kāraṇa*) of the Mahānubhāva sect, 92, 101; Purāṇic connections with Arjuna Kārtavīrya, 48 n. 12; *pūrṇa-avatāra,* 230, 249; *pūrṇa-devatā,* 230; recommends Viṣṇu's worship, 82 n. 37; related to *Śaivism,* 128 n. 17; represented as Viṣṇu sculptured in Yogic posture, 227, 228; residence in Dhanuṣkoṭi and teaching to Durācāra, 39; restorer of *dharma* and of Vedic religion and rites, 44, 86 n. 77; Ṛṣi in the *Mahābhārata,* 28–29, 249; sacred day, 117; Sādhu-Sant *paramparā,* 154–56; *saguṇa* form, 145; *Śaiva* characterization, 47 n. 3, 263 n. 27; sandals and footprints (*pādukās*), 92, 93, 98, 117–22, 132 n. 59, 132 n. 60, 132 n. 66, 146, 150, 156, 164 n. 68, 164 n. 71, 164 n. 73, 201, 223, 230, 232, 237, 247 n. 81, 255;

Dattātreya *(continued)*
saved Indra and other gods from Daityas and Dānavas, 29, 30–31, 48 n. 11, 86 n. 77; school based on the chanting of Datta's name in Rāmdās's *Dāsa-bodha,* 146; "school of thought" as in the *Kathā-bodha,* 33; served as Eknāth's doorkeeper, 152–53; served by Siddhas, 62; seventh in Jaina list of nine Vāsudevas, 98, 106–7 n. 41; shrine at Mātāpur, 94; shrine at Sucindram, 19 n. 41; Siddheśvar, 97; Śiva's disciple, 255, 263 n. 27; Śiva's Guru, 105 n. 35, 226, 263 n. 27; *smartṛ-gāmin,* 240 n. 14; spoke the Muhammadan language, 144; sported in Merubāḷā, 94; Tantric aspect, 174, 258; taught *aṣṭāṅga-yoga* (*ānvīkṣikī, sutarka-vidyā*) to Alarka, 33–38, 49 n. 24, 50 n. 28, 54 n. 67; taught Dāsopant why he, though qualityless (*nirguṇa*), appeared as *saguṇa,* 150, 165 n. 75; taught detachment and equanimity to Prahlāda, 38–39; taught *Śākta* nondualism to Paraśurāma in the *Tripurā-rahasya,* 49 n. 22, 169–94, 249; teacher of Sādhyas, 29, 55 n. 78, 176; teacher of Sāṃkhya, 33; teacher of *tretā* age, 49 n. 26, 95; teacher of Yoga, 27, 33, 36, 45, 57, 77, 255; teachings on Yoga and the Avadhūta's nature to Sāṃkṛti, 60, 62, 65; temple in Bhatgāon, 224–26, 239 n. 10, 241 n. 21; temple in Śedgāo, 262 n. 18; temple in Vajreśvarī, 194 n. 39; temples in Paṇḍharpur, 223, 235, 246 n. 68; temples in Puṇe, 235–36, 246 n. 71; tendency to appear suddenly and unexpectedly, 94–95; Thursday (*guruvar*) as special day, 255; *trimukhī* (modern iconography; Brahmā, Viṣṇu, and Śiva all in one), 45, 145–46, 198, 227–30, 232, 233, 235, 237–39, 242 n. 31, 242 n. 32, 243 n. 40, 249, 251, 252, 254; tutelary deity of the Jūnā Akhāḍā, 97; twenty-four Gurus taught detachment to King Yadu, 40–42, 51–52 n. 49, 52 n. 50, 52 n. 53, 57, 250; unbound by Vedic injunctions, 254; united to the various forms of his Śakti, 71, 72, 73; upholder of the view that only Brahmins are entitled to renounce, 64; venerated within the Daśanāmī order, 95, 112; Vibhava, 43; won against Gorakhnāth in magical bouts, 197, 238, 248 n. 91; worshipped by Gorakhnāth and Matsyendranāth as well as by all nine Nāthas in iconography, 232; Yogin and lord of Yoga, 29, 45, 46, 54 n. 67, 62, 74, 75, 76, 95, 97, 98, 99, 100, 101, 105 n. 33, 116, 117, 148, 156, 166 n. 86, 170, 174, 223, 224, 226, 228, 232, 249, 259 n. 1
Dattātreya Hills, 245 n. 66
Dattātreya Saṃhitā, 53 n. 62
Dattātreya Upaniṣad, 57, 69, 70–77, 94, 172
Dattātreya-bhujaṃga-stotra, 95
Dattātreya-bodha, 77
Dattātreya-cakra, 77
Dattātreya-campū, 156
Dattātreya-daśa-nāma-stotra, 151
Dattātreya-dvādaśa-nāma-stotra, 151
Dattātreya-gāyatrī, 77, 156
Dattātreya-gītā. See Avadhūta-gītā
Dattātreya-janman, 129 n. 37
Dattātreya-kalpa, 77, 156, 242 n. 30
Dattātreya-kavaca, 77

Dattātreya-mālā-mantra, 77
Dattātreya-mantra, 77
Dattātreya-mudrā, 245 n. 62
Dattātreya-nāma-valī, 151
Dattātreya-pūjā-paddhati, 156
Dattātreya-sahasra-nāma-stotra, 151
Dattātreya-śata-nāma-stotra, 151
Dattātreya-ṣoḍaśa-nāma-stotra, 151
Dattātreya-tantra, 77, 87 n. 79, 156
Dattātreya-tīrtha, 50 n. 33
Dattātreya-utpatti, 133 n. 68
Dattātreya-vajra-kavaca, 77, 240 n. 14
Dattātreyins, 105 n. 32
Dattātri. *See* Dattātreya
Dattobā. *See* Dattātreya
Dattrima. *See* Datta (received by gift)
Daulatabad. *See* Devgiri
Dayadhvam, 257, 258, 264 n. 38
dayā-śānti, 243 n. 40
Deccan, 113, 130 n. 42, 132 n. 65, 157 n. 2, 161 n. 37, 242 n. 28, 246 n. 74
deer: one of Dattātreya's Gurus, 41, 52 n. 50
Dehu, 163 n. 57
Deleury, G. A., 162 n. 52
Delhi (New Delhi), 97, 242 n. 31, 262 n. 22
Descriptive Catalogue, 216 n. 5, 219 n. 26
Deshpande, Y. K., 102 n. 9
deśpāṇḍya, 147, 160 n. 61
Deussen, Paul, 57, 78 n. 1
Devabhāga, 51 n. 46
devāce māse ("god's fish"), 130 n. 47
Devadatta, 226, 241 n. 19, 250; opposed Atri, 241 n. 20
Devadeveśvara temple, 94
Devagad, 160 n. 25
Devagiri hill, 91
Devahūti, 5, 19 n. 32
Devajī, 163 n. 58
Devakī, 24 n. 83
Devas, 11, 23 n. 76, 48 n. 14, 118
devatā, 71, 73, 77, 97, 144, 254
deva-yāna, 205
Devgiri (Daulatabad), 102 n. 10, 130 n. 42, 138, 157 n. 2, 160 n. 25, 160 n. 28, 161 n. 31
Devī, 71, 72, 73, 93, 94, 98, 103 n. 22, 104 n. 23, 134 n. 78, 170, 171, 172, 173, 174, 175, 177, 186, 187, 189 n. 1, 227, 231, 243 n. 45, 243 n. 46, 246 n. 68, 249; as *ardha-nara*, 193 n. 37
Devī-bhāgavata Purāṇa, 20 n. 48, 43
Devī-gītā, 197, 217 n. 13
Devī-kośa, 103 n. 22, 104 n. 23
Devī-māhātmya, 171, 191 n. 9
Devī-nāma-vilāsa, 191 n. 12
dhākṭen devghar, 146
dhamma, 28
Dhangar caste, 263 n. 24
Dhanuṣkoṭi, 39
dhāraṇā, 37, 220 n. 34
Dharma, 11, 23 n. 77
dharma, 42, 44, 46, 64, 67, 105 n. 34, 113, 117, 167 n. 97
Dharma Nārāyaṇa, 53 n. 61
Dharmarāja, 19 n. 38
dharma-śālās, 118
Dhataraṭṭha (Nāga King), 28
Dhenuka, 24 n. 83
Dhere, R. C., 44, 98, 99, 100, 102 n. 9, 145, 154, 163 n. 60, 227, 262 n. 20
dhikr, 167 n. 99
dhotī, 92, 93
Dhṛtarāṣṭra, 168 n. 104
dhūma-mārga, 220 n. 41
dhūta-saṃsāra-bandhana, 65, 214
dhyāna, 37, 60, 79 n. 16, 177, 220 n. 31, 220 n. 34
dhyāna-ślokas, 242 n. 30
digambara, 28, 62, 74, 230, 250
Digambara-anucara. *See* Dāsopant
Digambaras, 106 n. 41, 260 n. 3

Digambarrāya (Digambarpant), 147, 163 n. 58
dīkṣā, 112, 174, 175
Dikshit, T. R. C., 81 n. 27
Dīkṣit Svāmin, 154
dīpti-mārga, 220 n. 41
Diti, 20 n. 47
Divanji, P. C., 80 n. 20
divya-dṛṣṭi, 97
divya-śarīra, 58
dogs: association of various deities with, 244 n. 47; Dattātreya's connection with, 8, 9, 10, 93, 97, 144, 145, 227, 230, 231–32, 243 n. 40, 244 n. 49, 244 n.53, 255; identified as Kāmadhenu, 144; identified with the *Vedas*, 8, 9, 10, 228, 231, 237; Indian perception of, 243 n. 43; Mahānubhāva association with, 244 n. 48; not figuring among Dattātreya's twenty-four Gurus, 41; Tukārām's association with, 243 n. 42; within Eknāth's works, 142, 243 n. 42
draṃ, 70, 71, 72
drāṃ, 70, 71, 72
draṃ (drāṃ) dattātreyāya namaḥ, 72
Droṇa, 15 n. 4
dṛṣṭi, 205, 208
Dubhe (star), 2
Dumézil, Georges, 229, 242 n. 35, 242 n. 36
Durācāra, 39
Durgā, 171, 248 n. 88
Durvāsas: Ātreya as one of his names, 27; blessed gods and men, 23 n. 76; born to Atri and Anasūyā, 1, 5, 7, 9, 20 n. 44, 236; brought down the *Bhairava-tantra* along with other sages, 24 n. 84; credited with authorship of *Lalitā-stava-ratna* and *Śakti-mahimna-stava*, 25 n. 92; cursed gods and men, 23 n. 74, 24 n. 81; descended from Prabhākara's Svastyātreyas, 28; known as Krodha-bhaṭṭāraka in the Devī *Āgamas*, 14; linked to the *mantra* of *Śrī-vidyā*, 25 n. 92; mythological origins and personality, 12–14, 22 n. 72; Paramahaṃsa, 65, 69; practiced penance by remaining under water for ten thousand years, 20 n. 47; *raudra* nature and *unmatta* portrayal, 20 n. 46, 23 n. 78, 32, 185; relation with Tripurā, 25 n. 93, 170
Duṣyanta, 12, 23 n. 75
Dūta-kāvyas, 196
Dvaita, 198, 199
dvaita-advaita-vivarjita, 198, 199
dvandva, 208, 210
dvāpara-yuga, 24 n. 85, 95
Dvārakā, 24 n. 82, 40, 89, 90, 97, 102 n. 9
dvāras, 55 n. 78
dveśa, 20 n. 44
dvi-bāhu, 224, 226
dvīpas, 192 n. 27
Dvi-sahasrī, 155
Dvivedi, Hajariprasad, 90, 98, 100, 197, 218 n. 15
Dyaus, 16 n. 9
Dyczkowski, Mark S. G., 219 n. 31
'Dzam-gling-rgyas-bshad, 241 n. 21

Egypt, 256, 257
ehi, 72
eka-daṇḍīs, 83 n. 46
Eka-Janārdan, 141, 144
ekāka (period of solitude), 89
ekatva, 143
Ekavīrā. *See* Reṇukā
ekmukhī, 122, 223, 224, 226, 227, 228
Eknāth, 51 n. 49, 135, 136, 137, 138, 139, 140–45, 146, 159 n. 17, 159 n. 18, 160 n. 25, 160 n. 27,

160 n. 29, 160 n. 30, 161 n. 31, 161 n. 32, 161 n. 33, 161 n. 34, 161 n. 40, 162 n. 42, 162 n. 50, 162 n. 51, 163 n. 59, 166 n. 97, 227; and Dāsopant, 151–54, 166 n. 88, 168 n. 105; *bhārūḍ* celebrating the dog, 243 n. 42; connection with Nāthism, 141; identification with Janārdan, 160 n. 28; identification with Mahānubhāvas, 141; identified as Avatāra of Śrī Pāṇḍuraṅga by Dattātreya, 152–53, 166 n. 91; Islamic influence, 160 n. 26; unorthodox behavior, 141–42, 153–54, 161 n. 35
Eknāthī Bhāgavata, 51 n. 49, 138, 139, 140, 141, 159 n. 17, 160 n. 29
Eknāth-pañcaka, 146
ekoddiṣṭa-śrāddha, 84 n. 46
elephant (male): one of Dattātreya's twenty-four Gurus, 41
Eliade, Mircea, 73
Eliot, T. S., 257, 259, 264 n. 35, 264 n. 38
England, 255
Enopion. *See* Irieus
Etvah district, 167 n. 99

Faqīr (Fakir), 116, 131 n. 53, 140, 155, 156, 157 n. 2, 167 n. 99, 247 n. 79, 250, 259–60 n. 1
fanā-fi-sh-Shaykh, 160 n. 28
Fasana, E., 133 n. 71
Feuerstein, Georg, 36, 60
fish: one of Dattātreya's twenty-four Gurus, 41
folk religion, 125

gadā, 226, 233, 240 n. 12
Gadya-rāja, 92
gagana, 206, 212, 220 n. 40
gagana-ākāra, 212
gagana-maṇḍala, 206
Gahinī (Gahinīnāth), 58, 99, 107 n. 48
Gajānan Mahārāj of Śegāon, 246 n. 69, 251, 255, 261 n. 11, 261 n. 12
gaṃ, 53 n. 57, 86 n. 67
Gambhīrarāya, 190 n. 4
Gāṇagāpūr, 109, 113, 115, 117, 118–25, 131 n. 55, 132 n. 61, 133 n. 71, 155, 156, 158 n. 11, 167 n. 97, 232, 237, 238, 246 n. 72, 252
Gaṇapati. *See* Gaṇeśa
gaṇas, 132 n. 62
Gaṇḍ Mahārāj. *See* Yogānanda Sarasvatī
Gandhak river, 246 n. 74
Gandhamādana mountain, 174, 175
Gandharvas, 254
Gandharva-tantra, 77, 86 n. 78
Gandhi, M. K., 127 n. 12
Gaṇeśa (Gaṇapati), 71, 132 n. 62, 133 n. 68, 135, 235; as Śrī Vighnahar Cintāmaṇi, 119, 121; as Vakratuṇḍa, 53 n. 57; *mūla-mantra*, 86 n. 67
Gaṇeśa Purāṇa, 103 n. 18, 218 n. 13
Gaṇeśa-caturthī, 133 n. 68
Gaṇeśa-gītā, 197, 218 n. 13
Ganeshpuri, 78 n. 4, 194 n. 39
Gaṅgā (Jāhnavī), 4, 5, 17–18 n. 25, 106 n. 37, 131 n. 55, 145, 161 n. 35, 162 n. 54, 174, 192 n. 23, 230, 238, 257
Gaṅgābāī, 162 n. 41
Ganganath Maharaj, 235
garbha-gṛha, 119, 121
Garga, 29, 30, 31, 48 n. 10
Gargī, 80 n. 20
Gargī Vācaknavī, 193 n. 32
Garuḍa, 226, 227, 228
Garuḍa Purāṇa, 33, 38, 42, 50 n. 30
Garuḍeśvar, 238, 248 n. 94
gāthās, 243 n. 42
Gauḍapāda, 191 n. 11, 236, 247 n. 77

Gautama, 4, 23 n. 76
Gaviṣṭhira (*gotra*), 28
Gāyā, 112, 232
Gāyatrī (*gāyatrī*), 61, 73, 77, 238, 248 n. 90
geruā cloth, 238, 247 n. 82
Gheraṇḍa Saṃhitā, 81 n. 25
Ghṛtācī, 28
Ghurye, G. S., 130 n. 43, 133 n. 68, 133 n. 75, 154, 163 n. 56, 235, 242 n. 26, 247 n. 78, 262 n. 20
Giridhara, 165 n. 80
Girijābāī, 161 n. 31
giri-prasravaṇa, 59
Girnār, 94, 97–98, 105 n. 31, 106 n. 38, 145, 155, 235, 238, 245 n. 59, 250, 255, 256; Dattātreya meditates here, 162 n. 54; locus of Dattātreya's original footprints, 232
Gītāñjali, 264 n. 31
Gītārṇava, 150, 151, 165 n. 80
Gītārtha-candrikā, 151
Gītās: attempt to "imitate" the *Bhagavad-gītā*, 216–17 n. 7; collections of, 218 n. 13; contrasted with *Māhātmyas*, 217 n. 8; "label," 196
Giuseppe Felice da Morro, 240 n. 16
glauṃ, 71, 86 n. 67
glīṃ, 86 n. 67
Goa, 82 n. 40
Godāvarī, 16 n. 7, 89, 90, 103 n. 12, 136, 148, 150, 162 n. 54
Godāvarī district (east), 110
Godāvarī-māhātmya, 261 n. 11
Godubāī, 144
Gokarṇa, 111, 243 n. 40
Golden Dawn (Hermetic Order), 256
Gomatī, 25 n. 87
Gonda, Jan, 155, 197, 198, 229
Gopāl-kālā, 153
gopāṣṭamī, 243 n. 45
Gopatha Brāhmaṇa, 17 n. 14, 79 n. 16
Gopicandra, 58
Gorakh-bodh, 219 n. 28
Gorakha-gītā, 99, 107 n. 48
Gorakhnāth (Gorakṣa), 51 n. 48, 58, 98, 99, 100, 105 n. 34, 106 n. 40, 107 n. 46, 107 n. 48, 154, 158 n. 5, 163 n. 56, 166 n. 97, 216 n. 2, 218 n. 16, 230, 236, 240 n. 11; Dattātreya as his teacher, 100, 197, 198, 218 n. 14, 220 n. 33; lost in magical bouts with Dattātreya, 197, 238, 248 n. 91; supposed author of *Avadhūta-gītā*, 197, 218 n. 15; worships Dattātreya in iconography, 232
Gorakhpur, 164 n. 67; district of, 246 n. 74
Gorakṣa. *See* Gorakhnāth
Gorakṣa Saṃhitā (*Gorakṣa-paddhati*), 197, 218 n. 16
Gorakṣa-siddhānta-saṃgraha, 197, 198, 218 n. 15, 244 n. 52
Gosāvī. *See* Cakradhar
Gosāvīs, 103 n. 11
Gotama, 2, 15 n. 4
Govinda (Govinda Bhagavatpāda), 216 n. 1, 236, 247 n. 77
Govindaprabhu. *See* Guṇḍam Rāuḷ
Grantha-rāja, 151
"great tradition," 125
Greece, 256, 257
gṛhastha, 63
Gṛhastha (Avadhūtas), 84 n. 49
Group of Jacob (three stars of Orion's belt), 21 n. 53
Group of Peter (three stars of Orion's belt), 21 n. 53
Gujarat, 24 n. 82, 89, 106 n. 41, 107 n. 42, 110, 189, 233, 235, 245 n. 65, 255
Gulavani Mahārāj, 167 n. 97
Gulbarga district, 113
Guṇabhadra, 106 n. 41

guṇas, 28, 36, 37, 61, 150, 165 n. 75, 210, 243 n. 40
Guṇḍam Rāuḷ (Govindaprabhu), 89, 90, 98, 100, 102 n. 3, 102 n. 9, 154, 166 n. 97
Gurkhas, 239 n. 9, 240 n. 17
"Guru": preceptor of the gods, 40
Guru Nānak, 137
Guru Saṃhitā, 155
Guru Shikhar. *See* Mount Abu
guru-bhakta, 141
guru-bīja, 72
Gurubovā, 163 n. 58
Guru-caritra, 101, 109–15, 116, 118, 123, 125, 129 n. 34, 132 n. 66, 136, 138, 146, 155, 227, 253, 254, 260 n. 5
guru-paramparā, 104 n. 30, 126 n. 5, 128 n. 20, 130 n. 44, 135, 170
Guru-pūrṇimā, 20 n. 44, 260 n. 10
Guruvaṃśa-kāvya, 95
Guruvāyur, 39, 40
Gwalior, 192 n. 25

hādi-vidyā. *See* Lopāmudrā *vidyā*
Haihayas, 7, 20 n. 45, 29, 50 n. 33, 185
ḥāl, 140
Hālāsya (Madurai), 170
Haḷebīḍ, 227, 237, 241 n. 25
Hampi, 159 n. 24
Haṃsa, 66, 67, 84 n. 46, 84 n. 47, 85 n. 57
haṃsa, 70
Haṃsa, Bhagavan Śrī, 255
Hanumān (Māruti), 69, 121, 132 n. 65, 158 n. 5, 236
Hara. *See* Śiva
Hari (= Viṣṇu, Viṣṇu-Kṛṣṇa), 22 n. 62, 53 n. 55, 74, 146, 152, 153, 236, 241 n. 23
Haridvār, 105 n. 31; Dattātreya takes his morning bath here, 162 n. 54
Hari-gītā. *See Uddhava-gītā*
Harihara, 82 n. 40
Hari-Hara, 229
Hari-Hara-Pitāmaha, 227–28, 241 n. 23, 241 n. 25
Harināth, 102 n. 9
Haripāḷa (Haripāḷadeva). *See* Cakradhar
Haripaṇḍit, 162 n. 41
Hariścandra Ghāṭ, 106 n. 37
Hārītaka, 69, 85 n. 57
Hāritāyana. *See* Sumedha Hāritāyana
Harivaṃśa, 10, 14, 17 n. 21, 22 n. 62, 23 n. 79
Harṣa, 43
Haṭha-Yoga, 58, 61, 62, 78 n. 5, 80 n. 20, 80 n. 23, 81 n. 25, 197, 198, 210, 218 n. 15, 218 n. 16
Haṭha-yoga-pradīpikā, 80 n. 23, 81 n. 25, 221 n. 46
Hayagrīva, 92
Hazra, R. C., 45
Heka (star), 9
Hemacandra, 106–7 n. 41
Hemacūḍa, 176, 177, 178
Hemalekhā, 176, 177, 178
Hemāṅgada, 176, 188
Hermes, 8
Hilālpur, 148
Himachal Pradesh, 194 n. 40
Hindu rule, 167 n. 97
Hinduism, 58, 116, 125, 136, 138, 142, 143, 154, 157 n. 4, 242 n. 32, 249, 255
Hindu-Muslim unity, 137
Hindu-Muslim syncretism, 157 n. 2
Hindu-Turk Saṃvād, 143–44, 168 n. 105
Hiraṇyakaśipu, 50 n. 39
hlīṃ, 71
homo religiosus, 250
homo viator, 127 n. 12
honey gatherer: one of Dattātreya's twenty-four Gurus, 41

Hoyṣaḷeśvara temple, 227
hrāṃ, 72
hrīṃ, 71, 72, 75, 85 n. 66, 86 n. 67, 172, 188
Hṛṣīkeśa (= Viṣṇu), 18 n. 31
hrūṃ, 72
Hubli, 247 n. 78
huṃ, 72, 75, 76
Hyderabad State, 163 n. 57

icchā, 243 n. 40
ichneumon: one of Dattātreya's Gurus, 52 n. 50
iḍā channel, 60, 80 n. 17
Ilā, 18 n. 27
illa'llāh, 262 n. 22
Indo-Aryan languages, 161 n. 35
Indra, 2, 3, 4, 10, 11, 16 n. 9, 21 n. 60, 22 n. 64, 23 n. 74, 23 n. 77, 24 n. 81, 29, 30, 48 n. 11, 131 n. 50, 213, 229, 241 n. 20, 261 n. 10
Indranīla gem, 62
Indumatī, 39
Iraq, 157 n. 2
Irieus (Enopion), 8, 21 n. 55
īśitṛtva, 193 n. 29
Islam, 109, 116, 125, 136, 138, 141, 142, 143, 147, 154, 160 n. 26, 237, 250
Island of Jewels, 186
iṣṭa-devatā, 117, 139, 154, 244 n. 47, 244 n. 53, 246 n. 72, 255
Īśvara, 186, 199
īśvara (as a *tattva*), 181
Īśvara (as Parameśvara in the Mahānubhāva sect), 91
Īśvara-gītā, 196, 217 n. 13
Īśvara-pratyabhijñā-kārikā, 25 n. 87
Itihāsas, 216 n. 7

Jābāla Upaniṣad, 57, 62, 65–66, 77, 84 n. 54, 85 n. 57
Jaḍa, 50 n. 28
Jaḍabharata, 65, 69, 84 n. 54
Jagadambā, 162 n. 54
Jagadānanda, 160 n. 25
Jagadguru, 95
jāgīr, 105 n. 31
jagrat, 220 n. 35
jāgṛt, 71, 122
jāgṛt-sthāna, 123
Jāhnavī. *See* Gaṅgā
Jahnu, 18 n. 25
Jaimini, 49 n. 28, 165 n. 75
Jainism, 89, 98, 101, 106 n. 40, 106–7 n. 41, 245 n. 56, 250, 259 n. 1, 260 n. 3
Jaiswal, S., 55 n. 79
Jālandhara, 118, 131 n. 56
jalpa, 182
Jalvankar, Nārāyaṇ Mahārāj, 154, 155, 167 n. 97
Jamadagni, 2, 15 n. 4, 32, 42, 47–48 n. 9, 93, 102 n. 11, 145, 162 n. 51, 192 n. 21
Jāmadagnya, 53 n. 61
Jamb, 163 n. 57
Jambha, 29, 30, 48 n. 11
jambha-bhedin (= Indra), 48 n. 11
Janaka, 65; king of Videha, 176, 181, 182, 183, 184, 192 n. 24, 193 n. 32, 193 n. 33
Janamejaya, 39
Janārdan, 135, 136, 137, 138–40, 144, 145, 154, 157 n. 2, 158 n. 11, 158 n. 13, 159 n. 15, 159 n. 17, 160 n. 25, 160 n. 27, 160 n. 28, 160 n. 30, 161 n. 31, 166 n. 97; identification with Mahānubhāvas, 141; meaning of the name, 158 n. 9
Jaṅgam school, 219 n. 30
Janī Janārdan, 163 n. 59
japa, 74, 86 n. 74, 172
Jaras, 13
jaṭā, 228, 238
Jātakas, 28
jaṭā-mukuṭa, 227, 228, 241 n. 24
Jayadrathayāmala canon, 24 n. 84
Jayākhyā Saṃhitā, 53 n. 62

Jayamalla, 226, 240 n. 13
Jayasiṃha, 232
Jayasingpur station, 118
Jayasthiti Malla, 226, 240 n. 17
Jayayakṣa Malla, 226, 240 n. 17
Jejuri, 244 n. 47
jholī, 197, 248 n. 87
Jinasena, 106 n. 41
jīva, 70
jīvanmukta, 178, 184, 196
Jīvanmukta–gītā, 196, 217 n. 12
jīvanmukti, 58, 68, 78 n. 7, 201, 221 n. 46
Jīvanmukti-viveka, 67, 84 n. 51
jīvātman, 37, 193 n. 29, 210, 231
jñāna, 37, 57, 62, 67, 70, 76, 113, 117, 217 n. 8
Jñāna-Agni, 238
jñāna-mārga, 117
jñāna-mūrti, 117, 215
jñāna-saṃnyāsa, 84 n. 47
jñāna-vairāgya-saṃnyāsa, 84 n. 47
jñāna-yoga, 36
Jñāndev, 99, 102 n. 7, 135, 140, 141, 151, 159 n. 17, 160 n. 29; connection with Nāthism, 136
Jñāneśvarī, 99, 110, 136, 141, 160 n. 29
Jogāī, 104 n. 23
Jogeśvarī, 104 n. 23
Joshi, Hariprasad Shivprasad, 9, 129 n. 34, 154, 163 n. 60, 164 n. 66, 164 n. 71, 164 n. 72, 233, 236, 246 n. 74, 247 n. 76
Joshi, P. N., 103 n. 20
Judas Iscariot: as Devadatta, 241 n. 20
julāhā, 157 n. 4
Jumnā river, 246 n. 74
Jūnā Akhāḍā, 97, 105 n. 31, 244 n. 47
Junagadh, 97
Jyālendra, 58
jyotir-liṅga, 244 n. 50
Ka, 1
Kabīr, 137–38, 140, 154, 157 n. 2, 157 n. 4, 158 n. 5, 158 n. 7, 158 n. 8, 159 n. 18, 210, 213
Kabīr-panthī motto, 158 n. 5
kadamba trees (*Nauclea Cadamba*), 186, 193 n. 36
kādi-vidyā. *See* Kāmarāja *vidyā*
Kādrī school (Qādiri, Qādiriyya school), 130 n. 44, 137, 140, 157 n. 2
Kafir, 143
Kahoḍa, 192 n. 24
Kahola, 182
Kailāsa, 14, 25 n. 88, 93, 192 n. 22
kaivalya, 37
Kaivalya Upaniṣad, 242 n. 31
kākaḍā, 132 n. 67
kākaḍ-āratī, 121, 132 n. 67
Kakudmatī, 24 n. 83
Kāḷ Bhairav (Śvāśva; = Śiva), 25 n. 86, 123, 231; association with dogs, 244 n. 47
kāla (as a *tattva*), 181
kalā (as a *tattva*), 181
Kala Datta Mandir, 235
Kāla-cakra school, 219 n. 30
Kaḷagi, 237, 247 n. 78
kalās, 173
kalaśa, 43
Kālaṭi, 127 n. 13
Kālī, 171
Kālidāsa, 23 n. 75, 196, 221 n. 42
Kālikā Purāṇa, 244 n. 49
Kālikā-tantra, 77
kali-yuga, 14, 24 n. 85, 95, 138, 139, 152, 157 n. 4, 248 n. 92
Kalka, 98
Kalkin, 42, 53 n. 61
kalpa, 24 n. 85
Kālūrām: identified as Dattātreya, 106 n. 37
Kalyāṇa, 242 n. 28
Kalyāṇa Kalpataru, 86 n. 74, 102 n. 11, 127 n. 12

Kalyāṇī, 130 n. 44
Kāma, 48 n. 14, 71, 72
kāma, 34
kāma-bīja, 71
Kāmada forest, 5, 18 n. 29
Kāmadhenu: carried away by Arjuna Kārtavīrya, 32, 93; identified as dog, 144; identified as Mother Earth, 8, 9, 228, 231; owned by Vasiṣṭha, 15 n. 4, 230; presentation of, 243 n. 44; within Dattātreya's modern iconography, 227, 228, 230–31, 232, 233, 238 (as Gāyatrī), 242 n. 30, 243 n. 40 (as representing the *pañca-bhūtas*), 255
kamaṇḍalu, 49 n. 21, 97, 233
Kāmarāja *vidyā* (*kādi-vidyā*), 172
kāma-vāsanās, 185
Kāmeśvara, 172
kāmya rites, 82 n. 32
Kāñcīpuram, 78 n. 4
kanda, 80 n. 17
Kandalī, 23 n. 74
Kandesh district, 138
Kane, P. V., 54 n. 74
Kañjāsana. *See* Brahmā
Kāntimatī, 39
Kaṇva, 23 n. 75
kapāla-kuhara, 81 n. 25
Kāpālikas, 105 n. 34, 244 n. 52
Kapila, 43; "supreme sage" within the Sāṃkhya tradition and teacher of the *satya* age, 49 n. 26, 95
Kapila-gītā, 196, 217 n. 13
Karandikar, N. S., 154
Karañjā, 110, 113
Kardama, 5, 16 n. 8, 19 n. 32
Kārina-pā, 58
karma-bhūmi, 250
karman, 37, 46, 55 n. 78, 113, 117, 177, 185; paths of, 220 n. 41
karma-saṃnyāsa, 84 n. 47
karma-vāsanās, 185
karma-vipāka, 110
Karṇa, 23 n. 77
Karnataka. *See* Mysore
karṇī, 122
Karpātrī, Svāmin, 190 n. 4
Kārtavīrya, Kārtavīryārjuna. *See* Arjuna Kārtavīrya
Kārtavīryārjuna-kalpa, 49 n. 20
Kārtavīryārjuna-pañjara, 49 n. 20
Kārtavīryārjuna-sahasranāma, 49 n. 20
Kārtavīryārjuna-yantra-lakṣaṇa, 49 n. 20
Karvīr. *See* Kolhāpur
Kasba Peth, 235
Kashmir, 25 n. 93, 232
Kashmiri *Kaulism*, 171
Kashmiri *Śaivism*, 14, 24 n. 86, 25 n. 89, 57, 76, 128 n. 18, 171, 172, 181, 183, 200
Kāśī. *See* Benares
kāṣṭha-maṇḍap, 226
Kasturi, N., 251, 260 n. 8
Kaśyapa, 2, 16 n. 4, 16 n. 8, 20 n. 47, 22 n. 67, 32
Kāśyapa (as disciple of sage Astaka), 188
Kaṭha Upaniṣad, 218 n. 19
Kathā-bodha, 33
Kaṭha-śruti Upaniṣad, 62
Kathmandu, 226, 239 n. 9, 240 n. 11
Kaula, 72
Kaula, Sahib, 191 n. 12
Kaula-Vāma contexts, 171
Kauravas, 168 n. 104
Kauśika, 6, 19 n. 35, 19 n. 36
Kauṣītaki Brāhmaṇa, 17 n. 14
Kauṭilya, 33
kauṭilya, 214
kavacas, 155
kāvaḍī, 92, 93
Kāvaḍībovā, 155
Kāverī, 38
Kavirāj, Gopīnāth, 87 n. 79, 200, 216 n. 2, 219 n. 30

Kāvya. *See* Uśanas
kāya-daṇḍa, 83 n. 46
kāya-sādhana, 58
kāya-siddhi, 58
Kedāra, 60
Keḍgāokar, Nārāyaṇ Mahārāj, 154, 155, 167 n. 97
Kerala, 39, 48, 189, 235
Keśava (author of *Life of Eknāth*), 160 n. 25
Keśirāja, 91, 102 n. 10
Kevala, 199
kevala, 186
kevalādvaita-vāda. *See* Advaita Vedānta
kha, 75, 76
Khamgāon, 252
Khandesh, 154
Khaṇḍobā (Mārtaṇḍa) 148, 163 n. 61, 231, 263 n. 24; association with dogs, 244 n. 47
Khaṇḍya, Śrī. *See* Kṛṣṇa
Khare, G. H., 228, 242 n. 26
khecarī-mudrā, 62, 81 n. 25
Kho-khom, 241 n. 21
Kīnārām, Bābā (Kīnārām Aghorī), 97, 106 n. 36, 166 n. 97
Kings (three stars of Orion's belt), 21 n. 53
kīrtanas, 129 n. 37, 152, 153, 261 n. 11
kīrtankārs, 126
klīṃ, 71, 72
klūṃ, 72
ko'ham, 177
Kolaba district, 235
Kolhāpur (Karvīr), 91, 94, 103 n. 13, 104 n. 23, 162 n. 54; Dattātreya takes his meal here, 146; district of, 235
Koḷī tribe, 239 n. 4
Kolte, V. B., 92, 103 n. 15
Konkan district, 243 n. 40
Krama, 57, 78 n. 4, 221 n. 42
Kramrisch, Stella, 173
krāthana, 55 n. 78
Kratu, 2, 16 n. 8
krīṃ, 71
kriyā, 37
kriyā-yoga, 36
krodha, 20 n. 44
Krodha-bhaṭṭāraka. *See* Durvāsas
kroṃ, 72, 75
kṛpā, 247 n. 85
Kṛṣṇa (Krishna), 12, 13, 14, 18 n. 31, 23 n. 74, 23 n. 79, 24 n. 81, 24 n. 82, 24 n. 83, 39, 40, 42, 44, 51 n. 46, 51 n. 48, 74, 90, 98, 146, 152, 158 n. 5, 164 n. 68, 166 n. 91, 200, 202, 203, 213, 232, 244 n. 52, 254; as Śrī Khaṇḍya, 153
Kṛṣṇā (river), 111, 113, 117, 118, 128 n. 15, 130 n. 47, 131 n. 55, 138
Kṛṣṇa Sarasvatī, 112
Kṛṣṇa Sarasvatī (within the Datta *paramparā*), 167 n. 97
Kṛṣṇadās Jagadānanda, 158 n. 13
Kṛṣṇa-Gopāla, 164 n. 68, 166 n. 94
Kṛṣṇaism, 136
Kṛṣṇa-janmaṣṭamī, 166 n. 89
Kṛṣṇājīpant, 148
Kṛṣṇendra Guru, 167 n. 97
Kṛtavīrya, 29
kṛta-yuga (*satya-yuga*), 24 n. 85, 39, 95, 138
Kṛttikā constellation, 148
Kṣamā, 16 n. 8
Kṣemarāja, 78 n. 4, 219 n. 31
kṣetra, 117, 118, 131 n. 55
kṣetra-jña, 36
Kubjikā Upaniṣad, 79 n. 16
Kulārṇava-tantra, 73, 77, 130 n. 48, 198
Kulkarnee, Narayan H., 115, 116
kumbhaka, 61
kuṇḍ, 102 n. 11
Kuṇḍ Aghorī Śila, 97
kuṇḍalinī, 61, 76, 78 n. 5

kuṇḍalinī-śakti, 78 n. 5, 81 n. 25, 218 n. 16
Kuṇḍalinī-Yoga, 57, 58, 78 n. 5, 80 n. 23
Kuṇḍikā Upaniṣad, 62
Kuntī, 12, 23 n. 77
Kuntibhoja, 23 n. 77
Kuravapur, 111, 238
Kurda, 246 n. 74
Kūrma, 42, 53 n. 61
Kūrma Purāṇa, 50 n. 33, 217 n. 13
Kurukṣetra, 32; as an "internal place of pilgrimage," 60
Kuśarava, 168 n. 104
Kuśikas, 47 n. 9
Kuṭīcaka, 66, 67, 84 n. 46, 84 n. 47, 85 n. 57
Kuvera, 16 n. 8

Laghu-avadhūta Upaniṣad, 62
Laghu-saṃnyāsa Upaniṣad, 62
Lakhamundul, 246 n. 74
Lakṣmaṇa, 4, 39, 224
Lakṣmī (Śrī-Lakṣmī), 7, 25 n. 93, 48 n. 14, 71, 73, 169, 248 n. 89, 254; as Dattātreya's wife she forsakes the demons who had seized her placing her above their heads, 30, 48 n. 16; auspicious bodily parts, 48 n. 16; seated on Dattātreya's left lap in the *Agni Purāṇa*'s representation, 224
lakṣmī-bīja, 71
Lakṣmī-Nārāyaṇa, Śrī, 226, 242 n. 31
Lakulīśa, 25 n. 88
Lāl Pādrīs: followers of Dattātreya, 105 n. 33
Lalitā, Lalitā Tripurasundarī. *See* Tripurā
Lalitā-māhātmya (*Lalitopākhyāna*), 171, 191 n. 9, 192 n. 20
Lalitā-sahasra-nāma, 190 n. 4, 191 n. 12
Lalitā-stava-ratna, 25 n. 92
Lalitā-triśatī-bhāṣya, 171
Lalitopākhyāna. See *Lalitā-māhātmya*
langoṭī, 230
Laṅkā, 32
Larson, Gerald James, 33, 165 n. 75
Lavāsā, 255
laya, 80 n. 23, 221 n. 46
Laya-Yoga, 62, 80 n. 23
Lepakṣi, 233
Lepus (constellation), 10
Līlā-caritra, 90, 91, 98, 100, 102 n. 10, 231, 244 n. 48
līlās, 103 n. 14, 155, 181
Līlā-viśvambhara: epithet of Dattātreya, 144
liṅga, 7, 20 n. 49, 25 n. 87, 131 n. 50, 139, 158 n. 14, 233; *nāga-naṭeśa*, 132 n. 65; origin of its worship, 245 n. 63
Liṅga Purāṇa, 17 n. 17, 50 n. 33
lizard: one of Dattātreya's Gurus, 52 n. 50
lobha, 20 n. 44
Lokāyatas, 33
London, 256
Lopāmudrā, 170, 191 n. 8; *vidyā* (*hādi-vidyā*), 172
Lupus (constellation), 9, 10

Macchendra, Macchindranāth, Machhandranāth. *See* Matsyendranāth
mada, 31
Madālasā, 33, 34, 92
Mādhav, 112
Mādhava. *See* Vidyāraṇya
mādhūkara, 52 n. 51, 126 n. 7
mādhūkarin, 110
Madhya Pradesh, 126 n. 6
Madhya-deśa, 50 n. 42
Madhyārjunakṣetra. *See* Tiruvidyai Marudur
Madra, 5, 18 n. 28

Madurai. *See* Hālāsya
madya-pa, 45
Māgha, 43
Magi (three stars of Orion's belt), 21 n. 53
Mahābalipuram inscription, 42, 53 n. 59
Mahābhārata, 3, 4, 5, 11, 12, 15–16 n. 4, 17 n. 18, 17 n. 23, 17 n. 24, 19 n. 32, 19 n. 33, 19 n. 36, 19 n. 37, 19 n. 38, 22 n. 62, 22 n. 70, 23 n. 76, 23 n. 77, 24 n. 81, 24 n. 83, 25 n. 93, 27, 28, 29, 43, 47 n. 6, 47 n. 7, 47 n. 8, 48 n. 9, 49 n. 23, 51 n. 45, 55 n. 78, 83 n. 46, 86 n. 77, 131 n. 57, 158 n. 9, 168 n. 104, 169, 170, 176, 192 n. 25, 193 n. 33, 216 n. 7, 231
Mahādāisā, 92, 94, 95
Mahādeva. *See* Śiva
Mahālakṣmī, 94, 246 n. 68; Dattātreya begs for alms at midday in the courtyard's temple, 162 n. 54
mahā-māyā, 165 n. 76
mahā-mudrā, 62, 81 n. 25
mahā-muni, 46
mahā-naivedya, 122, 132 n. 67
Mahā-nāthas: Dattātreya as seventh in rank, 197
Mahā-nirvāṇa-tantra, 51 n. 48, 77
Mahānubhāvas, 89–95, 97, 101 n. 1, 102 n. 4, 102 n. 8, 103 n. 12, 103 n. 15, 116, 136, 140, 141, 145, 154, 155, 156, 162 n. 49, 172, 195, 231, 244 n. 48, 262 n. 17; assimilation of Muslim views and practices, 133 n. 76; attainment of liberation, 100–101; connection with Dattātreya, 90–95, 124, 223, 226, 236, 249, 250, 253; temples as healing centers, 123–24, 133 n. 75; ties with Nāthism, 98–99, 100, 101, 107 n. 43, 227
mahā-pūjā, 246 n. 71
Mahā-purāṇas, 98, 106 n. 41
Mahār: caste, 113, 163 n. 64; Dattātreya's appearance as, 147; within Eknāth's works, 142
Mahārājas of Mysore, 237
Maharashtra, 78 n. 4, 89, 90, 94, 99, 103 n. 11, 103 n. 17, 103 n. 22, 104 n. 23, 107 n. 45, 109, 112, 116, 123, 126 n. 4, 131 n. 52, 132 n. 65, 133 n. 75, 133 n. 77, 135, 136, 140, 146, 154, 156, 161 n. 32, 162 n. 54, 189, 190 n. 4, 195, 218 n. 14, 220 n. 33, 220 n. 39, 235, 239 n. 4, 243 n. 40, 246 n. 69, 251, 252, 253, 261 n. 11, 262 n. 14, 263 n. 24
Mahārāṣṭra-dharma, 116, 146
mahā-rudra, 77
Mahāsena, 176, 179, 180, 181, 193 n. 30
Mahā-śiva-rātri festival, 226
Mahātīts, 104 n. 29
Māhātmyas, 217 n. 8
mahā-vākya, 150
mahā-vidyās, 71, 85 n. 66
mahā-yajña, 32
mahā-yuga, 24 n. 85
Mahendra mountain, 32, 175
Maheśa, Maheśvara. *See* Śiva
Mahī, 110, 126 n. 6
Mahīpati, 115, 129 n. 37, 137, 139, 144, 145, 146, 151, 153, 154, 158 n. 13, 160 n. 25, 161 n. 31
Mahīpatidās Yogin, 166 n. 97
Mahiṣa, 191 n. 9
Mahī-sāgara-saṅgam, 110
Māhiṣmatī, 32
mahoṃ, 75, 76
Mahur. *See* Mātāpur
maiden: one of Dattātreya's twenty-four Gurus, 41
maithuna, 29
Maitreya, 156, 168 n. 104
Maitreya Upaniṣad, 62

Majorca, 255
makara, 164 n. 68
makara-kuṇḍala, 228
mālā-mantra, 70, 74–76
Malaṅg, 137, 145, 157 n. 2
mālās, 247 n. 84
Malaya mount, 170
Malla (demon), 244 n. 47
Malla dynasty, 240 n. 17
Mallāri-māhātmya, 244 n. 47
manana, 40, 184
manas, 60, 181, 221 n. 46
Mānasa lake, 25 n. 88
Maṇḍala-brāhmaṇa Upaniṣad, 51 n. 48
mandana, 55 n. 78
Māṇḍavya, 6, 19 n. 37, 19 n. 38
Māndhātṛ, 53 n. 61
Māṇḍūkya Upaniṣad, 37, 79 n. 16
Mandya district, 251
Māṅg, 92, 94
Maṇi, 244 n. 47
maṇi-karṇikā ghāṭ, 231
Māṇiknagar, 238, 248 n. 94
Māṇikprabhu, 154, 155, 167 n. 97, 167 n. 100, 238
maṇipūra-cakra, 70
Manīṣā-pañcaka hymn, 231, 244 n. 51
mano-daṇḍa, 83 n. 46
mano-hara, 118
manonmanī, 221 n. 46
manovācam agocaram, 199
māṅsa, 31
mantra, 12, 25 n. 92, 49 n. 21, 53 n. 57, 67, 68, 71, 72, 74, 75, 76, 77, 80 n. 23, 85 n. 64, 85 n. 65, 86 n. 70, 97, 112, 117, 130 n. 48, 155, 165 n. 74, 170, 172, 173, 180, 188, 191 n. 19, 219 n. 30, 224, 248 n. 90, 252; formation, 70; function, 73. *See* also *bīja-mantra*
Mantra-mahodadhi, 49 n. 20
mantra-pīṭha, 24 n. 84
Mantra-śāstras, 57
mantra-vīrya, 73
Mantra-Yoga, 62, 80 n. 23
Manu, 2, 17 n. 10, 63
Manu Svāyambhuva, 17 n. 10, 19 n. 32
Manu Vaivasvata, 17 n. 10
Manu-smṛti, 28, 83 n. 46, 132 n. 64
manvantara, 11, 17 n. 10
māraṇa, 87 n. 79
Marehra, 167 n. 99
mārga, 175
Māriammai, 131 n. 53
Marīci, 2, 16 n. 8
Mārkaṇḍeya: Dattātreya's precursor, 53 n. 61
Mārkaṇḍeya Purāṇa, 5, 15 n. 3, 18 n. 29, 19 n. 40, 27, 29, 31, 33, 37, 42, 44, 45, 46, 48 n. 15, 48 n. 16, 50 n. 32, 52 n. 50, 54 n. 74, 55 n. 77, 57, 60, 61, 71, 74, 94, 128 n. 17, 165 n. 75, 171, 215, 254
Mārtaṇḍa. *See* Khaṇḍobā
Māruti. *See* Hanumān
Maruts (Rudras), 16 n. 8, 21 n. 59, 25 n. 87
Mātāṅg, 162 n. 48
Mātāṅgī, 103 n. 22
mātā-pitṛ-bhakti, 18 n. 31
Mātāpur (Mahur), 91, 102 n. 11, 103 n. 20, 103 n. 22, 104 n. 23, 124, 162 n. 54, 164 n. 67, 172, 238, 248 n. 94, 255; Dattātreya's *āśrama*, 94, 95; Dattātreya's sleeping place, original seat of manifestation and privileged abode, 146, 147, 148, 223
Mate, M. S., 121, 122
Mathurā, 23 n. 77, 24 n. 83, 158 n. 5
Mātṛkā-cakra-viveka, 219 n. 30
mātṛkās, 72, 80 n. 23
Mātsaryāsura demon, 53 n. 57
Matsya, 42
Matsya Purāṇa, 4, 10, 17 n. 22, 18 n. 26, 42, 43, 48 n. 12, 223–24, 243 n. 37

Matsyendranāth (Macchendra, Macchindranāth, Machhandranāth, Matsyendra), 58, 100, 106 n. 40, 107 n. 46, 158 n. 5, 220 n. 33; worships Dattātreya in iconography, 232
mauñjī-bandhana, 112
māyā (Māyā): as goddess, 144, 165 n. 76; principle of illusion, 62, 150, 165 n. 75, 174, 186
Māyā-Bhuvaneśvarī, 71
māyā-bīja, 71
Māyāvatī, 24 n. 83
megha-dhvani, 59
Megha-dūta, 196
Megrez (star), 2
Mehad lake, 126 n. 6
Meher Bābā, 251, 260 n. 6
Menakā, 23 n. 75
menstruation, 7, 20 n. 42
Merak (star), 2
Meru, 179, 192 n. 27, 256, 257
Meru, 256
Merubāḷā, 94
Mhāibhaṭa, 90, 91
Mintaka (star), 8
Mirzam (star), 10
Mitchiner, John E., 15 n. 2
Mitra, 191 n. 8
Mizar (star), 2
mleccha, 136
Mokashi-Punekar, Shankar, 44, 45, 195, 198, 216 n. 2, 218 n. 14, 218 n. 15, 219 n. 23, 219 n. 26, 254, 256, 262 n. 20
mokṣa (*mukti*), 29, 36, 37, 42, 63, 68, 74, 76, 100, 113, 121, 128 n. 14, 128 n. 17, 129 n. 33, 140, 148, 166 n. 87, 170, 174, 176, 177, 183, 184, 187, 188, 210, 219 n. 30, 247 n. 81
Mominabad. *See* Ambā Jogāī
Moropant, 151
Moshan Fani, 95, 197
moth: one of Dattātreya's twenty-four Gurus, 40–41
Mount Abu (Abu, Guru Shikhar), 94, 98, 107 n. 42, 250
Mṛga, Mṛga-śiras. *See* Orion
Mṛttikāvatī, 192 n. 25
Mṛtyuñjaya (Muntojī), 130 n. 44
Mudgala. *See* Mukteśvar
Mudgala (*gotra*), 28
Mudgala (king), 23 n. 76
Mudgala Purāṇa, 53 n. 57
mudrā, 80 n. 23, 81 n. 25, 227, 228, 233, 245 n. 62
Muhammad Ghawth, 157 n. 2
mukha, 133 n. 69
Muktācūḍa, 176
Muktānanda, Svāmin, 78 n. 4, 194 n. 39
Mukteśvar (Mudgala), 144, 154, 162 n. 42, 162 n. 43, 166 n. 97
mukti. See *mokṣa*
Muktikā Upaniṣad, 69–70, 85 n. 59
Mukundarāj, 102 n. 9; link to Nāthism, 136, 159 n. 21
mūḷa-darī, 94
mūla-jharī, 103 n. 20
mūḷa-pīṭha, 94
mūla-prakṛti, 150, 165 n. 75
Mūḷa-stambha: attributed to "Dattātreya Avadhūta," 159 n. 21; Mukundarāj's, 159 n. 21
Muliphein (star), 10
mumukṣā, 185
mumukṣāṃ prati, 34
muni-śreṣṭha, 46
Muntojī. *See* Mṛtyuñjaya
murīd, 160 n. 28
mūrti, 90, 119, 122, 125, 132 n. 61, 132 n. 65, 136, 163 n. 56, 201, 223, 224, 226, 228, 232, 233, 242 n. 30, 242 n. 31, 246 n. 68, 248 n. 88, 253
Muslim: attack, 105 n. 31; converts to Hinduism, 116; Dattātreya's appearance as, 137, 144–45; descent, 106 n. 36; encounter with Hinduism, 143; family, 111,

Muslim: family *(continued)* 130 n. 44; historians, 143; holy men, 123, 124, 160 n. 26, 168 n. 107; impurity, 116; king, 118, 146, 147; localities, 130 n. 43; *mleccha*, 136; Pir, 130 n. 43; poet-saints, 130 n. 42; presence in Eknāth's works, 142–44; religiosity, 130 n. 43; rule and rulers, 115, 116, 130 n. 42, 138, 157 n. 2, 159 n. 21; saint, 155; tide, 143; tomb, 157 n. 2; views and practices (assimilated by Mahānubhāvas), 133 n. 76; weaver, 157 n. 4
Mysore (Karnataka), 106 n. 41, 118, 227, 228, 235, 236, 237, 246 n. 69, 247 n. 78, 247 n. 79, 251

nāda, 59, 79 n. 13, 209
Nāda-Brahman, 60, 79 n. 13
nāḍī, 60, 61, 205
Nāgadeva. *See* Bhaṭobāsa
Nāganāth, 121, 132 n. 65
Nāgas, 97, 104 n. 29, 105 n. 31, 244 n. 47; similarity with Nāthas, 97, 105 n. 32; women ascetics, 105 n. 31
Nāgpur, 89, 146
Nahuṣa, 39
naimittika rites, 82 n. 32
Naiṣadha-carita, 23 n.74, 43, 54 n. 67
naiṣkarmya, 159 n. 16
nakṣatra, 8
Nāmadhāraka, 109
namaḥ, 72
nāma-rūpa complex, 207
nāmasmaraṇa, 86 n. 74
Nāmdev, 132 n. 67, 135, 136, 137, 159 n. 17
Nāndeḍ, 148
Nandimitra: Datta's Baladeva, 107 n. 41
Nandin, 227
Nārada, 7, 170, 175, 241 n. 20
Nārada Purāṇa, 103 n. 22
Nārada-parivrājaka Upaniṣad, 52 n. 53, 57, 62, 63, 67, 68–69, 82 n. 39, 83 n. 46, 84 n. 48, 85 n. 57
Narahari. *See* Nṛsiṃha Sarasvatī
Narasiṁha, 42, 53 n. 61, 128 n. 23, 244 n. 52
Nārāyaṇ Gurudatta Mahārāj, 167 n. 97
Nārāyaṇ Svāmin, 166–67 n. 97
Nārāyaṇa (= Viṣṇu), 41, 60, 83 n. 46, 95; as Dattātreya, 70, 74, 76; Avatāra, 53 n. 61
Nārāyaṇas (= Nāthas), 58, 99
Nārāyaṇīya lists, 43
Nārāyaṇpeṭh, 147
nārī, 214
Narmadā, 5, 18 n. 29, 19 n. 37, 32, 54 n. 74, 233
Narsobāvāḍī (Vāḍī), 109, 113, 117, 118, 122, 129 n. 34, 232, 238
Nāsik, 104 n. 23, 105 n. 31, 218 n. 14, 224, 246 n. 68, 252
Nātha Yogins (Nāth Siddhas), 44, 46, 51 n. 48, 58, 78, 79 n. 8, 101, 105 n. 32, 107 n. 46, 107 n. 48, 155, 164 n. 67, 192 n. 28, 214, 235, 250, 251, 252, 262 n. 14; accompanied by cows, 230; accompanied by dogs, 231; adepts of *guru-vāda*, 220 n. 33; assimilation to Muslims, 116; Dattātreya as *ādi-guru* (takes Śiva's place), 198, 236; Dattātreya as eternal Guru, 105 n. 35; Dattātreya as Nātha Yogin, 89, 90; Dattātreya as presiding the western region, 102 n. 6, 197; drinking of "*soma* nectar" and link to alchemy (*rasāyana*), 100, 108 n. 53; fond of music, 263 n. 23; Harināth, identified as Cakradhar, 102 n. 9, 136; identification of Dattajī with

Dattātreya, 197; immortality of Dattātreya as a Nātha Yogin, 101, 104 n. 26, 250; placing *pādukās* on *samādhi*, 117; sanctuaries, 252; similarity with Nāgas, 97, 105 n. 32; Śiva as first Nātha and tutelary deity, 105 n. 35, 202, 205; Śiva as teacher of *Haṭha-Yoga*, 198; ties with Mahānubhāvas, 98–99, 100, 101, 107 n. 43, 227; Vallinātha, 110; worship Dattātreya in iconography, 232
nātha-pada. See *parama-pada*
Nathapanthi centres, 130 n. 43
Nāthism, 78 n. 6, 79 n. 8, 89, 90, 94, 98, 155, 156; *Avadhūta-gītā*, 195–221; bodily immortality, 100, 201, 206; *cakras*, 206; concept of *sahaja*, 202–3, 210, 212; cross-fertilization of Hindu and Muslim religiosity, 130 n. 43, 157 n. 4; Dāsopant's initiation in, 164 n. 72; Dattātreya's connections with, 89, 90, 99–100, 101, 102 n. 6, 104 n. 26, 105 n. 35, 163 n. 56, 164 n. 67, 197–99, 198, 220 n. 33, 224, 226, 232, 235, 236, 250, 251–52; Eknāth's link with, 141; essential *nāda* (*anāhata*), 209; importance of deified Guru, 201, 220 n. 33; influence on Kabīr, 157 n. 4; influence on Nṛsiṃha Sarasvatī, 129 n. 29; influence upon Marāṭhī religion and literature, 99; Jñāndev's link with, 136; link with Śāktism, 164 n. 67; Mukundarāj's link with, 136; mythology, 106 n. 40; *nirañjana* state, 210; phase of the Siddha cult, 58; reform movement against Tantric excesses, 107 n. 43; *Śaiva* orientation, 207; *sama-rasya* as goal, 198, 199–200; texts and their link with Dattātreya, 107 n. 48, 107 n. 51, 108 n. 52, 159 n. 21, 216 n. 2, 219 n. 28, 244 n. 52, 245 n. 60, 252; tradition of nine Nāthas, 58, 99, 100, 218–19 n. 21, 232, 236, 242 n. 30, 252–53
Nauclea Cadamba. See *kadamba* trees
Nava-ratna-mālā, 159 n. 21
nav-nāth, 58, 99
Navnāth *sampradāya*, 252–53
Nav-nāth-bhakti-sār, 100
Nav-nāth-caritra va Kathā, 245 n. 60, 261 n. 13
Nemināth (Nīmnāth), 98, 106 n. 40, 250, 259 n. 1
Nepal, 58, 95, 189, 220 n. 33, 224, 226, 239 n. 9, 240 n. 13, 240 n. 17, 240 n. 18, 241 n. 20, 241 n. 21, 250, 263 n. 27
Netra-tantra, 210, 221 n. 48
New Delhi. *See* Delhi
nibandha, 63
Nidāgha, 65, 69
nididhyāsana, 184
Nihal (star), 10
Nijānanda, 116
Nīlakaṇṭha, Śrī, 33, 49 n. 26
Nilgiri mountains, 260 n. 9
Nimi, 4, 29, 47
Nīmnāth. *See* Nemināth
Nīmnāthīs, 106 n. 40
Nipāt Nirañjan, 166 n. 97
nirākārī, 99
nirālamba, 221 n. 46
Nirañjan Raghunāth, 154, 155, 167 n. 97
nirañjana, 136, 210, 221 n. 44, 221 n. 45, 221 n. 46
nirañjana-siddhi, 210
Nirañjanī sect, 210
nirguṇa, 28, 36, 37, 132 n. 59, 136, 150, 165 n. 75, 202, 248 n. 96
nirguṇa-bhakti, 99, 136, 137, 157 n. 4

nirguṇa-brahman, 165 n. 75, 210
nirguṇa-pādukās, 119, 132 n. 59, 132 n. 60
nirguṇī literature and tradition, 157 n. 4, 213
nirīha, 213
Nirukta, 1
nirutthāna, 201
nirvāṇa, 198, 207
Nirvāṇa Upaniṣad, 62
nirvikalpa-samādhi, 51 n. 48
Nirvindhyā, 5
Nisargadatta Mahārāj, Śrī (Māruti Kampli), 252, 262 n. 15
niṣkala, 61
nitya rites, 82 n. 32
Nityānanda, 194 n. 39
Nityās, 173
Nivṛtti, 99
nivṛtti-mārga, 34
niyama, 61, 220 n. 34
niyati (as a *tattva*), 181
non-Aryan gods, 125
Nṛsiṃha Sarasvatī (Narahari, Nrsimha Saraswati, "Śrī Guru"), 44, 107 n. 46, 110, 111–16, 117, 118, 119, 121, 122, 123, 125, 128 n. 20, 128 n. 26, 129 n. 29, 129 n. 34, 129 n. 36, 132 n. 60, 135, 136, 138, 154, 158 n. 11, 158 n. 14, 165 n. 74, 167 n. 100, 171, 216 n. 2, 232, 238, 248 n. 92, 248 n. 93, 249
Nṛsiṃha Sarasvatī of Āḷandī, 167 n. 97
Nṛsiṃhānandanāth, 190 n. 4
nūr, 167 n. 99
Nūri, Abdul Husein, 167 n. 99
Nūri Mahārāj, 154, 155, 167 n. 99
nyāsa, 73, 86 n. 72
Nyatapole temple, 240 n. 13
Nyaya, 199

O'Flaherty, Wendy Doniger, 11
Oghad Shikhar, 98
Olcott, W. S., 256
Olivelle, Patrick, 63, 81 n. 27, 81 n. 29
oṃ syllable: discussion in chapter 42 of the *Mārkaṇḍeya Purāṇa*, 36, 37–38; fundamental *bīja-mantra*, 71; *mantra* of Paramahaṃsa renouncers, 67; practising *dhyāna* on, 79 n. 16; recitation in the *Gorakṣa Saṃhitā*, 218 n. 16; recited by Nṛsiṃha Sarasvatī, 112; within *Avadhūta-gītā*, 209; within Dattātreya's *mālā-mantra*, 74, 75, 76; within Gaṇeśa's *mūla-mantra*, 86 n. 67; within *Yoga Upaniṣads*, 59–60, 61
oṃ aiṃ kroṃ klīṃ klūṃ hrāṃ hrīṃ hrūṃ sauḥ dattātreyāya svāhā, 72
oṃ āṃ hrīṃ kroṃ ehi dattātreyāya svāhā, 72
oṃ namaḥ śivāya, 76
oṃ śrīṃ hrīṃ klīṃ glauṃ drāṃ, 71
Oṃkār, 105 n. 31
Orion (Mṛga, Mṛga-śiras): constellation, 8–9
Orissa, 210
osprey: one of Dattātreya's twenty-four Gurus, 41
oṭās, 253
ovīs, 109, 141, 150, 151, 157 n. 2

Padārṇava, 151, 166 n. 82
padārthas, 33
padas, 144
Padmā, 238
padma, 226, 233, 238, 240 n. 12
Padma Purāṇa, 19 n. 37, 20 n. 47, 22 n. 63, 23 n. 74, 23 n. 76, 39, 48 n. 12, 48 n. 14, 48 n. 15, 131 n. 56, 196, 217 n. 13
Padmapāda, 244 n. 52
padmāsana, 227, 228
Padma-tantra, 43
pādukā-mantra, 117, 219 n. 30
pādukāṃ pūjayāmi, 117

pādukās: of Dattātreya, 150, 164 n. 68, 164 n. 71, 164 n. 73, 223, 232, 237, 247 n. 81, 255; of Janārdan, 161 n. 31; of Nṛsiṃha Sarasvatī, 117–22, 132 n. 59, 132 n. 66, 232; within Dattātreya's cult, 156, 201
pāgal, 23 n. 78
Pain, Charles, 99, 100, 235, 236, 243 n. 41, 262 n. 20, 263 n. 23
Paiṭhaṇ. *See* Pratiṣṭhāna
pālkhī, 30, 107 n. 46, 117, 122
pallavas, 75
pañca-bhūtas, 243 n. 40
Pañcadaśī, 65, 82 n. 40
pañca-gavya, 243 n. 45
Pañca-Kṛṣṇas, 90, 101, 102 n. 9, 103 n. 14, 253
Pañcāḷeśvara, 91, 99, 136; Dattātreya takes his morning bath here, 162 n. 54
Pāñcarātra: literature, 116; texts classified into three groups, 53 n. 62; tradition, 43, 80 n. 19
pañca-śikha, 25 n. 93
Pañcaviṃśa Brāhmaṇa, 17 n. 14
Pañcī-karaṇa (*Pāsoḍī*), 151, 164 n. 73, 166 n. 82
Pāṇḍava-gītā, 217 n. 10
Pāṇḍavas, 15 n. 4, 23 n. 77, 24 n. 83, 168 n. 104
Paṇḍharpur, 18 n. 31, 99, 102 n. 7, 107 n. 46, 110, 131 n. 55, 136, 144, 159 n. 24, 223, 235, 246 n. 68, 252
Pāṇḍu, 23 n. 77, 168 n. 104
Pāṇḍuraṅga, Śrī, 152, 153
Pangarkar, 161 n. 40
Pāṇini, 194 n. 41
pāṇi-pātrin, 83 n. 46
pānsupārī, 145, 162 n. 45
pāpa, 77
Parabrahma Upaniṣad, 62
Paramahaṃsa, 37, 51 n. 48; description of, 65–69, 74, 84 n. 47, 84 n. 48, 84 n. 52, 85 n. 57, 154; disposal of the body at the time of death, 84 n. 46; Nṛsiṃha Sarasvatī, 115; *udara-pātrin* (eats like a cow), 83 n. 46
Paramahaṃsa Upaniṣad, 62, 67, 68
Paramahaṃsa-parivrājaka Upaniṣad, 62
parama-pada (*nātha-pada*), 200, 201, 202, 210
para-mārga, 89
parama-ṛṣi (= Kapila), 49 n. 26
Paramaśiva, 202
paramātman, 37, 60, 70
Parameśvara (Parameshwar), 90, 100, 101, 249, 253; as Śiva, 175
parā-mukti, 201
para-pada, 221 n. 46
Parāśara, 28, 168 n. 104
Paraśiva, 174
Pārasnāth, 106 n. 40
Pārasnāthīs, 106 n. 40
Paraśurāma, 15 n. 4, 29, 92, 145, 235; Avatāra of Viṣṇu, 42, 47–48 n. 9; beheaded his mother Reṇukā, 48 n. 9; created Kerala, 48 n. 9; had *darśana* of Dattātreya who appeared with a pair of dogs in his hands, 231; immortal living in a cave, 48 n. 9; instructed by Dattātreya in the *Tripurā-rahasya*, 49 n. 22, 169–94, 249; killed Arjuna Kārtavīrya and his sons and eliminated the Kṣatriya race for the following twenty-one generations, 32; Mahānubhāva story, 92, 93–94; performed the *śrāddha* ceremony with Dattātreya as priest, 49 n. 22; Prādurbhāvāntara, 43; sacred pool (*kuṇḍ*), 102 n. 11; went to Dattātreya's *āśrama* with Reṇukā, 49 n. 22
Paraśurāma (an author), 102 n. 10
Paraśurāma-kalpa-sūtra, 170, 190 n. 5

parganā, 163 n. 61
Pargiter, F. Eden, 28, 45, 54 n. 74
Parikṣit, 51 n. 45
pariṇāma, 165 n. 75
Parivrājaka, 51 n. 48
Parvatas, 188
Pārvatī, 7, 12, 22 n. 71, 25 n. 93, 227
Pārvatī (Dāsopant's mother), 147
pāśa, 25 n. 89
Pāsoḍī. See *Pañcī-karaṇa*
paśu, 25 n. 89
Pāśupatas: courting dishonor, 20 n. 46, 46, 55 n. 78, 190 n. 7
Paśupatināth *mandir*, 224
Pāṭaṇ, 233
Patañjali, 50 n. 36, 57, 58, 60, 80 n. 23, 192 n. 26, 193 n. 29, 199, 255
Pathan, 145
pati, 25 n. 89
Pauṣkara Saṃhitā, 53 n. 62
Pellegrini, A. Sannino, 216 n. 2, 219 n. 24
Phadke, Sadashiv Krishna, 254, 264 n. 40
Phadke, Vāsudev Balvant, 167 n. 97
Phalahāradeva *maṭha*, 247 n. 78
phala-śruti, 175, 215
phaṭ, 72, 75, 76
Phatta, 226, 240 n. 13
Phekda (star), 2
pigeons: one of Dattātreya's twenty-four Gurus, 40, 41
pilgrimage, 111, 112–13, 127 n. 12, 141, 161 n. 31
piṇḍas, 127 n. 8
piṇḍa-siddhi, 200, 201
Piṅgalā: a courtesan and one of Dattātreya's twenty-four Gurus, 41, 42
piṅgalā channel, 60, 80 n. 17
Pīr (*pīr*), 123, 124, 130 n. 43
piśāca, 69, 74, 122, 133 n. 73
Pitāmaha. *See* Brahmā
pītāmbara, 164 n. 68
Pīṭhāpur, 110
pitṛ, 127 n. 8
pitṛ-loka, 127 n. 8
pitṛ-yāna, 205
Pollux (star), 9
polytheism, 256, 263 n. 30
Poona. *See* Puṇe
Poseidon, 8
possession and exorcism, 109, 122–25, 133 n. 75, 133 n. 75, 133–34 n. 77, 134 n. 78, 226, 235
Prabhākara (called Atri or Ātreya), 28
Prabhākara (of Atri's race), 11
prabhu, 103 n. 11
Prādurbhāva manifestations, 42, 43; shorter lists, 53 n. 58
Prādurbhāvāntara manifestations, 43
Pradyumna, 14, 24 n. 79, 24 n. 83, 60
Prahlāda: Datta's Prati-vāsudeva, 107 n. 41; Dattātreya taught him detachment and the code of conduct pertaining to ascetics, 38–39; in Kabīr-panthī motto, 158 n. 5
praiṣa formula (*saṃnyastaṃ mayā*), 63, 82 n. 32
Prajāpati, 1, 258
Prajāpatis (lords of creation), 1, 16 n. 8, 17 n. 10, 19 n. 32, 22 n. 69
prajñāna-ghana, 193 n. 34
prajñānaṃ brahma, 97
prākāmya, 192 n. 26
prakaraṇa, 198
prakāśa, 172, 183, 200
Prakṛti, 36, 37, 150, 200, 211, 218 n. 19
pramāṇas, 176
prāṇa, 2, 50 n. 37, 59, 60, 81 n. 25, 177
praṇava, 59, 71, 72, 77
Praṇava Upaniṣads, 79 n. 16

Praṇava-Japa, 60
prāṇāyāma, 37, 60, 62, 80 n. 23, 205, 220 n. 34
Prapañca-sāra, 171
prapatti, 168 n. 106
prārabdha-karman, 184
prasāda, 48 n. 16, 94, 115
Prasenajit, 15 n. 4
Prasūti, 5, 19 n. 32
Pratiṣṭhāna (Paiṭhaṇ), 6, 16 n. 7, 89, 90, 94, 102 n. 9, 103 n. 12, 140, 142, 151, 152, 153, 159 n. 24, 161 n. 31
Pratiṣṭhāna-caritra, 158 n. 13, 160 n. 27, 161 n. 31
Prati-vāsudevas, 98, 107 n. 41
pratyabhijñā, 259
Pratyabhijñā school, 14, 25 n. 87, 171
pratyabhijñāna, 174
pratyāhāra, 37, 220 n. 34
Pravarā, 104 n. 24
pravṛtti-mārga, 34
Prayāg, 15 n. 4, 105 n. 31, 112, 118, 131 n. 55; as an "internal place of pilgrimage," 60
preman, 20 n. 44
Preman Sāī Bābā, 251; as Śakti, 260–61 n. 10
Prempur, 148
preta, 122, 133 n. 72
Priyavrata, 19 n. 32
Prometheus Unbound, 256
prostitutes, 247 n. 85, 262 n. 19; caste and role of, 52 n. 52; devotion to Dattātreya, 235–36, 246 n. 72, 253; in Eknāth's works, 140, 142
pūjā, 73, 74, 86 n. 78, 98, 121, 122, 128 n. 16, 132 n. 66, 139, 159 n. 24, 220 n. 31, 232, 246 n. 71
pujārī, 113, 118, 129 n. 35
Pulaha, 2, 16 n. 8, 19 n. 32
Pulakeśin I, 242 n. 28
Pulastya, 2, 16 n. 8
Punarvasu (constellation), 9, 10
Puṇḍalīka, 18 n. 31
Puṇe (Poona), 106 n. 35, 133 n. 75, 224, 235, 236, 246 n. 70, 246 n. 71, 251, 252; district of, 244 n. 47
Punjab, 137
puṇya, 153, 160 n. 30
puṇya-smaraṇa, 122
puraḥsara, 53 n. 61
Purī, 97
pūrṇa-avatāra, 230, 249
pūrṇa-devatā, 230
Pūrṇānanda, 116, 216 n. 2
Purohit Svāmin, Śrī (Śaṅkar Gajānan Purohit, Shri Purohit Swami), 98, 250, 259 n. 1, 261 n. 12, 262 n. 19, 263 n. 30; brought Hinduism and Dattātreya to the West, 255, 256; works, 263 n. 29, 264 n. 35
Puru, 23 n. 75, 51 n. 48
Purūravas, 4, 5, 10, 18 n. 25, 22 n. 61
Puruṣa, 82 n. 36
Puruṣa, 36, 165 n. 75, 169, 200, 211, 218 n. 19
Pūṣan, 10, 21 n. 59
Pustaka, 233
Puttaparthi, 251, 261 n. 10
python: offering a lesson in contentment, 38; one of Dattātreya's twenty-four Gurus, 40

Qādiri, Qādiriyya school. *See* Kādrī school
Qutubshahs, 115

Raeside, I. M. P., 27, 47 n. 7, 65, 70, 89, 92, 101 n. 1, 103 n. 15, 107 n. 43, 109, 136, 162 n. 49, 242 n. 32
rāga (as a *tattva*), 181
rāgas (in music), 254
Rāghava Caitanya, Śrī, 145

Raghunāth Bhātajī of Nāsik, 167 n. 97
Rahūgaṇa, 15 n. 4
Rahuri, 104 n. 24
Raidās, 140, 159 n. 18
Raivataka, 65, 69
Rajahmundry, 110
rajas, 243 n. 40
rajas (female ejaculate), 81 n. 25
Rajasthan, 107 n. 42, 210
Rajasthan Oriental Research Institute, 216 n. 5
rāja-sūya, 11, 22 n. 66
Rajavade, 103 n. 15
Rāja-Yoga, 62, 80 n. 23, 221 n. 46
Rāje Muhammad, 157 n. 2
Rājputānā Museum, 241 n. 25
Rājvāḍe, Viśvanāth Kāśīnāth, 163 n. 57, 163 n. 60
Rākṣasa-bhuvana, 150
rākṣasas, 16 n. 8, 133 n. 73
raṃ, 70
Rām (as God supreme), 160 n. 30
Rām Janārdan, 163 n. 59
Rāma, 4, 15 n. 4, 23 n. 76, 39, 42, 48 n. 9, 53 n. 61, 69, 70, 132 n. 65, 146, 224, 233, 254
rāma-bīja, 71
Rāmacandra Yogin, 118
Rāma-gītā, 197, 218 n. 13
ramainī, 137, 158 n. 5
Ramaṇa Maharṣi (Veṅkaṭaramaṇa Ayyār), 169, 190 n. 4; Guru is absolutely necessary, 52 n. 53; realization of the pure "I," 193 n. 34
Rāmānanda, 137, 157 n. 4
Rāmānanda Bīḍkar, 154
Rāmānandīs, 51 n. 48
Rāmānujīya schools, 168 n. 106
Rāmāyaṇa, 4, 5, 11, 15 n. 4, 17 n. 25, 19 n. 34, 22 n. 64, 32, 39, 47 n. 6, 132 n. 65, 144, 224, 231
Rāmdās, 116, 135, 146, 151, 163 n. 56, 163 n. 57, 165 n. 80
Rāmeśvara, 102 n. 10
Rāmṭek, 89
Rāṇaḍe, Lakṣmaṇ, 190 n. 5
Ranade, R. D., 138, 139, 141, 161 n. 31
Raṅga Avadhūta, Śrī, 154, 155, 167 n. 97, 237, 248 n. 91, 248 n. 92, 248 n. 94, 248 n. 95
Raṅganāth, 116
Rao, T. A. Gopinatha, 227, 228, 241 n. 25, 242 n. 30, 247 n. 76
rasa, 100, 207
rasāyana, 58, 100, 108 n. 53
Rastogi, N., 221 n. 42
Rāṣṭrakūṭa court, 106 n. 41
rat: one of Dattātreya's Gurus, 52 n. 50
Ratnāṅgada, 188
Raudrāśva. *See* Bhadrāśva
Rāuḷ (low caste), 101 n. 2
Ravaḷobāsa, 92, 103 n. 15
Rāvaṇa, 16 n. 8, 132 n. 65; defeated by Arjuna Kārtavīrya, 32, 49 n. 21; went to Dattātreya's *āśrama*, 49 n. 21
Rāvaṇārjunīya, 49 n. 21
Ravivar Peth, 236
Ṛbhu, 65, 69
Ṛcīka, 15 n. 4, 32
Ṛddhipur, 89, 90
renouncers (Saṃnyāsins): antifeminine conviction, 41, 64, 214–15, 221 n. 51; *āśrama*, 63–64; begging rules, 52 n. 51, 68, 126 n. 7; classification, 66–69, 84 n. 47, 84 n. 50, 85 n. 57; death, 84 n. 46; discard all exterior insigna, 83 n. 46; emblems, 64, 66, 83 n. 45, 83 n. 46; homelessness, 41, 68, 83 n. 46; hospitality offered to them, 126 n. 8; imitation of animals, 40–41, 52 n. 50, 52 n. 54, 69, 83 n. 46; madness, 69, 85 n. 56; not following any common duty, 95; possessions, 83 n. 45;

seeking of dishonor, 69; wandering behavior, 83 n. 46; women renouncers in contemporary India, 82 n. 38; women renouncers in the Mahānubhāva sect, 90; worship of, 122
Reṇukā (Ekavīrā), 15 n. 4, 32, 47–48 n. 9, 49 n. 22, 92, 93, 94, 102 n. 11, 103 n. 19, 104 n. 23, 145, 162 n. 51, 162 n. 54, 164 n. 67, 192 n. 21
Reṇukā-māhātmya, 103 n. 18, 162 n. 51
renunciation (*saṃnyāsa*): Brahminical literature, 81 n. 30; Brahminical theology, 63–64, 68; definition and link to detachment, 63, 66, 67, 82 n. 35, 214; *praiṣa* proclamation, 82 n. 32; revitalized by Nṛsiṃha Sarasvatī, 113; to be resorted to at the earliest, 42; within the Dattātreya movement, 156
Revaṇa (Revaṇanāth), 58, 252
Ṛg Veda, 2, 3, 10, 15 n. 4, 16 n. 5, 16 n. 8, 16 n. 9, 17 n. 13, 17 n. 25, 18 n. 27, 21 n. 59, 21 n. 60, 22 n. 66, 82 n. 36, 85 n. 60, 158 n. 10, 191 n. 8, 194 n. 41, 232, 242 n. 31, 248 n. 90
Ṛkṣakula mountain, 5, 18 n. 29
Rohiṇī, 11
Roy, Dilip Kumar, 52 n. 53
Ṛṣis, 17 n. 19, 93, 94, 196; giving birth through mind/inner eye, 20 n. 43; *Mahābhārata* list, 28; nature and functions of, 15 n. 2; origins and lists of, 1–2
Ṛtadhvaja Kuvalayāśva, 33, 34
Rudra, 10, 18 n. 28, 21 n. 59, 61, 236; lord of dogs (*śva-pati*), 244 n. 47
rudrākṣa rosary, 238, 247 n. 84
Rudrākṣa-jābāla Upaniṣad, 66, 247 n. 84
Rudras. *See* Maruts
Rudra-Śiva. *See* Śiva
Rudra-yāmala-tantra, 77, 86 n. 78, 240 n. 14
Rukmāṅgada, 188
Rukmin, 24 n. 83
Rukmiṇī, 13, 23 n. 74, 24 n. 79, 24 n. 83
Rukmiṇībāī, 141
Rukmiṇī-svayaṃvara, 161 n. 34
Ruṇḍa Mālā, 233
Russell, Bertrand, 264 n. 36

śabda, 165 n. 76
Śabda-Brahman, 71
sabhā-maṇḍap, 236
saccidānanda. See *sat-cit-ānanda*
Saccidānanda Bhāratī, 95
Sadāśiva, 73, 186, 202
sadā-śiva (as a *tattva*), 181
Sadāśiva (Avadhūta), 84 n. 49
Sadguru, 200, 202
*sādhaka,*173, 186
sādhana, 140, 164 n. 69, 175, 178, 207, 219 n. 30, 238, 248 n. 96, 252
Sādhu Mahārāj Kandharkar, 167 n. 97
Sādhu-Sant Datta *paramparā,* 154
Sādhyas, 29, 47 n. 6, 55 n. 78, 176
saguṇa, 165 n. 75, 202
saguṇa-bhakti, 136
sahaja, 202–3, 210, 215, 220 n. 36, 221 n. 46
sahaja pūrṇa nijānandī raṅgalā, 130 n. 46
sahaja-ānanda, 212
sahaja-ātmā, 220 n. 36
Sahajānanda, 116, 130 n. 44
Sahajiyā sect, 90, 220 n. 33
sahana, 20 n. 44
sahasranāma-stotras, 155
sahasrāra-cakra, 206
Sahasrārjuna. *See* Arjuna Kārtavīrya

Sahiṣṇu, 16 n. 8
saḥw, 140
Sahyādra-līḷā, 92, 94, 95
Sahyādri mountains, 38, 92, 93, 145, 148, 195
Sahyādri-varṇana, 92, 103 n. 15, 223
Sāī Bābā: lineage, 261 n. 10; movement, 251, 260 n. 4
Sāī Bābā of Śirḍī (Shirdi), 154, 155, 167 n. 97, 167 n. 100, 168 n. 107, 239 n. 6, 246 n. 69, 260 n. 5, 261 n. 11, 261 n. 12, 263 n. 23; as Śiva, 261 n. 10; link with Kabīr, 158 n. 8; Muslim origins, 251
Said Cāndasāheb Kādrī. *See* Cānda Bodhale
Śaiva Siddhānta, 14, 171, 172
Śaiva Upaniṣads, 66
Śaiva Vedānta, 25 n. 88
Śaivāgama, 25 n. 88
Śaivism, 136, 220 n. 39, 226, 229, 230; dualist, 24 n. 86; Nepali, 240 n. 16
śaka age, 113, 138
sakala, 61
sakaḷa-lipī, 103 n. 15
sakala-niṣkala, 61
sakāma-bhakti, 123, 133 n. 74
sākṣātkāra, 155, 255
Śākta Upaniṣads, 77, 78 n. 1, 87 n. 80
Śakti, 169, 172, 174, 186, 200, 261 n. 10
Śakti (world mother, Dattātreya's wife), 32, 46, 73
śakti, 25 n. 89, 71, 91, 165 n. 76; stored in the feet, 117, 232
śakti (as a *tattva*), 181
śakti-bīja, 71
Śakti-mahimna-stava, 25 n. 92
śakti-pīṭhas, 89, 94, 100, 104 n. 23, 124, 162 n. 54, 164 n. 67, 172
Śaktis, 170, 174, 192 n. 20
Śakti-saṅgama, 77
Śāktism, 14, 37, 94, 169, 171, 172, 189, 189 n. 1, 190 n. 4, 214, 235, 242 n. 32, 246 n. 68, 249; link with Nāthism, 164 n. 67
Śakuntalā, 12, 23 n. 75
Śakuntalā (play), 23 n. 75
Sākurī, 252
śalākā-puruṣas, 98, 106–7 n. 41
Salām: Dattātreya's utterance in the *Dāsopant-caritra*, 147
sama, 199
samā', 254, 263 n. 23
Sāma Veda, 60, 76
saṃbandhī pāśāṇs, 253
śama-dama, 243 n. 40
sama-darśana, 200
samādhi, 37, 80 n. 23, 179, 180, 183, 184, 185, 206, 220 n. 34, 221 n. 46
samādhi (tomb), 102 n. 11, 117, 123, 138, 146, 168 n. 107
sama-dṛṣṭi, 200
samāna, 50 n. 37
samarasī-karaṇa, 201
sama-rasya, 198, 200, 205, 206, 208, 213, 215, 219 n. 30, 219 n. 31
Samarth *sampradāya*, 163 n. 56
Samartha-pratāpa, 165 n. 80
samatā, 199, 200
samatva, 199, 200, 218 n. 15
śambala, 93
śambali, 91, 93
Śambara, 24 n. 83
Saṃkarṣaṇa, 60
Sāṃkhya *darśana*, 33, 36, 49 n. 26, 165 n. 75, 181, 199
sāṃkhya-prasādaḥ, 33
Sāṃkhya-Yoga, 33, 37
Sāṃkṛti, 60, 62, 65
saṃnyāsa. *See* renunciation
Saṃnyāsa Upaniṣads, 51 n. 48, 57, 62–69, 74, 77, 81 n. 27, 214, 215
Saṃnyāsins. *See* renouncers
saṃsāra, 7, 38, 50 n. 28, 65, 68, 70, 73, 91, 129 n. 32, 174, 205, 214, 259
samuccaya, 63

Samuddajā, 28
samudra-mathana, 231
Saṃvarta, 170, 173, 174, 175, 190 n. 7, 191 n. 20
Saṃvartaka, 65, 69
saṃvid, 207
Sanathana Sarathi, 20 n. 44
Sanatkumāra, 4
Śāṇḍilī, 6, 19 n. 36
Śāṇḍilya, 61, 80 n. 19
Śāṇḍilya Upaniṣad, 27, 57, 61–62, 223
saṅga, 34
saṅgama, 118, 123, 131 n. 55; as Dattātreya, 188
Sāṅglī, 117
Saṅgvī Havelī, 133 n. 75
śani-pradoṣa, 111, 128 n. 16
sāñjana, 221 n. 44
saṅkalpa, 180, 193 n. 29, 193 n. 34
saṅkalpa-śakti, 179, 193 n. 29
Śaṅkara, 49 n. 26, 83 n. 46, 89, 101, 104 n. 30, 112, 113, 127 n. 11, 127 n. 12, 127 n. 13, 171, 181, 190 n. 7, 191 n. 11, 199, 216 n. 1, 231, 244 n. 52; meeting with Dattātreya, 95–97; teacher of the *kali* age, 49 n. 26, 95
Śaṅkarācāryas, 78 n. 4, 104 n. 30
Śaṅkara-dig-vijaya, 49 n. 26, 95, 104 n. 27, 231, 244 n. 52
Śaṅkara-vijaya-vilāsa, 95
śaṅkha, 226, 227, 228, 233, 240 n. 12
śaṅkha-dhvani, 59
"Sanskritization," 125
sant, 107 n. 45
Santa-līlāmṛta, 129 n. 37
Santa-vijaya, 129 n. 37
śānti, 70, 85 n. 59
śānti (for inflicting injury on enemies), 87 n. 79
Santism, 99, 107 n. 45, 135, 136, 137, 138, 140, 145, 159 n. 17, 159 n. 18, 210; link with Nāthism, 157 n. 4
sānubhūti, 20 n. 44
sapiṇḍī-karaṇa, 84 n. 46
saptāha-parāyaṇa, 132 n. 66
Saptaśṛṅgī, 104 n. 23, 162 n. 54
Sarasijasambhava. *See* Brahmā
Sarasvatī, 7, 72, 115, 190 n. 4
Sarasvatī (river), 131 n. 55, 197
Sarasvatī Gaṅgādhar, 101, 109, 136, 146
sarpa-kuṇḍala (= *nāga-kuṇḍala*), 228, 242 n. 28
Sarva-darśana-saṃgraha, 83 n. 40
sarva-sama, 209
Sarva-tīrtha, 93
sarva-tīrtha, 118
sāṣṭāṅga-namaskāra, 152
śāstra-dhārīs, 105 n. 31
Śāstras, 112, 126 n. 8, 127 n. 11, 128 n. 26, 174
Sastri, A. Mahadeva, 79 n. 11
Śatapatha Brāhmaṇa, 2, 16 n. 6, 17 n. 14
Satārā district, 138
Śatarudrīya-mantra, 23 n. 76, 65
Śatarūpā, 17 n. 10
Sātavāhanas, 2, 16 n. 7
sat-cit-ānanda (*saccidānanda*), 72, 150, 238
Satī, 22 n. 71, 71, 104 n. 23
satī, 49 n. 22
Sātī Āsarās, 134 n. 78
Sat-kula, 118
Śatrumardana, 34
satsaṅga, 176
sattva-guṇa, 53 n. 55, 140, 243 n. 40, 254
Sāttvata Saṃhitā, 43, 53 n. 62, 54 n. 63, 116
Saturn, 128 n. 16
Satya Sāī Bābā, Svāmin, 20 n. 44, 251, 260 n. 7, 260 n. 9, 260 n. 10; as Śiva and Śakti, 261 n. 10
satya-loka, 186
Satyāmalanāth, 159 n. 21
Satyatapas, 23 n. 76

Śāṭyāyanīya Upaniṣad, 62, 63, 81 n. 27
satya-yuga. See *kṛta-yuga*
Saubhāgya *sampradāya*, 25 n. 93
Saubhāgya-ratnākara, 78 n. 4
sauḥ, 72–73, 75, 86 n. 70
Śaunaka, 158 n. 10
Saundarya-laharī, 171
Sawai, Yoshitsugu, 104 n. 27
Sāyaṇa, 82 n. 40
sāyujya, 77
Schoterman, Jan A., 79 n. 16
Schrader, F. O., 43, 54 n. 63, 54 n. 64, 62, 63, 78 n. 1, 81 n. 27
Śedgão, 262 n. 18
Śegāon, 251, 252
semboli, 93, 94
serpent: one of Dattātreya's twenty-four Gurus, 41
Setu-bandha, 190 n. 4
sevā, 246 n. 71
sex: greatest pitfall for the ascetic, 41, 64; woman as dangerous and destructive, 214–15, 221 n. 51
Shāh, Bābā Qālandār, 237
Shāhā Datta, 154
shaykh, 160 n. 28
Sheikh Muhammad, 137; Avatāra of Kabīr, 157 n. 2
Shimoga, 236
Shiva. *See* Śiva
Siddha, 109
Siddha-dattātreya-stotra, 151
Siddhānta-rahasya, 159 n. 21
Siddhānta-ratnākara, 53 n. 62
Siddharāmeśvar Mahārāj, Śrī, 252
Siddhas, 62, 104 n. 29, 163 n. 56, 184, 186, 187, 191 n. 15, 198, 200; cult, 58, 219 n. 30; environment, 135
Siddha-siddhānta-paddhati, 51 n. 48, 201, 216 n. 2
Siddha-Yoga, 194 n. 39
Siddheśvar Mahārāj, 166 n. 97
Siddheśvarī, 95
siddhis, 115, 156, 187, 192 n. 26, 194 n. 39, 197, 201, 210, 247 n. 83
Sijrā-i-kādrī line, 137
Śīlavatī, 19 n. 35
Silburn, Lilian, 72, 76
Singh, Mohan, 197
Singh, Sheo Bahadur, 227, 241 n. 25
Śirḍī, 252
Sirius, 9, 10, 21 n. 57
Sirmor district, 246 n. 74
Sistān, 262 n. 22
Śiśupāla-vadha, 43
śiṣya-paramparā, 138
Sītā, 4, 15 n. 4, 39, 192 n. 24, 224
Śītalā, 131 n. 53
Śiva (Agajāvara, Hara, Mahādeva, Maheśa, Maheśvara, Rudra-Śiva, Shiva), 1, 5, 6, 7, 8, 10, 11, 12, 14, 18 n. 28, 19 n. 32, 19 n. 41, 20 n. 44, 21 n. 59, 22 n. 71, 25 n. 87, 25 n. 88, 25 n. 93, 33, 47 n. 9, 65, 66, 69, 71, 72, 73, 75, 93, 97, 104 n. 23, 105 n. 32, 111, 117, 128 n. 16, 131 n. 50, 131 n. 56, 132 n. 65, 136, 146, 158 n. 5, 158 n. 14, 169, 170, 172, 178, 179, 185, 186, 198, 200, 205, 212, 213, 221 n. 45, 226, 227, 228, 229, 230, 233, 236, 241 n. 20, 241 n. 23, 241 n. 24, 242 n. 28, 243 n. 40, 244 n. 47, 245 n. 63, 246 n. 75, 247 n. 84, 249, 252, 255, 259 n. 1, 261 n. 10, 261 n. 11, 263 n. 26; *anāmaya*, 207; *ardha-nārī*, 193 n. 37; Avadhūta supreme, 213; Dattātreya as his Avatāra, 61, 223; Dattātreya as his Guru, 226, 263 n. 27; Dattātreya as his worshiper, 255, 263 n. 27; emblems, 227, 228; first Nātha and disciple of Dattātreya, 105 n. 35; identified with Dattātreya, 61–62, 76, 97, 174, 263 n. 27;

initiated all Nāthas in *Haṭha-Yoga*, 198; instructed Dattātreya, 87 n. 79, 255; *nirañjana*, 210; portrayed as a Śvapaca like Dattātreya, 231; vehicle, 227, 228
śiva, 25 n. 89
śiva (as a *tattva*), 181
Śiva Purāṇa, 18 n. 29, 19 n. 34, 20 n. 48, 23 n. 76
Śiva Upaniṣads, 78 n. 1
Śiva-dṛṣṭi, 25 n. 87
Śiva-gītā, 197, 217 n. 13
Śivājī, 167 n. 97
Śiva-Śakti, 72, 173
Śiva-svarodaya, 221 n. 45
sixteen: number symbolism, 111, 127 n. 12, 164 n. 66
Skanda Purāṇa, 17 n. 17, 18 n. 29, 19 n. 37, 19 n. 38, 20 n. 48, 23 n. 74, 39, 50 n. 33, 110, 224
śloka meter, 224
smārta: communities, 171; rites, 63, 81–82 n. 32
smartṛ-gāmin: a characteristic of Dattātreya, 240 n. 14
smṛti, 63, 64
Smṛti-sthaḷa, 101, 108 n. 56
snāna, 99, 122
Solāpur, 118, 252
Soma: born to Atri and Anasūyā, 1, 4, 5, 7, 9, 20 n. 44, 27, 236, 247 n. 76; descendant of Atri (Ātreya), 27; identified as Bhagnātma, 11; mythological origins, 10–12, 15 n. 2, 21 n. 58, 21 n. 59; prone to sensual pleasures, 185
soma, 4, 10, 16 n. 9, 21 n. 58, 76, 86 n. 77, 100
Somānanda, 14, 25 n. 87
Sontheimer, Günther D., 125
spanda, 70
Spanda school, 171
spandana, 55 n. 78
Spanda-saṃdoha, 219 n. 31
sparrow: one of Dattātreya's Gurus, 52 n. 50
sphurat, 172
spider: one of Dattātreya's twenty-four Gurus, 41
Sprockhoff, J. F., 62, 63
śrāddha, 4, 34, 110, 126–27 n. 8
śraddhā (faith), 176
śrauta rites, 63, 81–82 n. 32
śravaṇa, 184
Śrī, 190 n. 6
Śrī Datta Purāṇa, 49 n. 22
Śrī Guru-līlāmṛta, 49 n. 22
Śrī Parvata, 60
Śrī Sāī Satcarita, 260 n. 5
Śrī-cakra, 172, 173, 175, 191 n. 16
Śrī-dattātreya-jñān-koś, 103 n. 20, 162 n. 47
Śrīgonde, 157 n. 2
Śrīkaṇṭha, 14, 25 n. 88
Śrī-Lakṣmī. *See* Lakṣmī
śrīṃ, 71, 75, 86 n. 67
Śrīmat, 47 n. 6
Śrīnātha, 14
Śrī-nav-nāth-bhakti-kathā-sār, 198
Śrī-nav-nāth-kathā-sār, 218–19 n. 21, 245 n. 60, 261 n. 13
Śrīpāda Śrīvallabha (Śrīpād Śrīvallabh, Śrīpāda Vallabha), 44, 110–11, 112, 115, 117, 122, 123, 125, 127 n. 11, 127 n. 12, 133 n. 68, 138, 167 n. 100, 238
Śrīśaila Veṅkaṭasudhi, 53 n. 62
Śrī-Vaiṣṇava, 81 n. 27
Śrīvatsa, 221 n. 42
Śrī-vidyā, 14, 57, 78 n. 4, 170, 171, 190 n. 2, 190 n. 4, 191 n. 10, 191 n. 11, 191 n. 16; *mantra*, 25 n. 92, 172–73
Śrīvidyānandanāth, 78 n. 4
Śrī-vidyā-ratna-sūtra, 191 n. 11
Śrī-yantras, 191 n. 19
śṛṅgāraṇa, 55 n. 78
Śṛṅgeri, 78 n. 4, 82 n. 40, 95, 97, 164–65 n. 74, 171, 237

śrutis, 211
stambhana, 87 n. 79
Sthāna-pothī, 103 n. 20
stotra, 77, 144, 155, 189 n. 1, 221 n. 42
strīṃ, 71
Subāhu, 34, 38
Subhagodaya, 191 n. 11
Subhāṣitārṇava, 221 n. 50
Sucindram, 19 n. 41, 20 n. 49, 241 n. 20
Sudarśana (= Viṣṇu's disc), 49 n. 19
śuddha, 156
śuddha-caitanya, 200
śuddha-vidyā (as a *tattva*), 181
Sufism, 99, 112, 116, 124, 130 n. 42, 130 n. 44, 131 n. 51, 137, 138, 140, 155, 156, 157 n. 2, 157 n. 4, 159 n. 16, 160 n. 28, 167 n. 99, 168 n. 105, 168 n. 106, 250, 254, 262 n. 22
Śuka, 69, 85 n. 57
Śukra, 22 n. 67
Sumatī, 110, 111, 127 n. 8
Śumbha, 48 n. 11
Sumedha Hāritāyana (Hāritāyana), 170, 175, 190 n. 5, 191 n. 20
Sundara, 178
Sundaradās the younger, 157 n. 4
sundarī (secret script), 103 n. 15
śūnya (Śūnya), 198, 202, 207
śūnya-aśūnya, 221 n. 46
Supernatural Songs, 256
Supratīka, 39
Śūra, 23 n. 77
Surabhi. *See* Suśīlā
Śūrasenas, 23 n. 77
sūrya, 80 n. 17
Sūrya-gītā, 197, 218 n. 13
Sūryanārāyaṇ, 141
Suṣeṇa, 178
Suśīlā (= Kāmadhenu), 32
suṣumnā-nāḍī, 80 n. 17, 81 n. 25
suṣupti, 220 n. 35
sutarka-vidyā, 33
Sūtra-pāṭha, 90, 91, 92, 93, 100, 101, 102 n. 10
Sūtra-tattva-vimarśinī, 190 n. 5
svabhāva, 29
Svacchanda-tantra, 219 n. 30
svadhā, 68, 84 n. 53
svāhā, 66, 72, 75, 76, 83 n. 46, 86 n. 67
Śvapaca: as lord Śiva, 231
svapna, 220 n. 35
svar, 61, 83 n. 46
Svarbhānu, 3, 17 n. 12
svarūpa, 136, 173
svarūpa-nirvāṇa, 207
Svastyātreyas, 15 n. 2, 28
Śvāśva. *See* Kāḷ Bhairav
Svatantrānandanāth, 219 n. 30
svātantrya, 206
Svayambhū, 17 n. 10
Śvetaketu, 65, 69
Śvetāmbaras, 106 n. 41, 260 n. 3
śyāma-sundara, 164 n. 68
Śyāvāśva (*gotra*), 28

Tagare, G. V., 161 n. 35
Tagore, Rabindranath, 264 n. 31
Taharabad, 129 n. 37
Taittirīya Saṃhitā, 86 n. 68
Taittirīya Upaniṣad, 219 n. 28
Takṣaka, 39
tamas, 187, 243 n. 40
Tamiḷ: literature, 172; saint, 169; Siddhas, 191 n. 15
Tamilnadu, 19 n. 41, 189, 190 n. 4, 235
Taṅgaṇa, 176, 178, 179, 180, 193 n. 29
Tantra-kaumudī, 77
Tantrāloka, 25 n. 88, 25 n. 90
Tantra-mahārṇava, 90, 197
Tantras, 33, 75, 77, 86 n. 77, 171, 174, 175; *Śaiva*, 249; Śivaite and Buddhist, 198
Tantra-sāra-saṅgraha, 43
Tantra-tattva, 77

Tantrism, 27, 46, 94, 97, 98, 100, 107 n. 43, 123, 125, 128 n. 17, 129 n. 29, 156, 170, 171, 174, 190 n. 4, 191 n. 12, 193 n. 31, 198, 199, 200, 202, 206, 210, 213, 219 n. 30, 224, 233, 258
tapas, 3, 4, 5, 7, 10, 15 n. 2, 20 n. 43, 28, 32, 47 n. 4, 61, 129 n. 34, 146, 164 n. 71, 214, 236, 241 n. 20
tapo-dhana, 46
Tārā, 11
tāraka-mantra, 68, 70, 72, 73
tarka, 208
tat tvam asi, 97, 137
tathāstu, 111
tattva, 221 n. 46; as supreme *sahaja*, 202
tat-tvam-asyādi-lakṣya, 65, 214
tattvas, 33, 37, 165 n. 75, 181
tawakkul, 168 n. 106
tejas, 4
telos, 259
ṭha, 75, 76
Thañjavūr district, 190 n. 4
The Herne's Egg, 256
The Indian to His Love, 256
The Indian upon God, 256
The Waste Land, 257, 259
Theosophical Society, 256
thorlen devghar, 146
Tibet, 58, 239 n. 9
Tibetan text, 241 n. 21
tiger: guise under which Dattātreya passed his *śakti* to Cāṅgadeva Rāuḷ, 91
Ṭiḷak, Bāl Gaṅgādhar, 8, 9
tīrtha, 60, 95, 99, 102 n. 11, 112, 118, 122, 127 n. 12, 131 n. 55
Tīrthaṅkara, 98, 106 n. 41, 245 n. 56, 250
Tiruchendur, 246 n. 67
Tiru-mantiram, 172
Tirumūlar, 172
Tirumūrtti-malai Purāṇa, 20 n. 49
Tiruvaṇṇāmalai, 169
Tiruvidyai Marudur (Madhyārjunakṣetra), 190 n. 4
traiguṇya, 165 n. 75
Traipurī-vidyā, 191 n. 8
Trasadasyu, 4
tretā-yuga, 24 n. 85, 95
tribal religion, 125
tri-daṇḍin, 83 n. 46
Trika, 14, 25 n. 89
trīṃ, 71
trimukhī, 45, 223, 230, 232, 233, 242 n. 31, 243 n. 40
trimūrti, 1; absence of, 122; born from Atri and Anasūyā, 7, 20 n. 44, 236; development, 229–30, 242 n. 33, 243 n. 37; granted rain to Atri, 241 n. 20; identification with Dattātreya, 76, 106 n. 35, 226–30, 249, 263 n. 26; identification with *oṃ*, 38; identification with stars of Orion, 8, 9; identification with three *liṅgas* at the temple of Sucindram, 20 n. 49; inscriptions, 246 n. 74
Tripurā (Lalitā, Lalitā Tripurasundarī, Tripurasundarī, Tripura-sundarī), 14, 25 n. 93, 71, 77, 164 n. 67, 169, 170, 171, 172, 173, 174, 175, 177, 180, 181, 182, 183, 185, 186, 187, 188, 189 n. 1, 190 n. 2, 190 n. 4, 191 n. 8, 191 n. 12, 192 n. 20, 194 n. 39, 242 n. 32; granted a vision of Dattātreya to Dāsopant, 148
Tripura (city), 25 n. 93, 169
Tripurā Ambikā, 192 n. 20
Tripurā Upaniṣad, 172, 190 n. 4
Tripurā-rahasya, 37, 49 n. 22, 77, 94, 169–94, 249
Triṣaṣṭi-śalākā-puruṣa-caritra, 106 n. 41
Tripurā-tāpinī Upaniṣad, 25 n. 92
triśūla, 11

Trivandrum Library, 195, 216 n. 5
triveṇī, 131 n. 55
Trivikrama Śāstri, 161 n. 31
tṛṣṇā, 243 n. 40
Tryambaka, 14, 25 n. 87
Tryaruṇa Aikṣvāka, 4
Tukārām, 135, 140, 145, 146, 159 n. 17, 162 n. 52, 162 n. 53, 163 n. 57, 230; association with dogs, 243 n. 42
Tuḷjāpūr, 103 n. 22, 162 n. 54, 252
Tulpule, S. G., 99, 103 n. 15, 109, 112, 137, 140, 151, 162 n. 42
Tulsīdās, 138
turīya, 169, 220 n. 35, 255
Turīyātīta, 67
Turīyātīta-avadhūta Upaniṣad, 62, 67
Turk, 143, 168 n. 105
turya, 221 n. 46
twelve: number symbolism, 51 n. 48, 163 n. 63, 164 n. 71
tyāga-amṛtam, 208

uccāṭana, 87 n. 79
udāna, 50 n. 37
udara-pātreṇa, 66
udara-pātrin, 83 n. 46
uddhāra, 254
Uddhava, 40, 51 n. 48, 152, 153, 166 n. 91
Uddhava-gītā (*Hari-gītā*), 197, 217 n. 13
udgātṛ, 76
Udhalināth, 99
uḍumbara tree (*Ficus glomerata*), 117, 118, 130 n. 47, 134 n. 78, 138, 238; loved by Datta, 255
Ugrabhairava, 244 n. 52
Ugraśravas, 19 n. 35
Ujjāin, 25 n. 86, 105 n. 31
unmanī, 221 n. 46
unmatta, 7, 23 n. 78, 69, 74, 155, 167 n. 100
unmattavad-ācarantaḥ, 66
upacāras, 121, 132 n. 67
upanayana, 127 n. 11, 190 n. 4
Upaniṣad-Brahma-Yogin, Śrī, 79 n. 11, 81 n. 27
Upaniṣads, 59, 69, 84 n. 52, 85 n. 57, 85 n. 59, 137, 164 n. 74, 193 n. 32, 249, 255, 259
upāsana, 160 n. 28
Upāsanī Mahārāj of Sākurī (Upāsanī Bābā), 224, 239 n. 6, 251
upāya, 208
Ursa Major, 2
Urvaśī, 18 n. 27, 22 n. 61, 191 n. 8
Uśanas, 11, 22 n. 67
Utpaladeva, 25 n. 87
utsavas, 122
Uttar Pradesh, 167 n. 99, 227
Uttara-gītā, 217 n. 10

Vāc, 1
vāc, 2, 71, 165 n. 76
vacanarūpa parameśvara, 101
Vāḍī. *See* Narsobāvāḍī
Vadi-Narasimha, 235
vāg-bhava, 72
vāg-daṇḍa, 83 n. 46
Vāghyās, 244 n. 47
vahni-jāyā, 72
Vaijanātha-kalā-nidhi, 159 n. 21
vaikharī, 71
Vainya, 4
vairāgya, 37, 52 n. 50, 64, 70, 166 n. 88, 185; levels of detachment, 67
vairāgya-saṃnyāsa, 84 n. 47
Vaiśampāyana, 51 n. 45
Vaiṣṇava Upaniṣads, 57, 70
Vaiṣṇavism, 136, 229, 230
Vaiyāghrapadya family, 79 n. 15
Vājasaneyī branch, 112
vajra (secret script), 103 n. 15
vajra-kavaca, 240 n. 14
Vajrayānas, 220 n. 33
Vajra-Yoga, 219 n. 30
Vajreśvarī, 194 n. 39
vajrolī-mudrā, 62, 81 n. 25

Vākya-vṛtti, 216 n. 1
Vaḷḷi's Cave, 246 n. 67
Vallinātha: partial manifestation (*aṃśa*) of Dattātreya, 110
valmī, 224
vālmīka, 224
Vālmīki, 144, 224, 230, 239 n. 4
Vāmadeva, 69, 85 n. 57
Vāmadeva (competing Yogin in the *Līlā-caritra*), 91
Vāmana, 42, 53 n. 61, 107 n. 41
Vāmana Purāṇa, 18 n. 29, 22 n. 70
Vāmanrav Vaidya Vāmorikar, 167 n. 97
vānaprastha, 63
vāra, 102 n. 7
varada pose, 233, 245 n. 62
Varāha, 42, 247 n. 77
Varāha Purāṇa, 23 n. 76, 39
Vārakarī. *See* Vārkarī
vārakarī, 102 n. 7
Vārāṇasī. *See* Benares
vareṇya, 65, 214
Varivasyā-rahasya, 190 n. 4
Vārkarī (Vārakarī) movement, 90, 99, 102 n. 7, 110, 116, 135, 136, 138, 145, 156, 188, 261 n. 11
varman, 76
varṇa: born from Puruṣa (*Ṛg Veda* 10.90), 82 n. 36; distinctions having *tapas* as criterion, 47 n. 4; rules, 34
varṇāśrama-dharma, 109, 115
Varuṇa, 10, 21 n. 60, 181, 182, 191 n. 8
Varuṇa-Mitra, 229
vāsanā, 70, 80 n. 23, 185, 187, 214, 243 n. 40
vaṣaṭ, 68, 75, 76, 84 n. 53
Vasiṣṭha, 2, 15 n. 4, 191 n. 8, 231
Vasudeva, 23 n. 77, 51 n. 46, 53 n. 62
Vāsudeva, 60, 165 n. 75, 166 n. 91
Vāsudevānanda Sarasvatī, 118, 154, 155, 167 n. 97, 238
Vāsudevas, 98, 107 n. 41
Vāsudevāśrama, 63, 64, 67, 83 n. 46
Vasumān, 176, 188
Vasus, 11, 22 n. 64
vaśya, 87 n. 79
Vātāpī. *See* Bādāmi
Vaudeville, Charlotte, 90, 98, 100, 136, 202, 210, 220 n. 33
vauṣaṭ, 75, 76
Vāyu, 1, 23 n. 77, 40
Vāyu Purāṇa, 32, 49 n. 22, 53 n. 61
Vedānta, 58, 61, 64, 69, 82 n. 40, 95, 99, 104 n. 30, 136, 195, 196, 199
Vedānta Upaniṣads, 69
Vedānta-sāra. See *Avadhūta-gītā*
Veda-Puruṣas, 233
Vedas, 15 n. 4, 16 n. 9, 18 n. 27, 37, 47 n. 6, 49 n. 28, 61, 110, 111, 112, 113, 127 n. 11, 133 n. 73, 138, 153, 158 n. 10, 169, 174, 199, 205, 229, 233, 248 n. 90; identification as dogs, 8, 9, 228, 231, 237; representing the *oṃ*, 38
Vedavyāsa. *See* Vyāsa
Vedic: injunctions, 254; literature, 243 n. 46; liturgy, 76; religion, 115; ritual, 116, 125; sacrifice, 243 n. 46; texts, 229; times, 125, 130 n. 47
Vetāla, 39
Vibhava manifestations, 42, 43, 53 n. 58, 54 n. 63
vicāra, 176, 177
Vidarbha, 23 n. 79, 251
Videha, 4, 181, 182
videha-mukti, 69
vidhi-niṣedha, 254
Vidura, 19 n. 38, 156, 168 n. 104
vidveṣa, 87 n. 79
Vidyāraṇya (Mādhava), 65, 67, 82 n. 40, 95, 104 n. 27, 231
vidyās, 86 n. 78
Vidyāśaṅkara, Śrī, 237

vidyeśvara, 172
Vidyutprabhā, 39
Vijayanagar, 82 n. 40
vikalpa, 63
Vikrama, 18 n. 27
Vikrānta, 34
vimarśa, 172, 183
Vindhya mountains, 50 n. 33, 126 n. 6, 240 n. 14
Vipāśā river (Beas), 188, 194 n. 40
Vīrabhadra temple, 233
viraha, 101
Vīra-śaivas, 219 n. 30
virudas, 240 n. 17
Virūpākṣabuvā Nāgnāth, 166 n. 97
Viṣṇu (Vishnu), 1, 6, 7, 8, 18 n. 25, 19 n. 41, 20 n. 44, 22 n. 62, 23 n. 76, 24 n. 83, 27, 28, 30, 39, 40, 45, 47–48 n. 9, 48 n. 14, 49 n. 19, 61, 70, 71, 104 n. 23, 122, 128 n. 23, 131 n. 50, 136, 146, 158 n. 9, 164 n. 68, 169, 170, 179, 185, 186, 198, 223, 226, 227, 228, 236, 237, 240 n. 17, 241 n. 20, 241 n. 23, 243 n. 40, 245 n. 63, 249, 252, 255, 259 n. 1, 263 n. 26; as Dattātreya, 70, 74, 76, 223, 224, 227, 228, 229, 230, 233; Dattātreya as his Avatāra, 27, 28, 30, 42–44, 45, 46, 47 n. 3, 53 n. 61, 54 n. 67, 54 n. 69, 74, 95, 110, 116, 122, 148, 164 n. 68, 226, 228, 236, 245 n. 65, 249, 250, 255; Dattātreya recommends his worship, 82 n. 37; emblems, 64, 226, 227, 228; lists of Avatāras, 42–44, 53 n. 55, 53 n. 59, 53 n. 61; Trivikrama, 232; vehicle, 226, 227, 228
Viṣṇu Purāṇa, 20 n. 45, 20 n. 46, 23 n. 74, 24 n. 81, 32, 48 n. 12, 52 n. 54, 128 n. 23
Viṣṇubavā Brahmacārin, 167 n. 97
Viṣṇudās (Viṣṇudās Mahurkar), 154, 167 n. 97
Viṣṇudatta, 244 n. 53
Viṣṇu-dharma Purāṇa, 48 n. 12
Viṣṇu-dharmottara Purāṇa, 44, 224
Viṣṇu-Nārāyaṇa, 70
Viṣṇupada temple, 232
viśrānti-kaṭṭā, 118
Viśravas, 16 n. 8
Viśvadevas, 2, 16 n. 9
Viśvak-sena Saṃhitā, 43
Viśvambhara (members of Dāsopant's family line), 163 n. 58
Viśvāmitra, 2, 15 n. 4, 23 n. 75, 79 n. 15, 86 n. 78, 194 n. 41
Viśvanāth temple, 231, 244 n. 50
vital airs, 50 n. 37
vitaṇḍā, 182
Vitatha, 48 n. 10
Viṭhā Reṇukānandana, 163 n. 59
Viṭṭhala (Viṭhobā), 18 n. 31, 99, 102 n. 7, 107 n. 46, 126 n. 4, 136, 140, 141, 144, 146, 154, 159 n. 24, 161 n. 40, 166 n. 91, 166 n. 93, 246 n. 68
Vivasvat, 17 n. 10
Viveka-darpaṇa, 99, 107 n. 48
viveka-khyāti, 37
Vivekānanda, Svāmin, 195
Viveka-sindhu, 136
viyoga, 208, 213
Vṛṣabha, 69, 84 n. 54
Vṛtra, 16 n. 9
vṛtti, 193 n. 34
Vyāghrapāda, 176
vyākhyāna-mudrā, 233, 245 n. 62
vyakta, 165 n. 75
vyana, 50 n. 37
vyāpti, 184
Vyāsa (Vedavyāsa, Vyās), 43, 161 n. 35, 168 n. 104, 192 n. 26, 193 n. 29, 194 n. 39; Avatāra, 53 n. 61; saying of Kabīr mentioning him, 158 n. 5; teacher of the *dvāpara* age, 49 n. 26, 95

Vyāsa-gītā, 196, 217 n. 13
vyutthāna, 200

Wadiyar dynasty, 237
waḥdat al-wujūd, 168 n. 105
Wāī, 246 n. 70
wasp: one of Dattātreya's Gurus, 41, 52 n. 53
Weber, A., 78 n. 1
Wezen (star), 10
What the Thunder Said, 257, 259, 264 n. 36
White, Charles S. J., 260 n. 4
Wilson, H. H., 112
woman: greatest danger for ascetics and renouncers, 41, 64; reduced to dangerous, destructive sexuality, 214–15, 221 n. 51, 249
World War II, 255

Yādava Prakāśa, 82 n. 36; 82 n. 37, 83 n. 46
Yādavas, 13, 14, 20 n. 45, 24 n. 82, 29, 50 n. 33, 51 n. 48, 166 n. 91; kingdom of, 102 n. 10
Yadu: Dattātreya's teaching in detachment through the enumeration of his twenty-four Gurus, 40–42, 51 n. 48; within Dattātreya's lineage, 138
yajña-bhūmi, 116
yajñas, 115
Yājñavalkya, 65, 80 n. 20, 128 n. 22, 193 n. 32
Yājñavalkya Upaniṣad, 57, 62, 66, 82 n. 39
Yajur Veda: *Kṛṣṇa*, 64, 80 n. 24; *Śukla*, 65, 69, 84 n. 52, 85 n. 57, 128 n. 22
Yallāmmā, 104 n. 23
yama, 61, 220 n. 34
yāmala, 72
yama-niyama, 243 n. 40
Yamunā, 23 n. 77, 131 n. 55
yantras, 75, 77, 86 n. 76, 170, 172, 173, 191 n. 18
Yati-dharma-prakāśa, 63, 64, 83 n. 46
Yati-dharma-samuccaya, 82 n. 36, 82 n. 37, 83 n. 46
yātrā, 112
Yayāti, 51 n. 48
Yeats, William Butler, 255, 256, 262 n. 19, 263 n. 29, 263 n. 30, 264 n. 31, 264 n. 32, 264 n. 35
Yekhehal, 151
Yoga, 27, 29, 33, 36, 37, 45, 46, 49 n. 23, 50 n. 28, 50 n. 32, 50 n. 33, 54 n. 67, 57, 58, 60, 62, 69, 78 n. 3, 80 n. 23, 81 n. 25, 90, 94, 97, 98, 105 n. 33, 107 n. 48, 110, 111, 127 n. 12, 135, 164 n. 69, 172, 180, 192 n. 28, 192–93 n. 29, 193 n. 31, 194 n. 39, 196, 198, 199, 201, 202, 203, 205, 206, 208, 210, 213, 218 n. 16, 224, 227, 228, 247 n. 83, 250, 255; defined as *samatva*, 200
Yoga Upaniṣads, 57, 58–62, 77, 78 n. 6, 79 n. 11, 79 n. 13, 215
yoga-bhraṣṭa, 148
Yoga-mārtaṇḍa, 159 n. 21
yoga-mudrā, 228
Yogānanda Sarasvatī (Gaṇḍ Mahārāj), 154
yoga-nātha, 228
Yoga-rāja-ṭilaka, 62
Yoga-saṅgrāma, 137, 157 n. 2
Yoga-śāstra, 62, 80 n. 23
Yoga-sūtra, 50 n. 36, 58, 60, 80 n. 23, 192 n. 26, 193 n. 29, 193 n. 31, 193 n. 38, 194 n. 39, 255
Yoga-tattva Upaniṣad, 62, 80 n. 23
Yoga-vāsiṣṭha, 82 n. 39, 193 n. 29
yoga-vit, 46
Yoga-yājñavalkya-gītā, 61
yoga-yukta, 46

Yogin: connection with animals and the wilderness, 40; livelihood according to chapter 41 of *Mārkaṇḍeya Purāṇa*, 37
Yoginī, 34, 118
Yoginī-hṛdaya, 190 n. 4
Yogisampradāyāviṣkṛti, 99
yogīśvara, 46, 228
yoni, 215
Yudhiṣṭhira, 23 n. 77
yugas, 24 n. 85, 91, 101
yūpa, 130 n. 47

zamīndārs, 105 n. 31
Zelliot, Eleanor, 90, 99, 100, 142, 262 n. 20, 263 n. 23
Zeus, 8

www.ingramcontent.com/pod-product-compliance
Lightning Source LLC
Chambersburg PA
CBHW030127240426
43672CB00005B/46
* 9 7 8 0 7 9 1 4 3 6 9 6 7 *